MODERN CURRICULUM PR
MATHEMA

MW01015262

Teacher's Edition   Level B

Royce Hargrove   Richard Monnard

Acknowledgments

Content Writers   Babs Bell Hajdusiewicz
                      Phyllis Rosner
                      Laurel Sherman

Contributors   Linda Gojak
                      William Hunt
                      Christine Bhargava
                      Jean Laird
                      Roger Smalley
                      Erdine Bajbus
                      Rita Kuhar
                      Vicki Palisin
                      Jeanne White
                      Kathleen M. Becks
                      Jean Antonelli
                      Sandra J. Heldman
                      Susan McKenney
                      Nancy Toth
                      Nancy Ross
                      Connie Gorius
                      Denise Smith

Project Director Dorothy A. Kirk

Editors   Martha Geyen
                      Phyllis Sibbing

Editorial Staff   Sharon M. Marosi
                      Ann Marie Murray
                      Patricia Kozak
                      Ruth Ziccardi

Design   John K. Crum
                      The Remen-Willis
                       Design Group

Cover Art . . . . © 1993 Adam Peiperl

Copyright © **1994 by Modern Curriculum Press, Inc.**

MODERN CURRICULUM PRESS
13900 Prospect Road, Cleveland, Ohio 44136

A Paramount Communications Company

ISBN 0–8136–3117–3 (Teacher's Edition)   **ISBN 0–8136–3110–6** (Pupil's Edition)

4 5 6 7 8 9 10   98 97 96

Modern Curriculum Press

Mathematics

Modern Curriculum Press

Mathematics

Modern Curriculum Press

Mathematics

Modern Curriculum Press

Mathematics

Modern Curriculum Press

Mathematics

Modern Curriculum Press

Mathematics

Modern Curriculum Press

Mathematics

Teacher's Guide

Modern Curriculum Press

Mathematics

INTRODUCING MODERN CURRICULUM PRESS MATHEMATICS

A COMPLETE, ECONOMICAL MATH SERIES TEACHING PROBLEM-SOLVING STRATEGIES, CRITICAL-THINKING SKILLS, ESTIMATION, MENTAL-MATH SKILLS, AND ALL BASIC MATH CONCEPTS AND SKILLS!

Modern Curriculum Press Mathematics is an alternative basal program for students in grades K-6. This unique developmental series is perfect for providing the flexibility teachers need for ability grouping. Its design encourages thinking skills, active participation, and mastery of skills within the context of problem-solving situations, abundant practice to master those skills, developed models students actively work with to solve problems, and reinforcement of problem-solving and strategies. Other features like these provide students with solid math instruction.

Each lesson begins with a developed model that teaches algorithms and concepts in a problem-solving situation.

Students are required to interact with the model by gathering data needed to solve the problem.

A developmental sequence introduces and extends skills taught in the basal curriculum—including statistics, logic, and probability.

An abundant practice of math skills ensures true mastery of mathematics.

Estimation and mental math skills are stressed in all computational and problem-solving activities.

Calculator activities introduce students to basic calculator skills and terms.

Comprehensive **Teacher's Editions** provide abundant additional help for teachers in features like **Correcting Common Errors, Enrichment,** and **Extra Credit,** and the complete **Table of Common Errors.**

Modern Curriculum Press Mathematics is a comprehensive math program that will help students develop a solid mathematics background. This special sampler will show you how:

Developed Models begin each lesson, demonstrate the algorithm and concept in a problem-solving situation, and get students actively involved with the model.

Getting Started provides samples of the concept or skill that is taught and allows the teacher to observe students' understanding.

■ **Practice, Apply,** and **Copy and Do** activities develop independent skills where students practice the algorithm and apply what they have learned in the lesson or from a previous lesson. **Excursion** activities extend the math skill and are fun to do.

■ **Problem Solving** pages introduce students to the techniques of problem solving using a four-step model. **Apply** activities on these pages allow students to use problem-solving strategies they have learned in everyday situations. The second half of the page focuses on higher-order thinking skills.

■ **Chapter Test** pages provide both students and teachers with a checkpoint that tests all the skills taught in the chapter. There are alternative Chapter Tests based on the same objectives at the end of each student book.

■ **Cumulative Review** pages maintain skills that have been taught not only in the previous chapter, but all skills taught up to this point. A standardized test format is used beginning at the middle of the second grade text.

■ **Calculator** pages teach students the various functions and the basic skills needed to use calculators intelligently.

■ **Teacher Edition** pages feature reduced student pages with answers, objectives, suggestions for **Teaching the Lesson, Materials, Correcting Common Errors, Enrichment,** and more.

A Developed Model Gets Students To Think, Actively Participate, And Understand Math Skills!

The major difference between *Modern Curriculum Press Mathematics* and other math programs is the developed model in which students actively work. Every lesson of *Modern Curriculum Press Mathematics* features concept development based on this developed model. Students are required to interact with this model discriminating what data is needed to solve the problem. This process teaches and reinforces their thinking skills and gets them actively involved providing the motivation to read and understand. The four-step teaching strategy of SEE, PLAN, DO, CHECK successfully increases students' understanding and provides a firm foundation for total math master of skills.

■ One major objective is the focus of every two-page lesson.

■ An algorithm or a model word problem keeps students interested and involved and provides a purpose for learning.

Dividing by 4

Therese is using baskets of flowers to decorate the tables

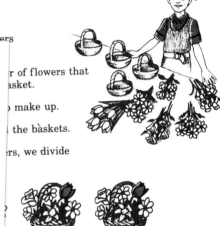

r of flowers that asket.

make up.

the baskets.

rs, we divide

wers into each basket.

nplete the number sentences.

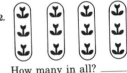

2.

How many in all? _____

_____ How many groups? _____

How many in each group? _____

$12 \div 4 =$ _____

nces.

4 = _____   5. $8 \div 4 =$ _____   6. $32 \div 4 =$ _____

Reviewing Addition Facts

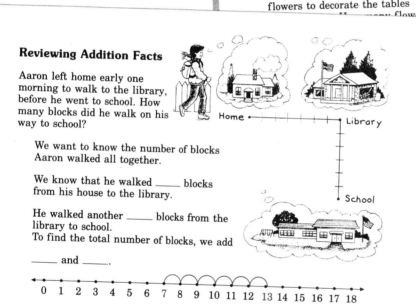

Aaron left home early one morning to walk to the library, before he went to school. How many blocks did he walk on his way to school?

We want to know the number of blocks Aaron walked all together.

We know that he walked _____ blocks from his house to the library.

He walked another _____ blocks from the library to school.
To find the total number of blocks, we add

_____ and _____.

0 1 2 3 4 5 6 7 8 9 10 11 12 13 14 15 16 17 18

$7 + 6 =$ _____
addends   sum

$\begin{array}{r} 7 \\ + 6 \end{array}$ addends
← sum

$7 + 6 = 13$ is called a **number sentence.**

Aaron walked _____ blocks from his home to school.

Getting Started

Complete the number sentences.

1. $4 + 2 =$ _____   2. $7 + 9 =$ _____   3. $8 + 3 =$ _____

4. $2 + 9 =$ _____   5. $5 + 6 =$ _____   6. $8 + 8 =$ _____

Add.

7. $\begin{array}{r} 8 \\ + 7 \end{array}$ 8. $\begin{array}{r} 4 \\ + 1 \end{array}$ 9. $\begin{array}{r} 9 \\ + 9 \end{array}$ 10. $\begin{array}{r} 5 \\ + 5 \end{array}$ 11. $\begin{array}{r} 3 \\ + 6 \end{array}$ 12. $\begin{array}{r} 9 \\ + 4 \end{array}$

3

- Students interact with the artwork to gather data needed to solve problems. This interaction helps develop higher-order thinking skills.

- Each objective is introduced in a problem-solving setting developing problem-solving thinking skills.

- The four-step teaching method of SEE, PLAN, DO, CHECK guides students easily through the development of each skill.

- Students SEE the "input" sentences and the artwork and use them to help solve the problems. This allows them to be actively involved in their work.

- Students PLAN how they are going to solve problems using their reasoning skills to determine what operations are needed.

- Students use the model to help DO the problem. Each developed model shows students how to do the algorithm.

- To CHECK understanding of the math skill, a concluding sentence reinforces the problem-solving process.

- Important math vocabulary is bold-faced throughout the text and defined in context and in the glossary.

- A check (√) points out important concepts to which students should give special attention.

Place Value through Thousands

The government space agency plans to sell used moon buggies to the highest bidders. What did Charley pay for the one he bought?

We want to understand the cost of Charley's moon buggy.

Charley paid exactly ————.
To understand how much money this is, we will look at the place value of each digit in the price.

✔ The numbers 0, 1, 2, 3, 4, 5, 6, 7, 8 and 9 are called **digits**. The position of the digit decides its place value.

thousands	hundreds	tens	ones
——	——	——	——

In 7,425, the digit 4 represents hundreds, and the digit 7 represents ————.
Numbers can be written in **standard** or **expanded form**.

Standard Form
7,425

Expanded Form
7,000 + 400 + 20 + 5

We say Charley paid **seven thousand, four hundred twenty-five dollars**. We write ————.

Getting Started

Write in standard form.

1. five thousand, six hundred fifty-eight ————

2. 3,000 + 50 + 8 ————

Write in words.

3. 6,497

4. 823

5. 9,045

Write the place value of the red digits.

6. 3,948

7. 9,603

8. 7,529

9. $5,370

7

Subtracting Fractions with Unlike

Duncan is feeding the chickens on his uncle's farm. When he started, there were $4\frac{1}{2}$ buckets of chicken feed. How much feed has he used?

We want to know how much chicken feed Duncan has used.

We know that he started with ____ buckets of feed, and he has ____ buckets left.

To find the amount used, we subtract the amount left from the original amount.

We subtract ____ from ____.

To subtract fractions with unlike denominator follow these steps:

Rename the fractions as equivalent fractions with the least common denominator

$$4\frac{1}{2} = 4\frac{2}{4}$$
$$-1\frac{1}{4} = 1\frac{1}{4}$$

Subtract the fractions.

$$4\frac{1}{2} = 4\frac{2}{4}$$
$$-1\frac{1}{4} = 1\frac{1}{4}$$
$$\frac{1}{4}$$

Duncan has used ____ buckets of feed.

Getting Started

Subtract.

1. $15\frac{5}{8}$
   $-7\frac{1}{3}$

2. $87\frac{2}{3}$
   $-39\frac{1}{6}$

3.

Copy and subtract.

5. $\frac{7}{8} - \frac{1}{4} =$ ____

6. $\frac{5}{6} - \frac{1}{2} =$ ____

7. $\frac{9}{10} - \frac{6}{15} =$ ____

127

TEACHER-GUIDED PRACTICE ACTIVITIES CHECK STUDENTS' UNDERSTANDING OF MATH CONCEPTS!

Getting Started activities provide the opportunity for students to try to do what they've just learned and for teachers a chance to check understanding. These activities also allow the teacher to evaluate students' progress in a particular objective before continuing on in the lesson. A complete **Table of Common Errors** can be found in the **Teacher's Editions.** This list helps the teacher diagnose and correct those errors identified by research to be the most common. Lesson plans offer specific suggestions for dealing with each individual error, so the teacher can concentrate on those area where students need help. Showing th teacher ways to keep errors from happening by alerting to common mistakes, will make teaching math go more smoothly.

Multiplying, the Factor 2

Sun Li is helping her mother pack eggs in cartons. How many eggs does she pack into each carton?

_____ 6 groups of _____ eggs each.

2 + 2 + 2 = _____

$6 \times 2 =$ _____ $\begin{array}{r} 2 \\ \times 6 \\ \hline \end{array}$

s 2 groups of _____ eggs

$2 \times 6 =$ _____ $\begin{array}{r} 6 \\ \times 2 \\ \hline \end{array}$

s into each carton.

tiplication to show how many

2. $\bigcirc\bigcirc\bigcirc\bigcirc\bigcirc$
$\bigcirc\bigcirc\bigcirc\bigcirc\bigcirc$

2 + 2 + 2 + 2 + 2 = _____

$5 \times 2 =$ _____

$2 \times 5 =$ _____

4. $2 \times 6 =$ _____   5. $\begin{array}{r} 4 \\ \times 2 \\ \hline \end{array}$ 6. $\begin{array}{r} 2 \\ \times 2 \\ \hline \end{array}$

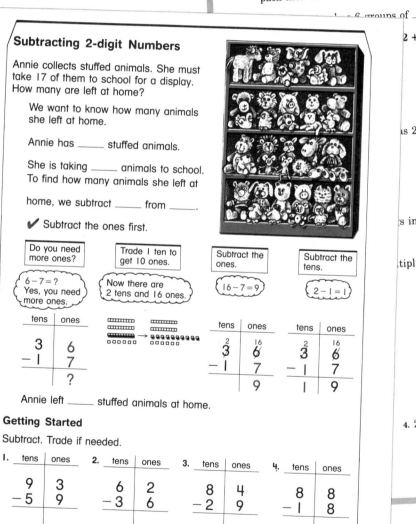

Subtracting 2-digit Numbers

Annie collects stuffed animals. She must take 17 of them to school for a display. How many are left at home?

We want to know how many animals she left at home.

Annie has _____ stuffed animals.

She is taking _____ animals to school. To find how many animals she left at home, we subtract _____ from _____.

✔ Subtract the ones first.

Do you need more ones?	Trade 1 ten to get 10 ones.	Subtract the ones.	Subtract the tens.
6 − 7 = ? Yes, you need more ones.	Now there are 2 tens and 16 ones.	(16 − 7 = 9)	(2 − 1 = 1)

tens	ones
3	6
−1	7
	?

tens	ones
²3	¹⁶6
−1	7
	9

tens	ones
²3	¹⁶6
−1	7
1	9

Annie left _____ stuffed animals at home.

Getting Started

Subtract. Trade if needed.

1.
tens	ones
9	3
−5	9

2.
tens	ones
6	2
−3	6

3.
tens	ones
8	4
−2	9

4.
tens	ones
8	8
−1	8

Subtracting 2-digit numbers, with trading

T-6

- Samples that the students work allow the teacher to check students' understanding of the skill.

- Students gain both confidence and competence in working these problems.

- If the objective is not fully grasped by the student, the **Table of Common Errors** will help the teacher deal with each individual type of error.

- Students gain a deeper understanding of the basic algorithm introduced in the developed model.

- New skills are reinforced through the sample problems students work right on the spot.

- Teachers observe any typical student errors before continuing additional work in the lesson.

- Teacher-guided practice activities will encourage classroom discussion.

- **Getting Started** activities help the teacher to single out predictable errors quickly.

- All samples found in the **Getting Started** activities prepare students to work the exercises found in the next part of the lesson.

Using Customary Units of Length

Robert, Janis and Jonathan are being measured for band uniforms. What is Robert's height in inches?

We want to rename Robert's height in inches.

We know that he is ____ feet ____ inches tall.

| 12 inches (in.) = 1 foot (ft) |
| 3 feet = 1 yard (yd) |
| 36 inches = 1 yard |
| 5,280 feet = 1 mile (mi) |
| 1,760 yards = 1 mile |

...ches as inches, we multiply ...the number of inches in a ...extra inches.

____ and add ____.

...ll.

...ber like $5\frac{1}{2}$ feet as inches, we

____ inches

...as larger units, like 48 inches

...___.

...o rename larger units as ...name smaller units as larger ones.

...easurements of length.

3 yd 1 ft
− 1 yd 2 ft
‾‾‾‾‾‾‾
1 yd 2 ft

(1 yd = 3 ft
3 ft + 1 ft = 4 ft)

2 in.

$1\frac{8}{9}$ yd

Add or subtract.

3. 6 ft 9 in.
     − 2 ft 11 in.

4. 7 yd 2 ft 3 in.
     − 5 yd 1 ft 6 in.

217

Addition and Subtraction Properties

Properties are like special tools. They make the job of adding and subtracting much easier.

Twelve minus nine is three.

That's right because nine plus three is twelve.

| **Addition** | | **Subtraction** | |

Order Property
We can add in any order.

5 + 2 = 7   2 + 5 = 7

3 + 6 + 7 = ____   7 + 3 + 6 = ____

Grouping Property
We can change the grouping.
✔ Remember to add the numbers in parentheses first.

(6 + 3) + 5 = 14   6 + (3 + 5) = 14

(8 + 2) + 4 = ____   8 + (2 + 4) = ____

Zero Property
Adding zero makes the sum the same as the other addend.

5 + 0 = 5   0 + 7 = 7

0 + 1 = ____   8 + 0 = ____

Subtracting Zero
Subtracting zero makes the difference the same as the minuend.

9 − 0 = 9   7 − 0 = ____

Subtracting a Number from Itself
Subtracting a number from itself leaves zero.

8 − 8 = 0   3 − 3 = ____

Checking Subtraction
Subtracting is the reverse of adding.

15 − 9 = 6 because 6 + 9 = 15

12 − 7 =

because ____ + ____ = ____

✔ **Solving for _n_** is finding the value for the _n_ in the equation.

Getting Started

Solve for _n_.

1. 0 + 0 = n   **2.** 0 + 6 = n

  n = ____   n = ____

Subtract. Check by adding.

3. 15   **4.** 12   **5.** 18
     − 9   − 7   − 9

Add. Check by grouping the addends another way.

6. 5   **7.** 2   **8.** 6   **9.** (5 + 2) + 6 = n   **10.** 3 + (5 + 4) = n
     3   6   3
   + 4   + 3   + 4   n = ____   n = ____

3

T-7

INDEPENDENT PRACTICE ACTIVITIES PROVIDE PLENTY OF DRILL, PRACTICE, AND EXTENSION IN A VARIETY OF FORMATS!

The purpose of building skills is to ensure that students can use and apply those skills. That goal can only be reached when skills are clearly and systematically taught and then practiced. With *Modern Curriculum Press Mathematics,* the teacher can be as-sured that students will have abundant opportunities to practice their newly-learned math skills. The variety of practice activities allows the teacher to meet the needs of every student. Working independently helps students strengthen new skills, become more confident, and increase their under-standing. Practice helps students lear Some students need more practice th others to help them catch on. *Moder Curriculum Press Mathematics* offers variety of practice situations so that students stay on target with what the are learning.

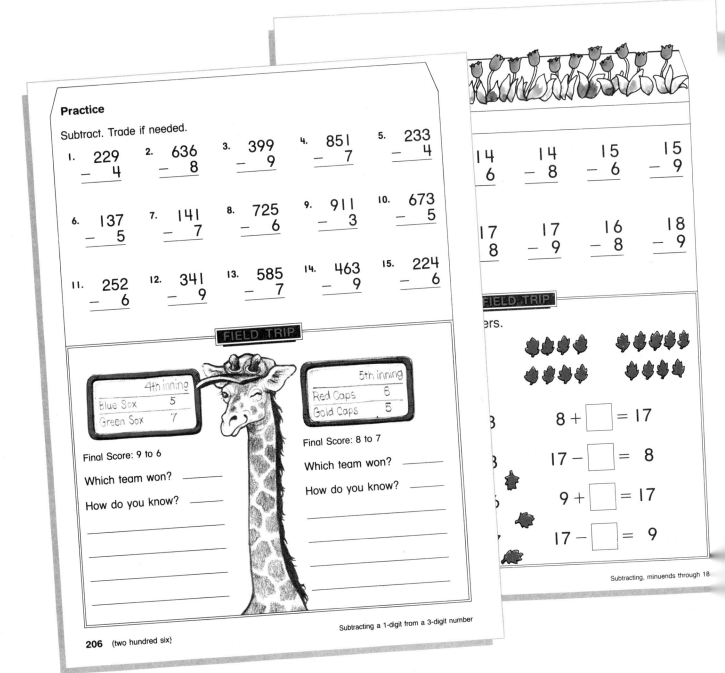

Practice

Subtract. Trade if needed.

1. 229 − 4	2. 636 − 8	3. 399 − 9	4. 851 − 7	5. 233 − 4
6. 137 − 5	7. 141 − 7	8. 725 − 6	9. 911 − 3	10. 673 − 5
11. 252 − 6	12. 341 − 9	13. 585 − 7	14. 463 − 9	15. 224 − 6

FIELD TRIP

4th inning
Blue Sox 5
Green Sox 7

Final Score: 9 to 6

Which team won? _____

How do you know? _____

5th inning
Red Caps 6
Gold Caps 5

Final Score: 8 to 7

Which team won? _____

How do you know? _____

Subtracting a 1-digit from a 3-digit number

206 (two hundred six)

14 − 6	14 − 8	15 − 6	15 − 9
17 − 8	17 − 9	16 − 8	18 − 9

FIELD TRIP

ers.

8 + ☐ = 17

17 − ☐ = 8

9 + ☐ = 17

17 − ☐ = 9

Subtracting, minuends through 18

T-8

The teacher can begin the process of individual mastery by assigning **Practice** exercises that students can work independently.

■ *Modern Curriculum Press Mathematics* integrates problem solving into the practice activities with **Apply** problems. Some of these problems relate to the algorithm. However, some require previously-learned skills encouraging students to think and maintain skills.

Both vertical and horizontal forms of problems are used making students more comfortable with forms found in standardized test formats.

■ An emphasis on practical skills encourages learning by applying math to everyday situations.

■ Independent practice provides more opportunities for application and higher-order thinking skills.

■ The variety of practice activities keeps students motivated and interested in learning.

■ **Copy and Do** exercises check students' ability to assemble an algorithm from an equation and gives them practice in transferring information.

■ **Excursion** activities extend the basic skill work and are fun to do. The teacher can challenge the more capable students with these mind-stretching activities.

■ Giving students ample opportunities to practice and strengthen new skills builds solid skill development and helps the teacher more easily measure the results.

Practice

Estimate the sum by rounding the addends to the greatest common place value.

1. 736
    + 475

2. $3,694
    +   587

3.   8,439
    + 6,650

4. 9,245
    + 8,273

5. 3,865
    + 7,256

6. 13,475
    + 9,150

7. $162.45
    +   73.95

8. 49,725
    + 75,212

9. 127,247
    + 438,500

10. 38,725
    + 73,689

11. $217.75
    + 468.52

12. $3,275.16
    +   789.50

13. 745,925
    + 627,215

14. $13,795.92
    +   8,227.75

15. 136,795
    +   8,500

Copy and Do

16. 478 + 569

17. $3,942 + $687

18. 9,645 + 4,509

19. 6,973 + 4,768

20. 39,040 + 55,389

21. 209,349 + 567,499

22. 35,462 + 7,096

23. 16,494 + 6,095

24. $555.99 + $62.85

The clock-5 arithmetic system uses only the five digits on the clock to answer all addition and subtraction problems. Use this clock to find the answers.

1. 3 + 4 = ____

2. 4 − 3 = ____

3. 2 + 3 = ____

4. 2 − 4 = ____

5. 4 + 4 + 4 = ____

6. 1 − 2 = ____

---

3. 4)80   4. 4)96   5. 2)56

8. 5)80   9. 6)96   10. 9)90

13. 4)56   14. 7)91   15. 6)84

18. 7)98   19. 3)90   20. 4)76

)0 ÷ 2   23. 85 ÷ 5   24. 72 ÷ 6

50 ÷ 2   27. 72 ÷ 4   28. 88 ÷ 4

76 ÷ 2   31. 87 ÷ 3   32. 96 ÷ 8

you
uch did

3 apples
y many
eat in 27

34. Lemons cost 8¢ each. Sally has 96¢. How many lemons can Sally buy?

36. The tennis club used 45 tennis balls in a tournament. Tennis balls are sold 3 in a can. How many cans did the club use?

MATH COMES ALIVE WHEN STUDENTS LEARN TO INTEGRATE COMPUTATION, PROBLEM-SOLVING STRATEGIES, AND REASONING TO MAKE DECISIONS FOR THEMSELVES!

Problem-solving pages present lessons that increase understanding with a four-step teaching strategy: SEE, PLAN, DO, CHECK. *Modern Curriculum Press Mathematics* offers step-by-step instruction in how to understand word problems as well as varied practice in actually using the skills learned. Each lesson focuses on a different problem-solving strategy. These strategies develop students' higher-order thinking skills and help them successfully solve problems. Step-by-step, students will understand the question, find the information needed, plan a solution, and then check it for accuracy. This develops students' critical-thinking skills and ability to apply what they've learned to solve problem that go beyond basic operations.

■ Word problems utilize high-interest information and focus on everyday situations.

PROBLEM SOLVING

Drawing a Picture

A parking lot has 9 rows of 8 parking spaces each. The fourth and fifth spaces in every third row have trees in them. The outside spaces in every row are reserved for the handicapped or for emergency vehicles. How many regular parking spaces are there in the lot?

★ SEE

We want to know how many spaces are left for regular parking.

There are _____ rows of parking spaces.

There are _____ spaces in each row.

In every third row, _____ spaces are lost to trees.

In every row _____ spaces are used for special vehicles.

★ PLAN

We can draw a picture of the parking lot, crossing out the closed parking spaces. Then we can count the regular spaces left.

★ DO

We count _____ spaces left for regular parking.

★ CHECK

We can check by adding the spaces open in each row.

$4 + 6 + 6 + 4 + 6 + 6 + 4 + 6 + 6 =$ _____

173

---

ach problem.

2. A Super-Duper ball bounces twice its height when it is dropped. Carl dropped a Super-Duper ball from the roof of a 12-foot garage. How high will the ball bounce after 5 bounces?

4. The distance around a rectangle is 10 centimeters. The length of each of the two longer sides is 3 centimeters. What is the length of each of the two shorter sides?

6. What 7 coins together make 50 cents?

- Step by step, students learn to understand the question, find the information they need, plan a method of solution, find an answer, and check it for accuracy.

- Every step of the process is organized so that students truly understand how to arrive at the solution.

- The problem-solving banner alerts students that they are involved in a problem-solving lesson. These focused lessons remind students how to approach problems and how to use skills and specific strategies already learned.

- Learning to integrate computation, problem-solving strategies, and reasoning makes math come alive for students.

- Problems incorporate previously taught computational skills—focusing students' minds on the problem-solving process itself.

- Problem-solving applications appear in every problem-solving lesson. This frequent practice reduces apprehension and builds confidence.

- Practice in applying the strategies gives students a chance to use skills in routine and non-routine problems.

- In every chapter, problem-solving strategies and critical-thinking skills are developed, applied, and reinforced.

- Students choose appropriate strategies to solve problems and are challenged to formulate their own problems and to change the conditions in existing problems.

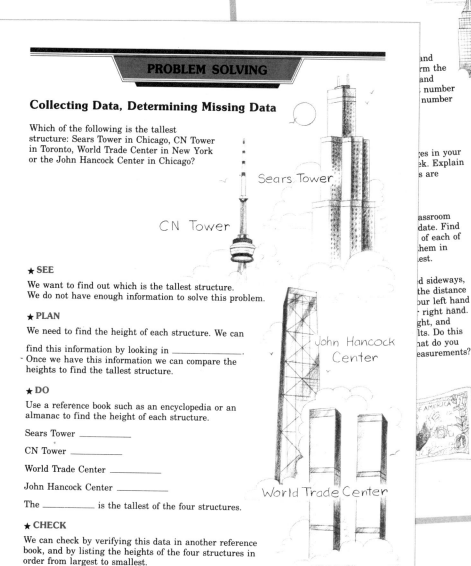

PROBLEM SOLVING

Collecting Data, Determining Missing Data

Which of the following is the tallest structure: Sears Tower in Chicago, CN Tower in Toronto, World Trade Center in New York or the John Hancock Center in Chicago?

★ SEE

We want to find out which is the tallest structure.
We do not have enough information to solve this problem.

★ PLAN

We need to find the height of each structure. We can

find this information by looking in _____.
Once we have this information we can compare the heights to find the tallest structure.

★ DO

Use a reference book such as an encyclopedia or an almanac to find the height of each structure.

Sears Tower _____

CN Tower _____

World Trade Center _____

John Hancock Center _____

The _____ is the tallest of the four structures.

★ CHECK

We can check by verifying this data in another reference book, and by listing the heights of the four structures in order from largest to smallest.

2. Roll a pair of dice 30 times and record the number of times each sum appears. Perform the experiment a second time. What sum appears most often? What sum appears least often?

4. Toss a coin 50 times and record the number of heads and tails. Which side of the coin appears most often?

6. Record the dates of the coins available in your classroom. How many years difference exist between the newest and oldest coin?

8. An arithmetic game is created by adding the values of certain U.S. currency. Since a portrait of George Washington appears on a $1 bill and a portrait of Abraham Lincoln appears on the $5 bill, we say that George Washington + Abraham Lincoln = $6. Find the value of Thomas Jefferson + Alexander Hamilton + Woodrow Wilson.

CHAPTER TEST PAGES PROVIDE A VEHICLE FOR STUDENT EVALUATION AND FEEDBACK!

Every chapter in *Modern Curriculum Press Mathematics* concludes with a **Chapter Test.** These tests provide the opportunity for students to demonstrate their mastery of recently acquired skills. **Chapter Test** pages enable the teacher to measure all the basic skills students have practiced in the lesson and evaluate their understanding. The focus of these pages is the assessing of mastery of algorithms. An adequate number of sample problems are provided to accomplish this. This important checkpoint helps the teacher to better meet individual student-computational needs.

■ **Chapter Test** pages are carefully correlated to what has been taught throughout the entire series.

■ **Chapter Test** pages assess students' mastery of all the skills taught in the lesson.

■ All directions are written in an easy-to-follow format.

■ Both vertical and horizontal forms of problems are used making students more comfortable with exercises found in standardized tests.

■ In the back of each student book, there is an alternate **Chapter Test** for each chapter based on the same objectives covered in the first test.

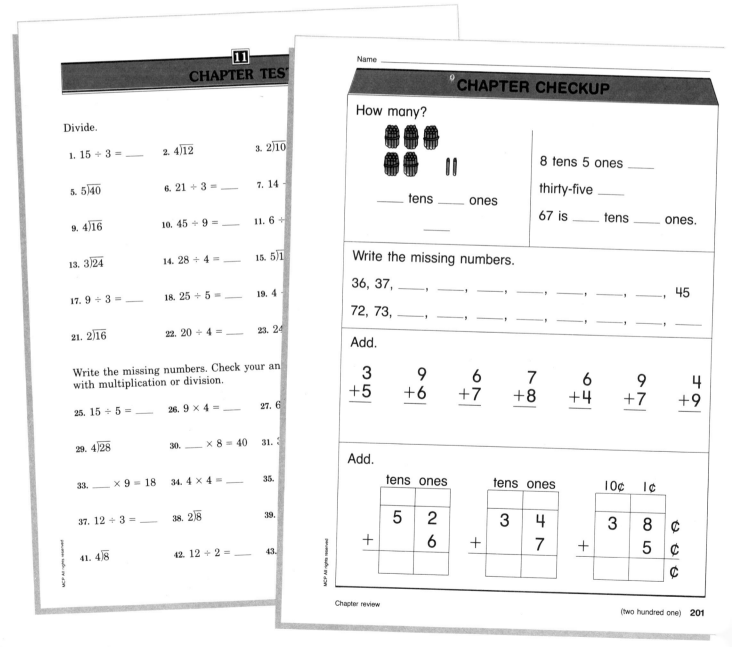

SYSTEMATIC MAINTENANCE IS PROVIDED AT EVERY LEVEL WITH CUMULATIVE REVIEW PAGES!

Every chapter contains a **Cumulative Review** page that provides an on-going refresher course in basic skills. These pages maintain the skills that have been taught in the chapter plus the skills learned in previous chapters.

Cumulative Review pages actually reach back into the text for a total maintenance of skills. **Cumulative Review** pages are progressive instruction because they build on the foundation laid earlier for a thorough and sequential program of review. A standardized test format is used beginning at the middle of the second grade. Students will benefit by gaining experience in dealing with this special test format.

■ A variety of problems done in standardized test format give students a better chance to score well on these tests.

■ Directions are minimal and easy to understand.

■ Design elements on every test are the same found on standardized tests.

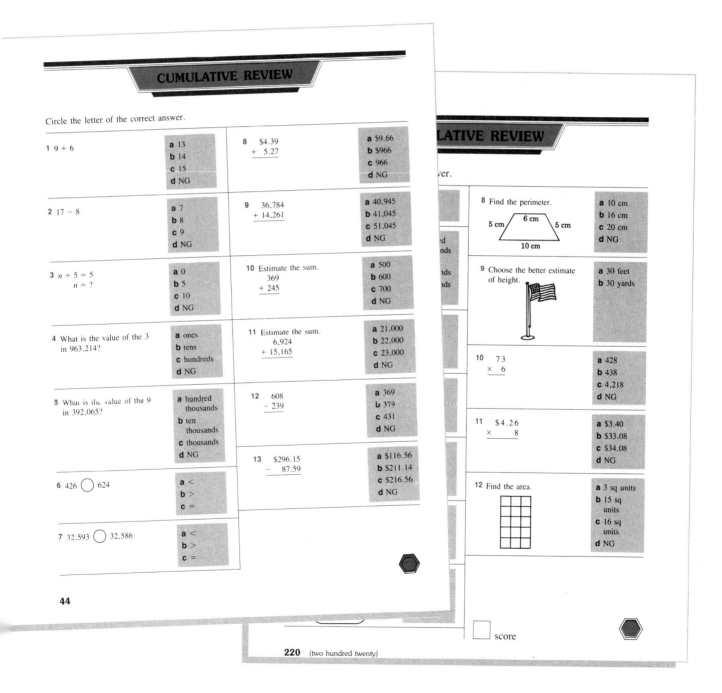

CUMULATIVE REVIEW

Circle the letter of the correct answer.

1 9 + 6
a 13
b 14
c 15
d NG

2 17 − 8
a 7
b 8
c 9
d NG

3 $n + 5 = 5$
   $n = ?$
a 0
b 5
c 10
d NG

4 What is the value of the 3 in 963,214?
a ones
b tens
c hundreds
d NG

5 What is the value of the 9 in 392,065?
a hundred thousands
b ten thousands
c thousands
d NG

6 426 ◯ 624
a <
b >
c =

7 32,593 ◯ 32,586
a <
b >
c =

8 $4.39
 + 5.27
a $9.66
b $966
c 966
d NG

9 36,784
 + 14,261
a 40,945
b 41,045
c 51,045
d NG

10 Estimate the sum.
   369
 + 245
a 500
b 600
c 700
d NG

11 Estimate the sum.
   6,924
 + 15,165
a 21,000
b 22,000
c 23,000
d NG

12 608
  − 239
a 369
b 379
c 431
d NG

13 $296.15
  − 87.59
a $116.56
b $211.14
c $216.56
d NG

8 Find the perimeter.
a 10 cm
b 16 cm
c 20 cm
d NG

9 Choose the better estimate of height.
a 30 feet
b 30 yards

10   7 3
   × 6
a 428
b 438
c 4,218
d NG

11 $4.26
  × 8
a $3.40
b $33.08
c $34.08
d NG

12 Find the area.
a 3 sq units
b 15 sq units
c 16 sq units
d NG

score

CALCULATOR LESSONS PROVIDE EXCITING LEARNING ACTIVITIES AND ADD INTEREST AND PRACTICALITY TO MATH!

Calculator lessons are found throughout *Modern Curriculum Press Mathematics*. The activities are used in many ways—to explore number patterns, to do calculations, to check estimations, and to investigate functions. Each **Calculator** lesson is designed to help students learn to use and operate calculators while they reinforce and improve their mathematical skills.

■ **Calculator** lessons teach students to use simple calculators while reinforcing chapter content.

■ **Calculator** lessons introduce students to basic calculator skills and terms.

■ Practical calculator activities promote student involvement as they take an active part in what they are learning.

■ Students learn, practice, and apply critical-thinking skills as they use calculators.

Practice

Complete these calculator codes.

1. 85 [÷] 5 [=] [____]

2. 57 [÷] 3 [=] [____]
4. 96 [÷] 6 [=] [____]
6. 90 [÷] 9 [=] [____]
8. 63 [÷] 7 [×] 8 [=] [____]
10. 75 [÷] 5 [×] 6 [=] [____]
12. 216 [−] 158 [÷] 2 [=] [____]

14. Nathan can jog 5 miles in 65 minutes. How long will it take Nathan to jog 8 miles?

16. Bananas are on sale at 6 for 96¢. How much do 8 bananas cost?

2. The sum of 2 numbers is 60. Their difference is 12. What are the numbers?

4. Five times one number is three more than six times another number. The difference between the numbers is 1. What are the numbers?

Calculators, the Division Key

Natalie is packing lunches for a picnic. She needs to buy 5 apples. How much will Natalie pay for the 5 apples?

Apples 3 for 51¢

We want to know the price for 5 apples.

We know that _____ apples cost _____.

To find the cost of 5 apples, we first find the cost of 1 by dividing _____ by _____. Then, we multiply the cost of 1 apple by _____.

This can be done on the calculator in one code.

[·] 51 [÷] 3 [×] 5 [=] [____]

Natalie will pay _____ for 5 apples.

Complete these calculator codes.

1. 42 [÷] 7 [=] [____]
3. 96 [÷] 4 [=] [____]
5. 36 [÷] 9 [×] 7 [=] [____]
7. 72 [÷] 6 [×] 9 [=] [____]

2. 76 [÷] 2 [=] [____]
4. 52 [÷] 4 [=] [____]
6. 84 [÷] 4 [×] 3 [=] [____]
8. 75 [÷] 5 [×] 9 [=] [____]

139

PLAN CLASSROOM-READY MATH LESSONS IN MINUTES WITH COMPREHENSIVE TEACHER'S EDITIONS!

The **Teacher's Editions** of *Modern Curriculum Press Mathematics* are designed and organized with the teacher in mind. The full range of options provides more help than ever before and guarantees efficient use of the teacher's planning time and the most effective results for efforts exerted.

Each **Teacher's Edition** provides an abundance of additional **Enrichment, Correcting Common Errors** and application activities. Plus they contain a complete **Error Pattern Analysis.** The teacher will also find reduced student pages with answers, objectives, suggestions for teaching lessons, materials, **Mental Math** exercises, and more.

■ There's no need for the teacher to struggle with two separate books because student pages are reduced in the **Teacher's Edition.**

■ Clear headings and notes make it easy for the teacher to find what is needed before teaching the lesson.

■ The teacher will be more effective with lesson plans that are always complete in two pages and include everything needed.

■ Student **Objectives** set a clear course for the lesson goal.

Time to the Half-hour
pages 163-164

Objective
To practice telling time to the hour and half-hour

Materials
* Demonstration clock
* Two pencils of different lengths

Mental Math
Which is less?
1. 2 dimes or 5 nickels (2 dimes)
2. 14 pennies or 2 nickels (2 nickels)
3. 5 nickels or 4 dimes (5 nickels)
4. 1 quarter or 2 dimes (2 dimes)
5. 6 nickels or 1 quarter (1 quarter)

Skill Review
Show times to the hour and half hour on the demonstration clock. Have students write the time on the board. Now have a student set the clock to show an hour or half-hour. Have the student ask another student to write the time on the board. Have a student write a time for the hour or half-hour and invite another student to place the hands on the clock to show the times.

Name _____

Match the clocks

Telling time to the hour and half-hour

Teaching page 163
On the demonstration clock, start at 12:00 and slowly move the minute hand around the clock. Ask students to tell what the hour hand does as the minute hand moves around the clock face. (moves slowly toward the next number) Tell students the minute hand moves around the clock face 60 minutes while the hour hand moves from one number to the next. Tell students there are 60 minutes in 1 hour.

Ask students to tell where the hour hand is on the first clock. (between 5 and 6) Ask where the minute hand is. (on 6) Ask the time. (5:30) Tell students to find 5:30 in the center column and trace the line from the clock to 5:30. Tell students to draw a line from each clock to its time.

Multiplying, the Factor 5
pages 125-126

Objective
To multiply by the factor 5

Materials
none

Mental Math
Ask students to multiply 4 by:
1. the number of ears one person has. ($4 \times 2 = 8$)
2. the number of feet two students have. ($4 \times 4 = 16$)
3. the number of noses in a crowd of 7. ($4 \times 7 = 28$)
4. the number of their toes. ($4 \times 10 = 40$)

Skill Review
Have students make up a multiplication chart. Tell them to write 2, 3, 4 along the top, 2 through 10 along the side. Tell them to fill in the chart by multiplying each top number by each side number.

Multiplying, the Factor 5

Each key on a calculator has a special job to do. How many keys are there on the calculator keyboard?

We need to find the total number of keys on the calculator.

We can see there are __5__ rows of keys.

Each row has __5__ keys.

We can add. $5 + 5 + 5 + 5 + 5 =$ __25__

We can also multiply.

$5 \times 5 =$ __25__ $\begin{array}{r} 5 \\ \times 5 \\ \hline 25 \end{array}$

There are __25__ keys on the calculator keyboard.

Getting Started

Use both addition and multiplication to show how many are in the picture.

1. 🗝🗝🗝🗝🗝
   🗝🗝🗝🗝🗝
   🗝🗝🗝🗝🗝
   🗝🗝🗝🗝🗝

   $5 + 5 + 5 + 5 =$ __20__
   $4 \times 5 =$ __20__
   $5 \times 4 =$ __20__

Multiply.

2. $\begin{array}{r} 3 \\ \times 5 \\ \hline 15 \end{array}$

3. $\begin{array}{r} 8 \\ \times 5 \\ \hline 40 \end{array}$

4. $5 \times 6 =$ __30__

5. $9 \times 5 =$ __45__

(one hundred twenty-five) **125**

Teaching the Lesson

Introducing the Problem Have students look at the calculator illustrated while you read the problem. Identify the question and explain that there are several ways they could answer it. Have students read the information sentences, filling in the information required. (5 rows, 5 keys) Read each sentence and tell students to do the indicated operation in their text while one student writes it on the board. Read the solution sentence aloud and have a student give the answer while the others complete that sentence in their texts. (30)

Developing the Skill Have students start at 5 and count aloud by five's through 50. Ask a volunteer to continue through 100. Explain that this may seem easy because they are used to counting out nickels. Because five is also half of ten, and when counting by fives, every other number will be a multiple of ten. Now write these addition problems on the board and have students work them: $5 + 5 =$, $5 + 5 + 5 =$, $5 + 5 + 5 + 5 =$. (10, 15, 20) Next to each of these problems write the multiplication problem that corresponds. ($5 \times 2, 5 \times 3, 5 \times 4$) Have volunteers put the rest of the addition and multiplication problems for the factor five on the board, 5×5 through 5×10.

■ A list of **Materials** helps the teacher reduce class preparation time.

■ The **Mental Math** exercise gives the teacher an opportunity to brush-up on skills at the beginning of each day's lesson.

■ **Skill Review** bridges new skills with previously-taught skills for total reinforcement.

■ The **Teaching the Lesson** section is meant to give practical suggestions for introducing the problem and developing the skill. Specific suggestions for an effective presentation of the model are made in **Introducing the Problem.**

■ In **Developing the Skill,** the teacher is given suggestions for presenting and developing the algorithm, skill, and/or concept. Where practical, recommendations are made for the use of manipulatives.

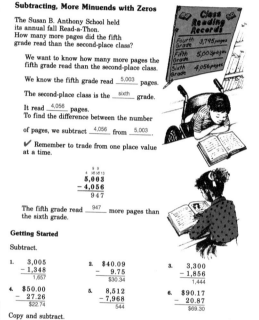

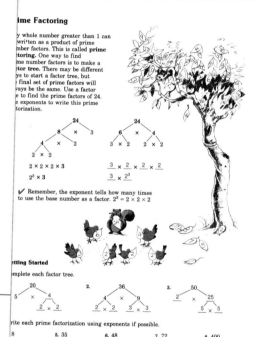

Zeros in Minuend

pages 69-70

Objective

To subtract 4- or 5-digit numbers when minuends have zeros

Materials

* thousands, hundreds, tens, ones jars
* place value materials

Mental Math

Tell students to answer true or false:

1. 776 has 77 tens. (T)
2. 10 hundreds < 1,000. (F)
3. 46 is an odd number. (F)
4. 926 can be rounded to 920. (F)
5. 72 hours = 3 days. (T)
6. 42 ÷ 6 > 7 × 1. (F)
7. 1/3 of 18 = 1/2 of 12. (T)
8. perimeter = L × W. (F)

Skill Review

Write 4 numbers of 3- to 5-digits each on the board. Have students arrange the numbers in order, from the least to the greatest, and then read the numbers as they would appear if written from the greatest to the least. Repeat for more sets of 4 or 5 numbers.

Teaching the Lesson

Introducing the Problem Have a student read the problem. Ask students what 2 problems are to be solved. (which class read the second-highest number of pages and how many more pages the first-place fifth graders read) Ask students how we can find out which class came in second place. (arrange numbers from the table in order from greatest to least) Ask a student to write the numbers from greatest to least on the board. (5,003, 4,056, 3,795) Have students complete the sentences and work through the model problem with them.

Developing the Skill Write **4,000–2,875** vertically on the board. Ask students if a trade is needed to subtract the ones column. (yes) Tell students that since there are no tens and no hundreds, we must trade 1 thousand for 10 hundreds. Show the 3 thousands and 10 hundreds left. Now tell students we can trade 1 hundred for 10 tens. Show the trade with 9 hundreds and 10 tens left. Tell students we can now trade 1 ten for 10 ones. Show the trade so that 9 tens and 10 ones are left. Tell students we can now subtract each column beginning with the ones column and working to the left. Show students the subtraction to a solution of **1,125.** Remind students to add the subtrahend and the difference to check the work. Repeat for more problems with zeros in the minuend.

Subtracting, More Minuends with Zeros

The Susan B. Anthony School held its annual fall Read-a-Thon. How many more pages did the fifth grade read than the second-place class?

We want to know how many more pages the fifth grade read than the second-place class.

We know the fifth grade read ___5,003___ pages.

The second-place class is the ___sixth___ grade.

It read ___4,056___ pages.
To find the difference between the number of pages, we subtract ___4,056___ from ___5,003___.

✔ Remember to trade from one place value at a time.

$$\begin{array}{r} \overset{9\ 9}{\cancel{5},\overset{9}{\cancel{0}}\overset{9\ 13}{\cancel{0}3}} \\ -\ 4,056 \\ \hline 947 \end{array}$$

The fifth grade read ___947___ more pages than the sixth grade.

Getting Started

Subtract.

1. $\begin{array}{r} 3,005 \\ -1,348 \\ \hline 1,657 \end{array}$
2. $\begin{array}{r} \$40.09 \\ -\ \ 9.75 \\ \hline \$30.34 \end{array}$
3. $\begin{array}{r} 3,300 \\ -1,856 \\ \hline 1,444 \end{array}$
4. $\begin{array}{r} \$50.00 \\ -\ 27.26 \\ \hline \$22.74 \end{array}$
5. $\begin{array}{r} 8,512 \\ -7,968 \\ \hline 544 \end{array}$
6. $\begin{array}{r} \$90.17 \\ -\ 20.87 \\ \hline \$69.30 \end{array}$

Copy and subtract.

7. 26,007 − 18,759
   7,248
8. 70,026 − 23,576
   46,450
9. $900.05 − $267.83
   $632.22

69

Prime Factoring

...y whole number greater than 1 can ...written as a product of prime ...mber factors. This is called **prime ...ctoring.** One way to find ...me number factors is to make a ...ctor tree. There may be different ...ys to start a factor tree, but ...final set of prime factors will ...ways be the same. Use a factor ...e to find the prime factors of 24. ...e exponents to write this prime ...torization.

```
     24              24
    /  \            /  \
   8    × 3        6   ×  4
  / \              / \   / \
 4  × 2          3 × 2 2 × 2
/ \
2 × 2
```

2 × 2 × 2 × 3   3 × 2 × 2 × 2
2³ × 3   3 × 2³

✔ Remember, the exponent tells how many times to use the base number as a factor. 2³ = 2 × 2 × 2

Getting Started

Complete each factor tree.

1. ```
      20
     /  \
    5 ×  4
        / \
       2 × 2
   ```
2. ```
      36
     /  \
    4  ×  9
   / \   / \
  2 × 2 3 × 3
   ```
3. ```
      50
     /  \
    2 ×  25
        / \
       5 × 5
   ```

Write each prime factorization using exponents if possible.

4. 8   5. 35   6. 48   7. 72   8. 400
   2³   5 × 7   2⁴ × 3   2³ × 3²   2⁴ × 5²

99

Developing the Skill Point out that when a prime number is used more than once in the prime factoring, it can be expressed with an **exponent.** Remind students that 2³ is the same as 2 × 2 × 2. Stress that the 3 in 2³ is an exponent, and that this exponent tells the number of times 2 is used as a factor. Have students complete each of the following factor trees and then write each prime factorization using exponents:

```
        50                  28
       /  \                /  \
      2 ×  (25)           7 × (4)
          / \                 / \
 (2) × (5) × (5)   (7) × (2) × (2)
      (2 × 5²)          (7 × 2²)
```

...omposite ...ctors. Tell ...e factor- ...h aloud. ...he tree ...r tree on ...at a num- ...of prime

...d. Have ...f each

```

FREQUENT ATTENTION IS GIVEN TO CORRECTING COMMON ERRORS, ENRICHMENT AND OPTIONAL EXTRA-CREDIT ACTIVITIES!

These comprehensive **Teacher's Editions** are intended to provide the teacher with a convenient, well-structured approach to teaching mathematics. From motivating introductory exercises to challenging extension activities, *Modern Curriculum Press*

Mathematics **Teacher's Editions** suggest a complete step-by-step plan to insure successful learning. The succinct lesson plans help the teacher provide solid math instruction to students.

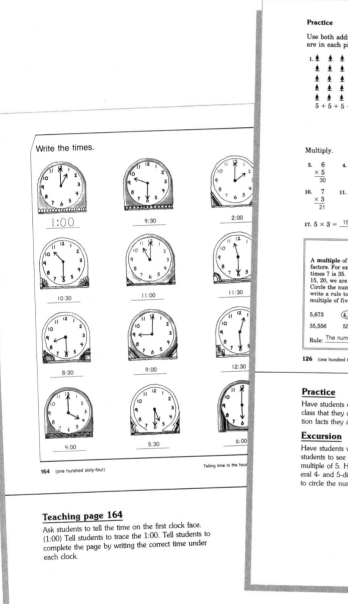

Practice

Use both addition and multiplication to show how many are in each picture.

1. 5 + 5 + 5 + 5 + 5 + 5 + 5 = __35__

7 × 5 = __35__

5 × 7 = __35__

2. 5 + 5 + 5 + 5 + 5 + 5 = __30__

6 × 5 = __30__

5 × 6 = __30__

Multiply.

3. 6 × 5 = 30	4. 4 × 3 = 12	5. 3 × 5 = 15	6. 5 × 7 = 35	7. 8 × 5 = 40	8. 9 × 4 = 36	9. 4 × 8 = 32
10. 7 × 3 = 21	11. 4 × 5 = 20	12. 5 × 9 = 45	13. 5 × 5 = 25	14. 2 × 5 = 10	15. 6 × 4 = 24	16. 5 × 2 = 10

17. 5 × 3 = __15__   18. 6 × 5 = __30__   19. 5 × 7 = __35__   20. 5 × 9 = __45__

EXCURSION

A **multiple** of 5 is a number that has 5 as one of its factors. For example, 35 is a multiple of 5 because 5 times 7 is 35. When we count by fives, like 5, 10, 15, 20, we are naming some more multiples of five. Circle the numbers that are multiples of five. Then write a rule to use for deciding if a number is a multiple of five.

5,673   (4,220)   (7,110)   (3,245)   (23,320)   4,373   (77,770)

35,556   55,551   (47,315)   2,222   (40,000)   21,502   (1,115)

Rule: The number must end in 0 or 5.

126 (one hundred twenty-six)

Correcting Common Errors

If students have difficulty learning facts of 5, have them practice with partners. Have them draw a vertical number line from 0 through 50, marking it in intervals of 5. Have one partner write the addition problem to the left of each multiple of five on the number line while the other partner writes the corresponding multiplication problem.

|0
5 |5   (5 × 1)
5 + 5 |10   (5 × 2)
5 + 5 + 5 |15   (5 × 3)
5 + 5 + 5 + 5 |20   (5 × 4)

Enrichment

Ask students how many fives are in 55 if, there are 10 fives in 50. (11) Tell them to complete a multiplication table for fives that goes up to the product 150. Have them use the table to figure the number of nickels in $4.00. (80)

Write the times.

1:00	9:30	2:00
10:30	11:00	11:30
8:30	9:00	12:30
4:00	5:30	6:00

164 (one hundred sixty-four)   Telling time to the hour

Teaching page 164

Ask students to tell the time on the first clock face. (1:00) Tell students to trace the 1:00. Tell students to complete the page by writing the correct time under each clock.

Practice

Have students do all the problems on the page. Remind the class that they can use addition to figure out any multiplication facts they are not sure of.

Excursion

Have students write the multiples of 5 through 200. Help students to see that any number that ends in 0 or 5 is a multiple of 5. Have students write the rule. Now write several 4- and 5-digit numbers on the board and ask students to circle the numbers that are multiples of 5.

Extra Credit   *Logic*

Write the following on the board:

WOW	TOT	POP	BIB
525	969	343	5445

Ask students what all of these have in common. Explain they are palindromes, or words or numbers which are the same whether they are read forward or backward. Also, explain 302 is not a palindrome, but if you reverse the numbers and add, it will make a palindrome:

302
+203
505

Using this method, ask students what palindrome they can make with these numbers: 36; (99) 342; (585) 4,205; (9,229) 3,406 (9,449). Have students list some other numbers which, when reversed and added, will form a palindrome.

126

- Follow up activities focus on **Correcting Common Errors, Enrichment,** and **Extra Credit** suggestions.

- In the **Correcting Common Errors** feature, a common error pattern is explored and a method of remediation is recommended. Collectively, all the **Correcting Common Errors** features in any chapter constitute a complete set of the common errors likely to be committed by the students when working in that area of mathematics.

- **Enrichment** activities are a direct extension of the skills being taught. Students can do these activities on their own while the teacher works with those students who need more help.

- **Extra Credits** are challenging independent activities to expand the mathematical experiences of the students. The **Extra Credit** section encompasses a wide variety of activities and projects and introduces and extends skills taught in the normal basal curriculum—including statistics, logic, and probability.

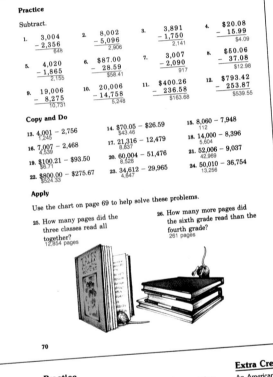

Practice

Subtract.

1. 3,004 − 2,356	2. 8,002 − 5,096	3. 3,891 − 1,750	4. $20.08 − 15.99
648	2,906	2,141	$4.09
5. 4,020 − 1,865	6. $87.00 − 28.59	7. 3,007 − 2,090	8. $50.06 − 37.08
2,155	$58.41	917	$12.98
9. 19,006 − 8,275	10. 20,006 − 14,758	11. $400.26 − 236.58	12. $793.42 − 253.87
10,731	5,248	$163.68	$539.55

Copy and Do

13. 4,001 − 2,756
1,245
14. $70.05 − $26.59
$43.46
15. 8,060 − 7,948
112
16. 7,007 − 2,468
4,539
17. 21,316 − 12,479
8,837
18. 14,000 − 8,396
5,604
19. $100.21 − $93.50
$6.71
20. 60,004 − 51,476
8,528
21. 52,006 − 9,037
42,969
22. $800.00 − $275.67
$524.33
23. 34,612 − 29,965
4,647
24. 50,010 − 36,754
13,256

Apply

Use the chart on page 69 to help solve these problems.

25. How many pages did the three classes read all together?
12,854 pages

26. How many more pages did the sixth grade read than the fourth grade?
261 pages

70

Correcting Common Errors

Some students may bring down the numbers that are being subtracted when there are zeros in the minuend.

INCORRECT   CORRECT

3,006   3,006
− 1,425   − 1,425
2,421   1,581

Have students work in pairs and use play money to model a problem such as $300 − $142, where they see that they must trade 3 hundreds for 2 hundreds, 9 tens, and 10 ones before they can subtract.

Enrichment

Tell students to find out the year in which each member of their family was born, and make a chart to show how old each will be in the year 2000.

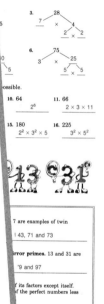

3. 28
7 × 4
2² × 2

6. 75
3 × 25
5 × 5

10. 64
2⁶
11. 66
2 × 3 × 11
15. 180
2² × 3² × 5
16. 225
3² × 5²

7 are examples of twin
43, 71 and 73
rror primes. 13 and 31 are
9 and 97
f its factors except itself.
f the perfect numbers less

Correcting Common Errors

Some students do not write the prime factorization of a number correctly because they cannot identify prime numbers. Have them work with partners to name all the prime numbers from 1 to 50 and write them on an index card. The students can use these cards as a guide for this work.

Enrichment

Provide this alternative method of dividing to find prime factorization of a number. Tell students they must always divide by a prime number.

2 | 36   36 = 2² × 3²
2 | 18
3 | 9
3

Have students use this method to find the prime factorization of:
120 (2³ × 3 × 5); 250 (5³ × 2); 1,000 (2³ × 5³); 72 (3² × 2³)

Practice

Remind students to begin with the ones column, work to the left and trade from one place value at a time. Have students complete the page independently.

Extra Credit   *Biography*

An American inventor, Samuel Morse, struggled for many years before his inventions, the electric telegraph and Morse code were recognized. Morse was born in Massachusetts in 1791, and studied to be an artist. On a trip home from Europe, Morse heard his shipmates discussing the idea of sending electricity over wire. Intrigued, Morse spent the rest of the voyage formulating his ideas about how this could be accomplished. Morse taught at a university in New York City, and used his earnings to continue development of his telegraph. After five years, Morse demonstrated his invention, but found very little support. After years of requests for support, Congress finally granted Morse $30,000 to test his invention. He dramatically strung a telegraph wire from Washington, D.C. to Baltimore, Maryland, and relayed the message, "What hath God wrought" using Morse code. Morse's persistence finally won him wealth and fame. A statue honoring him was unveiled in New York City one year before his death in 1872.

prob-
tly.

enes as
ct num-
o com-

Extra Credit   *Applications*

Have a student write the primary United States time zones across the board. Discuss how this pattern continues around the world. Divide students into groups and provide them with globes or flat maps. Have students choose various cities in the United States and elsewhere in the world, and determine what the time would be in those cities when it is 6:00 AM in their home city. Have students make another list of cities without times indicated to exchange with classmates to figure time comparisons.

100

Bibliography

Grades K-3

Bake and Taste. Tucson, AZ: MindPlay, 1990. (Apple, IBM)

Educators looking for a slightly different program might be interested in *Bake and Taste.* Students are guided through the process of making a dessert of their choosing. In the course of the baking fun, students work on the skills of measuring, counting, and figuring fractions. The desserts can really be baked and eaten. Teacher or parent involvement is necessary for nonreaders.

Elastic Lines: The Electronic Geoboard. Education Development Center. Pleasantville, NY: Sunburst Communications, 1989. (Apple, IBM)

This is a simulation of rubber bands being stretched over pegboards of variable size and type. Students can practice the skills of visualizing shapes in space and estimating. Primary students will enjoy the most elementary of the concepts in this program that is recommended for Grades 2 through 8.

Exploring Measurement, Time, and Money, Level II. Dayton, NJ: IBM, 1990. (IBM)

This program combines a tutorial with drill and practice focusing on linear measurement, time measurement, and money. Students practice such skills as comparing measurements and making change.

Hop to It! Pleasantville, NY: Sunburst Communications, 1990. (Apple)

This program focuses on using problem solving skills to better understand addition, subtraction, and the number line. Students must choose the operation that will help animals capture objects along a number line. The number line can begin anywhere between −10 and 10.

KidsMath. Scotts Valley, CA: Great Wave Software, 1989. (Macintosh)

KidsMath offers eight games to help students learn basic math skills such as addition, subtraction, multiplication, division, and fractions. Students will be delighted with the attractive graphics and animations.

Math Rabbit. Fremont, CA: The Learning Company, 1989. (Apple, IBM, Macintosh)

A colorful program which introduces basic number concepts such as counting, addition, subtraction, and number relationships. Recommended for preschool to Grade 1.

Math Shop Jr. Jefferson City, MO: Scholastic, 1989. (Apple, IBM, Mac)

As they pretend to run stores in a mall, students work on real-life situations in which they use addition, subtraction, multiplication, division, odd and even numbers, estimation, and coins.

New Math Blaster Plus. Torrance, CA: Davidson & Associates, 1990. (Apple, IBM, Mac)

With its fast-paced, arcade-like games, this program will be a favorite of all students. It includes problems in addition, subtraction, multiplication, division, fractions, decimals, and percents. Teachers can print customized tests.

Number Munchers. Minneapolis, MN: MECC, 1986. (Apple, IBM, Mac)

Students control a number-munching monster. If the monster eats the correct answer, the student moves on to the next level. The program drills concepts such as multiples 2–20, factoring of numbers 3–99, prime numbers 1–99, equality and inequality.

NumberMaze. Scotts Valley, CA: Great Wave Software, 1988. (Mac)

To travel through the mazes, students must answer questions involving basic math concepts. Some word problems are included.

Picture Chompers. Minneapolis, MN: MECC, 1990. (Apple)

Students practice classification skills in this fast-paced game. User guides a pair of teeth around a grid and the teeth eat objects of specified color, pattern, size, or shape.

Stickybear Math. Norfolk, CT: Optimum Resource, Inc., 1984. (Apple, IBM)

Students solve simple addition and subtraction problems to get the colorful Stickybear out of sticky situations.

Super Solvers: Treasure Mountain! Fremont, CA: The Learning Company, 1990. (IBM)

This program builds problem-solving skills as students try to foil the prankster Morty Maxwell who has stolen the enchanted crown. Math, reading, thinking, and science skills are required.

Winker's World of Patterns. Scotts Valley, CA: Wings for Learning, 1990. (Apple, IBM)

Students practice recognizing and remembering patterns involving colors, numbers, and words.

Scope and Sequence

	K	1	2	3	4	5	6
READINESS							
Attributes	■						
Shapes	■	■					
Colors	■	■	■				
NUMERATION							
On-to-one correspondence	■						
Understanding numbers	■	■	■				
Writing numbers	■	■					
Counting objects	■	■	■				
Sequencing numbers	■	■	■	■	■		
Numbers before and after	■	■	■	■	■		
Ordering numbers			■	■	■	■	■
Comparing numbers	■	■	■	■	■	■	■
Grouping numbers	■	■	■	■	■		
Ordinal numbers	■	■	■	■			
Number words		■	■	■	■	■	■
Expanded numbers		■	■	■	■	■	■
Place value		■	■	■	■	■	■
Skip-counting		■	■	■	■	■	
Roman numerals			■	■	■		
Rounding numbers				■	■	■	■
Squares and square roots				■			

Scope and Sequence

	K	1	2	3	4	5	6
Primes and composites				■	■	■	■
Multiples					■	■	■
Least common multiples						■	■
Greatest common factors						■	■
Exponents							■
ADDITION							
Addition facts	■	■	■	■	■	■	■
Fact families		■	■	■	■	■	
Missing addends	■	■	■	■	■		
Adding money	■	■	■	■	■	■	■
Column addition		■	■	■	■	■	■
Two-digit addends		■	■	■	■	■	
Multidigit addends			■	■	■	■	■
Addition with trading		■	■	■	■	■	■
Basic properties of addition				■	■	■	■
Estimating sums				■	■	■	■
Addition of fractions				■	■	■	■
Addition of mixed numbers				■	■	■	■
Addition of decimals				■	■	■	■
Rule of order				■	■	■	■
Addition of customary measures						■	■

Scope and Sequence

	K	1	2	3	4	5	6
Addition of integers							■
SUBTRACTION							
Subtraction facts	■	■	■	■	■	■	■
Fact families		■	■	■	■	■	
Missing subtrahends		■	■				
Subtracting money	■	■	■	■	■	■	■
Two-digit numbers		■	■	■	■	■	
Multidigit numbers			■	■	■	■	■
Subtraction with trading		■	■	■	■	■	■
Zeros in the minuend				■	■	■	■
Basic properties of subtraction				■	■	■	■
Estimating differences				■	■	■	■
Subtraction of fractions				■	■	■	■
Subtraction of mixed numbers						■	■
Subtraction of decimals				■	■	■	■
Rule of order				■	■	■	■
Subtraction of customary measures						■	■
Subtraction of integers							■
MULTIPLICATION							
Multiplication facts			■	■	■	■	■
Fact families			■	■	■		

Scope and Sequence

	K	1	2	3	4	5	6
Missing factors					■		
Multiplying money			■	■	■	■	■
Multiplication by powers of ten				■	■	■	■
Multidigit factors				■	■	■	■
Multiplication with trading				■	■	■	■
Basic properties of multiplication			■	■	■	■	■
Estimating products				■	■	■	■
Rule of order				■	■	■	■
Multiples					■	■	■
Least common multiples						■	■
Multiplication of fractions						■	■
Factorization						■	■
Multiplication of mixed numbers							■
Multiplication of decimals					■	■	■
Exponents							■
Multiplication of integers							■
DIVISION							
Division facts				■	■	■	■
Fact families				■	■		
Divisibility rules				■		■	■
Two-digit quotients				■	■	■	■

Scope and Sequence

	K	1	2	3	4	5	6
Remainders				■	■	■	■
Multidigit quotients					■	■	■
Zeros in quotients					■	■	■
Division by multiples of ten					■	■	■
Two-digit divisors					■	■	■
Properties of division					■	■	
Averages				■	■	■	■
Greatest common factors						■	■
Division of fractions						■	■
Division of mixed numbers						■	■
Division of decimals						■	■
Division by powers of ten						■	■
MONEY							
Counting pennies	■	■	■	■	■		
Counting nickels	■	■	■	■	■		
Counting dimes	■	■	■	■	■		
Counting quarters		■	■	■	■		
Counting half-dollars			■	■	■		
Counting dollar bills		■	■	■	■		
Writing dollar and cents signs		■	■	■	■	■	■
Matching money with prices	■	■	■				

Scope and Sequence

	K	1	2	3	4	5	6
Determining amount of change	■	■	■				
Determining sufficient amount		■	■				
Determining which coins to use		■	■				
Addition	■	■	■	■	■	■	■
Subtraction	■	■	■	■	■	■	■
Multiplication			■	■	■	■	■
Division					■	■	■
Rounding amounts of money				■	■	■	■
Finding fractions of amounts					■	■	■
Buying from a menu or ad			■	■	■	■	■
FRACTIONS							
Understanding equal parts	■	■	■	■			
One half	■	■	■	■			
One fourth	■	■	■	■			
One third	■	■	■	■			
Identifying fractional parts of figures			■	■	■	■	■
Identifying fractional parts of sets			■	■	■	■	■
Finding unit fractions of numbers				■	■	■	
Equivalent fractions				■	■	■	■
Comparing fractions				■	■	■	■
Simplifying fractions					■	■	■

Scope and Sequence

	K	1	2	3	4	5	6
Renaming mixed numbers					■	■	■
Addition of fractions				■	■	■	■
Subtraction of fractions				■	■	■	■
Addition of mixed numbers					■	■	■
Subtraction of mixed numbers						■	■
Multiplication of fractions						■	■
Factorization						■	■
Multiplication of mixed numbers						■	■
Division of fractions						■	■
Division of mixed numbers						■	■
Renaming fractions as decimals							■
Renaming fractions as percents							■
DECIMALS							
Place value				■	■	■	■
Reading decimals				■	■	■	■
Writing decimals				■	■	■	■
Converting fractions to decimals				■	■	■	■
Writing parts of sets as decimals				■	■	■	
Comparing decimals				■	■	■	■
Ordering decimals							■
Addition of decimals				■	■	■	■

Scope and Sequence

	K	1	2	3	4	5	6
Subtraction of decimals				■	■	■	■
Rounding decimals				■		■	■
Multiplication of decimals					■	■	■
Division of decimals						■	■
Renaming decimals as percents							■
GEOMETRY							
Polygons	■	■	■	■	■	■	■
Sides and corners of polygons			■	■	■		
Lines and line segments					■	■	■
Rays and angles					■	■	■
Measuring angles						■	■
Symmetry			■			■	■
Congruency				■	■	■	■
Similar figures					■	■	■
Circles						■	■
MEASUREMENT							
Non-standard units of measure	■	■					
Customary units of measure		■	■	■	■	■	■
Metric units of measure	■	■	■	■	■	■	■
Renaming customary measures					■	■	■
Renaming metric measures					■	■	■

Scope and Sequence

	K	1	2	3	4	5	6
Selecting appropriate units			■	■	■	■	
Estimating measures		■	■	■	■	■	
Perimeter by counting	■	■	■				
Perimeter by formula			■	■	■	■	■
Area of polygons by counting			■	■			
Area of polygons by formula					■	■	■
Volume by counting				■			
Volume by formula					■	■	■
Addition of measures						■	■
Subtraction of measures						■	■
Circumference of circles							■
Area of circles							■
Surface area of space figures							■
Estimating temperatures				■			
Reading temperature scales			■	■			
TIME							
Ordering events	■						
Relative time	■						
Matching values	■	■	■	■	■		
Calendars	■	■	■	■			
Days of the week	■	■	■	■			

Scope and Sequence

	K	1	2	3	4	5	6
Months of the year	■	■	■	■			
Telling time to the hour	■	■	■	■			
Telling time to the half-hour		■	■	■			
Telling time to the five-minutes			■	■	■		
Telling time to the minute			■	■	■		
Understanding AM and PM					■		
Time zones					■		
GRAPHING							
Tables		■	■	■	■	■	■
Bar graphs	■	■	■	■	■	■	■
Picture graphs			■	■	■		■
Line graphs					■	■	■
Circle graphs						■	■
Tree diagrams						■	
Histograms							■
Ordered pairs				■	■	■	■
PROBABILITY							
Understanding probability					■	■	■
Listing outcomes					■	■	■
Means and medians						■	
Circle graphs						■	■

Scope and Sequence

	K	1	2	3	4	5	6
Tree diagrams						■	■
Histograms							■
RATIOS AND PERCENTS							
Understanding ratios					■	■	■
Equal ratios						■	■
Proportions							■
Scale drawings						■	■
Ratios as percents						■	■
Percents as fractions						■	■
Fractions as percents						■	■
Finding the percents of numbers						■	■
INTEGERS							
Understanding integers							■
Addition of integers							■
Subtraction of integers							■
Multiplication of integers							■
Graphing integers on coordinate planes							■
PROBLEM SOLVING							
Creating an algorithm from a word problem		■	■	■	■	■	■
Selecting the correct operation		■	■	■	■	■	■
Using data			■	■	■	■	■

Scope and Sequence

	K	1	2	3	4	5	6
Reading a chart			■	■	■	■	■
Using a four-step plan				■	■	■	■
Drawing a picture				■	■	■	■
Acting it out				■	■	■	■
Making a list				■	■	■	■
Making a tally				■	■	■	
Making a table				■	■	■	■
Making a graph				■	■	■	
Guessing and checking					■	■	■
Looking for a pattern					■	■	■
Making a model					■		
Restating the problem					■	■	■
Selecting notation					■	■	■
Writing an open sentence					■	■	■
Using a formula					■	■	■
Identifying a subgoal						■	■
Working backwards						■	■
Determining missing data						■	■
Collecting data						■	■
Solving a simpler but related problem						■	■
Making a flow chart							■

Scope and Sequence

	K	1	2	3	4	5	6
CALCULATORS							
Calculator codes				■	■	■	■
Equal key				■	■	■	■
Operation keys				■	■	■	■
Square root key				■			
Clear key				■	■	■	■
Clear entry key				■	■	■	■
Money				■	■	■	■
Unit prices				■	■	■	
Fractions				■	■		
Percents					■		
Banking				■	■	■	
Inventories					■		
Averages					■		
Rates						■	■
Formulas						■	■
Cross multiplication							■
Functions							■
Binary numbers							■
Repeating decimals							■
Statistics							■

Table of Common Errors

This **Table of Common Errors** is designed to help the teacher understand the thinking patterns and potential errors that students commonly commit in the course of learning the content in *Modern Curriculum Press Mathematics.* Familiarity with this list can help the teacher forestall errant thinking and save much time used in reteaching.

In the **Correcting Common Errors** feature in each lesson in *Modern Curriculum Press Mathematics,* abundant suggestions are made to remediate situations where students might have misconceptions of other difficulties with a skill. These suggestions make frequent use of manipulatives and cooperative learning.

Numeration

1. The student transposes digits when writing the number of objects in a picture.

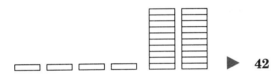

▶ **42**

2. When counting objects in an array, the student counts some objects twice or fails to count each object in the array.

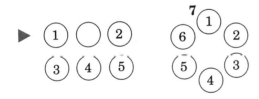

3. The student mistakes one number for another because it has been carelessly written.

4. When writing numerals for a number that is expressed in words, the student fails to write zeros as placeholders where they are needed.

Write five hundred four in numerals.

▶ **54**

5. The student confuses the names of place values.

6. The student fails to write the money sign and/or decimal point in an answer involving money.

$3.52
+   2
▶ **804**

7. The student does not relate money to what has been learned about place value.

For example, the student does not relate dimes to tens place.

8. When ordering whole numbers, the student incorrectly compares single digits regardless of place value.

For example, the student thinks that **203 is less than 45** because 2 is less than 4 and 3 is less than 5.

9. The student rounds down when the last significant digit is 5.

▶   75 ≈ **70**

10. The student rounds progressively from digit to digit until the designated place value is reached.

   Round $3.45 to dollars.

   ▶ **$3.45 ≈ $3.50 ≈ $4**

11. When counting past twenty, the student incorrectly repeats the number pattern between ten and twenty.

   ▶ . . . eighteen, nineteen, twenty, **twenty-eleven, twenty-twelve** . . .

12. The student changes the common interval when skip-counting.

   ▶ 2, 4, 6, 8, **11, 14, 17**

13. The student starts off skip-counting but reverts to a counting series after a few numbers.

   ▶ 3, 6, 9, **10, 11, 12,** . . .

14. The student fails to count money from the largest bills and coins to the smallest.

15. The student thinks since five pennies equal a nickel, that other coin relationships are also based on a five to one ratio.

   ▶ **5** quarters = 1 dollar

16. The student counts all coins as one cent regardless of their value.

17. The student confuses the greater than and less than signs.

   ▶ 56 < 29
       34 > 55

Addition and Subtraction

1. The student is unsure of the basic facts of addition and/or subtraction.

2. The student copies the problem incorrectly.

   Find the sum of 6, 5, and 9.

   ▶
   $$\begin{array}{r} 6 \\ \mathbf{4} \\ +9 \\ \hline \mathbf{19} \end{array}$$

3. The student makes simple addition errors when adding numbers with two or more digits.

   $$\begin{array}{r} 25 \\ +63 \\ \hline \end{array}$$
   ▶ **87**

4. The student thinks that a number plus zero is zero.

   ▶ **6 + 0 = 0**

5. The student adds during a subtraction computation, or vice versa.

   $$\begin{array}{rr} 56 & 75 \\ +23 & -28 \\ \hline \end{array}$$
   ▶ **33   103**

6. The student computes horizontal equations from left to right regardless of the operation.

   ▶ **3 + 2 × 5 = 25**

7. The student adds or subtracts before multiplying or dividing in a horizontal equation.

▶ $3 \times \mathbf{4 + 6} \times 2 = 60$

8. When doing a computation involving several numbers, the student omits a number.

Find the sum of 23, 36, 54, and 75.

$$
\begin{array}{r}
23 \\
36 \\
+75 \\
\hline
\mathbf{134}
\end{array}
$$

9. The student forgets the partial sum when adding a column of addends.

$$
\begin{array}{r}
\mathbf{3} \\
\mathbf{9} \\
+4 \\
\hline
\mathbf{4}
\end{array}
$$

10. The student omits the regrouped value.

$$
\begin{array}{r}
75 \\
+46 \\
\hline
\mathbf{111}
\end{array}
$$

11. The student fails to rename and places more than one digit in a column in an addition problem.

$$
\begin{array}{r}
36 \\
+78 \\
\hline
\mathbf{1,014}
\end{array}
$$

12. In an addition problem, the student writes the tens digit as part of the sum and regroups the ones.

$$
\begin{array}{r}
\mathbf{4} \\
36 \\
+78 \\
\hline
\mathbf{141}
\end{array}
$$

13. The student renames when it is not necessary.

$$
\begin{array}{r}
\mathbf{1} \\
32 \\
+45 \\
\hline
\mathbf{87}
\end{array}
$$

14. In an addition problem with a zero in the first addend, the student aligns the digits of the second addend with the nonzero digits in the first.

Add 307 and 12.

$$
\begin{array}{r}
307 \\
+1\ 2 \\
\hline
\mathbf{409}
\end{array}
$$

15. The student does not align the numbers properly when adding or subtracting whole numbers.

$$
\begin{array}{r}
62 \\
+39 \\
\hline
\mathbf{659}
\end{array}
$$

16. The student rounds the answer rather than the components of the problem.

Estimate the sum of 35 and 49.

$$
\begin{array}{r}
35 \\
+49 \\
\hline
\mathbf{84} \approx \mathbf{80}
\end{array}
$$

17. The student incorrectly adds from left to right.

$$
\begin{array}{r}
1 \\
37 \\
+82 \\
\hline
\mathbf{110}
\end{array}
$$

18. The student confuses addition and subtraction by one with either addition and subtraction of zero or with multiplication by one.

▶ $5 + 1 = \mathbf{5}$
$5 - 1 = \mathbf{5}$

19. The student makes simple subtraction errors when subtracting numbers with two or more digits.

$$
\begin{array}{r}
116 \\
\cancel{26} \\
-19 \\
\hline
\mathbf{6}
\end{array}
$$

20. The student thinks that a number minus zero is zero.

▶ $6 - \mathbf{0} = \mathbf{0}$

21. The student thinks that zero minus another number is zero.

▶ $\mathbf{0} - 6 = \mathbf{0}$

22. When creating fact families, the student incorrectly applies commutativity to subtraction.

$8 - 5 = 3$
$8 - 3 = 5$
▶ $\mathbf{5 - 8 = 3}$
$\mathbf{3 - 8 = 5}$

23. The student brings down the digit in the subtrahend when the corresponding minuend digit is a zero.

$$\begin{array}{r} 50 \\ +36 \\ \hline 26 \end{array}$$
▶

24. In a multidigit subtraction problem, the student correctly renames the zero in the tens place but does not decrease the digit to the left of the zero.

▶ $$\begin{array}{r} {}^{9\,13} \\ 4\,\cancel{0}\,\cancel{3} \\ -2\,5\,6 \\ \hline 2\,4\,7 \end{array}$$

25. In a multidigit subtraction problem, the student ignores the zero and regroups from the digit to the left of the zero.

▶ $$\begin{array}{r} {}^{3\ \ 13} \\ \cancel{4}\,0\,\cancel{3} \\ -2\,5\,6 \\ \hline 5\,7 \end{array}$$

26. In a multidigit subtraction problem, the student correctly regroups from the digit to the left of the zero and renames the zero as ten, but fails to reduce the ten by one when the second regrouping is done.

▶ $$\begin{array}{r} {}^{1\,10\,14} \\ \cancel{2}\,\cancel{0}\,\cancel{4} \\ -1\,5\,5 \\ \hline 5\,9 \end{array}$$

27. The student does not regroup, but finds the difference between the smaller digit and the larger one regardless of their position and function.

$$\begin{array}{r} 35 \\ -29 \\ \hline 14 \end{array}$$
▶

28. The student does not decrease the digit to the left after regrouping.

▶ $$\begin{array}{r} {}^{15} \\ 3\,\cancel{5} \\ -2\,9 \\ \hline 1\,6 \end{array}$$

29. Instead of regrouping in a subtraction problem, the student incorrectly thinks that if you take a larger digit from a smaller one, there will be nothing left.

$$\begin{array}{r} 35 \\ -29 \\ \hline 10 \end{array}$$
▶

30. In regrouping, the student thinks that the renamed value is found by subtracting the two digits of the same place value.

▶ $$\begin{array}{r} {}^{5\,13} \\ 4\,\cancel{9}\,\cancel{3} \\ -\ \ 4\,5 \\ \hline 4\,1\,8 \end{array}$$

Multiplication

1. The student does not understand the connection between repeated addition and multiplication.

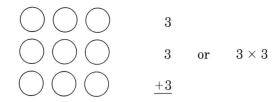

$$
\begin{array}{r}
3 \\
3 \quad \text{or} \quad 3 \times 3 \\
+3 \\
\end{array}
$$

2. The student is unsure of the basic multiplication facts.

3. The student mistakes a multiplication sign for an addition sign, or vice versa.

   ▶ $6 \times 3 = 9$
       $6 + 3 = 18$

4. The student thinks that one times any number is one.

   ▶ $35 \times 1 = 1$

5. The student confuses multiplication by zero with multiplication by one thinking that any number times zero is that number.

   ▶ $36 \times 0 = 36$

6. The student makes simple multiplication mistakes in multidigit multiplication problems.

   $$
   \begin{array}{r}
   \$3.46 \\
   \times 2 \\
   \hline
   \end{array}
   $$
   ▶ $\$6.72$

7. The student is unsure of how many zeros should be in the product when multiplying by a multiple of ten.

   $$
   \begin{array}{r}
   20 \\
   \times 3 \\
   \hline
   \end{array}
   $$
   ▶ 600

8. The student multiplies the digits from left to right.

   $$
   \begin{array}{r}
   36 \\
   \times 3 \\
   \hline
   \end{array}
   $$
   ▶ 918

9. The student fails to regroup and writes both digits in the product.

   $$
   \begin{array}{r}
   45 \\
   \times 3 \\
   \hline
   \end{array}
   $$
   ▶ 1,215

10. The student writes the tens digit as part of the product and regroups the ones.

    $$
    \begin{array}{r}
    2 \\
    36 \\
    \times 2 \\
    \hline
    \end{array}
    $$
    ▶ 81

11. The student does not regroup or fails to add the regrouped value.

    $$
    \begin{array}{r}
    36 \\
    \times 2 \\
    \hline
    \end{array}
    $$
    ▶ 62

12. When multiplying numbers, the student adds the regrouped digit before multiplying.

    $$
    \begin{array}{r}
    1 \\
    36 \\
    \times 2 \\
    \hline
    \end{array}
    $$
    ▶ 82

1. The student fails to understand the connection between division and multiplication.

   For example, the student does not see the relationship between the fact $3 \times 2 = 6$ and $6 \div 2 = 3$.

2. The student is unsure of the basic division facts.

3. In a division problem, if either term is one, the student thinks the answer must be one.

   ▶ $6 \div 1 = 1$
   ▶ $1 \div 6 = 1$

4. The student confuses division by one with division by the same number.

   ▶ $6 \div 6 = 6$
      $6 \div 1 = 1$

5. The student does not realize that division by zero has no meaning.

   ▶ $6 \div 0 = 6$
      $0 \div 0 = 0$

6. The student places the initial quotient digit over the wrong place value in the dividend.

   ▶
   $$
   \begin{array}{r}
   77\ \text{R1} \\
   2\overline{)15} \\
   14 \\
   \hline
   15 \\
   14 \\
   \hline
   1
   \end{array}
   $$

7. The student ignores initial digits in the dividend that are less than the divisor.

   ▶
   $$
   \begin{array}{r}
   2\ \text{R1} \\
   2\overline{)15} \\
   4 \\
   \hline
   1
   \end{array}
   $$

8. The first estimated partial quotient is too low so the student subtracts and divides again and places the extra digit in the quotient.

   ▶
   $$
   \begin{array}{r}
   1\,14 \\
   3\overline{)72} \\
   3 \\
   \hline
   4 \\
   3 \\
   \hline
   12 \\
   12 \\
   \hline
   \end{array}
   $$

9. The student fails to subtract the last time or fails to record the remainder as part of the quotient.

   ▶
   $$
   \begin{array}{r}
   11 \\
   3\overline{)35} \\
   3 \\
   \hline
   5 \\
   3 \\
   \hline
   \end{array}
   $$

10. The student records the remainder as the last digit of the quotient.

   ▶
   $$
   \begin{array}{r}
   112 \\
   3\overline{)35} \\
   3 \\
   \hline
   5 \\
   3 \\
   \hline
   2
   \end{array}
   $$

11. The student records a remainder that is larger than the divisor.

   ▶
   $$
   \begin{array}{r}
   11\ \text{R5} \\
   3\overline{)38} \\
   3 \\
   \hline
   8 \\
   3 \\
   \hline
   5
   \end{array}
   $$

12. When checking a division problem, the student fails to add the remainder after multiplying the quotient by the divisor.

$$
\begin{array}{r}
15 \text{ R1} \\
3\overline{)46} \\
3 \\
\overline{16} \\
15 \\
\overline{1}
\end{array}
$$

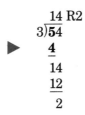

$$
\begin{array}{r}
15 \\
\times 3 \\
\overline{45}
\end{array}
$$

13. The student incorrectly subtracts in a division problem.

$$
\begin{array}{r}
16 \\
3\overline{)38} \\
3 \\
\end{array}
$$

▶
$$
\begin{array}{r}
18 \\
\underline{18}
\end{array}
$$

14. The student fails to subtract before bringing down the next digit in a division problem.

$$
\begin{array}{r}
11 \text{ R1} \\
3\overline{)54} \\
3 \\
\end{array}
$$

▶
$$
\begin{array}{r}
4 \\
3 \\
\overline{1}
\end{array}
$$

15. The student incorrectly multiplies in a division problem.

$$
\begin{array}{r}
14 \text{ R2} \\
3\overline{)54} \\
\end{array}
$$

▶
$$
\begin{array}{r}
4 \\
14 \\
12 \\
\overline{2}
\end{array}
$$

T-39

Measurement

1. The student is confused about how to read fractional measures on a ruler.

   Measure the tape to the nearest quarter-inch.

   ▶ **2** inches

2. The student does not properly align the object to be measured with the point that represents zero on the ruler.

3. The student reads the small hand of a standard clock as minutes and the large hand as hours.

   ▶ **1:15**

4. When the hour hand is between two numbers, the student reads the time for the next hour.

   ▶ **7:50**

5. The student counts the minutes after the hour by starting at the hour hand.

   ▶ **4:20**

6. The student becomes confused about identifying days beyond those in the first week on a calendar.

7. The student uses an incorrect frame of reference when relating temperatures with real-life activities.

8. The student is unfamiliar with the object for which he or she must make an estimate.

Geometry

1. The student does not understand the concept of a two-dimensional figure.

2. The student does not understand the concept of surface area.

3. The student confuses the names of basic polygons.

4. The student thinks any figure is a square if it has 4 equal sides.

For example, the student thinks that figure A and **B** are both squares.

5. The student does not understand that the relative position of a figure has no effect on the figure's shape.

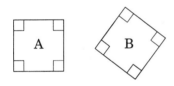

For example, the student thinks that figure **B** is **not** a square.

6. The student identifies a line as a line of symmetry, even though it does not create two congruent parts.

7. The student thinks that right angles must always have the same orientation.

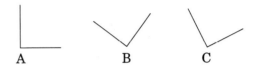

For example, the student thinks that **only** angle A is a right angle.

8. The student omits one or more of the dimensions of a polygon when computing its perimeter.

9. The student confuses the names of basic solid figures.

Fractions

1. The student counts the wrong number of parts of a picture when naming equivalent fractions.

   Write a fraction to represent the shaded parts.

     $\dfrac{3}{4}$

2. The student transposes the numerator and the denominator of a fraction.

3. To find equivalent fractions, the student uses addition or subtraction instead of multiplication or division.

   ▶ $\dfrac{2}{3} + \dfrac{3}{3} = \dfrac{5}{3}$

4. When comparing fractions, the student compares only the numerators.

   ▶ $\dfrac{2}{3} < \dfrac{3}{5}$

5. When comparing fractions with the same numerator, the student compares only the denominators.

   ▶ $\dfrac{1}{4} > \dfrac{1}{3}$

6. When adding fractions, the students add both the numerators and the denominators.

   ▶ $\dfrac{1}{3} + \dfrac{1}{3} = \dfrac{2}{6}$

7. The student fails to multiply by the numerator when finding a fractional part of a number.

   ▶ $\dfrac{2}{5}$ of 15 = 3

Decimals

1. The student confuses the terms used for place values in decimal numbers with those in whole numbers.

   Find the place value of the underlined digit in 4.6̲3.

   ▶ **tens**

2. When writing decimal numbers, the student misplaces the nonzero digit.

   Write three and four hundredths in numerals.

   ▶ 3.4

3. The student omits the decimal point in a decimal number.

   Write fourteen hundredths in numerals.

   ▶ **14**

4. When ordering decimal numbers, the student's answer is based on the number of digits rather than their value.

   For example, the student thinks that 0.23 **is larger than** 0.4 because 23 is larger than 4.

5. When rounding decimal numbers, the student replaces values beyond the designated place value with zeros.

   Round 0.65 to tenths.

   ▶ 0.60

6. When adding or subtracting decimal numbers, the student operates on the whole number parts and the decimal parts of the numbers separately.

   $$\begin{array}{r} 4.6 \\ +3.9 \\ \hline 7.\mathbf{15} \end{array}$$

7. The student places the decimal point in the wrong place in a decimal answer.

   $$\begin{array}{r} 4.6 \\ +3.9 \\ \hline \mathbf{.715} \end{array}$$

Graphing

1. The student fails to divide by the number of addends when computing the average of a group of numbers.

   Find the average of 16, 25, 80, 44, and 90.

   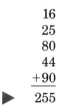

   ```
       16
       25
       80
       44
      +90
   ▶  255
   ```

2. The student always divides by 2 or some other constant number when calculating an average.

   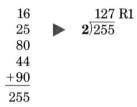

   ```
    16           127 R1
    25    ▶   2)255
    80
    44
   +90
    255
   ```

3. The student reverses the numbers in an ordered pair.

   For example, the student thinks that (3,2) **is the same as** (2,3).

   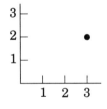

4. The student reads the next larger interval on the scale when reading a bar graph.

   ▶ **6**

5. The student does not refer to a scale when interpreting a picture graph.

   How many books does Tony have?

   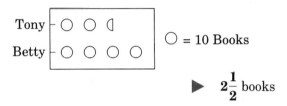

   ○ = 10 Books

   ▶ $2\frac{1}{2}$ books

Problem Solving

1. The student's answer is based only on the size of the objects.

   For example, the student thinks a nickel is worth more than a dime.

2. The student uses the wrong operation or operations to solve a problem.

3. The student does not read the problem but chooses the operation based on the relative size of the numbers in the problem.

4. The student does not read the problem carefully, but selects key words to determine the operation or operations.

5. The student thinks that all numbers in a word problem must be used to get the solution.

6. The student does not use all the relevant information given in a problem.

7. When comparing cost, the student does not find the unit cost of each product.

8. The student thinks that a lower cost always means the better buy.

9. The student does not answer the question posed in the problem.

10. The student is confused because the problem contains unfamiliar words or situations.

    For example, the student does not know that there are 52 cards in a standard deck of cards.

11. The student does not find all the possible solutions because he or she does not create a systematic list.

12. The student does not collect enough data to establish a pattern.

13. The student misreads a chart or table used in a problem.

14. The student's diagram does not faithfully depict the situation in the problem.

15. The student does not check if the data that is being tested makes sense in the problem.

16. The student is confused about what to do with a remainder in a real situation involving division.

17. The student does not check to see that the answer is reasonable.

Calculators

1. The student enters the incorrect codes into the calculator.

2. The student does not enter the codes into the calculator in the correct order.

3. The student does not relate the equal sign on a calculator with the repeated addition function.

4. When entering a subtraction into a calculator, the student enters the subtrahend before the minuend.

5. When entering a division into a calculator, the student enters the divisor before the dividend.

6. The student fails to enter a decimal point at the appropriate place in a calculator code.

MODERN CURRICULUM PRESS

MATHEMATICS

Level B

Richard Monnard   Royce Hargrove

Project Editor............................Dorothy A. Kirk
Editor.....................................Phyllis Sibbing
Design and Production............Remen-Willis Design Group
Illustration ....Roberta Holmes-Landers, Doug Roy,
    Sharron O'Neil, D J Simison, Susan Jaekel, Cynthia Brodie,
                        Victoria Marugg, Valerie Felts
Cover Art...........................© 1993 Adam Peiperl

This book is the property of:

Book No. _____ **Enter information in spaces below as instructed.**

State _____

Province _____

County _____

Parish _____

School district _____

Other _____

Issued to	Year Used	CONDITION	
		ISSUED	RETURNED

PUPILS to whom this textbook is issued must not write on any page or mark any part of it in any way, consumable textbooks excepted.

1. Teachers should see that the pupil's name is clearly written in ink in the spaces above in every book issued.
2. The following items should be used in recording the condition of this book: New, Good; Fair; Poor; Bad.

MODERN CURRICULUM PRESS
13900 Prospect Road, Cleveland, Ohio 44136

A Paramount Communications Company

ISBN 0-8136-3110-6 (Pupil's Edition)
ISBN 0-8136-3117-3 (Teacher's Edition)

Table of Contents

Numbers
0 through 10

pages 1-2

Objectives

To read numbers and number names 0 through 10

To count 0 through 10 and write the number

Materials

*number and number name cards for 0 through 10

Mental Math

Have students name the number that:

1. tells their age.
2. tells how many people are in their family.
3. tells how many children are in their family.
4. rhymes with eleven. (7)
5. names no objects. (0)
6. rhymes with sticks. (6)

Skill Review

Have students count in unison from 0 through 10. Now have a student name a number from 0 through 10. Have students begin with that number and count on through 10. Repeat for more review of counting on to 10. Repeat the exercise to have students write the numbers on the board.

1 BASIC FACTS, SUMS THROUGH 10

Match the set to the number.
Match the number to the number name.

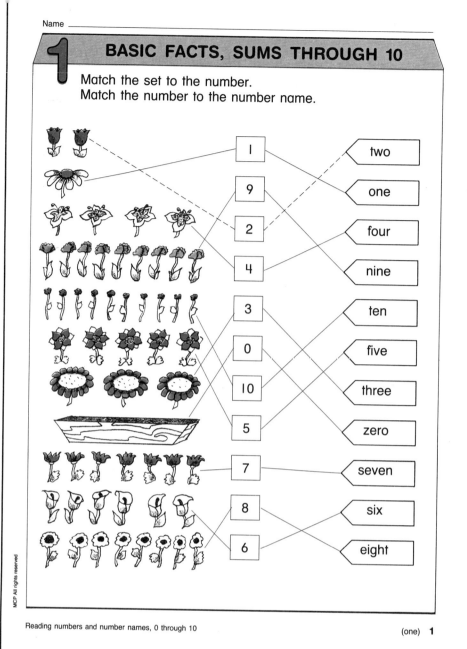

Reading numbers and number names, 0 through 10

(one) **1**

Teaching page 1

Draw 6 circles on the board. Ask students to tell how many circles are drawn. Write **6** and **six** on the board and have students read the number and the number word. Write **four** on the board and have a student draw circles and write the number. (4) Continue for the other numbers from 0 through 10. When all numbers have been represented on the board, have students locate the numbers and number names on the board as you say them in random order.

Have students count the objects in the first group and trace the line to the 2. Tell students to trace the line from the number 2 to its number name. Tell students they are to draw a line from each group to the number which tells how many objects are in the group. Tell students they are then to draw a line from

the number to its number name. Have students complete the page independently.

1

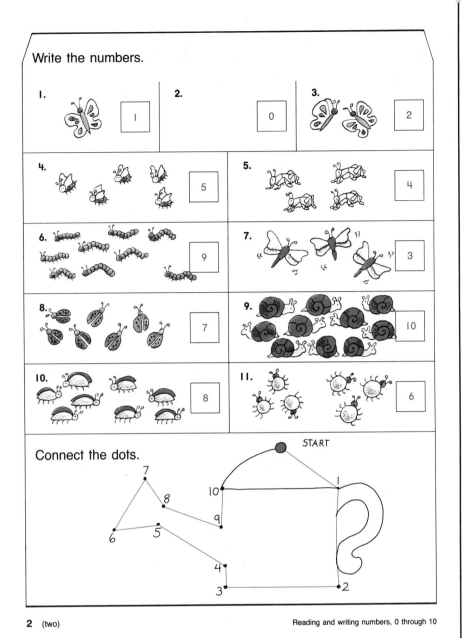

Write the numbers.

1. [butterfly] 1

2. 0

3. [butterflies] 2

4. [flies] 5

5. [grasshoppers] 4

6. [caterpillars] 9

7. [butterflies] 3

8. [ladybugs] 7

9. [snails] 10

10. [beetles] 8

11. [spiders] 6

Connect the dots.

START
7
8
10
9
6 5
4
3 2
1

Reading and writing numbers, 0 through 10

Enrichment

1. Have students cut pictures of objects from catalogs or magazines to show each number from 0 through 10. They should then write the number beside each group.
2. Ask students to make a dot-to-dot picture for the numbers 0 through 10. Then tell them to have a friend connect the dots.
3. Have students play "Concentration" with a friend. They should lay all number and number name cards for 0 through 10 face down. The player who turns over and matches the most numbers to their names wins.

Teaching page 2

Tell students to write in each box the number that tells how many objects there are. Tell students to begin at zero and connect the dots in order from 0 through 10. Have students complete the page independently.

Extra Credit   *Numeration*

Play Simon Says using directions that require counting movements a specified number of times. For example say **Simon says jump 10 times,** and have students count aloud. Then say, **Simon says clap 8 times. Hold up 4 fingers.** Students holding up fingers would be out of the game because it was not prefaced with "Simon says." Continue playing and counting until only one person remains.

As a variation, do a movement such as touching shoulders many times in succession while children count silently. Have a student imitate the movement the same number of times while students count aloud. Continue having one student lead the movements a number of times and another student try to duplicate the movements.

2

Sums through 5

pages 3-4

Objective

To review addition facts for sums through 5

Materials

5 counters

Mental Math

Have students name the number that:
1. comes before 6. (5)
2. follows 9. (10)
3. comes first in their phone number.
4. comes last in their phone number.
5. is 1 more than 8. (9)
6. comes before 1. (0)
7. rhymes with late. (8)
8. is at the bottom of a clock face. (6)

Skill Review

Combine number and number name cards for 0 through 10. Have a student draw a card and illustrate the number on the board by drawing x's, circles or other objects. Continue until all students have participated.

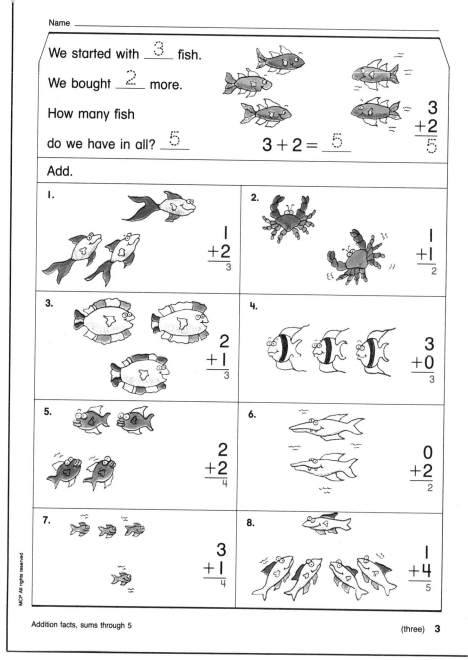

Addition facts, sums through 5

(three) **3**

Teaching page 3

Have students put out 3 counters. Tell students to put the 3 counters into 2 groups. Ask how many are in each group. Write a vertical and horizontal number sentence on the board for each grouping as students name them. If all possible groupings are not given, have students find others until the following are written on the board: **0 + 3 = 3, 1 + 2 = 3, 2 + 1 = 3, 3 + 0 = 3.** Repeat for sums of 1, 2, 4 and 5. Have students tell about the picture at the top of the page. Read the first sentence telling how many fish we started with. Have students trace the 3. Continue reading with students as they trace the 2 and 5. Help students read the number sentence and vertical problem. Then have them trace the 5 in each. Tell students to write the sum for each problem on the page. Have students complete the problems independently.

3

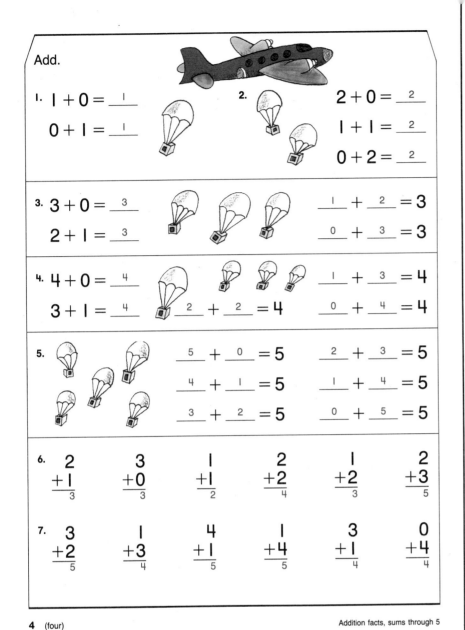

Add.

1. $1 + 0 = \underline{1}$
   $0 + 1 = \underline{1}$

2. $2 + 0 = \underline{2}$
   $1 + 1 = \underline{2}$
   $0 + 2 = \underline{2}$

3. $3 + 0 = \underline{3}$
   $2 + 1 = \underline{3}$
   $\underline{1} + \underline{2} = 3$
   $\underline{0} + \underline{3} = 3$

4. $4 + 0 = \underline{4}$
   $3 + 1 = \underline{4}$
   $\underline{2} + \underline{2} = 4$
   $\underline{1} + \underline{3} = 4$
   $\underline{0} + \underline{4} = 4$

5. $\underline{5} + \underline{0} = 5$
   $\underline{4} + \underline{1} = 5$
   $\underline{3} + \underline{2} = 5$
   $\underline{2} + \underline{3} = 5$
   $\underline{1} + \underline{4} = 5$
   $\underline{0} + \underline{5} = 5$

6.
$$\begin{array}{ccccccccccc} 2 & & 3 & & 1 & & 2 & & 1 & & 2 \\ +1 & & +0 & & +1 & & +2 & & +2 & & +3 \\ \hline 3 & & 3 & & 2 & & 4 & & 3 & & 5 \end{array}$$

7.
$$\begin{array}{ccccccccccc} 3 & & 1 & & 4 & & 1 & & 3 & & 0 \\ +2 & & +3 & & +1 & & +4 & & +1 & & +4 \\ \hline 5 & & 4 & & 5 & & 5 & & 4 & & 4 \end{array}$$

4 (four)

Addition facts, sums through 5

Correcting Common Errors

Some students may have difficulty with the concept of addition. Have 3 students stand. Have another student join the 3. Ask, "How many are there in all?" (4) Write $3 + 1 = 4$ on the chalkboard. Have 2 of the students stand apart from the other 2. Write $2 + 2 = 4$ on the chalkboard. Ask students how the 4 students could be grouped other ways into 2 groups to model more number sentences where the sum is 4. ($1 + 3 = 4$, $4 + 0 = 4$, $0 + 4 = 4$) Write the number sentences on the chalkboard as students answer.

Enrichment

1. Have students use number names to write 6 different addition sentences for the sum of 5.
2. Tell students to cut pictures of objects from catalogs or magazines to illustrate 5 different addition sentences for the sum of 4.

Teaching page 4

Have students complete the number sentences to find all the ways to show a sum of 1, 2, 3, 4 and 5. Tell students to find the sums for each problem in the two rows at the bottom. Have students complete the page independently.

Extra Credit   *Numeration*

Provide each student with an egg carton with the top removed and some small plastic bags filled with objects like beans, beads, macaroni, buttons or paper clips. Number the egg carton sections with random numerals such as 12, 17, 9, 22 and 3. Have students count and place the correct number of objects in each section. They can exchange egg cartons to count and check for any mistakes. Empty the cartons and exchange cartons with another student refill them. After several exchanges, see who can correctly fill an entire egg carton the fastest.

4

Sums through 10

pages 5-6

Objective

To review addition facts for sums through 10

Materials

10 counters
addition fact cards for sums through 10

Mental Math

Ask students who is older:
1. Ted is 18, Ned is 19. (Ned)
2. Rick is 16, Nick is 15. (Rick)
3. Mary is 2, Teri is 8. (Teri)
4. Darin is 13, Taryn is 12. (Darin)
5. Kyle is 11, Lyle is 14. (Lyle)
6. Juan is 8, Jon is 18. (Jon)
7. Phil is 27, Lil is 37. (Lil)
8. Kara is 21, Sarah is 11. (Kara)

Skill Review

Have students work in groups with counters to lay out facts for sums of 1 through 5. Have groups rotate to check another group's work.

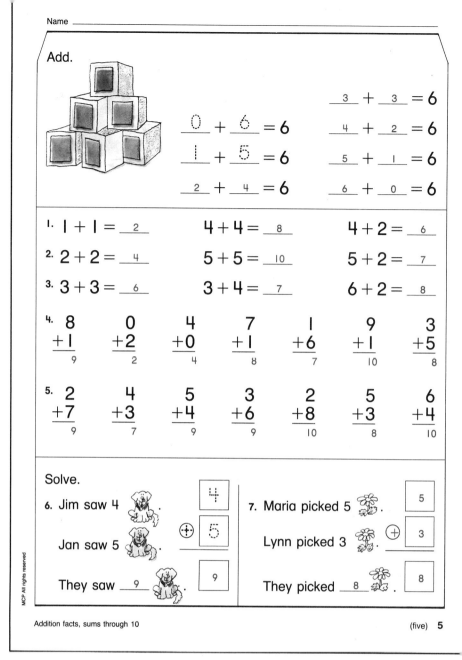

Add.

$\underline{0} + \underline{6} = 6$
$\underline{1} + \underline{5} = 6$
$\underline{2} + \underline{4} = 6$

$\underline{3} + \underline{3} = 6$
$\underline{4} + \underline{2} = 6$
$\underline{5} + \underline{1} = 6$
$\underline{6} + \underline{0} = 6$

1. $1 + 1 = \underline{2}$ 　 $4 + 4 = \underline{8}$ 　 $4 + 2 = \underline{6}$
2. $2 + 2 = \underline{4}$ 　 $5 + 5 = \underline{10}$ 　 $5 + 2 = \underline{7}$
3. $3 + 3 = \underline{6}$ 　 $3 + 4 = \underline{7}$ 　 $6 + 2 = \underline{8}$

4.
$\begin{array}{r} 8 \\ +1 \\ \hline 9 \end{array}$
$\begin{array}{r} 0 \\ +2 \\ \hline 2 \end{array}$
$\begin{array}{r} 4 \\ +0 \\ \hline 4 \end{array}$
$\begin{array}{r} 7 \\ +1 \\ \hline 8 \end{array}$
$\begin{array}{r} 1 \\ +6 \\ \hline 7 \end{array}$
$\begin{array}{r} 9 \\ +1 \\ \hline 10 \end{array}$
$\begin{array}{r} 3 \\ +5 \\ \hline 8 \end{array}$

5.
$\begin{array}{r} 2 \\ +7 \\ \hline 9 \end{array}$
$\begin{array}{r} 4 \\ +3 \\ \hline 7 \end{array}$
$\begin{array}{r} 5 \\ +4 \\ \hline 9 \end{array}$
$\begin{array}{r} 3 \\ +6 \\ \hline 9 \end{array}$
$\begin{array}{r} 2 \\ +8 \\ \hline 10 \end{array}$
$\begin{array}{r} 5 \\ +3 \\ \hline 8 \end{array}$
$\begin{array}{r} 6 \\ +4 \\ \hline 10 \end{array}$

Solve.

6. Jim saw 4 .

Jan saw 5 .

They saw $\underline{9}$.

$\begin{array}{r} 4 \\ \oplus\ 5 \\ \hline 9 \end{array}$

7. Maria picked 5 .

Lynn picked 3 .

They picked $\underline{8}$.

$\begin{array}{r} 5 \\ \oplus\ 3 \\ \hline 8 \end{array}$

Addition facts, sums through 10

(five) **5**

Teaching page 5

Have students lay out 8 counters in 2 groups. Ask students how many are in each group as you develop all 9 addition facts for 8. Have a student write each fact on the board as it is developed. Have another student write the fact on the board in another way, such as horizontally if the first student wrote a vertical problem. Repeat the activity for sums of 6, 7, 9 and 10.

Have students cover all of the blocks on the top of the page with their hand or a piece of paper and tell how many blocks. (0) Have students remove the cover and tell how many blocks. (6) Ask students the sum of 0 and 6. (6) Have students trace the 0 and 6 and read the number sentence. Repeat for $1 + 5 = 6$. Tell students they are to complete the facts for a sum of 6

and then work the number sentences below those facts. Remind students that a fact can be written vertically. Tell students to work the 2 rows of vertical problems. Work through the first story problem with students and have them trace the numbers and the addition sign, and write the answer in the problem and in the solution statement. Tell students they are to write the addition sign in the circle of the second problem. Help students complete the problem.

5

Add.

1.
| 1
+9
10 | 3
+6
9 | 4
+2
6 | 1
+2
3 | 6
+1
7 | 3
+7
10 | 2
+2
4 |

2.
| 3
+2
5 | 6
+2
8 | 4
+1
5 | 5
+2
7 | 2
+6
8 | 5
+1
6 | 1
+8
9 |

3.
| 2
+1
3 | 7
+2
9 | 2
+8
10 | 4
+6
10 | 1
+7
8 | 8
+2
10 | 3
+1
4 |

Complete the tables.

4.

Add 3	
2	5
4	7
1	4
3	6
6	9
5	8
7	10

5.

Add 4	
1	5
3	7
0	4
2	6
6	10
5	9
4	8

6.

Add 5	
3	8
0	5
2	7
5	10
1	6
4	9

Addition facts, sums through 10

Some students may have difficulty remembering addition facts for sums through 10. Make 2 sets of cards with the addends for a fact on one side and the other side blank. Have students work in pairs with the cards. Tell then to lay out the cards face down in an array. Have one partner turn one card over and tell the sum. This partner then tries to turn over another card with the same sum. A match wins both cards and another turn. If there is no match, both cards are returned to the array face down and the other partner tries for a match. The winner is the partner with the most cards at the end.

Enrichment

1. Have students write a story problem of their own like those at the bottom of page 5. Have a friend solve the problem.
2. Tell students to draw pictures to show an addition fact that tells how many animals they and a friend have all together.
3. Tell students they have 10¢ to buy 2 items. Have them list all the possible prices of the items they could buy.

Teaching page 6

Tell students to find the sum of each problem in the first three rows. Now have students look at the first table at the bottom of the page. Tell students that if we have 2 and add 3 more, we have 5 all together. Have students trace the 5. Ask students to tell the sum if we have 4 and add 3 more. (7) Have students write the 7. Tell students the next table asks them to give the sum if 4 is added and, in the last table, they are to add 5 to each number. Have students complete all 3 tables.

Extra Credit   Sets

Ask students to bring old buttons in many different styles from home. Place them in a box and mix them. Divide the class into small groups. One person from each group takes a large handful of buttons from the box. This student spreads the buttons out for the group to see. Each person in the group takes a turn sorting the buttons into two groups such as those with two holes and those with four, etc. The other students in the group guess what system of sorting was used to make these subsets. They continue taking turns until they have found as many different subsets as they can. Have the groups repeat the activity this time sorting the set into three subsets. Again, the others guess what system of sorting was used. Stress the fact that as these subsets emerge, they are distinctly separate and no button can be placed in more than one pile.

Minuends through 5

pages 7-8

Objective

To review subtraction facts for minuends through 5

Materials

*addition fact cards for sums through 10
5 counters

Mental Math

Have students give the following numbers:
1. numbers on a clock face (12)
2. digits on a clock face (15)
3. days in a week (7)
4. 0 + 0 (0)
5. 4 + 0 (4)
6. 3 and 2 more (5)
7. 6 plus 4 (10)
8. add 3 and 6 (9)

Skill Review

Have students give the sum of addition facts as you show them in random order. As the sum of each fact is given, have students place fact cards in groups of common sums. For example, put all sums of 8 in a group, etc.

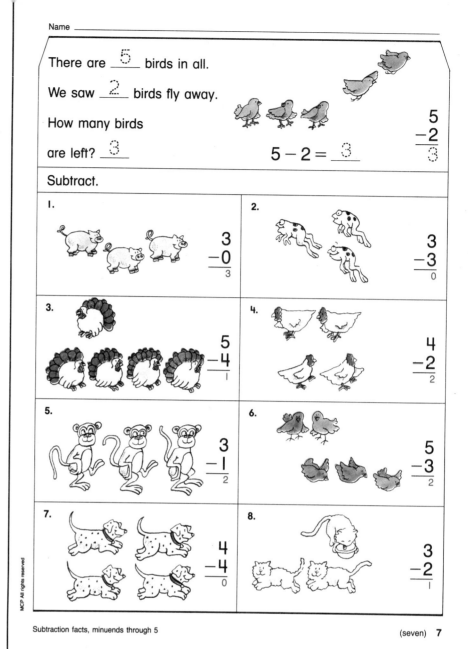

Name _____

There are __5__ birds in all.

We saw __2__ birds fly away.

How many birds are left? __3__

$5 - 2 = $ __3__

$$\begin{array}{r} 5 \\ -2 \\ \hline 3 \end{array}$$

Subtract.

1. $$\begin{array}{r} 3 \\ -0 \\ \hline 3 \end{array}$$

2. $$\begin{array}{r} 3 \\ -3 \\ \hline 0 \end{array}$$

3. $$\begin{array}{r} 5 \\ -4 \\ \hline 1 \end{array}$$

4. $$\begin{array}{r} 4 \\ -2 \\ \hline 2 \end{array}$$

5. $$\begin{array}{r} 3 \\ -1 \\ \hline 2 \end{array}$$

6. $$\begin{array}{r} 5 \\ -3 \\ \hline 2 \end{array}$$

7. $$\begin{array}{r} 4 \\ -4 \\ \hline 0 \end{array}$$

8. $$\begin{array}{r} 3 \\ -2 \\ \hline 1 \end{array}$$

Subtraction facts, minuends through 5

(seven) **7**

Teaching page 7

Have students lay out 5 counters. Tell students to group the counters into 2 groups with 3 in 1 group and 2 in the other. Write **3 + 2 = 5** on the board. Have students remove the group of 2 counters and tell how many are left. (3) Write **5 take away 2 is 3** on the board. Remind students that we can write this sentence a shorter way as you write **5 − 2 = 3** on the board. Have students replace the 2 counters and take the group of 3 away. Write **5 take away 3 is 2** and **5 − 3 = 2** on the board. Remind students that take-away problems are called **subtraction**. Continue to develop the subtraction facts for minuends of 5 and then have students find facts for minuends of 4, 3, 2 and 1. Have students write the number sentences on the board as facts are found.

Have students tell about the picture at the top of the page. Help students count the birds and read the sentence telling how many birds in all. Have students trace the 5. Continue reading with the students as they trace the 2 and 3. Help students read the number sentence and vertical problem. Then have them trace the 3 in each. Tell students to find the number of animals left in each box and write the number under the problem. Have students solve the problems independently.

7

Subtract.

1. $5 - 1 = 4$

2. $3 - 2 = 1$

3. $2 - 0 = 2$

4. $4 - 0 = 4$

5. $2 - 1 = 1$

6. $5 - 4 = 1$

7. $2 - 2 = 0$

8. $5 - 3 = 2$

9. $1 - 0 = 1$

10. $4 - 1 = 3$

11. $4 - 3 = 1$

12. $5 - 2 = 3$

FIELD TRIP

Write two addition and two subtraction sentences.

$2 + 3 = 5$ $5 - 3 = 2$

$3 + 2 = 5$ $5 - 2 = 3$

8 (eight)   Subtraction facts, minuends through 5

Teaching page 8

Ask students how many there are in all. (5) Have students draw a line through 1 object to show that 1 object is to be subtracted. Ask how many are left. (4) Have students trace the 4. Work through another problem with the students. Have students complete the problems independently.

Field Trip

Draw 4 x's in a group and 3 x's in another group on the board. Tell students we can write four different number sentences about the x's. Write **4 + 3 = 7, 3 + 4 = 7, 7 − 4 = 3** and **7 − 3 = 4** on the board. Discuss each problem with the students. Tell students they are to write 4 number sentences which tell about the picture. Tell students they will use only the numbers 2, 3 and 5. Have students complete the problems independently.

Extra Credit *Numeration*

Use cardboard "footprints" as a number line. Cut out 13 footprints and label them 0-12. Possibly have students make them by tracing around one of their shoes. Tape the footprints to the floor about 6 inches apart. Have students use the number line to solve addition and subtraction problems, by acting out the problems, moving back and forth along the number line.

Minuends through 10

pages 9-10

Objective

To review subtraction facts for minuends through 10

Materials

*addition fact cards for sums
 through 10
*subtraction fact cards for minuends
 through 5

Mental Math

Ask students to count backward
from:
1. 20 to 10.
2. 13 to 0.
3. 22 to 11.
4. 19 to 9.
5. 10 to 0.
6. 24 to 12.
7. 12 to 2.
8. 18 to 4.

Skill Review

Have students give the answer for
each addition or subtraction fact card
as you show them in random order.
As the sum or difference is given,
have students place fact cards in
groups of fact families.

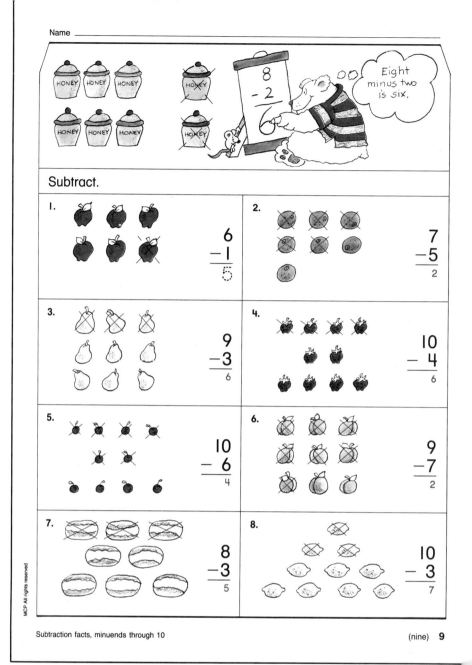

Subtraction facts, minuends through 10

(nine) **9**

Teaching page 9

Remind students that **8 + 2 = 10** as you write the
number sentence on the board. Ask students how
many would be left if 2 were taken away from 10. (8)
Write **10 − 2 = 8** on the board. Now ask how many
would be left if 8 were taken away from 10. (2) Have
a student write the number sentence or vertical
problem on the board. (10 − 8 = 2) Continue to
develop more subtraction facts for 10 and some of the
facts for 6, 7, 8 and 9.

Have students tell about the picture and trace the lines
through the 2 objects to show that 2 are taken away
from 8. Have students tell the number left. (6) Work
the next problem with the students and then have
them complete the page independently.

9

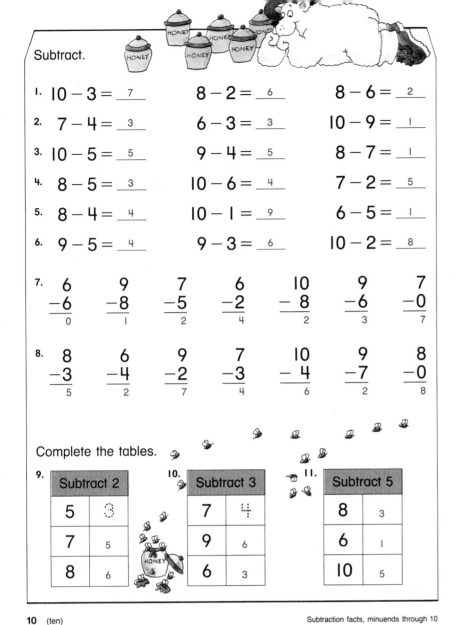

Subtract.

1. $10 - 3 = \underline{7}$ $8 - 2 = \underline{6}$ $8 - 6 = \underline{2}$

2. $7 - 4 = \underline{3}$ $6 - 3 = \underline{3}$ $10 - 9 = \underline{1}$

3. $10 - 5 = \underline{5}$ $9 - 4 = \underline{5}$ $8 - 7 = \underline{1}$

4. $8 - 5 = \underline{3}$ $10 - 6 = \underline{4}$ $7 - 2 = \underline{5}$

5. $8 - 4 = \underline{4}$ $10 - 1 = \underline{9}$ $6 - 5 = \underline{1}$

6. $9 - 5 = \underline{4}$ $9 - 3 = \underline{6}$ $10 - 2 = \underline{8}$

7.
$$\begin{array}{r} 6 \\ -6 \\ \hline 0 \end{array} \quad \begin{array}{r} 9 \\ -8 \\ \hline 1 \end{array} \quad \begin{array}{r} 7 \\ -5 \\ \hline 2 \end{array} \quad \begin{array}{r} 6 \\ -2 \\ \hline 4 \end{array} \quad \begin{array}{r} 10 \\ -8 \\ \hline 2 \end{array} \quad \begin{array}{r} 9 \\ -6 \\ \hline 3 \end{array} \quad \begin{array}{r} 7 \\ -0 \\ \hline 7 \end{array}$$

8.
$$\begin{array}{r} 8 \\ -3 \\ \hline 5 \end{array} \quad \begin{array}{r} 6 \\ -4 \\ \hline 2 \end{array} \quad \begin{array}{r} 9 \\ -2 \\ \hline 7 \end{array} \quad \begin{array}{r} 7 \\ -3 \\ \hline 4 \end{array} \quad \begin{array}{r} 10 \\ -4 \\ \hline 6 \end{array} \quad \begin{array}{r} 9 \\ -7 \\ \hline 2 \end{array} \quad \begin{array}{r} 8 \\ -0 \\ \hline 8 \end{array}$$

Complete the tables.

9.
Subtract 2	
5	3
7	5
8	6

10.
Subtract 3	
7	4
9	6
6	3

11.
Subtract 5	
8	3
6	1
10	5

10   (ten)   Subtraction facts, minuends through 10

Correcting Common Errors

Some students may have difficulty remembering subtraction facts for minuends through 10. Practice by whispering to each student a number from 6 through 10. Have them write a subtraction sentence using that number as a minuend, another number for the subtrahend, and a blank line for the answer. They then can take turns writing their facts on the chalkboard with other students supplying the answers.

Enrichment

1. Have students use a spinner with numbers 0 through 10. Tell them to take turns with a friend giving one addition and one subtraction fact for each number they spin.
2. Have students name as many situations as they can where subtraction is used. For example, if they have 9 pencils and 4 are not sharpened, they have 5 sharp pencils.

Teaching page 10

Remind students that subtraction problems can be written as number sentences or as vertical problems. Tell students they will work problems of both kinds on this page. Have students look at the first table at the bottom of the page. Ask what number is left if we have 5 and take 2 away. (3) Have students trace the 3. Repeat for the first problem in the next table and then tell students to complete the page independently.

Extra Credit   Sets

Draw the following group of sets on the board: 2 triangles, 3 circles, 4 squares, 6 stars and 5 rectangles. From this group of sets have students identify the set that has:

the fewest objects; the most objects; one more than the square; two less than the half circles; more than the triangles, but less than the stars and more than the half circles and the squares.

Now have some of the students ask their classmates to identify these sets by properties. Are any of the sets equivalent? Have students draw a set that is equivalent to the triangles.

10

Mixed Practice

pages 11-12

Objectives

To practice addition facts for sums through 10

To practice subtraction facts for minuends through 10

Materials

10 counters

Mental Math

Have students name a subtraction fact related to:

1. $4 + 5 = 9$ ($9 - 5 = 4$, $9 - 4 = 5$)
2. $3 + 7 = 10$ ($10 - 3 = 7$, $10 - 7 = 3$)
3. $2 + 6 = 8$
4. $4 + 6 = 10$

Have them name an addition fact related to:

5. $10 - 2 = 8$ ($8 + 2 = 10$, $2 + 8 = 10$)
6. $6 - 4 = 2$ ($4 + 2 = 6$, $2 + 4 = 6$)
7. $10 - 5 = 5$
8. $9 - 0 = 9$

Skill Review

Write **4 + 5 =** on the board. Have students show the problem with their counters and give the sum. Have a student write the sum on the board. Repeat for more facts for sums and minuends through 10.

Teaching page 11

Tell students to find the sum of each problem on this page. Students may wish to use counters to work the problems. Have students complete the page independently.

Add.

1.	2 +2 4	1 +1 2	5 +2 7	3 +2 5	6 +1 7	1 +4 5	7 +2 9

1. $\begin{array}{r}2\\+2\\\hline 4\end{array}$ $\begin{array}{r}1\\+1\\\hline 2\end{array}$ $\begin{array}{r}5\\+2\\\hline 7\end{array}$ $\begin{array}{r}3\\+2\\\hline 5\end{array}$ $\begin{array}{r}6\\+1\\\hline 7\end{array}$ $\begin{array}{r}1\\+4\\\hline 5\end{array}$ $\begin{array}{r}7\\+2\\\hline 9\end{array}$

2. $\begin{array}{r}4\\+1\\\hline 5\end{array}$ $\begin{array}{r}6\\+3\\\hline 9\end{array}$ $\begin{array}{r}2\\+6\\\hline 8\end{array}$ $\begin{array}{r}5\\+1\\\hline 6\end{array}$ $\begin{array}{r}3\\+7\\\hline 10\end{array}$ $\begin{array}{r}4\\+2\\\hline 6\end{array}$ $\begin{array}{r}1\\+9\\\hline 10\end{array}$

3. $\begin{array}{r}0\\+4\\\hline 4\end{array}$ $\begin{array}{r}3\\+3\\\hline 6\end{array}$ $\begin{array}{r}8\\+1\\\hline 9\end{array}$ $\begin{array}{r}1\\+6\\\hline 7\end{array}$ $\begin{array}{r}5\\+0\\\hline 5\end{array}$ $\begin{array}{r}2\\+1\\\hline 3\end{array}$ $\begin{array}{r}4\\+5\\\hline 9\end{array}$

4. $\begin{array}{r}1\\+2\\\hline 3\end{array}$ $\begin{array}{r}8\\+0\\\hline 8\end{array}$ $\begin{array}{r}4\\+3\\\hline 7\end{array}$ $\begin{array}{r}2\\+8\\\hline 10\end{array}$ $\begin{array}{r}7\\+1\\\hline 8\end{array}$ $\begin{array}{r}6\\+4\\\hline 10\end{array}$ $\begin{array}{r}2\\+5\\\hline 7\end{array}$

5. $\begin{array}{r}3\\+4\\\hline 7\end{array}$ $\begin{array}{r}5\\+3\\\hline 8\end{array}$ $\begin{array}{r}1\\+8\\\hline 9\end{array}$ $\begin{array}{r}5\\+5\\\hline 10\end{array}$ $\begin{array}{r}6\\+2\\\hline 8\end{array}$ $\begin{array}{r}8\\+2\\\hline 10\end{array}$ $\begin{array}{r}3\\+1\\\hline 4\end{array}$

6. $\begin{array}{r}7\\+3\\\hline 10\end{array}$ $\begin{array}{r}4\\+4\\\hline 8\end{array}$ $\begin{array}{r}2\\+3\\\hline 5\end{array}$ $\begin{array}{r}3\\+5\\\hline 8\end{array}$ $\begin{array}{r}0\\+7\\\hline 7\end{array}$ $\begin{array}{r}1\\+3\\\hline 4\end{array}$ $\begin{array}{r}9\\+1\\\hline 10\end{array}$

7. $\begin{array}{r}2\\+4\\\hline 6\end{array}$ $\begin{array}{r}3\\+6\\\hline 9\end{array}$ $\begin{array}{r}1\\+5\\\hline 6\end{array}$ $\begin{array}{r}4\\+6\\\hline 10\end{array}$ $\begin{array}{r}1\\+7\\\hline 8\end{array}$ $\begin{array}{r}5\\+4\\\hline 9\end{array}$ $\begin{array}{r}2\\+7\\\hline 9\end{array}$

Addition facts, sums through 10

(eleven) **11**

11

Subtract.

1.	4 −2 2	2 −1 1	7 −2 5	5 −3 2	7 −1 6	5 −4 1	9 −2 7
2.	5 −1 4	9 −3 6	8 −6 2	6 −5 1	10 − 3 7	6 −2 4	10 − 1 9
3.	8 −2 6	6 −3 3	9 −8 1	7 −6 1	5 −5 0	3 −1 2	9 −4 5
4.	3 −2 1	8 −0 8	7 −4 3	10 − 8 2	8 −1 7	10 − 4 6	7 −5 2
5.	7 −3 4	8 −5 3	9 −1 8	10 − 5 5	5 −2 3	10 − 2 8	4 −3 1
6.	10 − 7 3	8 −4 4	4 −0 4	8 −3 5	7 −7 0	4 −1 3	10 − 9 1
7.	6 −4 2	9 −6 3	6 −1 5	10 − 6 4	8 −7 1	9 −5 4	9 −7 2

Subtraction facts, minuends through 10

Correcting Common Errors

Some students may need practice with their facts. Have them work with partners with addition and subtraction fact cards through sums of 10. They can take turns showing each other a fact card and asking for the answer identifying it as a sum or difference. Be sure students read aloud all parts of each fact.

Enrichment

1. Tell students to write a story about 4 cats and 5 cats. They should then write a subtraction or addition problem that goes with the story.
2. Have students work in pairs. Tell one student to affix an addition or subtraction fact to the back of a partner. The student should then tell a story as a clue for the partner to guess the fact.

Teaching page 12

Tell students to subtract in all the problems on this page. Allow students to use counters if they choose. Have students complete the page independently.

Extra Credit   *Numeration*

Distribute six 5-in. square tagboard cards to each student. Students work with partners. Each pair decides on a number greater than 10 and less than 30. Both students draw a set with that number on one of their cards. For example, if one pair chooses 16 as their first number, they each draw a set with 16 objects on their card. The students continue selecting a number and drawing matching sets on the cards. When all six cards have matching, equivalent sets, the two students shuffle their cards and place them facedown on the table. Students take turns playing Concentration by turning over 2 cards and counting to see if the numbers are equivalent. If they match, the student keeps the cards and takes another turn. When all cards are matched, the student with the most cards wins.

12

Mixed Problem Solving

pages 13-14

Objective

To add or subtract to solve problems

Materials

10 counters
laminated index cards
*fact cards for sums and minuends through 10

Mental Math

Ask students if they should add or subtract the following:
1. 3 plus 6 (add)
2. 9 take away 2 (subtract)
3. 8 and 1 more (add)
4. 4 minus 2 (subtract)
5. 5 less than 7 (subtract)
6. 4 and 7 more (add)
7. 2 plus 8 (add)
8. 10 minus 6 (subtract)

Skill Review

Write **7 + 2 = 9** on the board and ask a student to write a related subtraction fact (9 − 2 = 7, 9 − 7 = 2) Continue to write other addition or subtraction facts on the board and have students write related facts for each.

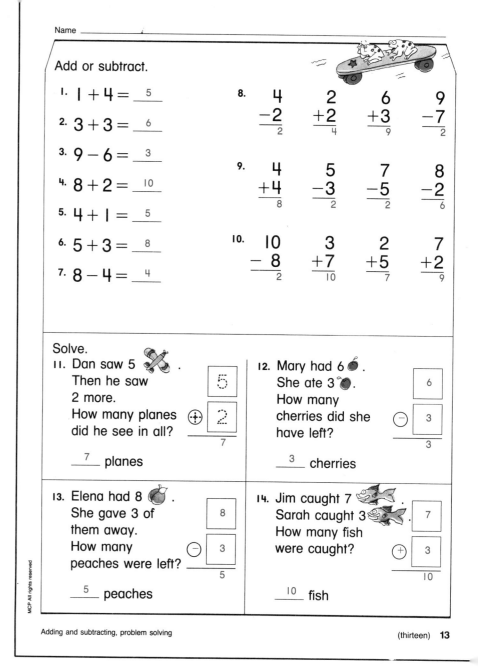

Name _____

Add or subtract.

1. $1 + 4 = \underline{5}$
2. $3 + 3 = \underline{6}$
3. $9 - 6 = \underline{3}$
4. $8 + 2 = \underline{10}$
5. $4 + 1 = \underline{5}$
6. $5 + 3 = \underline{8}$
7. $8 - 4 = \underline{4}$

8.
$$\begin{array}{c} 4 \\ -2 \\ \hline 2 \end{array} \qquad \begin{array}{c} 2 \\ +2 \\ \hline 4 \end{array} \qquad \begin{array}{c} 6 \\ +3 \\ \hline 9 \end{array} \qquad \begin{array}{c} 9 \\ -7 \\ \hline 2 \end{array}$$

9.
$$\begin{array}{c} 4 \\ +4 \\ \hline 8 \end{array} \qquad \begin{array}{c} 5 \\ -3 \\ \hline 2 \end{array} \qquad \begin{array}{c} 7 \\ -5 \\ \hline 2 \end{array} \qquad \begin{array}{c} 8 \\ -2 \\ \hline 6 \end{array}$$

10.
$$\begin{array}{c} 10 \\ -8 \\ \hline 2 \end{array} \qquad \begin{array}{c} 3 \\ +7 \\ \hline 10 \end{array} \qquad \begin{array}{c} 2 \\ +5 \\ \hline 7 \end{array} \qquad \begin{array}{c} 7 \\ +2 \\ \hline 9 \end{array}$$

Solve.

11. Dan saw 5 ✈. Then he saw 2 more. How many planes did he see in all? ⊕ 5 2 / 7

   _7_ planes

12. Mary had 6 🍒. She ate 3 🍒. How many cherries did she have left? ⊖ 6 3 / 3

   _3_ cherries

13. Elena had 8 🍑. She gave 3 of them away. How many peaches were left? ⊖ 8 3 / 5

   _5_ peaches

14. Jim caught 7 🐟. Sarah caught 3 🐟. How many fish were caught? ⊕ 7 3 / 10

   _10_ fish

Adding and subtracting, problem solving

(thirteen) **13**

Teaching page 13

Write **4 + 6 =** and **3 − 2 =** on the board and ask students which problem tells them to subtract. (3 − 2 =) Ask how they know to subtract. (the minus sign) Ask students what the other problem tells them to do. (add) Ask how they know to add. (the plus sign) Dictate addition and subtraction problems for students to write and solve on the board. Remind students to look at the sign in a problem before doing anything with the numbers.

Go down the first column of problems and ask students to tell what operation they will do in each problem. Allow students to use counters if they choose as they complete the top half of the page. Read through the first word problem with the students as they trace the addends and the plus sign. Have

students write the sum in the box and in the solution statement. Have students complete the remaining story problems.

Add or subtract.

1.
$$\frac{4}{-2} = 2 \qquad \frac{6}{-3} = 3 \qquad \frac{8}{-4} = 4 \qquad \frac{10}{-3} = 7 \qquad \frac{9}{-3} = 6 \qquad \frac{8}{-5} = 3 \qquad \frac{7}{-4} = 3$$

2.
$$\frac{5}{+2} = 7 \qquad \frac{3}{+3} = 6 \qquad \frac{4}{+4} = 8 \qquad \frac{7}{+2} = 9 \qquad \frac{5}{+5} = 10 \qquad \frac{7}{-3} = 4 \qquad \frac{9}{-4} = 5$$

3.
$$\frac{10}{-4} = 6 \qquad \frac{2}{+7} = 9 \qquad \frac{8}{+2} = 10 \qquad \frac{6}{+4} = 10 \qquad \frac{5}{-2} = 3 \qquad \frac{7}{-6} = 1 \qquad \frac{6}{+2} = 8$$

FIELD TRIP

Write the missing numbers.

1.
2	3	4	7	3	5
+ [2]	+ [3]	+ [4]	+ [3]	+ [6]	+ [3]
4	6	8	10	9	8

2.
4	7	6	8	9	10
− [1]	− [2]	− [3]	− [4]	− [2]	− [5]
3	5	3	4	7	5

14 (fourteen)

Practice, adding and subtracting

Problem Solving with Money

pages 15-16

Objective

To add or subtract to solve money problems

Materials

10 real or play pennies
*addition fact cards
*subtraction fact cards

Mental Math

Ask students which is more:
1. 5 + 3 or 9 − 2? (5 + 3)
2. 8 − 2 or 7 + 2? (7 + 2)
3. 3 + 3 or 3 + 5? (3 + 5)
4. 6 − 0 or 5 − 4? (6 − 0)
Ask which is less:
5. 8 − 2 or 5 + 0 (5 + 0)
6. 4 + 5 or 6 + 4? (4 + 5)
7. 8 − 3 or 9 − 5? (9 − 5)
8. 10 − 3 or 10 − 4? (10 − 4)

Skill Review

Have students give the sum or difference as you randomly show addition and subtraction fact cards.

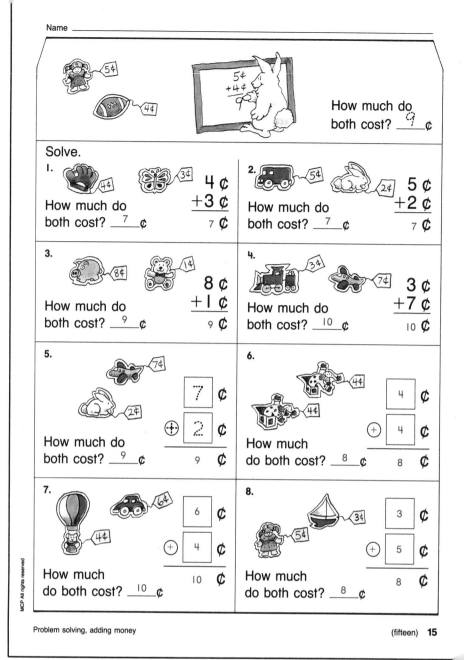

Problem solving, adding money

(fifteen) 15

Teaching page 15

Tell students to lay out 4 pennies as you tell them that Ryan bought a toy which cost 4¢. Tell students that Ryan also bought another toy which cost 6¢. Have students lay out 6 more pennies. Tell students we want to know how much both toys cost. Ask students if we would add or subtract. (add) Have a student write and solve an addition problem on the board to find Ryan's total cost. (6¢ + 4 = 10¢ or 4¢ + 6 = 10¢) Repeat for more addition problems. Then have students lay out 8¢ to show how much money Sarah had before she bought a piece of gum which cost 4¢. Ask students if we would add or subtract the 4 pennies to find how much money Sarah has left. (subtract) Have a student write and solve the problem on the board. (8¢ − 4 = 4¢) Repeat for more subtraction problems.

Ask students to tell the price of each of the items in the problem at the top of the page. (5¢ and 4¢) Have a student read the question. Have students read the problem, trace the 9 and then trace the 9 after the question. Go through the first problem with the students. Have students look at the fifth problem to see that they are to write the addends and plus signs in each of the last 4 problems. Have students complete the page independently.

15

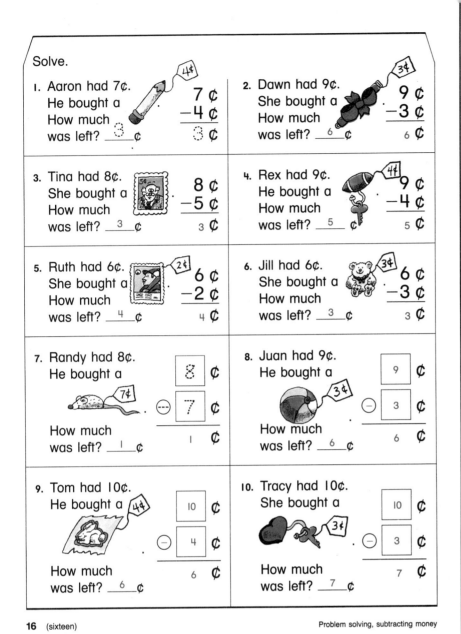

Solve.

1. Aaron had 7¢.
He bought a
How much
was left? __3__ ¢

7 ¢
−4 ¢
3 ¢

2. Dawn had 9¢.
She bought a
How much
was left? __6__ ¢

9 ¢
−3 ¢
6 ¢

3. Tina had 8¢.
She bought a
How much
was left? __3__ ¢

8 ¢
−5 ¢
3 ¢

4. Rex had 9¢.
He bought a
How much
was left? __5__ ¢

9 ¢
−4 ¢
5 ¢

5. Ruth had 6¢.
She bought a
How much
was left? __4__ ¢

6 ¢
−2 ¢
4 ¢

6. Jill had 6¢.
She bought a
How much
was left? __3__ ¢

6 ¢
−3 ¢
3 ¢

7. Randy had 8¢.
He bought a
How much
was left? __1__ ¢

8 ¢
− 7 ¢
1 ¢

8. Juan had 9¢.
He bought a
How much
was left? __6__ ¢

9 ¢
− 3 ¢
6 ¢

9. Tom had 10¢.
He bought a
How much
was left? __6__ ¢

10 ¢
− 4 ¢
6 ¢

10. Tracy had 10¢.
She bought a
How much
was left? __7__ ¢

10 ¢
− 3 ¢
7 ¢

16 (sixteen)

Problem solving, subtracting money

Teaching page 16

Tell students to subtract in each problem to find the amount of money left. Work through the first problem with the students. Have them look at the seventh problem as you tell them they are to write the problem and the minus sign in the last 4 problems. Have students complete the page independently.

Extra Credit   *Statistics*

Take an inventory in the classroom. Have students compile a list of things to count, for example: chairs, desks, pieces of chalk, windows, reading books, electrical outlets, clocks, blue pencils, etc. Students may work independently or in small groups to complete the tally. Count together to check for accuracy when the count is complete.

16

More Problem Solving

pages 17-18

Objective

To choose an operation to solve a problem

Materials

10 counters

Mental Math

Ask students how many:
1. letters in their first names.
2. letters in their last names.
3. total letters in their names.
4. a's in their first and last names.
5. letters in their school's name.
6. more letters in one of their names than the other.
7. more letters in their name than a friend's name.

Skill Review

Tell students that Jerry found 3 shells in the morning and 5 shells in the afternoon. Ask them what operation would be used to find the total number of shells. (addition) Then ask them to solve the problem. (8) Write **3 + 5 = 8** on the board. Give students other addition and subtraction word problems and ask them to name the operation to be used.

Name _____

Solve.

1. Maria picked 3 🍎.
   Sonja picked 4.
   How many apples were picked?

   3
   ⊕ 4
   ___
   7

   __7__ apples

2. Jack had 6 🍐.
   He ate 2.
   How many pears are left?

   6
   ⊖ 2
   ___
   4

   __4__ pears

3. Leah found 10 🐚.
   She gave 3 to Sarah.
   How many shells are left?

   10
   ⊖ 3
   ___
   7

   __7__ shells

4. Eve had 9 🐟.
   She gave 3 to Alan.
   How many goldfish are left?

   9
   ⊖ 3
   ___
   6

   __6__ goldfish

5. Larry found 6 🌰.
   Dino found 3.
   How many acorns were found?

   6
   ⊕ 3
   ___
   9

   __9__ acorns

6. There are 10 🍌.
   The monkey ate 6.
   How many bananas are left?

   10
   ⊖ 6
   ___
   4

   __4__ bananas

7. Mike has 7 pets.
   3 of them are cats.
   How many pets are not cats?

   7
   ⊖ 3
   ___
   4

   __4__ pets

8. Jan walked 5 blocks.
   She ran 4 blocks.
   How far did Jan go?

   5
   ⊕ 4
   ___
   9

   __9__ blocks

Problem solving, choosing the operation

(seventeen) **17**

Teaching page 17

Write **7 − 3 =** on the board. Have a student silently act out having 7 objects and laying 3 down. Ask how the student knew to lay 3 down instead of picking up 3 more. (The minus sign means to take away.) Have a student solve the problem. (4) Repeat for more addition and subtraction problems.

Work through the first 2 problems with the students as they trace the numbers and signs. Then have students write the answers on the answer lines. Remind students to decide which operation will be used before beginning to work each problem. Allow students to use counters if they choose.

17

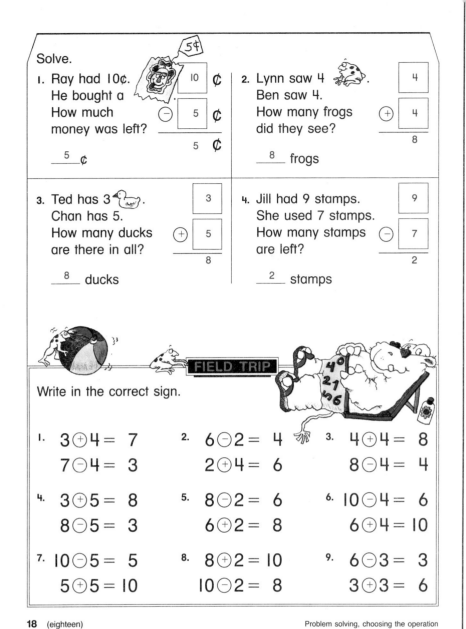

Solve.

1. Ray had 10¢.
He bought a
How much
money was left?

10	¢
⊖ 5	¢
5	¢

___5___ ¢

2. Lynn saw 4 .
Ben saw 4.
How many frogs
did they see?

| 4 |
| ⊕ 4 |
| 8 |

___8___ frogs

3. Ted has 3 .
Chan has 5.
How many ducks
are there in all?

| 3 |
| ⊕ 5 |
| 8 |

___8___ ducks

4. Jill had 9 stamps.
She used 7 stamps.
How many stamps
are left?

| 9 |
| ⊖ 7 |
| 2 |

___2___ stamps

FIELD TRIP

Write in the correct sign.

1. 3 ⊕ 4 = 7
   7 ⊖ 4 = 3

2. 6 ⊖ 2 = 4
   2 ⊕ 4 = 6

3. 4 ⊕ 4 = 8
   8 ⊖ 4 = 4

4. 3 ⊕ 5 = 8
   8 ⊖ 5 = 3

5. 8 ⊖ 2 = 6
   6 ⊕ 2 = 8

6. 10 ⊖ 4 = 6
   6 ⊕ 4 = 10

7. 10 ⊖ 5 = 5
   5 ⊕ 5 = 10

8. 8 ⊕ 2 = 10
   10 ⊖ 2 = 8

9. 6 ⊖ 3 = 3
   3 ⊕ 3 = 6

18 (eighteen)   Problem solving, choosing the operation

Correcting Common Errors

Some students may have difficulty choosing addition or subtraction to solve a problem. Have them work with partners. One partner reads the problem out loud and then they discuss what words in the problem help them decide what operation to use. Encourage them to circle these words. They should then choose the operation and solve the problem.

Enrichment

1. Have students work in pairs with 2 dice. They should throw the dice and subtract 1 number from the other. They may keep score with the highest number winning another throw.

2. Have the class play, "What's My Number?" with addition and subtraction facts for sums and minuends through 10. One student should give a fact. The student who responds correctly will get the next turn.

3. Have students name situations where they need to know several ways to make 10 for example, sharing 10 pennies between 2 people.

Teaching page 18

Tell students they are to decide which operation they will use and then write the problem and the sign. Tell students to solve the problem and write the answer under the problem, and again on the line following the question. Have students complete the page independently.

Field Trip

Write **11 ◯ 6 = 5** on the board and have a student write the sign in the circle which makes the problem true. (−) Write **6 ◯ 6 = 12** on the board and have a student write the correct sign. (+) Tell students to write the sign in each circle to make the problems true.

Extra Credit   *Statistics*

Assemble a bulletin board entitled, "OUR CLASS HAS:" Under the title list things to count in the class. For example, count how many: blue eyes? thumbs? toes? pockets? January birthdays? Students count the total number of each for the class and write the number next to the questions. These poster questions can be changed periodically.

Review

pages 19-20

Objectives

To review addition and subtraction facts for sums through 10
To maintain skills learned previously this year

Materials

10 counters

Mental Math

Ask students how many people are at the party if there were:

1. 9 and 2 left. (7)
2. 10 and 10 left. (0)
3. 6 and 4 more came. (10)
4. 8 and 5 left. (3)
5. 7 and 3 left. (4)
6. 2 and 6 more came. (8)
7. 7 and 4 went home. (3)
8. 6 and 3 more came. (9)

Skill Review

Write on the board: **Bret had 4 books. Alan had 5 books. How many books did the boys have in all?** Ask if we will add or subtract in this problem. (add) Have a student write and solve a fact to answer the problem. (4 + 5 = 9 or 5 + 4 = 9) Repeat for more word problems for sums or minuends through 10.

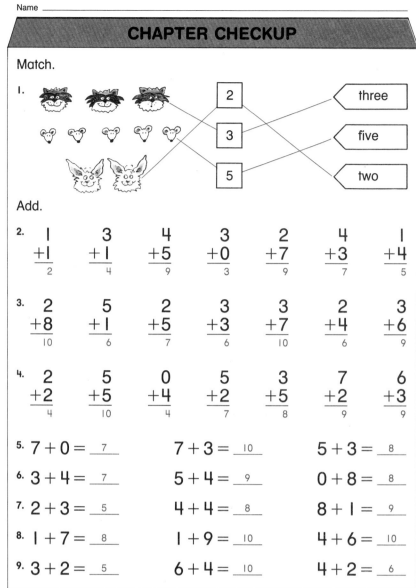

Name ______

CHAPTER CHECKUP

Match.

1.

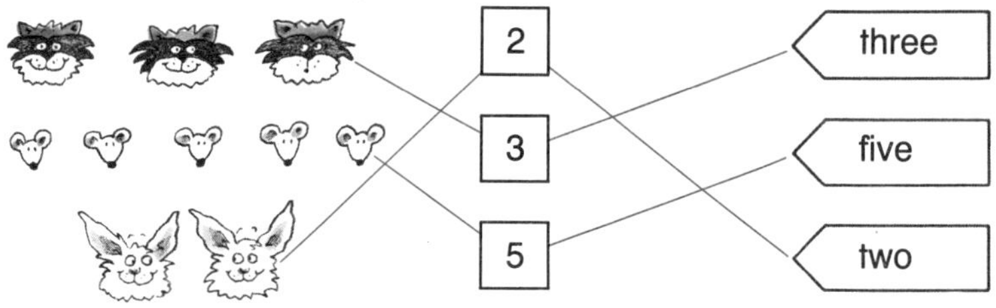

Add.

2.	1 + 1 = 2	3 + 1 = 4	4 + 5 = 9	3 + 0 = 3	2 + 7 = 9	4 + 3 = 7	1 + 4 = 5
3.	2 + 8 = 10	5 + 1 = 6	2 + 5 = 7	3 + 3 = 6	3 + 7 = 10	2 + 4 = 6	3 + 6 = 9
4.	2 + 2 = 4	5 + 5 = 10	0 + 4 = 4	5 + 2 = 7	3 + 5 = 8	7 + 2 = 9	6 + 3 = 9

5. 7 + 0 = 7   7 + 3 = 10   5 + 3 = 8
6. 3 + 4 = 7   5 + 4 = 9   0 + 8 = 8
7. 2 + 3 = 5   4 + 4 = 8   8 + 1 = 9
8. 1 + 7 = 8   1 + 9 = 10   4 + 6 = 10
9. 3 + 2 = 5   6 + 4 = 10   4 + 2 = 6

Teaching page 19

Ask students what they are to do at the top of the page. (Draw a line from the objects to the number and from the number to its number name.) Tell students to complete the matching and then write the sum of each problem to complete the page. Allow students to use counters if needed.

Subtract.

1.
$$
\begin{array}{r} 3 \\ -1 \\ \hline 2 \end{array}
\qquad
\begin{array}{r} 2 \\ -0 \\ \hline 2 \end{array}
\qquad
\begin{array}{r} 4 \\ -2 \\ \hline 2 \end{array}
\qquad
\begin{array}{r} 7 \\ -4 \\ \hline 3 \end{array}
\qquad
\begin{array}{r} 6 \\ -3 \\ \hline 3 \end{array}
\qquad
\begin{array}{r} 8 \\ -6 \\ \hline 2 \end{array}
\qquad
\begin{array}{r} 5 \\ -3 \\ \hline 2 \end{array}
$$

2.
$$
\begin{array}{r} 6 \\ -4 \\ \hline 2 \end{array}
\qquad
\begin{array}{r} 9 \\ -2 \\ \hline 7 \end{array}
\qquad
\begin{array}{r} 10 \\ -1 \\ \hline 9 \end{array}
\qquad
\begin{array}{r} 6 \\ -2 \\ \hline 4 \end{array}
\qquad
\begin{array}{r} 9 \\ -5 \\ \hline 4 \end{array}
\qquad
\begin{array}{r} 8 \\ -3 \\ \hline 5 \end{array}
\qquad
\begin{array}{r} 10 \\ -5 \\ \hline 5 \end{array}
$$

3. $10 - 2 = \underline{8} \qquad 10 - 3 = \underline{7} \qquad 6 - 6 = \underline{0}$

4. $8 - 4 = \underline{4} \qquad 7 - 0 = \underline{7} \qquad 10 - 6 = \underline{4}$

Solve.

5. Alex had 9 .
He gave Liz 3.
How many leaves
are left?

$\boxed{9}$
$\ominus \boxed{3}$
$\overline{\quad 6 \quad}$

$\underline{6}$ leaves

6. Jeff saw 4 .
Bill saw 4.
How many butterflies
were seen?

$\boxed{4}$
$\oplus \boxed{4}$
$\overline{\quad 8 \quad}$

$\underline{8}$ butterflies

7. Hal bought a 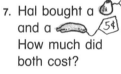 5¢
and a 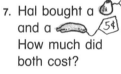 5¢.
How much did
both cost?

$\boxed{5}$ ¢
$\oplus \boxed{5}$ ¢
$\overline{\quad 10 \quad}$ ¢

$\underline{10}$ ¢

8. Rose had 8¢.
She bought a 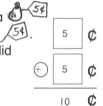 2¢.
How much
is left?

$\boxed{8}$ ¢
$\ominus \boxed{2}$ ¢
$\overline{\quad 6 \quad}$ ¢

$\underline{6}$ ¢

Chapter review

1. Have students make a number book for the numbers 1 through 10. They should then write addition and related subtraction facts for each number on each page.
2. Have students draw 2 priced items they might buy with 9¢.
3. Have students write in order all subtraction facts for minuends of 10 from 10-1 through 10-9.

Teaching page 20

This page reviews subtraction facts and word problems for minuends through 10.

Tell students they are to find the difference in each subtraction problem. Tell students that some of the word problems are addition and some are subtraction problems. Remind students to write the + or − sign in the circle and to write each answer on the line under the question. Have students complete the page independently.

Sums through 12

pages 21-22

Objective

To review addition facts for sums through 12

Materials

12 counters

Mental Math

Dictate the following problems:
1. 3 + 5 (8)
2. 6 − 2 (4)
3. 5 + 0 (5)
4. 9 − 2 (7)
5. 6 + 3 (9)
6. 4 − 2 (2)
7. 7 + 3 (10)
8. 9 − 3 (6)

Skill Review

Write on the board addition or subtraction facts such as **7 ◯ 3 = 4** and have students write the sign in the circle that makes the fact true.

BASIC FACTS, SUMS THROUGH 12

Add.

I is I ten and I one

$$\begin{array}{r} 8 \\ +3 \\ \hline 11 \end{array}$$

1.
$$\begin{array}{r} 7 \\ +5 \\ \hline 12 \end{array}$$

2.
$$\begin{array}{r} 5 \\ +6 \\ \hline 11 \end{array}$$

3.
$$\begin{array}{r} 6 \\ +6 \\ \hline 12 \end{array}$$

4.
$$\begin{array}{r} 9 \\ +3 \\ \hline 12 \end{array}$$

5.
$$\begin{array}{r} 8 \\ +4 \\ \hline 12 \end{array} \quad \begin{array}{r} 5 \\ +7 \\ \hline 12 \end{array} \quad \begin{array}{r} 4 \\ +4 \\ \hline 8 \end{array} \quad \begin{array}{r} 9 \\ +2 \\ \hline 11 \end{array} \quad \begin{array}{r} 7 \\ +4 \\ \hline 11 \end{array} \quad \begin{array}{r} 9 \\ +3 \\ \hline 12 \end{array} \quad \begin{array}{r} 3 \\ +8 \\ \hline 11 \end{array}$$

6.
$$\begin{array}{r} 4 \\ +7 \\ \hline 11 \end{array} \quad \begin{array}{r} 4 \\ +8 \\ \hline 12 \end{array} \quad \begin{array}{r} 5 \\ +6 \\ \hline 11 \end{array} \quad \begin{array}{r} 3 \\ +9 \\ \hline 12 \end{array} \quad \begin{array}{r} 2 \\ +9 \\ \hline 11 \end{array} \quad \begin{array}{r} 6 \\ +5 \\ \hline 11 \end{array} \quad \begin{array}{r} 7 \\ +5 \\ \hline 12 \end{array}$$

Addition facts, sums through 12

(twenty-one) **21**

Teaching page 21

Have students write the numbers from 0 through 12 along a number line on the board. Draw 11 triangles on the board. Have a student count the triangles and tell how many. (11) Have a student circle 10 of the triangles to form a group. Ask how many tens and ones. (1,1) Repeat for 12 triangles (1 ten 2 ones) Write **3 + 8** vertically on the board and have a student find 3 on the number line and go forward 8 more to tell the sum. (11) Repeat for **2 + 9** and **4 + 7.** Now write **3 + 9** on the board and repeat the activity to have students find the sum. (12) Continue for sums of 11 or 12 until all sums are found. Tell students to trace the circle around the group of 10 and trace the 11 to show that the sum of 8 and 3 is 1 ten 1 one or 11. Repeat for the second problem. Tell students to circle the group of ten in each of the next 3 problems and then work the 2 rows of problems at the bottom. Allow students to use counters if needed. Have students complete the page independently.

21

Complete the wheels.

1.

Add.

2.
$$\begin{array}{r} 7 \\ +2 \\ \hline 9 \end{array}$$
$$\begin{array}{r} 9 \\ +1 \\ \hline 10 \end{array}$$
$$\begin{array}{r} 8 \\ +4 \\ \hline 12 \end{array}$$
$$\begin{array}{r} 5 \\ +5 \\ \hline 10 \end{array}$$
$$\begin{array}{r} 4 \\ +7 \\ \hline 11 \end{array}$$
$$\begin{array}{r} 6 \\ +6 \\ \hline 12 \end{array}$$
$$\begin{array}{r} 9 \\ +3 \\ \hline 12 \end{array}$$

3.
$$\begin{array}{r} 4 \\ +5 \\ \hline 9 \end{array}$$
$$\begin{array}{r} 6 \\ +3 \\ \hline 9 \end{array}$$
$$\begin{array}{r} 2 \\ +7 \\ \hline 9 \end{array}$$
$$\begin{array}{r} 8 \\ +2 \\ \hline 10 \end{array}$$
$$\begin{array}{r} 3 \\ +9 \\ \hline 12 \end{array}$$
$$\begin{array}{r} 7 \\ +5 \\ \hline 12 \end{array}$$
$$\begin{array}{r} 3 \\ +6 \\ \hline 9 \end{array}$$

4.
$$\begin{array}{r} 8 \\ +3 \\ \hline 11 \end{array}$$
$$\begin{array}{r} 5 \\ +6 \\ \hline 11 \end{array}$$
$$\begin{array}{r} 4 \\ +6 \\ \hline 10 \end{array}$$
$$\begin{array}{r} 7 \\ +4 \\ \hline 11 \end{array}$$
$$\begin{array}{r} 3 \\ +8 \\ \hline 11 \end{array}$$
$$\begin{array}{r} 6 \\ +4 \\ \hline 10 \end{array}$$
$$\begin{array}{r} 9 \\ +2 \\ \hline 11 \end{array}$$

5.
$$\begin{array}{r} 4 \\ +8 \\ \hline 12 \end{array}$$
$$\begin{array}{r} 6 \\ +5 \\ \hline 11 \end{array}$$
$$\begin{array}{r} 3 \\ +7 \\ \hline 10 \end{array}$$
$$\begin{array}{r} 5 \\ +4 \\ \hline 9 \end{array}$$
$$\begin{array}{r} 7 \\ +3 \\ \hline 10 \end{array}$$
$$\begin{array}{r} 2 \\ +8 \\ \hline 10 \end{array}$$
$$\begin{array}{r} 5 \\ +7 \\ \hline 12 \end{array}$$

22 (twenty-two)   Addition facts, sums through 12

Correcting Common Errors

Some students may have difficulty working with sums greater than 10. Have them work with partners and counters. Have them use the counters to model problems for sums of 11 ($9 + 2 = 11$, $2 + 9 = 11$, $8 + 3 = 11$, $3 + 8 = 11$, $7 + 4 = 11$, $4 + 7 = 11$, $6 + 5 = 11$, $5 + 6 = 11$) and sums of 12 ($9 + 3 = 12$, $3 + 9 = 12$, $8 + 4 = 12$, $4 + 8 = 12$, $7 + 5 = 12$, $5 + 7 = 12$, $6 + 6 = 12$). They can use counters to model each addend, join them, and count to find the sum. Then they can write the fact.

Enrichment

1. Have students write and solve problems of doubles from $0 + 0$, $1 + 1$, etc. as far as they can.
2. Have students use an egg carton and counters to find all the ways to use addition to make 1 dozen.
3. Tell students to draw a clock face and write the numbers in place. They should then write addition problems such as $1 + 11 = 12$, $2 + 10 = 12$, etc., until a pattern is seen. Have them tell about the pattern for finding 2 addends whose sum is 12.

Teaching page 22

Have students find the 3 in the center of the first circle. Tell students they will begin with 3 and add a number in the next ring, to write a sum in the outer ring. Have students add $3 + 3$ and trace the 6. Have students work $3 + 6$ and record the sum of 9. Tell students to begin with 5 in the second wheel and add the numbers to write the sums. Have students complete the page independently.

Extra Credit   *Creative Drill*

Clap count math facts. For example, clap 10 times, pause, and state **plus** or **minus.** Then clap 6 more times. Have a student clap the correct answer. (16) Invite students to take turns clapping their own math problems and ask another student to indicate the correct answer. If a student gives the correct answer, they are the next clapper. Variations can include stamping feet, humming, etc.

22

Practice
Sums through 12

pages 23-24

Objectives

To practice addition for sums through 12

To add for sums through 12 to solve problems

Materials

12 counters

Mental Math

Dictate the following problems:
1. 0 + 1 + 2 (3)
2. 9 + 0 + 1 (10)
3. 6 + 2 + 1 (9)
4. 2 + 2 + 3 (7)
5. 3 + 4 + 1 (8)
6. 1 + 0 + 3 (4)
7. 2 + 1 + 3 (6)
8. 2 + 2 + 1 (5)

Skill Review

Write addition and subtraction problems on the board such as **3 ◯ 9 = 12** or **8 ◯ 3 = 5** and have students write the correct sign in the circle. Use subtraction problems for minuends through 10 only at this time.

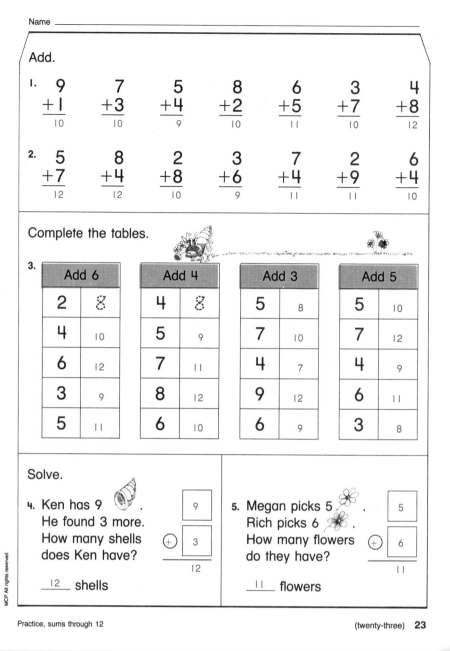

Name _____

Add.

1.
$$9 + 1 = 10$$ $$7 + 3 = 10$$ $$5 + 4 = 9$$ $$8 + 2 = 10$$ $$6 + 5 = 11$$ $$3 + 7 = 10$$ $$4 + 8 = 12$$

2.
$$5 + 7 = 12$$ $$8 + 4 = 12$$ $$2 + 8 = 10$$ $$3 + 6 = 9$$ $$7 + 4 = 11$$ $$2 + 9 = 11$$ $$6 + 4 = 10$$

Complete the tables.

3.

Add 6	
2	8
4	10
6	12
3	9
5	11

Add 4	
4	8
5	9
7	11
8	12
6	10

Add 3	
5	8
7	10
4	7
9	12
6	9

Add 5	
5	10
7	12
4	9
6	11
3	8

Solve.

4. Ken has 9. He found 3 more. How many shells does Ken have?

9 ⊕ 3 = 12

__12__ shells

5. Megan picks 5. Rich picks 6. How many flowers do they have?

5 ⊕ 6 = 11

__11__ flowers

Practice, sums through 12

(twenty-three) **23**

Teaching page 23

Tell students to lay out 7 counters to show that Pete fed 7 carrots to his rabbits in the morning. Tell students that Pete fed his rabbits 4 more carrots that evening. Ask students to lay out 4 counters to show the rabbits' evening meal. Ask how many carrots the rabbits ate that day. (11) Have students make up a similar word problem where 5 and 7 more are to be added. Continue acting out word problems for students to practice sums of 11 and 12. Tell students they are to write the sums for the problems at the top of the page. Have students look at the tables in the middle of the page. Ask what is to be done in such a table. (add 6 to each number in the first table, then add 4 to each number, etc.) Help students read the word problems if necessary. Remind students to write the sum of the

problem and in the solution statement. Have students complete the page independently.

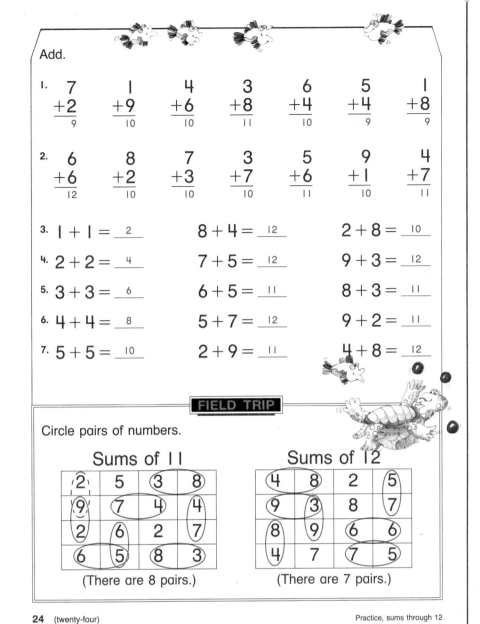

Add.

1.
$$7 + 2 = 9$$
$$1 + 9 = 10$$
$$4 + 6 = 10$$
$$3 + 8 = 11$$
$$6 + 4 = 10$$
$$5 + 4 = 9$$
$$1 + 8 = 9$$

2.
$$6 + 6 = 12$$
$$8 + 2 = 10$$
$$7 + 3 = 10$$
$$3 + 7 = 10$$
$$5 + 6 = 11$$
$$9 + 1 = 10$$
$$4 + 7 = 11$$

3. $1 + 1 = 2$ $8 + 4 = 12$ $2 + 8 = 10$

4. $2 + 2 = 4$ $7 + 5 = 12$ $9 + 3 = 12$

5. $3 + 3 = 6$ $6 + 5 = 11$ $8 + 3 = 11$

6. $4 + 4 = 8$ $5 + 7 = 12$ $9 + 2 = 11$

7. $5 + 5 = 10$ $2 + 9 = 11$ $4 + 8 = 12$

FIELD TRIP

Circle pairs of numbers.

Sums of 11

2	5	3	8
9	7	4	4
2	6	2	7
6	5	8	3

(There are 8 pairs.)

Sums of 12

4	8	2	5
9	3	8	7
8	9	6	6
4	7	7	5

(There are 7 pairs.)

24 (twenty-four)   Practice, sums through 12

Teaching page 24

Tell students to write the sum in each vertical problem and in each number sentence. Have students complete the problems independently.

Field Trip

Write on the board:
$$\begin{matrix} 2 & 4 & 6 & 1 \\ 8 & 1 & 5 & 5 \\ 0 & 9 & 3 & 2 \\ 6 & 3 & 7 & 4 \end{matrix}$$

Tell students to circle 2 numbers next to each other whose sum is 10. Circle the pair of 5's as you tell students that 5 plus 5 more equals 10. Have students circle other pairs of numbers until 6 pairs are found. Have students trace the circle in the first problem. Ask how many pairs are in each problem. (8, 7) Tell students that some pairs may share a number. Have students complete the activity independently.

Extra Credit *Numeration*

Duplicate matrix squares, such as the following for students.

+	0	1	2	3	4	. . . 9
0	0	1	2	3	4	
1	1	2	3	4	5	
2	2	3	4	5	6	
3	3	4	5	6	7	
4	4	5	6	7	8	
⋮						
9						

Explain that the numbers across the top and down the left side are the addends. To find a sum of 2 addends, tell students to find one addend along the top, and follow down the row to match the second addend on the left. The number marking their match point is the sum. Give students several addition problems to solve using the matrix.

Minuends through 12

pages 25-26

Objective

To subtract from minuends through 12

Materials

*subtraction fact cards for minuends 9 through 12
12 counters

Mental Math

Dictate the following money problems:
1. 7¢ + 2 (9¢)
2. 4¢ + 2 (2¢)
3. 3¢ + 4 + 7 (14¢)
4. 4¢ + 8 (12¢)
5. 9¢ + 8 (17¢)
6. 6¢ + 2 − 1 (7¢)

Skill Review

Dictate the following problems for students to write and solve on the board: 7 − 4 = (3), 10 − 2 = (8), 7 + 4 = (11), 9 + 3 = (12), 9 − 6 = (3), 6 + 6 = (12), 5 + 7 = (12), 10 − 4 = (6), 9 − 4 = (5). Allow students to write the problems in vertical or horizontal form. Vary the dictation to include the different ways to denote addition and subtraction; for example minus, take away, and 6 more, plus, etc.

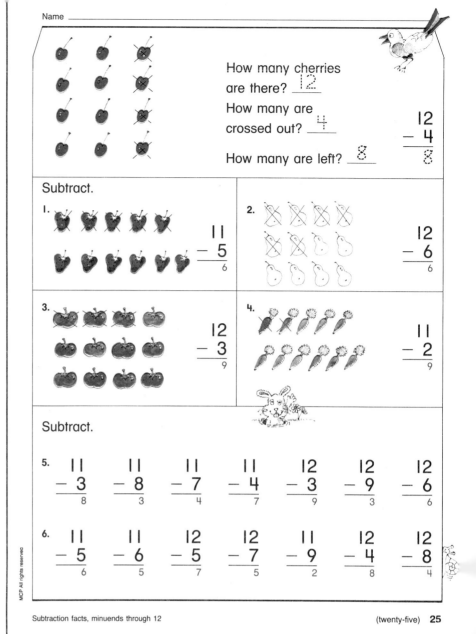

Subtraction facts, minuends through 12

(twenty-five) **25**

Teaching page 25

Review the take-away concept of subtraction by drawing 10 objects on the board. Write **10 − 7 −** on the board and have a student cross out 7 of the objects and tell how many are left. (3) Repeat for more subtraction problems for minuends through 10. Now draw 12 objects on the board and have students tell how many. (12) Write **12 − 4 =** on the board and have a student cross out 4 of the objects and tell how many are left. (8) Repeat for more problems for minuends of 12 and 11. Read each question at the top of the page with students as they trace the answers. Tell students to cross out the number of objects to be taken away and then write the number left in the problem. Tell students to complete all the problems on the page. Allow use of counters as needed.

25

Subtract.

1. $8 - 1 = \underline{7}$ $11 - 6 = \underline{5}$ $10 - 1 = \underline{9}$

2. $10 - 2 = \underline{8}$ $9 - 1 = \underline{8}$ $12 - 8 = \underline{4}$

3. $11 - 4 = \underline{7}$ $12 - 7 = \underline{5}$ $8 - 2 = \underline{6}$

4. $9 - 0 = \underline{9}$ $10 - 9 = \underline{1}$ $10 - 4 = \underline{6}$

5. $11 - 5 = \underline{6}$ $8 - 7 = \underline{1}$ $12 - 5 = \underline{7}$

6. $10 - 3 = \underline{7}$ $12 - 6 = \underline{6}$ $8 - 3 = \underline{5}$

7. $12 - 9 = \underline{3}$ $9 - 5 = \underline{4}$ $11 - 2 = \underline{9}$

8.
$\begin{array}{r} 9 \\ -2 \\ \hline 7 \end{array}$
$\begin{array}{r} 10 \\ -8 \\ \hline 2 \end{array}$
$\begin{array}{r} 9 \\ -9 \\ \hline 0 \end{array}$
$\begin{array}{r} 11 \\ -3 \\ \hline 8 \end{array}$
$\begin{array}{r} 9 \\ -4 \\ \hline 5 \end{array}$
$\begin{array}{r} 11 \\ -8 \\ \hline 3 \end{array}$
$\begin{array}{r} 8 \\ -6 \\ \hline 2 \end{array}$

9.
$\begin{array}{r} 9 \\ -8 \\ \hline 1 \end{array}$
$\begin{array}{r} 10 \\ -5 \\ \hline 5 \end{array}$
$\begin{array}{r} 8 \\ -4 \\ \hline 4 \end{array}$
$\begin{array}{r} 9 \\ -3 \\ \hline 6 \end{array}$
$\begin{array}{r} 12 \\ -4 \\ \hline 8 \end{array}$
$\begin{array}{r} 10 \\ -6 \\ \hline 4 \end{array}$
$\begin{array}{r} 9 \\ -7 \\ \hline 2 \end{array}$

10.
$\begin{array}{r} 8 \\ -8 \\ \hline 0 \end{array}$
$\begin{array}{r} 11 \\ -7 \\ \hline 4 \end{array}$
$\begin{array}{r} 9 \\ -6 \\ \hline 3 \end{array}$
$\begin{array}{r} 10 \\ -7 \\ \hline 3 \end{array}$
$\begin{array}{r} 12 \\ -3 \\ \hline 9 \end{array}$
$\begin{array}{r} 8 \\ -5 \\ \hline 3 \end{array}$
$\begin{array}{r} 11 \\ -9 \\ \hline 2 \end{array}$

Subtraction facts, minuends through 12

Correcting Common Errors

If students have difficulty subtracting from 11 and 12, have them write related addition sentences. For a subtraction sentence, such as
$$11 - 6 = \square$$
have them write
$$\square + 6 = 11$$
and find the addend that makes the number sentence true. Encourage students to model these sentences with markers. Once they know that $5 + 6 = 11$, then they should know that $11 - 6 = 5$.

Enrichment

1. Working in pairs, have one student point to 1 on a clock face. The other student should point to the number that is 12 take away 1. Tell them to continue through 12 take away 11.
2. Have one student give a related addition fact for each subtraction fact card that another student shows.
3. Have students make a subtraction fact table for minuends through 12.

Teaching page 26

Have students complete the page independently.

Extra Credit *Numeration*

Duplicate matrix squares, such as the following for students:

```
+ | 0 1 2 3 4  5 . . 9
0 | 0 1 2 3 4  5
1 | 1 2 3 4 5  6
2 | 2 3 4 5 6  7
3 | 3 4 5 6 7  8
4 | 4 5 6 7 8  9
5 | 5 6 7 8 9 10
: |
9 |
```

Remind students about the addition problems they used the matrix for, in the previous extra credit. Now, have students do the following, and look for patterns:
1. count by ones from the top
2. count by ones from the left side
3. count by two's diagonally, left to right
4. trace the diagonal from right to left
5. look for other patterns

More Minuends through 12

pages 27-28

Objective

To practice subtraction from minuends through 12

Materials

*subtraction fact cards for minuends through 12
*addition fact cards for sums through 12

Mental Math

Have students name the number for:
1. 1 ten 2 ones (12)
2. 2 tens 1 one (21)
3. 1 ten 6 ones (16)
4. 9 ones (9)
5. 2 tens 0 ones (20)
6. 1 ten 5 ones (15)

Skill Review

Group subtraction fact cards into minuends through 8, minuends 9 through 12 and facts related to doubles. Select several facts from the first group and have students work problems at the board. Help students see that all the facts are related to sums through 8. Repeat for facts related to sums of 9 through 12 and facts related to doubles.

Subtract.

1.
$$11 - 3 = 8 \qquad 11 - 5 = 6 \qquad 11 - 9 = 2 \qquad 11 - 4 = 7 \qquad 11 - 7 = 4 \qquad 11 - 6 = 5 \qquad 11 - 8 = 3$$

2.
$$12 - 3 = 9 \qquad 12 - 5 = 7 \qquad 12 - 6 = 6 \qquad 12 - 8 = 4 \qquad 12 - 4 = 8 \qquad 12 - 7 = 5 \qquad 12 - 9 = 3$$

Complete the wheels.

3.

Solve.

4. Janice has 11 📖.
   She read 5 of them.
   How many books
   are left to read?

   $11 \ominus 5 = 6$

   __6__ books

5. Jim had 12 🍇.
   He ate 7 of them.
   How many grapes
   are left?

   $12 \ominus 7 = 5$

   __5__ grapes

Teaching page 27

Tell students they are to write the answer to each subtraction fact in the 2 rows of problems. Ask students if they can tell what they will do with the 2 wheels. Have students tell the number left when 8 is taken away from 12. (4) Have students trace the 4 and then help students work another problem, and 1 problem on the second wheel if necessary. Have students read through the 2 word problems and give help if needed. Have students then complete the page independently.

Subtract.

1. $10 - 3 = \underline{7}$ $8 - 2 = \underline{6}$ $10 - 8 = \underline{2}$

2. $9 - 1 = \underline{8}$ $11 - 3 = \underline{8}$ $11 - 5 = \underline{6}$

3. $11 - 4 = \underline{7}$ $10 - 4 = \underline{6}$ $9 - 3 = \underline{6}$

4. $10 - 7 = \underline{3}$ $12 - 3 = \underline{9}$ $12 - 5 = \underline{7}$

5. $8 - 7 = \underline{1}$ $10 - 5 = \underline{5}$ $12 - 6 = \underline{6}$

6. $11 - 2 = \underline{9}$ $12 - 8 = \underline{4}$ $10 - 2 = \underline{8}$

7. $12 - 4 = \underline{8}$ $10 - 9 = \underline{1}$ $11 - 6 = \underline{5}$

8. $10 - 1 = \underline{9}$ $11 - 7 = \underline{4}$ $12 - 9 = \underline{3}$

9. $11 - 8 = \underline{3}$ $12 - 7 = \underline{5}$ $10 - 6 = \underline{4}$

10. $9 - 7 = \underline{2}$ $9 - 5 = \underline{4}$ $11 - 9 = \underline{2}$

FIELD TRIP

Use these numbers to write four number sentences.

| 5 | 11 | 6 | | 4 | 12 | 8 |

$5 + 6 = 11$ $4 + 8 = 12$

$6 + 5 = 11$ $8 + 4 = 12$

$11 - 6 = 5$ $12 - 8 = 4$

$11 - 5 = 6$ $12 - 4 = 8$

Correcting Common Errors

Some students may need more practice subtracting from minuends of 11 and 12. Have them practice with partners and fact cards with minuends of 11 and 12. They can take turns showing each other the fact cards, asking for the answers. They should repeat more often those facts that their partner has difficulty remembering.

Enrichment

1. Have students sort subtraction fact cards into a group having even numbered answers and a group having answers which are odd numbers.
2. Tell students to write all the subtraction facts which are related to sums of 11 and 12.

Teaching page 28

Tell students to complete the 3 columns of problems independently.

Field Trip

Write **2, 6, 4** on the board and tell students we can use these 3 numbers to write 4 number sentences. Write **2 + 4 = 6** on the board and help students develop and write 3 more. (4 + 2 = 6, 6 − 2 = 4, 6 − 4 = 2) Repeat the activity for 4 sentences using the numbers 2, 5 and 3. (2 + 3 = 5, 3 + 2 = 5, 5 − 2 = 3, 5 − 3 = 2) Have students trace the numbers in the first problem and then complete the activity independently.

Extra Credit   *Numeration*

Have a Mystery Day. Have students write answers to a brief numerical questionnaire about themselves. Sample questions might include: how many buttons on dress or shirt? how many missing teeth? how many pockets? how many years old? how many brothers? how many letters in last name?, etc. Collect the completed questionnaires and read them aloud. Have students guess each mystery student. Provide more counting practice by having students count the letters in their first and last names. Have them discover who has the most letters. Then, have them count how many of each letter are in the names of the entire class, and record the number next to each letter on an alphabet chart. Have students write their names with crayons and incorporate them into colorful designs to be displayed.

28

Mixed Practice

pages 29-30

Objective

To practice addition and subtraction

Materials

12 counters

Mental Math

Have students count on to 19 from:
1. 6 (7, . . . ,19)
2. 11
3. 9
4. 14
5. 10
6. 12
7. 8
8. 4

Skill Review

Write on the board:

4 + 6	9
3 + 6	8
12 − 6	11
6 + 5	12
11 − 3	3
5 + 7	10
12 − 9	6

Have students draw a line from the problem to its answer.

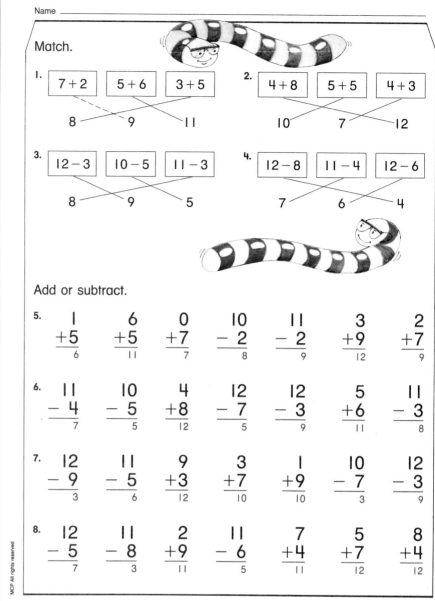

Name _____

Match.

1. | 7 + 2 | 5 + 6 | 3 + 5 |

8   9   11

2. | 4 + 8 | 5 + 5 | 4 + 3 |

10   7   12

3. | 12 − 3 | 10 − 5 | 11 − 3 |

8   9   5

4. | 12 − 8 | 11 − 4 | 12 − 6 |

7   6   4

Add or subtract.

5.
1	6	0	10	11	3	2
+5	+5	+7	− 2	− 2	+9	+7
6	11	7	8	9	12	9

6.
11	10	4	12	12	5	11
− 4	− 5	+8	− 7	− 3	+6	− 3
7	5	12	5	9	11	8

7.
12	11	9	3	1	10	12
− 9	− 5	+3	+7	+9	− 7	− 3
3	6	12	10	10	3	9

8.
12	11	2	11	7	5	8
− 5	− 8	+9	− 6	+4	+7	+4
7	3	11	5	11	12	12

Practice, adding and subtracting

(twenty-nine) **29**

Teaching page 29

Discuss the following or other situations where students use addition or subtraction: Wanting 10 players to begin a game of soccer and having only 6, collecting 12 students' papers and counting only 9 so far, having a group of 8 students join a group of 4 students, etc. Have students tell which operation they would use in each situation. Tell students they are to find the answer to the problem in each box at the top of the page and draw a line from the box to the answer. Have students work the first problem and trace the line to the 9. Tell students to write the answer to each problem in the next section. Remind students to look at the sign in each problem to see if they are to add or subtract. Have students complete the page independently.

29

Add or subtract.

1. $2 + 9 = \underline{11}$

2. $5 + 7 = \underline{12}$

3. $8 + 3 = \underline{11}$

4. $10 - 1 = \underline{9}$

5. $11 - 4 = \underline{7}$

6. $12 - 6 = \underline{6}$

7. $7 + 5 = \underline{12}$

8. $8 + 2 = \underline{10}$

9. $4 + 7 = \underline{11}$

10. $10 - 5 = \underline{5}$

11. $12 - 9 = \underline{3}$

12. $6 + 5 = \underline{11}$

13.
$$\begin{array}{r} 9 \\ +1 \\ \hline 10 \end{array} \quad \begin{array}{r} 4 \\ +8 \\ \hline 12 \end{array} \quad \begin{array}{r} 11 \\ -9 \\ \hline 2 \end{array} \quad \begin{array}{r} 3 \\ +8 \\ \hline 11 \end{array}$$

14.
$$\begin{array}{r} 6 \\ +4 \\ \hline 10 \end{array} \quad \begin{array}{r} 12 \\ -7 \\ \hline 5 \end{array} \quad \begin{array}{r} 11 \\ -5 \\ \hline 6 \end{array} \quad \begin{array}{r} 12 \\ -8 \\ \hline 4 \end{array}$$

15.
$$\begin{array}{r} 12 \\ -3 \\ \hline 9 \end{array} \quad \begin{array}{r} 3 \\ +7 \\ \hline 10 \end{array} \quad \begin{array}{r} 9 \\ +3 \\ \hline 12 \end{array} \quad \begin{array}{r} 5 \\ +5 \\ \hline 10 \end{array}$$

16.
$$\begin{array}{r} 8 \\ +4 \\ \hline 12 \end{array} \quad \begin{array}{r} 10 \\ -6 \\ \hline 4 \end{array} \quad \begin{array}{r} 12 \\ -5 \\ \hline 7 \end{array} \quad \begin{array}{r} 11 \\ -3 \\ \hline 8 \end{array}$$

17.
$$\begin{array}{r} 10 \\ -8 \\ \hline 2 \end{array} \quad \begin{array}{r} 3 \\ +9 \\ \hline 12 \end{array} \quad \begin{array}{r} 11 \\ -7 \\ \hline 4 \end{array} \quad \begin{array}{r} 6 \\ +6 \\ \hline 12 \end{array}$$

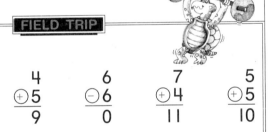

FIELD TRIP

Write the correct sign.

$$\begin{array}{r} 8 \\ \ominus 3 \\ \hline 5 \end{array} \quad \begin{array}{r} 12 \\ \ominus 7 \\ \hline 5 \end{array} \quad \begin{array}{r} 4 \\ \oplus 5 \\ \hline 9 \end{array} \quad \begin{array}{r} 6 \\ \ominus 6 \\ \hline 0 \end{array} \quad \begin{array}{r} 7 \\ \oplus 4 \\ \hline 11 \end{array} \quad \begin{array}{r} 5 \\ \oplus 5 \\ \hline 10 \end{array}$$

Practice, adding and subtracting

Correcting Common Errors

If students continue to have difficulty mastering their addition or subtraction facts through sums of 12, have them create fact families with fact cards. Have students work in pairs. Give them the fact cards mixed up for 5 fact families and have them form the fact families by placing the related fact cards in groups. After the five groups are correctly formed, encourage students to read each set aloud to see the relationships.

Enrichment

1. Tell one student to say a number. Have another student silently add or subtract a number and give the sum or difference. Tell the first student to guess the number and tell if it had been added or subtracted to the first number.
2. Have students use grid paper and 2 different-colored crayons to show any facts through sums and minuends of 12.

Teaching page 30

Remind students to look at the sign in each problem before beginning to work the problem. Have students complete the page independently.

Field Trip

Tell students they are to write a plus or minus sign in each circle to make the problem true. Have students complete the problems independently.

Extra Credit *Sets*

Make a bulletin board that illustrates the intersection and union of sets. Use different colors of yarn to outline large shapes. The regions should overlap each other. For example:

Cut out stars and place them at random across the board. Use 30 to 50 stars depending on the size of the board. Ask students to tell how many stars are in the set hearts, the set circle, in the union of half-moon and heart, in the intersection of circle and rectangle? Have students create questions to ask other students.

Problem Solving with Money

pages 31-32

Objective

To add or subtract to solve money problems

Materials

2 nickels
12 pennies

Mental Math

Tell students to name the number that comes:
1. before 26.
2. before 12.
3. after 19.
4. between 10 and 12.
5. before 16.
6. between 19 and 21.

Skill Review

Draw a number line on the board and write **5, 10, 15, 20** and **25** in their respective places. Have students count with you by 5's through 25. Have students write in the missing numbers from 0 through 24. Point to the 8 and have students begin at 5 and count on to 8 to tell the number. Repeat for other points on the number line, having students count by 5's through 20, for example, and then count on by 1's to 23.

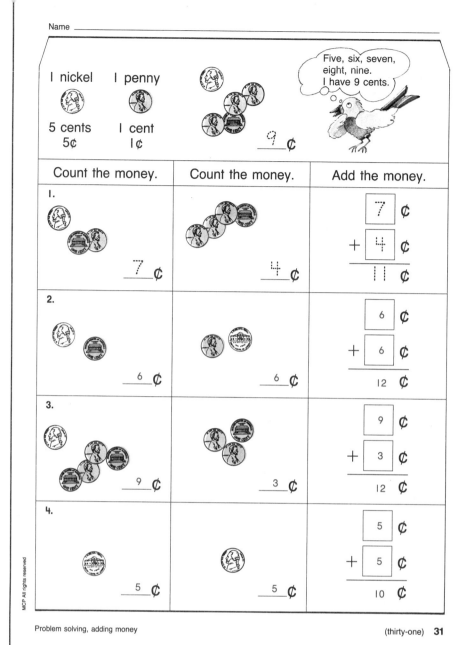

Problem solving, adding money

(thirty-one) **31**

Teaching page 31

Have students lay out 2 nickels. Ask students how many pennies are in 1 nickel. (5) Ask students to tell the total amount. (10¢) Write **5¢ + 5¢ = 10¢** vertically on the board. Have students lay out 1 nickel and 6 pennies. Ask students what money problem they can write to find the sum of these coins. (5¢ + 6 =) Have a student write and solve the problem on the board. (11¢) Now draw 2 groups of coins on the board to show 8¢ + 4¢ and have students tell the amount of money in each group. (8¢, 4¢) Have a student write and solve the problem on the board. (8¢ + 4 = 12¢) Repeat for more examples of 2 amounts through totals of 12¢. Now have students lay out 11¢. Tell students to remove 6¢ and tell how much money is left. (5¢) Have a student write and solve the problem on the board. (11¢ − 6 = 5¢) Repeat for more subtraction

problems of minuends through 12¢.
Read through the coin names and amounts with the students. Have students count the coins on the right and trace the 9. Remind students to begin with 5 and count on. Have students count the money in the first box and trace the 7. Have students count the 4 pennies and trace the 4. Tell students to trace the 7 and 4 in the problem and trace the 11 to show the sum of the 2 groups of coins. Tell students to count the money and write the amount in each box and then solve the problem to find the sum. Have students complete the problems independently.

31

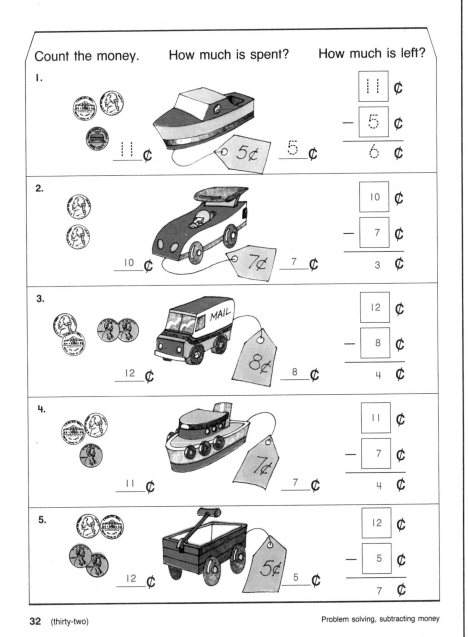

Count the money.   How much is spent?   How much is left?

1.
  11 ¢
  5¢   5 ¢
  11 ¢
  | 11 | ¢
  − | 5 | ¢
  ‾‾‾‾‾‾
  6 ¢

2.
  10 ¢
  7¢   7 ¢
  | 10 | ¢
  − | 7 | ¢
  ‾‾‾‾‾‾
  3 ¢

3.
  MAIL
  12 ¢
  8¢   8 ¢
  | 12 | ¢
  − | 8 | ¢
  ‾‾‾‾‾‾
  4 ¢

4.
  11 ¢
  7¢   7 ¢
  | 11 | ¢
  − | 7 | ¢
  ‾‾‾‾‾‾
  4 ¢

5.
  12 ¢
  5¢   5 ¢
  | 12 | ¢
  − | 5 | ¢
  ‾‾‾‾‾‾
  7 ¢

Problem solving, subtracting money

Correcting Common Errors

Some students may add or subtract money incorrectly because they have difficulty counting money. For a group of coins, such as 1 nickel and 3 pennies, have them start with the coin that has the greater value, the nickel, and count on the 3 pennies: 5¢ . . . 6¢, 7¢, 8¢ to find the total value of the group. They can write this amount as one of the addends in the problem. Then they should count in a similar manner to find the value of the second group of coins and write the other addend.

Enrichment

1. Have students draw 3 objects and their price tags of 4¢, 6¢ and 2¢. Tell them to write and solve a problem to find the total cost of all 3 objects.
2. Have students write subtraction facts for minuends of 11 or 12 whose answers are 7 or more. Then tell them to write 2 related addition facts for each subtraction fact.
3. Have students write addition problems to show why Marika and Pilar have the same amount of money when Marika has 2 nickels and 6 pennies and Pilar has only 1 nickel and 11 pennies.

Teaching page 32

Remind students that 1 nickel is 5¢ so they should count by 5's and count on by 1's to find how much money in all. Have students count the coins in the first box and trace the 11. Ask students the cost of the item in the first box. (5¢) Have students trace the 5. Tell students they have 11¢ and spend 5¢. They need to find out how much money is left. Have students trace the numbers in the problem to find the answer. Tell students to complete the 4 problems independently.

Extra Credit   *Numeration*

Take a counting walk outside. Make each group of students responsible for counting specific items such as: houses, cars, traffic lights, telephone poles, dogs, lines in sidewalks, etc. Have students write their results on the board and compare. Back in the classroom, have groups count how many steps from the door to the wastebasket, how many times a student can jump in one minute, how many days until vacation, etc. Compare results tallied by different groups to see how much they differ. If totals counted by each group are not the same, have students suggest reasons to explain the differences.

More Problem Solving

pages 33-34

Objective

To add or subtract to solve word problems

Materials

2 nickels
12 pennies

Mental Math

Dictate the following problems:
1. 6 + 6 (12)
2. 7 + 4 (11)
3. 12 − 5 (7)
4. 11 − 6 (5)
5. 10 − 3 (7)
6. 4 − 2 + 3 (5)
7. 6 + 5 + 1 (12)

Skill Review

Have students lay out 12¢ and group the coins into 2 groups. Ask students to write addition problems on the board to show different ways to make 12¢. Encourage students to use a nickel to show 5¢. Ask a student to tell a story of having an amount of money through 12¢ and spending some of the money. Have other students lay out the money to show the story as one student writes and solves the subtraction problem on the board.

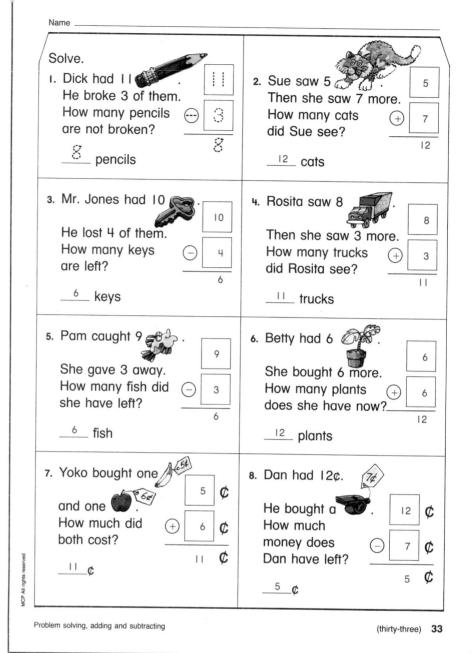

Solve.

1. Dick had 11 [pencil]. He broke 3 of them. How many pencils are not broken?

   11
   ⊙ 3
   8

   __8__ pencils

2. Sue saw 5 [cat]. Then she saw 7 more. How many cats did Sue see?

   5
   ⊕ 7
   12

   __12__ cats

3. Mr. Jones had 10 [key]. He lost 4 of them. How many keys are left?

   10
   ⊖ 4
   6

   __6__ keys

4. Rosita saw 8 [truck]. Then she saw 3 more. How many trucks did Rosita see?

   8
   ⊕ 3
   11

   __11__ trucks

5. Pam caught 9 [fish]. She gave 3 away. How many fish did she have left?

   9
   ⊖ 3
   6

   __6__ fish

6. Betty had 6 [plant]. She bought 6 more. How many plants does she have now?

   6
   ⊕ 6
   12

   __12__ plants

7. Yoko bought one [banana 5¢] and one [apple 6¢]. How much did both cost?

   5 ¢
   ⊕ 6 ¢
   11 ¢

   __11__ ¢

8. Dan had 12¢. He bought a [whistle 7¢]. How much money does Dan have left?

   12 ¢
   ⊖ 7 ¢
   5 ¢

   __5__ ¢

Problem solving, adding and subtracting

(thirty-three) **33**

Teaching page 33

Tell a story of having 12 objects or 12¢ in coins and taking some away. Ask students if they would add or subtract to solve the problem. (subtract) Have a student write and solve the problem on the board. Now tell a story of having 7¢ and earning 4¢ more. Ask students if they would add or subtract to solve the problem. (add) Have a student write and solve the problem on the board. (7¢ + 4 = 11¢) Repeat for more word problems.

Read through the first word problem with the students as they trace the numbers and the minus sign. Remind student to trace the 8 in the solution statement. Help students read each problem, if necessary, as they complete the work independently. Remind students to write the plus or minus sign in the circle in each problem to show what operation they will use to solve

the problem. Also remind students again to write their answer in the solution statement.

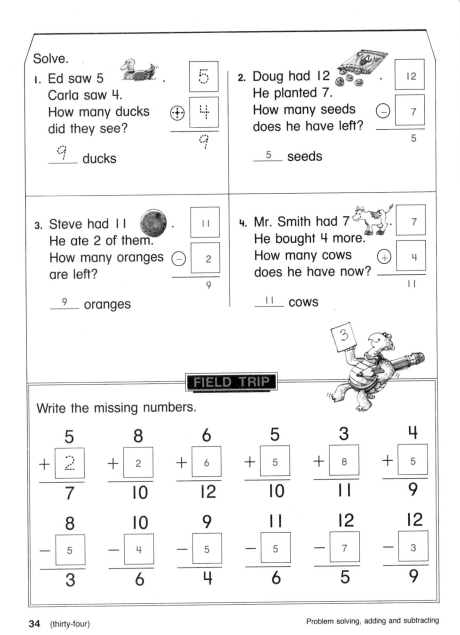

Solve.

1. Ed saw 5 🐕.
   Carla saw 4.
   How many ducks
   did they see?

   $\begin{array}{r} 5 \\ \oplus\ 4 \\ \hline 9 \end{array}$

   __9__ ducks

2. Doug had 12 🫘.
   He planted 7.
   How many seeds
   does he have left?

   $\begin{array}{r} 12 \\ \ominus\ 7 \\ \hline 5 \end{array}$

   __5__ seeds

3. Steve had 11 🍊.
   He ate 2 of them.
   How many oranges
   are left?

   $\begin{array}{r} 11 \\ \ominus\ 2 \\ \hline 9 \end{array}$

   __9__ oranges

4. Mr. Smith had 7 🐄.
   He bought 4 more.
   How many cows
   does he have now?

   $\begin{array}{r} 7 \\ \oplus\ 4 \\ \hline 11 \end{array}$

   __11__ cows

FIELD TRIP

Write the missing numbers.

$\begin{array}{r} 5 \\ +\ 2 \\ \hline 7 \end{array}$
$\begin{array}{r} 8 \\ +\ 2 \\ \hline 10 \end{array}$
$\begin{array}{r} 6 \\ +\ 6 \\ \hline 12 \end{array}$
$\begin{array}{r} 5 \\ +\ 5 \\ \hline 10 \end{array}$
$\begin{array}{r} 3 \\ +\ 8 \\ \hline 11 \end{array}$
$\begin{array}{r} 4 \\ +\ 5 \\ \hline 9 \end{array}$

$\begin{array}{r} 8 \\ -\ 5 \\ \hline 3 \end{array}$
$\begin{array}{r} 10 \\ -\ 4 \\ \hline 6 \end{array}$
$\begin{array}{r} 9 \\ -\ 5 \\ \hline 4 \end{array}$
$\begin{array}{r} 11 \\ -\ 5 \\ \hline 6 \end{array}$
$\begin{array}{r} 12 \\ -\ 7 \\ \hline 5 \end{array}$
$\begin{array}{r} 12 \\ -\ 3 \\ \hline 9 \end{array}$

34 (thirty-four)   Problem solving, adding and subtracting

Teaching page 34

Tell students to work the word problems independently. Help students read the problems where necessary. Remind students to write the plus or minus sign in each problem and record each answer in its solution statement.

Field Trip

Remind students that they have worked problems like this before. Ask students what number is added to 5 to have a sum of 7. (2) Have students trace the 2. Ask what operation is to be used in each problem in the first row. (addition) Ask what operation they will use in the second row. (subtraction) Have students complete the problems independently.

Extra Credit *Logic*

Read these sentences aloud: Ruth is taller than John. John is shorter than Ruth. True or False? (True) Now read: Sara got to school first. Sid arrived after Martin. Martin got to school last. (False) Give students the following to identify as true or false:

1. Mrs. Morgan is John's mother. John is Mrs. Morgan's son. (true)
2. It is three miles from school to the police station. It is two miles from the police station to school. (false)
3. Allen is Mark's brother. Shirley is Allen's sister. Mark is Shirley's brother. (true)
4. Mount Hope is in Ohio. Ohio is in the United States. Mount Hope is in the United States. (true)
5. Susan and Inge have the same number of dolls. Inge has three dolls. Susan has one doll. (false)

34

Review

pages 35-36

Objectives

To review addition and subtraction facts for sums through 12
To maintain skills learned previously this year

Materials

2 nickels
12 pennies

Mental Math

If $10 - 3 = 7$ is the reverse of $7 + 3 = 10$, have students tell the reverse of:
1. $4 + 5 = 9$ ($9 - 5 = 4$ or $9 - 4 = 5$)
2. $12 - 4 = 8$ ($8 + 4 = 12$ or $4 + 8 = 12$)
3. $6 + 6 = 12$
4. $11 - 1 = 10$
5. $2 + 7 = 9$
6. $5 + 5 = 10$
7. $11 - 5 = 6$

Skill Review

Write several addition and subtraction problems on the board for sums and minuends through 12. Do not write the signs. Have students look at each problem and tell the operation to be used. Then have students copy and solve the problems.

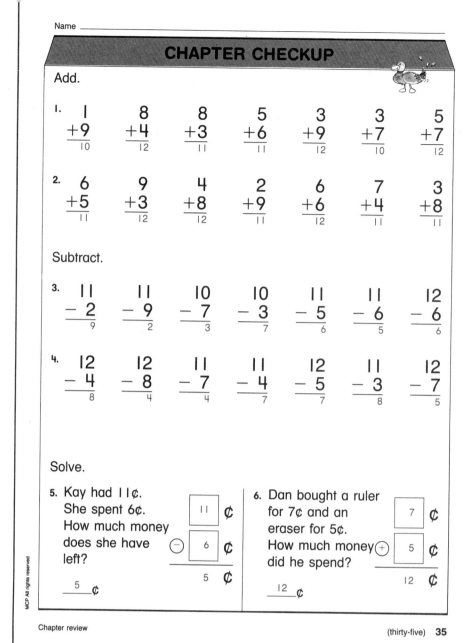

Name _____

CHAPTER CHECKUP

Add.

1.
$\begin{array}{r} 1 \\ +9 \\ \hline 10 \end{array}$
$\begin{array}{r} 8 \\ +4 \\ \hline 12 \end{array}$
$\begin{array}{r} 8 \\ +3 \\ \hline 11 \end{array}$
$\begin{array}{r} 5 \\ +6 \\ \hline 11 \end{array}$
$\begin{array}{r} 3 \\ +9 \\ \hline 12 \end{array}$
$\begin{array}{r} 3 \\ +7 \\ \hline 10 \end{array}$
$\begin{array}{r} 5 \\ +7 \\ \hline 12 \end{array}$

2.
$\begin{array}{r} 6 \\ +5 \\ \hline 11 \end{array}$
$\begin{array}{r} 9 \\ +3 \\ \hline 12 \end{array}$
$\begin{array}{r} 4 \\ +8 \\ \hline 12 \end{array}$
$\begin{array}{r} 2 \\ +9 \\ \hline 11 \end{array}$
$\begin{array}{r} 6 \\ +6 \\ \hline 12 \end{array}$
$\begin{array}{r} 7 \\ +4 \\ \hline 11 \end{array}$
$\begin{array}{r} 3 \\ +8 \\ \hline 11 \end{array}$

Subtract.

3.
$\begin{array}{r} 11 \\ -2 \\ \hline 9 \end{array}$
$\begin{array}{r} 11 \\ -9 \\ \hline 2 \end{array}$
$\begin{array}{r} 10 \\ -7 \\ \hline 3 \end{array}$
$\begin{array}{r} 10 \\ -3 \\ \hline 7 \end{array}$
$\begin{array}{r} 11 \\ -5 \\ \hline 6 \end{array}$
$\begin{array}{r} 11 \\ -6 \\ \hline 5 \end{array}$
$\begin{array}{r} 12 \\ -6 \\ \hline 6 \end{array}$

4.
$\begin{array}{r} 12 \\ -4 \\ \hline 8 \end{array}$
$\begin{array}{r} 12 \\ -8 \\ \hline 4 \end{array}$
$\begin{array}{r} 11 \\ -7 \\ \hline 4 \end{array}$
$\begin{array}{r} 11 \\ -4 \\ \hline 7 \end{array}$
$\begin{array}{r} 12 \\ -5 \\ \hline 7 \end{array}$
$\begin{array}{r} 11 \\ -3 \\ \hline 8 \end{array}$
$\begin{array}{r} 12 \\ -7 \\ \hline 5 \end{array}$

Solve.

5. Kay had 11¢. She spent 6¢. How much money does she have left?

11 ¢
⊖ 6 ¢
_____
5 ¢

___5___ ¢

6. Dan bought a ruler for 7¢ and an eraser for 5¢. How much money did he spend?

7 ¢
⊕ 5 ¢
_____
12 ¢

___12___ ¢

Chapter review

(thirty-five) **35**

Teaching page 35

Ask students what operation they will use to solve each problem in the first group. (addition) Repeat for the second group. (subtraction) Have students read and tell what they will do in each of the word problems. Be sure students write the sign in the circle and the answer in the solution statement. Help students read the word problems if necessary. Allow students to use the coins as counters if they choose. Have students complete the page independently.

ROUNDUP REVIEW

Add or subtract.

1. $1 + 2 = \underline{3}$ $9 - 3 = \underline{6}$ $1 + 5 = \underline{6}$

2. $7 - 4 = \underline{3}$ $8 - 2 = \underline{6}$ $3 + 3 = \underline{6}$

3. $2 + 4 = \underline{6}$ $6 - 1 = \underline{5}$ $9 + 3 = \underline{12}$

4. $5 + 3 = \underline{8}$ $7 + 5 = \underline{12}$ $6 + 4 = \underline{10}$

5.
$$\begin{array}{c} 9 \\ -4 \\ \hline 5 \end{array} \quad \begin{array}{c} 4 \\ +4 \\ \hline 8 \end{array} \quad \begin{array}{c} 2 \\ +7 \\ \hline 9 \end{array} \quad \begin{array}{c} 5 \\ +5 \\ \hline 10 \end{array} \quad \begin{array}{c} 8 \\ -5 \\ \hline 3 \end{array} \quad \begin{array}{c} 9 \\ -6 \\ \hline 3 \end{array} \quad \begin{array}{c} 10 \\ -5 \\ \hline 5 \end{array}$$

6.
$$\begin{array}{c} 11 \\ -3 \\ \hline 8 \end{array} \quad \begin{array}{c} 12 \\ -5 \\ \hline 7 \end{array} \quad \begin{array}{c} 10 \\ -2 \\ \hline 8 \end{array} \quad \begin{array}{c} 9 \\ +1 \\ \hline 10 \end{array} \quad \begin{array}{c} 6 \\ +3 \\ \hline 9 \end{array} \quad \begin{array}{c} 11 \\ -6 \\ \hline 5 \end{array} \quad \begin{array}{c} 12 \\ -8 \\ \hline 4 \end{array}$$

7.
$$\begin{array}{c} 5 \\ -5 \\ \hline 0 \end{array} \quad \begin{array}{c} 8 \\ +3 \\ \hline 11 \end{array} \quad \begin{array}{c} 6 \\ +5 \\ \hline 11 \end{array} \quad \begin{array}{c} 4 \\ +8 \\ \hline 12 \end{array} \quad \begin{array}{c} 3 \\ +7 \\ \hline 10 \end{array} \quad \begin{array}{c} 10 \\ -7 \\ \hline 3 \end{array} \quad \begin{array}{c} 12 \\ -9 \\ \hline 3 \end{array}$$

Solve.

8. Adam saw 4  and 5 . How many animals did Adam see?

$\boxed{4}$ $\oplus$ $\boxed{5}$ $\underline{9}$

__9__ animals

9. Molly had 11 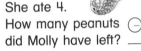. She ate 4. How many peanuts did Molly have left?

$\boxed{11}$ $\ominus$ $\boxed{4}$ $\underline{7}$

__7__ peanuts

Cumulative review

1. Have students draw a picture that shows why $8 + 3$ and $8 - 3$ have different answers.
2. Have students use the numbers 6, 5 and 11 to write and solve 4 different addition or subtraction facts.
3. Have students act out a story where they subtracted when they should have added. Then tell them to write the 2 problems and tell how they differ.

Teaching page 36

This page reviews addition, subtraction and problem solving for sums and minuends through 12. Ask students what they should do first before problems like the ones on this page. (look at the sign to see what operation to use) Ask students what operation to use in each of the word problems. Help students read the problems if necessary. Have students complete the page independently.

Numbers through 19

pages 37-38

Objectives

To read and write numbers through 19
To add 1 ten and ones for sums through 19

Materials

*blank addition table
ten-sticks and ones

Mental Math

Ask students what number is added to:
1. 10 to have a sum of 15. (5)
2. 12 to have a sum of 12. (0)
3. 9 to have a sum of 12. (3)
4. 15 to have a sum of 20. (5)
What number is subtracted from:
5. 12 to have 3 left. (9)
6. 15 to have 10 left. (5)
7. 20 to have 15 left. (5)

Skill Review

Draw a number line on the board and have students fill in the numbers 0 through 19. Have students circle every other number from 0 through 18. Have students read the circled numbers to count by 2's. Have students read the odd numbers in order.

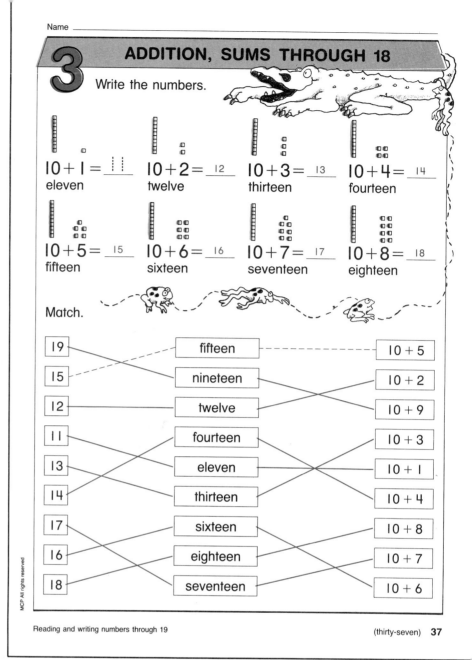

Reading and writing numbers through 19   (thirty-seven) **37**

Teaching page 37

Write **8 + 3 =** on the board and have a student write the sum. (11) Have a student draw 11 objects on the board and circle 10 of them. Ask students how many tens are in 11. (1) Ask how many ones. (1) Write **10 + 1 =** on the board and have a student write the sum. (11) Write **eleven** on the board and remind students that this is the number name for 11. Repeat the activity to develop more numbers from 12 through 19 and write the number name for each number. Have students write the sums through 12 on the addition table. Have students then count the blank squares to find out how many addition facts have sums of more than 10. (36) Tell students to count the tens and ones and write the sum for each problem at the top of the page. Have students complete the first

problem and trace the 11. On the second half of the page, tell students to draw a line from the number name in the middle column to its number on the left. Have students trace the line to match fifteen to 15. Then tell students to match the number name to the box on the right which tells the number of tens and ones in the number. Have students trace the line from fifteen to 10 + 5. Have students complete the page independently.

Write the numbers.

1. eleven ___11___ 2. eighteen ___18___ 3. fourteen ___14___

4. twelve ___12___ 5. ten ___10___ 6. seventeen ___17___

7. nineteen ___19___ 8. thirteen ___13___ 9. sixteen ___16___

10. fifteen ___15___ 11. zero ___0___ 12. nine ___9___

Add. Color by answers.

11	red	12	blue	13	green
14	black	15	orange	16	brown
17	yellow	18	purple	19	pink

$10 + 3 = 13$

$10 + 9 = 19$

$10 + 2 = 12$

$10 + 6 = 16$

$10 + 8 = 18$

$10 + 4 = 14$

$10 + 1 = 11$

$10 + 7 = 17$

$10 + 5 = 15$

Reading and writing numbers through 19

Correcting Common Errors

Some students may have difficulty with the numbers 11 through 19. Have them work with partners to model these numbers. For example, have them use a ten strip and a single to model eleven writing $10 + 1 = 11$ to show what they have done. Then have them continue in this manner with the numbers in order through 19. Encourage students to also count out an array of single counters to match each number.

Enrichment

1. Have students write the numbers and number names from 0 through 19 on cards. Tell them to match the numbers to their names with a partner.
2. Have students use grid paper and crayons to make a ten-strip and strips of 1 through 9 squares. Tell them to cut out the strips and then lay out a number from 11 through 19 for a friend to name their number.

Teaching page 38

Have students read the word, eleven, and trace the number. Tell students to read the number name and write its number on the line in each problem in this section. Then have students read the number and color pairs. Tell them to find the sum for each problem, match each sum to a color and color that part of the picture with that color.

Extra Credit   *Numeration*

Ask students to think about the way they use numbers every day. Write their ideas on the board. Then ask students to think about what life would be like without a numbering system. Tell students to draw a picture showing one way the absence of numbers would make a difference in their lives. Have them write a few sentences to describe their picture on the back. Have students explain their pictures to the rest of the class. Put all the pages together, add a cover and title, and share the book with other classes.

More Sums through 12

pages 39-40

Objective

To practice sums through 12

Materials

*addition fact cards for sums through 12
*cards numbered 0 through 12
egg carton
12 counters

Mental Math

Ask students which day comes before:

1. Monday (Sunday)
2. Thursday
3. Friday
4. Tuesday
5. Sunday
6. Wednesday
7. Saturday

Skill Review

Show the addition fact cards which are doubles and doubles plus 1, in random order. Have students give the sum of each and place them in a doubles or doubles-plus-1 group. Now show the double fact cards and have students find the double-plus-1 fact. Then show a double-plus-1 fact for students to find the double fact.

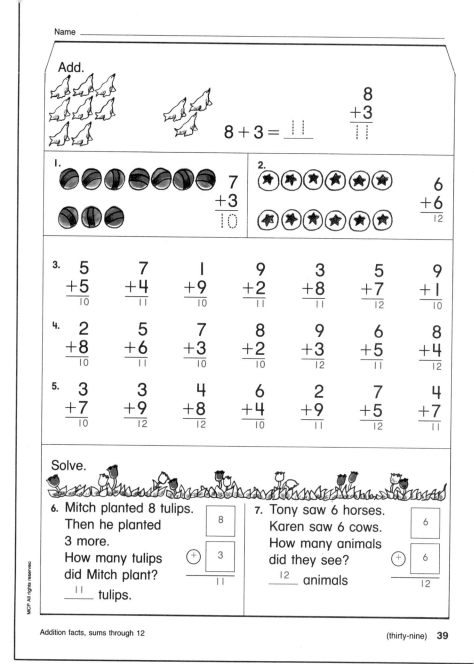

Addition facts, sums through 12

(thirty-nine) **39**

Teaching page 39

Have students place 1 counter in each compartment of the egg carton. Ask students how many counters in all. (12) Tell students that 12 of anything can be called a **dozen.** Discuss buying eggs by the dozen. Have students remove all counters and then place 1 counter in each of 3 compartments. Ask how many more counters will make 1 dozen. (9) Have a student write 3 + 9 = 12 on the board. Continue to review the facts for 12 and 11 in this way. Have students count how many in each picture and tell the total. (11) Have students trace the 11 in both problems. Ask students the number of objects in each group in the next problem. (7, 3) Ask students how many in all. (10) Remind students there are 1 ten 0 ones in 10 as they draw a circle around the 10 objects. Repeat the procedure for the next problem and have students complete the next set of problems. Read through the 2 word problems with the students, if necessary. Remind students they must write the sign in each problem and record the answer in the solution statement when they complete it.

Add.

1.
$$\begin{array}{r}3\\+9\\\hline 12\end{array}\qquad\begin{array}{r}5\\+5\\\hline 10\end{array}\qquad\begin{array}{r}3\\+6\\\hline 9\end{array}\qquad\begin{array}{r}8\\+2\\\hline 10\end{array}\qquad\begin{array}{r}5\\+3\\\hline 8\end{array}\qquad\begin{array}{r}9\\+1\\\hline 10\end{array}\qquad\begin{array}{r}8\\+4\\\hline 12\end{array}$$

2.
$$\begin{array}{r}5\\+7\\\hline 12\end{array}\qquad\begin{array}{r}1\\+9\\\hline 10\end{array}\qquad\begin{array}{r}7\\+3\\\hline 10\end{array}\qquad\begin{array}{r}6\\+5\\\hline 11\end{array}\qquad\begin{array}{r}4\\+8\\\hline 12\end{array}\qquad\begin{array}{r}3\\+3\\\hline 6\end{array}\qquad\begin{array}{r}7\\+5\\\hline 12\end{array}$$

3.
$$\begin{array}{r}3\\+4\\\hline 7\end{array}\qquad\begin{array}{r}7\\+4\\\hline 11\end{array}\qquad\begin{array}{r}8\\+3\\\hline 11\end{array}\qquad\begin{array}{r}4\\+5\\\hline 9\end{array}\qquad\begin{array}{r}7\\+2\\\hline 9\end{array}\qquad\begin{array}{r}4\\+4\\\hline 8\end{array}\qquad\begin{array}{r}2\\+9\\\hline 11\end{array}$$

4.
$$\begin{array}{r}6\\+6\\\hline 12\end{array}\qquad\begin{array}{r}9\\+3\\\hline 12\end{array}\qquad\begin{array}{r}4\\+7\\\hline 11\end{array}\qquad\begin{array}{r}5\\+3\\\hline 8\end{array}\qquad\begin{array}{r}2\\+8\\\hline 10\end{array}\qquad\begin{array}{r}9\\+2\\\hline 11\end{array}\qquad\begin{array}{r}4\\+6\\\hline 10\end{array}$$

FIELD TRIP

Answer the riddles.

My double is 8.

Who am I? 4

My double is between

4 and 8. Who am I? 3

My double is 10.

Who am I? 5

When you double me,

you get 12. Who am I? 6

Addition facts, sums through 12

Correcting Common Errors

Some students may need additional practice with sums through 12. Have students work in pairs. Give each pair a card with a number from 8 through 12 on it. Each pair looks at their card and the partners take turns writing on a separate piece of paper a fact whose sum is the number on the card. When all the facts for the number are written correctly, the pair trades cards with another pair, continuing in this manner until all the facts are practiced.

Enrichment

1. Tell students to have a friend guess the addition fact they are thinking of if the sum is 11, and one of the numbers is 2, etc.
2. Tell students to roll 2 dice and give the sum and have a friend roll and give a sum. The higher sum wins a point. The first player to earn 10 points wins.
3. Tell students to use toothpicks to illustrate all the different addition groupings for the sum of 12.

Teaching page 40

Have students complete the 4 rows of problems independently.

Field Trip

Have students tell the number whose double is 4. (2) If students have difficulty with this statement, ask them to think of a number that would be 4 if it were doubled. Now have students think of a number that would be 2 if it were doubled. (1) Help students find the first double and then have students complete the doubles independently.

Extra Credit   *Numeration*

Place different numbers of objects with interesting shapes in 10 small paper bags. Select a student to find the bag that has the number of objects in it from 1 through 10 that you name. Have students feel the bags to determine which one holds the specified number of objects. Students may not look inside the bags. When students think they have found the correct bag, empty the bag and have the students count the objects. Mix the order of the bags and repeat the activity several times. This game can be played with 2 teams. Call out a number. One person from each team runs forward and feels the objects in each bag. The first to find the correct bag scores 1 point for their team. The first team to total 10 points wins.

Sums through 14

pages 41-42

Objective

To add for sums through 14

Materials

*addition fact cards for sums through 14
14 counters

Mental Math

Have students give the sum:
1. 4 + 3 + 2 (9)
2. 1 + 9 + 6 (16)
3. 4 + 8 + 3 (15)
4. 2 + 2 + 6 (10)
5. 5 + 5 + 5 (15)
6. 2 + 5 + 7 (14)
7. 4 + 0 + 8 (12)

Skill Review

Have students name the sum of each addition fact for sums through 12 when shown in random order. A correct sum earns the card. When all cards have been earned, write across the board: **Double, Double-Plus 1, Sum of 0 through 8, Sum of 0 through 12.** Have students place their cards on the chalk tray under the proper headings.

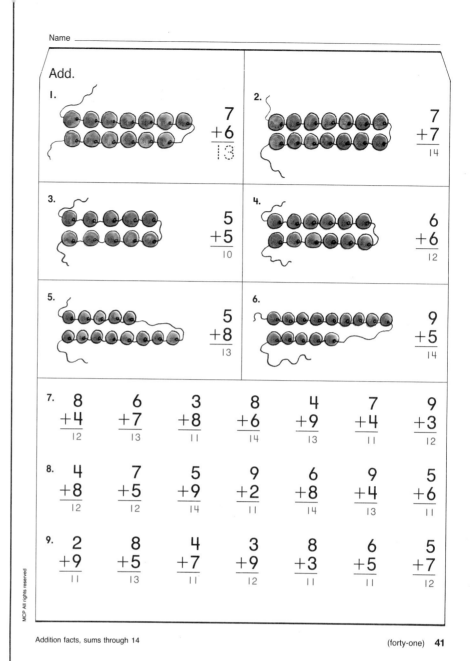

Add.

1. 7
   +6
   ___
   13

2. 7
   +7
   ___
   14

3. 5
   +5
   ___
   10

4. 6
   +6
   ___
   12

5. 5
   +8
   ___
   13

6. 9
   +5
   ___
   14

7.
8	6	3	8	4	7	9
+4	+7	+8	+6	+9	+4	+3
12	13	11	14	13	11	12

8.
4	7	5	9	6	9	5
+8	+5	+9	+2	+8	+4	+6
12	12	14	11	14	13	11

9.
2	8	4	3	8	6	5
+9	+5	+7	+9	+3	+5	+7
11	13	11	12	11	11	12

Addition facts, sums through 14

Teaching page 41

Write **9 + 3 =** on the board and have a student write the sum. (12) Have a student draw a group of 9 x's and a group of 3 x's on the board. Have another student circle a group of 10 and tell how many tens and ones are in 12. (1, 2) Draw another x on the board in the group of 3 x's and ask students how many tens and ones in all. (1, 3) Write **13** on the board. Ask students what 2 numbers have a sum of 13. (10 and 3 or 9 and 4) Help students develop other facts for sums of 13 by drawing 13 x's and ask students to circle two groups of x's. Repeat the procedure to develop sums of 14.

Have students tell the 2 numbers to be added. (7, 6) Ask students to name the sum and trace the 13. Have students draw a circle around ten and tell how many

tens and ones in 13. (1, 3) Repeat for the problem of 7 + 7. Tell students to find the sum of each problem and circle a group of 10 where necessary. Then have them write the sums for the last section of problems.

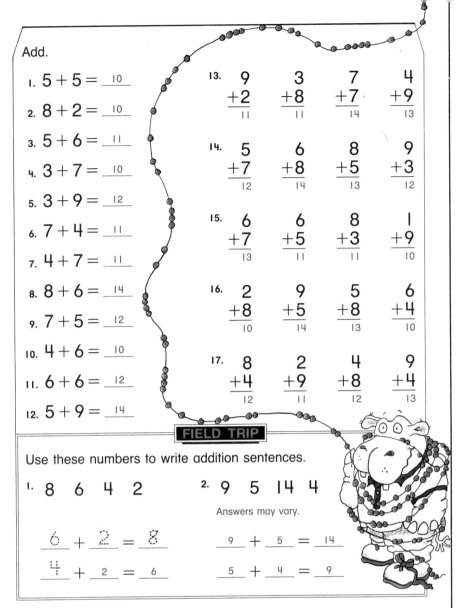

Add.

1. $5 + 5 = $ __10__
2. $8 + 2 = $ __10__
3. $5 + 6 = $ __11__
4. $3 + 7 = $ __10__
5. $3 + 9 = $ __12__
6. $7 + 4 = $ __11__
7. $4 + 7 = $ __11__
8. $8 + 6 = $ __14__
9. $7 + 5 = $ __12__
10. $4 + 6 = $ __10__
11. $6 + 6 = $ __12__
12. $5 + 9 = $ __14__

13.
$$\begin{array}{r}9\\+2\\\hline 11\end{array} \quad \begin{array}{r}3\\+8\\\hline 11\end{array} \quad \begin{array}{r}7\\+7\\\hline 14\end{array} \quad \begin{array}{r}4\\+9\\\hline 13\end{array}$$

14.
$$\begin{array}{r}5\\+7\\\hline 12\end{array} \quad \begin{array}{r}6\\+8\\\hline 14\end{array} \quad \begin{array}{r}8\\+5\\\hline 13\end{array} \quad \begin{array}{r}9\\+3\\\hline 12\end{array}$$

15.
$$\begin{array}{r}6\\+7\\\hline 13\end{array} \quad \begin{array}{r}6\\+5\\\hline 11\end{array} \quad \begin{array}{r}8\\+3\\\hline 11\end{array} \quad \begin{array}{r}1\\+9\\\hline 10\end{array}$$

16.
$$\begin{array}{r}2\\+8\\\hline 10\end{array} \quad \begin{array}{r}9\\+5\\\hline 14\end{array} \quad \begin{array}{r}5\\+8\\\hline 13\end{array} \quad \begin{array}{r}6\\+4\\\hline 10\end{array}$$

17.
$$\begin{array}{r}8\\+4\\\hline 12\end{array} \quad \begin{array}{r}2\\+9\\\hline 11\end{array} \quad \begin{array}{r}4\\+8\\\hline 12\end{array} \quad \begin{array}{r}9\\+4\\\hline 13\end{array}$$

FIELD TRIP

Use these numbers to write addition sentences.

1. 8 6 4 2

2. 9 5 14 4

Answers may vary.

$6 + 2 = 8$

$4 + 2 = 6$

$9 + 5 = 14$

$5 + 4 = 9$

42 (forty-two)

Addition facts, sums through 14

Correcting Common Errors

If students have difficulty with the new facts with sums of 13 and 14, have them work in pairs with counters to model each problem and count to find the sum:
$4 + 9 = 13$, $5 + 8 = 13$, $6 + 7 = 13$,
$7 + 6 = 13$, $8 + 5 = 13$, $9 + 4 = 13$,
$5 + 9 = 14$, $6 + 8 = 14$, $7 + 7 = 14$,
$8 + 6 = 14$, and $9 + 5 = 14$.
Encourage students to discuss the "one more" and "one less" patterns that they see in the addends.

Enrichment

1. Tell students to write the facts whose sums are even numbers less than 14, and then circle the doubles.
2. Tell students to write the facts whose sums are odd numbers less than 14 and circle the double-plus-1 facts.
3. Have students complete an addition table through sums of 14.

Teaching page 42

Encourage students to work the column of problems first. Have students complete the page independently.

Field Trip

Have a student read the 4 numbers. Tell students they are to use all 4 numbers to write 2 addition sentences. Have students trace the numbers in the first sentence as they read aloud with you. Have students complete the next sentence and then work the second problem independently.

Extra Credit *Creative Drill*

Have a special place on the chalk board to write a daily riddle that involves mathematical concepts, or numbers in general. Put an envelope beneath it.

Tell students to solve the riddle before the end of day, write their solution on a piece of paper and put it in the envelope. Read all the answers aloud, giving a point to each student giving the correct one. Here are some examples:

1. What has eight legs and sings? (4 canaries)
2. If two is company and three's a crowd, what is four and five? (nine)
3. What grows larger each time you take something from it? (a hole)
4. How can you pick up a ton with one hand? (Pick it up one pound at a time.)

After you have done this activity for several days, ask students to bring in daily math riddles to share with the class.

42

Money
Sums through 14

pages 43-44

Objective

To add money amounts through 14¢

Materials

*addition fact cards for sums of 13 and 14
*items priced 2¢, 6¢, 3¢, 8¢ and 7¢
2 nickels
12 pennies

Mental Math

Have students count backwards to 0 from:
1. 12 (12, 11, . . . ,0)
2. 16
3. 20
4. 11
5. 9
6. 15
7. 17
8. 13

Skill Review

Have students display coins in 2 groups for a sum of 11¢. Have students write addition problems on the board to tell about their coin groups. Repeat for other sums through 12¢.

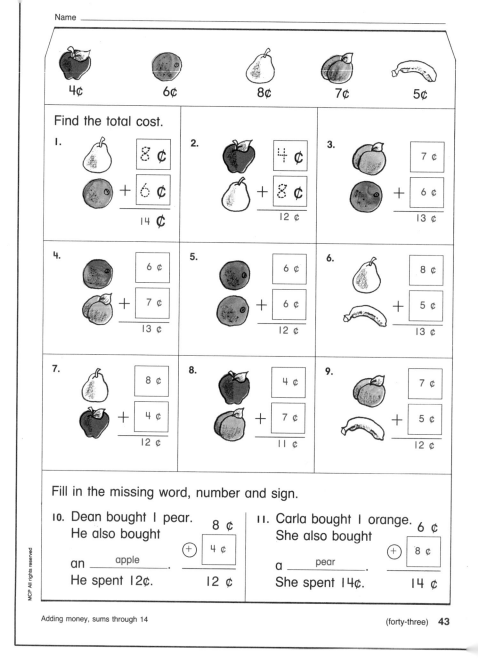

4¢   6¢   8¢   7¢   5¢

Find the total cost.

1. 8 ¢
    + 6 ¢
    14 ¢

2. 4 ¢
    + 8 ¢
    12 ¢

3. 7 ¢
    + 6 ¢
    13 ¢

4. 6 ¢
    + 7 ¢
    13 ¢

5. 6 ¢
    + 6 ¢
    12 ¢

6. 8 ¢
    + 5 ¢
    13 ¢

7. 8 ¢
    + 4 ¢
    12 ¢

8. 4 ¢
    + 7 ¢
    11 ¢

9. 7 ¢
    + 5 ¢
    12 ¢

Fill in the missing word, number and sign.

10. Dean bought 1 pear.
    He also bought
    an ___apple___ .
    He spent 12¢.
    8 ¢
    ⊕ 4 ¢
    12 ¢

11. Carla bought 1 orange.
    She also bought
    a ___pear___ .
    She spent 14¢.
    6 ¢
    ⊕ 8 ¢
    14 ¢

Adding money, sums through 14

(forty-three) **43**

Teaching page 43

Show students the 5 priced items. Ask a student to write and solve a problem on the board to find the sum of any 2 of the items. Continue to have students write and solve problems until each item has been paired with another. Now have students put out coins to show each purchase of 2 items.

Have students name each item across the top of the page and tell its price. Tell students they are to write the price of each item in the box next to the item and find the total cost of the 2 items. Have students trace the numbers in the first problem and write the sum. Repeat for the second problem and remind students to write the cent sign in the sum. Tell students it is very important that the cent sign be written beside each price and each sum so that anyone would know the

problem is about money. Now have students read the first word problem. Ask students what item Dean would buy from the top of the page if he paid 12¢ in all. (apple) Have students write the word and its cost in the problem. Help students complete the next problem, if necessary.

Add.

1. $5¢ + 5¢ = \underline{10}¢$ $4¢ + 6¢ = \underline{10}¢$ $7¢ + 4¢ = \underline{11}¢$

2. $2¢ + 8¢ = \underline{10}¢$ $8¢ + 4¢ = \underline{12}¢$ $6¢ + 4¢ = \underline{10}¢$

3. $5¢ + 4¢ = \underline{9}¢$ $1¢ + 9¢ = \underline{10}¢$ $5¢ + 6¢ = \underline{11}¢$

4. $9¢ + 1¢ = \underline{10}¢$ $8¢ + 2¢ = \underline{10}¢$ $6¢ + 6¢ = \underline{12}¢$

5. $4¢ + 7¢ = \underline{11}¢$ $6¢ + 5¢ = \underline{11}¢$ $1¢ + 9¢ = \underline{10}¢$

6.
$6¢$	$8¢$	$7¢$	$7¢$	$5¢$	$8¢$	$4¢$
$+8¢$	$+3¢$	$+5¢$	$+6¢$	$+7¢$	$+5¢$	$+9¢$
14 ¢	11 ¢	12 ¢	13 ¢	12 ¢	13 ¢	13 ¢

7.
$5¢$	$9¢$	$3¢$	$8¢$	$9¢$	$6¢$	$7¢$
$+9¢$	$+3¢$	$+7¢$	$+6¢$	$+2¢$	$+7¢$	$+3¢$
14 ¢	12 ¢	10 ¢	14 ¢	11 ¢	13 ¢	10 ¢

8.
$4¢$	$9¢$	$3¢$	$5¢$	$9¢$	$7¢$	$3¢$
$+8¢$	$+4¢$	$+9¢$	$+8¢$	$+5¢$	$+7¢$	$+8¢$
12 ¢	13 ¢	12 ¢	13 ¢	14 ¢	14 ¢	11 ¢

Solve.

9. There were 9 children on the playground. 4 more children joined them. How many children are on the playground?

	9
$+$	4
	13

$\underline{13}$ children

10. Eric has 7 aunts. He has 7 uncles. How many aunts and uncles does Eric have?

	7
$+$	7
	14

$\underline{14}$ aunts and uncles.

Adding money, sums through 14

Correcting Common Errors

If students have difficulty adding amounts of money, have them work in pairs using pennies to model each problem. Help them see the facts in pairs; for example, if 3¢ + 9¢ = 12¢, then 9¢ + 3¢ is also equal to 12¢.

Enrichment

1. Tell students to write and solve 4 different addition or subtraction problems using the numbers 6, 7 and 13.
2. Have students write and solve addition problems to show all the total costs if they could buy only 2 items at a time, of things priced 6¢, 5¢, 8¢ and 4¢.
3. Tell students to suppose they have 14¢ and buy an item for 6¢ and another item for 7¢. Ask if they would have enough left to buy gum that costs 3¢?

Teaching page 44

Have students find the sum for each money problem. Then read through the first word problem with them and ask what operation they will use to solve the problem. (addition) Have students write the plus sign in the circle. Ask students what numbers will be added and have them write the numbers in the boxes and find the sum. Accept 9 + 4 or 4 + 9 and discuss why either order is correct. Have students write the sum in the solution statement. Have students complete the second word problem independently.

Extra Credit   *Numeration*

Have students work with partners to count to a specified number. The first player in each pair begins counting and says either one or two numbers. The other player begins where the first player left off and may also say one or two numbers. Players continue counting until one of the players wins by counting to the specified number. Strategy is required to determine whether a student will say one or two numbers at each turn in an effort to be the student who says the final number.

As a variation, the children can count by even or odd numbers, by 5's, 10's, or in fractional increments of ¼ (¼, ½, ¾, 1, 1¼, etc.) depending on their skill level.

Sums through 16

pages 45-46

Objective

To add for sums through 16

Materials

16 counters

Mental Math

Have students name the number:
1. 2 tens 6 ones. (26)
2. 4 tens 0 ones. (40)
3. 1 ten 1 one. (11)
4. 7 tens 5 ones. (75)
5. 3 tens 3 ones. (33)
6. 2 tens 4 ones. (24)
7. 5 tens 0 ones. (50)
8. 0 tens 9 ones. (9)

Skill Review

Write groups of 4 addition facts such as **4 + 9, 3 + 6, 6 + 7, 8 + 5** on the board. Have students circle all the facts in the group that have the same sum. Repeat for more groups of 4 facts where students are asked to find facts having sums of 13 or 14.

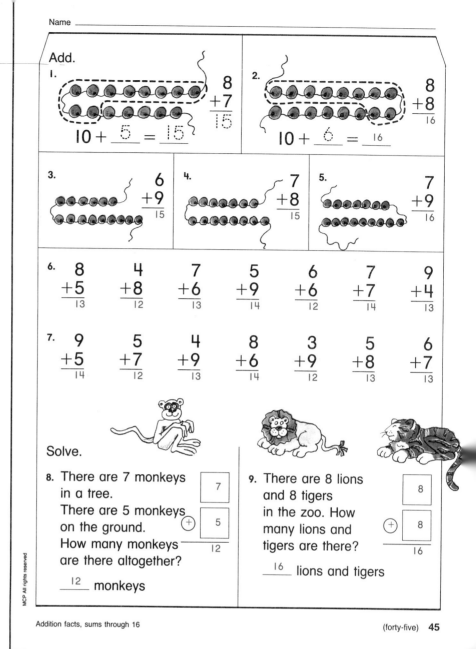

Name _____

Add.

1. 8 +7 = 15   10 + 5 = 15

2. 8 +8 = 16   10 + 6 = 16

3. 6 +9 = 15

4. 7 +8 = 15

5. 7 +9 = 16

6.
| 8 +5 = 13 | 4 +8 = 12 | 7 +6 = 13 | 5 +9 = 14 | 6 +6 = 12 | 7 +7 = 14 | 9 +4 = 13 |

7.
| 9 +5 = 14 | 5 +7 = 12 | 4 +9 = 13 | 8 +6 = 14 | 3 +9 = 12 | 5 +8 = 13 | 6 +7 = 13 |

Solve.

8. There are 7 monkeys in a tree. There are 5 monkeys on the ground. How many monkeys are there altogether?

7 (+) 5 = 12

__12__ monkeys

9. There are 8 lions and 8 tigers in the zoo. How many lions and tigers are there?

8 (+) 8 = 16

__16__ lions and tigers

Addition facts, sums through 16

(forty-five) **45**

Teaching page 45

Have students display a group of 9 counters and another group of 5. Ask how many in all. (14) Have students add 1 counter to the group of 5 and tell how many are in each group now. (9 and 6) Have a student write 9 + 6 on the board. Ask students how many counters in all. (15) Have a student write the sum on the board. Tell students they have found 1 addition fact for 15. Ask students how many tens and ones are in 15. (1, 5) Have students group the counters as 1 ten and 5 ones. Have a student write 10 + 5 = 15 on the board. Ask students how many of the 15 counters would be in 1 group if they had 8 in the other. (7) Have a student write 8 + 7 = 15 on the board. Continue to develop facts for 15 and then repeat the procedure to develop the facts for 16. Ask students how many objects are in each group in

the first box. (8 and 7) Have students circle 10 of the objects and then trace the numbers to complete the problem. Repeat for the next problem and have students write the sums. Tell students to circle 10 objects where necessary in each of the problems and write the sums for the rest of the page. Then help students read the word problems and remind them to write in the sign of operation. Have students complete them independently.

45

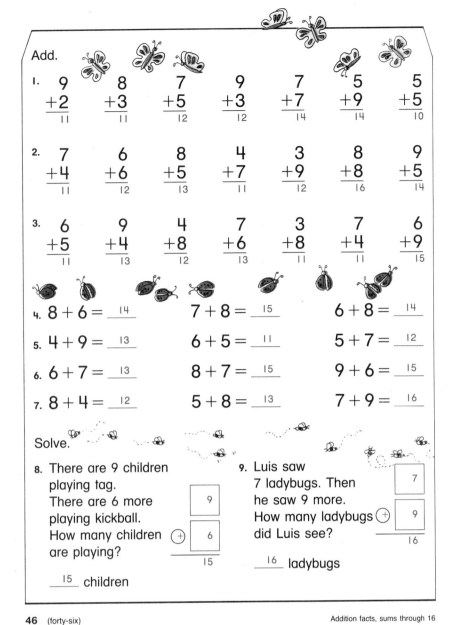

Add.

1.
$$9 + 2 = 11$$ $$8 + 3 = 11$$ $$7 + 5 = 12$$ $$9 + 3 = 12$$ $$7 + 7 = 14$$ $$5 + 9 = 14$$ $$5 + 5 = 10$$

2.
$$7 + 4 = 11$$ $$6 + 6 = 12$$ $$8 + 5 = 13$$ $$4 + 7 = 11$$ $$3 + 9 = 12$$ $$8 + 8 = 16$$ $$9 + 5 = 14$$

3.
$$6 + 5 = 11$$ $$9 + 4 = 13$$ $$4 + 8 = 12$$ $$7 + 6 = 13$$ $$3 + 8 = 11$$ $$7 + 4 = 11$$ $$6 + 9 = 15$$

4. 8 + 6 = __14__   7 + 8 = __15__   6 + 8 = __14__

5. 4 + 9 = __13__   6 + 5 = __11__   5 + 7 = __12__

6. 6 + 7 = __13__   8 + 7 = __15__   9 + 6 = __15__

7. 8 + 4 = __12__   5 + 8 = __13__   7 + 9 = __16__

Solve.

8. There are 9 children playing tag. There are 6 more playing kickball. How many children are playing?

⊕ 9
6
___15___

__15__ children

9. Luis saw 7 ladybugs. Then he saw 9 more. How many ladybugs did Luis see?

7
⊕ 9
16

__16__ ladybugs

Addition facts, sums through 16

Sums through 18

pages 47-48

Objective

To add for sums through 18

Materials

*addition facts table
18 counters

Mental Math

Ask students how much money in:
1. 2 dimes. (20¢)
2. 2 dimes and 1 penny. (21¢)
3. 4 dimes and 6 pennies. (46¢)
4. 1 dime and 2 pennies. (12¢)
5. 2 dimes and 9 pennies. (29¢)
6. 1 dime and 8 pennies. (18¢)
7. 3 dimes and 0 pennies. (30¢)
8. 5 dimes. (50¢)

Skill Review

Have students fill in all sums through 16 on an addition facts table. Have students note that only 3 facts are missing.

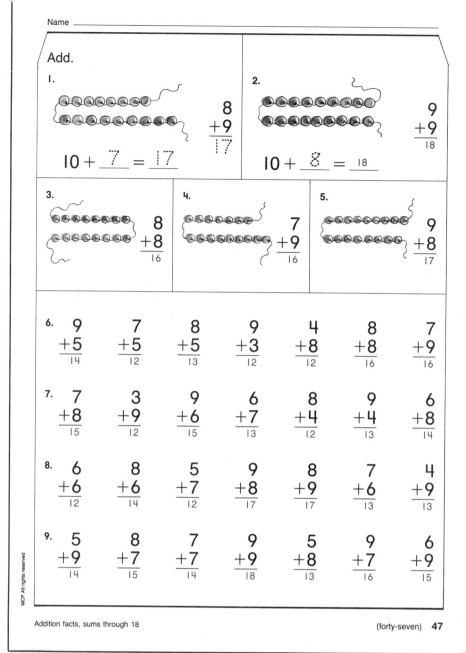

Addition facts, sums through 18

(forty-seven) **47**

Teaching page 47

Write **9+8 =** and **9+9 =** on the board and tell students these are 2 of the remaining 3 facts to complete the addition table. Have students think of the sums of the double, 8+8, and count on 1 to tell the sum of 9+8. Have a student write the sum. (17) Have students tell the number of tens and ones in 17. (1, 7) Have students think of the double-plus-1 fact of 9+8 and count on 1 to tell the sum of 9+9. Have a student write the sum. (18) Have students tell the number of tens and ones in 18. (1, 8) Ask students what 1 more fact is known if 9+8 = 17. (8+9 = 17) Have students write the sums of 17 and 18 in the correct place on the facts table.

Discuss the number of objects in each group and have students draw a circle around 10 of them. Have

students trace the numbers. Repeat for the second problem and have students write the sum. Have students complete the page independently.

47

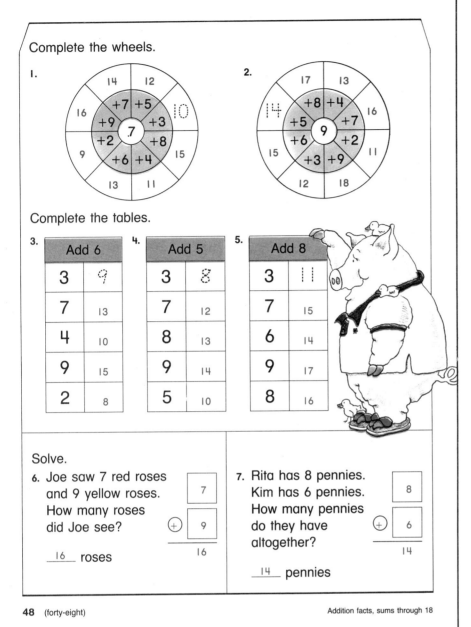

Complete the wheels.

1.

	14	12	
16	+7 +5		10
	+9 +3		
	7		
	+2 +8		
9	+6 +4		15
	13	11	

2.

	17	13	
14	+8 +4		16
	+5 +7		
	9		
	+6 +2		
15	+3 +9		11
	12	18	

Complete the tables.

3.
Add 6	
3	9
7	13
4	10
9	15
2	8

4.
Add 5	
3	8
7	12
8	13
9	14
5	10

5.
Add 8	
3	11
7	15
6	14
9	17
8	16

Solve.

6. Joe saw 7 red roses and 9 yellow roses. How many roses did Joe see?

7
(+) 9
___
16

16 roses

7. Rita has 8 pennies. Kim has 6 pennies. How many pennies do they have altogether?

8
(+) 6
___
14

14 pennies

Addition facts, sums through 18

Correcting Common Errors

Encourage students who have difficulty with some of the sums through 18 to use the double and double plus one strategies to help them remember their facts.

Double	Double Plus One
5 + 5 = 10	5 + 6 = 10 + 1, or 11
6 + 6 = 12	6 + 7 = 13
7 + 7 = 14	7 + 8 = 15
8 + 8 = 16	8 + 9 = 17

Enrichment

1. Tell students to write all facts that are doubles or doubles-plus-1 for sums through 18.
2. Have students make their own set of addition fact cards for sums through 18.
3. Tell students to draw a picture to help them remember each fact they cannot quickly recall.

Teaching page 48

Remind students that they have completed wheels and tables before. Ask students what they will do in the wheels. (add the number in the second ring to the number in the center, and write the sum in the outer ring) Ask what they will do in the tables. (add 6 to each number and write the sum, then add 5 to each number in the next table and add 8 to each number in the last table) Ask students what they will do in the word problems. By this time students should remember to write the sign of operation and record the answer in the solution statement. Have students complete the page independently.

Extra Credit   Creative Drill

Prepare four gameboards for students to play Button Toss Addition and Subtraction. Divide the board into 11 rectangles and mark each with a number 0 through 10. Divide the class into four groups, each having two buttons. Each player takes a turn tossing the 2 buttons onto the board and subtracts the smaller number landed on, from the larger number. That is their score. Have students take several turns, and add all individual scores to get a total, and a winner. You can extend the activity by using numbers 9 through 18 on the boards.

Column Addition

pages 49-50

Objective

To add three or four 1-digit numbers for sums through 18

Materials

*addition fact cards for sums 9 through 18
18 counters

Mental Math

Tell students to count to 100 by 10's from:
1. 40 (50, 60, . . ., 100)
2. 10
3. 60
4. 30
5. 70
6. 20
7. 50
8. 0

Skill Review

Display all fact cards for sums 9 through 18 on the chalk tray. Group students in pairs and assign each pair a number from 9 through 18. Tell students they are to collect all the fact cards that have their number as a sum. When all cards are collected, have groups trade cards to check each other's work.

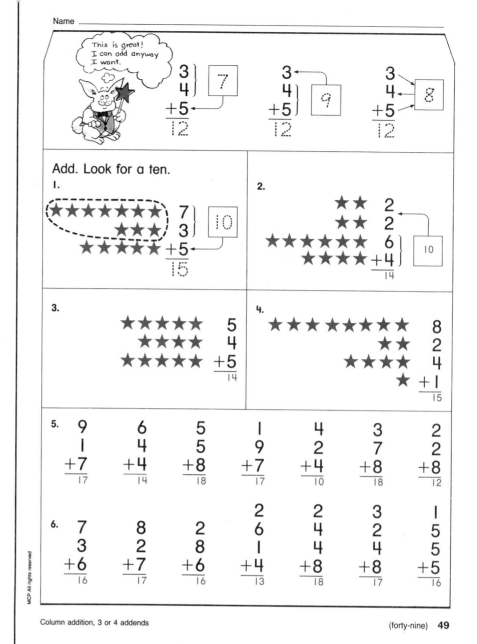

Column addition, 3 or 4 addends

(forty-nine) **49**

Teaching page 49

Write **3+2+7** vertically on the board. Remind students we can add only 2 numbers at a time. Ask students the sum of 3 and 2. (5) Tell them they now can add 5 and 7 to find the total sum. (12) Now ask students the sum of 7 and 2 as you start at the bottom of the problem. (9) Ask the sum of 9 and 3. (12) Tell students we added down the column of numbers and then added up the column to check the work. Ask students the sum of 7 and 3 as you point out the numbers. (10) Ask students the sum of 10 and 2. (12) Tell students it is often easier to add a column of numbers if we look for 2 numbers whose sum is 10. Repeat for more problems of 3 addends. Now write **7+6+1+4** vertically on the board and help students find a sum of 10 and continue adding to find the sum. (18) Have students check by adding up the column.

Have students add 3 and 4 and trace the 7 and sum of 12. Remind students they can add the numbers in any order. Point out the next 2 problems are the same but are to be added in a different order. Have students write the sum of 4 and 5 in the box (9) and then add 3 and write the sum. (12) Have students compare the sums to check their work. Have students complete the third problem. Remind students to add up the column to check their work. Have students complete the page independently.

49

Add. Look for a ten.

1.

2	2	3	3	7	7	1
3	7	2	7	2	3	1
+7	+3	+7	+2	+3	+2	+1
12	12	12	12	12	12	3

2.

2	3	4	5	6	7	8
2	3	4	5	6	3	2
+2	+3	+4	+5	+4	+7	+8
6	9	12	15	16	17	18

3.

4	5	2	3	7	6	4
2	1	3	6	1	2	4
3	2	4	1	1	1	1
+7	+6	+8	+5	+6	+7	+3
16	14	17	15	15	16	12

FIELD TRIP

Write two addition number sentences using each number only once.

1. △1 △2 △3 △4 △5 △7

1 + 3 = 4

2 + 5 = 7

2. [2] [3] [4] [5] [6] [8]

2 + 4 = 6

3 + 5 = 8

50 (fifty)   Column addition, 3 or 4 addends

Money Sums through 18¢

pages 51-52

Objective

To add money through sums of 18¢

Materials

2 nickels
18 pennies

Mental Math

Dictate the following:
1. 2+3+2 (7)
2. 1+5+4 (10)
3. 10+4 (14)
4. 1 ten 2 ones (12)
5. 2 tens 6 ones (26)
6. 5¢+4¢ (9¢)
7. 8+8+2 (18)

Skill Review

Draw a nickel and 4 pennies on the board and ask students to tell the amount. (9¢) Have students show another way to make 9¢ with their coins. (9 pennies) Have students show other amounts through 18¢ in 1 or 2 ways, with coins available. Then have students put out 18¢ in 3 groups of coins and write and solve a 3-addend problem on the board.

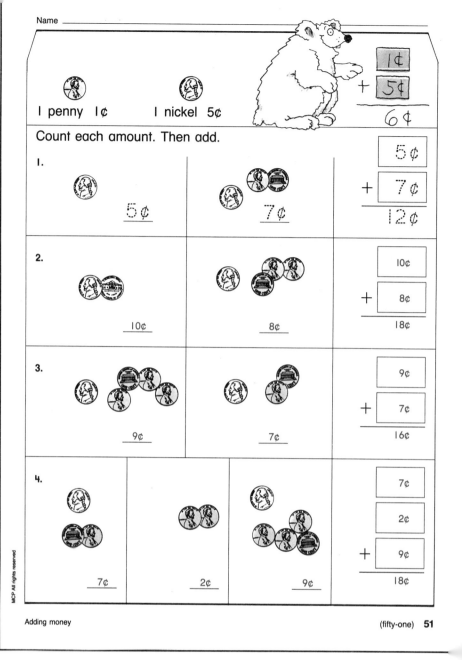

Adding money   (fifty-one) **51**

Teaching page 51

Have students put out a nickel and 3 pennies in 1 group and a nickel and 4 pennies in another. Tell a student to write and solve a problem to add the amount of money in each group remembering the cent signs. (8¢+9 = 17¢) Repeat for a group of 2 nickels and a group of 1 nickel and 1 penny. (10¢+6 = 16¢) Tell students the cent sign must be written when we are talking about cents. Now repeat for 3 groups of coins for a 3-addend problem of 1-digit amounts, whose sum is 18¢ or less.

Have students trace the 5¢, 7¢ and the sum of 12¢ in the problem. Tell students to write the cent sign in each addend and in the sum for every problem on this page. Have students complete the page independently.

51

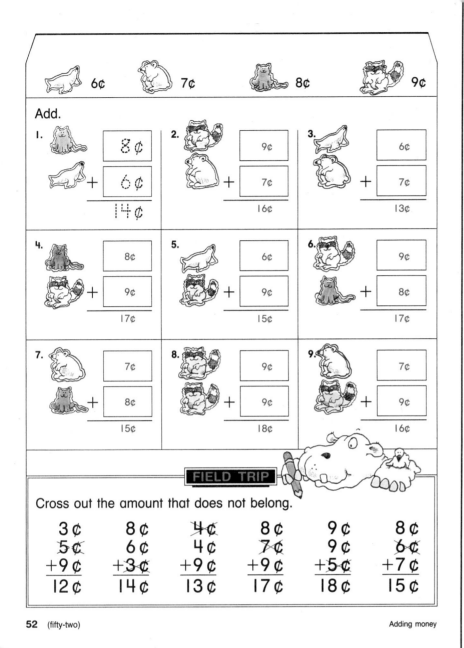

6¢   7¢   8¢   9¢

Add.

1. 8¢
    + 6¢
    14¢

2. 9¢
    + 7¢
    16¢

3. 6¢
    + 7¢
    13¢

4. 8¢
    + 9¢
    17¢

5. 6¢
    + 9¢
    15¢

6. 9¢
    + 8¢
    17¢

7. 7¢
    + 8¢
    15¢

8. 9¢
    + 9¢
    18¢

9. 7¢
    + 9¢
    16¢

FIELD TRIP

Cross out the amount that does not belong.

3 ¢	8 ¢	4̶ ¢	8 ¢	9 ¢	8 ¢
5̶ ¢	6 ¢	4 ¢	7̶ ¢	9 ¢	6̶ ¢
+9 ¢	+3̶ ¢	+9 ¢	+9 ¢	+5̶ ¢	+7 ¢
12 ¢	14 ¢	13 ¢	17 ¢	18 ¢	15 ¢

Adding money

Correcting Common Errors

Some students may have difficulty with adding money. Have them work in pairs with real coins or play money. Each partner puts out an amount of money equal to 9¢ or less. The partners count each other's money, join the amounts and find the sum. They can repeat the activity with other amounts of money less than 10¢.

Enrichment

1. Have students draw coins to show 3 equal amounts whose total sum is 18¢. Then have them draw 18¢ in 2 equal amounts.
2. Tell students to write the addition problem that shows how much money in a club treasury if there were 5 members and each paid 3¢ dues.
3. Tell students to make an illustration to explain why they and a friend each have 9¢ but their coins are not the same.

Teaching page 52

Have students tell the name of each object and its price. Remind students that they have done this activity before, as you tell them to trace the 8¢ for the price of the cat, 6¢ for the price of the seal and 14¢ for the total amount spent. Remind students that we always write cents to show we are talking about money. Have students complete the page independently.

Field Trip

Ask students to tell the sum of the first problem. (12¢) Tell students that 1 of the addends does not belong in the problem. Ask students to find which 2 addends have a sum of 12¢. (3¢ and 9¢) Tell students to cross out the 5¢. Help students complete the next problem before assigning the rest of the problems to be completed independently.

Extra Credit *Creative Drill*

Draw a triangle, circle, square and rectangle on the floor with chalk or tape. Make them large enough for a child to stand inside and bounce a ball. Tell four students to choose their home shape. Tell the students that when you clap your hands they are to start bouncing the ball. They can continue as long as they stay within their shapes. If they do not, they take their seats. As they bounce, they count. The student who has the highest number of bounces and stays within his shape, wins. Continue play until all the students have had a turn.

Problem Solving Sums through 18

pages 53-54

Objective

To solve problems using sums through 18

Materials

18 counters

Mental Math

Ask students which is more:
1. 13 or 31. (31)
2. 26 or 62. (62)
3. 45 or 15. (45)
4. 16 or 61. (61)
5. 11 or 21. (21)
6. 33 or 23. (33)
7. 24 or 34. (34)

Skill Review

Write **5+7 =** on the board and have a student write the sum. (12) Write **12 = __+2** on the board and have a student complete the sentence. (10) Write **5+7 = 10+2** on the board and tell students that 5 of the group of 7, joined the 5 to make 10 and left only 2 of the 7. Have students act out this movement from 1 group to the other. Repeat the procedure for 8+7 and 9+8.

Name _____

Solve.

1. There were 8 cars in the parking lot. Then 9 more drove in. How many cars are now in the parking lot?

   8
   $\oplus$ 9
   ___17___

   __17__ cars

2. Sally found 8 shells. Trudy found 7 shells. How many shells did they find?

   8
   $+$ 7
   ___15___

   __15__ shells

3. There were 6 children playing a video game. 5 more children joined them. Now how many are playing?

   6
   $+$ 5
   ___11___

   __11__ children

4. Mike used 5 tickets for the roller coaster. He used 9 tickets for the rocket. How many tickets did he use?

   5
   $+$ 9
   ___14___

   __14__ tickets

5. There are 7 dogs on the grass. 5 more dogs join them. How many dogs are on the grass?

   7
   $+$ 5
   ___12___

   __12__ dogs

6. Father used 5 apples and 8 bananas in a salad. How many pieces of fruit did he use?

   5
   $+$ 8
   ___13___

   __13__ pieces of fruit

7. Kyle ate 9 crackers. Chris ate 7 crackers. How many crackers did they eat?

   9
   $+$ 7
   ___16___

   __16__ crackers

8. Doyle counted 4 blue trucks and 8 red trucks. How many trucks did Doyle count?

   4
   $+$ 8
   ___12___

   __12__ trucks

Problem solving, addition

(fifty-three) **53**

Teaching page 53

Tell students a story of having 8 days off from school for vacation and then 2 snow days off. Ask what operation should be used to find how many days the school was closed for vacation and weather conditions. (addition) Have a student write the problem with its sign on the board. (8+2) Have students check to see if the problem is written correctly to answer the question and then have a student solve the problem. (10 days) Repeat the procedure for more addition word problems for sums through 18.

Tell students they are to read each problem, decide what operation to use and write that sign in the circle. Have a student read the first problem aloud. Have students trace the plus sign and the addends, write the sum and record it in the answer statement. Ask

students to check by counting on. Help students read the problems if necessary as they solve each independently. When the page is completed have students work in pairs to act out the problems to check their work.

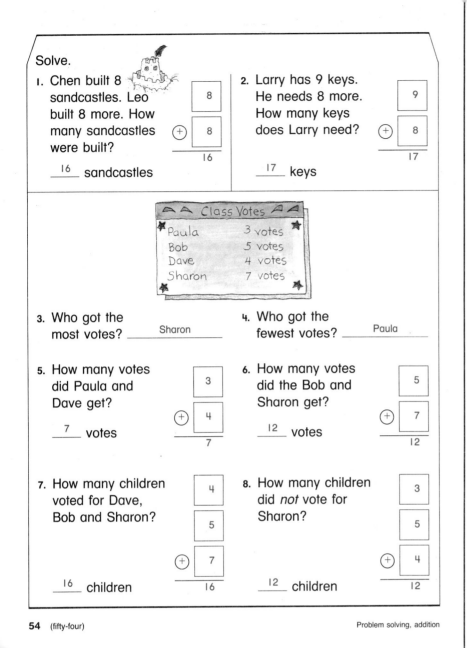

Solve.

1. Chen built 8 sandcastles. Leo built 8 more. How many sandcastles were built?

$$\begin{array}{r} 8 \\ + \ 8 \\ \hline 16 \end{array}$$

___16___ sandcastles

2. Larry has 9 keys. He needs 8 more. How many keys does Larry need?

$$\begin{array}{r} 9 \\ + \ 8 \\ \hline 17 \end{array}$$

___17___ keys

Class Votes

Paula	3 votes
Bob	5 votes
Dave	4 votes
Sharon	7 votes

3. Who got the most votes? ___Sharon___

4. Who got the fewest votes? ___Paula___

5. How many votes did Paula and Dave get?

$$\begin{array}{r} 3 \\ + \ 4 \\ \hline 7 \end{array}$$

___7___ votes

6. How many votes did the Bob and Sharon get?

$$\begin{array}{r} 5 \\ + \ 7 \\ \hline 12 \end{array}$$

___12___ votes

7. How many children voted for Dave, Bob and Sharon?

$$\begin{array}{r} 4 \\ 5 \\ + \ 7 \\ \hline 16 \end{array}$$

___16___ children

8. How many children did *not* vote for Sharon?

$$\begin{array}{r} 3 \\ 5 \\ + \ 4 \\ \hline 12 \end{array}$$

___12___ children

54 (fifty-four)

Problem solving, addition

Correcting Common Errors

Some students may have difficulty solving word problems. Have them work with partners. One partner should read the problem aloud and the other partner can retell it in his or her own words. They should discuss what words or actions described in the problem indicate that they should add. Then they should solve the problem. They can continue in the same manner, reversing roles with each new problem.

Enrichment

1. Tell students to write an addition word problem of 2 or 3 addends and present the problem to other students.
2. Have students find the total number of pets owned by 5 classmates.
3. Tell students to use the information on page 54 to find out how many students did not vote for Paul. Repeat for Bob and then Dave.

Teaching page 54

Have students complete the word problems. Now tell students a story about a soccer team voting for a team captain. Have students tell about the picture. Ask how many votes each player received. (Paula 3, Bob 5, Dave 4, Sharon 7) Have a student read the first problem. Tell students to compare the numbers to find the number that is the greatest. (7) Have students write the answer. (Sharon) Ask them to decide what operation is needed to solve each problem. Have students write and solve the problems and record their answers in the solution statement. Help students see that in number 8, they need to add all the votes except Sharon's since any vote for another player is not a vote for Sharon. Have students complete the page.

Extra Credit *Creative Drill*

Draw a large circle on the chalk board with smaller circles around it to look like a Ferris Wheel. Randomly place numbers 1–9 in the smaller circles and one number in the center of the wheel. Ask students to see how quickly they can go around the Ferris Wheel by adding the middle number to each number around the edge. Students may take turns and time themselves. Repeat and change the number in the center. This could also be used for practice of subtraction.

Review

pages 55-56

Objectives

To review sums through 18
To maintain skills learned previously
this year

Materials

18 counters

Mental Math

Tell students to name the day after:
1. Tuesday.
2. Saturday.
3. Monday.
4. Wednesday.
Ask students what day of the week:
5. is today?
6. was yesterday?
7. is tomorrow?
8. is the day after tomorrow?

Skill Review

Have a student write an addition
problem using two 1-digit numbers
whose sum is 14. Have students
write other problems with sums of
14. Encourage students to use 3 or 4
addends to find a sum of 14.

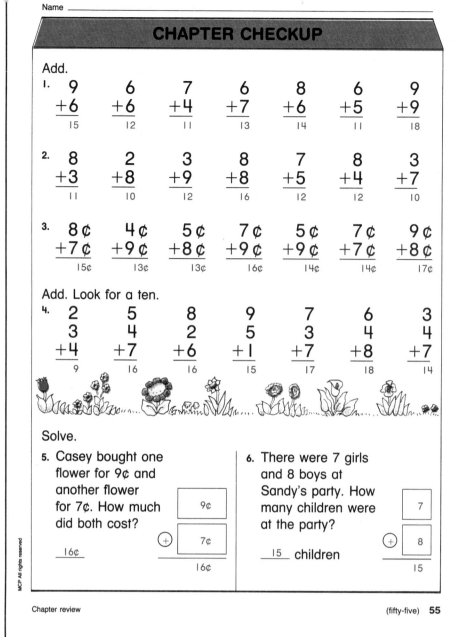

CHAPTER CHECKUP

Add.

1.
$$\begin{array}{r} 9 \\ +6 \\ \hline 15 \end{array} \quad \begin{array}{r} 6 \\ +6 \\ \hline 12 \end{array} \quad \begin{array}{r} 7 \\ +4 \\ \hline 11 \end{array} \quad \begin{array}{r} 6 \\ +7 \\ \hline 13 \end{array} \quad \begin{array}{r} 8 \\ +6 \\ \hline 14 \end{array} \quad \begin{array}{r} 6 \\ +5 \\ \hline 11 \end{array} \quad \begin{array}{r} 9 \\ +9 \\ \hline 18 \end{array}$$

2.
$$\begin{array}{r} 8 \\ +3 \\ \hline 11 \end{array} \quad \begin{array}{r} 2 \\ +8 \\ \hline 10 \end{array} \quad \begin{array}{r} 3 \\ +9 \\ \hline 12 \end{array} \quad \begin{array}{r} 8 \\ +8 \\ \hline 16 \end{array} \quad \begin{array}{r} 7 \\ +5 \\ \hline 12 \end{array} \quad \begin{array}{r} 8 \\ +4 \\ \hline 12 \end{array} \quad \begin{array}{r} 3 \\ +7 \\ \hline 10 \end{array}$$

3.
$$\begin{array}{r} 8¢ \\ +7¢ \\ \hline 15¢ \end{array} \quad \begin{array}{r} 4¢ \\ +9¢ \\ \hline 13¢ \end{array} \quad \begin{array}{r} 5¢ \\ +8¢ \\ \hline 13¢ \end{array} \quad \begin{array}{r} 7¢ \\ +9¢ \\ \hline 16¢ \end{array} \quad \begin{array}{r} 5¢ \\ +9¢ \\ \hline 14¢ \end{array} \quad \begin{array}{r} 7¢ \\ +7¢ \\ \hline 14¢ \end{array} \quad \begin{array}{r} 9¢ \\ +8¢ \\ \hline 17¢ \end{array}$$

Add. Look for a ten.

4.
$$\begin{array}{r} 2 \\ 3 \\ +4 \\ \hline 9 \end{array} \quad \begin{array}{r} 5 \\ 4 \\ +7 \\ \hline 16 \end{array} \quad \begin{array}{r} 8 \\ 2 \\ +6 \\ \hline 16 \end{array} \quad \begin{array}{r} 9 \\ 5 \\ +1 \\ \hline 15 \end{array} \quad \begin{array}{r} 7 \\ 3 \\ +7 \\ \hline 17 \end{array} \quad \begin{array}{r} 6 \\ 4 \\ +8 \\ \hline 18 \end{array} \quad \begin{array}{r} 3 \\ 4 \\ +7 \\ \hline 14 \end{array}$$

Solve.

5. Casey bought one
flower for 9¢ and
another flower
for 7¢. How much
did both cost?

<u>16¢</u>

$\boxed{9¢}$
$\oplus \boxed{7¢}$
$16¢$

6. There were 7 girls
and 8 boys at
Sandy's party. How
many children were
at the party?

<u>15</u> children

$\boxed{7}$
$\oplus \boxed{8}$
15

Chapter review

(fifty-five) **55**

Teaching page 55

Have students scan the rows of problems to tell what
operation they will use on this page. (addition) Ask
students what they will look for in each problem in the
last row. (a ten) Have students tell what they will do
first in each word problem. (decide on the operation)
Have students complete the page independently.

ROUNDUP REVIEW

Add or subtract.

1. $12 - 3 = \underline{9}$ $12 - 8 = \underline{4}$ $11 - 2 = \underline{9}$

2. $11 - 5 = \underline{6}$ $11 - 4 = \underline{7}$ $8 + 4 = \underline{12}$

3. $5 + 5 = \underline{10}$ $12 - 5 = \underline{7}$ $3 + 8 = \underline{11}$

Add.

4.
$\begin{array}{r} 7 \\ +7 \\ \hline 14 \end{array}$
$\begin{array}{r} 8 \\ +8 \\ \hline 16 \end{array}$
$\begin{array}{r} 9 \\ +9 \\ \hline 18 \end{array}$
$\begin{array}{r} 6 \\ +7 \\ \hline 13 \end{array}$
$\begin{array}{r} 7 \\ +8 \\ \hline 15 \end{array}$
$\begin{array}{r} 8 \\ +9 \\ \hline 17 \end{array}$
$\begin{array}{r} 7 \\ +6 \\ \hline 13 \end{array}$

5.
$\begin{array}{r} 8 \\ +7 \\ \hline 15 \end{array}$
$\begin{array}{r} 9 \\ +8 \\ \hline 17 \end{array}$
$\begin{array}{r} 9 \\ +7 \\ \hline 16 \end{array}$
$\begin{array}{r} 6 \\ +8 \\ \hline 14 \end{array}$
$\begin{array}{r} 8 \\ +5 \\ \hline 13 \end{array}$
$\begin{array}{r} 9 \\ +6 \\ \hline 15 \end{array}$
$\begin{array}{r} 7 \\ +9 \\ \hline 16 \end{array}$

6.
$\begin{array}{r} 9 \\ +5 \\ \hline 14 \end{array}$
$\begin{array}{r} 5 \\ +8 \\ \hline 13 \end{array}$
$\begin{array}{r} 6 \\ +9 \\ \hline 15 \end{array}$
$\begin{array}{r} 5 \\ +7 \\ \hline 12 \end{array}$
$\begin{array}{r} 5 \\ 3 \\ +5 \\ \hline 13 \end{array}$
$\begin{array}{r} 3 \\ 2 \\ +7 \\ \hline 12 \end{array}$
$\begin{array}{r} 6 \\ 4 \\ +7 \\ \hline 17 \end{array}$

Solve.

7. There were 12 frogs. 7 hopped away. How many frogs were left?

$\begin{array}{r} \boxed{12} \\ \ominus \boxed{7} \\ \hline \end{array}$ 5

$\underline{5}$ frogs

8. Bruce saved 9¢ on Monday and 5¢ on Friday. How much money did he save?

$\begin{array}{r} \boxed{9 \text{ ¢}} \\ \oplus \boxed{5 \text{ ¢}} \\ \hline \end{array}$ 14 ¢

$\underline{14¢}$

Cumulative review

1. Tell students to use the same numbers to write and solve 2 problems of addition with 1 of the problems involving money.
2. Have students write an addition problem with 3 addends where a ten can be used to make the addition easier. Then tell them to write a problem of 3 addends where a ten is not found.
3. Have students write 5 addition problems of 1-digit numbers whose sum is 18. Tell them they may need to use more than 2 addends.

Teaching page 56

This page reviews sums and minuends through 18, finding a sum of 10 in column addition and problem solving. Remind students to look at the sign in each problem before beginning to work, and decide on the operation they will use in each word problem. Ask students how they will show that the second word problem talks about money. (use the cent sign) Have students complete the page independently.

Minuends through 12

pages 57-58

Objective

To subtract minuends through 12

Materials

*subtraction fact cards for minuends through 12
12 counters

Mental Math

Ask students which is less:
1. 1 ten 1 one or 9 (9)
2. 26 or 21 (21)
3. 11 or 13 (11)
4. 2 + 9 or 3 + 5 (3 + 5)
5. 9 − 2 or 8 (9 − 2)
6. 17 − 9 or 4 + 3 (4 + 3)

Skill Review

Have students lay out 10 counters and take away 9. Ask how many are left. (1) Have a student write the problem on the board. (10 − 9 = 1) Repeat to find other facts for the minuend 10. Write each fact on the board. Repeat for minuends 8 and 6.

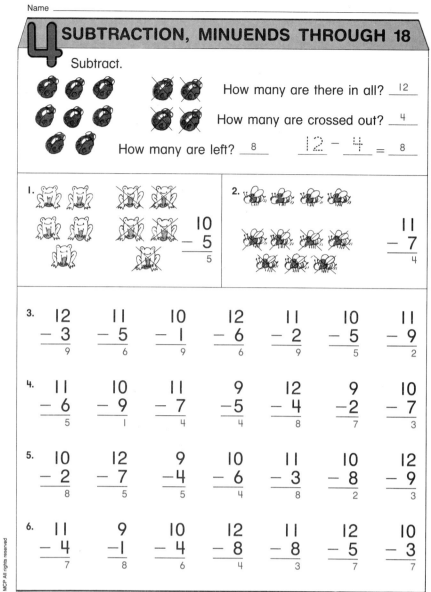

4 **SUBTRACTION, MINUENDS THROUGH 18**

Subtract.

How many are there in all? __12__

How many are crossed out? __4__

How many are left? __8__   12 − 4 = 8

1.   10
      − 5
      ___
       5

2.   11
      − 7
      ___
       4

3. 12   11   10   12   11   10   11
   − 3   − 5   − 1   − 6   − 2   − 5   − 9
   ___   ___   ___   ___   ___   ___   ___
    9   6   9   6   9   5   2

4. 11   10   11   9   12   9   10
   − 6   − 9   − 7   − 5   − 4   − 2   − 7
   ___   ___   ___   ___   ___   ___   ___
    5   1   4   4   8   7   3

5. 10   12   9   10   11   10   12
   − 2   − 7   − 4   − 6   − 3   − 8   − 9
   ___   ___   ___   ___   ___   ___   ___
    8   5   5   4   8   2   3

6. 11   9   10   12   11   12   10
   − 4   − 1   − 4   − 8   − 8   − 5   − 3
   ___   ___   ___   ___   ___   ___   ___
    7   8   6   4   3   7   7

Subtraction facts, minuends through 12   (fifty-seven) **57**

Teaching page 57

To show that subtraction is the inverse of addition tell students we want to find all the numbers which are addends for the sum of 11, and then write the related subtraction facts. Have students lay out 11 counters, remove 9 and tell how many are left. (2) Have a student write the problem on the board. (11 − 9 = 2) Have a student write the 2 addends of 11. (9, 2) Follow this procedure for all other addends of 11. Repeat for addends of 12.

Have a student read the first question on the page and tell the number of objects in all. (12) Have students write the answer. Continue for the next 2 questions and then have students trace the 12 and 4 and write the answer to the problem. (8) Remind students we use the minus sign to mean take-away

subtraction. Have students complete the page independently.

Complete the tables.

1. Subtract 3

9	6
7	4
12	9
10	7
8	5
11	8

2. Subtract 4

11	7
8	4
4	0
10	6
12	8
9	5

3. Subtract 5

12	7
7	2
9	4
11	6
8	3
10	5

4. Subtract 6

7	1
9	3
6	0
10	4
8	2
11	5

Subtract.

5.

$$8 - 7 = 1 \qquad 9 - 2 = 7 \qquad 10 - 9 = 1 \qquad 11 - 7 = 4 \qquad 9 - 9 = 0 \qquad 12 - 9 = 3 \qquad 11 - 2 = 9$$

6.

$$10 - 1 = 9 \qquad 12 - 8 = 4 \qquad 8 - 0 = 8 \qquad 9 - 7 = 2 \qquad 10 - 2 = 8 \qquad 12 - 6 = 6 \qquad 11 - 9 = 2$$

7.

$$9 - 8 = 1 \qquad 10 - 7 = 3 \qquad 12 - 7 = 5 \qquad 11 - 8 = 3 \qquad 9 - 1 = 8 \qquad 10 - 8 = 2 \qquad 7 - 4 = 3$$

Subtraction facts, minuends through 12

Correcting Common Errors

Some students may need practice with subtraction. Have them work with partners and subtraction fact cards. Have students group the cards into those facts related to doubles, such as $6 - 3 = 3$, $8 - 4 = 4$, etc., and facts related to sums of 9, 10, 11, or 12 like $9 - 4 = 5$.

Enrichment

1. Tell students to fold a paper in half and draw a picture on one side to show an addition fact. Using the same 3 numbers they should illustrate a related subtraction fact on the other half of the paper. Then have them write each fact under its picture.
2. Tell students to work in pairs using addition and subtraction fact cards for sums of 9 through 12. They should draw 2 cards and tell if the facts are related.
3. Tell students to write a story to tell about a dozen eggs and how some were broken.

Teaching page 58

Work through the first problem in the first 2 tables with the students. Remind students to subtract in each problem on this page. Have students complete the tables and rows of problems independently.

Extra Credit   Sets

Give the students a sheet of paper with 12 circles on it. Ask them to design sets having three members each, that have these properties:

  3 sets of the same color
  3 sets of the same shapes
  2 sets of the same color, different shapes
  2 sets of the same shapes, different colors
  2 sets of different shapes and different colors

Then ask students questions such as the following: Do you need to use all twelve circles to complete the list of properties? Can you make a set that is not identical to one of the sets, but has size, shape and color in common? Can you make a set that has an element in common with all the other sets?

58

Minuends through 14

pages 59-60

Objective

To subtract from minuends through 14

Materials

14 counters

Mental Math

Tell students to name 3 addends whose sum is:

1. 14
2. 15
3. 17
4. 11
5. 18
6. 12
7. 9
8. 13

Skill Review

Have students give answers for subtraction facts for minuends of 11 and then place the cards in order along the chalk tray from the greatest answer to the least. Repeat for minuends of 12.

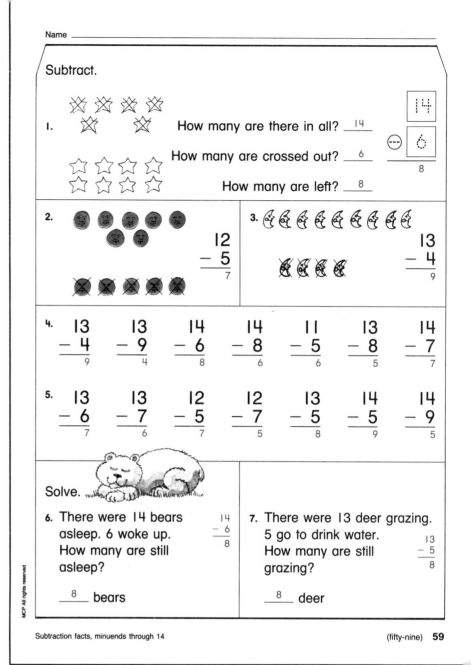

Name _____

Subtract.

1. How many are there in all? __14__

   How many are crossed out? __6__

   How many are left? __8__

   $$\begin{array}{r} 14 \\ \ominus \quad 6 \\ \hline 8 \end{array}$$

2. $$\begin{array}{r} 12 \\ -5 \\ \hline 7 \end{array}$$

3. $$\begin{array}{r} 13 \\ -4 \\ \hline 9 \end{array}$$

4. $$\begin{array}{r} 13 \\ -4 \\ \hline 9 \end{array}\quad\begin{array}{r} 13 \\ -9 \\ \hline 4 \end{array}\quad\begin{array}{r} 14 \\ -6 \\ \hline 8 \end{array}\quad\begin{array}{r} 14 \\ -8 \\ \hline 6 \end{array}\quad\begin{array}{r} 11 \\ -5 \\ \hline 6 \end{array}\quad\begin{array}{r} 13 \\ -8 \\ \hline 5 \end{array}\quad\begin{array}{r} 14 \\ -7 \\ \hline 7 \end{array}$$

5. $$\begin{array}{r} 13 \\ -6 \\ \hline 7 \end{array}\quad\begin{array}{r} 13 \\ -7 \\ \hline 6 \end{array}\quad\begin{array}{r} 12 \\ -5 \\ \hline 7 \end{array}\quad\begin{array}{r} 12 \\ -7 \\ \hline 5 \end{array}\quad\begin{array}{r} 13 \\ -5 \\ \hline 8 \end{array}\quad\begin{array}{r} 14 \\ -5 \\ \hline 9 \end{array}\quad\begin{array}{r} 14 \\ -9 \\ \hline 5 \end{array}$$

Solve.

6. There were 14 bears asleep. 6 woke up. How many are still asleep?

   $$\begin{array}{r} 14 \\ -6 \\ \hline 8 \end{array}$$

   __8__ bears

7. There were 13 deer grazing. 5 go to drink water. How many are still grazing?

   $$\begin{array}{r} 13 \\ -5 \\ \hline 8 \end{array}$$

   __8__ deer

Subtraction facts, minuends through 14   (fifty-nine) **59**

Teaching page 59

Tell students we want to find all the numbers which are addends for the sum of 13, and then write the related subtraction facts. Allow students to use counters to develop each fact. Have students write 2 subtraction sentences for each pair of addends for the sum of 13. $(13 - 9 = 4, 13 - 4 = 9,$ etc.) Repeat for addends of 14. Have a student read the first question and tell the answer. (14) Tell students to write the answer after the question. Repeat for the next 2 questions. Ask students what operation is necessary in this problem. (subtraction)

Have students trace the minus sign in the problem and then trace 14 and 6 and write the answer. Have students complete the next 2 problems independently. Have students read the word problems at the bottom

of the page and tell what operation is needed in each. (subtraction) Remind students to write out and solve the problem for each and then record the answer in the solution statement. Have students complete the page independently.

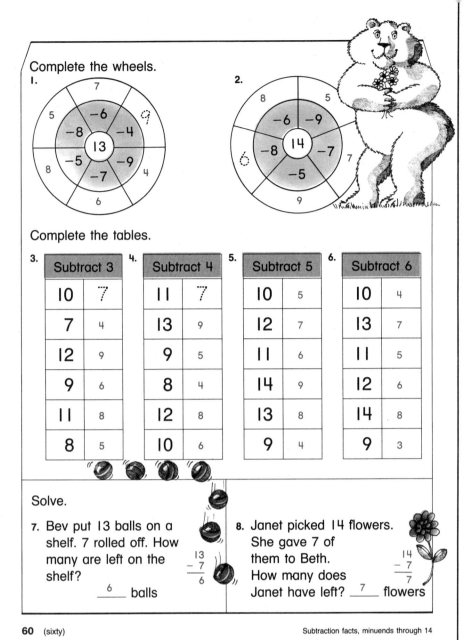

Complete the wheels.

1.
Center: 13, with -6, -4, -9, -7, -5, -8
Outer: 7, 5, 8, 8, 6, 4, 9

2.
Center: 14, with -6, -9, -7, -5, -8
Outer: 8, 5, 6, 7, 9

Complete the tables.

3. Subtract 3		4. Subtract 4		5. Subtract 5		6. Subtract 6	
10	7	11	7	10	5	10	4
7	4	13	9	12	7	13	7
12	9	9	5	11	6	11	5
9	6	8	4	14	9	12	6
11	8	12	8	13	8	14	8
8	5	10	6	9	4	9	3

Solve.

7. Bev put 13 balls on a shelf. 7 rolled off. How many are left on the shelf?

$$\begin{array}{r} 13 \\ -\ 7 \\ \hline 6 \end{array}$$

___6___ balls

8. Janet picked 14 flowers. She gave 7 of them to Beth. How many does Janet have left? ___7___ flowers

$$\begin{array}{r} 14 \\ -\ 7 \\ \hline 7 \end{array}$$

Subtraction facts, minuends through 14

Correcting Common Errors

To practice subtraction from minuends through 14, have students work with partners and subtraction fact cards. For each card, have them take turns writing the entire fact with the difference and then writing the related addition fact.

Enrichment

1. Tell students to write all subtraction facts through minuends of 14 which have an answer of 9.
2. Have students write and solve a problem which tells how they would find the number of strawberry plants they have already planted if they started with 14 and have 6 left.
3. Tell students to draw a picture which shows that at 4:00 there were 13 children at a party. At 6:00 there were 7 children, and at 7:00 there were only 2 children left. They should then write 2 subtraction problems to explain their work.

Teaching page 60

Ask students how many would be left from 13 if 4 were taken away. (9) Have students trace the 9. Go through another problem with students if necessary. In the next section have students subtract 3 from 10 in the first table and trace the 7. Remind students to subtract the number at the top. Tell students to decide which operation to do in each of the word problems before beginning to solve the problem. Have students complete the page independently.

Extra Credit *Sets*

Make a master set of different colored geometric shapes, in two different sizes. You could use construction paper or poster board in blue, red and yellow. Make patterns of large and small circles, triangles, squares, rectangles and hexagons. Have students trace the large and small patterns onto colored paper, cutting out a large and small set in each color. Start the activities by first having students sort the pieces by size, shape and then color. Then have students find a set of pieces that are the same size and color but different shapes. Ask them what other sets they can find and describe, and share them with the class.

Problem Solving Subtraction

pages 61-62

Objective

To use comparative subtraction to solve problems

Materials

14 counters

Mental Math

Have students name a fact in the family of:
1. 9 (12 − 3, 6 + 3, 8 + 1, etc.)
2. 14
3. 18
4. 12
5. 6
6. 11
7. 17
8. 15

Skill Review

Review take-away subtraction by acting out situations where some objects are taken away from a group. Have students write and solve subtraction problems for each situation. Stress with the students the terms **subtraction, take-away** and **number left.**

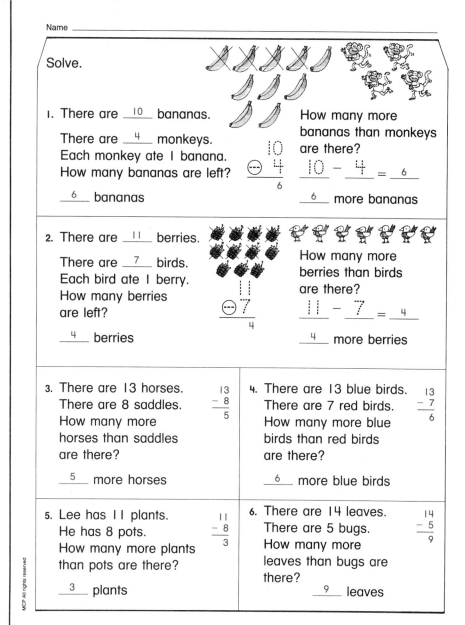

Solve.

1. There are __10__ bananas.

   There are __4__ monkeys.
   Each monkey ate 1 banana.
   How many bananas are left?

   ⊖ 4
      —
      6

   __6__ bananas

   How many more bananas than monkeys are there?

   10 − 4 = 6

   __6__ more bananas

2. There are __11__ berries.

   There are __7__ birds.
   Each bird ate 1 berry.
   How many berries are left?

   ⊖ 7
      —
      4

   __4__ berries

   How many more berries than birds are there?

   11 − 7 = 4

   __4__ more berries

3. There are 13 horses.
   There are 8 saddles.
   How many more horses than saddles are there?

   13
   − 8
   ——
     5

   __5__ more horses

4. There are 13 blue birds.
   There are 7 red birds.
   How many more blue birds than red birds are there?

   13
   − 7
   ——
     6

   __6__ more blue birds

5. Lee has 11 plants.
   He has 8 pots.
   How many more plants than pots are there?

   11
   − 8
   ——
     3

   __3__ plants

6. There are 14 leaves.
   There are 5 bugs.
   How many more leaves than bugs are there?

   14
   − 5
   ——
     9

   __9__ leaves

Problem solving, comparative subtraction

(sixty-one) **61**

Teaching page 61

Have students lay out 11 counters in a row. Tell students to lay out 6 more counters in a row under the first 6 of the 11 counters. Ask students how they can find out how many more counters are in the first group. (subtract) Help students see that by matching the first 6 counters in the top group to the first 6 in the second group, they can see how many are not matched.

Ask students how many are not matched. (5) Ask students how many more counters are in the group of 11 than in the group of 6. (5) Write **11 − 6 = 5** on the board. Tell students they can also use subtraction to compare numbers to see which is more. Write on the board: **There are 12 nuts and 5 squirrels. How many more nuts are there than squirrels?** Tell students to compare the numbers 12

and 5 to see how many more nuts there are than squirrels. Have a student write and solve the problem on the board. (12 − 5 = 7) Repeat for more similar subtraction word problems to compare numbers for minuends through 14.

Work through the first problem with the students. Help students see that the 2 questions are asked differently. Encourage discussion of the 2 types of questions as you work. Remind students to write the sign of operation and record each answer in the solution statement. Then have students complete the page independently.

61

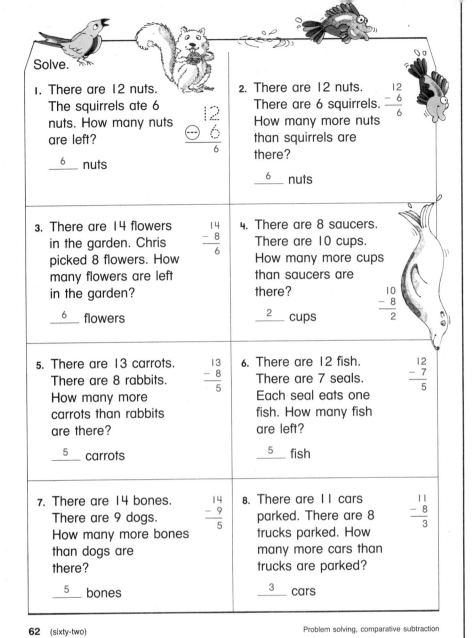

Solve.

1. There are 12 nuts. The squirrels ate 6 nuts. How many nuts are left?

$12 \ominus 6 \over 6$

___6___ nuts

2. There are 12 nuts. There are 6 squirrels. How many more nuts than squirrels are there?

$12 \over -6 \over 6$

___6___ nuts

3. There are 14 flowers in the garden. Chris picked 8 flowers. How many flowers are left in the garden?

$14 \over -8 \over 6$

___6___ flowers

4. There are 8 saucers. There are 10 cups. How many more cups than saucers are there?

$10 \over -8 \over 2$

___2___ cups

5. There are 13 carrots. There are 8 rabbits. How many more carrots than rabbits are there?

$13 \over -8 \over 5$

___5___ carrots

6. There are 12 fish. There are 7 seals. Each seal eats one fish. How many fish are left?

$12 \over -7 \over 5$

___5___ fish

7. There are 14 bones. There are 9 dogs. How many more bones than dogs are there?

$14 \over -9 \over 5$

___5___ bones

8. There are 11 cars parked. There are 8 trucks parked. How many more cars than trucks are parked?

$11 \over -8 \over 3$

___3___ cars

62 (sixty-two)   Problem solving, comparative subtraction

Correcting Common Errors

Some students may have difficulty writing their own subtraction problems to solve word problems. Have them work with partners. One partner should read the word problem aloud, and the other partner can identify the words in the problems that indicate subtraction (how many are left, how many more). Remind students that the larger number is written first in a subtraction problem. Then they should write the subtraction problem and solve it.

Enrichment

1. Have students write a take-away subtraction word problem for a friend to solve.
2. Have students write a subtraction word problem comparing 2 numbers for a friend to solve.
3. Tell students to write and solve a problem to find out how many more days are in 2 weeks than in 1 week.

Teaching page 62

Have students tell how the question in each problem differs. (The words how many more or how many . . . left are different) Ask what operation each type of question asks them to do. (subtract) Have students complete the page independently.

Extra Credit   *Measurement*

Give each student a strip of one-inch graph paper. Have students print their names, one letter per square, on the strip, and cut off any blank squares. Have students count the squares and measure with a ruler the length of their names. Arrange the name strips in a class graph on the bulletin board, to compare lengths.

Minuends through 16

pages 63-64

Objective

To subtract from minuends through 16

Materials

16 counters

Mental Math

Tell students to name the number that:
1. comes after 10, 20, 30. (40)
2. is 2 more than 20. (22)
3. comes before 40. (39)
4. tells today's date.
5. comes after 8, 10, 12. (14)
6. is the double of 9. (18)

Skill Review

Have 2 students hold up 10 fingers and match their hands palm-to-palm. Ask how many more fingers 1 student is showing than the other. (none) Write **10 − 10 = 0** on the board. Have 1 student fold down 3 fingers and match palms with the other student. Ask how many more fingers are extended on 1 student's hand. (3) Have a student write and solve the subtraction problem on the board. (10 − 7 = 3) Continue for other examples.

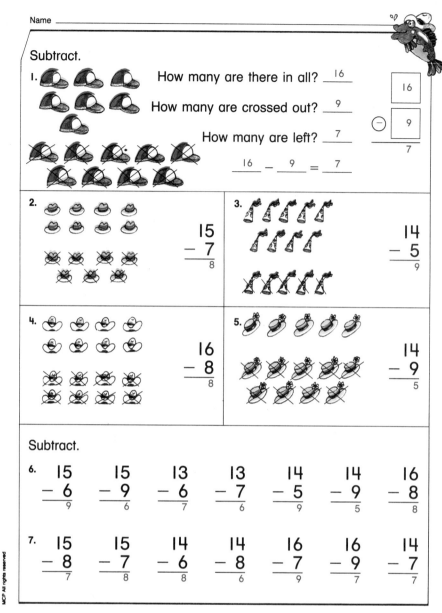

Subtraction facts, minuends through 16

(sixty-three) **63**

Teaching page 63

Tell students we want to find all the numbers which are addends for the sum of 13, and then write the related subtraction facts. Allow students to use counters to develop each fact. Have students write 2 subtraction sentences for each pair of addends for 15. (15 − 9 = 6, 13 − 6 = 7, etc.) Remind students that all addends should be 9 or less. Ask students how many subtraction facts for 15 there are. (4) Repeat for addends of 16. Ask students how many subtraction facts for 16 there are. (3) Ask students how many more subtraction facts there are for 15 than for 16. (1) Help students work through the example crossing out as they count. Have students complete the page independently.

63

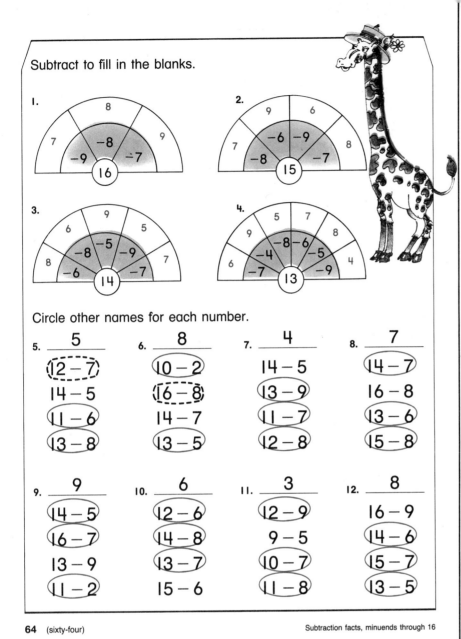

Subtract to fill in the blanks.

1.

8
7 —8 9
—9 —7
16

2.

9 6
7 —6 —9 8
—8 —7
15

3.

9
6 5
—8 —5 —9
8 —7
—6 7
14

4.

5 7
9 —8 —6 8
—4 —5
6 —7 —9 4
13

Circle other names for each number.

5. 5
⟨12 − 7⟩ (dashed)
14 − 5
⟨11 − 6⟩
⟨13 − 8⟩

6. 8
⟨10 − 2⟩
⟨16 − 8⟩ (dashed)
14 − 7
⟨13 − 5⟩

7. 4
14 − 5
⟨13 − 9⟩
⟨11 − 7⟩
⟨12 − 8⟩

8. 7
⟨14 − 7⟩
16 − 8
⟨13 − 6⟩
⟨15 − 8⟩

9. 9
⟨14 − 5⟩
⟨16 − 7⟩
13 − 9
⟨11 − 2⟩

10. 6
⟨12 − 6⟩
⟨14 − 8⟩
⟨13 − 7⟩
15 − 6

11. 3
⟨12 − 9⟩
9 − 5
⟨10 − 7⟩
⟨11 − 8⟩

12. 8
16 − 9
⟨14 − 6⟩
⟨15 − 7⟩
⟨13 − 5⟩

64 (sixty-four)   Subtraction facts, minuends through 16

Correcting Common Errors

Some students may need more practice subtracting from minuends of 15 and 16. Have students work with partners and fact cards for minuends of 15 and 16. One partner can draw objects to represent the minuend, and the other partner can cross out the number indicated by the subtrahend. Then they should each write the fact. They can then reverse roles and follow the same procedure for the other facts.

Enrichment

1. Have students use facts for sums and minuends through 16 to write all the names for 9. Tell students there should be 18 facts.
2. Have students make a half-circle subtraction activity like those on page 64. They should write 11 in the circle and have a friend solve the problems. Tell them to check their friend's work.

Teaching page 64

Have students complete the 4 half-circles independently. Now have students trace the ring around 12 − 7 to show it is a name for the number 5. Ask students if 14 − 5 is a name for 5. (no) Tell students it is not to be circled. Continue through the next 2 facts as students see they are both names for 5 and should be circled. Continue with names for 8 and then have students complete the page independently.

Extra Credit   Sets

Have students make two circles by cutting two lengths of string 2 feet long and tying the ends. Have students overlap the circles on their desks to form a Venn diagram.

Have them practice with buttons or colored shapes, placing sets within the circles. Demonstrate the property that some sets have elements in common. For example, put all of the yellow pieces in one circle and all of the triangles in another. Have students decide where the yellow triangle will be placed. Let students practice making sets that have elements in common and placing them within the circles.

Minuends through 18

pages 65-66

Objective

To subtract from minuends through 18

Materials

*addition fact cards for sums 12 through 18
18 counters

Mental Math

Ask students what ordinal number comes after:
1. third (fourth)
2. ninth (tenth)
3. first (second)
4. eighth (ninth)
5. seventh (eighth)
6. second (third)
7. fifth (sixth)
8. nineteenth (twentieth)

Skill Review

Review addition facts for sums 12 through 18. Have students give the sums and then put the cards on the chalk tray under the headings of Sums 12 through 14 and Sums 15 through 18.

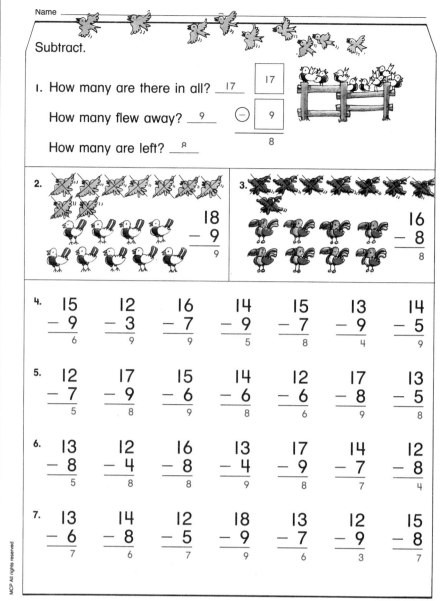

Subtraction facts, minuends through 18

(sixty-five) **65**

Teaching page 65

Have students lay out 18 counters in 2 groups of 9 or less. Ask students what the addends are. (9,9) Have a student write the related subtraction fact on the board. (18 − 9 = 9) Students should note that there is only 1 subtraction fact for 18. Repeat for addends of 17 to show 17 − 9 = 8 and 17 − 8 = 9. Help students to see that basic facts have only 1-digit numbers so there are only 2 subtraction facts for 17.

Have students read each question and write the answers. Have students decide the operation to be used and write the sign in the circle. (−) Have students write and solve the problem. Have students complete the subtraction problems on the page independently.

65

Subtract.

1.
$$\begin{array}{r}15\\-9\\\hline 6\end{array}\quad\begin{array}{r}12\\-5\\\hline 7\end{array}\quad\begin{array}{r}14\\-6\\\hline 8\end{array}\quad\begin{array}{r}9\\-9\\\hline 0\end{array}\quad\begin{array}{r}15\\-6\\\hline 9\end{array}\quad\begin{array}{r}12\\-9\\\hline 3\end{array}\quad\begin{array}{r}13\\-5\\\hline 8\end{array}$$

2.
$$\begin{array}{r}12\\-4\\\hline 8\end{array}\quad\begin{array}{r}17\\-8\\\hline 9\end{array}\quad\begin{array}{r}14\\-9\\\hline 5\end{array}\quad\begin{array}{r}15\\-8\\\hline 7\end{array}\quad\begin{array}{r}12\\-6\\\hline 6\end{array}\quad\begin{array}{r}16\\-9\\\hline 7\end{array}\quad\begin{array}{r}12\\-8\\\hline 4\end{array}$$

3.
$$\begin{array}{r}10\\-6\\\hline 4\end{array}\quad\begin{array}{r}13\\-8\\\hline 5\end{array}\quad\begin{array}{r}17\\-9\\\hline 8\end{array}\quad\begin{array}{r}12\\-3\\\hline 9\end{array}\quad\begin{array}{r}14\\-7\\\hline 7\end{array}\quad\begin{array}{r}12\\-7\\\hline 5\end{array}\quad\begin{array}{r}16\\-7\\\hline 9\end{array}$$

4.
$$\begin{array}{r}16\\-8\\\hline 8\end{array}\quad\begin{array}{r}14\\-5\\\hline 9\end{array}\quad\begin{array}{r}15\\-7\\\hline 8\end{array}\quad\begin{array}{r}18\\-9\\\hline 9\end{array}\quad\begin{array}{r}13\\-7\\\hline 6\end{array}\quad\begin{array}{r}14\\-8\\\hline 6\end{array}\quad\begin{array}{r}13\\-6\\\hline 7\end{array}$$

FIELD TRIP

Answer the riddles.

1. When you add me to 5, the sum is 11.

   $$\begin{array}{r}5\\+6\\\hline 11\end{array}$$

   Who am I? __6__

2. When you double me, the sum is 16.

   $$\begin{array}{r}8\\+8\\\hline 16\end{array}$$

   Who am I? __8__

3. When you add me to 8, the sum is 17.

   $$\begin{array}{r}8\\+9\\\hline 17\end{array}$$

   Who am I? __9__

4. When you double me and add 1, you get 13.

   $$\begin{array}{r}6\\+6\\\hline 12\end{array}\quad\begin{array}{r}12\\+1\\\hline 13\end{array}$$

   Who am I? __6__

Subtraction facts, minuends through 18

Correcting Common Errors

Some students may have difficulty with certain subtraction facts. Have them work with partners to practice the subtraction facts. Give each pair of students fact-family cards similar to the one shown below.

$$\boxed{17\ \begin{array}{|c}9\\\hline 8\end{array}}$$

For each such card, the partners should write two addition and two subtraction facts.

$$\begin{array}{r}9\\+8\\\hline 17\end{array}\quad\begin{array}{r}8\\+9\\\hline 17\end{array}\quad\begin{array}{r}17\\-9\\\hline 8\end{array}\quad\begin{array}{r}17\\-8\\\hline 9\end{array}$$

Enrichment

1. Have students write addition and subtraction problems for sums and minuends through 18 to show all the ways to name 9. Tell students there should be 20 facts.
2. Have students draw a picture showing 9 objects being removed from 17. They should then write a subtraction problem to tell how many are removed and a second problem to show how many are left.

Teaching page 66

Have students write the answers to the problems independently.

Field Trip

Read the first problem and have students discuss what is being asked. Ask students what operation is suggested. (addition) Ask students to think of an addition fact which has a 5 and another number for a sum of 11. (5 + 6 = 11) Have students complete the next 3 problems independently. Then discuss the solutions and how they were found.

Extra Credit   *Applications*

Bring a stopwatch to school. Discuss with students its use for timing a race. Take students outside and help them measure a distance of 50 yards. Have them line up behind the starting point and tell them they will run a 50-yd dash. Have one student give the "ready, set, go" and time each runner. Have other students take turns writing down the times. When all students have had a chance to run, post the times on a board so the class can compare. Have students identify the most frequently run time.

More Minuends through 18

pages 67-68

Objective

To practice subtraction from minuends through 18

Materials

18 counters

Mental Math

Tell students that Monday is the second day of the week. Then ask which day is:

1. Wednesday (fourth)
2. first (Sunday)
3. third (Tuesday)
4. Saturday (seventh)
5. Thursday (fifth)
6. sixth (Friday)

Skill Review

Pair students with counters. Students should use a divider so they cannot see each other's counters. Tell each student to lay out a subtraction fact for a minuend of 12 or more. Have students remove their divider and tell their fact with the answer. Vary the requirements for winning each time, such as, the fact with the largest answer, the fact with the smallest answer, doubles winning over any fact, etc. Students score one point for each win, or one each for a tie.

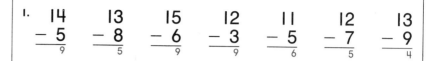

Name _____

Subtract.

1.
14	13	15	12	11	12	13
-5	-8	-6	-3	-5	-7	-9
9	5	9	9	6	5	4

2.
12	11	16	11	10	12	14
-4	-6	-8	-2	-7	-5	-7
8	5	8	9	3	7	7

3.
13	10	11	13	10	11	16
-4	-1	-7	-5	-8	-3	-7
9	9	4	8	2	8	9

4.
17	12	11	15	10	13	14
-8	-6	-4	-9	-2	-6	-8
9	6	7	6	8	7	6

Complete the tables.

5.
Subtract 9	
11	2
15	6
18	9
13	4
17	8
14	5
16	7

6.
Subtract 8	
11	3
15	7
17	9
14	6
12	4
16	8
13	5

7.
Subtract 7	
13	6
10	3
15	8
12	5
16	9
14	7
11	4

8.
Subtract 6	
9	3
14	8
11	5
12	6
13	7
10	4
15	9

Practice, minuends through 18

(sixty-seven) **67**

Teaching page 67

Write on the board:

Subtract 4		Subtract 5	
8	(4)	**11**	(6)
12	(8)	**14**	(9)
(10)	**6**	(13)	**8**
13	(9)	**10**	(5)
(7)	**3**	(12)	**7**

Have students complete the tables, using addition or subtraction facts.

Have students complete the page independently.

Subtract.

1. $11 - 8 = \underline{3}$ $16 - 9 = \underline{7}$ $10 - 6 = \underline{4}$
2. $10 - 3 = \underline{7}$ $10 - 5 = \underline{5}$ $15 - 8 = \underline{7}$
3. $14 - 6 = \underline{8}$ $12 - 8 = \underline{4}$ $9 - 9 = \underline{0}$
4. $18 - 9 = \underline{9}$ $10 - 9 = \underline{1}$ $8 - 5 = \underline{3}$
5. $10 - 4 = \underline{6}$ $13 - 7 = \underline{6}$ $14 - 9 = \underline{5}$
6. $12 - 9 = \underline{3}$ $9 - 3 = \underline{6}$ $9 - 0 = \underline{9}$
7. $15 - 7 = \underline{8}$ $17 - 9 = \underline{8}$ $11 - 9 = \underline{2}$

Complete the wheels.

8.
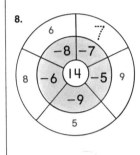

9.
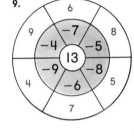

FIELD TRIP

Write in the correct sign.

1. $13 \ominus 6 = 7$ $16 \ominus 8 = 8$ $8 \oplus 5 = 13$
2. $9 \oplus 9 = 18$ $13 \ominus 7 = 6$ $11 \ominus 5 = 6$
3. $8 \oplus 8 = 16$ $5 \oplus 9 = 14$ $12 \ominus 6 = 6$
4. $17 \ominus 9 = 8$ $7 \oplus 2 = 9$ $14 \ominus 5 = 9$

68 (sixty-eight)   Practice, minuends through 18

Some students may need more practice with certain subtraction facts. Have them work in pairs. Give each pair cards on which two numbers are written, such as shown below.

7	8

For each card, the pair of students write four facts.

$$\begin{array}{cccc} 7 & 8 & 15 & 15 \\ +8 & +7 & -\ 8 & -\ 7 \\ \hline 15 & 15 & 7 & 8 \end{array}$$

Enrichment

1. Tell students to make a table with **Subtract ?** at the top. Have them write minuends down the left side. On the right side, tell them to write numbers to show what would be left if the secret number were subtracted from each minuend. Have students trade with a classmate to tell the secret number.

2. Tell students to find this mystery number. If it is doubled, has 7 subtracted from it, and then has 4 added to it, the number will equal 13. Hint: Start with 13 and work backward. (8)

Teaching page 68

Ask students what operation they will use in the first 2 parts of the page. Have students complete the page independently.

Field Trip

Tell students to write a plus or minus sign in each sentence to make it true. Have students trace the minus sign in the first problem and read the problem to tell if it is true. (yes) Ask if a plus sign would make the problem true. (no) Ask why. (13 + 6 would not be 7) Remind students to check each problem to be sure it is true. Have students complete the problems independently.

Extra Credit *Numeration*

Fill containers with small items such as counters, buttons, beads, dried peas, small toys, etc. Place the containers in various locations around the room. Give each pair of students a card with a numerical value printed on it; for examples include: less than 8, more than 50, between 25 and 30. Have students look for the container having their set number, then count the items to check. Tell them to label each container with its identifying card. As a conclusion, students can arrange the containers in order from the least to greatest numbers.

Problem Solving Using Money

pages 69-70

Objective

To solve addition and subtraction word problems for sums and minuends through 18¢

Materials

*objects priced through 9¢
3 nickels
18 pennies

Mental Math

Have students tell the tens and ones in:
1. 78 (7 tens 8 ones)
2. 46 (4 tens 6 ones)
3. 99 (9 tens 9 ones)
4. 65 (6 tens 5 ones)
5. 80 (8 tens 0 ones)
6. 29 (2 tens 9 ones)
7. 35 (3 tens 5 ones)

Skill Review

Have students lay out 2 nickels and tell the total money. (10¢) Have students add another nickel and count by fives to find the sum. (15¢) Have students find other sums of money made with combinations of nickels and pennies through 18¢.

Solve.

1. Carlos had 15¢.
He bought a bear.
How much money
is left?

$$\begin{array}{r} 15¢ \\ -\ 6¢ \\ \hline 9¢ \end{array}$$

_9¢_

2. A truck costs _9¢_.

A ring costs _7¢_.
How much more does
the truck cost?

$$\begin{array}{r} 9¢ \\ -7¢ \\ \hline 2¢ \end{array}$$

_2¢_

3. Joan had 17¢.
She bought a truck.
How much money
is left?

$$\begin{array}{r} 17¢ \\ -\ 9¢ \\ \hline 8¢ \end{array}$$

_8¢_

4. Donna had 15¢.
She bought a train.
How much money
does she have left?

$$\begin{array}{r} 15¢ \\ -\ 8¢ \\ \hline 7¢ \end{array}$$

_7¢_

5. Chuck gave the clerk
10¢ to pay for a ring.
How much change did
he get?

$$\begin{array}{r} 10¢ \\ -\ 7¢ \\ \hline 3¢ \end{array}$$

_3¢_

6. Marge gave the clerk
10¢ to pay for a car.
How much change did
she get?

$$\begin{array}{r} 10¢ \\ -\ 5¢ \\ \hline 5¢ \end{array}$$

_5¢_

7. Dorothy had 18¢.
She bought a truck.
How much does she
have left?

$$\begin{array}{r} 18¢ \\ -\ 9¢ \\ \hline 9¢ \end{array}$$

_9¢_

8. How much did Cal pay
for a car and a train?

$$\begin{array}{r} 5¢ \\ +8¢ \\ \hline 13¢ \end{array}$$

_13¢_

Problem solving, adding and subtracting money

(sixty-nine) **69**

Teaching page 69

Have students lay out 18¢. Show students an object priced at 9¢ and ask how much money they would have left if they bought the item. (9¢) Have a student write and solve the subtraction problem on the board. (18¢ − 9¢ = 9¢) Repeat for other amounts and other priced objects. Show students 2 objects priced at 9¢ and 8¢. Ask students how to find how much more the 9¢ object costs than the 9¢ object. (subtract) Have a student write and solve the problem. (9¢ − 8¢ = 1¢) Repeat for more comparisons of costs. Ask students to write a problem to tell how much change they would receive if an item costs 6¢ and they gave the clerk 10¢. (10¢ − 6¢ = 4¢) Now show students 2 objects priced 8¢ and 6¢ and ask how to find their total cost. (add) Have a student write and solve the problem

(8¢ + 6¢ = 14¢) Repeat for more addition problems of 2 prices.

Have students tell the name and price of each item. Help students solve the first problem. Remind students to first decide which operation to use. Remind them to use cent signs, operation signs and to write their answer in the solution statement. Have students complete the page independently. Then discuss each problem and talk through its solution.

69

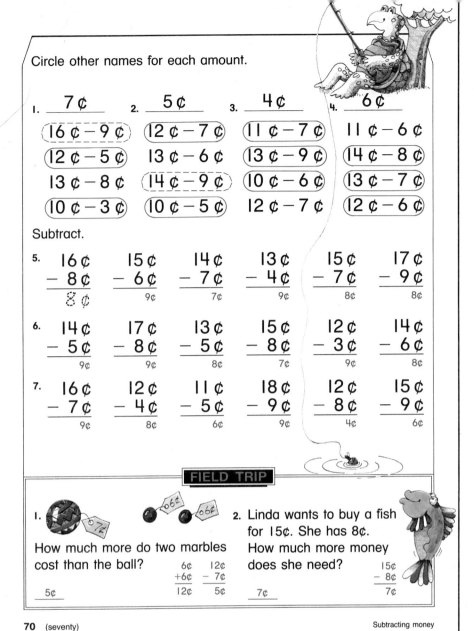

Circle other names for each amount.

1. __7 ¢__

(16 ¢ − 9 ¢)
(12 ¢ − 5 ¢)
13 ¢ − 8 ¢
(10 ¢ − 3 ¢)

2. __5 ¢__

(12 ¢ − 7 ¢)
13 ¢ − 6 ¢
(14 ¢ − 9 ¢)
(10 ¢ − 5 ¢)

3. __4 ¢__

(11 ¢ − 7 ¢)
(13 ¢ − 9 ¢)
(10 ¢ − 6 ¢)
12 ¢ − 7 ¢

4. __6 ¢__

11 ¢ − 6 ¢
(14 ¢ − 8 ¢)
(13 ¢ − 7 ¢)
(12 ¢ − 6 ¢)

Subtract.

5.
16 ¢ − 8 ¢ = 8 ¢
15 ¢ − 6 ¢ = 9 ¢
14 ¢ − 7 ¢ = 7 ¢
13 ¢ − 4 ¢ = 9 ¢
15 ¢ − 7 ¢ = 8 ¢
17 ¢ − 9 ¢ = 8 ¢

6.
14 ¢ − 5 ¢ = 9 ¢
17 ¢ − 8 ¢ = 9 ¢
13 ¢ − 5 ¢ = 8 ¢
15 ¢ − 8 ¢ = 7 ¢
12 ¢ − 3 ¢ = 9 ¢
14 ¢ − 6 ¢ = 8 ¢

7.
16 ¢ − 7 ¢ = 9 ¢
12 ¢ − 4 ¢ = 8 ¢
11 ¢ − 5 ¢ = 6 ¢
18 ¢ − 9 ¢ = 9 ¢
12 ¢ − 8 ¢ = 4 ¢
15 ¢ − 9 ¢ = 6 ¢

FIELD TRIP

1. How much more do two marbles cost than the ball?

6¢   12¢
+6¢   − 7¢
12¢   5¢

__5¢__

2. Linda wants to buy a fish for 15¢. She has 8¢. How much more money does she need?

15¢
− 8¢
7¢

__7¢__

Subtracting money

Correcting Common Errors

For students who need practice adding and subtracting with money, have them work with partners and pennies to model each problem. One partner should read the problem aloud and use the pennies to model it. The other partner should write and solve the addition or subtraction fact that matches the first partner's action.

Enrichment

1. Tell students to draw the change you would receive from 18¢ if they bought gum for 5¢ and a toy for 8¢.
2. Ask students how much change they would get from 50¢ if they bought items costing 2¢, 11¢, 5¢, 9¢ and 3¢. (20¢)

Teaching page 70

Remind students they have done this first activity before but now the cent sign has been added. Help students complete the names for 7¢ and then have students complete the page independently.

Field Trip

Draw 2 kites on the board and write **8¢** under each to show their costs. Draw a piece of candy priced at **7¢**. Ask a student to write and solve a problem on the board to show the total cost of 2 kites. (8¢ + 8¢ = 16¢) Ask students how they could find out how much more 2 kites would cost than the 1 piece of candy. (subtract) Have a student write and solve the problem on the board. (16¢ − 7¢ = 9¢) Discuss with the students how to solve each of the 2 problems and then have students complete them independently.

Extra Credit   *Logic*

Play the game "Guess Who's Missing." Write the names of all the students and the teacher on small pieces of paper and put them in a bag. One student is picked to be Witness, and another is called Detective. The Witness draws a name out of the bag and keeps the name secret from everyone. The Witness then gives the Detective clues that will point to the Missing Person. For example, the person is not an adult, the person was last seen wearing tennis shoes, the person is female. As each clue is given, the Detective sorts out the groups of possible missing persons. As the subsets get smaller, and sets are eliminated, the clues will be more specific: the person has brown hair and blue eyes. Eventually, the Detective will be able to find the Missing Person, and reveal the name that the Witness has drawn.

70

Mixed Practice

pages 71-72

Objective

To practice addition and subtraction for sums and minuends through 18

Materials

*addition and subtraction fact cards for sums and minuends through 18
18 counters

Mental Math

Ask how many pennies are in a:
1. dime (10)
2. quarter (25)
3. dollar (100)
4. nickel (5)
5. nickel and dime (15)
6. dime and another dime (20)
7. quarter and 1 penny (26)

Skill Review

Show fact cards randomly and have students look for facts which use the same numbers, for example; 6 + 3 = 9, 3 + 6 = 9, 9 − 6 = 3, 9 − 3 = 6. Have students group some of the facts in this way until several groups have been formed. Then distribute the remaining facts for students to continue building families until all cards are grouped.

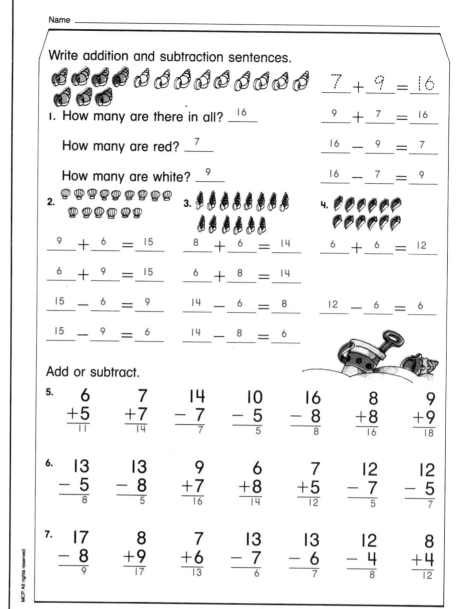

Name _____

Write addition and subtraction sentences.

$7 + 9 = 16$
1. How many are there in all? 16 $9 + 7 = 16$
   How many are red? 7 $16 − 9 = 7$
   How many are white? 9 $16 − 7 = 9$

2. $9 + 6 = 15$ 3. $8 + 6 = 14$ 4. $6 + 6 = 12$
   $6 + 9 = 15$ $6 + 8 = 14$
   $15 − 6 = 9$ $14 − 6 = 8$ $12 − 6 = 6$
   $15 − 9 = 6$ $14 − 8 = 6$

Add or subtract.

5.
$\begin{array}{r} 6 \\ +5 \\ \hline 11 \end{array}$
$\begin{array}{r} 7 \\ +7 \\ \hline 14 \end{array}$
$\begin{array}{r} 14 \\ -7 \\ \hline 7 \end{array}$
$\begin{array}{r} 10 \\ -5 \\ \hline 5 \end{array}$
$\begin{array}{r} 16 \\ -8 \\ \hline 8 \end{array}$
$\begin{array}{r} 8 \\ +8 \\ \hline 16 \end{array}$
$\begin{array}{r} 9 \\ +9 \\ \hline 18 \end{array}$

6.
$\begin{array}{r} 13 \\ -5 \\ \hline 8 \end{array}$
$\begin{array}{r} 13 \\ -8 \\ \hline 5 \end{array}$
$\begin{array}{r} 9 \\ +7 \\ \hline 16 \end{array}$
$\begin{array}{r} 6 \\ +8 \\ \hline 14 \end{array}$
$\begin{array}{r} 7 \\ +5 \\ \hline 12 \end{array}$
$\begin{array}{r} 12 \\ -7 \\ \hline 5 \end{array}$
$\begin{array}{r} 12 \\ -5 \\ \hline 7 \end{array}$

7.
$\begin{array}{r} 17 \\ -8 \\ \hline 9 \end{array}$
$\begin{array}{r} 8 \\ +9 \\ \hline 17 \end{array}$
$\begin{array}{r} 7 \\ +6 \\ \hline 13 \end{array}$
$\begin{array}{r} 13 \\ -7 \\ \hline 6 \end{array}$
$\begin{array}{r} 13 \\ -6 \\ \hline 7 \end{array}$
$\begin{array}{r} 12 \\ -4 \\ \hline 8 \end{array}$
$\begin{array}{r} 8 \\ +4 \\ \hline 12 \end{array}$

Practice, adding and subtracting

(seventy-one) **71**

Teaching page 71

Draw 15 objects on the board and circle 6 of them. Ask students how many objects in all. (15) Ask how many objects are circled. (6) Ask how many are not circled. (9) Write **15, 6** and **9** on the board. Tell students there are 4 sentences which can be written with these 3 numbers to tell about the objects. Encourage students to help discover and write the following on the board: **15 − 9 = 6, 15 − 6 = 9, 6 + 9 = 15** and **9 + 6 = 15.** Repeat for 16 objects and then for 17 objects. Have students read the questions at the top of the page and write the answers. Have students trace the first number sentence and then write 3 more number sentences using the same numbers. Help students work the next problem if necessary before having them complete the page independently.

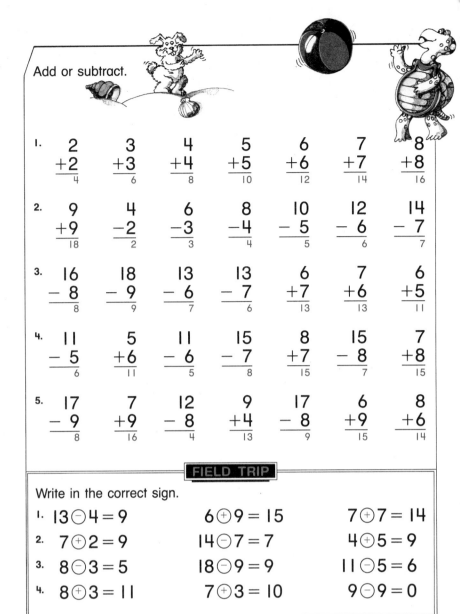

Add or subtract.

1.
$$\begin{array}{r} 2 \\ +2 \\ \hline 4 \end{array}$$
$$\begin{array}{r} 3 \\ +3 \\ \hline 6 \end{array}$$
$$\begin{array}{r} 4 \\ +4 \\ \hline 8 \end{array}$$
$$\begin{array}{r} 5 \\ +5 \\ \hline 10 \end{array}$$
$$\begin{array}{r} 6 \\ +6 \\ \hline 12 \end{array}$$
$$\begin{array}{r} 7 \\ +7 \\ \hline 14 \end{array}$$
$$\begin{array}{r} 8 \\ +8 \\ \hline 16 \end{array}$$

2.
$$\begin{array}{r} 9 \\ +9 \\ \hline 18 \end{array}$$
$$\begin{array}{r} 4 \\ -2 \\ \hline 2 \end{array}$$
$$\begin{array}{r} 6 \\ -3 \\ \hline 3 \end{array}$$
$$\begin{array}{r} 8 \\ -4 \\ \hline 4 \end{array}$$
$$\begin{array}{r} 10 \\ -5 \\ \hline 5 \end{array}$$
$$\begin{array}{r} 12 \\ -6 \\ \hline 6 \end{array}$$
$$\begin{array}{r} 14 \\ -7 \\ \hline 7 \end{array}$$

3.
$$\begin{array}{r} 16 \\ -8 \\ \hline 8 \end{array}$$
$$\begin{array}{r} 18 \\ -9 \\ \hline 9 \end{array}$$
$$\begin{array}{r} 13 \\ -6 \\ \hline 7 \end{array}$$
$$\begin{array}{r} 13 \\ -7 \\ \hline 6 \end{array}$$
$$\begin{array}{r} 6 \\ +7 \\ \hline 13 \end{array}$$
$$\begin{array}{r} 7 \\ +6 \\ \hline 13 \end{array}$$
$$\begin{array}{r} 6 \\ +5 \\ \hline 11 \end{array}$$

4.
$$\begin{array}{r} 11 \\ -5 \\ \hline 6 \end{array}$$
$$\begin{array}{r} 5 \\ +6 \\ \hline 11 \end{array}$$
$$\begin{array}{r} 11 \\ -6 \\ \hline 5 \end{array}$$
$$\begin{array}{r} 15 \\ -7 \\ \hline 8 \end{array}$$
$$\begin{array}{r} 8 \\ +7 \\ \hline 15 \end{array}$$
$$\begin{array}{r} 15 \\ -8 \\ \hline 7 \end{array}$$
$$\begin{array}{r} 7 \\ +8 \\ \hline 15 \end{array}$$

5.
$$\begin{array}{r} 17 \\ -9 \\ \hline 8 \end{array}$$
$$\begin{array}{r} 7 \\ +9 \\ \hline 16 \end{array}$$
$$\begin{array}{r} 12 \\ -8 \\ \hline 4 \end{array}$$
$$\begin{array}{r} 9 \\ +4 \\ \hline 13 \end{array}$$
$$\begin{array}{r} 17 \\ -8 \\ \hline 9 \end{array}$$
$$\begin{array}{r} 6 \\ +9 \\ \hline 15 \end{array}$$
$$\begin{array}{r} 8 \\ +6 \\ \hline 14 \end{array}$$

FIELD TRIP

Write in the correct sign.

1. $13 \ominus 4 = 9$ $6 \oplus 9 = 15$ $7 \oplus 7 = 14$
2. $7 \oplus 2 = 9$ $14 \ominus 7 = 7$ $4 \oplus 5 = 9$
3. $8 \ominus 3 = 5$ $18 \ominus 9 = 9$ $11 \ominus 5 = 6$
4. $8 \oplus 3 = 11$ $7 \oplus 3 = 10$ $9 \ominus 9 = 0$

72 (seventy-two)   Practice, adding and subtracting

Teaching page 72

Help students see that each of the problems in the first row concerns a double. Have students note that some problems on the page are addition and some require them to subtract. Remind students to look at the sign before beginning to work each problem. Have students complete the page independently.

Field Trip

Tell students they are to write a plus or minus sign in each problem. Remind students to check each problem to be certain it is true. Have students complete the problems independently.

Extra Credit   *Numeration*

Have students form two teams of 10 players with each member holding a number card from 0 through 9. A leader calls out any number from 10-99. The players on each team who are holding the cards with the correct numerals go to the front of the room, face the class and arrange themselves to show the correct number. The team that first holds up the correct number scores one point. There will be only one player from each team for "double numbers"-11, 22, 33, etc. Have the two players go together to form the number and award each team one point. Vary this activity by using three-digit numbers.

72

Mixed Problem Solving

pages 73-74

Objective

To solve problems for sums and minuends through 18

Materials

18 counters

Mental Math

Tell students to name the hour that comes after:
1. 2:00 (3:00)
2. 9:00
3. 4:00
4. 12:00
5. 10:00
6. 6:00
7. 3:00
8. Noon

Skill Review

Write **13 − 6 =** on the board and have students solve the problem. (7) Then tell them to write 3 related addition or subtraction sentences. (13 − 7 = 6, 6 + 7 = 13, 7 + 6 = 13) Repeat for more addition or subtraction facts for sums or minuends through 18.

Name _____

Solve.

1. Fido ate 6 dog treats. Then he ate 5 more. How many did he eat in all?

$$\begin{array}{r} 6 \\ +5 \\ \hline 11 \end{array}$$

___11___ treats

2. Ben saw 16 ladybugs. 8 flew away. How many were left?

$$\begin{array}{r} 16 \\ -8 \\ \hline 8 \end{array}$$

___8___ ladybugs

3. Lois has 8 bananas and 9 apples. How many pieces of fruit does she have?

$$\begin{array}{r} 8 \\ +9 \\ \hline 17 \end{array}$$

___17___ pieces of fruit

4. Mario saw 6 frogs on a rock. He saw 8 frogs in the water. How many frogs were there altogether?

$$\begin{array}{r} 6 \\ +8 \\ \hline 14 \end{array}$$

___14___ frogs

5. There are 16 cherries and 7 strawberries. How many more cherries than strawberries are there?

$$\begin{array}{r} 16 \\ -7 \\ \hline 9 \end{array}$$

___9___ cherries

6. Jerry counted 15 cows in the field. 6 of them went into the barn. How many cows are left in the field?

$$\begin{array}{r} 15 \\ -6 \\ \hline 9 \end{array}$$

___9___ cows

7. Allen fed 6 squirrels. Ramona fed 7 squirrels. How many squirrels did they feed?

$$\begin{array}{r} 6 \\ +7 \\ \hline 13 \end{array}$$

___13___ squirrels

8. There are 16 ducks in the pond. There are 9 ducks on land. How many more ducks are in the pond?

$$\begin{array}{r} 16 \\ -9 \\ \hline 7 \end{array}$$

___7___ ducks

Problem solving, adding and subtracting

(seventy-three) **73**

Teaching page 73

Have students lay out 9 counters and 7 counters to form 2 groups. Ask students what operation they would use to find the number of counters in all. (addition) Have a student write and solve the problem on the board. (9 + 7 = 16) Ask students what operation they would use to find how many more counters are in 1 group than the other. (subtraction) Have a student write and solve the problem. (9 − 7 = 2) Ask what operation they would use to find how many counters are in 1 of the groups. (subtraction) Have a student write and solve the problem on the board. (16 − 9 = 7 or 16 − 7 = 9) Repeat the activities for 15 counters in groups of 6 and 9.

Have students complete the problems independently after a reminder to first decide on the operation. Then discuss all problems and their solutions with the students.

Answer the riddles.

1. If you double me, you get 10. Who am I? __5__	$\begin{array}{r} 5 \\ +5 \\ \hline 10 \end{array}$
2. If you add 4 to me, you get 12. Who am I? __8__	$\begin{array}{r} 8 \\ +4 \\ \hline 12 \end{array}$
3. If you subtract 9 from me, you get 5. Who am I? __14__	$\begin{array}{r} 14 \\ -9 \\ \hline 5 \end{array}$
4. If you double me, you get 16. Who am I? __8__	$\begin{array}{r} 8 \\ +8 \\ \hline 16 \end{array}$
5. If you add me to myself, you get 14. Who am I? __7__	$\begin{array}{r} 7 \\ +7 \\ \hline 14 \end{array}$
6. If you add 2 to me, and then add 3 more, you get 8. Who am I? __3__	$\begin{array}{r} 3 \\ 2 \\ +3 \\ \hline 8 \end{array}$

FIELD TRIP

Add or subtract.

Start (15) −8 (7) +3 (10) −5 (5) +3 (8) +7 (15) −9 (6) −6 (0) End

Start (18) −9 (9) −3 (6) +8 (14) −7 (7) −7 (0) +5 (5) −5 (0) End

74 (seventy-four)   Problem solving, adding and subtracting

Correcting Common Errors

Some students may have difficulty deciding whether to add or subtract. Have them work with partners, discussing each story problem. They should identify the words that suggest whether they should add (e.g., in all, altogether, etc.) or subtract (e.g., are left, many more, etc.). Encourage them to circle these words before deciding what operation to perform.

Enrichment

1. Tell students to use the numbers 17 and 9 to write a puzzle problem for a friend to solve.
2. Tell students to write a problem about sharing 18 pennies with 2 friends. One friend will have only 2 pennies.

Teaching page 74

Remind students they have worked this type of puzzle problem before. Tell students to think of the operation they will use before beginning to work each problem. Have students solve the puzzles independently. Discuss each solution with the students and show the work on the board.

Field Trip

Tell students they are to start at 15 and subtract 8 to get to the next circle. Ask students what number they will trace in the circle. (7) Tell students they must now add 7 and 3 to get to the next circle. Ask the sum of 7 and 3. (10) Have students write 10 in the circle. Ask students what problem they will work to get to the next circle. (10 − 5) Have students complete the path to the circle marked End. Ask students if they ended with

zero. (yes) Tell students to start at 18 and work their way to the word End on the second path. Then have students work the problems of the second path on the board to check their work.

Extra Credit *Numeration*

Tell the students that you are thinking of a number between 1 and 20. To guess the number, they may ask you only 20 yes or no questions. Also, the questions they ask must be in the form of a mathematical problem. For example: Can the number be subtracted from 10, leaving a whole number? Can it be added to 5 and get a sum of 15? Have students take turns asking questions until they guess your number. Extend the activity by choosing a student to pick a number and answer the questions.

74

Review

pages 75-76

Objectives

To review addition and subtraction for sums and minuends through 18
To maintain skills learned previously this year

Materials

18 counters

Mental Math

Name the next number:
1. 5, 10, 15 (20)
2. 17, 18, 19 (20)
3. 2, 4, 6, 8 (10)
4. 10, 20, 30 (40)
5. 1, 3, 5, 7 (9)
6. 27, 28, 29 (30)
7. 82, 83, 84 (85)
8. 47, 48, 49 (50)

Skill Review

Divide the students into two groups. Use a complete set of subtraction fact flash cards to play the game of *Football*. One team gives the facts until they make a mistake, receiving a point for each correct answer. The other team then goes on the **offensive** to answer. The game ends when a special point total is reached.

CHAPTER CHECKUP

Subtract.

1.
$$10 - 7 = 3 \qquad 13 - 5 = 8 \qquad 12 - 3 = 9 \qquad 15 - 6 = 9 \qquad 8 - 0 = 8 \qquad 13 - 4 = 9 \qquad 14 - 7 = 7$$

2.
$$14 - 6 = 8 \qquad 11 - 5 = 6 \qquad 13 - 7 = 6 \qquad 16 - 8 = 8 \qquad 15 - 9 = 6 \qquad 13 - 8 = 5 \qquad 15 - 7 = 8$$

3.
$$17 - 8 = 9 \qquad 13 - 9 = 4 \qquad 9 - 9 = 0 \qquad 16 - 7 = 9 \qquad 14 - 8 = 6 \qquad 11 - 4 = 7 \qquad 12 - 7 = 5$$

4.
$$18 - 9 = 9 \qquad 14 - 5 = 9 \qquad 16 - 9 = 7 \qquad 15 - 8 = 7 \qquad 13 - 6 = 7 \qquad 14 - 9 = 5 \qquad 17 - 9 = 8$$

Solve.

5. Brenda saw 14 lightning bugs. Elmer saw 9. How many more lightning bugs did Brenda see?

$$14 - 9 = 5$$

__5__ lightning bugs

6. Matt has 17 marbles. Paul has 9 marbles. How many more marbles does Matt have?

$$17 - 9 = 8$$

__8__ marbles

7. Sonja had 15¢. She bought a balloon for 8¢. How much money does she have left?

$$15¢ - 8¢ = 7¢$$

__7¢__

8. Roy counted 16 crows. 8 of them flew away. How many are left?

$$16 - 8 = 8$$

__8__ crows

Chapter review

(seventy-five) **75**

Teaching page 75

Ask students what kind of problems they will be doing at the top of the page. (subtraction) Ask students what they will need to do in any problem concerning money. (write the cent sign) Have students complete the page independently.

ROUNDUP REVIEW

Add or subtract.

1.
$$\begin{array}{r} 7 \\ +0 \\ \hline 7 \end{array}\quad \begin{array}{r} 9 \\ +1 \\ \hline 10 \end{array}\quad \begin{array}{r} 6 \\ -5 \\ \hline 1 \end{array}\quad \begin{array}{r} 7 \\ -5 \\ \hline 2 \end{array}\quad \begin{array}{r} 4 \\ -0 \\ \hline 4 \end{array}\quad \begin{array}{r} 8 \\ +2 \\ \hline 10 \end{array}\quad \begin{array}{r} 9 \\ +7 \\ \hline 16 \end{array}$$

2.
$$\begin{array}{r} 9 \\ -3 \\ \hline 6 \end{array}\quad \begin{array}{r} 10 \\ -5 \\ \hline 5 \end{array}\quad \begin{array}{r} 8 \\ -7 \\ \hline 1 \end{array}\quad \begin{array}{r} 10 \\ -9 \\ \hline 1 \end{array}\quad \begin{array}{r} 7 \\ +3 \\ \hline 10 \end{array}\quad \begin{array}{r} 9 \\ +5 \\ \hline 14 \end{array}\quad \begin{array}{r} 7 \\ +6 \\ \hline 13 \end{array}$$

3.
$$\begin{array}{r} 11 \\ -4 \\ \hline 7 \end{array}\quad \begin{array}{r} 12 \\ -7 \\ \hline 5 \end{array}\quad \begin{array}{r} 8 \\ +4 \\ \hline 12 \end{array}\quad \begin{array}{r} 9 \\ +3 \\ \hline 12 \end{array}\quad \begin{array}{r} 8 \\ +8 \\ \hline 16 \end{array}\quad \begin{array}{r} 13 \\ -5 \\ \hline 8 \end{array}\quad \begin{array}{r} 14 \\ -7 \\ \hline 7 \end{array}$$

4.
$$\begin{array}{r} 15 \\ -6 \\ \hline 9 \end{array}\quad \begin{array}{r} 7 \\ +9 \\ \hline 16 \end{array}\quad \begin{array}{r} 8 \\ +6 \\ \hline 14 \end{array}\quad \begin{array}{r} 9 \\ +9 \\ \hline 18 \end{array}\quad \begin{array}{r} 16 \\ -7 \\ \hline 9 \end{array}\quad \begin{array}{r} 17 \\ -9 \\ \hline 8 \end{array}\quad \begin{array}{r} 15 \\ -8 \\ \hline 7 \end{array}$$

Solve.

5. Nancy counted 9 deer and 5 wild turkeys. How many animals did she count?

$$\begin{array}{r} 9 \\ +5 \\ \hline 14 \end{array}$$

__14__ animals

6. Bert picked 11 tulips. Fay picked 8 tulips. How many more tulips did Bert pick?

$$\begin{array}{r} 11 \\ -8 \\ \hline 3 \end{array}$$

__3__ tulips

7. Bill ran 7 blocks. Then he ran 6 blocks more. How many blocks did Bill run?

$$\begin{array}{r} 7 \\ +6 \\ \hline 13 \end{array}$$

__13__ blocks

8. There were 12 dogs in the park. 7 dogs ran home. How many dogs are left in the park?

$$\begin{array}{r} 12 \\ -7 \\ \hline 5 \end{array}$$

__5__ dogs

76 (seventy-six)   Cumulative review

Enrichment

1. Have students draw books in 2 stacks to show that 1 group has 7 more than the other. They should then write and solve a problem to explain their illustration.
2. Tell students to draw their family dinner table to show that they are expecting 4 guests. Have them write and solve a problem to tell how many people will be having dinner.
3. Tell students to arrange all addition and subtraction fact cards in groups having the same answer. Ask how many fact cards are in each group.

Teaching page 76

This page reviews addition and subtraction problems and story problems related to sums through 18. Remind students to look at the sign in each problem before beginning to work with the numbers. Have students complete the page independently.

Numbers through 100

pages 77-78

Objective

To read and write numbers through 100

Materials

*number chart 0 through 100 with number names
counting sticks
rubber bands

Mental Math

Ask students how many tens and ones in the number that comes:
1. before 20. (1,9)
2. after 82. (8,3)
3. after 89. (9,0)
4. before 50. (4,9)
5. next in the sequence: 45, 50, 55. (6,0)
6. before 11. (1,0)
7. next in the sequence: 77, 78, 79. (8,0)

Skill Review

Write **12 = 10+2** on the board and ask students how many tens are in the number. (1) Ask how many ones. (2) Have students tell a basic addition fact which has a sum of 12. (8+4, 9+3, etc.) Continue for numbers 11 through 18.

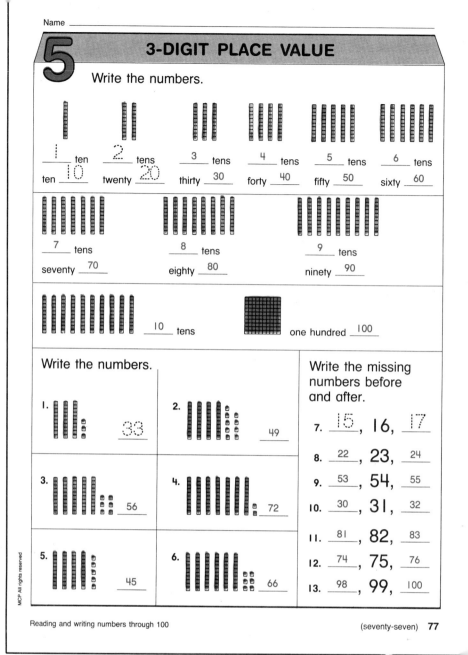

Teaching page 77

Have students work in pairs to count out 26 sticks and use rubber bands to make bundles of 10. Ask how many tens are left. (6) Write **2 tens 6 ones = 26** on the board. Point to the 2 and the 6 in 26 as the students read the number as 2 tens 6 ones. Write **twenty-six** on the board and have students read the number name. Repeat for the number of tens and ones in other numbers through 99. Have students lay out 100 sticks, bundle them into tens and tell how many tens and ones. (10,0) Remind students that 10 tens, 0 ones is 1 hundred as you write **one hundred** and **100** on the board. Write a 2-digit number on the board and have students tell information about the number such as the number of tens and ones, the number that comes before and after, the number that is 10 more or 10 less, etc.

Have students trace the 1, 10, 2 and 20. Tell students to write how many tens are shown and then write the number. Tell students that in the following problems they are to write the number shown. Tell students that in problems in the last section they are to fill in the missing numbers before and after each number in the middle column. Have students complete the page independently.

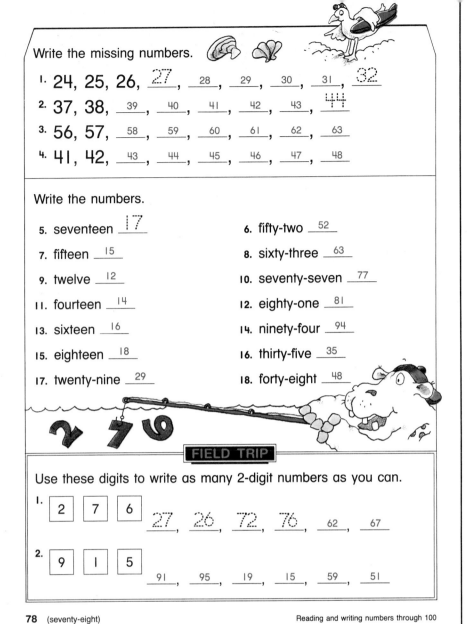

Write the missing numbers.

1. 24, 25, 26, _27_, _28_, _29_, _30_, _31_, _32_
2. 37, 38, _39_, _40_, _41_, _42_, _43_, _44_
3. 56, 57, _58_, _59_, _60_, _61_, _62_, _63_
4. 41, 42, _43_, _44_, _45_, _46_, _47_, _48_

Write the numbers.

5. seventeen _17_
6. fifty-two _52_
7. fifteen _15_
8. sixty-three _63_
9. twelve _12_
10. seventy-seven _77_
11. fourteen _14_
12. eighty-one _81_
13. sixteen _16_
14. ninety-four _94_
15. eighteen _18_
16. thirty-five _35_
17. twenty-nine _29_
18. forty-eight _48_

FIELD TRIP

Use these digits to write as many 2-digit numbers as you can.

1. | 2 | 7 | 6 | _27_, _26_, _72_, _76_, _62_, _67_

2. | 9 | 1 | 5 | _91_, _95_, _19_, _15_, _59_, _51_

Reading and writing numbers through 100

Teaching page 78

Have students read the first 3 numbers, trace the dotted numbers and write in the missing numbers to complete the sequence. Have students complete the next sequences. In the next group of problems, help students read the number names if necessary as they write the numbers.

Field Trip

Write **8** and **4** on the board. Ask students what 2-digit numbers can be made using an 8 and a 4. (84 and 48) Now write **1, 2** and **3** on the board and have students make 2-digit numbers. Tell students to use each digit only 1 time in each 2-digit number. (12, 13, 21, 23, 31, 32) Repeat for the numbers 3, 4 and 5. (34, 35, 43, 45, 53, 54) Have students trace the 4

numbers and then write 2 more. (62,67) Have students complete the second problem independently.

Extra Credit   *Creative Drill*

Have students draw a large clock on the floor with chalk, omitting the hands. Take two pieces of rope or yarn to use for the hands. Have a student sit in the center of the clock to hold one end of each rope. Make one rope the minute hand extending to the rim of the clock. Make the other rope the hour hand to be noticeably shorter. Choose two students to be Mr. Hour and Miss Minute. Tell students different times to the quarter-hour they must act out by walking around the circle holding the rope and stopping at the correct number. Repeat for all students to participate.

Correcting Common Errors

Some students may have difficulty writing missing numbers in a sequence. Have them work with partners on number charts from 0 through 100. Have one partner point to a number on the chart and the other partner say the numbers before and after it. They should repeat this procedure taking turns. Then have a partner point to a number, such as 24, and the other partner read it two ways; e.g., 2 tens 4 ones, and twenty-four.

Enrichment

1. Tell students to write all the 2-digit numbers that have the same number of tens in them as ones.
2. Have students write all the number words they would say if they counted by tens from 10 through 100.
3. Tell students to write all the 2-digit numbers that are 1 less than each number they would say if they were counting by 5's from 0 through 100.

78

3-digit Numbers

pages 79-80

Objective

To understand and write 3-digit numbers

Materials

*hundred-flats
*ten-strips and ones
centimeter graph paper
crayons

Mental Math

Have students count by:
1. 1's from 40 through 60.
2. 10's from 10 through 100.
3. 5's from 25 through 50.
4. 2's from 4 through 18.
5. 5's from 70 through 100.
6. 1's from 76 through 92.
7. 2's from 18 through 30.
8. 5's from 35 through 70.

Skill Review

Have students use ten-strips and ones to show various 2-digit numbers. Have students write the numbers and their number names on the board.

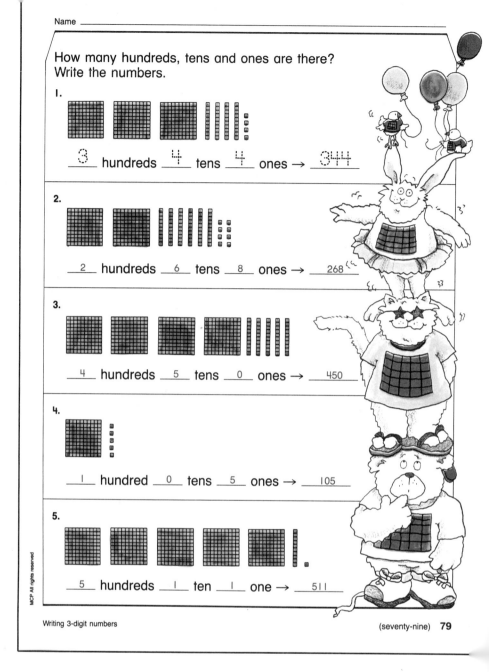

Name _____

How many hundreds, tens and ones are there? Write the numbers.

1.
    _3_ hundreds _4_ tens _4_ ones → _344_

2.
    _2_ hundreds _6_ tens _8_ ones → _268_

3.
    _4_ hundreds _5_ tens _0_ ones → _450_

4.
    _1_ hundred _0_ tens _5_ ones → _105_

5.
    _5_ hundreds _1_ ten _1_ one → _511_

Writing 3-digit numbers

(seventy-nine) **79**

Teaching page 79

Have students put out 10 ten-strips and tell how many tens and ones. (10,0) Remind students the number represented is **100** or **one-hundred** as you write both on the board. Show students a hundred-flat. Have students place 10 ten-strips on the flat to see that 10 ten-strips equal 1 hundred-flat. Tell students that 100 is 1 hundred 0 tens 0 ones since the 10 tens can be traded for 1 hundred. Help students see that the 1 hundred-flat is easier to use than the 10 ten-strips to represent 100. Now display 1 hundred-flat, 2 ten-strips and 6 ones and ask students to tell how many of each there are. (1 hundred 2 tens 6 ones) Have a student write the number on the board. (126) Continue for other 3-digit numbers through 999. Lay out 1 hundred-flat and 1 ten-strip and have students write the number. (110) Continue to add 1 ten-strip at a time to

have students count by 10's. Show students the trading of 10 tens for another hundred-flat and continue through 300 or 400.

Tell students to trace the numbers to tell how many hundreds, tens and ones there are and then trace the 344. Have students complete the page independently.

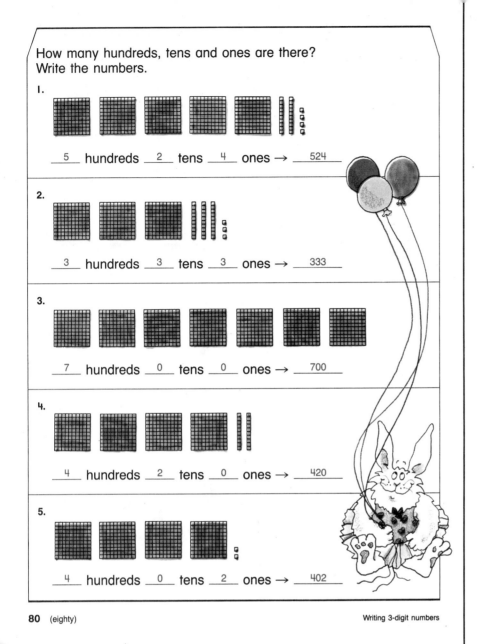

How many hundreds, tens and ones are there?
Write the numbers.

1.

___5___ hundreds ___2___ tens ___4___ ones → ___524___

2.

___3___ hundreds ___3___ tens ___3___ ones → ___333___

3.

___7___ hundreds ___0___ tens ___0___ ones → ___700___

4.

___4___ hundreds ___2___ tens ___0___ ones → ___420___

5.

___4___ hundreds ___0___ tens ___2___ ones → ___402___

Writing 3-digit numbers

Correcting Common Errors

Some students may write a number like four hundred twenty-eight as 4028. Use a place-value chart to show that numbers in the hundreds (those less than 1,000) have only three digits. Have students write the numbers on a place-value chart before they write the standard numeral.

Enrichment

1. Have students write the largest 3-digit number in hundreds, tens and ones. Then have them write the smallest 3-digit number.
2. Tell students to write all the 3-digit numbers that have no ones beginning with 800. What sequence have they written?
3. Have students write all the 3-digit numbers that have no tens. How many numbers did they write?

Teaching page 80

Have students complete the page independently. Remind them to write the correct number in the last answer blank.

Extra Credit   *Applications*

Bring several decks of cards to class and teach students how to play *Go Fish*. Go through a deck with them, pointing out that there are four kinds of cards (hearts, diamonds, clubs and spades) and that there are 13 of each kind (from the ace through the king). Divide the class into groups of three or four. Show them how to deal the cards, giving each player the same number. Explain that the game begins with one player asking one of the others for a card, by number and kind or suit. In order to request a card, the player must have at

least one of this kind already in his hand. If players get the requested card, they take another turn. Explain that they are trying to get all four kinds of a given number and that as soon as they reach their goal they put the four matching cards down in front of them. The winner is the player who has the most sets down when all the cards have been played.

More 3-digit Numbers

pages 81-82

Objective

To understand and write 3-digit numbers

Materials

*numbered cards 0 through 9
*hundred-flats
*ten-strips and ones
*blank cards

Mental Math

Ask students what operation is used to go from:

1. 62 to 72. (addition)
2. 42 to 40. (subtraction)
3. 20 to 25. (addition)
4. 16 to 15. (subtraction)
5. 80 to 70. (subtraction)
6. 52 to 49. (subtraction)
7. 30 to 36. (addition)
8. 0 to 20. (addition)

Skill Review

Write **176** on the board and have students tell how many ones, hundreds and tens. (6,1,7) Having students tell the values out of order helps to put emphasis on the place value of each number. Repeat for more 3-digit numbers.

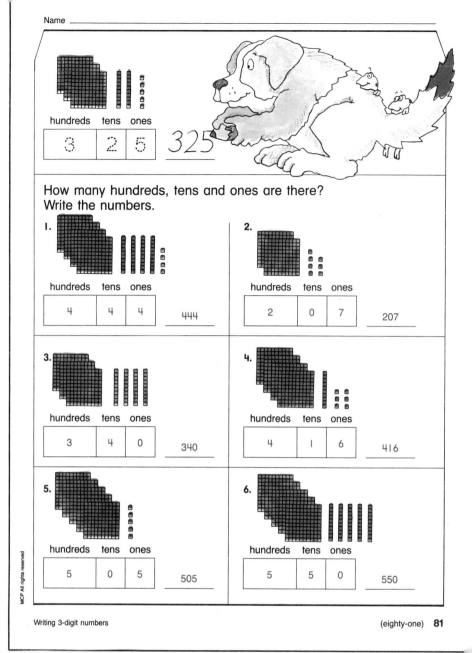

Writing 3-digit numbers

(eighty-one) **81**

Teaching page 81

Lay out 3 hundred-flats, 8 ten-strips and 4 ones. Write (3) **hundreds** (8) **tens** (4) **ones** = (384) on the board and have a student complete the sentence. Repeat for more 3-digit numbers and then have students lay out the manipulatives for any 3-digit numbers they write on the board. Now have students write the number that comes before and after 200. (199,201) Repeat to have students tell the numbers before and after more 3-digit numbers. Write **998** on the board and help students write the numbers before and after it. Tell students to write the number of hundreds, tens and ones in each number and then write the number.

Have students look at the page, count and trace the 325. Have students complete the page independently.

81

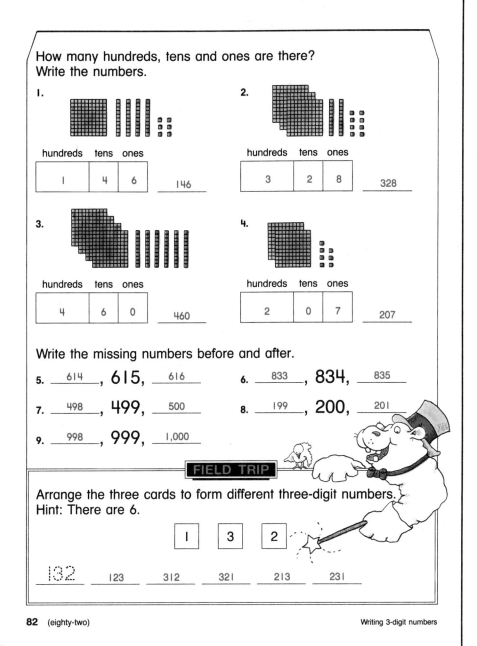

How many hundreds, tens and ones are there?
Write the numbers.

1.

hundreds	tens	ones
1	4	6

146

2.

hundreds	tens	ones
3	2	8

328

3.

hundreds	tens	ones
4	6	0

460

4.

hundreds	tens	ones
2	0	7

207

Write the missing numbers before and after.

5. __614__, 615, __616__

6. __833__, 834, __835__

7. __498__, 499, __500__

8. __199__, 200, __201__

9. __998__, 999, __1,000__

FIELD TRIP

Arrange the three cards to form different three-digit numbers.
Hint: There are 6.

| 1 | 3 | 2 |

132   123   312   321   213   231

82 (eighty-two)   Writing 3-digit numbers

Counting Money through $5

pages 83-84

Objective

To count dollars, dimes and pennies through $5

Materials

*hundred-flats
*ten-strips and ones
dollars, dimes and pennies

Mental Math

Dictate the following:
1. 4+9+2+1 (16)
2. 16 − 4+2 (14)
3. 7+17+4 (28)
4. 9 − 9+9 (9)
5. 0+7+10 (17)
6. 12 − 4+10 (18)

Skill Review

Dictate a 2- or 3-digit number and have a student show the number using the hundred-flats, ten-strips and ones. Then have a student rename the number in hundreds, tens and ones and write the number on the board. Have another student write the number before and the number after. Repeat for more 2- or 3-digit numbers.

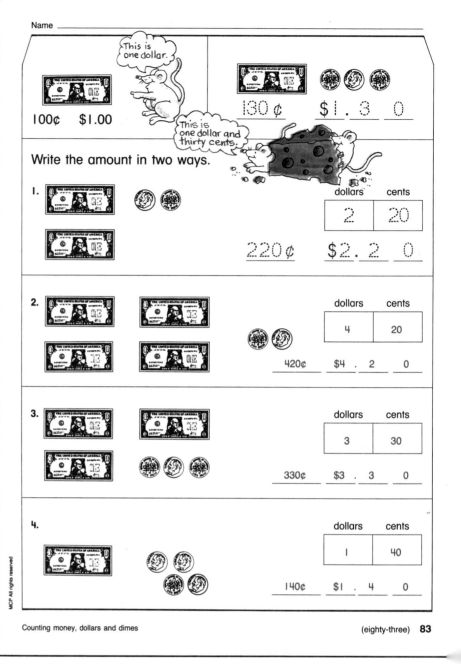

Counting money, dollars and dimes

(eighty-three) **83**

Teaching page 83

Show a dime and remind students that it is worth 10¢ or 10 pennies. Have students count by tens as you put out 10 dimes. Tell students that 10 dimes can be traded for $1 because $1 is equal to 100 pennies, just as 1 hundred is equal to 10 tens. Write on the board: **10 dimes = 100 cents = 1 dollar.** Write **$1.00** on the board and tell students that the decimal point separates the dollars from the cents. Remind students that we say the word **and** at the decimal point. Now write **$1.25 = 125¢** on the board and have a student read the sentence. Lay out 2 dollars 4 dimes and 6 pennies and have a student write and read the amount. ($2.46, two dollars and forty-six cents) Put out 4 dimes and 2 pennies and have a student write and read the amount. ($0.42, forty-two cents) Remind students we can also write this as 42¢ as you write

42¢ on the board. Repeat for more amounts through $5.

Go through the example with the students as they count the money and write it in two ways. Help students complete problem 1 and then have students complete the page independently.

83

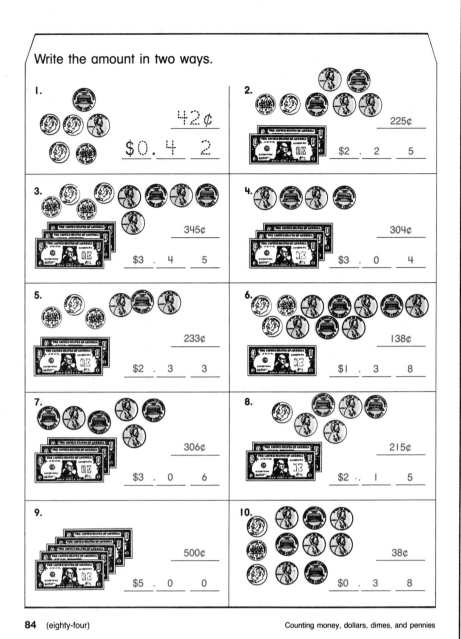

Write the amount in two ways.

1.
42¢
$0. 4 2

2.
225¢
$2 . 2 5

3.
345¢
$3 . 4 5

4.
304¢
$3 . 0 4

5.
233¢
$2 . 3 3

6.
138¢
$1 . 3 8

7.
306¢
$3 . 0 6

8.
215¢
$2 . 1 5

9.
500¢
$5 . 0 0

10.
38¢
$0 . 3 8

Counting money, dollars, dimes, and pennies

Correcting Common Errors

Some students may forget to write the dollar sign and cents point when writing amounts of money such as $3.20. Stress that the cents point separates the dollars from the dimes; that is, the dollars from the cents and that, without it, the amount of money has a different value.

Enrichment

1. Tell students to write the number of dimes they would have if they had each of these amounts all in dimes: 320¢, 460¢, $5.20, 150¢, $7.90, 60¢.
2. Have students see how many ways they can make $2.26 with dimes, pennies and a dollar.
3. Tell students to use grid paper, crayons and money to show why 1 hundred 2 tens 9 ones is equal to 1 dollar, 2 dimes and 9 pennies.

Teaching page 84

Help students complete the first problem and ask them what difference there is between the two answer lines. (one shows the decimal point) Have them complete the page independently.

Extra Credit   *Applications*

Read aloud the story of *Goldilocks and the Three Bears*. This tale is easily remembered by children because each bear has its own bowl, chair and bed. This one-to-one correspondence is very important in graphing. To reinforce students' understanding of this idea, ask them to draw the three bowls of porridge, the three chairs, the three beds and the three bears. Now have them connect each bear with it's own bowl, chair and bed. Post these illustrations so that students can see each other's work.

Counting through 1,000

pages 85-86

Objectives

To count by 1's, 5's, 10's and 100's through 1,000
To recognize place value through hundreds

Materials

*hundred-flats
*ten-strips and ones

Mental Math

Have students tell the time when the long hand is on:
1. 12 and short hand is on 11. (11:00)
2. 12 and short hand is on 2. (2:00)
3. 6 and short hand is between 12 and 1. (12:30)
4. 6 and short hand is between 5 and 6. (5:30)

Skill Review

Have students write the numbers for counting by 10's through 100 on the board, leaving spaces between. (10, 20, 30, . . . , 100) Have students fill in the numbers to change the sequence to counting by 5's. (5, 15, . . . , 95) Help students write the numbers through 100 for counting by 2's.

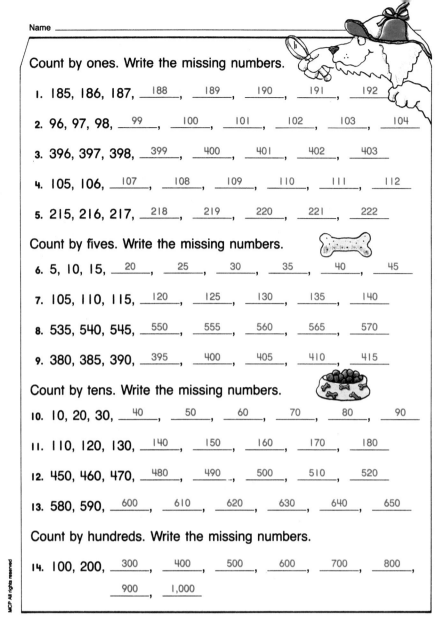

Name _____

Count by ones. Write the missing numbers.

1. 185, 186, 187, __188__, __189__, __190__, __191__, __192__

2. 96, 97, 98, __99__, __100__, __101__, __102__, __103__, __104__

3. 396, 397, 398, __399__, __400__, __401__, __402__, __403__

4. 105, 106, __107__, __108__, __109__, __110__, __111__, __112__

5. 215, 216, 217, __218__, __219__, __220__, __221__, __222__

Count by fives. Write the missing numbers.

6. 5, 10, 15, __20__, __25__, __30__, __35__, __40__, __45__

7. 105, 110, 115, __120__, __125__, __130__, __135__, __140__

8. 535, 540, 545, __550__, __555__, __560__, __565__, __570__

9. 380, 385, 390, __395__, __400__, __405__, __410__, __415__

Count by tens. Write the missing numbers.

10. 10, 20, 30, __40__, __50__, __60__, __70__, __80__, __90__

11. 110, 120, 130, __140__, __150__, __160__, __170__, __180__

12. 450, 460, 470, __480__, __490__, __500__, __510__, __520__

13. 580, 590, __600__, __610__, __620__, __630__, __640__, __650__

Count by hundreds. Write the missing numbers.

14. 100, 200, __300__, __400__, __500__, __600__, __700__, __800__, __900__, __1,000__

Counting by ones, fives, tens, and hundreds through 1,000

(eighty-five) **85**

Teaching page 85

Display 1 hundred-flat and add ones as students count by 1's through 120. Write each number on the board in sequence. Now have students use the manipulatives to count from 100 through 120 by 2's, 5's and 10's as you write the sequences on the board. Repeat for counting from 570 through 590 and from 790 through 810. Now have students put out the hundred-flats and count by hundreds through 1,000. Have students tell the number before and after 999, and write these on the board. Note: Place value is not extended beyond 1,000 in second grade.

Have a student read the directions aloud for each problem section. Have them complete the page independently.

85

What does the red digit mean? Circle the correct word.

1. 275 — (tens) / ones / hundreds	**2.** 341 — hundreds / tens / (ones)	**3.** 204 — ones / tens / (hundreds)
4. 526 — tens / hundreds / (ones)	**5.** 973 — (hundreds) / ones / tens	**6.** 858 — (tens) / ones / hundreds

Write the number of hundreds, tens and ones.

7. 732 — _7_ hundreds, _3_ tens, _2_ ones	**8.** 467 — _6_ tens, _7_ ones, _4_ hundreds	**9.** 618 — _6_ hundreds, _8_ ones, _1_ tens
10. 279 — _2_ hundreds, _9_ ones, _7_ tens	**11.** 312 — _1_ tens, _3_ hundreds, _2_ ones	**12.** 103 — _3_ ones, _0_ tens, _1_ hundreds

FIELD TRIP

Solve.

1. I am thinking of a number. It has 2 tens, 3 hundreds and 5 ones. What is my number?

   _325_

2. My number has no ones, two hundreds and no tens. What is my number?

   _200_

86 (eighty-six)   Place value, recognizing ones, tens, and hundreds

---

Correcting Common Errors

Some students may name the place value of a digit incorrectly. Have them place each three-digit number, such as 356, on a place-value chart and give the place value names for all 3 digits.

Hundreds	Tens	Ones
3	5	6

3 hundreds
5 tens
6 ones

Enrichment

1. Have students draw a street with 6 houses on each side and number the first house on one side 464 and the last house 474. Tell them to number the first 2 houses on the other side 463 and 465 and have a friend write in the missing house numbers.

2. Tell students to number backward from 1,000, counting by 100's.

3. Have students draw an office building with 10 floors. Then tell them to draw a sign on each floor that tells the office numbers if the third floor sign reads: 300–330.

Teaching page 86

Have students tell the value of each of the digits in 275. (2 hundreds 7 tens 5 ones) Have them tell again what the 7 means (tens) and trace the circle around the word. Tell students to circle the word which tells the value of the red digit in each box in the first section and write the correct value in the second section. Have students complete all problems independently.

Field Trip

Tell students to think of a number that has 2 tens and 0 ones. Have a student write the number. (20) Continue for more 2- and 3-digit numbers. Have students complete the 2 problems independently.

Extra Credit   *Creative Drill*

Tell the students they are going to play a game called Fox and Goose. Have them form a circle of Geese with the Fox in the center. The Fox calls a student by name and gives a single-digit addition or subtraction for them to solve. If the sum or difference is not given correctly, the Goose is caught and joins the Fox in the center of the circle. Another Goose is named and play continues. A caught Goose may escape by: giving a correct answer when the Fox accepts a wrong answer; or by giving the answer before the named Goose can give it. Periodically choose a new Fox, and allow the caught Geese to go back to the ring. Extend the activity to include 2-digit problems.

Multiples of Ten

pages 87-88

Objectives

To write numbers that are 10 more and 10 less than a number
To write numbers that are 100 more and 100 less than a number

Materials

*hundred-flats
*ten-strips and ones

Mental Math

Have students tell the number that comes:
1. between 49 and 51.
2. before 210.
3. after 400.
4. before 1,000.
5. between 376 and 378.
6. after 750.
7. between 126 and 124.
8. between 206 and 204.

Skill Review

Review counting by 10's by having a student write a decade number such as 110, on the board. Have the next 3 or 4 students count on by 10's and write the numbers on the board. Repeat until all students have contributed. Leave the sequences on the board for later use in this lesson.

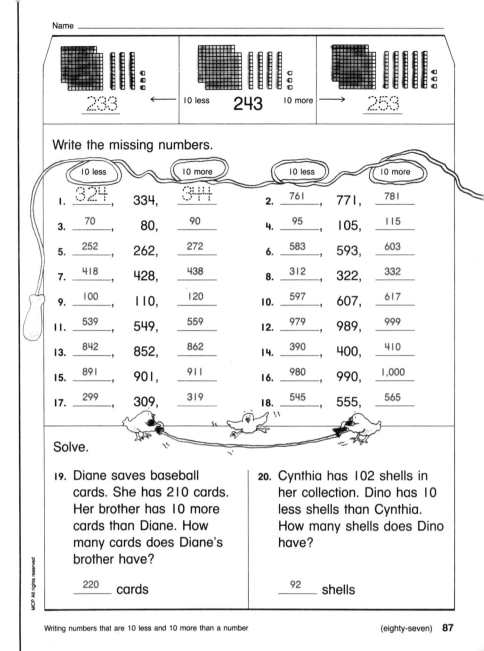

Teaching page 87

Put out 3 hundred-flats, 4 ten-strips and 2 ones. Have a student write the number. (342) Remove a ten-strip and have a student write the number in front of the 342. (332) Tell students that 332 is 10 less than 342. Replace the ten-strip to show 342 and ask students what the number would be if we added a ten-strip. (352) Have a student write 352 after 342. Now write **332, 342, 352** vertically for students to easily see the change in the tens digits. Repeat for more examples as needed. Now repeat the activity for 232, 332 and 432 to have students see the change in the hundreds digit. Have students trace the 233 to tell the number shown. Repeat for 243 and 253. Ask students what number is 10 less than 243 (233) and 10 more than 243. (253) Have students tell how each number shown differs

from the next one. (10 less or 10 more) Read the word problems with students and have them complete the page independently.

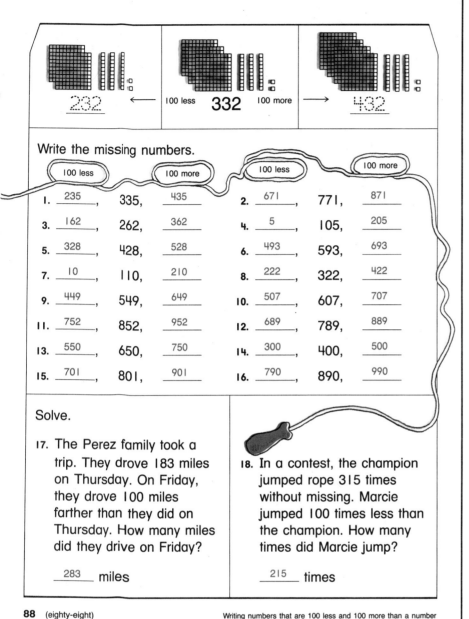

232 ← 100 less 332 100 more → 432

Write the missing numbers.

	100 less		100 more		100 less		100 more

1. 235 , 335, 435
2. 671 , 771, 871
3. 162 , 262, 362
4. 5 , 105, 205
5. 328 , 428, 528
6. 493 , 593, 693
7. 10 , 110, 210
8. 222 , 322, 422
9. 449 , 549, 649
10. 507 , 607, 707
11. 752 , 852, 952
12. 689 , 789, 889
13. 550 , 650, 750
14. 300 , 400, 500
15. 701 , 801, 901
16. 790 , 890, 990

Solve.

17. The Perez family took a trip. They drove 183 miles on Thursday. On Friday, they drove 100 miles farther than they did on Thursday. How many miles did they drive on Friday?

   283 miles

18. In a contest, the champion jumped rope 315 times without missing. Marcie jumped 100 times less than the champion. How many times did Marcie jump?

   215 times

Writing numbers that are 100 less and 100 more than a number

Correcting Common Errors

When students are asked to write the number that is 10 more or 10 less, or 100 more or 100 less, they may change the digit in the wrong place. Have them first draw an arrow above the place with which they are working; e.g., above the tens place for 10 more or 10 less, and above the hundreds place for 100 more or 100 less. Then have them add 1 to or subtract 1 from that digit.

Enrichment

1. Tell students to write the numbers of the runners who finished 10 ahead and 10 behind runner 267.
2. Have students tell how much money each of 3 friends would have if one has $472 and one friend is $100 poorer while the other friend is $100 richer than the first.

Teaching page 88

Tell students they are to find the number that is 100 more or less than another number. Go through the example with the students as they trace the numbers. Read the word problems with students and have them complete the page independently.

Extra Credit   Statistics

Introduce the idea of a many-to-one correspondence. Ask each student to draw any collection of special things they have. This could well be combined with a show-and-tell day when students bring in their collections. Have them draw themselves in the picture as well. Explain that unlike the story of *Goldilocks and the Three Bears* where there was one bed, one bowl or one chair for each bear, there are times when there are many items all corresponding to the same person. Ask one student to hold up the drawing of their collection. Point out that the objects in the picture all belong to the same person. Ask them to draw lines from the objects to themselves in the pictures. See if students can think of other examples of a many-to-one correspondence. Examples might include: a tree with many leaves, a wagon with four wheels, a book with many pages.

Comparing 2-digit Numbers

pages 89-90

Objectives

To find the greater or lesser of 2-digit numbers

To use the > and < signs to compare 2-digit numbers

Materials

*ten-strips and ones

Mental Math

Have students tell the number:
1. 2 hundreds 2 tens (220)
2. 4 tens 9 ones (49)
3. 9 ones 3 hundreds (309)
4. 6 tens 6 hundreds 2 ones (662)
5. 7 ones 9 tens (97)
6. 2 ones 1 ten (12)

Skill Review

Write **756** on the board. Have a student write the number that is 100 less than 756 above the number. (656) Have a student write the number that is 100 more, below 756. (856) Write **756** again on the board and have a student write the number that is 10 less. (746) Have a student write the number that is 10 more. Repeat for more numbers.

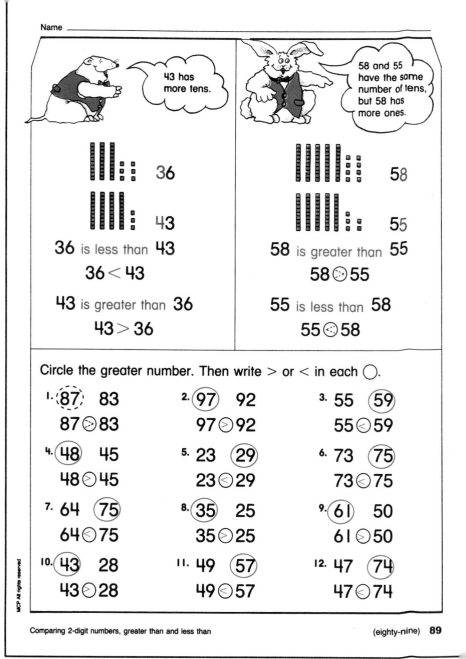

Name _____

43 has more tens.

58 and 55 have the same number of tens, but 58 has more ones.

36

43

36 is less than 43

$$36 < 43$$

43 is greater than 36

$$43 > 36$$

58

55

58 is greater than 55

$$58 > 55$$

55 is less than 58

$$55 < 58$$

Circle the greater number. Then write > or < in each ◯.

1. (87) 83
   87 > 83

2. (97) 92
   97 > 92

3. 55 (59)
   55 < 59

4. (48) 45
   48 > 45

5. 23 (29)
   23 < 29

6. 73 (75)
   73 < 75

7. 64 (75)
   64 < 75

8. (35) 25
   35 > 25

9. (61) 50
   61 > 50

10. (43) 28
    43 > 28

11. 49 (57)
    49 < 57

12. 47 (74)
    47 < 74

Comparing 2-digit numbers, greater than and less than

(eighty-nine) **89**

Teaching page 89

Have a student put out 32 in ten-strips and ones. Have another student lay out 36 in ten-strips and ones. Ask how many tens each number has. (3, 3) Ask how many ones each number has. (2 and 6) Ask which number is greater. (36) Ask why. (36 has more ones) Write **32 is less than 36** on the board and tell students that this can be written a shorter way as you write **32 < 36** on the board. Write **36 is greater than 32** on the board and tell students that this can also be written a shorter way as you write **36 > 32** on the board. Tell students that the point of the sign always points to the smaller number. Write **92 ◯ 87** on the board and have a student write the sign to compare the numbers. (>) Now write **87 ◯ 92** and have a student write the sign. (<) Have students tell why 92 is greater than 87. (9 tens is more than 8 tens)

Repeat for more comparisons as you emphasize comparing the tens digits first. Now write **62, 43** and **78** on the board and have students place them in order from least to greatest. (43, 62, 78) Repeat for more groups of three 3-digit numbers.

Help students read and complete the 2 problems at the top of the page reading the words aloud for each sign. Then help students work problems 1 and 2. Have students complete the page independently.

89

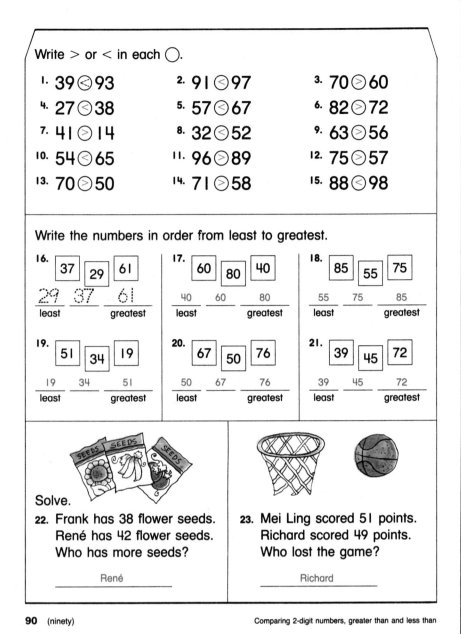

Write > or < in each ◯.

1. 39 ⬸ 93
2. 91 ⬸ 97
3. 70 ⬹ 60
4. 27 ⬸ 38
5. 57 ⬸ 67
6. 82 ⬹ 72
7. 41 ⬹ 14
8. 32 ⬸ 52
9. 63 ⬹ 56
10. 54 ⬸ 65
11. 96 ⬹ 89
12. 75 ⬹ 57
13. 70 ⬹ 50
14. 71 ⬹ 58
15. 88 ⬸ 98

Write the numbers in order from least to greatest.

16. 37 29 61

<u>29</u>   <u>37</u>   <u>61</u>
least   greatest

17. 60 80 40

40   60   80
least   greatest

18. 85 55 75

55   75   85
least   greatest

19. 51 34 19

19   34   51
least   greatest

20. 67 50 76

50   67   76
least   greatest

21. 39 45 72

39   45   72
least   greatest

Solve.

22. Frank has 38 flower seeds. René has 42 flower seeds. Who has more seeds?

<u>   René   </u>

23. Mei Ling scored 51 points. Richard scored 49 points. Who lost the game?

<u>   Richard   </u>

Comparing 2-digit numbers, greater than and less than

Correcting Common Errors

Some students may have difficulty comparing two numbers. Have them work with partners to compare two numbers such as 29 and 35. Have them use ten-strips and ones to model each number and decide, after discussing why, which number is greater. Repeat the activity with other numbers, including those where the digits in the tens place are identical.

Enrichment

1. Tell students to use > and < signs to compare 46 to each of the following numbers: 29, 45, 82, 56, 39.
2. Have students use > and < signs to compare their age with that of each member of their family.
3. Tell students to illustrate the > and < signs in a way that may help someone remember them. (A sign could be an alligator's mouth or an arrow.)

Teaching page 90

Tell students to write the > or < sign in each circle to show how the numbers compare. Tell them to arrange the numbers in the next section so that the smallest number is first and the greatest number is last. Read through the 2 word problems with the students and then assign the page to be completed independently.

Extra Credit   *Numeration*

Tell students to write as many correct addition and subtraction problems as they can in five minutes, using the numbers 0–50. Have students work in pairs, one computing and the other timing. Have them repeat the activity after each has had a turn, to try to better their time. Extend the activity by having students create the same problems, but to use each number 0–50, only once.

Comparing 3-digit Numbers

pages 91-92

Objectives

To find the greater or lesser of two
2- or 3-digit numbers
To use the > and < signs to
compare 2 numbers

Materials

*hundred-flats
*ten-strips and ones
*cards numbered 0 through 9

Mental Math

Tell students to find the sum or
difference:
1. 16 + 2 (18)
2. 9 + 8 + 3 (20)
3. 18¢ − 2 − 4 (12¢)
4. 10 + 20 (30)
5. 8 + 8 + 2 (18)
6. 14 − 9 + 13 (18)
7. 2 tens + 6 tens (8 tens or 80)

Skill Review

Have each of 4 students select a
number card. Ask students to hold
the cards to form two 2-digit
numbers for the rest of the students
to compare. Have a student write the
numbers on the board with the > or
< sign. Continue for more students
to form numbers to be compared.

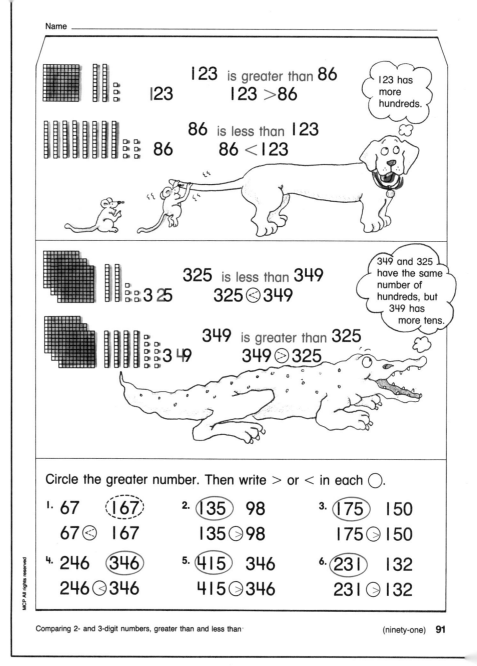

Name _____

123 is greater than 86
123 > 86

86 is less than 123
86 < 123

123 has more hundreds.

325 is less than 349
325 ⊙ 349

349 is greater than 325
349 ⊙ 325

349 and 325 have the same number of hundreds, but 349 has more tens.

Circle the greater number. Then write > or < in each ◯.

1. 67 (167)
   67 ⊙ 167

2. (135) 98
   135 ⊙ 98

3. (175) 150
   175 ⊙ 150

4. 246 (346)
   246 ⊙ 346

5. (415) 346
   415 ⊙ 346

6. (231) 132
   231 ⊙ 132

Comparing 2- and 3-digit numbers, greater than and less than

(ninety-one) **91**

Teaching page 91

Write **512** ◯ **826** on the board and have students put
out manipulatives to show the numbers. Ask students
which number has more hundreds. (826) Ask which
number is larger. (826) Have a student write < in the
circle. Repeat for more comparisons of two 3-digit
numbers having a different number of hundreds. Then
write **423** ◯ **416** on the board as you remind
students to compare the digits in the largest place first.
Ask how many hundreds each number has. (4, the
same) Tell students to then compare the next digits and
tell which number has more tens. (423) Ask students if
the ones need to be compared. (no) Have a student
write > in the circle. Continue for students to compare
two 3-digit numbers having the same number of
hundreds, but different digits in the ones place. Write

172 ◯ **98** on the board and help students see that
172 is larger because there are no hundreds in 98.
Repeat for more examples.
Remind students to compare the highest digits first as
you work through the 2 problems at the top with
them. Then tell students that in the following problems
they are to circle the greater number and write the
sign in the circle to compare the numbers. Have
students complete the page independently.

91

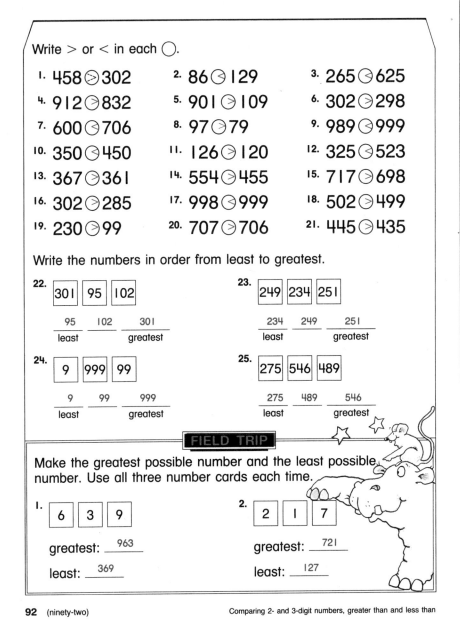

Write > or < in each ◯.

1. 458 ⊜ 302   2. 86 ⊜ 129   3. 265 ⊜ 625
4. 912 ⊜ 832   5. 901 ⊜ 109   6. 302 ⊜ 298
7. 600 ⊜ 706   8. 97 ⊜ 79   9. 989 ⊜ 999
10. 350 ⊜ 450   11. 126 ⊜ 120   12. 325 ⊜ 523
13. 367 ⊜ 361   14. 554 ⊜ 455   15. 717 ⊜ 698
16. 302 ⊜ 285   17. 998 ⊜ 999   18. 502 ⊜ 499
19. 230 ⊜ 99   20. 707 ⊜ 706   21. 445 ⊜ 435

Write the numbers in order from least to greatest.

22. | 301 | 95 | 102 |

95   102   301
least   greatest

23. | 249 | 234 | 251 |

234   249   251
least   greatest

24. | 9 | 999 | 99 |

9   99   999
least   greatest

25. | 275 | 546 | 489 |

275   489   546
least   greatest

FIELD TRIP

Make the greatest possible number and the least possible number. Use all three number cards each time.

1. | 6 | 3 | 9 |

greatest: ___963___

least: ___369___

2. | 2 | 1 | 7 |

greatest: ___721___

least: ___127___

Comparing 2- and 3-digit numbers, greater than and less than

Teaching page 92

Ask students what they are to do in each of the problems in the first section. (compare the numbers and write > or < in the circle) Have a student read aloud the instruction sentence in the next section. Help students complete the first problem and then complete the page independently.

Field Trip

Write **3, 1** and **2** on the board. Tell students to use each digit to make all the 3-digit numbers possible. Help students discover and write on the board the following numbers: 312, 321, 132, 123, 231, 213. Tell students to find the smallest and largest of the 6 numbers. Ask how this should be done. (arrange the numbers in order from least to greatest) Remind students to compare the hundreds digits first, then the

tens and then the ones. Tell students to write each number on a slip of paper to make it easy to move the numbers around.

Extra Credit *Applications*

Set up a small store in the classroom as a continuing project. Have students decide what kind of store it will be. Students can price the items and use buttons or bottle caps to represent coins. Muffin tins make good cash registers. Appoint a cashier and a bagger. Allow small groups to make purchases. Give each student a different number of "coins" and challenge them to make purchases so they will have a specific number of coins left. Encourage students to count their change carefully.

Ordinal Numbers

pages 93-94

Objectives

To read ordinal numbers through 32nd

To use ordinal numbers to tell about days on a calendar

Materials

*numbered cards 1 through 32

*ordinal cards first through thirty-second

*calendar of present month

Mental Math

Have students tell the number that is:
1. 2 more than 41. (43)
2. 1 quarter and 1 dime. (35¢)
3. 7 hundreds 4 ones. (704)
4. between 140 and 142. (141)
5. 10 more than 470. (480)

Skill Review

Have students write a 2- or 3-digit number on paper. Have 2 students show their numbers and tell which is greater or lesser and why. Continue with more numbers. Help students order all the numbers by asking for those less than 100, those with 9 tens, 8 tens, etc. Continue until all numbers have been placed in order.

Name _____

Mrs. Jones wants to put her class role in order for the school party. Write each name in order.

3.	Bill	first	Adam
2.	Beverly	second	Beverly
4.	Chan	third	Bill
1.	Adam	fourth	Chan
6.	Diane	fifth	Cheryl
5.	Cheryl	sixth	Diane
8.	Dorothy	seventh	Dick
10.	George	eighth	Dorothy
7.	Dick	ninth	Emma
13.	Jack	tenth	George
11.	Harry	eleventh	Harry
9.	Emma	twelfth	Isaac
14.	Jean	thirteenth	Jack
12.	Isaac	fourteenth	Jean
16.	Ken	fifteenth	Juan
15.	Juan	sixteenth	Ken

21.	Mike	seventeenth	Leah
18.	Linda	eighteenth	Linda
20.	Me Lin	nineteenth	Mary
17.	Leah	twentieth	Me Lin
19.	Mary	twenty-first	Mike
24.	Paul	twenty-second	Noah
22.	Noah	twenty-third	Opal
26.	Rosa	twenty-fourth	Paul
23.	Opal	twenty-fifth	Raul
27.	Sarah	twenty-sixth	Rosa
25.	Raul	twenty-seventh	Sarah
30.	Tom	twenty-eighth	Stacey
28.	Stacey	twenty-ninth	Terry
32.	Wade	thirtieth	Tom
29.	Terry	thirty-first	Vera
31.	Vera	thirty-second	Wade

Reading ordinal numbers through thirty-second

(ninety-three) **93**

Teaching page 93

Review first through tenth with students by placing the ordinal number cards first through tenth along the chalk tray. Help students write the corresponding number above each ordinal number. Now place the ordinal numbers eleventh through twentieth on the chalk tray and repeat the activity. Have students count by ordinal numbers from first through twentieth. Repeat the activity for the ordinal numbers twenty-first through thirty-second. Show students the calendar and have them locate the twenty-fifth day, the seventeenth day, etc. Have students locate any of their birthdays in the month shown and tell the dates in ordinal numbers. Have a student read about Mrs. Jones. Ask what is to be done. (write the students' names in order) Have a student read the first 5 names and the numbers beside each. Have students find the word first and trace Adam

beside it. Help students see that Adam is number 1 so his name goes beside the word first. Help students locate several more numbered names and then have them complete the page independently.

93

January						
Sunday	Monday	Tuesday	Wednesday	Thursday	Friday	Saturday
		1	2	3	4	5
6	7	8	9	10	11	12
13	14	15	16	17	18	19
20	21	22	23	24	25	26
27	28	29	30	31		

Use the calendar to write the day of the month.

1. first Monday ___7___
2. fourth Saturday ___26___
3. second Sunday ___13___
4. fifth Tuesday ___29___
5. third Wednesday ___16___
6. second Friday ___11___

Use the calendar to write the day of the week.

7. January first ___Tuesday___
8. January sixteenth ___Wednesday___
9. January tenth ___Thursday___
10. January twelfth ___Saturday___
11. January eleventh ___Friday___
12. January fifteenth ___Tuesday___
13. January thirteenth ___Sunday___
14. January twenty-first ___Monday___
15. January eighteenth ___Friday___
16. January seventh ___Monday___
17. January thirty-first ___Thursday___
18. January twenty-sixth ___Saturday___
19. January thirtieth ___Wednesday___
20. January twentieth ___Sunday___
21. January seventeenth
   ___Thursday___
22. January twenty-eighth
   ___Monday___

94 (ninety-four)   Reading ordinal numbers using the calendar

Number Names

pages 95-96

Objectives

To read 3-digit number names
To write 2- and 3-digit numbers to solve problems

Materials

*cards with 2- and 3-digit numbers
*cards with number names of above
2- and 3-digit numbers

Mental Math

Tell students to name two numbers that are between:
1. 726 and 729. (727, 728)
2. 106 and 103.
3. 48 and 51.
4. 98 and 104.
5. 78 and 90.
6. 450 and 472.
7. 106 and 92.

Skill Review

Have students form a line and name their place in line, using ordinal numbers. Have students change places and tell their new ordinal number. Now assign the number 32 to the last person and ask students to tell their place in ordinal numbers.

Match the number name with the number.

1. two hundred   400
2. six hundred   900
3. nine hundred   200
4. four hundred   700
5. seven hundred   600

6. three hundred seventy   130
7. one hundred thirty   490
8. five hundred ten   860
9. eight hundred sixty   370
10. four hundred ninety   510

11. two hundred fifty-three   255
12. five hundred sixty-six   998
13. nine hundred ninety-eight   566
14. five hundred sixteen   516
15. two hundred fifty-five   253

16. eight hundred seventy-two   344
17. three hundred forty-four   872
18. eight hundred twenty-seven   418
19. three hundred four   827
20. four hundred eighteen   304

Reading 3-digit numbers and number names

(ninety-five) **95**

Teaching page 95

Write **two hundred forty-six** on the board for a student to read and then write the number. (246) Continue for more 3-digit numbers. Now tell students to guess the 3-digit number you are thinking of if all its digits are 9's. Have a student write the number. (999) Have a student write the number which is less than 9 tens 4 ones but greater than 9 tens 2 ones. (93) Ask a student to write the 3-digit number which is greater than 476, less than 500 and has 8 tens and 4 ones. (484) Continue for other puzzles to have students write 2- and 3-digit numbers.

Tell students to draw a line from each number name to its number. Help students complete two matches and then assign the page to be completed independently.

Write the numbers.

1. forty-five ___45___

2. nine hundred ninety ___990___

3. one hundred forty-five ___145___

4. four hundred five ___405___

5. two hundred nineteen ___219___

6. seven hundred eighteen ___718___

7. five hundred ___500___

8. ninety-nine ___99___

9. three hundred ten ___310___

10. eight hundred eight ___808___

11. six hundred fifty ___650___

12. five hundred twenty ___520___

Solve.

13. I am a number greater than 8 tens and 5 ones. I am less than 8 tens and 7 ones.
Who am I? ___86___

14. We are two numbers. We are both less than 8 tens. We are both greater than 77.
Who are we? ___78___ ___79___

15. We are two numbers. We are both less than 2 hundreds, 5 tens, and 6 ones. We are both greater than 2 hundreds, 5 tens, 3 ones.
Who are we?
___254___ ___255___

16. I am a 3-digit number. All my digits are the number 3.
Who am I? ___333___

17. I am a number 1 less than 1,000.
Who am I? ___999___

Reading 3-digit number names, problem solving

Correcting Common Errors

Students may need practice with identifying numbers from number names. Give a different number-name card to each student. Place a number card on the chalk tray and ask the student who has that number-name card to place it next to the number card on the tray.

Enrichment

1. Tell students to write the number that is 200 more and the number which is 200 less than two hundred fifty-six.
2. Have students write all 3-digit numbers that are more than 900 and have 9 ones. Ask them what is the sequence?
3. Have students write the number name to tell the total number of students in your school.

Teaching page 96

Tell students to read each number name and write the number. Have students complete the first section independently. Work through the first word problem with the students pointing out that each one is a puzzle. Have them complete the page independently.

Extra Credit   Statistics

Introduce many-to-many correspondence in this lesson. Ask for three volunteers. Write their names in a circle on the board. In another circle write these words: **cookies, milk, pizza, hamburgers, apples.** Now ask each of the volunteers to come to the board and draw an arrow from their name to each of the items they like to eat. Explain that they will draw from one to five arrows, depending on the number of different kinds of food they like. After all three have shown their preferences, ask another student to point to foods liked by more than one person. Have students construct their own many-to-many correspondence by listing three forms of transportation in one circle on a piece of paper. Now have them list at least three destinations in another circle. Have students draw lines between modes of transportation and destinations.

Review

pages 97-98

Objectives

To review comparisons, sequencing and place value of 2- and 3-digit numbers
To maintain skills learned previously this year

Materials

Mental Math

Ask students which number comes first:
1. 76 or 34. (34)
2. 216 or 261. (216)
3. 300 or 298. (298)
Ask them which number comes second.
4. 187 or 87. (187)
5. 303 or 333. (333)
6. 201 or 199. (201)

Skill Review

Write on the board:

two hundred seventy-six	third
five hundred twelve	second
nine hundred eighty	fourth
ninety-seven	first
four hundred twenty-two	fifth

Have students write the number for each number name, place the numbers in order from least to greatest and then draw a line from the number name to its ordinal.

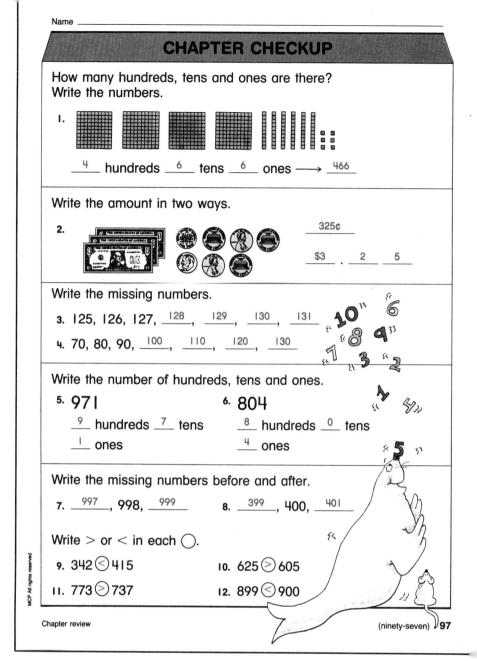

CHAPTER CHECKUP

How many hundreds, tens and ones are there? Write the numbers.

1. ____4____ hundreds ___6___ tens ___6___ ones ⟶ __466__

Write the amount in two ways.

2.   325¢

$3 . 2 5

Write the missing numbers.

3. 125, 126, 127, __128__, __129__, __130__, __131__

4. 70, 80, 90, __100__, __110__, __120__, __130__

Write the number of hundreds, tens and ones.

5. 971   6. 804
   __9__ hundreds __7__ tens   __8__ hundreds __0__ tens
   __1__ ones   __4__ ones

Write the missing numbers before and after.

7. __997__, 998, __999__   8. __399__, 400, __401__

Write > or < in each ◯.

9. 342 ◁ 415   10. 625 ▷ 605
11. 773 ▷ 737   12. 899 ◁ 900

Chapter review

(ninety-seven) **97**

Teaching page 97

Have students tell what they will do in each section of problems. Then have students complete the page independently.

ROUNDUP REVIEW

Add or subtract.

1.
$$\begin{array}{r} 2 \\ +7 \\ \hline 9 \end{array}$$
$$\begin{array}{r} 5 \\ +5 \\ \hline 10 \end{array}$$
$$\begin{array}{r} 8 \\ +3 \\ \hline 11 \end{array}$$
$$\begin{array}{r} 3 \\ +6 \\ \hline 9 \end{array}$$
$$\begin{array}{r} 11 \\ -7 \\ \hline 4 \end{array}$$
$$\begin{array}{r} 14 \\ -6 \\ \hline 8 \end{array}$$
$$\begin{array}{r} 15 \\ -8 \\ \hline 7 \end{array}$$

2.
$$\begin{array}{r} 12 \\ -5 \\ \hline 7 \end{array}$$
$$\begin{array}{r} 17 \\ -8 \\ \hline 9 \end{array}$$
$$\begin{array}{r} 2 \\ +9 \\ \hline 11 \end{array}$$
$$\begin{array}{r} 9 \\ +7 \\ \hline 16 \end{array}$$
$$\begin{array}{r} 8 \\ +8 \\ \hline 16 \end{array}$$
$$\begin{array}{r} 11 \\ -5 \\ \hline 6 \end{array}$$
$$\begin{array}{r} 15 \\ -6 \\ \hline 9 \end{array}$$

3.
$$\begin{array}{r} 11 \\ -8 \\ \hline 3 \end{array}$$
$$\begin{array}{r} 13 \\ -7 \\ \hline 6 \end{array}$$
$$\begin{array}{r} 10 \\ -6 \\ \hline 4 \end{array}$$
$$\begin{array}{r} 7 \\ +7 \\ \hline 14 \end{array}$$
$$\begin{array}{r} 9 \\ +3 \\ \hline 12 \end{array}$$
$$\begin{array}{r} 8 \\ +5 \\ \hline 13 \end{array}$$
$$\begin{array}{r} 16 \\ -7 \\ \hline 9 \end{array}$$

4.
$$\begin{array}{r} 18 \\ -9 \\ \hline 9 \end{array}$$
$$\begin{array}{r} 14 \\ -8 \\ \hline 6 \end{array}$$
$$\begin{array}{r} 16 \\ -9 \\ \hline 7 \end{array}$$
$$\begin{array}{r} 2 \\ +8 \\ \hline 10 \end{array}$$
$$\begin{array}{r} 7 \\ +7 \\ \hline 14 \end{array}$$
$$\begin{array}{r} 9 \\ +9 \\ \hline 18 \end{array}$$
$$\begin{array}{r} 5 \\ +7 \\ \hline 12 \end{array}$$

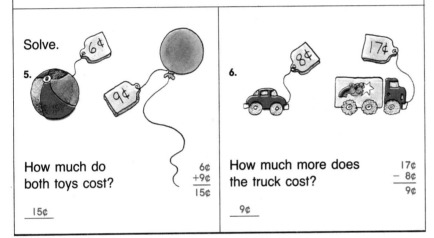

Solve.

5. How much do both toys cost?

$$\begin{array}{r} 6¢ \\ +9¢ \\ \hline 15¢ \end{array}$$

15¢

6. How much more does the truck cost?

$$\begin{array}{r} 17¢ \\ -8¢ \\ \hline 9¢ \end{array}$$

9¢

Cumulative review

Enrichment

1. Have students copy 10 number words from any 10 different pages in this book on cards. Tell them to have a friend arrange their number name cards in order from least to greatest.
2. Tell students to write 10 different 3-digit numbers on cards and place them in order from least to greatest, naming the ordinal number for each.
3. Have students write a different 3-digit number on each of 20 cards. Tell them to take turns drawing 2 cards with a partner, each telling which number is greater and why.

Teaching page 98

This page reviews sums and minuends through 18 and problem solving with money. Have students complete the page independently.

Telling Time to the Hour

pages 99-100

Objective

To tell time to the hour

Materials

*demonstration clock
clock faces

Mental Math

Have students tell the next number:
1. 47, 48, 49, (50)
2. 800, 700, 600, (500)
3. 92, 91, 90 (89)
4. 14, 16, 18, (20)
5. 1, 3, 5, 7, (9)
6. 262, 362, 462, (562)
7. 90, 95, 100, (105)
8. 120, 110, 100, (90)

Skill Review

Write on the board:

> nineteenth
> thirtieth
> twenty-first
> tenth
> twenty-ninth
> thirty-second
> fifth

Have students write the number beside its ordinal number and then place the numbers in order from least to greatest.

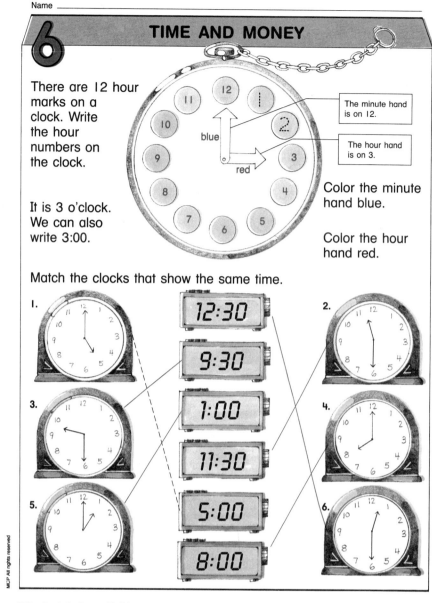

TIME AND MONEY

There are 12 hour marks on a clock. Write the hour numbers on the clock.

blue

red

The minute hand is on 12.

The hour hand is on 3.

It is 3 o'clock. We can also write 3:00.

Color the minute hand blue.

Color the hour hand red.

Match the clocks that show the same time.

1.

12:30

9:30

2.

3.

1:00

11:30

4.

5.

5:00

8:00

6.

Telling time to the hour and half-hour

(ninety-nine) **99**

Teaching page 99

Have students identify the hour and minute hands on the demonstration clock. Place a minute hand on 12 and the hour hand on 4. Have a student tell the time. (4:00) Write **four o'clock, 4 o'clock** and **4:00** on the board and tell students the 3 ways of writing this time are all read the same. Ask students to tell what happens to the hour or short hand as you move the minute or long hand around the clock once and back to 12. (It moves slowly to 5.) Ask the time now. (5:00) Have a student write 5 o'clock, five o'clock, and 5:00 on the board. Continue to move the minute hand one revolution and have students write the 3 ways to tell the time on the board. Remind students that digital clocks show the time as 3:00, etc. Have students read the paragraph about the hour marks aloud and then write the hour numbers on the clock face. Have

students color the hands according to the directions. Have a student read the remaining information about the hour and minute hands and ways to write an o'clock. Tell students they are to draw a line from each clock face to the digital clock which tells the same time. Have students complete the page independently.

99

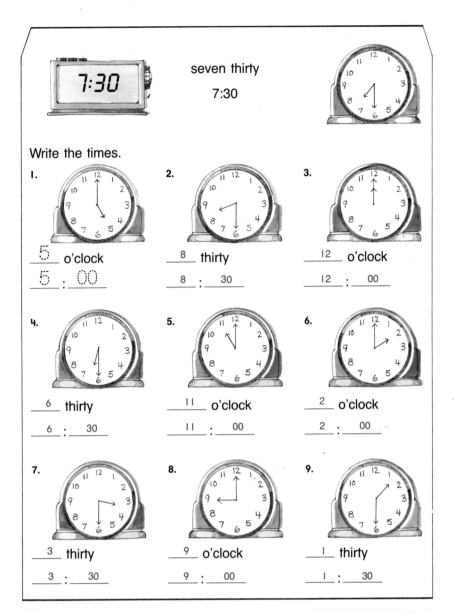

seven thirty
7:30

Write the times.

1. _5_ o'clock
_5_ : _00_

2. _8_ thirty
_8_ : _30_

3. _12_ o'clock
_12_ : _00_

4. _6_ thirty
_6_ : _30_

5. _11_ o'clock
_11_ : _00_

6. _2_ o'clock
_2_ : _00_

7. _3_ thirty
_3_ : _30_

8. _9_ o'clock
_9_ : _00_

9. _1_ thirty
_1_ : _30_

Telling time to the hour and half-hour

Correcting Common Errors

Some students may confuse the hour hand and the minute hand. Have them work with partners to draw hands on a clock face for times such as 2:00, 7:00, and 11:00. Discuss how the short hand shows the hour; hence, it is the hour hand. Some may be helped by thinking that, in an hour, the shorter hand goes the shorter distance from one hour to the next, and the longer hand goes the longer distance, completely around the clock face.

Enrichment

1. Tell students to draw a clock face and a digital clock to show that they go to bed at 8:00.
2. Have students show any o'clock on a clock face. Then have a friend tell the time and show the next o'clock.
3. Ask students to draw a clock face and a digital clock to show the time, to the nearest hour, when they eat lunch, go to school and come home from school. Have them label each clock with the activity they are doing at that time.

Teaching page 100

Have students read the time on the digital clock and the clock face and then read the 3 ways to write an o'clock. Tell students they are to write the number under each clock to tell the o'clock and then write the time as it would look on a digital clock. Have students complete the page.

Extra Credit   *Statistics*

Showing a correspondence between things is often called **mapping.** Give students a paper arranged in the following way:

sponge		bath towel
peanut butter		soap
dish cloth	kitchen	knife
toilet		milk
frying pan		plate
sugar	bathroom	glass

Ask students to draw lines of correspondence connecting the item with the room in which it is found. See if students recognize that while many of the items belong in one room or the other, some could be found in either.

100

Telling Time to 5 minutes

pages 101-102

Objective

To tell time in 5-minute intervals

Materials

*demonstration clock

Mental Math

Have students name 2 addition facts for:
1. 17. (8 + 9 = 17, 9 + 8 = 17)
2. 13. (6 + 7 = 13, 9 + 4 = 13, etc.)
3. 15.
4. 16.

Have them name 2 subtraction facts for:
5. 15. (15 − 8 = 7, 15 − 9 = 6, etc.)
6. 17. (17 − 9 = 8, 17 − 8 = 9)
7. 11.
8. 12.

Skill Review

Have students count by 5's through 100 in unison. Now have 1 student begin with 5 and count on by 5's for 3 or 4 numbers. Have the next student continue from there to say the next 3 or 4 numbers by 5's. Continue until students reach 100. Have students repeat the activity by writing the 3 or 4 numbers on the board as they count by 5's.

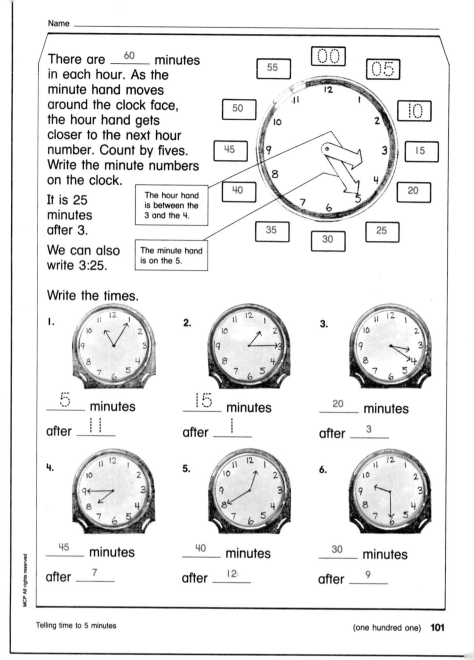

Name _____

There are __60__ minutes in each hour. As the minute hand moves around the clock face, the hour hand gets closer to the next hour number. Count by fives. Write the minute numbers on the clock.

The hour hand is between the 3 and the 4.

It is 25 minutes after 3.

We can also write 3:25.

The minute hand is on the 5.

Write the times.

1. __5__ minutes after __11__

2. __15__ minutes after __1__

3. __20__ minutes after __3__

4. __45__ minutes after __7__

5. __40__ minutes after __12__

6. __30__ minutes after __9__

Telling time to 5 minutes

(one hundred one) **101**

Teaching page 101

Have students notice the 1 minute marks on the clock face. Tell students there are 60 of these on a clock face for 60 minutes in 1 hour. Tell students to count by 5's as you move the minute hand around the clock from 1 number to the next. Help students see that the hour hand moved slowly from the 5 to the 6 as 60 minutes went by. Now place the minute hand on the 1 and tell students it is 5 minutes after 6:00. Write **6:05** on the board and tell students we write five minutes after 6 this way. Continue to move the minute hand around the clock as you tell students it is 10 minutes after 6:00, 15 minutes after 6:00, etc. through 55 minutes after 6:00. Then show 7:00 because 60 minutes or 1 whole hour has passed. Write each time on the board as it is found. Place the hour hand on 7 and the minute hand on the 5 and ask a student to count by

5's to see how many minutes after 7:00 it is. (25 minutes) It is important to refer to all times as after the hour in this lesson since reading time after and before the hour in the same lesson is confusing to students. Help students write in the numbers for counting by 5's in their texts. Have students read the sentences about 3:25 aloud with you. Have students write 69 in the sentence. Have them read the information and directions aloud with you. Help students work each of the problems, if necessary, or assign the page to be completed independently.

101

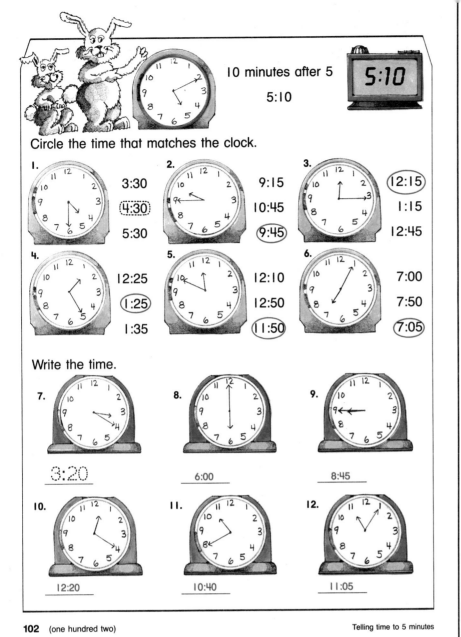

10 minutes after 5
5:10

5:10

Circle the time that matches the clock.

1. 3:30
(4:30)
5:30

2. 9:15
10:45
(9:45)

3. (12:15)
1:15
12:45

4. 12:25
(1:25)
1:35

5. 12:10
12:50
(11:50)

6. 7:00
7:50
(7:05)

Write the time.

7. 3:20

8. 6:00

9. 8:45

10. 12:20

11. 10:40

12. 11:05

Telling time to 5 minutes

Teaching page 102

Have students read the times on the 2 clocks. Tell students that in the first section they are to circle 1 of the 3 times to show the correct time on the clock. Then tell them they are to write the time for each of the next clocks. Have students complete the problems. Now have students show on the demonstration clock, all times in each of the first problems to check their answers.

Extra Credit *Probability*

Give each student a penny and a piece of paper. Have them fold the paper in half, the long way. Now write the words **heads** and **tails** on the board. Ask a student to explain what the head and tail of a penny means. Have students predict how many heads and tails they will get if they flip the penny 20 times. (Answers will vary, but many students will say 10 of each.) Now have each student flip the penny 20 times. Explain that each time they toss the coin they are to mark the result on one side of the paper or the other. Some may illustrate each head or tail, others will just make an X or a slash mark. At the end of the activity ask students how many actually got exactly 10 heads and 10 tails. Explain that on the average they will expect equal numbers of heads and tails, but that for any single trial of 20 coin tosses, they may expect any answer.

Telling Time, Before-After

pages 103-104

Objective

To solve problems by telling time hours earlier or later

Materials

*demonstration clock

Mental Math

Have students say the numbers in order from least to greatest:
1. 6, 4, 8, 9
2. 212, 201, 215
3. 50, 10, 100
4. 900, 400, 800
5. 20, 0, 200
6. 18, 24, 14
7. 151, 51, 91
8. 3, 7, 11, 9, 5

Skill Review

Have a student move the hands of the clock to read any hour, half-hour or 5-minute interval. Have a student read the times and write it one way on the board. Have students write the time another way. Repeat for students to practice positioning the hands and then saying and writing the times.

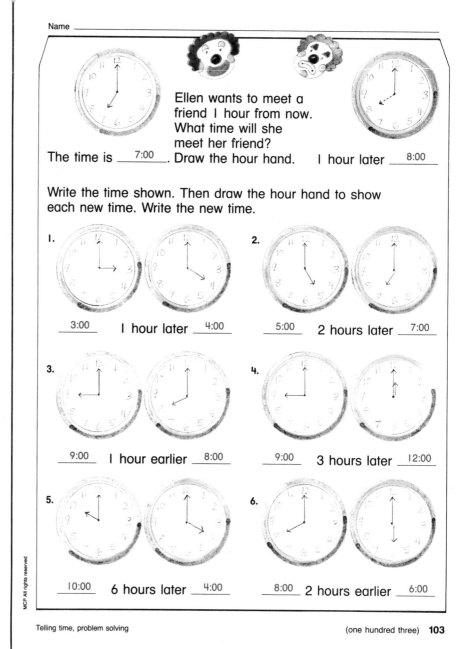

Name _____

Ellen wants to meet a friend 1 hour from now. What time will she meet her friend?

The time is ___7:00___. Draw the hour hand.   1 hour later ___8:00___

Write the time shown. Then draw the hour hand to show each new time. Write the new time.

1. ___3:00___ 1 hour later ___4:00___
2. ___5:00___ 2 hours later ___7:00___
3. ___9:00___ 1 hour earlier ___8:00___
4. ___9:00___ 3 hours later ___12:00___
5. ___10:00___ 6 hours later ___4:00___
6. ___8:00___ 2 hours earlier ___6:00___

Telling time, problem solving   (one hundred three) **103**

Teaching page 103

Remind students that there are 60 minutes in 1 hour as you move the minute hand one full revolution to go from 12:00 to 1:00. Tell students that each time the minute hand goes around the clock, 1 hour has passed. Ask students what time is shown now. (1:00) Ask students to tell how much later 1:00 is than 12:00. (1 hour) Ask students to tell how many hours later than 12:00 it is now as you show 4:00. (4 hours) Repeat for more on-the-hour times. Give students some times where they must count beyond the 12, such as 4 hours later than 9:00, etc. Now show 9:00 on the clock and ask students how many hours from 9:00 to 10:00. (1 hour) Tell students that 9:00 is 1 hour earlier than 10:00. Show 12:00 and ask students how many hours ago the clock showed 4:00. (8 hours)

Repeat for other numbers of hours. Include some questions where students must count back past the 12:00. Help students read the problem, if necessary. Ask what is to be solved. (the time Ellen will meet her friend) Ask what time it is now. (7:00) Have students write 7:00. Ask how many hours from now the friends will meet. (1 hour) Ask what time it will be 1 hour later than 7:00. (8:00) Have students trace the hour hand and write 8:00. Have a student read the directions. Ask what is to be done. (draw the hour hand in the second clock and write both times) Have students complete the page independently.

103

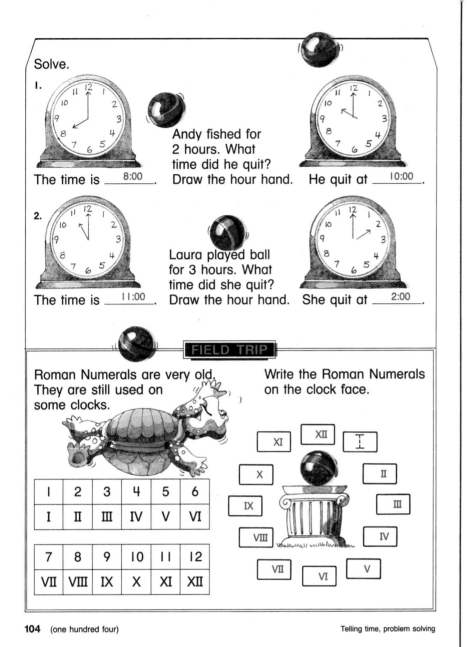

Solve.

1.

The time is ___8:00___.

Andy fished for 2 hours. What time did he quit? Draw the hour hand.

He quit at ___10:00___.

2.

The time is ___11:00___.

Laura played ball for 3 hours. What time did she quit? Draw the hour hand.

She quit at ___2:00___.

FIELD TRIP

Roman Numerals are very old. They are still used on some clocks.

Write the Roman Numerals on the clock face.

1	2	3	4	5	6
I	II	III	IV	V	VI

7	8	9	10	11	12
VII	VIII	IX	X	XI	XII

Telling time, problem solving

Correcting Common Errors

Some students may have difficulty determining previous and relapsed time. Have them practice with partners by completing a chart like the following. When they have finished, ask them to choose one line on the chart and draw clocks to show the times.

1 hour earlier	TIME	1 hour later
(3:00)	4:00	(5:00)
(6:00)	7:00	(8:00)
(10:00)	11:00	(12:00)
(12:00)	1:00	(2:00)
(11:00)	12:00	(1:00)

Enrichment

1. Tell students to draw clocks to show the time they get up in the morning and when they have dinner in the evening. Then have them tell how many hours earlier than dinner they rise and how many hours it is after they rise until they eat dinner.

2. Have students draw a picture of themselves playing in the yard at 12:00 noon. Tell them to show the sun at the top of their picture at noon. Have them draw a second picture showing the sun setting 6 hours later. Tell them to draw clocks to show both times.

Teaching page 104

Tell students to read each problem, draw the hour hand and write the times in the first section.

Field Trip

Show students a clock or picture of a clock with Roman numerals. Have students compare the Roman numerals to the numbers on the classroom clock. Tell students that the Roman Numeral I means 1, V means 5 and X means 10. Write **IV** and **VI** on the board and tell students the IV means 5-1 or 4 and VI means 5 + 1 or 6. Repeat for **IX** and **XI**. Have students write the numbers from 1 through 12 with their corresponding Roman numerals. Have students write the Roman numerals on the clock face independently.

Extra Credit *Applications*

Set up a shop in class where students can trade tokens for actual items. Invent your own token system. You may want to give students a certain number of tokens to spend. Or students can earn tokens by doing their homework, keeping their desk tidy, or being a good citizen for a week. The items for sale in the shop might include pencils, small notebooks or packs of paper or stickers. Have students help set the prices for the various items in the shop and rotate the job of shopkeeper. Have other students act as the book-keepers, recording the items sold each day and the number of tokens taken in.

Problem Solving
Telling Time

pages 105-106

Objectives

To tell the time that is 5 minutes later
To solve problems by telling time in
5-minute intervals

Materials

*2 demonstration clocks
*clock cards for every 5-minute
interval in 1 hour

Mental Math

Ask students how are they counting?
1. 193, 194, 195, 196 (by 1's)
2. 4th, 6th, 8th, 10th (by 2's)
3. 215, 220, 225, 230 (by 5's)
4. 680, 780, 880, 980 (by 100's)
5. 25, 35, 45, 55 (by 10's)
6. 35, 40, 45, 50 (by 5's)
7. 82, 92, 102, 112 (by 10's)

Skill Review

Have students begin at the 1 on the
clock and count the minutes by 5's
around the clock through 60
minutes. Now point to the 4 and
have students begin at 20 and count
on by 5's through 60. Repeat for
counting on by 5's through 60 from
any number on the clock.

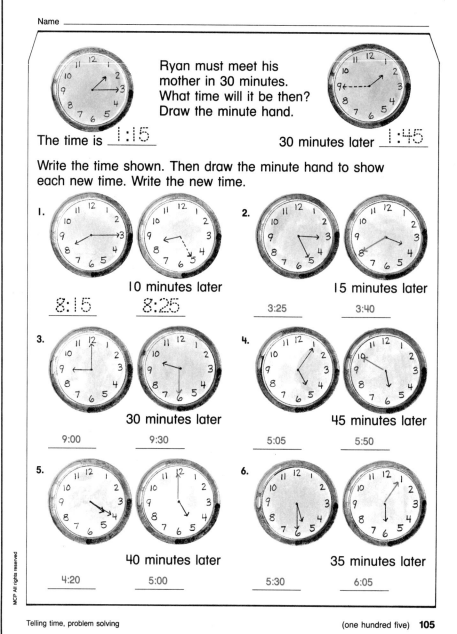

Ryan must meet his
mother in 30 minutes.
What time will it be then?
Draw the minute hand.

The time is __1:15__   30 minutes later __1:45__

Write the time shown. Then draw the minute hand to show
each new time. Write the new time.

1.   10 minutes later
   __8:15__   __8:25__

2.   15 minutes later
   3:25   3:40

3.   30 minutes later
   9:00   9:30

4.   45 minutes later
   5:05   5:50

5.   40 minutes later
   4:20   5:00

6.   35 minutes later
   5:30   6:05

Telling time, problem solving   (one hundred five) **105**

Teaching page 105

Review the o'clocks for 2 hours later or earlier than
10:00, by having students tell the number of hours
later or earlier and the new time. Now show the
present time on 1 demonstration clock and tell students
that in 20 minutes they will go out to play or go to
lunch. Have a student set the second demonstration
clock at the present time and then move the minute
hand 20 minutes ahead. Ask students the new time.
Set the first clock at other times and tell stories which
ask the students to add on minutes in increments of 5's
through 55 minutes. Have students show the new
times on the second clock and tell the time. Now set
the clock to show 10 minutes later than the first and
have students tell how many minutes later. Repeat for
more examples of less than 60 minutes later.
Have students read the problem aloud and tell what is

to be solved. (the time when Ryan will meet his
mother) Ask the time on the first clock and have
students trace the 1:15. Ask students how many
minutes until Ryan is to meet his mother. (30) Have
students trace the minute hand, tell the time that is 30
minutes later and trace the 1:45. Help students
complete the first problem and then assign the page to
be completed independently.

105

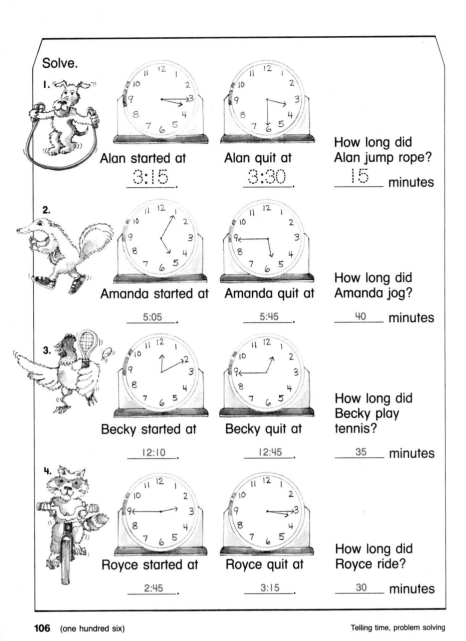

Solve.

1. Alan started at
3:15.

Alan quit at
3:30.

How long did Alan jump rope?
15 minutes

2. Amanda started at
5:05.

Amanda quit at
5:45.

How long did Amanda jog?
40 minutes

3. Becky started at
12:10.

Becky quit at
12:45.

How long did Becky play tennis?
35 minutes

4. Royce started at
2:45.

Royce quit at
3:15.

How long did Royce ride?
30 minutes

Telling time, problem solving

Correcting Common Errors

For students who need more practice, have them work with partners
and the clock cards described under
Materials. Have them take turns
selecting two cards, telling the two
times on the cards, and giving the
interval of time between them.

Enrichment

1. Tell students to draw 5 clocks in
a row with each clock showing a
time that is 20 minutes later than
the one before it.
2. Draw 2 clocks to show one
activity from rising in the morning
to arriving at school. Tell them to
show the start of the activity on 1
clock, and the time it takes to do
the activity on the other.
3. Have students draw a clock which
shows the present time, and then
draw a second clock which shows
90 minutes later.

Teaching page 106

Help students complete the first problem and then
have students complete the page independently.
Remind students to answer the question for each
problem.

Extra Credit   *Creative Drill*

Have each player draw a playing grid with 15 squares,
3 across and 5 down. Have a student call out a sum
less than 50. Each player fills in each horizontal row by
writing numbers that when added across, equal the
sum given. For example, if the sum is 18, students may
write 8, 1, 9 in the first row.
Each player receives one point for each different
combination of numbers that correctly equals the sum.
Repeat for other sums.
A variation could be to have 16 squares (4 across and
4 down) with 4 addends for each sum.

106

Telling Time to the Minute

pages 107-108

Objective

To tell time to the minute

Materials

*demonstration clock
clock faces

Mental Math

Ask students where the minute hand is when it is:
1. 1:15. (on the 3)
2. 5:05. (on the 1)
3. 20 minutes after 4. (on the 4)
4. 55 minutes after 10. (on the 11)
5. 12:40. (on the 8)
6. 7:25. (on the 5)
7. 9:00. (on the 12)

Skill Review

Have a student write 4:45 on the board and show the time on the clock. Have another student show the time that is 20 minutes later and write the new time on the board. Have a third student show the time that is 40 minutes later and write the new time on the board. Continue until all students have participated.

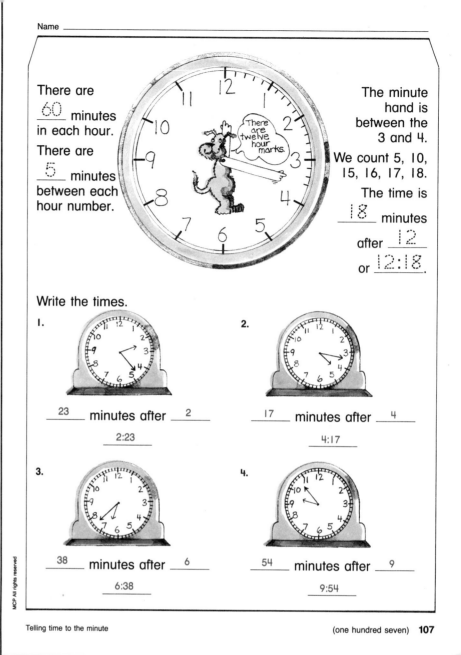

Name _____

There are __60__ minutes in each hour.

There are __5__ minutes between each hour number.

There are twelve hour marks.

The minute hand is between the 3 and 4.
We count 5, 10, 15, 16, 17, 18.
The time is __18__ minutes after __12__ or __12:18__.

Write the times.

1. __23__ minutes after __2__
    2:23

2. __17__ minutes after __4__
    4:17

3. __38__ minutes after __6__
    6:38

4. __54__ minutes after __9__
    9:54

Telling time to the minute

(one hundred seven) **107**

Teaching page 107

Ask students the number of minutes in 1 hour. (60) Have students count by 5's from 5 through 60 as 1 student moves the minute hand accordingly around the clock. Now show students the minute marks between each number on the clock as you remind students that there are 5 minutes between each number. Have a student begin at the 12 and point to each minute mark as students count by 1's through 8. Have other students point to the minute marks as students continue to count by 1's through 60. Move the hour hand to the 10 and the minute hand to the 3 and ask students how many minutes after 10:00. (15) Have a student write 10:15 on the board. Move the minute hand to 22 minutes after 10 and have students count 5, 10, 15, 20, 21, 22 to tell the number of minutes after 10:00. (22) Have a student write 10:22 on the

board. Continue for more times after the hour. Now write **3:06** on the board and have a student show the time on the clock and say the time. (6 minutes after 3) Repeat for more practice.

Have students read the information as they trace the answers to find 6:18. Remind students to count by 5's as far as possible and then count by 1's. Help students count the minutes on each clock and have students complete the page independently.

107

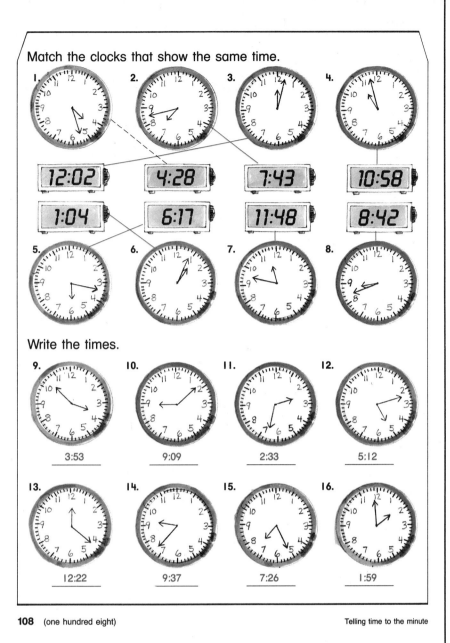

Match the clocks that show the same time.

1. 2. 3. 4.

12:02 4:28 7:43 10:58

1:04 6:17 11:48 8:42

5. 6. 7. 8.

Write the times.

9. 10. 11. 12.

3:53   9:09   2:33   5:12

13. 14. 15. 16.

12:22   9:37   7:26   1:59

Telling time to the minute

Correcting Common Errors

If students have difficulty telling time to the minute, have them work with partners and a demonstration clock. One partner can write a time for the other partner to show on the clock. They can then reverse roles and continue showing other times.

Enrichment

1. Have students write 5 times as they would look on a digital clock and have a friend show the times on a clock face.
2. Tell students to draw clocks to show 4:22 and 9:49. Ask them how the hands are positioned on each.
3. Tell students to draw clocks to show 5 different times when the minute and hour hands point to the same place on the clock.

Teaching pages 108

Tell students that in the first section of problem 1 they are to draw a line from each clock face to the digital clock reading the same time. Tell students to write the time under each clock in the last section. Have students complete the page independently.

Extra Credit   *Logic*

Bring a lunch bag and five small objects to class. Examples might be a crayon, paper clip, rubber band, rock and band-aid. Show students the objects and then put them in the bag. Now draw out four of the things and ask students to name the fifth. Replace the objects and have a student come up and draw four out. Ask another student to name the fifth. Make the game harder by pulling three objects out. Ask them to name the two that remain in the bag. This can be repeated with different objects. Each time you play, have a student withdraw a different number of things from the bag.

An alternate activity with the bag is to describe a hidden object with two words. If you said that the object you were thinking of was straight and colorful, they should guess you are thinking of the crayon. Have one student describe and another guess the mystery object.

Days and Months

pages 109-110

Objectives

To write the days of the week
To write the months of the year

Materials

*calendar
*cards of days of the week
*cards of months of the year

Mental Math

Have students name the number:
1. 10 less than 902. (892)
2. 100 more than 216. (316)
3. 10 more than 4 tens 2 ones. (52)
4. 376 plus 100 more. (476)
5. 777 minus 10. (767)
6. 1 ten more than 5 hundreds. (510)
7. 1 ten less than 400. (390)
8. 8 hundreds 9 tens 8 ones and 1 ten more. (908)

Skill Review

Have students tell the day of the week for the second Tuesday, the first Wednesday, the third Saturday, etc. of the present month. Have students name the day of the week for the 30th, the 16th, the 7th, etc. day of the present month.

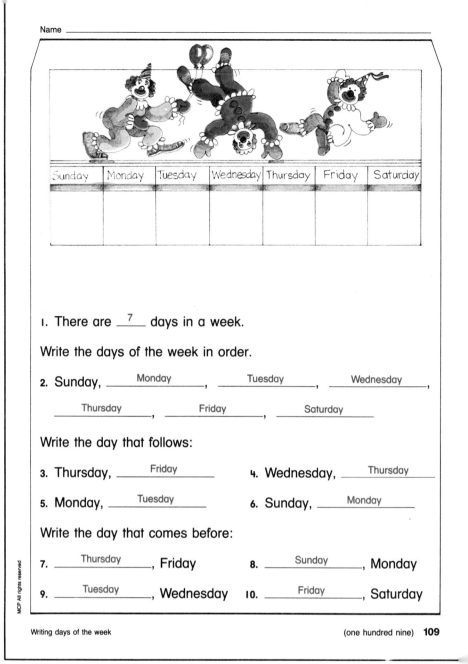

Name _____

Sunday	Monday	Tuesday	Wednesday	Thursday	Friday	Saturday

1. There are __7__ days in a week.

Write the days of the week in order.

2. Sunday, ___Monday___, ___Tuesday___, ___Wednesday___,
___Thursday___, ___Friday___, ___Saturday___

Write the day that follows:

3. Thursday, ___Friday___   4. Wednesday, ___Thursday___

5. Monday, ___Tuesday___   6. Sunday, ___Monday___

Write the day that comes before:

7. ___Thursday___, Friday   8. ___Sunday___, Monday

9. ___Tuesday___, Wednesday   10. ___Friday___, Saturday

Writing days of the week   (one hundred nine) **109**

Teaching page 109

Show the present month on the calendar and have students read the days of the week in order. Name a day of the week and have students begin with that day and write the days in order through the named day again. Repeat for more practice. Place the day cards in order on the chalk tray and have students say the days in order. Scramble the cards and have students place them in order again. Ask the day that comes third, sixth, before Tuesday, after Saturday, between Monday and Wednesday, etc. Now have students name the months of the year in order, as you flip the calendar pages from January through December. Place the month cards in order on the chalk tray and have students say them in order. Scramble the cards and have students use the calendar if necessary to place the months in order again. Now put the cards in order again and have students tell the month which comes before September, after December, between April and June, etc. Have students write the third month, twelfth month, etc. on the board.

Have students complete the page independently.

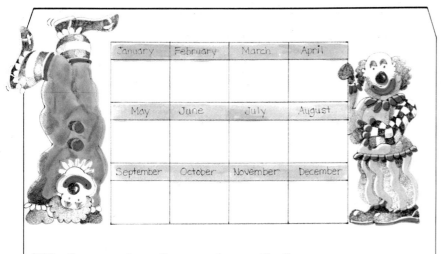

January	February	March	April
May	June	July	August
September	October	November	December

Write the correct month or number on the line.

1. There are ___12___ months in one year.

2. The first month of the year is _January_ .

3. The last month of the year is _December_ .

4. The fourth month of the year is _April_ .

5. Which month comes before June? _May_

6. Which month comes before November? _October_

7. Which month comes before March? _February_

8. Which month comes after April? _May_

9. Which month comes after February? _March_

10. Which month comes after December? _January_

110 (one hundred ten)   Writing months of the year

Teaching page 110

Have students read the months in order and then complete the page independently.

Extra Credit   *Geometry*

Give students a brief description of the meaning of symmetry. Take a square piece of paper and fold it in half. Open the paper and hold it up for students to see. Explain that one side is the same as the other. They can prove it by superimposing one on the other as they fold it. Point out that the line through the square is a line of symmetry and that we say that the figure is symmetrical. Have a student stand before the class and ask if people are symmetrical. (yes) Draw an imaginary line down the middle of the student and point out that the student is the same on either side of the line. Illustrate a spoon on the board and sketch a line through the drawing to show the spoon's symmetry. Have students bring an object from home that is symmetrical, and explain their choice to the class.

Calendars

pages 111-112

Objective

To make and read a calendar

Materials

*calendar
*cards of months of the year
*cards of days of the week

Mental Math

Dictate the following:
1. $7 + 6 + 3$ (16)
2. $14 - 7 + 6$ (13)
3. 100 less than 100 (0)
4. $15 + 1 - 8$ (8)
5. $9 + 9 + 9 + 9$ (36)
6. $18 - 1 - 9$ (8)
7. minutes in 1 hour (60)
8. days in 1 week (7)

Skill Review

Distribute the month cards to students and have them place the cards in order on the chalk tray. Repeat for more students to participate. Repeat the activity for the day cards. Now distribute the month cards and call for September to be placed on the chalk tray. Have students place the cards in order from September through August. Repeat for a different beginning month and then repeat the activity using the day cards.

Name _____

January

Sunday	Monday	Tuesday	Wednesday	Thursday	Friday	Saturday
				1	2	3
4	5	6	7	8	9	10
11	12	13	14	15	16	17
18	19	20	21	22	23	24
25	26	27	28	29	30	31

1. January has __31__ days.

Write the dates for each day of the week.

2. Monday: __5__, __12__, __19__, __26__

3. Friday: __2__, __9__, __16__, __23__, __30__

4. Saturday: __3__, __10__, __17__, __24__, __31__

5. What day of the week does this month begin with? __Thursday__

Write the day of the week for each of the following.

6. January fourth: __Sunday__

7. January twelfth: __Monday__

8. January nineteenth: __Monday__

9. January thirtieth: __Friday__

10. January twenty-third: __Friday__

11. January fifteenth: __Thursday__

Reading a calendar   (one hundred eleven) **111**

Teaching page 111

Show the present month on the classroom calendar and ask students the name of the month. Ask a student to find the year and the present day. Ask students to find the first and last days of the month and tell the day of the week for each. Ask how many Saturdays, Tuesdays, etc. in the month. Ask how many days in the month. Have students tell the date and the day of the week of any holidays or students' birthdays in the month. Ask students to tell the day of the week of the 29th day, the 14th day, etc.

Tell students to use the calendar at the top of the page to complete the questions. Have students complete the page independently.

111

Complete the calendar for this month.

Sunday	Monday	Tuesday	Wednesday	Thursday	Friday	Saturday

_____ Month _____ Year

1. How many days are in this month? _____   Answers will vary depending on the month and the year.

2. _____ is the first day of the month.

3. _____ is the last day of the month.

4. There are _____ holidays in this month.

How many of each of the following days are there in this month?

5. Sundays _____   6. Mondays _____

7. Tuesdays _____   8. Wednesdays _____

9. Thursdays _____   10. Fridays _____

11. Saturdays _____

112 (one hundred twelve)   Making a calendar

Teaching page 112

Help students complete the calendar, if necessary. Tell students to use their calendar month to complete the page independently.

Extra Credit   *Geometry*

Ask each student to bring three different leaves to class. Remind the class of the meaning of symmetry. Then trace a large leaf on the board and, if the leaf is symmetric, draw the line of symmetry through the center of the tracing.

Have students trace their three leaves and draw in the line of symmetry if they can. Some may bring in leaves that are not symmetrical. The begonia has asymmetric leaves, for example. If they have time, let students trade leaves and trace several more. If students have trouble tracing leaves, you can have them make crayon rubbings which will give them the same outline.

Counting Money through Dimes

pages 113-114

Objective

To count dimes, nickels and pennies through 99¢

Materials

*items priced through 99¢
pennies, nickels, dimes

Mental Math

Have students name the day or month:

1. third month of the year (March)
2. second day of the week (Monday)
3. sixth day of the week (Friday)
4. months beginning with letter M (March, May)
5. days beginning with letter T (Tuesday, Thursday)

Skill Review

Have students count by 10's aloud through 200. Have a student start at 10 and say the first 3 numbers for counting by 10's. Have the next student say the next 3 numbers and continue for all students to say 3 numbers. Repeat for counting by 5's and by 1's.

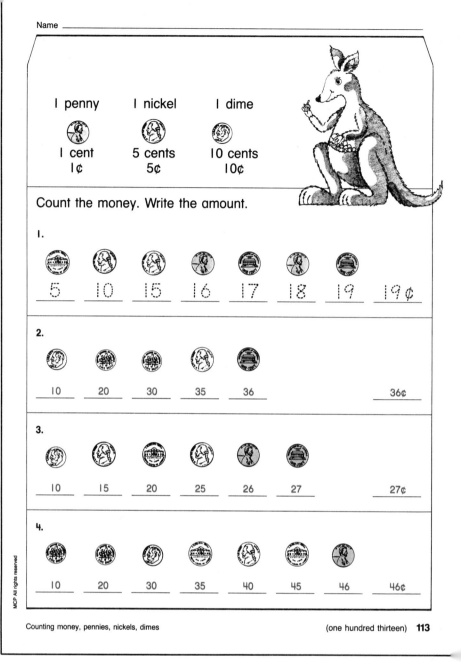

Count the money. Write the amount.

1. 5 10 15 16 17 18 19 19¢

2. 10 20 30 35 36 36¢

3. 10 15 20 25 26 27 27¢

4. 10 20 30 35 40 45 46 46¢

Counting money, pennies, nickels, dimes   (one hundred thirteen) **113**

Teaching page 113

Have students put out 2 dimes, 1 nickel and 1 penny. Tell students we count the dimes by 10's, nickels by 5's and pennies by 1's as you count out 10, 20, 25, 26¢. Have students repeat the counting through 26¢. Have a student write 26¢ on the board. Have students lay out other amounts of coins and practice counting on by 10's, then by 5's and then by 1's. Encourage students to sort coins for easier counting, with dimes first, then nickels and then pennies. Have a student write each amount on the board with the cent sign. Hold up a priced item and draw coins on the board as you count by 10's, then 5's and 1's to show the coins needed to buy the item. Continue to show priced items and have students display coins to show the costs. Remind students the cent sign must be used to denote money.

Help students complete the first problem tracing the numbers, before assigning the page to be completed independently.

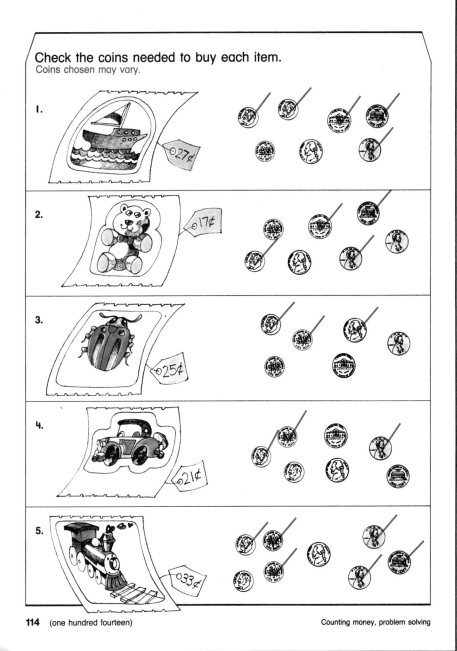

Check the coins needed to buy each item.
Coins chosen may vary.

1.

2.

3.

4.

5.

Counting money, problem solving

Correcting Common Errors

Some students may have difficulty switching from counting one kind of coin to counting another kind when a group of coins are given. Have them work with partners, counting aloud, pausing when they finish counting one type of coin before they count another.

Enrichment

1. Have students draw coins in order to show this counting sequence: 10, 20, 30, 35, 36, 46, 47, 57¢.
2. Tell students to cut an item priced less than 99¢ from a grocery ad and draw the coins they would need to buy it.
3. Ask students to draw the coins they would have left if they bought an item priced at 47¢, and had 8 dimes, 3 nickels and 4 pennies to spend.

Teaching page 114

Help students complete the first problem before assigning the page to be completed independently. Remind students there will be coins not used in each problem.

Extra Credit   *Logic*

Read or duplicate for students:

A dog has a 10-foot chain attached to his collar. He sees a bone 11 feet from where he is standing. He is very hungry! He looks at the bone, and finally figures out a way to get it. How does he get the bone?

(He simply walks over and takes it. One end of the chain is attached to his collar, but the other end is not attached to anything.)

114

Counting Money through Quarters

pages 115-116

Objective

To count quarters, dimes, nickels and pennies through 99¢

Materials

*items priced through 99¢
1 quarter
dimes, nickels, pennies

Mental Math

Have students tell how they are counting from:
1. 4 to 14 to 24 to 34 (10's)
2. 20 to 25 (5's)
3. 85 to 86 (1's)
4. 400 to 500 (100's)
5. 70 to 75 (5's)
6. 60 to 70 (10's)
7. 26 to 36 (10's)

Skill Review

Have students tell the total amount of money they would have if they had 4 dimes, 2 nickels and 6 pennies. (56¢) Repeat for more amounts of dimes, nickels and pennies. Have students lay out 70¢ in dimes, nickels and pennies and tell what coins make the amount. (Coins will vary.) Repeat for more amounts through 99¢.

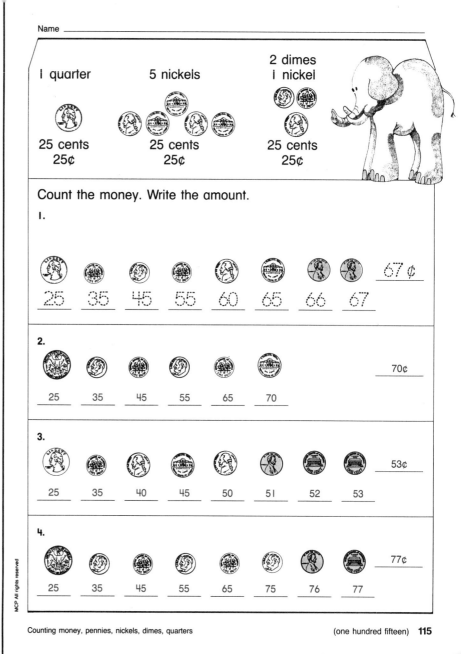

1 quarter   5 nickels   2 dimes 1 nickel

25 cents 25¢   25 cents 25¢   25 cents 25¢

Count the money. Write the amount.

1.   25   35   45   55   60   65   66   67   67¢

2.   25   35   45   55   65   70   70¢

3.   25   35   40   45   50   51   52   53   53¢

4.   25   35   45   55   65   75   76   77   77¢

Counting money, pennies, nickels, dimes, quarters   (one hundred fifteen) **115**

Teaching page 115

Draw a circle on the board and write **25¢** in it. Tell students that a **quarter** has a value of 25¢. Discuss the heads and tails sides of the quarter and other coins. Draw a dime on the board and write **10¢** in it. Tell students we want to know the total amount of money in a quarter and dime. Write **25¢** and **35¢** under the coins as you tell students to begin at 25 and count by 10's to 35¢ to find the total. Draw another 2 dimes and write **45¢** and **55¢** under them. Have students begin at 25 and count by 10's to tell the total money. (55¢) Now add 2 nickels and 2 pennies to the row of coins and write **60¢, 65¢, 66¢** and **67¢** under them. Have students begin at 25 and count the coins with you. (25, 35, 45, 55, 60, 65, 66, 67¢) Repeat for more amounts using 1 quarter and any number of other coins for amounts through 99¢. Have students

lay out an amount of coins using 1 quarter. Hold up a priced item and ask students if they have enough money to buy the item. Continue for more items priced less and more than their coins.

Have students read the values of the coins at the top of the page and help them complete the first problem. Then have students work the next problems independently. When they have completed the page, have them count the amounts of money out loud.

115

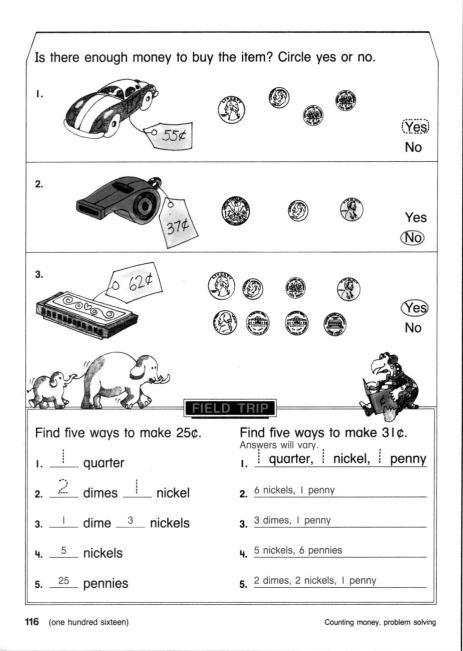

Is there enough money to buy the item? Circle yes or no.

1. 55¢ — **Yes** / No

2. 37¢ — Yes / **No**

3. 62¢ — **Yes** / No

FIELD TRIP

Find five ways to make 25¢.

1. __1__ quarter
2. __2__ dimes __1__ nickel
3. __1__ dime __3__ nickels
4. __5__ nickels
5. __25__ pennies

Find five ways to make 31¢.
Answers will vary.

1. __1__ quarter, __1__ nickel, __1__ penny
2. 6 nickels, 1 penny
3. 3 dimes, 1 penny
4. 5 nickels, 6 pennies
5. 2 dimes, 2 nickels, 1 penny

Counting money, problem solving

Correcting Common Errors

Some students will need more practice counting with money. Place a number of priced items around the room. Give each student a different amount of real or play money with which to shop. Ask them to count the amount of money that they have and then make a list of all purchases that they could make.

Enrichment

1. Tell students to draw 92¢ in coins. Then have them draw a priced item they could buy and one they could not buy with their coins.
2. Tell students to draw coins to show 4 ways to pay for an item costing 46¢.
3. Ask students to draw the change they would have left if they had 1 quarter, 4 dimes, 2 nickels and 8 pennies and bought an item for 53¢.

Teaching page 116

Ask students how much the first item costs? (55¢) Tell students to count the money in the first problem. (55¢) Ask if there is 55¢ or more. (yes) Have students trace the circle to answer the question. Tell students to complete the next problems independently.

Field Trip

Have students use coins to find and record all 5 ways to make 25¢. Tell students to now find and record 5 ways to make 31¢. Help students see that a systematic way to find coins to equal 31¢ is to start with 31 pennies and then trade 5 pennies for a nickel, 10 pennies for 2 nickels, 2 nickels for 1 dime, etc. Accept any reasonable answer.

Extra Credit   *Applications*

Write these sentences on the board:

A truck is longer than a car.
A house is smaller than a school.
A baby is shorter than a second-grader.

Ask students to think of their own sentence that compares the size of two objects. Tell students to write and illustrate their comparison. Help them with words they do not know how to spell. This can be assigned as homework. When students bring their sentences and drawings in, post them in a place where they can look at the comparisons other students have made.

116

Counting Money through Half-dollars

pages 117-118

Objective

To count a half-dollar, quarters, dimes, nickels and pennies through 99¢

Materials

1 half-dollar, 2 quarters dimes, nickels, pennies

Mental Math

Have students name a related fact for:
1. $15 - 8 = 7$ ($8 + 7 = 15$, etc.)
2. $6 + 7 = 13$ ($7 + 6 = 13$, etc.)
3. $17 - 8 = 9$
4. $18 - 9 = 9$
5. $9 - 0 = 9$
6. $10 - 1 = 9$
7. $12 - 3 = 9$
8. $11 - 6 = 5$

Skill Review

Have students put out 76¢ using a quarter, dimes, nickels and pennies and then draw the coins on the board. Repeat for other amounts through 99¢. Discuss with students why it's easier to use larger denomination coins rather than all nickels and pennies, etc.

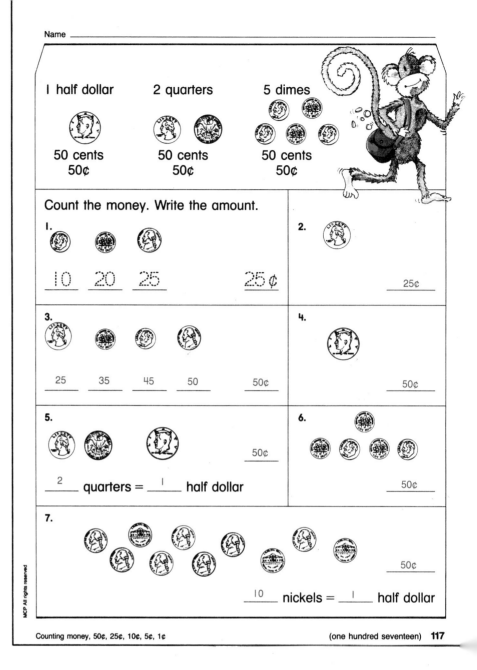

Teaching page 117

Have students put out 5 dimes and write the amount on the board. (50¢) Tell students they could use 2 quarters to show 50¢ also. Have students lay out 2 quarters and write the amount on the board. (50¢) Show students a **half-dollar** or **50 cent piece** as you tell the 2 names for the coin. Tell students the half-dollar is our largest coin whose value is less than one dollar and it can be used in place of 5 dimes or 2 quarters. Remind students there are 2 nickels in 1 dime as you ask students to lay out nickels to make 50¢. Ask how many nickels. (10) Now ask students to draw coins on the board to show all the ways to use 1 kind of coin to make 50¢. (1 half-dollar, 2 quarters, 5 dimes, 10 nickels, 50 pennies) Discuss the convenience of having 1 or 2 coins versus 5, 10 or 50. Have students note the heads and tails sides of the half-

dollar. Have students lay out a half-dollar and 2 dimes. Tell students to begin at 50 and count by 10's to tell the total. (70¢) Repeat for other amounts using a half-dollar or 2 quarters.

Read through the coin values at the top of the page with the students before having them complete the page independently.

117

Count the money. Write the amount.
Is there enough money to buy the item? Circle yes or no.

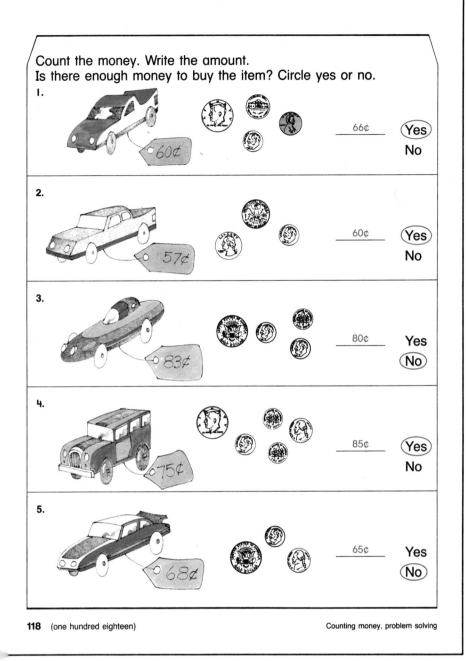

1. 60¢   66¢   (Yes)
                                           No

2. 57¢   60¢   (Yes)
                                           No

3. 83¢   80¢   Yes
                                          (No)

4. 75¢   85¢   (Yes)
                                           No

5. 68¢   65¢   Yes
                                          (No)

Counting money, problem solving

Correcting Common Errors

Some students will have difficulty
counting with a half-dollar. Have students work with partners and coins
or play money. Give them 3 different
cards with an item and its price pictured on each. Ask them to use their
coins, beginning with a half-dollar, to
show the amount of money they
would need to buy the item pictured
on each card. Remind students that
this means they start counting at 50¢.

Enrichment

1. Tell students to draw coins to
   show as many ways to make 50¢
   as they can.
2. Tell students to draw coins to
   show 91¢ without using any coin
   twice.
3. Ask students if they had 2 of each
   kind of coin, how much money
   would they have? Tell them to
   draw the coins.

Teaching page 118

Tell students they are to count the money, write the
amount and then decide if there is enough money to
purchase the priced item. Tell students to circle the
word that answers the question. Have students
complete the page.

Extra Credit *Probability*

Give each pair of students a coin and two pieces of
graph paper. Ask each pair to flip the coin 10 times
and make a simple bar graph of the results. Remind
them to use one square to represent one toss on their
graphs. Then ask each pair to tell how many heads
and how many tails they got in 10 flips. List these
results on the board:

    heads   tails   pairs with this result
      5   5
      4   6   (Numbers will vary.)
      6   4
    and so on. . .

Then ask each pair to graph the class results on
another graph and compare it to the first.

118

Counting Money through Dollars

pages 119-120

Objective

To count 1 dollar, half-dollars, quarters, dimes, nickels and pennies through $4.99

Materials

paper dollars
2 half-dollars
quarters, dimes
nickels, pennies

Mental Math

Have students tell the amount of money:
1. 50¢ more than 2 dimes. (70¢)
2. 25¢ more than 4 nickels. (45¢)
3. 10¢ less than 50¢. (40¢)
4. 3 dimes more than 20¢. (50¢)
5. 1 quarter plus 1 quarter. (50¢)
6. 1 quarter less than 85¢. (60¢)
7. 5 dimes and 1 quarter. (75¢)
8. 1 of each kind of coin. (91¢)

Skill Review

Have students work in pairs. Give each group an amount of money through 99¢. Have students see how many different ways they can draw their amount of money. Have one group check another group's work.

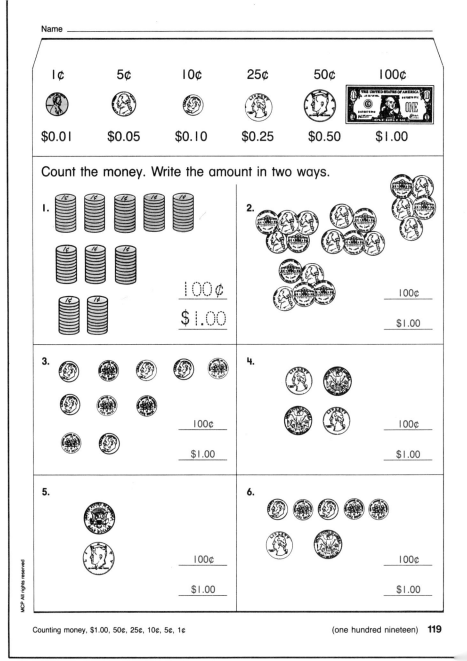

Teaching page 119

Have students display coins to show 99¢. Have students lay out 1 more penny to make 100¢. Write **100¢** on the board. Remind students to use the cent sign to show money amounts. Tell students that 100¢ or more can be written another way as you write **$1.00** on the board. Tell students the **dollar sign** and **decimal point** are used together instead of the cent sign. Tell students that less than 100¢ can also be written using the dollar sign and decimal point. Write **92¢** and **$0.92** on the board and have students read each as 92 cents. Have students notice that a zero is written to show there are no dollars. Repeat for other amounts less than $1. Show students a paper dollar and discuss the convenience of holding 1 piece of money rather than many coins. Write **$1.00** on

the board. Now have students draw on the board some ways to make $1.00 using coins. Have students lay out 1 dollar and 2 quarters. Tell students we can write this amount of money as **150¢** or **$1.50** as you write each on the board. Have students lay out another dollar and 2 dimes and tell the total cents as you write **270¢** on the board. Have a student write $2.70 on the board. Continue for amounts of money less than $1.00 through $4.99.

Read through the money amounts across the top of the page with the students and then have students complete the page independently.

119

Count the money. Write the amount in two ways.

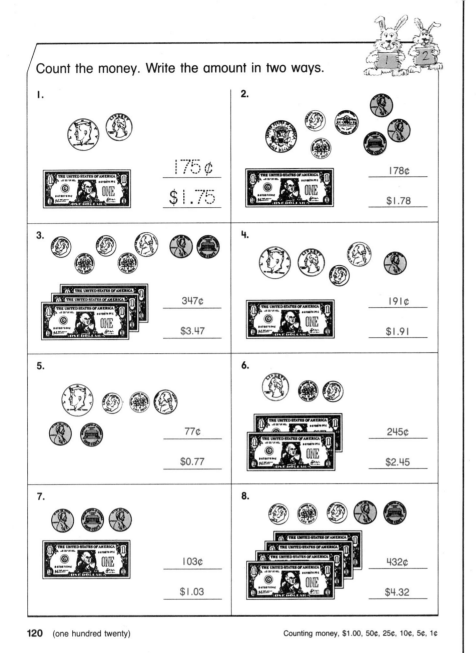

1. 175¢
   $1.75

2. 178¢
   $1.78

3. 347¢
   $3.47

4. 191¢
   $1.91

5. 77¢
   $0.77

6. 245¢
   $2.45

7. 103¢
   $1.03

8. 432¢
   $4.32

Counting money, $1.00, 50¢, 25¢, 10¢, 5¢, 1¢

Correcting Common Errors

Students may have trouble writing amounts of money with a dollar sign and cents point. Dictate amounts of money from $1.00 through $4.99 for students to write two ways, using the cents sign and then using the dollar sign and cents point. Then have them draw pictures or use play money of the dollars and coins to show the amount of money. Be sure they understand that an amount like $2.45 is always written with the dollar sign and cents point and that only amounts less than a dollar are written with the cents sign.

Enrichment

1. Have students use paper dollars and coins to draw as many ways as they can to show $2.50. Then tell them to write the total for each amount in 2 ways.
2. Have students work with a friend as each of them lays out an amount of money through $4.99 behind a cover. Tell them to remove the covers and read each other's amounts.
3. Tell students to work with a friend to lay out coins and dollars for the least number of coins possible to show an amount of money through $4.99.

Teaching page 120

Tell students to count the money and use the cent sign to write the amount in total cents. Tell students to write the amount of money using the dollar sign and decimal point. Help students write the amount in the first problem before assigning the page to be completed independently.

Extra Credit *Applications*

Invite a student who has a paper route to come to your classroom. Ask the paper carrier to demonstrate and discuss the math skills needed to run a successful route. Some of these might include counting, record keeping, scheduling and making change. Ask him to discuss the hardest and easiest parts of his job, and allow students to ask questions.

Problem Solving Counting Money

pages 121-122

Objective

To count money to solve problems

Materials

*items priced through $4.99
dollars, half-dollars
quarters, dimes, pennies

Mental Math

Tell students to name the coins if:
1. 3 coins equal 75¢. (25, 25, 25)
2. 5 coins equal 25¢. (5, 5, 5, 5, 5)
3. 5 coins equal 91¢. (50, 25, 10, 5, 1)
4. 5 coins equal 50¢. (10, 10, 10, 10, 10)
5. 3 coins equal 25¢. (10, 10, 5)
6. 3 coins equal 45¢. (25, 10, 10)
7. 2 coins equal 50¢. (25, 25)
8. 2 coins equal 75¢. (50, 25)

Skill Review

Show a priced item and have students lay out the amount of money shown on the price tag. Have students count their money to check the amount. Repeat for more practice.

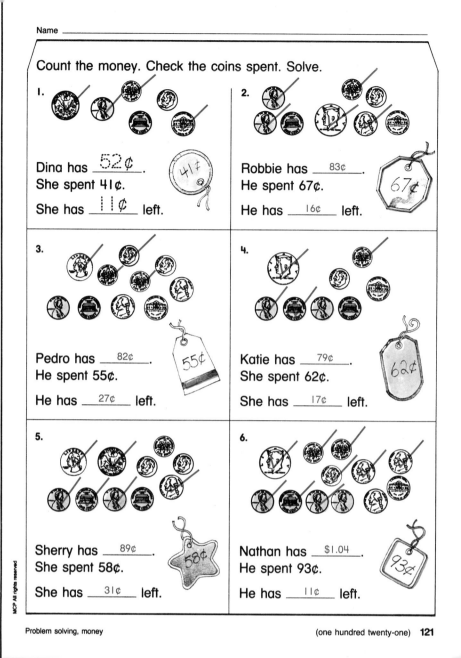

Name _____

Count the money. Check the coins spent. Solve.

1. Dina has __52¢__. She spent 41¢.
She has __11¢__ left. 41¢

2. Robbie has __83¢__. He spent 67¢.
He has __16¢__ left. 67¢

3. Pedro has __82¢__. He spent 55¢.
He has __27¢__ left. 55¢

4. Katie has __79¢__. She spent 62¢.
She has __17¢__ left. 62¢

5. Sherry has __89¢__. She spent 58¢.
She has __31¢__ left. 58¢

6. Nathan has __$1.04__. He spent 93¢.
He has __11¢__ left. 93¢

Problem solving, money

(one hundred twenty-one) **121**

Teaching page 121

Have students lay out 1 half-dollar, 2 quarters, 2 dimes and 4 nickels. Ask students the amount. ($1.40) Have a student write the amount on the board in dollar notation. Show students an item priced less than $1.40 and ask students to move aside the coins they would need to purchase the item. Ask a student to write the cost of the item on the board. Have another student write the amount of money that would be left after purchasing the item. Repeat for more amounts of money and priced items for students to practice selecting the money needed to buy an item and counting the money left.

Have a student read aloud the directions above the first problem. Ask students what they are to do. (count the money and check the coins spent) Ask students the total amount of money. (52¢) Have students read

the first sentence and trace the 52 to tell how much money Dina has. Ask students to read the next sentence to find out how much money Dina spent. (41¢) Tell students to draw the check marks through the coins that make 41¢. Ask students which coins were not used. (dime and penny) Ask students how much money Dina has left. (11¢) Tell students to trace the 11 to show that Dina has 11¢ left. Go through the next problem similarly with the students before assigning the page to be completed independently.

121

Count the money. Check the money spent. Solve.

1.

Chan has $ _1.28_ .
He spent $1.02.
He has _26 ¢_ left.

$1.02

2.

Julie has _$2.39_ .
She spent $2.32.
She has _7¢_ left.

$2.32

3.

Lory has _$2.28_ .
She spent $1.16.
She has _$1.12_ left.

$1.16

4.

Sam has _$1.89_ .
He spent 17¢.
He has _$1.72_ left.

17¢

FIELD TRIP

1. 50¢ is the same as:

_1_ half-dollar
_2_ quarters
_5_ dimes
_10_ nickels
_50_ pennies

2. $1.00 is the same as:

_2_ half-dollars
_4_ quarters
_10_ dimes
_20_ nickels
_100_ pennies

Problem solving, money

Correcting Common Errors

Students may have difficulty figuring out how much they have left after they make a purchase. Have them work with partners with 3 quarters, 1 dime, 1 nickel, and 5 pennies. Give them index cards showing items that cost $0.32, $0.51, and $0.84. Have them count their money aloud ($0.95) and tell how much they would have left if they bought the first item ($0.63), the second item ($0.44), and the third item ($0.11). Encourage students to model the price of the item and the change with extra coins. Then they can show that the amounts are correct by counting the money in both groups together.

Enrichment

1. Tell students to draw $4.83 in dollars and coins. Have them cut ads from newspapers for items costing less than the amount you have drawn. Tell students to circle the money they would have left.
2. Have students draw money to show 4 different ways to make $4.25 and circle the way which uses the least number of coins. Then have them draw a box around the easiest way to use it to buy an item costing $3.98.

Teaching page 122

Ask students to read the directions and tell what they are to do. (count the money and check the money spent) Remind students to write the amount of money left and then tell students to complete the problems independently.

Field Trip

It is helpful to have students work in pairs and begin with 50 pennies, trade pennies for nickels, then nickels for dimes, etc. Have students complete problem 1 and then work the second problem.

Extra Credit *Creative Drill*

This activity is an addition ring-toss. Prepare a target by turning a chair upside down, and taping a card with any number 2–9 to each leg. Draw a chalk line on the floor about 6 feet away. Tell students they are to stand behind the line and toss jar rings, or similar circular items, over the legs. Tell them to add the numbers on any legs they successfully ring, and write their names and totals on the board. Any student adding incorrectly must record a zero. This activity can be repeated, with each student's totals added together at the end. Encourage students to try to ring the chair legs with the largest numbers, since the student with the largest cumulative total wins.

Review

pages 123-124

Objectives

To review time and money
To maintain skills learned previously this year

Materials

dollars and coins
clock faces

Mental Math

Have students tell the time for:
1. 25 minutes later than 1:20. (1:45)
2. 55 minutes earlier than 1:00. (12:05)
3. the hour hand on 6 and minute hand on 5. (6:05)
4. 20 minutes later than your bedtime.
5. 45 minutes before your bedtime.

Skill Review

Write **460** on the board. Have students write the number which comes before 460, after 460, the number which is 100 more, 100 less, 10 more and 10 less. Have students begin at 460 and write the next 5 numbers if counting by 2's, 5's, 10's or 100's.
Repeat the activity for 7 tens 3 hundreds 7 ones.

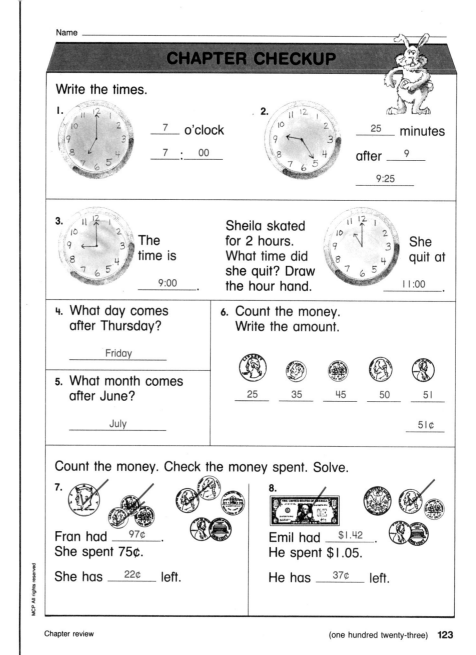

Teaching page 123

Have students tell what they are to do in each group of problems. Then have students complete the page independently.

ROUNDUP REVIEW

Add or subtract.

1.

$$\begin{array}{r} 7 \\ +4 \\ \hline 11 \end{array} \qquad \begin{array}{r} 8 \\ +7 \\ \hline 15 \end{array} \qquad \begin{array}{r} 5 \\ +5 \\ \hline 10 \end{array} \qquad \begin{array}{r} 14 \\ -6 \\ \hline 8 \end{array} \qquad \begin{array}{r} 10 \\ -9 \\ \hline 1 \end{array} \qquad \begin{array}{r} 15 \\ -6 \\ \hline 9 \end{array} \qquad \begin{array}{r} 12 \\ -5 \\ \hline 7 \end{array}$$

2.
$$\begin{array}{r} 11 \\ -6 \\ \hline 5 \end{array} \qquad \begin{array}{r} 13 \\ -5 \\ \hline 8 \end{array} \qquad \begin{array}{r} 6 \\ +6 \\ \hline 12 \end{array} \qquad \begin{array}{r} 8 \\ +5 \\ \hline 13 \end{array} \qquad \begin{array}{r} 16 \\ -8 \\ \hline 8 \end{array} \qquad \begin{array}{r} 8 \\ +6 \\ \hline 14 \end{array} \qquad \begin{array}{r} 9 \\ +9 \\ \hline 18 \end{array}$$

Write the number.

3. .... _____364_____

Count by ones. Write the numbers.

4. 96, 97, 98, __99__, __100__, __101__, __102__, __103__

5. 308, 309, __310__, __311__, __312__, __313__, __314__

6. 896, 897, __898__, __899__, __900__, __901__, __902__

Write the time.

7.

3:25

Count the money. Check the coins spent. Solve.

8.

Carl had __87¢__.

He spent 66¢. He has __21¢__ left.

Cumulative review

Teaching page 124

This page reviews basic addition and subtraction facts, counting sequences, place value, time and money. Have students tell what they are to do in each section before assigning the page to be completed independently.

Math Award Transition

pages 125-126

These two transition pages have been inserted to create a bridge for students from the format of Chapter 6, to the new format of Chapter 7. In chapters 7 through 15 of Level B, the format is similar to that used in Levels C through F of the MCP Mathematics Series. This change in lesson format allows for an easier-to-follow presentation of the increasingly difficult mathematics skills students will be learning.

page 125

The Math Award on page 125 signals the students' completion of the first portion of Level B. As students reach this point, fill in their Certificates of Completion and sign your name at the bottom. Emphasize to students that this is a significant accomplishment, and now they are ready for a new lesson approach. Have them color the page, if desired. Encourage students to take certificates home, so parents are also aware of changes in the lesson approach.

GET READY,
GET SET,
GO ON . . .

WATCH FOR . . .

MODEL PROBLEM
Work through the problem
with your teacher.

GETTING STARTED
Try the new math skill.
Ask questions.

PRACTICE
Complete the problems to practice
the new skill.

APPLY
Solve word problems using the
math skills you have learned.

FIELD TRIP
Have fun with mathematics.

page 126

This page will familiarize students with the new lesson format they will be using in the remainder of Level B. The **Model Problem** that will introduce most lessons, is designed to be worked by you and the students together. This model is representative of the kind of problem the student will be working in that particular lesson. The **Getting Started** section gives students sample problems to work, to practice the new skill being introduced. At this point you can immediately see if students have an understanding of the problems. The **Practice** page gives students ample practice to reinforce the skill they have learned. Students also learn to solve word problems in the **Apply** section, using both new and previously learned math skills. Finally, the **Field Trips** continue to offer students a chance to have fun with mathematics, while being challenged to extend mastered skills.

Have a student read each item description, as you explain them. Remind students that, like the bear with the magnifying glass, they must watch for each new item and read directions carefully.

2-digit Addition

pages 127-128

Objective

To add 2- and 1-digit numbers with no trading

Materials

ten-strips and ones

Mental Math

Tell students to name another fact with the same sum or difference as:

1. 7 + 6 (9 + 4, 8 + 5, etc.)
2. 12 − 9 (11 − 8, 10 − 7, etc.)
3. 8 + 5
4. 9 + 6
5. 15 − 9
6. 17 − 9
7. 8 + 6
8. 16 − 9

Skill Review

Write **46** on the board and have students show the number in ten-strips and ones. (4 tens 6 ones) Have students lay out ten-strips and ones for other 1- and 2-digit numbers. Now tell students to lay out ten-strips and ones for 5 tens 3 ones. Have students write the number on the board. Dictate more numbers for students to arrange on their desks. Have each number written on the board.

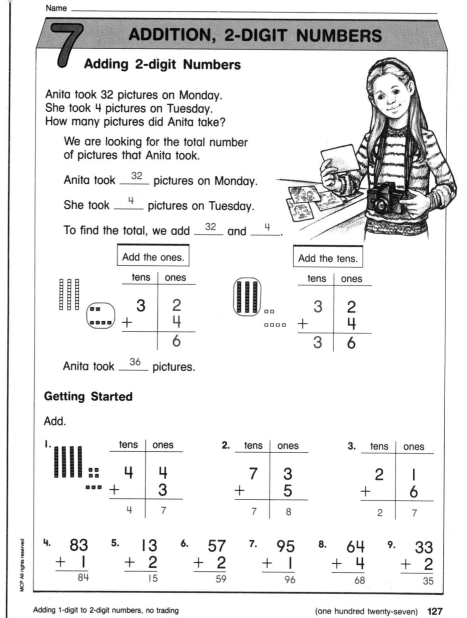

7

Adding 2-digit Numbers

Anita took 32 pictures on Monday.
She took 4 pictures on Tuesday.
How many pictures did Anita take?

We are looking for the total number of pictures that Anita took.

Anita took __32__ pictures on Monday.

She took __4__ pictures on Tuesday.

To find the total, we add __32__ and __4__.

Add the ones.

tens	ones
3	2
+	4
	6

Add the tens.

tens	ones
3	2
+	4
3	6

Anita took __36__ pictures.

Getting Started

Add.

1.
tens	ones
4	4
+	3
4	7

2.
tens	ones
7	3
+	5
7	8

3.
tens	ones
2	1
+	6
2	7

4. 83 + 1 = 84

5. 13 + 2 = 15

6. 57 + 2 = 59

7. 95 + 1 = 96

8. 64 + 4 = 68

9. 33 + 2 = 35

Adding 1-digit to 2-digit numbers, no trading

(one hundred twenty-seven) **127**

Teaching the Lesson

Introducing the Problem Have students tell about the picture. Read the problem aloud with the students and ask what is to be solved. (the number of pictures Anita took) Ask what information is given in the problem. (Anita took 32 pictures on Monday and 4 pictures on Tuesday.) Continue reading aloud with the students as they complete the information sentences. Work through the addition model with students and then have them complete the solution sentence. Have students count the photos in the picture to check their addition work.

Developing the Skill Tell students that Jack fed an elephant 15 peanuts. Have them lay out ten-strips and ones to show 15. Ask how many tens and ones there are. (1, 5) Make a tens and ones grid on the board and put 15 in the proper columns. Tell students that Jack then fed the elephant 4 more peanuts. Ask students how to find the total number of peanuts. (add) Tell students to add 4 ones to their counters. Write 4 under the 5 in the ones column. Tell students to add the ones first. Have a student write the sum on the board. (9) Have another student write the total number of tens in the tens column. (1) Ask how many peanuts in all. (19) Ask how many tens and ones in 19. (1, 9) Repeat for more problems of 1-digit numbers added to 2-digit numbers where no trade is needed.

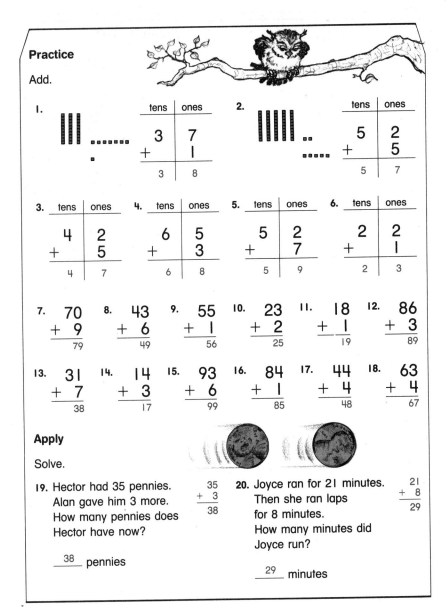

Practice

Add.

1.
tens	ones
3	7
+	1
3	8

2.
tens	ones
5	2
+	5
5	7

3.
tens	ones
4	2
+	5
4	7

4.
tens	ones
6	5
+	3
6	8

5.
tens	ones
5	2
+	7
5	9

6.
tens	ones
2	2
+	1
2	3

7.
```
  70
+  9
 79
```
8.
```
  43
+  6
 49
```
9.
```
  55
+  1
 56
```
10.
```
  23
+  2
 25
```
11.
```
  18
+  1
 19
```
12.
```
  86
+  3
 89
```

13.
```
  31
+  7
 38
```
14.
```
  14
+  3
 17
```
15.
```
  93
+  6
 99
```
16.
```
  84
+  1
 85
```
17.
```
  44
+  4
 48
```
18.
```
  63
+  4
 67
```

Apply

Solve.

19. Hector had 35 pennies. Alan gave him 3 more. How many pennies does Hector have now?

```
  35
+  3
 38
```

___38___ pennies

20. Joyce ran for 21 minutes. Then she ran laps for 8 minutes. How many minutes did Joyce run?

```
  21
+  8
 29
```

___29___ minutes

128 (one hundred twenty-eight)

Adding 1-digit to 2-digit numbers, no trading

Addition with Trading

pages 129-130

Objective

To add 1-digit numbers to 2-digit numbers with some trading

Materials

counting sticks and rubber bands
ten-strips and ones
graph paper

Mental Math

Ask students how many tens are in:

1. 264 (6)
2. 59 (5)
3. 40 (4)
4. 6 (0)

Ask students how many ones in:

5. 7 (7)
6. 189 (9)
7. 64 (4)
8. 490 (0)

Skill Review

Have students work the following vertical problems at the board as other students work with ten-strips and ones: 43 + 6 (49), 72 + 7 (79), 54 + 3 (57), 61 + 8 (69), 82 + 6 (88).

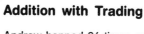

Addition with Trading

Andrew hopped 26 times on his left foot and 8 times on his right foot. How many times did Andrew hop?

We want to find out how many times Andrew hopped.

Andrew hopped __26__ times on his left foot.

He hopped __8__ times on his right foot. To find the total number of hops,

we add __26__ and __8__.

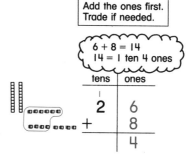

	Add the ones first. Trade if needed.		Add the tens.	

6 + 8 = 14
14 = 1 ten 4 ones

1 + 2 tens = 3 tens

	tens	ones
	2	6
+		8
		4

	tens	ones
	2	6
+		8
	3	4

Andrew hopped __34__ times.

Getting Started

Add. Trade if needed.

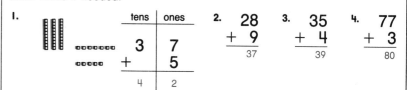

1.

	tens	ones
	3	7
+		5
	4	2

2. 28
   + 9
   ___
    37

3. 35
   + 4
   ___
    39

4. 77
   + 3
   ___
    80

Adding 1-digit to 2-digit numbers with trading

Teaching the Lesson

Introducing the Problem Have students tell about the picture. Have a student read the problem aloud. Ask students what is to be found. (number of times Andrew hopped) Ask what information is known. (He hopped 26 times on his left foot and 8 times on his right foot.) Ask students how to find the total number of hops. (add) Have students read aloud with you as they complete the information sentences. Work through the problem and then have students complete the solution sentence. Have students count the tens and ones pictured to check their work.

Developing the Skill Have students lay out 23 counting sticks and bundle the groups of 10. Ask how many tens and ones. (2, 3) Ask students how many ones in all if we add 8 more ones. (11) Ask if another ten can be bundled now. (yes) Have students bundle the ten and tell how many tens and ones. (3, 1) Repeat for more numbers. Now write **26 + 8** vertically on the board and have students lay out 26 sticks, bundle them into tens, add 8 and bundle another ten. Talk through the work as you write **4** in ones place and trade the 10 ones for 1 ten. Have a student write 3 in tens place and read the sum in tens and ones. (3, 4) Help students work more problems using the ten-strips and ones in place of counting sticks.

129

Practice

Add. Trade if needed.

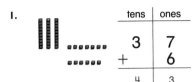

	tens	ones
1.	3	7
	+	6
	4	3

	tens	ones
2.	5	3
	+	9
	6	2

3. 34
  + 5
   39

4. 65
  + 6
   71

5. 83
  + 9
   92

6. 62
  + 7
   69

7. 29
  + 5
   34

8. 56
  + 8
   64

9. 23
  + 6
   29

10. 39
   + 3
    42

11. 28
   + 6
    34

12. 61
   + 8
    69

13. 75
   + 9
    84

14. 57
   + 4
    61

FIELD TRIP

Write the missing numbers.

1. 3 4
  + 2
   3 6

2. 1 7
  + 2
   1 9

3. 1 6
  + 4
   2 0

4. 3 1
  + 8
   3 9

5. 6 2
  + 5
   6 7

6. 2 3
  + 7
   3 0

7. 3 5
  + 6
   4 1

8. 6 3
  + 9
   7 2

9. 4 6
  + 7
   5 3

10. 5 7
   + 8
    6 5

130 (one hundred thirty)   Adding 1-digit to 2-digit numbers with trading

Correcting Common Errors

Some students may have difficulty trading. Have them work with partners to rewrite problems such as the following with ten less ones and one more ten.

3 tens 16 ones (4 tens 6 ones)
4 tens 19 ones (5 tens 9 ones)
2 tens 11 ones (3 tens 1 one)
8 tens 15 ones (9 tens 5 ones)
5 tens 10 ones (6 tens 0 ones)

Encourage students to use ten-strips and ones to show each regrouping.

Enrichment

Have students write and solve a problem to find how many desks would be in their classroom if 9 new students joined the class.

Practice

Remind students to add the ones first and make a trade if necessary before adding the tens. Have students complete the problems at the top of the page independently.

Field Trip

Write **18 + ___ = 21** vertically on the board. Ask students what number needs to be added to 8 to get 1 one and 1 ten. (3) Have students experiment with other numbers, if necessary, to see that 3 is the only number which satisfies the problem. Repeat for **34 + ___ = 43** (9), **56 + ___ = 63** (7) and **29 + ___ = 33** (4).
Tell students to complete each problem by finding the number which makes the problem true.

Extra Credit   *Geometry*

Have students experiment with mosaics. Provide many squares of construction paper in a variety of colors. Squares that are one inch on a side are easy to make with a paper cutter. Give each student plain paper and glue. Explain that they can arrange the squares any way they like to make a picture or a pattern. Encourage them to cover the entire paper.
This activity can be enhanced by bringing in pictures of real tile mosaics. The mosaics will be a good introduction to the idea of tessellations, the repetition of a simple shape forming a pattern. Display the finished creations.

130

More Addition with Trading

pages 131-132

Objective

To add two 2-digit numbers with some trading for sums through 99

Materials

ten-strips and ones

Mental Math

Tell students to name the number:

1. 2 tens + 3 tens + 4 tens (90)
2. 6 ones + 4 ones + 9 ones (19)
3. 7 hundreds + 2 hundreds (900)
4. 2 tens + 5 tens + 1 ten (80)
5. 0 hundreds 0 tens 0 ones (0)
6. 14 ones + 2 ones (16)
7. 1 one + 1 hundred (101)
8. 5 tens 6 ones 4 hundreds (456)

Skill Review

Dictate the following problems: 46 + 6 (52), 35 + 4 (39), 3 tens 8 ones + 9 (47), 75 + 5 (80), 8 tens 9 ones + 4 (93), 62 + 7 (69). Have students work with manipulatives or write and solve the problems on paper as other students work the problems on the board. Remind students to add the ones first and then the tens.

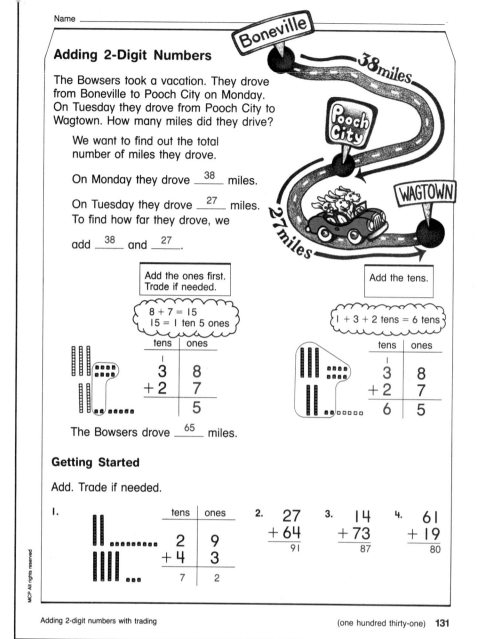

Name _____

Adding 2-Digit Numbers

The Bowsers took a vacation. They drove from Boneville to Pooch City on Monday. On Tuesday they drove from Pooch City to Wagtown. How many miles did they drive?

We want to find out the total number of miles they drove.

On Monday they drove __38__ miles.

On Tuesday they drove __27__ miles. To find how far they drove, we

add __38__ and __27__.

Add the ones first. Trade if needed.

8 + 7 = 15
15 = 1 ten 5 ones

tens	ones
3	8
+2	7
	5

Add the tens.

1 + 3 + 2 tens = 6 tens

tens	ones
3	8
+2	7
6	5

The Bowsers drove __65__ miles.

Getting Started

Add. Trade if needed.

1.

tens	ones
2	9
+4	3
7	2

2.   27
   +64
    91

3.   14
   +73
    87

4.   61
   +19
    80

Adding 2-digit numbers with trading

(one hundred thirty-one) **131**

Teaching the Lesson

Introducing the Problem Have students tell about the picture. Have a student read the problem aloud. Ask students what is to be solved. (the total number of miles the Bowsers drove) Ask what information is given in the picture. (38 miles from Boneville to Pooch City and 27 miles from Pooch City to Wagtown) Have students read and complete the information sentences. Remind students that the ones are always added first as you work through the problem together. Have students complete the solution statement. Have students check their work with manipulatives.

Developing the Skill Write **46 + 28** vertically on the board and have students lay out the numbers in ten-strips and ones. Ask how many ones in all. (14) Ask students what they need to do. (trade 10 ones for 1 ten) Have students make the trade and tell how many ones are left. (4) Have a student write 4 in the ones place and show the traded ten on the board. Ask how to find the number of tens in all. (add 4 + 2 + 1) Have a student write 7 in the tens column. Ask students to read the sum of 46 and 28 aloud. (74) Have students check by counting their ten-strips and ones. Repeat the procedure for 52 + 28 (80), 76 + 19 (95), 42 + 53 (95) and 73 + 18 (91).

131

Practice

Add. Trade if needed.

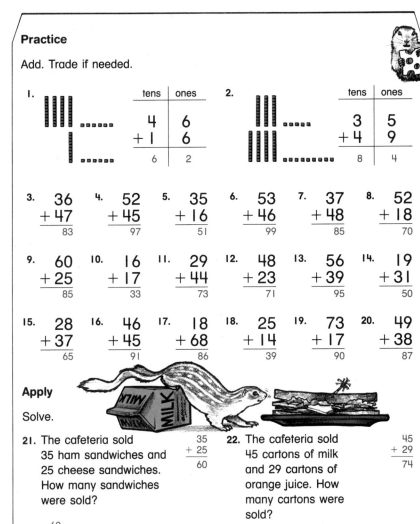

1.
tens	ones
4	6
+1	6
6	2

2.
tens	ones
3	5
+4	9
8	4

3.
```
  36
+ 47
  83
```

4.
```
  52
+ 45
  97
```

5.
```
  35
+ 16
  51
```

6.
```
  53
+ 46
  99
```

7.
```
  37
+ 48
  85
```

8.
```
  52
+ 18
  70
```

9.
```
  60
+ 25
  85
```

10.
```
  16
+ 17
  33
```

11.
```
  29
+ 44
  73
```

12.
```
  48
+ 23
  71
```

13.
```
  56
+ 39
  95
```

14.
```
  19
+ 31
  50
```

15.
```
  28
+ 37
  65
```

16.
```
  46
+ 45
  91
```

17.
```
  18
+ 68
  86
```

18.
```
  25
+ 14
  39
```

19.
```
  73
+ 17
  90
```

20.
```
  49
+ 38
  87
```

Apply

Solve.

21. The cafeteria sold 35 ham sandwiches and 25 cheese sandwiches. How many sandwiches were sold?

```
  35
+ 25
  60
```

__60__ sandwiches

22. The cafeteria sold 45 cartons of milk and 29 cartons of orange juice. How many cartons were sold?

```
  45
+ 29
  74
```

__74__ cartons

132 (one hundred thirty-two) Adding 2-digit numbers with trading

Adding 2-digit numbers with trading

Correcting Common Errors

Some students may add incorrectly because they add each column separately, failing to trade.

INCORRECT	CORRECT
	1
26	26
+18	+18
314	44

Correct by having them use place-value materials to model the problem.

Enrichment

Tell students to write and solve a problem which finds the number of people in 2 classes at their school. Tell them to include the teachers. Now have them write out and solve a problem which finds out how many pencils are needed if each person needs 2.

Practice

Remind students to add the ones first and make a trade if necessary before adding the tens. Tell students to complete the problems independently. Then go through each word problem to be sure students know what operation they will use. Have students work the 2 problems independently and then as a group at the board.

Mixed Practice

1. 3¢ + 5¢ (8¢)
2. 1¢ + 3¢ (4¢)
3. 9¢ − 6¢ (3¢)
4. 8¢ − 4¢ (4¢)
5. 3 + 3 (6)
6. 10 − 4 (6)
7. 5¢ + 5¢ (10¢)
8. 2 + 4 (6)
9. 1 + 9 (10)
10. 9 − 3 (6)

Extra Credit *Applications*

Introduce the application of mathematics to growing things. Bring to class a package of seeds, enough styrofoam cups so that each student will have one and a bag of potting soil. Plants that will grow reliably and quickly include: radish, marigolds, beans and grass. Read the directions for planting to the class. Explain that the **germination time** is the number of days it takes the plant to sprout from a seed. Have each student plant several different seeds in styrofoam cups filled with potting soil. Put the labeled cups in a sunny place and have students keep them watered until they germinate. Now have students measure their own plants using inches or centimeters every other day. Help them keep track of the height of their seedlings on a chart that lists Day 1 as the day the seed was planted. Remind them that until the seed actually sprouts, the height will be zero.

Adding Multiples of 10

pages 133-134

Objective

To add any two 2-digit multiples of 10

Materials

hundred-flat
ten-strips
graph paper

Mental Math

Tell students to name a related subtraction fact for:

1. $7 + 9$ $(16 - 7, 16 - 9)$
2. 6 ones + 8 ones, $(14 - 8, 14 - 6)$
3. $9 + 9$ $(18 - 9)$
4. $8 + 9$ $(17 - 9, 17 - 8)$
5. $6 + 4$, $(10 - 4, 10 - 6)$
6. $9 + 4$ $(13 - 4, 13 - 9)$
7. $8 + 8$ $(16 - 8)$

Skill Review

Have students count by 10's through 200. Write **80 + 10** vertically on the board for a student to find the sum. (90) Repeat for **60 + 30** (90), **20 + 40** (60), **30 + 40** (70), etc., for sums of 90 or less. Ask students how many ones are in each sum. (none)

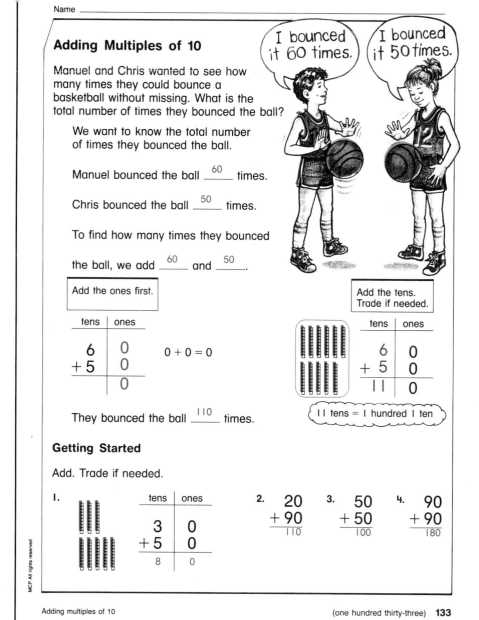

Adding Multiples of 10

Manuel and Chris wanted to see how many times they could bounce a basketball without missing. What is the total number of times they bounced the ball?

I bounced it 60 times.

I bounced it 50 times.

We want to know the total number of times they bounced the ball.

Manuel bounced the ball __60__ times.

Chris bounced the ball __50__ times.

To find how many times they bounced the ball, we add __60__ and __50__.

Add the ones first.

tens	ones
6	0
+ 5	0
	0

$0 + 0 = 0$

Add the tens. Trade if needed.

tens	ones
6	0
+ 5	0
1 1	0

11 tens = 1 hundred 1 ten

They bounced the ball __110__ times.

Getting Started

Add. Trade if needed.

1.
tens	ones
3	0
+ 5	0
8	0

2.
```
   20
 + 90
  110
```

3.
```
   50
 + 50
  100
```

4.
```
   90
 + 90
  180
```

Adding multiples of 10

(one hundred thirty-three) **133**

Teaching the Lesson

Introducing the Problem Have students tell about the picture. Ask a student to read the problem aloud and tell what is being asked. (the total number of bounces) Ask students what information is known. (Manuel bounced 60 times and Chris bounced 50 times.) Have students read aloud with you as they complete the sentences. Work through the problem with students and then have them complete the solution sentence. Have students lay out ten-strips to check their answer.

Developing the Skill Have students lay out 6 tens and 3 tens and tell the number. (90) Tell students to lay out another ten and tell the total number of tens. (10) Ask how many ones. (0) Write **100 = 10 tens 0 ones** on the board. Have students lay out another ten and tell the number of tens. (11) Ask how many ones. (0) Write **110 = 11 tens 0 ones = 1 hundred 1 ten 0 ones** on the board. Continue to develop 120, 130, etc. Write **60 + 40** vertically on the board and have a student add the ones column. (0) Have a student add the tens column. (10) Ask students to read the number. (one hundred) Ask students to tell the number of hundreds, tens and ones in 100. (1, 0, 0) Repeat for **90 + 20** (110), and other sums through 180 which are multiples of tens.

133

Practice

Add. Trade if needed.

1.

tens	ones
7	0
+ 6	0
13	0

2.
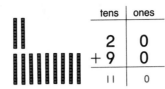

tens	ones
2	0
+ 9	0
11	0

3. 40
   + 30
   ___
    70

4. 60
   + 60
   ___
   120

5. 80
   + 80
   ___
   160

6. 30
   + 50
   ___
    80

7. 90
   + 90
   ___
   180

8. 50
   + 50
   ___
   100

9. 50
   + 40
   ___
    90

10. 90
    + 50
    ___
    140

11. 70
    + 80
    ___
    150

12. 10
    + 90
    ___
    100

13. 80
    + 40
    ___
    120

14. 70
    + 50
    ___
    120

15. 80
    + 90
    ___
    170

16. 90
    + 70
    ___
    160

17. 20
    + 30
    ___
     50

18. 70
    + 60
    ___
    130

19. 20
    + 80
    ___
    100

20. 60
    + 50
    ___
    110

Apply

Solve.

21. Phil took 30 steps to the door and 30 steps back. How many steps did Phil take?

    30
   + 30
   ___
    60

    __60__ steps

22. Myra rode her bike for 40 minutes. She played ball for 70 minutes. How many minutes did Myra play?

    40
   + 70
   ___
   110

   __110__ minutes

Adding multiples of 10

Correcting Common Errors

When adding multiples of 10, some students will omit the zero in ones place. One way to impress on them the importance of the place holder is for them to model a simple problem like 10 + 10 using first ones and then trading ones for ten-strips. Encourage them to verbalize how 2 is different than 20.

Enrichment

Tell students to write and solve problems to show 10 ways to add 2 or 3 multiples of ten to have a sum of 120.

Practice

Remind students to add the ones column first and then find the sum of the tens column. Have students read through the 2 word problems and tell what they will do in each. (add) Assign the page to be completed independently.

Mixed Practice

1. 8 + 3 (11)
2. 7 − 5 (2)
3. 7¢ + 2¢ (9¢)
4. 12¢ − 9¢ (3¢)
5. 5 − 5 (0)
6. 3¢ + 9¢ (12¢)
7. 4 + 8 (12)
8. 11 − 9 (2)
9. 7¢ − 1¢ (6¢)
10. 6 + 5 (11)

Extra Credit *Applications*

Have students display the charts they made for measuring their growing seeds. Hold up one of the charts and ask the class if it is easy to read at a distance. (probably not) Help them make a bar graph on graph paper, using their data. Put a sample graph on the board in this form:

	day 1			
DATE	**day 2**			
	day 3			
	day 4			
	day 5			
	1	2	3	4

HEIGHT IN INCHES

Help them see that before the seed has sprouted, they will not color in any squares. When the seed has sprouted, they will begin to color in one square for each inch or centimeter. Tell students to show that the sprout has grown more or less than an inch by coloring in a part of a square.

3-digit Sums

pages 135-136

Objective

To add two 2-digit numbers with trading for 2- or 3-digit sums

Materials

hundred-flat
ten-strips and ones

Mental Math

Ask students to tell the total amount of money for:

1. 5 dimes 2 nickels (60¢)
2. 4 pennies 1 quarter (29¢)
3. 1 dollar 4 nickels ($1.20)
4. 1 half-dollar 3 dimes (80¢)
5. 8 nickels 1 dime (50¢)
6. 2 quarters 1 nickel (55¢)
7. 1 dollar 1 half-dollar ($1.50)
8. 3 quarters 1 half-dollar ($1.25)

Skill Review

Have students work the following vertical problems at the board: 78 + 4 (82), 80 + 5 (85), 47 + 9 (56), 29 + 8 (37), 30 + 80 (110), 72 + 8 (80), 60 + 90 (150), 15 + 6 (21).

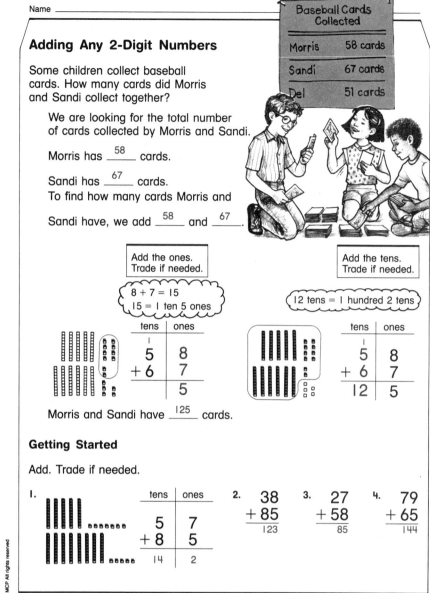

Teaching the Lesson

Introducing the Problem Have students tell about the picture and read the chart. Have a student read the problem. Ask what is to be found. (the number of cards Morris and Sandi collected) Ask students where information can be gained to solve the problem. (from the chart) Ask what information is needed from the chart. (Morris collected 58 and Sandi collected 67.) Ask if they will use the information about Del's cards to solve this problem. (no) Have students read aloud with you as they complete the information sentences. Work through the problem with the students and then have them complete the solution statement. Have students lay out ten-strips and ones to check their answer.

Developing the Skill Write **48 + 96** vertically on the board. Have students lay out ten-strips and ones to show each number. Ask how many ones in all. (14) Ask if a trade is needed. (yes) Have students trade 10 ones for 1 ten as you write **4** in the ones column. Tell students to add 4 tens and 9 tens plus the 1 traded ten for the total number of tens. (14) Ask if there are enough tens to trade for 1 hundred. (yes) Tell students to trade 10 tens for 1 hundred as you write **4** in the tens column. Ask students how many hundreds. (1) Write **1** in the hundreds column. Have students read the sum. (one hundred forty-four) Repeat for 79 + 85 (164), 37 + 48 (85), 56 + 99 (155) and 72 + 96 (168).

135

Practice

Add. Trade if needed.

		tens	ones			tens	ones
1.		2	9	**2.**		8	8
	+	7	4		+	7	7
		10	3			16	5

3. 34
    + 23
    ___
     57

4. 85
    + 57
    ___
    142

5. 29
    + 76
    ___
    105

6. 16
    + 37
    ___
     53

7. 43
    + 44
    ___
     87

8. 91
    + 26
    ___
    117

9. 35
    + 45
    ___
     80

10. 67
    + 78
    ___
    145

11. 38
    + 38
    ___
     76

12. 75
    + 75
    ___
    150

13. 41
    + 99
    ___
    140

14. 27
    + 98
    ___
    125

15. 57
    + 23
    ___
     80

16. 56
    + 65
    ___
    121

17. 99
    + 99
    ___
    198

18. 65
    + 85
    ___
    150

19. 36
    + 55
    ___
     91

20. 43
    + 75
    ___
    118

21. 25
    + 63
    ___
     88

22. 69
    + 32
    ___
    101

23. 47
    + 77
    ___
    124

24. 38
    + 95
    ___
    133

25. 67
    + 27
    ___
     94

26. 83
    + 79
    ___
    162

Adding 2-digit numbers with trading, 3-digit answers

Correcting Common Errors

Watch for students who rename incorrectly because they reverse the tens and ones.

INCORRECT	CORRECT
6	1
17	17
+29	+29
91	46

Correct by having students use place-value materials to model the problem and show the regrouping.

Enrichment

Use the information on page 135 to find out how many more cards Sandi and Morris collected than Sandi and Del collected. (7)

Practice

Remind students to add the ones column first. Help students complete the first few problems, if necessary, before assigning the page to be completed independently.

Mixed Practice

1. 3 + 4 (7)
2. 11 − 6 (5)
3. 7¢ − 2¢ (5¢)
4. 0 + 7 (7)
5. 12 − 5 (7)
6. 10 − 3 (7)
7. 10 + 3 (13)
8. ___ + 3 = 12 (9)
9. 12¢ − 6¢ (6¢)
10. 4 + ___ = 5 (1)

Extra Credit   *Geometry*

Provide a worksheet having several geometric shapes with many smaller geometric shapes within such as the following.

Have students count how many squares and how many triangles.

Have students color the geometric shapes after they count them. Encourage them to use a ruler and design their own geometric patterns and write related questions. Display the geometric designs and have students count the total number of squares, circles and triangles.

Problem Solving Addition

pages 137-138

Objective

To solve problems using addition of two 2-digit numbers with trading, for 2- or 3-digit sums

Materials

hundred-flat
ten-strips and ones

Mental Math

Ask students which hand on a clock is:

1. on 7 at 8:35. (minute)
2. on 2 at 2:00. (hour)
3. on 6 at 6:30. (minute)
4. on 12 at 4:00. (minute)
5. on 4 at 5:20. (minute)
6. between 2 and 3 at 2:30. (hour)
7. almost on 12 at 4:58. (minute)
8. almost on 9 at 8:52. (hour)

Skill Review

Dictate the following problems for students to work at the board: 4 tens 6 ones + 8 tens 4 ones (130), 78 + 14 (92), 7 tens 9 ones + 68 (147), 55 + 66 (121), 42 + 64 (106), 94 + 6 tens 9 ones (163).

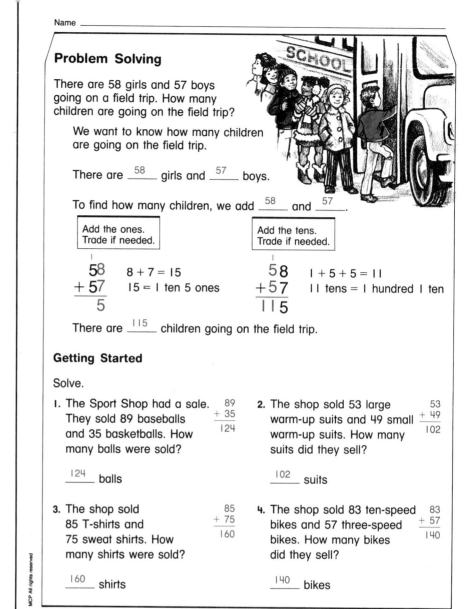

Name _____

Problem Solving

There are 58 girls and 57 boys going on a field trip. How many children are going on the field trip?

We want to know how many children are going on the field trip.

There are ___58___ girls and ___57___ boys.

To find how many children, we add ___58___ and ___57___.

Add the ones. Trade if needed.	Add the tens. Trade if needed.

$5\overset{1}{8}$
$+ 57$
_____
5

$8 + 7 = 15$
$15 = 1$ ten 5 ones

$\overset{1}{5}8$
$+ 57$
_____
115

$1 + 5 + 5 = 11$
11 tens $= 1$ hundred 1 ten

There are ___115___ children going on the field trip.

Getting Started

Solve.

1. The Sport Shop had a sale. They sold 89 baseballs and 35 basketballs. How many balls were sold?

   89
   $+ 35$
   _____
   124

   ___124___ balls

2. The shop sold 53 large warm-up suits and 49 small warm-up suits. How many suits did they sell?

   53
   $+ 49$
   _____
   102

   ___102___ suits

3. The shop sold 85 T-shirts and 75 sweat shirts. How many shirts were sold?

   85
   $+ 75$
   _____
   160

   ___160___ shirts

4. The shop sold 83 ten-speed bikes and 57 three-speed bikes. How many bikes did they sell?

   83
   $+ 57$
   _____
   140

   ___140___ bikes

Problem solving, addition

(one hundred thirty-seven) **137**

Teaching the Lesson

Introducing the Problem Have students tell about the picture. Have a student read the problem and tell what is to be found. (number of children going on a field trip) Ask what information is given. (There are 58 girls and 57 boys.) Have students read and complete the information sentences. Work through the model with students and then have them complete the solution sentence. Have students use manipulatives to check their solution.

Developing the Skill Tell students a story of 2 children counting car license plates having an A or B. Tell students that 1 child counted 48 plates with an A and the other child counted 59 with a B. Ask students what operation they will use to tell how many cars in all had an A or B on the license plate. (addition) Ask a student to write the problem on the board as you retell the story. (48 + 59) Ask students what they will do first. (add the ones) Have a student add the ones. (17) Ask if a trade is needed. (yes) Have the student record the trade and the ones left. (7) Ask students what they will do next. (add the tens) Have a student add the tens (10) and tell if a trade is needed. (yes) Have the student record the trade and the tens left. (0) Have students read the sum. (one hundred seven) Encourage students to create problems for more practice.

Solve.

1. The Jackson Ranch has 98 cows and 67 horses. How many cows and horses do they have?

$$\begin{array}{r} 98 \\ + 67 \\ \hline 165 \end{array}$$

_165_ cows and horses

2. The ranch has 65 wild turkeys and 89 wild pigs. How many pigs and turkeys do they have?

$$\begin{array}{r} 65 \\ + 89 \\ \hline 154 \end{array}$$

_154_ pigs and turkeys

3. Read exercise 1 again. What if the Jacksons sell 23 of their horses? Then how many cows and horses will they have?

_142_ cows and horses

4. Read exercise 2 again. What if the ranch got 21 more wild turkeys? Then how many pigs and turkeys would they have?

_175_ pigs and turkeys

FIELD TRIP

Add. Then write the answers in the puzzle.

Across:

1. $\begin{array}{r} 47 \\ + 44 \\ \hline 91 \end{array}$

3. $\begin{array}{r} 76 \\ + 85 \\ \hline 161 \end{array}$

5. $\begin{array}{r} 37 \\ + 47 \\ \hline 84 \end{array}$

6. $\begin{array}{r} 15 \\ + 16 \\ \hline 31 \end{array}$

8. $\begin{array}{r} 93 \\ + 79 \\ \hline 172 \end{array}$

9. $\begin{array}{r} 52 \\ + 25 \\ \hline 77 \end{array}$

Down:

2. $\begin{array}{r} 98 \\ + 16 \\ \hline 114 \end{array}$

4. $\begin{array}{r} 79 \\ + 58 \\ \hline 137 \end{array}$

7. $\begin{array}{r} 40 \\ + 82 \\ \hline 122 \end{array}$

Problem solving, addition

Correcting Common Errors

Some students may answer incorrectly because they add from left to right when they are computing.

INCORRECT
$$\begin{array}{r} 1 \\ 85 \\ + 57 \\ \hline 313 \end{array}$$

CORRECT
$$\begin{array}{r} 1 \\ 85 \\ + 57 \\ \hline 142 \end{array}$$

Remind students that when adding, they first add the ones, and then the tens. Encourage them to work the problem towards the plus sign, not away from it.

Enrichment

Tell students there are 48 hours in 2 days. Then ask them to find how many hours are in 3 days. In 4 days? In 5 days? In 6 days? In 1 week?

Practice

Remind students to show their work for each word problem. Have students complete the problems independently.

Field Trip

Tell students to work the 9 problems and check each sum using manipulatives or by adding up from the bottom of the problem. Tell students that they must be sure of the sum of each problem before completing the puzzle because one wrong number can affect other answers in a puzzle. Help students find the boxes in the puzzle for the Across problems and then the Down problems. Have students complete the puzzle independently.

Extra Credit *Applications*

Have the students make a list of all the occupations they can think of that use measurement: for example dressmaker, carpenter, rug layer, wallpaper hanger, baker, etc. Have them list the types of measuring tools they might use, if they know them, and whether or not they use the metric system. Extend the activity by having students draw a picture of one of these workers doing some measuring.

Adding Money

pages 139-140

Objective

To add money for sums through $1.99

Materials

dollar bill and coins

Mental Math

Ask students if a trade is needed for the following:

1. 7 tens + 2 tens (no)
2. 4 ones + 9 ones (yes)
3. 6 ones + 0 ones (no)
4. 8 tens + 2 tens (yes)
5. 5 tens + 9 tens (yes)
6. 2 ones + 9 ones (yes)
7. 6 tens + 6 tens (yes)
8. 1 one + 8 ones (no)

Skill Review

Show a dollar and ask students to write the amount of money on the board using the cent sign and then using the dollar sign and a decimal point. (100¢, $1.00) Repeat for a half-dollar, quarter, dime, nickel and penny. Now show 2 or 3 coins or a dollar and some coins and have students write the amount 2 ways. Repeat for more amounts of money.

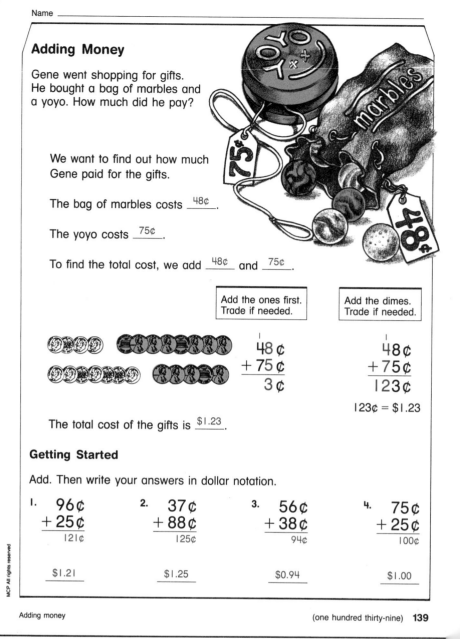

Adding Money

Gene went shopping for gifts. He bought a bag of marbles and a yoyo. How much did he pay?

We want to find out how much Gene paid for the gifts.

The bag of marbles costs __48¢__.

The yoyo costs __75¢__.

To find the total cost, we add __48¢__ and __75¢__.

Add the ones first. Trade if needed.	Add the dimes. Trade if needed.

$$\begin{array}{r} 48\ ¢ \\ +\ 75\ ¢ \\ \hline 3\ ¢ \end{array} \qquad \begin{array}{r} 48\ ¢ \\ +\ 75\ ¢ \\ \hline 123\ ¢ \end{array}$$

123¢ = $1.23

The total cost of the gifts is __$1.23__.

Getting Started

Add. Then write your answers in dollar notation.

1.
$$\begin{array}{r} 96\ ¢ \\ +\ 25\ ¢ \\ \hline 121¢ \end{array}$$
$1.21

2.
$$\begin{array}{r} 37\ ¢ \\ +\ 88\ ¢ \\ \hline 125¢ \end{array}$$
$1.25

3.
$$\begin{array}{r} 56\ ¢ \\ +\ 38\ ¢ \\ \hline 94¢ \end{array}$$
$0.94

4.
$$\begin{array}{r} 75\ ¢ \\ +\ 25\ ¢ \\ \hline 100¢ \end{array}$$
$1.00

Adding money   (one hundred thirty-nine) **139**

Teaching the Lesson

Introducing the Problem Have a student read the problem aloud and tell what is to be found. (how much Gene paid for a bag of marbles and a yoyo) Ask what information is needed. (the cost of each) Ask students where the cost is given. (in the picture) Have students read and complete the information sentences. Work through the model and then have students complete the solution sentence. Have students lay out coins and trade for 1 dollar to check their solution.

Developing the Skill Write **47¢ + 85¢** vertically on the board. Cover the cent signs and remind students that this problem is familiar to them. Have students use coins to show 47¢ and 85¢. Ask how many pennies or ones in all. (12) Ask if 10 pennies can be traded for 1 dime. (yes) Have students make the trade as you record it. Ask how many pennies are left as you record the 2. Have students add the dimes or tens (13) and tell if a trade is needed. (yes) Have

students make the trade as you record it. Ask how many dimes are left as you record the 3. Ask how many dollars or hundreds. (1) Record the 1 and write the cent sign. Have a student tell the amount. (132¢) Tell students this amount can also be written another way as you write **$1.32** on the board. Repeat for other sums with 2, 1 or no trades. Note: Have students record a zero in the dollar place when there are no dollars.

139

Practice

Add. Then write your answers in dollar notation.

1. $\begin{array}{r}30¢\\+30¢\\\hline 60¢\end{array}$ $\underline{\$0.60}$

2. $\begin{array}{r}45¢\\+56¢\\\hline 101¢\end{array}$ $\underline{\$1.01}$

3. $\begin{array}{r}62¢\\+76¢\\\hline 138¢\end{array}$ $\underline{\$1.38}$

4. $\begin{array}{r}79¢\\+75¢\\\hline 154¢\end{array}$ $\underline{\$1.54}$

5. $\begin{array}{r}8¢\\+99¢\\\hline 107¢\end{array}$ $\underline{\$1.07}$

6. $\begin{array}{r}81¢\\+93¢\\\hline 174¢\end{array}$ $\underline{\$1.74}$

7. $\begin{array}{r}84¢\\+68¢\\\hline 152¢\end{array}$ $\underline{\$1.52}$

8. $\begin{array}{r}91¢\\+65¢\\\hline 156¢\end{array}$ $\underline{\$1.56}$

9. $\begin{array}{r}87¢\\+26¢\\\hline 113¢\end{array}$ $\underline{\$1.13}$

10. $\begin{array}{r}58¢\\+82¢\\\hline 140¢\end{array}$ $\underline{\$1.40}$

11. $\begin{array}{r}40¢\\+87¢\\\hline 127¢\end{array}$ $\underline{\$1.27}$

12. $\begin{array}{r}55¢\\+98¢\\\hline 153¢\end{array}$ $\underline{\$1.53}$

13. $\begin{array}{r}90¢\\+71¢\\\hline 161¢\end{array}$ $\underline{\$1.61}$

14. $\begin{array}{r}73¢\\+68¢\\\hline 141¢\end{array}$ $\underline{\$1.41}$

15. $\begin{array}{r}64¢\\+63¢\\\hline 127¢\end{array}$ $\underline{\$1.27}$

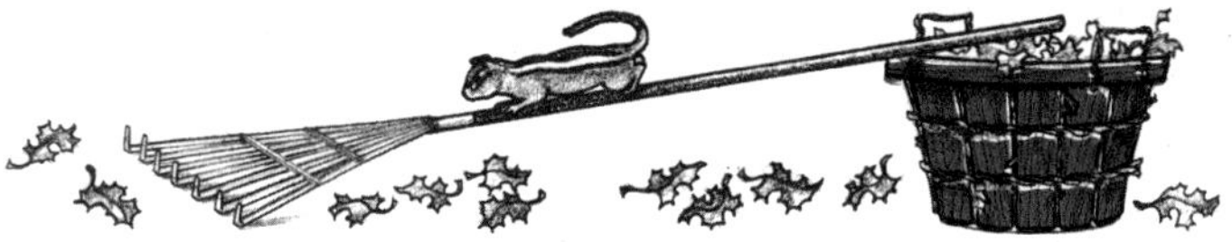

Apply

Solve. Then write your answers in dollar notation.

16. Lu had 50¢. She earned 75¢ raking leaves. How much money does she have now?

$\begin{array}{r}50¢\\+75¢\\\hline 125¢\end{array}$

$\underline{\$1.25}$

17. Walt bought one book for 89¢ and another book for 95¢. How much money did he spend?

$\begin{array}{r}89¢\\+95¢\\\hline 184¢\end{array}$

$\underline{\$1.84}$

Adding money

140

Problem Solving Addition

pages 141-142

Objective

To solve problems using addition of 2 amounts of money less than $1.00

Materials

hundred-flat
ten-strips and ones
dollar and coins

Mental Math

Ask students if each of the following is true or false:

1. 60¢ + 60¢ = $1.20 (T)
2. 6 ones + 7 ones requires a trade (T)
3. 12 tens = 1 hundred (F)
4. 2 quarters = 1 half-dollar (T)
5. $1.25 = 4 quarters (F)
6. 2 half-dollars > 1 dollar (F)

Skill Review

Write **72¢ + 49¢** on the board and have a student find the sum in total pennies and in dollars and cents. (121¢, $1.21) Repeat for the following: 69¢ + 2¢ (71¢, $0.71), 17¢ + 39¢ (56¢, $0.56), 44¢ + 96¢ (140¢, $1.40). Ask students which of the 2 ways should be used for sums over $1.00. (dollar notation)

Name _____

Problem Solving

Solve.

1. 65 girls and 72 boys attended Fun Day. How many children attended Fun Day?

    65
    + 72
    137

    ___137___ children

2. Tim rode the Roller Coaster for 75¢ and the Ferris Wheel for 80¢. How much did he spend?

    75¢
    + 80¢
    155¢

    $1.55

3. Wendy rode the Tilt-A-Whirl for 65¢ and the Hammer for 85¢. How much did both rides cost?

    65¢
    + 85¢
    150¢

    $1.50

4. Bill rode the Merry-Go-Round for 95¢ and the Snake for 55¢. How much money did he spend?

    95¢
    + 55¢
    150¢

    $1.50

5. Read exercise 3 again. What if Wendy rode the Hammer twice? How much would both rides cost?

    $1.70

6. Read exercise 4 again. Which would cost more, a ride on the Merry-Go-Round or two rides on the Snake?

    two rides on the Snake

Problem solving, addition

(one hundred forty-one) **141**

Teaching page 141

Have a student read the first problem aloud and tell what is to be found as you write **What is to be found?** on the board. (the number of children who attended Fun Day) Write the student's response on the board. Ask what information is known as you write **What do we know?** on the board. (There were 65 girls and 72 boys.) Write the student's response. Ask students what they will need to do with the numbers as you write **What needs to be done with the numbers?** on the board. (add) Write **add** on the board. Have a student write 65 + 72 on the board and find the sum. (137) Ask students what trading was needed to find the sum. (10 tens for 1 hundred) Have students read the sum. (one hundred thirty-seven) Tell students that they now need to check their answer to see if it makes sense as you write **Does the answer make sense?** on the board. Tell students to lay out ten-strips and ones to show 65 and 72 and tell the total number of hundreds, tens and ones. (1, 3, 7) Ask students if the sum shown is the same as the sum

they found earlier. (yes) Have students read in unison the questions from the board. Tell students these questions will help them solve each of the word problems on this page. Ask students what they will use to show an answer of a money amount. (dollar sign and decimal point) Assign the page to be completed independently. If necessary, go over each problem orally, having students answer the questions on the board for each problem.

141

Solve.

1. Willie spent 72¢.
   Stan spent 68¢.
   Who spent more
   money?

   _____Willie_____

2. Kiyo rode the Ferris Wheel
   for 80¢ and the Tilt-A-Whirl
   for 65¢. How much money
   did she pay for both?

   $\begin{array}{r} 80¢ \\ + \ 65¢ \\ \hline 145¢ \end{array}$

   _____$1.45_____

3. Read exercise 1 again. Decide if
   both boys together spent more
   or less than $1.50.

   _____less_____

4. Read exercises 1 and 2 again.
   Decide who spent more money,
   Kiyo or the two boys.

   _____Kiyo_____

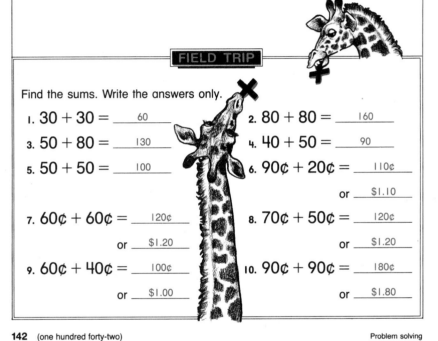

FIELD TRIP

Find the sums. Write the answers only.

1. 30 + 30 = _____60_____

2. 80 + 80 = _____160_____

3. 50 + 80 = _____130_____

4. 40 + 50 = _____90_____

5. 50 + 50 = _____100_____

6. 90¢ + 20¢ = _____110¢_____
   or _____$1.10_____

7. 60¢ + 60¢ = _____120¢_____
   or _____$1.20_____

8. 70¢ + 50¢ = _____120¢_____
   or _____$1.20_____

9. 60¢ + 40¢ = _____100¢_____
   or _____$1.00_____

10. 90¢ + 90¢ = _____180¢_____
    or _____$1.80_____

142 (one hundred forty-two)

Problem solving

Teaching page 142

Remind students to use the questions on the board to help
them solve the word problems. Have students tell what is to
be done with the numbers in problem 4. (subtract) Have
students complete the problems independently.

Field Trip

Write **20 + 30** on the board and tell students to think of the
problem as 2 tens plus 3 tens or 5 tens. Ask students what
number equals 5 tens. (50) Repeat for 60 + 70 (13 tens or
130), 40 + 80 (12 tens or 120) and 90¢ + 40¢ (13 dimes
or 130¢ or $1.30).
Tell students to think of each addend as a number of tens
or dimes and work the problems mentally if possible. Remind students to write each money amount as cents and
then in dollar notation.

Extra Credit   *Creative Drill*

Ask students to be detectives and investigate some missing
numbers. Read the following to the students:

1. We have a missing number. He is even. He has an older
   sister who is four. Can you identify him? (2)
2. A number is missing. It was last seen around the middle
   of the number line. It has five tens, is odd and is smaller
   than 53. Who is it? (51)
3. All cars be on the lookout for a missing number. His
   hundred's place is an even number between 6 and 10.
   His tens place is 7. His ones place is an odd number less
   than three. Who is he? (871)

Review

pages 143-144

Objectives

To review addition of 2-digit numbers with and without trading
To maintain skills learned previously this year

Materials

hundred-flat
ten-strips and ones
dollar and coins

Mental Math

Ask students how many pennies are in:

1. $1.84 (184)
2. 1 dollar and 1 dime (110)
3. 6 dimes and 2 nickels (70)
4. $1.96 (196)
5. 3 quarters (75)
6. 2 dollars (200)
7. $1.92 (192)
8. 1 dollar, 1 quarter and 1 dime (135)

Skill Review

Write **$0.26** on the board. Have a student read the amount. (twenty-six cents) Have a student write the amount using a cent sign. (26¢) Continue to write amounts of money in dollar or cent notation for students to read and then write in the other notation.

CHAPTER CHECKUP

Add. Trade if needed.

1.	2.	3.	4.	5.	6.
83 + 5 88	35 + 9 44	86 + 7 93	80 +50 130	30 +70 100	90 +40 130

7.	8.	9.	10.	11.	12.
57 +31 88	65 +29 94	34 +82 116	76 +77 153	99 +99 198	42 +38 80

13.	14.	15.	16.	17.	18.
16 + 7 23	56 +68 124	30 +80 110	76 +21 97	64 + 4 68	43 +17 60

19.	20.	21.	22.	23.	24.
45 +45 90	59 +84 143	38 +37 75	27 + 9 36	98 + 3 101	75 +83 158

Add. Then write your answers in dollar notation.

25.	26.	27.	28.	29.
68¢ + 7¢ 75¢	70¢ +50¢ 120¢	64¢ +24¢ 88¢	75¢ +18¢ 93¢	96¢ +89¢ 185¢
$0.75	$1.20	$0.88	$0.93	$1.85

Solve.

30. There were 65 girls and 77 boys on the skating rink. How many children were skating?

65
 + 77
 142

___142___ children

31. Cleve has 85¢. Lu Ann has 98¢. How much money do they have in all?

85¢
 + 98¢
 183¢

$1.83

Chapter review   (one hundred forty-three) **143**

Teaching page 143

Have students tell what is to be done in each section. Remind students that in word problems, they should ask what is to be done, what information is known, what operation needs to be done and does the answer make sense. Ask students what problems on this page involve money. Tell students that in some problems they are to write each answer using the cent sign and then write it using the dollar sign and a decimal point. Have students complete the page independently.

ROUNDUP REVIEW

Fill in the oval next to the correct answer.

1	$\begin{array}{r} 8 \\ + 7 \\ \hline \end{array}$	○ 16 ● 15 ○ 14 ○ NG
2	9 + 3	○ 10 ○ 16 ● 12 ○ NG
3	$\begin{array}{r} 15 \\ - 6 \\ \hline \end{array}$	● 9 ○ 7 ○ 6 ○ NG
4	$\begin{array}{r} 13 \\ - 7 \\ \hline \end{array}$	○ 5 ○ 7 ● 6 ○ NG
5	(clock)	○ 3:10 ● 2:15 ○ 2:03 ○ NG
6	(bills and coins)	○ $3.45 ○ $3.35 ● $3.40 ○ NG

7	What is the value of the 6 in 267?	○ hundreds ● tens ○ ones ○ NG
8	What is the value of the 7 in 750?	● hundreds ○ tens ○ ones ○ NG
9	364 ○ 446	○ > ● <
10	$\begin{array}{r} 37 \\ + 58 \\ \hline \end{array}$	○ 94 ○ 85 ● 95 ○ NG
11	$\begin{array}{r} 60 \\ + 60 \\ \hline \end{array}$	○ 12 ○ 102 ○ 130 ● NG
12	$\begin{array}{r} 35 \\ + 7 \\ \hline \end{array}$	● 42 ○ 32 ○ 47 ○ NG
13	$\begin{array}{r} 75 \\ + 88 \\ \hline \end{array}$	○ 153 ○ 165 ● 163 ○ NG

[ ] score

Cumulative review

Teaching page 144

This page reviews addition and subtraction facts, place value, time, money and addition with carrying. Tell students to solve each problem and then find the answer in the 4 choices to the right. Tell students to fill in the oval beside the correct answer. Tell students the NG means the answer is not given and they only mark that oval if none of the answers is the correct one. Help students complete the first problem before assigning the page to be completed independently.

144

2-digit Subtraction

pages 145-146

Objective

To subtract any two 2-digit numbers with no trading

Materials

*subtraction fact cards
ten-strips and ones

Mental Math

Ask if the following amounts are greater or less than $1.00:

1. 60¢ + 30¢ (less)
2. 75¢ + 50¢ (greater)
3. 4 dimes and 1 half-dollar (less)
4. 2 half-dollars and 1 dime (greater)
5. 6 quarters (greater)
6. 90¢ + 20¢ (greater)

Skill Review

Write the numbers 0 through 9 across the board. Give a subtraction fact card to a student to place on the chalk tray under the number which tells its answer. Have other students tell if the fact is correctly placed. Repeat until all facts have been placed on the chalk tray.

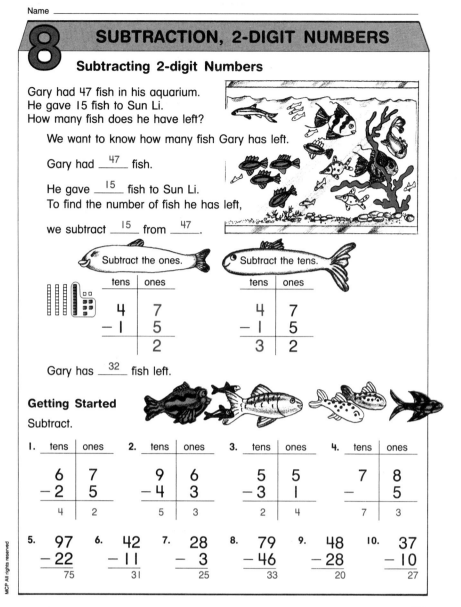

8 SUBTRACTION, 2-DIGIT NUMBERS

Subtracting 2-digit Numbers

Gary had 47 fish in his aquarium.
He gave 15 fish to Sun Li.
How many fish does he have left?

We want to know how many fish Gary has left.

Gary had __47__ fish.

He gave __15__ fish to Sun Li.
To find the number of fish he has left,

we subtract __15__ from __47__.

Subtract the ones.

tens	ones
4	7
− 1	5
	2

Subtract the tens.

tens	ones
4	7
− 1	5
3	2

Gary has __32__ fish left.

Getting Started

Subtract.

	tens	ones		tens	ones		tens	ones		tens	ones
1.	6	7	2.	9	6	3.	5	5	4.	7	8
	− 2	5		− 4	3		− 3	1		−	5
	4	2		5	3		2	4		7	3

5.	97	6.	42	7.	28	8.	79	9.	48	10.	37
	−22		−11		− 3		−46		−28		−10
	75		31		25		33		20		27

Subtracting 2-digit numbers, no trading   (one hundred forty-five) **145**

Teaching the Lesson

Introducing the Problem Have a student read the problem aloud and tell what is to be solved. (how many fish Gary has left) Ask students what information is given. (He had 47 fish and gave 15 fish away.) Ask what operation needs to be used to solve the problem. (subtraction) Have students read and complete the information sentences. Work through the model with the students and then have them complete the solution sentence.

Developing the Skill Write on the board:

tens	ones
8	9
− 4	5
(4)	(4)

Have a student subtract 5 ones from 9 ones and write the number left. (4) Have a student subtract 4 tens from 8 tens and write the number left. (4) Have students read the number. (forty-four) Repeat for 76 − 46 (30), 99 − 66 (33), 87 − 12 (75), 42 − 30 (12), and 79 − 25 (54), using a tens and ones grid. Erase all work from the board and work similar problems using no grid. Have students tell the number of tens and ones in each answer.

145

Practice

Subtract.

	tens	ones		tens	ones		tens	ones		tens	ones
1.	8	3	2.	5	7	3.	6	8	4.	2	9
	−2	1		−4	1		−6	4		−	9
	6	2		1	6			4		2	0

5.	78 −52	6.	35 − 2	7.	46 −22	8.	99 − 4	9.	76 − 6	10.	87 −83
	26		33		24		95		70		4

11.	47 −31	12.	75 −55	13.	18 − 7	14.	88 −46	15.	36 −26	16.	50 −20
	16		20		11		42		10		30

17.	56 −54	18.	22 − 1	19.	77 −50	20.	96 −36	21.	49 − 2	22.	58 −30
	2		21		27		60		47		28

Apply

Solve.

23. At the bake sale they sold 48 blueberry muffins and 36 bran muffins. How many more blueberry muffins were sold?

48
− 36
12

___12___ blueberry muffins

24. The sale started with 28 loaves of bread. They had 5 left. How many loaves of bread were sold?

28
− 5
23

___23___ loaves

146 (one hundred forty-six)　　　　　　　　Subtracting 2-digit numbers, no trading

---

146

Subtraction with Trading

pages 147-148

Objective

To subtract a 1-digit number from a 2-digit number with some trading

Materials

*subtraction fact cards
ten-strips and ones

Mental Math

Tell students to skip 2 numbers and say the next number:

1. 48 (51)
2. 761 (764)
3. 115 (118)
4. 0 (3)
5. 398 (401)
6. 969 (972)
7. 83 (86)
8. 500 (503)

Skill Review

Show students a subtraction fact card such as 15 − 8 and have students give the difference. (7) Ask students to give 3 related facts for 15 − 8. (8 + 7, 7 + 8 and 15 − 7) Write all 4 facts on the board and have students write the answers. Repeat for 17 − 9, 16 − 8, etc.

Trading a Ten to Subtract

The pet store had 34 puppies for sale. They sold 8 puppies. How many are left?

We want to know how many puppies are left?

There are __34__ puppies for sale.

The store sold __8__ puppies. To find out how many are left,

we subtract __8__ from __34__.

✔ Subtract the ones first.

Do you need more ones?	Trade 1 ten to get 10 ones.	Subtract the ones.	Subtract the tens.
4 − 8 = ? Yes, you need more ones.	Now there are 2 tens and 14 ones.	14 − 8 = 6	2 − 0 = 2

tens	ones
3	4
−	8
	?

→

tens	ones
³2̸	¹⁴4̸
−	8
	6

tens	ones
²3̸	¹⁴4̸
−	8
2	6

The pet store has __26__ puppies left.

Getting Started

Do you need more ones? Circle Yes or No. Then subtract and trade if needed.

1.
tens	ones	
5	6	(Yes)
−	9	No
4	7	

2.
tens	ones	
2	2	(Yes)
−	8	No
1	4	

3.
tens	ones	
6	8	Yes
−	7	(No)
6	1	

Trading 1 ten for 10 ones to subtract   (one hundred forty-seven) **147**

Teaching the Lesson

Introducing the Problem Have a student read the problem aloud and tell what is to be solved. (how many puppies are left in the store) Ask students what facts are known. (There were 34 and 8 were sold.) Ask students what operation needs to be used to find the number left. (subtraction) Have students read and complete the information sentences. Work through the model with students and then have them complete the solution sentence.

Developing the Skill Write on the board:

tens	ones
(8)	(17)
9	7
−	8
(8)	(9)

Ask students if 8 ones can be taken from 7 ones. (no) Tell students that to get more ones we can trade a ten for 10 ones. Show the trade and ask students if 8 ones can be taken from 17 ones. (yes) Have a student write the number of ones left. (9) Ask students how many tens. (8) Have students read the number that is left when 8 is subtracted from 97. (eighty-nine) Repeat for 46 − 8 (34), 72 − 6 (66), 34 − 7 (27), 96 − 8 (88) and 55 − 9 (46).

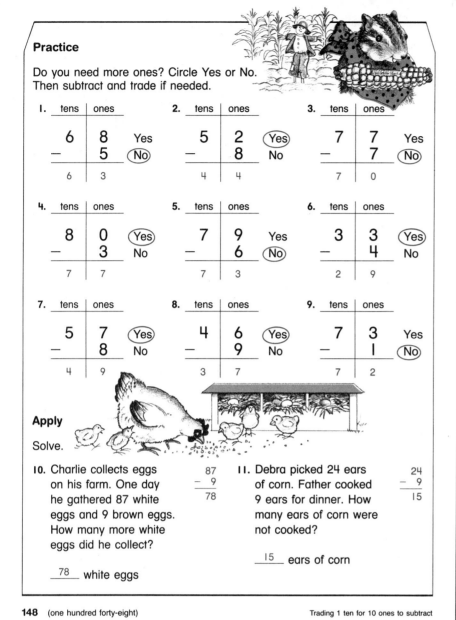

Practice

Do you need more ones? Circle Yes or No.
Then subtract and trade if needed.

1.

tens	ones
6	8
−	5
6	3

Yes
(No)

2.

tens	ones
5	2
−	8
4	4

(Yes)
No

3.

tens	ones
7	7
−	7
7	0

Yes
(No)

4.

tens	ones
8	0
−	3
7	7

(Yes)
No

5.

tens	ones
7	9
−	6
7	3

Yes
(No)

6.

tens	ones
3	3
−	4
2	9

(Yes)
No

7.

tens	ones
5	7
−	8
4	9

(Yes)
No

8.

tens	ones
4	6
−	9
3	7

(Yes)
No

9.

tens	ones
7	3
−	1
7	2

Yes
(No)

Apply

Solve.

10. Charlie collects eggs on his farm. One day he gathered 87 white eggs and 9 brown eggs. How many more white eggs did he collect?

```
  87
-  9
  78
```

__78__ white eggs

11. Debra picked 24 ears of corn. Father cooked 9 ears for dinner. How many ears of corn were not cooked?

```
  24
-  9
  15
```

__15__ ears of corn

Trading 1 ten for 10 ones to subtract

Correcting Common Errors

Some students may forget to decrease the tens by one when they are trading. Have them work with partners to rewrite problems such as the following with one less ten and ten more ones.

6 tens 4 ones (5 tens 14 ones)
3 tens 7 ones (2 tens 17 ones)
2 tens 2 ones (1 ten 12 ones)
5 tens 4 ones (4 tens 14 ones)
8 tens 1 one (7 tens 11 ones)
4 tens 0 ones (3 tens 10 ones)

They can model these problems with ten-strips and ones to demonstrate why the tens are reduced by one.

Enrichment

Tell students to write and solve a problem to find how many hours are left in the day when 8 hours have passed since midnight. Have them work another problem which tells how many hours are left when 6 hours have passed since midnight.

Practice

Tell students to circle the word yes or no to tell if more ones are needed. Tell students to then solve each problem independently. Remind students to decide what operation to use when solving the word problems.

Mixed Practice

1. 9 + 5 (14)
2. 2 + ___ = 9 (7)
3. 12¢ − 7¢ (5¢)
4. 10 + 3 (13)
5. 6 − 0 (6)
6. 6¢ + 2¢ (8¢)
7. 2 − 1 (1)
8. 10 + 7 (17)
9. 6 + ___ = 12 (6)
10. 6 + 9 (15)

Extra Credit *Logic*

Duplicate the following math riddle or write on the board:

How can a cat go into a basement with 4 feet, and come out with 8 feet? (by catching a mouse)

2-digit Subtraction

pages 149-150

Objective

To subtract a 2-digit number from a 2-digit number with some trading

Materials

*tens jar and ones jar
*large and small paper clips
ten-strips and ones

Mental Math

Tell students to name the following numbers:

1. 72 + 6 (78)
2. 90 − 10 − 10 (70)
3. 25¢ + 25¢ + 25¢ (75¢)
4. $1.40 + 1 nickel ($1.45)
5. $1.00 + 25¢ − 10¢ ($1.15)
6. 40 + 50 + 20 (110)
7. 91 − 2 (89)
8. 2 nickels + 6 dimes + 2 quarters ($1.20)

Skill Review

Write various problems of 2-digit numbers minus 1-digit numbers on the board and have students tell if trading is needed in each. Then have students write similar problems on the board for classmates to tell if trading is needed.

Subtracting 2-digit Numbers

Annie collects stuffed animals. She must take 17 of them to school for a display. How many are left at home?

We want to know how many animals she left at home.

Annie has __36__ stuffed animals.

She is taking __17__ animals to school. To find how many animals she left at home, we subtract __17__ from __36__.

✔ Subtract the ones first.

Do you need more ones?	Trade 1 ten to get 10 ones.	Subtract the ones.	Subtract the tens.
6 − 7 = ? Yes, you need more ones.	Now there are 2 tens and 16 ones.	16 − 7 = 9	2 − 1 = 1

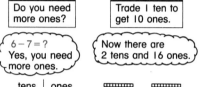

tens	ones
3	6
− 1	7
	?

tens	ones
³3	¹⁶6̸
− 1	7
	9

tens	ones
²3̸	¹⁶6̸
− 1	7
1	9

Annie left __19__ stuffed animals at home.

Getting Started

Subtract. Trade if needed.

1. tens	ones		2. tens	ones		3. tens	ones		4. tens	ones
9	3		6	2		8	4		8	8
− 5	9		− 3	6		− 2	9		− 1	8
3	4		2	6		5	5		7	0

Subtracting 2-digit numbers, with trading

(one hundred forty-nine) **149**

Teaching the Lesson

Introducing the Problem Have a student read the problem aloud and tell what is to be solved. (how many animals were left at home) Ask students what facts are given in the problem. (Annie took 17 to school.) Ask what information is not given in the problem. (number of animals in all) Have students study the picture, count by tens and count on to find how many animals Annie had in all. (36) Have students read and complete the information sentences. Work through the model with students and then have them complete the solution sentence. Now have students cross out 17 of the animals and count the remaining ones to check their solution.

Developing the Skill Have students lay out ten-strips and ones to show 45. Write on the board:

tens	ones
(3)	(15)
4	5
− 2	8
(1)	(7)

Ask if more ones are needed to subtract the 8 ones. (yes) Work through the trade with the students and record it on the board. Have students read the answer (17) and then tell the answer in tens and ones. (1,7) Repeat the procedure for 92 − 26 (66), 78 − 46 (32), 43 − 19 (24) and 61 − 39. (22)

149

Practice

Subtract. Trade if needed.

1.	tens	ones
	5	7
−	2	3
	3	4

2.	tens	ones
	8	0
−	3	0
	5	0

3.	tens	ones
	8	1
−	1	2
	6	9

4.	tens	ones
	4	2
−	1	7
	2	5

5.	tens	ones
	8	3
−	5	5
	2	8

6.	tens	ones
	5	0
−	2	9
	2	1

7.	tens	ones
	9	0
−	2	0
	7	0

8.	tens	ones
	7	5
−	4	5
	3	0

9.	tens	ones
	5	5
−		6
	4	9

10.	tens	ones
	7	9
−	3	0
	4	9

11.	tens	ones
	9	6
−	3	8
	5	8

12.	tens	ones
	6	7
−	4	9
	1	8

FIELD TRIP

Stacey has 15¢. How many pennies, nickels, and dimes would make 15¢ if she had:

1. 2 coins   1 dime, 1 nickel

2. 3 coins   3 nickels

3. 6 coins   1 dime, 5 pennies

4. 7 coins   2 nickels, 5 pennies

150 (one hundred fifty)   Subtracting 2-digit numbers, with trading

Correcting Common Errors

Some students may not trade when necessary but subtract the lesser digit from the greater digit.

INCORRECT	CORRECT
	1 13
23	23
− 8	− 8
25	15

Correct by having students work with partners and place-value materials to model each problem.

Enrichment

Tell students to write and solve a problem to find the number of minutes before 3:00 if it is 15 minutes after 2 o'clock.

Practice

Remind students to first see if a trade is needed to subtract the ones. Tell students that some problems on this page do not need a trade. Have students complete the problems independently.

Field Trip

Ask students to lay out 2 coins to equal 2¢. (2 pennies) Tell students to now lay out 2 coins to equal 10¢. (2 nickels) Continue for 2 coins to equal 50¢ (2 quarters), 3 coins to equal 60¢ (2 quarters 1 dime) and 4 coins to equal 20¢. (4 nickels)

Have a student read the problem and tell what is to be done. (find ways to make 15¢ using pennies, nickels and dimes) Help students complete the first problem, and assign the remaining problems.

Extra Credit   *Creative Drill*

Duplicate or write on the board the following puzzle.

1. (_ _ _ _ _ _)
   —
4. (_   2. (_ _ _ _ _ _ _ _ _)
   —
3. (_ _ _ _ _ _ _ _ _ _)
   —
   —
   _)

ACROSS

1. ☐ ◯ △ ▭   are all called (shapes).
2. What figure can you make with three toothpicks (triangle)?
3. The door is shaped like a (rectangle).

DOWN
1. A saltine cracker is usually in the shape of a (square).
4. A shape without any straight sides is the (circle).

More 2-digit Subtraction

pages 151-152

Objective

To subtract 2-digit numbers with some trading

Materials

*2 tens and 2 ones jars
*large and small paper clips
ten-strips and ones

Mental Math

Have students name the number that comes:

1. next after 14, 16, 18. (20)
2. before 10 tens. (99)
3. after 299. (300)
4. between 462 and 464. (463)
5. before 1,000. (999)
6. after 7 hundreds. (701)
7. before 8 hundreds 2 ones. (801)

Skill Review

Have students turn to page 67 in any book that has at least 100 pages. Ask students how many pages there are from page 67 to page 90. Have a student write $90 - 67$ on the board and solve the problem. (23) Continue the activity to find the number of pages from 26 to 82 (56), 16 to 41 (25), 48 to 99 (51) and 53 to 82 (29).

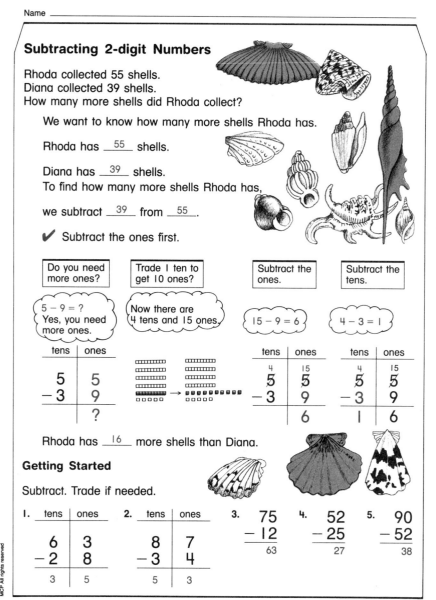

Subtracting 2-digit Numbers

Rhoda collected 55 shells.
Diana collected 39 shells.
How many more shells did Rhoda collect?

We want to know how many more shells Rhoda has.

Rhoda has __55__ shells.

Diana has __39__ shells.
To find how many more shells Rhoda has,

we subtract __39__ from __55__.

✔ Subtract the ones first.

Do you need more ones?	Trade 1 ten to get 10 ones?	Subtract the ones.	Subtract the tens.

$5 - 9 = ?$ Yes, you need more ones.

Now there are 4 tens and 15 ones.

$15 - 9 = 6$

$4 - 3 = 1$

tens	ones
5	5
−3	9
	?

tens	ones
4 / 5	15 / 5
−3	9
	6

tens	ones
4 / 5	15 / 5
−3	9
1	6

Rhoda has __16__ more shells than Diana.

Getting Started

Subtract. Trade if needed.

1.
tens	ones
6	3
−2	8
3	5

2.
tens	ones
8	7
−3	4
5	3

3. $\begin{array}{r} 75 \\ -12 \\ \hline 63 \end{array}$

4. $\begin{array}{r} 52 \\ -25 \\ \hline 27 \end{array}$

5. $\begin{array}{r} 90 \\ -52 \\ \hline 38 \end{array}$

Subtracting 2-digit numbers, with trading

(one hundred fifty-one) **151**

Teaching the Lesson

Introducing the Problem Have a student read the problem aloud and tell what is to be found. (how many more shells Rhoda collected) Ask students what information is given. (Rhoda collected 55 shells and Diana collected 39.) Have students read and complete the information sentences. Work through the model with students and then have them complete the solution statement. Have students lay out ten-strips and ones to check their solution.

Developing the Skill Have a student place large and small paper clips in the tens and ones jars to show 46. (4 large, 6 small) Have a student place clips in another set of jars to show 29. (2 large, 9 small) Tell students to find how many more are in the first student's jars than in the second student's jars. Write **46 − 29** on the board. Tell students to remove clips from the first student's jars until there are 29 left and then see how many were removed. Tell students we know there are going to be 9 small clips left and since we

only have 6 ones, a ten must be traded. Help students trade 1 large clip for 10 small clips and complete the problem. Ask how many more clips were in the first student's jars. (17) Show the trade on the board and talk through the subtraction to show 17 as the difference. Repeat the activity for $77 - 48$ (29), $52 - 28$ (24), $39 - 16$ (23), $82 - 57$ (25) and $41 - 12$ (29).

151

Practice

Subtract. Trade if needed.

1.	tens	ones
	6	8
−	2	3
	4	5

2.	tens	ones
	7	1
−	3	9
	3	2

3.	tens	ones
	5	2
−	2	6
	2	6

4.	tens	ones
	8	5
−	2	5
	6	0

5.
$$57 - 23 = 34$$

6.
$$75 - 29 = 46$$

7.
$$53 - 46 = 7$$

8.
$$79 - 30 = 49$$

9.
$$50 - 8 = 42$$

10.
$$32 - 18 = 14$$

11.
$$73 - 50 = 23$$

12.
$$57 - 45 = 12$$

13.
$$81 - 15 = 66$$

14.
$$77 - 39 = 38$$

15.
$$31 - 17 = 14$$

16.
$$64 - 9 = 55$$

17.
$$83 - 33 = 50$$

18.
$$61 - 34 = 27$$

19.
$$60 - 20 = 40$$

20.
$$77 - 18 = 59$$

21.
$$82 - 55 = 27$$

22.
$$53 - 47 = 6$$

Apply

Solve.

23. Martha had 80¢.
She lost 35¢.
How much was left?

$$80¢ - 35¢ = 45¢$$

45¢

24. Allan earned 68¢ on
Friday. He earned 25¢ on
Saturday. How much
money does
he have now?

$$68¢ + 25¢ = 93¢$$

93¢

Subtracting 2-digit numbers, with trading

Correcting Common Errors

Watch for students who reduce the tens digit by one even though they do not need to trade.

INCORRECT	CORRECT
4	
59	59
−32	−32
17	27

Correct by having students use place-value materials to model the problem.

Enrichment

Tell students to write and solve a problem to find out how many dimes they would have left from 8 dimes and 4 pennies if they gave 26¢ to a friend. (5 dimes)

Practice

Remind students that in the subtraction problems, they must first decide if a trade for more ones is needed. Tell students they will need to decide if addition or subtraction is needed in each of the word problems. Have students complete the page independently.

Mixed Practice

1. 14 − 8 (6)
2. 10¢ − 6¢ (4¢)
3. 8¢ + 1¢ (9¢)
4. 6 + ___ = 7 (1)
5. 13 − 7 (6)
6. 9¢ + 6¢ (15¢)
7. 14 − 7 (7)
8. 8 + 5 (13)
9. 11 − 8 (3)
10. 9¢ − 4¢ (5¢)

Extra Credit   *Applications*

Have students make a list of some common math skills such as counting, measuring, adding, subtracting, telling time, etc. Tell students to make a second list of occupations that would use some of these skills. From that list, choose one occupation students are most interested in. Have the class write an invitation to someone in your community having that occupation, to come to speak to your class about the math skills they use in their job. Discuss the importance of developing our individual math skills for use now and in the future.

More 2-digit Subtraction

pages 153-154

Objective

To subtract 2-digit numbers with some trading

Materials

*colored chalk
ten-strips and ones

Mental Math

Ask students if a trade is needed for the following:

1. 62 − 46 (yes)
2. 50 − 41 (yes)
3. 29 − 2 (no)
4. 68 − 59 (yes)
5. 21 − 6 (yes)
6. 82 − 30 (yes)
7. 53 − 12 (no)
8. 91 − 46 (yes)

Skill Review

Write **2 tens 8 ones** on the board and have students tell all the numbers of ones which can be subtracted from 8 ones without requiring a trade. (0 through 8) Repeat for 6 ones, 2 ones, 7 ones, 5 ones, 9 ones.

Subtracting 2-digit Numbers

Chip has fun riding his bike.
How many more blocks did he ride the first week than the second week?

CHIP
1st week   61 Blocks
2nd week   43 Blocks
3rd week   63 Blocks

We want to know how many more blocks he rode his bike the first week than the second week.

Chip rode his bike __61__ blocks the first week.

He rode his bike __43__ blocks the second week.
To find how many more blocks he rode his bike the

first week than the second week, we subtract __43__ from __61__.

✔ Remember to subtract the ones first.

Subtract the ones. Trade if needed.	Subtract the tens.
$\begin{array}{r} \overset{5}{\cancel{6}}\ \overset{11}{\cancel{1}} \\ -\ 4\ 3 \\ \hline 8 \end{array}$	$\begin{array}{r} \overset{5}{\cancel{6}}\ \overset{11}{\cancel{1}} \\ -\ 4\ 3 \\ \hline 1\ 8 \end{array}$

Chip rode his bike __18__ more blocks the first week than the second week.

Getting Started

Subtract. Trade if needed.

1. 90 −49	2. 87 −23	3. 45 −18	4. 67 −47	5. 54 −39	6. 90 −40
41	64	27	20	15	50

Subtracting 2-digit numbers, with trading   (one hundred fifty-three) **153**

Teaching the Lesson

Introducing the Problem   Have a student read the problem aloud and tell what is to be found. (how many more blocks Chip rode the first week than he rode the second week) Ask students what information is needed. (the number of blocks Chip rode each week) Ask students if any unnecessary information is given. (yes) Have students tell which information is needed. (61 blocks the first week and 43 blocks the second week) Have students read and complete the information sentences. Work through the model with students and then have them complete the solution sentence. Have students use ten-strips and ones to check their solution.

Developing the Skill   Tell students there were 45 guests at one party and 16 guests at another. We want to know how many more guests were at the first party. Ask students if we need to add or subtract. (subtract) Write **45 − 16** on the board. Use colored chalk to show the trade of 1 ten for 10 ones. Show that 4 tens 5 ones is renamed as 3 tens 15 ones. Have a student use regular chalk to solve the problem (29) Have students use colored chalk to show any trades before other students use regular chalk to solve the following problems on the board: 73 − 46 (27), 69 − 45 (24), 71 − 28 (43), 67 − 39 (28), 92 − 45 (47), 55 − 18 (37).

Practice

Subtract. Trade if needed.

1. 90 − 50 40	2. 65 − 35 30	3. 73 − 40 33	4. 65 − 9 56	5. 51 − 27 24	6. 86 − 28 58
7. 75 − 41 34	8. 48 − 24 24	9. 34 − 17 17	10. 56 − 37 19	11. 83 − 55 28	12. 51 − 19 32
13. 62 − 28 34	14. 97 − 65 32	15. 80 − 52 28	16. 45 − 25 20	17. 37 − 18 19	18. 64 − 57 7
19. 83 − 48 35	20. 77 − 56 21	21. 44 − 14 30	22. 32 − 16 16	23. 58 − 25 33	24. 33 − 18 15

Apply

Solve.

25. There are 35 bikes in the race. 17 bikes get flat tires. How many bikes did not get flat tires?

   35
   − 17
   18

   __18__ bikes

26. There were 25 prizes given. 19 got bike lights. How many children got other prizes?

   25
   − 19
   6

   __6__ children

Subtracting 2-digit numbers, with trading

Correcting Common Errors

Watch for students who simply bring down the number that is being subtracted when there is a zero in the minuend.

INCORRECT	CORRECT
	7 10
80	80
−34	−34
54	46

Have these students work with partners using place-value materials to model problems such as 30 − 12 and 40 − 28.

Enrichment

Ask students to find out how many more horses can be boarded on a farm which has barns with 16, 28 and 10 stalls than on a neighboring farm which has only 27 stalls in all. (27)

Practice

Remind students that trading is not needed in some of the problems on this page. Have students complete the page independently.

Mixed Practice

1. 11 − 2 (9)
2. 5 + 10 (15)
3. 10 − 7 (3)
4. 3¢ + 8¢ (11¢)
5. 10 + 9 (19)
6. ___ + 1 = 4 (3)
7. 7 − 4 (3)
8. 9¢ − 2¢ (7¢)
9. 12 − 4 (8)
10. 8 + 9 (17)

Extra Credit   *Probability*

Give each student 2 pennies and a piece of paper. Ask a student to explain all the possible ways the two coins could land if they are flipped at the same time. (head, tail; head, head; and tail, tail) Tell the class to toss the two coins together a total of 10 times, and mark each combination that turns up on a chart. Before they begin, ask them to guess how many of each combination they will get, writing their guess on paper.

	guess	actual
head/tail		
head/head		
tail/tail		

Give them time to try the experiment and to record their results.

Checking Subtraction

pages 155-156

Objective

To check subtraction by adding

Materials

*subtraction fact cards
ten-strips and ones

Mental Math

Have students name the number if
they start at:

1. 3, add 4, add 6 (13)
2. 8, add 7, subtract 7 (8)
3. 15, subtract 6, add 9 (18)
4. 12, add 2, subtract 7 (7)
5. 20, subtract 4, add 2 (18)
6. 32, subtract 12, add 4 (24)
7. 2, add 15, subtract 9 (8)
8. 26, subtract 14, add 0 (12)

Skill Review

Show the fact 15 − 6 and have students write the related facts on the
board. (15 − 9, 9 + 6, 6 + 9) Repeat
for other subtraction facts.

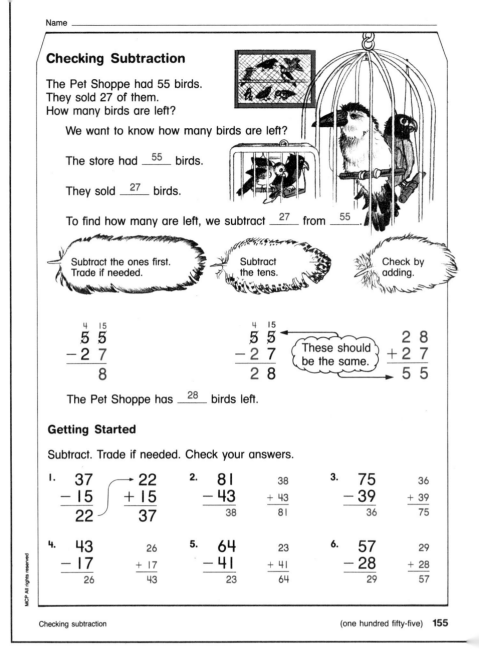

Checking subtraction

(one hundred fifty-five) **155**

Teaching the Lesson

Introducing the Problem Have a student read the
problem aloud and tell what is to be solved. (how many
birds are left) Ask students what information is given. (There
were 55 birds and 27 were sold.) Have students read and
complete the information sentences. Work through the
model with students emphasizing the checking procedure.
Then have students complete the solution sentence.

Developing the Skill Have students lay out 4 tens 3
ones. Tell students to take 2 tens 9 ones away as you write
43 − 29 on the board. Ask students the number left. (14)
Tell students the solution can be checked by adding 14 and
29. Write **14 + 29** on the board. Have students add and
tell the sum. (43) Ask students if the sum of the addition
problem is the same as the minuend in the subtraction
problem. (yes) Circle the 43 in each problem on the board
and connect the circles with a line. Tell students that if the
sum is the same as the minuend in the subtraction problem,

then the answer is correct. Tell students that if the sum of
the addition problem had not been 43, then we would
know an error had been made. Explain that this is a good
way to check their work in a subtraction problem. Repeat
the procedure for 88 − 26 (62), 29 − 12 (17), 77 − 48 (29)
and 90 − 66 (24). Ask students if an error has been made
as each problem is checked by adding.

155

Subtract. Trade if needed. Check your answers.

1.	75	50	2.	61	34	3.	38	25
	−25	+25		−27	+27		−13	+13
	50	75		34	61		25	38

4.	53	17	5.	85	26	6.	67	28
	−36	+36		−59	+59		−39	+39
	17	53		26	85		28	67

7.	42	27	8.	95	37	9.	51	8
	−15	+15		−58	+58		−43	+43
	27	42		37	95		8	51

10.	99	30	11.	64	39	12.	77	29
	−69	+69		−25	+25		−48	+48
	30	99		39	64		29	77

FIELD TRIP

Solve.

1. Subtract two numbers. One number is 25. The answer is 50. What is the other number?

50
+ 25
75

75

2. Subtract two numbers. The greater number is 60. The answer is 45. What is the other number?

60
− 45
15

15

Checking subtraction

Correcting Common Errors

Some students may add the answer to the minuend when they are checking subtraction. Correct by having them check using the form shown at the right where there is no need to recopy any numbers

46
−29
+17
46

Enrichment

Have students write and solve a problem which will show that an error was made when 29 was subtracted from 72 for a difference of 45. Tell them to correct the subtraction problem and then show their work to prove the solution is error-free.

Practice

Remind students to show the work that checks each answer. Have students complete the problems independently.

Field Trip

This exercise requires students to think of addition as a method of checking subtraction. Tell students that you are thinking of a number that, when added to 4, the sum will be 13. Write **4 + ___ = 13** and **13 − 4 =** on the board. Have students complete the sentences. (9) Ask students to name a number if the difference of that number and 70 is 30. Help students write 70 − ___ = 30 on the board. Have students solve the problem. (40) Have students work through each problem to find its missing number.

Extra Credit   *Creative Drill*

Tape 18-inch squares of heavy paper next to each other on the floor around the room, to resemble a gameboard. Mark the first square start. Have students write addition or subtraction math problems using 2-digit numbers less than 40 each on a separate card. Select a small group of students to play the first game. The first student selects a card and solves the problem. Starting at the marked square, the student walks the number of squares that are equivalent to the answer counting out loud. If a student answers incorrectly, he must sit down. Continue with each student in the group until one student passes the starting point. Each time a student passes the starting square, they choose another student to take their place. Continue playing until everyone has had a turn on the giant gameboard.

Subtracting Money

pages 157-158

Objective

To subtract 2-digit money amounts

Materials

dimes and pennies
ten-strips and ones

Mental Math

Tell students to rename the quantity to
show a trade of 1 ten for 10 ones in
the following:

1. 6 tens 4 ones. (5 tens 14 ones)
2. 9 tens 8 ones. (8 tens 18 ones)
3. 7 tens 0 ones. (6 tens 10 ones)
4. 2 tens 4 ones. (1 ten 14 ones)
5. 1 ten 6 ones. (0 tens 16 ones)
6. 9 tens 0 ones. (8 tens 10 ones)
7. 2 tens 1 one. (1 ten 11 ones)

Skill Review

Write **46 − 12** on the board. Have a
student solve the problem and check
the solution. (34, 34 + 12 = 46) Repeat for 70 − 16 (54), 58 − 19 (39),
44 − 17 (27), 36 − 24 (12) and 85 −
67 (18).

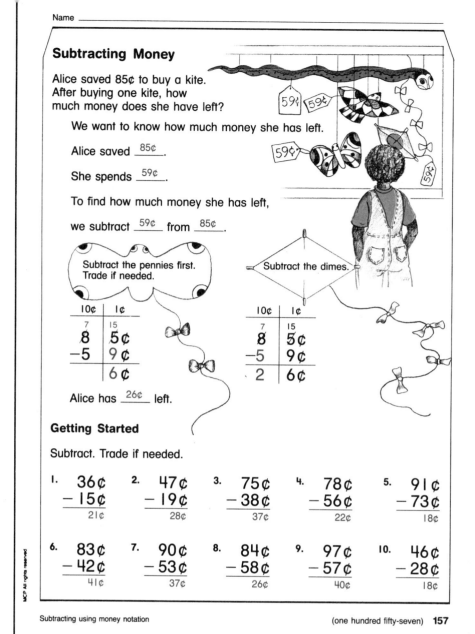

Subtracting Money

Alice saved 85¢ to buy a kite.
After buying one kite, how
much money does she have left?

We want to know how much money she has left.

Alice saved __85¢__.

She spends __59¢__.

To find how much money she has left,

we subtract __59¢__ from __85¢__.

Subtract the pennies first.
Trade if needed.

10¢	1¢
7 8	15 5¢
−5	9 ¢
	6 ¢

Subtract the dimes.

10¢	1¢
7 8	15 5¢
−5	9¢
2	6¢

Alice has __26¢__ left.

Getting Started

Subtract. Trade if needed.

1. 36¢ − 15¢ = 21¢
2. 47¢ − 19¢ = 28¢
3. 75¢ − 38¢ = 37¢
4. 78¢ − 56¢ = 22¢
5. 91¢ − 73¢ = 18¢

6. 83¢ − 42¢ = 41¢
7. 90¢ − 53¢ = 37¢
8. 84¢ − 58¢ = 26¢
9. 97¢ − 57¢ = 40¢
10. 46¢ − 28¢ = 18¢

Subtracting using money notation

(one hundred fifty-seven) **157**

Teaching the Lesson

Introducing the Problem Have a student read the
problem aloud and tell what is to be solved. (find the
amount of money Alice has left after buying a kite) Ask students what information is given in the problem. (Alice had
85¢.) Ask what information is needed yet. (the cost of the
kite) Ask students to use the picture to tell the cost of the
kite. (59¢) Have students read and complete the information
sentences. Work through the model with students and then
have them complete the solution sentence. Ask students
how the solution to this subtraction problem can be
checked. (add the solution and the money spent) Have students check by adding.

Developing the Skill Have student lay out 75 in ten-
strips and ones and 75¢ in dimes and pennies. Ask students
the number of ten-strips and dimes. (7) Ask how many ones
and pennies. (5) Tell students to take 4 tens and 8 ones
and 4 dimes and 8 pennies away and tell how many are
left. (2 tens and 7 ones, 2 dimes and 7 pennies) Remind
students that the problems are the same but money notation
is used in one problem. Write **75 − 48** and **75¢ − 48¢** on
the board. Have a student solve each problem on the board
(27, 27¢) Now have a student check each problem by adding. (27 + 48 = 75, 27¢ + 48¢ = 75¢) Repeat for more
subtraction problems using money.

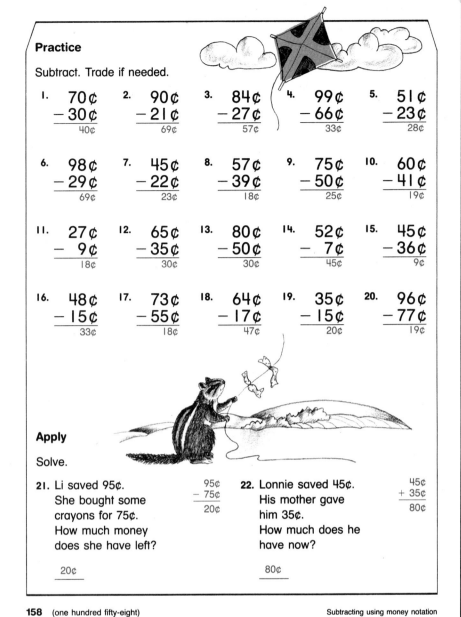

Practice

Subtract. Trade if needed.

1. $\begin{array}{r} 70¢ \\ -30¢ \\ \hline 40¢ \end{array}$
2. $\begin{array}{r} 90¢ \\ -21¢ \\ \hline 69¢ \end{array}$
3. $\begin{array}{r} 84¢ \\ -27¢ \\ \hline 57¢ \end{array}$
4. $\begin{array}{r} 99¢ \\ -66¢ \\ \hline 33¢ \end{array}$
5. $\begin{array}{r} 51¢ \\ -23¢ \\ \hline 28¢ \end{array}$

6. $\begin{array}{r} 98¢ \\ -29¢ \\ \hline 69¢ \end{array}$
7. $\begin{array}{r} 45¢ \\ -22¢ \\ \hline 23¢ \end{array}$
8. $\begin{array}{r} 57¢ \\ -39¢ \\ \hline 18¢ \end{array}$
9. $\begin{array}{r} 75¢ \\ -50¢ \\ \hline 25¢ \end{array}$
10. $\begin{array}{r} 60¢ \\ -41¢ \\ \hline 19¢ \end{array}$

11. $\begin{array}{r} 27¢ \\ -\ \ 9¢ \\ \hline 18¢ \end{array}$
12. $\begin{array}{r} 65¢ \\ -35¢ \\ \hline 30¢ \end{array}$
13. $\begin{array}{r} 80¢ \\ -50¢ \\ \hline 30¢ \end{array}$
14. $\begin{array}{r} 52¢ \\ -\ \ 7¢ \\ \hline 45¢ \end{array}$
15. $\begin{array}{r} 45¢ \\ -36¢ \\ \hline 9¢ \end{array}$

16. $\begin{array}{r} 48¢ \\ -15¢ \\ \hline 33¢ \end{array}$
17. $\begin{array}{r} 73¢ \\ -55¢ \\ \hline 18¢ \end{array}$
18. $\begin{array}{r} 64¢ \\ -17¢ \\ \hline 47¢ \end{array}$
19. $\begin{array}{r} 35¢ \\ -15¢ \\ \hline 20¢ \end{array}$
20. $\begin{array}{r} 96¢ \\ -77¢ \\ \hline 19¢ \end{array}$

Apply

Solve.

21. Li saved 95¢.
    She bought some
    crayons for 75¢.
    How much money
    does she have left?

    $\begin{array}{r} 95¢ \\ -75¢ \\ \hline 20¢ \end{array}$

    20¢

22. Lonnie saved 45¢.
    His mother gave
    him 35¢.
    How much does he
    have now?

    $\begin{array}{r} 45¢ \\ +35¢ \\ \hline 80¢ \end{array}$

    80¢

Subtracting using money notation

158

Mixed Problem Solving

pages 159-160

Objectives

To add or subtract to solve problems
To use a bar graph to solve problems

Materials

*large grid paper
ten-strips and ones

Mental Math

Ask students to name an addition problem to check the following subtraction problems:

1. 26 − 14 (12 + 14)
2. 72 − 2 (2 + 70)
3. 46 − 31 (15 + 31)
4. 77 − 44 (33 + 44)
5. 15 − 6 (6 + 9)
6. 41 − 38 (3 + 38)
7. 50 − 35 (15 + 35)

Skill Review

Write **84 − 46 = 38** vertically on the board. Have a student check the problem by adding. (38 + 46 = 84) Ask if the problem checks out to be correct. (no) Have the student correct the subtraction problem and check by adding. (84 − 46 = 38, 38 + 46 = 84) Continue for more subtraction problems which have correct or incorrect answers.

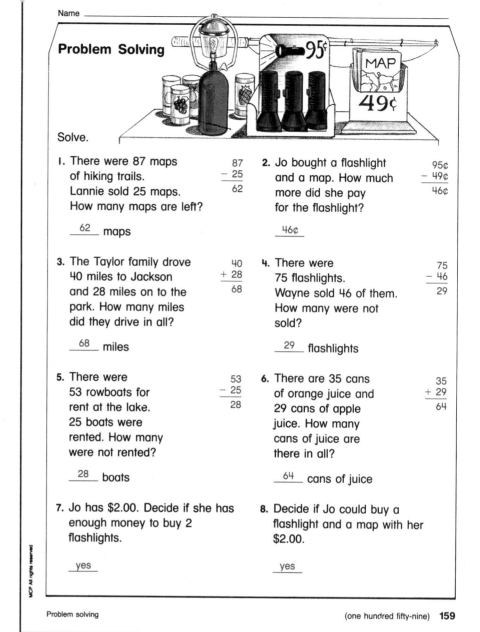

Problem Solving

Solve.

1. There were 87 maps of hiking trails. Lannie sold 25 maps. How many maps are left?

$$\begin{array}{r} 87 \\ -\ 25 \\ \hline 62 \end{array}$$

____62____ maps

2. Jo bought a flashlight and a map. How much more did she pay for the flashlight?

$$\begin{array}{r} 95¢ \\ -\ 49¢ \\ \hline 46¢ \end{array}$$

____46¢____

3. The Taylor family drove 40 miles to Jackson and 28 miles on to the park. How many miles did they drive in all?

$$\begin{array}{r} 40 \\ +\ 28 \\ \hline 68 \end{array}$$

____68____ miles

4. There were 75 flashlights. Wayne sold 46 of them. How many were not sold?

$$\begin{array}{r} 75 \\ -\ 46 \\ \hline 29 \end{array}$$

____29____ flashlights

5. There were 53 rowboats for rent at the lake. 25 boats were rented. How many were not rented?

$$\begin{array}{r} 53 \\ -\ 25 \\ \hline 28 \end{array}$$

____28____ boats

6. There are 35 cans of orange juice and 29 cans of apple juice. How many cans of juice are there in all?

$$\begin{array}{r} 35 \\ +\ 29 \\ \hline 64 \end{array}$$

____64____ cans of juice

7. Jo has $2.00. Decide if she has enough money to buy 2 flashlights.

____yes____

8. Decide if Jo could buy a flashlight and a map with her $2.00.

____yes____

Problem solving

(one hundred fifty-nine) **159**

Teaching page 159

Have students name the pictured items and their prices. Have a student read the first problem aloud and tell what is to be found as you write **What is to be found?** on the board. (number of maps left) Ask what information is given as you write **What do we know?** on the board. (There were 87 maps and 25 were sold.) Ask what operation needs to be done as you write **What needs to be done with the numbers?** on the board. (subtract) Tell students to write and solve the problem independently and record their answer on the line before the word "maps". Ask students how they can check to see if the answer makes sense as you write **Does the answer make sense?** on the board. (check by adding) Tell students to check by adding. Remind students to use the 4 questions on the board to help them solve each of the problems on this page. Tell students they may want to use ten-strips and ones to check problems which involve addition. Remind students to record each answer on the answer line.

159

Maria showed a list of four pets to her friends at school. She asked each friend to pick their favorite pet and then made a graph of their choices.

Use her graph to find the answers.

1. __27__ children chose a cat.

2. __35__ children chose a dog.

3. __22__ children chose a bird.

4. __9__ children chose a rabbit.

5. How many children chose a cat or a dog?

$$\begin{array}{r} 27 \\ + 35 \\ \hline 62 \end{array}$$

__62__

6. How many more children chose a dog than a cat?

$$\begin{array}{r} 35 \\ - 27 \\ \hline 8 \end{array}$$

__8__

7. How many children chose a bird or a rabbit?

$$\begin{array}{r} 22 \\ + 9 \\ \hline 31 \end{array}$$

__31__

8. How many children chose a dog or a rabbit?

$$\begin{array}{r} 35 \\ + 9 \\ \hline 44 \end{array}$$

__44__

9. How many more children chose a cat than a rabbit?

$$\begin{array}{r} 27 \\ - 9 \\ \hline 18 \end{array}$$

__18__

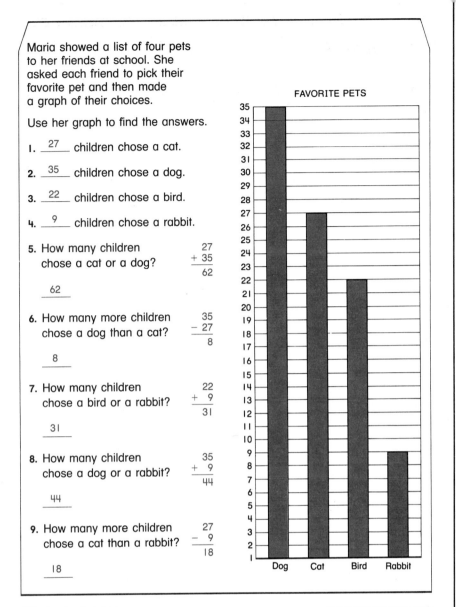

FAVORITE PETS

Dog   Cat   Bird   Rabbit

160 (one hundred sixty)

Using information from a graph

Correcting Common Errors

Some students may need additional work solving word problems. Change the prices of the pictured items and the numbers in the word problems on page 159 to give them additional practice.

Enrichment

Have students make a bar graph showing the number of students in each of 4 classrooms in your school. Then have students answer the following questions:

1. How many students are in each classroom?
2. Which class has the most students?
3. How many total students are in the 4 classrooms?
4. How many more students are in the class with the most students than in the class with the least students?

Teaching page 160

Have a student read the paragraph aloud. Help students read the graph to find and record how many of Maria's friends chose each pet. Have students fill in the first 4 statements. Have a student read problem 5 aloud. Help students recognize that this problem asks for the number of children who chose a cat and the number who chose a dog. Tell students to make a plan to solve each problem and then have them complete the problems independently. Remind students to check each problem to be sure their answers make sense.

Extra Credit   *Measurement*

Have students bring in various objects from home to be weighed. Weigh each object using an appropriate scale and make a chart showing each object's name and weight in pounds and ounces. Then put each object in an unmarked paper bag. Have students choose a bag, estimate its weight in pounds, and guess its contents based on its weight. Then have students weigh the bag to verify their guess. Repeat several times for students to estimate the weight of different bags and keep a chart of their responses.

160

Review

pages 161-162

Objectives

To review subtraction of 2-digit numbers

To maintain skills learned previously this year

Materials

*addition and subtraction fact cards
dollars and coins

Mental Math

Ask if the following are true or false:

1. $15 - 8$ is related to $8 + 7$ (T)
2. 3:30 is 30 minutes after 3 (T)
3. 440 is 4 ones more than 400 (F)
4. A half-dollar = 2 quarters (T)
5. At 6:25 the minute hand is on the 5 (T)
6. $7 + 9 > 10 + 6$ (F)
7. 11 is 6 more than 6 (F)

Skill Review

Place any addition or subtraction fact card on the chalk tray. Have students write all the related facts on the board. Repeat for more fact cards.

CHAPTER CHECKUP

Subtract. Trade if needed.

1. 25 − 3 22	2. 35 − 8 27	3. 71 − 5 66	4. 55 − 9 46
5. 80 −30 50	6. 90 −30 60	7. 60 −20 40	8. 85 −31 54
9. 45 −17 28	10. 71 −53 18	11. 64 −19 45	12. 97 −29 68
13. 83 −15 68	14. 98 −75 23	15. 81 −67 14	16. 35 −19 16
17. 75¢ −25¢ 50¢	18. 65¢ −48¢ 17¢	19. 92¢ −55¢ 37¢	20. 73¢ −15¢ 58¢

Solve.

21. Pat saved 35 marbles. She gave Dino 16 of them. How many marbles did she have left?

$$\begin{array}{r} 35 \\ -16 \\ \hline 19 \end{array}$$

__19__ marbles

22. The pet store had 75 goldfish. They sold 39 of them. How many did they have left?

$$\begin{array}{r} 75 \\ -39 \\ \hline 36 \end{array}$$

__36__ goldfish

Chapter review

(one hundred sixty-one) **161**

Teaching page 161

Tell students that some of the problems on this page require trading and some do not. Remind them to write a cent sign in the answers that require one. Tell students to read the word problems carefully before deciding which operation to use. Have students complete the page independently.

161

ROUNDUP REVIEW

Fill in the oval next to the correct answer.

1	15 − 9	○ 24 ● 6 ○ 14 ○ NG	8	80 + 70	○ 160 ● 150 ○ 10 ○ NG
2	7 + 4	● 11 ○ 3 ○ 4 ○ NG	9	76 + 97	○ 163 ○ 1,613 ● 173 ○ NG
3	(coins)	○ 81¢ ○ 80¢ ● 76¢ ○ NG	10	80 − 30	● 50 ○ 110 ○ 40 ○ NG
4	(clock)	○ 4:25 ● 3:25 ○ 5:15 ○ NG	11	59 − 15	● 44 ○ 74 ○ 54 ○ NG
5	(blocks)	○ 135 ○ 55 ● 145 ○ NG	12	98¢ − 35¢	○ 133¢ ○ 36¢ ● 63¢ ○ NG
6	51 + 37	○ 14 ○ 98 ○ 89 ● NG	13	71¢ − 23¢	○ 52¢ ● 48¢ ○ 94¢ ○ NG
7	29¢ + 34¢	● 63¢ ○ 53¢ ○ 513 ○ NG		score	

Cumulative review

Enrichment

1. Tell students to draw a clock that shows 40 minutes after 6. Then tell them to draw a second clock that shows the time that is 4 hours later.
2. Have students draw coins to show 92¢. Then tell them to draw another group of coins that would give $1.00 in all.
3. Tell students to write and solve a problem that tells how much more money than 5¢ they would need to buy an item that costs 92¢.

Teaching page 162

This page reviews time, money, place value, some basic facts and adding and subtracting 2-digit numbers. Tell students they are to solve each problem and then fill in the oval beside the correct answer. Remind students that NG means the answer is not given and they will only mark that oval if none of the answers is correct. Have students complete the page independently.

3-digit Sums

pages 163-164

Objective

To add two 2-digit numbers for a 3-digit sum

Materials

hundred-flat
ten-strips and ones

Mental Math

Ask students which number is more and how many more:

1. 78, 64 (78, 14 more)
2. 52, 59 (59, 7 more)
3. 91, 89 (91, 2 more)
4. 50, 82 (82, 32 more)
5. 45, 76 (76, 31 more)
6. 90, 75 (90, 15 more)
7. 50, 20 (50, 30 more)
8. 66, 99 (99, 33 more)

Skill Review

Write **28 + 16** on the board and ask students if a trade is needed. (yes) Ask what trade is needed. (10 ones for 1 ten) Write **47 − 26** on the board and ask if a trade is needed. (no) Continue to write 2-digit addition or subtraction problems on the board and ask if a trade is needed and, if so, what trade is needed.

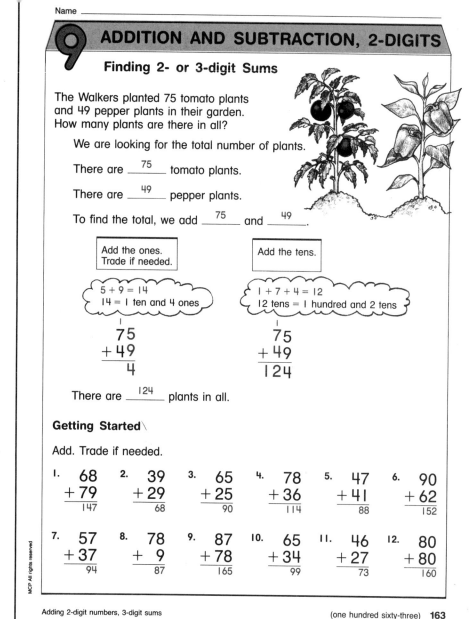

Finding 2- or 3-digit Sums

The Walkers planted 75 tomato plants and 49 pepper plants in their garden. How many plants are there in all?

We are looking for the total number of plants.

There are ___75___ tomato plants.

There are ___49___ pepper plants.

To find the total, we add ___75___ and ___49___.

Add the ones. Trade if needed.	Add the tens.

5 + 9 = 14
14 = 1 ten and 4 ones

$$\begin{array}{r} 75 \\ +49 \\ \hline 4 \end{array}$$

1 + 7 + 4 = 12
12 tens = 1 hundred and 2 tens

$$\begin{array}{r} 75 \\ +49 \\ \hline 124 \end{array}$$

There are ___124___ plants in all.

Getting Started

Add. Trade if needed.

1. $\begin{array}{r}68\\+79\\\hline 147\end{array}$	2. $\begin{array}{r}39\\+29\\\hline 68\end{array}$	3. $\begin{array}{r}65\\+25\\\hline 90\end{array}$	4. $\begin{array}{r}78\\+36\\\hline 114\end{array}$	5. $\begin{array}{r}47\\+41\\\hline 88\end{array}$	6. $\begin{array}{r}90\\+62\\\hline 152\end{array}$
7. $\begin{array}{r}57\\+37\\\hline 94\end{array}$	8. $\begin{array}{r}78\\+\ 9\\\hline 87\end{array}$	9. $\begin{array}{r}87\\+78\\\hline 165\end{array}$	10. $\begin{array}{r}65\\+34\\\hline 99\end{array}$	11. $\begin{array}{r}46\\+27\\\hline 73\end{array}$	12. $\begin{array}{r}80\\+80\\\hline 160\end{array}$

Adding 2-digit numbers, 3-digit sums

(one hundred sixty-three) **163**

Teaching the Lesson

Introducing the Problem Have a student read the problem aloud and tell what is to be solved. (the number of plants in all) Ask what information is given. (There are 75 tomato and 49 pepper plants.) Ask what operation is needed to find the total number of plants. (addition) Have students read and then complete the information sentences. Work through the model with students and then have them complete the solution sentence. Tell students to lay out ten-strips and ones to check their solution.

Developing the Skill Write **64 + 48** on the board and have students lay out ten-strips and ones to show each number. Have a student add 4 ones and 8 ones, show the trade and record the number of ones left as other students trade 10 ones for a ten-strip and count the ones left. (2 ones) Ask students the number of ten-strips in all as the student adds 6, 4 and 1. (11 tens) Tell students that 11 tens = 1 hundred and 1 ten. Tell students to trade 10 tens for 1 hundred and tell the number of tens left. (1) Have the student show the trade on the board and record the 1 ten left. Have students tell the total hundreds as 1 hundred is recorded in the problem on the board. Continue for the following problems where 1, 2 or no trades are needed: 26 + 93 (119), 64 + 21 (85), 45 + 66 (111), 87 + 87 (174), 36 + 90 (129), 76 + 85 (161), 40 + 60 (100), 72 + 9 (81).

Practice

Add. Trade if needed.

1. 11 +46 = 57	2. 80 +44 = 124	3. 49 + 6 = 55	4. 18 +44 = 62	5. 99 +33 = 132	6. 18 +15 = 33
7. 36 +64 = 100	8. 19 +22 = 41	9. 23 +39 = 62	10. 96 +32 = 128	11. 8 +48 = 56	12. 45 +74 = 119
13. 79 +89 = 168	14. 72 +77 = 149	15. 27 +17 = 44	16. 88 +33 = 121	17. 28 +45 = 73	18. 67 +70 = 137
19. 49 + 9 = 58	20. 63 +48 = 111	21. 48 +86 = 134	22. 82 +12 = 94	23. 67 +23 = 90	24. 85 +12 = 97
25. 56 +84 = 140	26. 37 +28 = 65	27. 44 +37 = 81	28. 62 +17 = 79	29. 59 +98 = 157	30. 26 + 6 = 32

Apply

Solve.

31. Ellie picked 50 tomatoes in the morning and 80 in the afternoon. How many tomatoes did she pick?

50
+ 80
130

130 tomatoes

32. Charley picked 75 green peppers and 65 yellow peppers. How many peppers did he pick?

75
+ 65
140

140 peppers

Adding 2-digit numbers, 3-digit sums

Correcting Common Errors

Some students may have difficulty adding when the sum is three digits. Have them work their problems on a place-value chart with columns for hundreds, tens, and ones. This will help them to see that an amount such as 14 tens is the same as and is written as 1 hundred 4 tens.

Enrichment

Tell students to find the sums of: 99 + 1, 99 + 11, 99 + 21, 99 + 31, 99 + 41, 99 + 51, 99 + 61, 99 + 71, 99 + 81 and 99 + 91. Ask what pattern they see in the tens place?

Practice

Tell students that some of the addition problems on this page require no trading, but they may need to trade 1 or 2 times in other problems. Tell students to make a plan to solve each of the word problems. Have students complete the page independently.

Mixed Practice

1. 10 + 8 (18)
2. 7 + 8 (15)
3. 15, 20, 25, 30, ____, (35)
4. 0 + 4 (4)
5. 4 hundred 8 tens 6 ones (486)
6. 1¢ + 7¢ (8¢)
7. 30, 40, 50, ____ (60)
8. 17 − 9 (8)
9. 8¢ + 6¢ (14¢)
10. 10 − 5 (5)

Extra Credit   *Applications*

Write a fairly simple recipe for granola bars on the board. Ask students to look at the recipe and tell how many people it will serve if each has one bar. How many if each has two bars. Ask students to list the abbreviations for measurements that they find in the recipe. Write the measurement words next to the abbreviations for students to copy. Discuss cup, teaspoon and tablespoon measures. Explain how the temperature of the oven is set and how to use a timer. Finally see if the class can list all the different ways they had to use math in order to make granola bars. Encourage them to try the recipe, with help, at home.

Adding Three 2-digit Numbers

pages 165-166

Objective

To add three 2-digit numbers for sums through 199

Materials

hundred-flat
tens-strips and ones

Mental Math

Tell students to name the number for:

1. 8 tens + 80. (160)
2. 70 − 2 tens. (50)
3. 53 − 4 tens. (13)
4. 9 tens − 6 ones. (84)
5. 40 + 8 tens. (120)
6. 96 + 5 ones. (101)
7. 8 tens 2 ones + 8 ones. (90)
8. 1 hundred 2 tens + 4 tens. (160)

Skill Review

Have a student write any 2-digit number on the board. Have a second student write another 2-digit number and add the numbers. Have students use manipulatives to check the work. Repeat for more problems of 2-digit numbers plus 1- or 2-digit numbers.

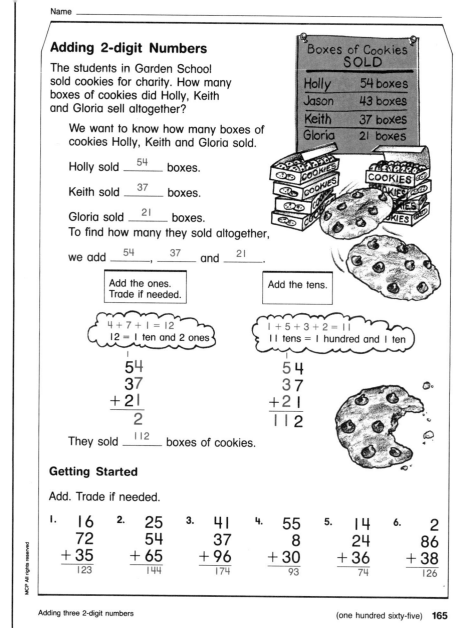

Adding 2-digit Numbers

The students in Garden School sold cookies for charity. How many boxes of cookies did Holly, Keith and Gloria sell altogether?

Boxes of Cookies SOLD

Holly	54 boxes
Jason	43 boxes
Keith	37 boxes
Gloria	21 boxes

We want to know how many boxes of cookies Holly, Keith and Gloria sold.

Holly sold __54__ boxes.

Keith sold __37__ boxes.

Gloria sold __21__ boxes.

To find how many they sold altogether,

we add __54__, __37__ and __21__.

| Add the ones. Trade if needed. | Add the tens. |

4 + 7 + 1 = 12
12 = 1 ten and 2 ones

$$
\begin{array}{r}
5\,4 \\
3\,7 \\
+\,2\,1 \\
\hline
2
\end{array}
$$

1 + 5 + 3 + 2 = 11
11 tens = 1 hundred and 1 ten

$$
\begin{array}{r}
5\,4 \\
3\,7 \\
+\,2\,1 \\
\hline
1\,1\,2
\end{array}
$$

They sold __112__ boxes of cookies.

Getting Started

Add. Trade if needed.

1.
$$
\begin{array}{r}
1\,6 \\
7\,2 \\
+\,3\,5 \\
\hline
1\,2\,3
\end{array}
$$

2.
$$
\begin{array}{r}
2\,5 \\
5\,4 \\
+\,6\,5 \\
\hline
1\,4\,4
\end{array}
$$

3.
$$
\begin{array}{r}
4\,1 \\
3\,7 \\
+\,9\,6 \\
\hline
1\,7\,4
\end{array}
$$

4.
$$
\begin{array}{r}
5\,5 \\
8 \\
+\,3\,0 \\
\hline
9\,3
\end{array}
$$

5.
$$
\begin{array}{r}
1\,4 \\
2\,4 \\
+\,3\,6 \\
\hline
7\,4
\end{array}
$$

6.
$$
\begin{array}{r}
2 \\
8\,6 \\
+\,3\,8 \\
\hline
1\,2\,6
\end{array}
$$

Adding three 2-digit numbers

(one hundred sixty-five) **165**

Teaching the Lesson

Introducing the Problem Have a student read the problem aloud and tell what is to be solved. (the total number of boxes of cookies sold by Holly, Keith and Gloria) Ask students what information is needed. (Holly sold 54 boxes, Keith sold 37 boxes and Gloria sold 21 boxes.) Ask what unnecessary information is given. (Jason sold 43 boxes.) Have students read and complete the information sentences. Work through the model with students and then have them complete the solution sentence. Have students add up the columns from the bottom up to check their solution.

Developing the Skill Write **86 + 17 + 45** vertically on the board. Have students lay out 86 in ten-strips and ones. Repeat for 17 and 45. Ask students how many ones in all. (18) Tell students to trade 10 ones for 1 ten and tell how many ones are left. (8) Ask the number of tens in all. (14) Tell students to trade 10 tens for 1 hundred-flat and tell how many tens are left. (4) Ask students how many hundreds. (1) Ask a student to write the sum in the problem on the board. (148) Remind students that looking for a ten is helpful in adding a column of numbers. Now have a student add the columns from the bottom up in the problem on the board and show any trades to check the solution. Repeat for 29 + 38 + 11 (78), 51 + 8 + 92 (151), 45 + 15 + 65 (125); and 27 + 81 + 90 (198).

Add. Trade if needed.

1. 23 37 +90 150	2. 40 30 +70 140	3. 6 70 +58 134	4. 13 33 +76 122	5. 11 37 +59 107	6. 49 10 +68 127
7. 10 69 +18 97	8. 59 61 + 3 123	9. 51 39 +97 187	10. 31 6 +52 89	11. 10 70 +80 160	12. 54 34 +25 113
13. 86 1 + 8 95	14. 35 30 +35 100	15. 83 6 +54 143	16. 30 19 +88 137	17. 82 14 +18 114	18. 72 23 +98 193

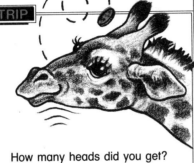

FIELD TRIP

If you toss a coin 30 times, guess how many times it will land tail up?

_____ times   Answers will vary.

Try it.

Toss a coin 30 times.

How many tails did you get?

_____

How many heads did you get?

_____

Was your guess close? _____

Adding three 2-digit numbers

Correcting Common Errors

Some students may have difficulty keeping their numbers aligned properly and their trades shown in the proper columns when performing column addition. Have them write their problems on a place-value chart which will help them keep hundreds, tens, and ones in the proper columns.

Enrichment

Tell students to write and solve an addition problem to find the number of months they have lived since their birth.

Practice

Remind students to add the ones first and look for a ten when adding each column. Have students complete the rows of problems independently.

Field Trip

Group students in pairs with 1 student tossing a coin and the other student recording the tosses. Write the following on the board to show students a recording method:

heads	//
tails	/

Have students record their guesses and then complete the activity and record their results by using tally marks in the chart. Discuss with students that there are 2 possible outcomes of heads or tails and the most accurate guess would be 15 of each because 15 + 15 = 30.

Extra Credit   *Applications*

Invite a chef or dietician to speak to students about one or two of their favorite recipes. After explaining the recipe to the class, ask them to demonstrate how to increase the recipe to serve 50 or more people. Have them chart the ingredients on the board to make it easier for students to understand. Ask the speaker to discuss other types of math problems they encounter in their work.

Subtracting 2-digit Numbers

pages 167-168

Objective

To subtract two 2-digit numbers

Materials

colored chalk

Mental Math

Ask students to name the following times:

1. 15 minutes after 2:00. (2:15)
2. 4 hours later than 6:25. (10:25)
3. 30 minutes after 6:26. (6:56)
4. 14 minutes later than 2:10. (2:24)
5. 15 minutes later than 11:50. (12:05)
6. 20 minutes after 4:30. (4:50)
7. 47 minutes after 3:00. (3:47)
8. 2 hours later than 7:36. (9:36)

Skill Review

Write **62 = 6 tens 2 ones = 5 tens 12 ones** on the board. Have a student similarly rename 78 on the board. (78 = 7 tens 8 ones = 6 tens 18 ones) Continue for more practice in renaming 2-digit numbers.

Subtracting 2-digit Numbers

Greg sold 75 adult tickets to the school play. He sold 48 student tickets. How many more adult tickets did Greg sell?

We want to know how many more adult tickets were sold.

Greg sold ___75___ adult tickets.

He sold ___48___ student tickets.

To find how many more adult tickets were sold,

we subtract ___48___ from ___75___.

✔ Remember to subtract the ones first.

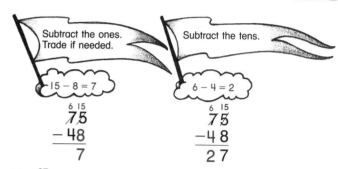

Greg sold ___27___ more adult tickets.

Getting Started

Subtract. Trade if needed.

1.	2.	3.	4.	5.	6.
74	47	71	89	80	91
−26	−33	−51	−76	−52	−27
48	14	20	13	28	64

Subtracting 2-digit numbers, with trading

(one hundred sixty-seven) **167**

Teaching the Lesson

Introducing the Problem Have a student read the problem aloud and tell what is to be found. (how many more adult tickets than student tickets Greg sold) Ask students what information is known. (He sold 75 adult and 48 student tickets.) Have students read and complete the information sentences. Work through the model with students and then have them complete the solution sentence. Tell students to check their answer by adding.

Developing the Skill Write **87 − 49** on the board and use colored chalk to show the trade of 1 ten for 10 ones. Have a student complete the problem. (38) Have another student check by adding. (38 + 49 = 87) Now write **92 − 59** on the board and have a student use colored chalk to show the trade and complete the problem. (33) Have another student check the work by adding. (33 + 59 = 92) Have students use colored chalk only if trading is needed as they continue practice with the following problems: 91 − 80 (11), 77 − 49 (28), 63 − 34 (29), 54 − 27 (27), 86 − 53 (33), 85 − 69 (16).

167

Practice

Subtract. Trade if needed.

1. 47 − 36 = 11
2. 66 − 34 = 32
3. 38 − 14 = 24
4. 75 − 68 = 7
5. 70 − 57 = 13
6. 61 − 44 = 17

7. 93 − 13 = 80
8. 32 − 15 = 17
9. 78 − 29 = 49
10. 61 − 28 = 33
11. 54 − 37 = 17
12. 63 − 29 = 34

13. 80 − 65 = 15
14. 52 − 30 = 22
15. 93 − 87 = 6
16. 17 − 11 = 6
17. 95 − 76 = 19
18. 75 − 59 = 16

19. 72 − 29 = 43
20. 87 − 42 = 45
21. 54 − 18 = 36
22. 31 − 29 = 2
23. 60 − 34 = 26
24. 82 − 20 = 62

25. 60 − 19 = 41
26. 55 − 23 = 32
27. 94 − 75 = 19
28. 27 − 20 = 7
29. 50 − 46 = 4
30. 37 − 11 = 26

Apply

Solve.

31. Martin found 37 shells. He gave 18 shells to Nell. How many shells does Martin have left?

37 − 18 = 19

__19__ shells

32. Rona poured 65 cups of juice. She sold 28 cups. How many cups of juice were not sold?

65 − 28 = 37

__37__ cups of juice

Subtracting 2-digit numbers, with trading

Correcting Common Errors

Some students may get confused deciding when or when not to trade. As they work each problem, have them first check to see whether the ones in the minuend are greater than the ones in the subtrahend. If not, then they know that they must trade. Encourage them to verbalize this decision in the case of each place value until they feel comfortable with this skill.

Enrichment

Tell students to write and solve four 2-digit subtraction problems that require trading and 4 problems that require no trading. Now tell them to erase the number in the ones column of each minuend, and have a friend find the missing numbers.

Practice

Remind students to make a plan to solve each word problem and then assign the page to be completed independently.

Mixed Practice

1. 5 hundreds 4 tens 0 ones (540)
2. 27 ○ 72 (<)
3. 5 + 4 (9)
4. 76, 77, 78, ___ (79)
5. 7¢ + 5¢ (12¢)
6. 8 − 5 (3)
7. 38 ○ 28 (>)
8. 12¢ − 6¢ (6¢)
9. ___ + 4 = 12 (8)
10. 10 + 4 (14)

Extra Credit   *Applications*

Bring in several different packages of crackers. Put a chart with these headings on the board:

type of cracker	number in package	weight of package	price

Have students work in groups to copy the chart and fill it in after examining all the different packages. Now ask them to compare the cost of the different kinds of crackers. Ask the following questions: Which package gives you the most crackers?, Which gives you the most weight?, Why do some cost more than others? Which is the best buy? Have students compare their answers.

Mixed Practice

pages 169-170

Objective

To add or subtract 2-digit numbers

Materials

*addition fact cards
*subtraction fact cards
ten-strips and ones

Mental Math

Have students name the number that is:

1. 100 less than 463. (363)
2. 10 more than 430. (440)
3. between 910 and 912. (911)
4. next in the sequence 18, 16, 14, 12 . . . (10)
5. 6 tens more than 50. (110)
6. 46 more than 200. (246)
7. less than 46, more than 40 and has the same number of tens and ones. (44)

Skill Review

Show fact cards randomly for students to tell the operation and then give the sum or difference. Encourage students to increase their speed in answering.

Mixed Practice

Add or subtract. Trade if needed.

1.	2.	3.	4.	5.	6.
35 +23 = 58	74 +96 = 170	90 +57 = 147	54 +29 = 83	58 +36 = 94	32 +99 = 131

7.	8.	9.	10.	11.	12.
49 −15 = 34	86 −34 = 52	90 −25 = 65	41 −28 = 13	72 −33 = 39	91 −59 = 32

13.	14.	15.	16.	17.	18.
63 +33 = 96	86 +46 = 132	57 −50 = 7	90 −67 = 23	75 +95 = 170	51 −26 = 25

19.	20.	21.	22.	23.	24.
53 24 +87 = 164	65 4 +38 = 107	40 21 +30 = 91	7 52 +73 = 132	32 14 +94 = 140	74 44 + 4 = 122

Solve.

25. There are 33 puppies in the pet store. There are 17 kittens. How many more puppies than kittens are there?

  33 − 17 = 16

  __16__ puppies

26. There are 75 goldfish and 85 guppies. How many fish are there altogether?

  75 + 85 = 160

  __160__ fish

27. There are 18 canaries and 26 parakeets. How many birds are there altogether?

  18 + 26 = 44

  __44__ birds

28. The pet store had 34 turtles. They sold 19. How many were not sold?

  34 − 19 = 15

  __15__ turtles

Mixed addition and subtraction practice   (one hundred sixty-nine) **169**

Teaching the Lesson

Introducing the Problem Write **67 + 28** and **67 − 28** on the board. Have 2 students work the problems. (67 + 28 = 95, 67 − 28 = 39) Ask students if the answers are the same. (no) Ask why. (One problem is addition and one is subtraction.)

Developing the Skill Tell students a story of having 67 collector's cards and giving 28 away. Ask which problem on the board tells how many cards are left. (67 − 28 = 39) Have a student tell a story that is answered by the problem 67 + 28 = 95. Repeat the activity for 26 − 18 and 26 + 18. Remind students to look at each operation sign before working the problems. Tell students to make a plan to solve each word problem. Assign the page to be completed independently.

More Mixed Practice

Add or subtract. Trade if needed.

1. $\begin{array}{r} 66 \\ +40 \\ \hline 106 \end{array}$ 2. $\begin{array}{r} 97 \\ +41 \\ \hline 138 \end{array}$ 3. $\begin{array}{r} 95 \\ -20 \\ \hline 75 \end{array}$ 4. $\begin{array}{r} 91 \\ -59 \\ \hline 32 \end{array}$ 5. $\begin{array}{r} 35 \\ +44 \\ \hline 79 \end{array}$ 6. $\begin{array}{r} 79 \\ +44 \\ \hline 123 \end{array}$

7. $\begin{array}{r} 95 \\ -70 \\ \hline 25 \end{array}$ 8. $\begin{array}{r} 73 \\ -26 \\ \hline 47 \end{array}$ 9. $\begin{array}{r} 64 \\ -17 \\ \hline 47 \end{array}$ 10. $\begin{array}{r} 79 \\ +74 \\ \hline 153 \end{array}$ 11. $\begin{array}{r} 56 \\ +40 \\ \hline 96 \end{array}$ 12. $\begin{array}{r} 69 \\ +64 \\ \hline 133 \end{array}$

13. $\begin{array}{r} 65 \\ -52 \\ \hline 13 \end{array}$ 14. $\begin{array}{r} 95 \\ +74 \\ \hline 169 \end{array}$ 15. $\begin{array}{r} 82 \\ -27 \\ \hline 55 \end{array}$ 16. $\begin{array}{r} 77 \\ -49 \\ \hline 28 \end{array}$ 17. $\begin{array}{r} 63 \\ +99 \\ \hline 162 \end{array}$ 18. $\begin{array}{r} 95 \\ -74 \\ \hline 21 \end{array}$

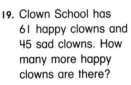

Solve.

19. Clown School has
61 happy clowns and
45 sad clowns. How
many more happy
clowns are there?

$\begin{array}{r} 61 \\ -45 \\ \hline 16 \end{array}$

___16___ happy clowns

20. The circus needs
23 horses, 14 lions
and 18 dogs. How many
animals do they need?

$\begin{array}{r} 23 \\ 14 \\ +18 \\ \hline 55 \end{array}$

___55___ animals

21. 89 girls and
94 boys went
to the circus.
How many children went
to the circus?

$\begin{array}{r} 89 \\ +94 \\ \hline 183 \end{array}$

___183___ children

22. Jumbo, the elephant, is
53 years old.
Atlas, the elephant, is
38 years old.
How many years older
is Jumbo?

$\begin{array}{r} 53 \\ -38 \\ \hline 15 \end{array}$

___15___ years

Mixed addition and subtraction practice

Correcting Common Errors

Some students may add when they should subtract or vice versa when working with a set of mixed problems. To help them become more aware of the operation signs, have them circle all the addition signs in one color and all the subtraction signs in another. This will help alert them to a change in operation.

Enrichment

Have students use a calendar to find the total number of days in the first 6 months of the year. Then tell them to find the number of days in the last 6 months of the year. Ask which 6-month period has more days. Why?

Practice

Remind students to look at the operation sign for each problem. Tell them to make a plan to solve each word problem and then assign the page to be completed independently.

Mixed Practice

1. 8¢ − 5¢ (3¢)
2. 400, 500, 600, ___ (700)
3. 2 + 5 (7)
4. 64 ◯ 68 (<)
5. 10 + 5 (15)
6. 6 hundreds 3 tens 0 ones (630)
7. 15 − 8 (7)
8. 137 ◯ 371 (<)
9. 6 + 8 (14)
10. 15 − 9 (6)

Extra Credit   *Numeration*

Provide students with a page from a monthly calendar. Have each student choose a 2 x 2 square of dates, for example Tuesday-Wednesday for 2 consecutive weeks. Have students add the numbers on one diagonal, then add the numbers for the other diagonal, and compare the sums. (The answers will be the same.) Ask students to choose other 2 x 2 squares and see if the results are the same. Challenge them to see if they can find any 2 x 2 square where the pattern does not exist.

This activity can be extended by using 3 x 3 and 4 x 4 squares.

Number Sentences

pages 171-172

Objective

To add or subtract when a problem is horizontal

Materials

ten-strips and ones

Mental Math

Tell students to give the sum and difference for:

1. 80, 20 (100, 60)
2. 66, 33 (99, 33)
3. 10¢, 8¢ (18¢, 2¢)
4. 19, 19 (38, 0)
5. 60, 50 (110, 10)
6. 42, 22 (64, 20)
7. 25¢, 10¢ (35¢, 15¢)

Skill Review

Write **86 + 45** and **86 − 45** on the board. Ask students which problem will have an answer less than 86. (86 − 45) Ask why. (because 45 is taken away from 86) Ask which will have an answer more than 86. (86 + 45) Ask why. (because 45 is added to 86) Continue for more problems having the same 2-digit numbers but different operational signs.

Addition and Subtraction Sentences

Adding and subtracting problems are sometimes written across as number sentences. To work the problems, you need to copy them as shown below. Then you can add or subtract.

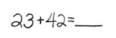

$$23 + 42 = \underline{\quad}$$

$$\begin{array}{r} 23 \\ +42 \\ \hline \end{array}$$

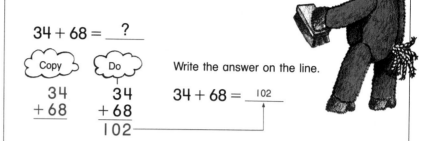

$$34 + 68 = \underline{\ ?\ }$$

Copy
$$\begin{array}{r} 34 \\ +68 \\ \hline \end{array}$$

Do
$$\begin{array}{r} 34 \\ +68 \\ \hline 102 \end{array}$$

Write the answer on the line.

$$34 + 68 = \underline{\ 102\ }$$

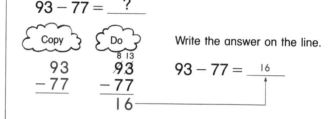

$$93 - 77 = \underline{\ ?\ }$$

Copy
$$\begin{array}{r} 93 \\ -77 \\ \hline \end{array}$$

Do
$$\begin{array}{r} {}^{8}\!\!\!\not{9}{}^{13}\!\!\!\not{3} \\ -77 \\ \hline 16 \end{array}$$

Write the answer on the line.

$$93 - 77 = \underline{\ 16\ }$$

Getting Started

Copy and do. Write the answer on the line.

1. $79 + 57 = \underline{\ 136\ }$

$$\begin{array}{r} 79 \\ +57 \\ \hline 136 \end{array}$$

2. $47 + 12 + 96 = \underline{\ 155\ }$

$$\begin{array}{r} 47 \\ 12 \\ +96 \\ \hline 155 \end{array}$$

Adding and subtracting sentences

(one hundred seventy-one) **171**

Teaching the Lesson

Introducing the Problem Have a student read the paragraph aloud and tell about the picture. Work through both problems with the students as they complete the sentences by writing the answers on the lines. Have students use ten-strips and ones to check both problems and then check the subtraction problem again by adding.

Developing the Skill Write **29 + 78 =** horizontally on the board. Tell students that a problem like this is easier to work if it is rewritten vertically. Rewrite the problem vertically on the board. Have a student solve the problem and then record the sum in the horizontal problem. (107) Repeat for 82 − 26. (56) Provide more horizontal addition and subtraction problems for students to copy vertically on the board and solve. Include some addition problems of 3 addends for sums less than 200.

171

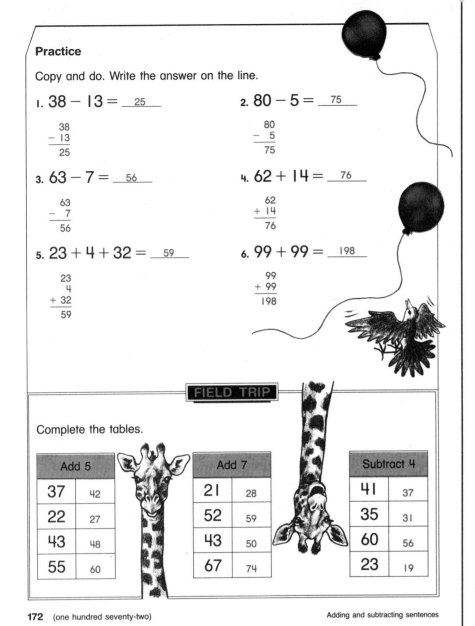

Practice

Copy and do. Write the answer on the line.

1. $38 - 13 =$ __25__

$$\begin{array}{r} 38 \\ -13 \\ \hline 25 \end{array}$$

2. $80 - 5 =$ __75__

$$\begin{array}{r} 80 \\ -\ 5 \\ \hline 75 \end{array}$$

3. $63 - 7 =$ __56__

$$\begin{array}{r} 63 \\ -\ 7 \\ \hline 56 \end{array}$$

4. $62 + 14 =$ __76__

$$\begin{array}{r} 62 \\ +14 \\ \hline 76 \end{array}$$

5. $23 + 4 + 32 =$ __59__

$$\begin{array}{r} 23 \\ 4 \\ +32 \\ \hline 59 \end{array}$$

6. $99 + 99 =$ __198__

$$\begin{array}{r} 99 \\ +99 \\ \hline 198 \end{array}$$

FIELD TRIP

Complete the tables.

Add 5	
37	42
22	27
43	48
55	60

Add 7	
21	28
52	59
43	50
67	74

Subtract 4	
41	37
35	31
60	56
23	19

Adding and subtracting sentences

Subtracting Money

pages 173-174

Objective

To subtract amounts of money less than $1

Materials

ten-strips and ones
dimes and pennies

Mental Math

Tell students to name the number that is:

1. 4 tens 16 ones. (56)
2. 11 tens and 8 ones. (118)
3. 6 ones 12 tens. (126)
4. 19 tens 10 ones. (200)
5. 2 hundreds 18 ones. (218)
6. 19 ones + 2 tens. (39)
7. 15 tens − 10 tens. (50)

Skill Review

Write **68 − 49** horizontally on the board and have a student write and solve the problem vertically. (19) Have another student check the problem by adding. Continue with the following horizontal problems: 74 + 85 (159), 83 − 64 (19), 58 + 58 (116), 92 − 86 (6), 60 − 49 (11).

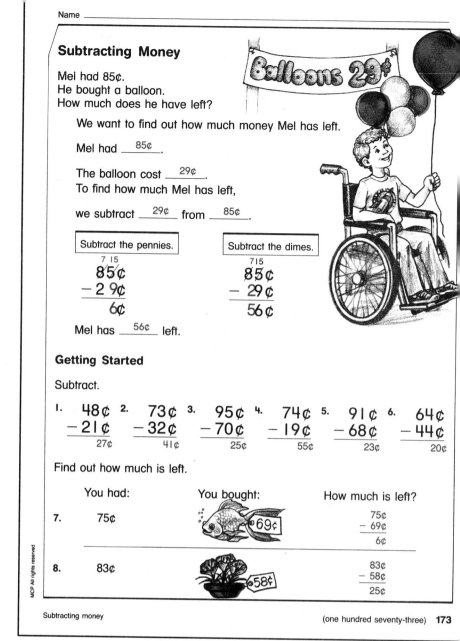

Name _____

Subtracting Money

Mel had 85¢.
He bought a balloon.
How much does he have left?

We want to find out how much money Mel has left.

Mel had ___85¢___.

The balloon cost ___29¢___.
To find how much Mel has left,

we subtract ___29¢___ from ___85¢___.

Subtract the pennies.		Subtract the dimes.
7 15		715
8̶5̶¢		85¢
− 2 9¢		− 29¢
6¢		56¢

Mel has ___56¢___ left.

Getting Started

Subtract.

1. 48¢
− 21¢
27¢

2. 73¢
− 32¢
41¢

3. 95¢
− 70¢
25¢

4. 74¢
− 19¢
55¢

5. 91¢
− 68¢
23¢

6. 64¢
− 44¢
20¢

Find out how much is left.

	You had:	You bought:	How much is left?
7.	75¢	69¢	75¢ − 69¢ 6¢
8.	83¢	58¢	83¢ − 58¢ 25¢

Subtracting money

(one hundred seventy-three) **173**

Teaching the Lesson

Introducing the Problem Have a student read the problem aloud and tell what is to be found. (how much money Mel has left) Ask students what information is needed. (amount of money Mel had and amount he spent) Ask what information is given. (Mel had 85¢ and spent 29¢.) Have students read and complete the information sentences. Work through the model with students and then have them complete the solution sentence. Have a student write and solve an addition problem on the board to check the solution. (56¢ + 29 = 85¢)

Developing the Skill Write **85 − 26** and **85¢ − 26¢** on the board. Ask students how the 2 problems differ. (One has cent signs.) Have half the class use ten-strips and ones to work the first problem and the other half of the class use dimes and pennies. Talk through the trade of 1 ten or 1 dime for 10 ones or 10 pennies. Have students tell their solutions. (59 or 59¢) Help students show the trades with colored chalk as they work the problems on the board. Now have 2 other students write and solve addition problems to check the subtraction. Have students alternate using coins and ten-strips and ones as you repeat the activity for the following: 91 − 45 (46) and 91¢ − 45¢ (46¢), 94 − 27 (67) and 94¢ − 27¢ (67¢), 83 − 56 (27) and 83¢ − 56¢ (27¢).

173

Practice

Subtract.

1. $\begin{array}{r} 90¢ \\ -30¢ \\ \hline 60¢ \end{array}$	2. $\begin{array}{r} 50¢ \\ -36¢ \\ \hline 14¢ \end{array}$	3. $\begin{array}{r} 87¢ \\ -82¢ \\ \hline 5¢ \end{array}$	4. $\begin{array}{r} 33¢ \\ -9¢ \\ \hline 24¢ \end{array}$	5. $\begin{array}{r} 96¢ \\ -49¢ \\ \hline 47¢ \end{array}$	6. $\begin{array}{r} 70¢ \\ -17¢ \\ \hline 53¢ \end{array}$
7. $\begin{array}{r} 61¢ \\ -24¢ \\ \hline 37¢ \end{array}$	8. $\begin{array}{r} 93¢ \\ -78¢ \\ \hline 15¢ \end{array}$	9. $\begin{array}{r} 62¢ \\ -6¢ \\ \hline 56¢ \end{array}$	10. $\begin{array}{r} 28¢ \\ -16¢ \\ \hline 12¢ \end{array}$	11. $\begin{array}{r} 74¢ \\ -39¢ \\ \hline 35¢ \end{array}$	12. $\begin{array}{r} 44¢ \\ -18¢ \\ \hline 26¢ \end{array}$

Find out how much is left.

	You had:	You bought:	How much is left?
13.	45¢	⬤18¢	$\begin{array}{r} 45¢ \\ -18¢ \\ \hline 27¢ \end{array}$
14.	88¢	45¢	$\begin{array}{r} 88¢ \\ -45¢ \\ \hline 43¢ \end{array}$
15.	67¢	38¢	$\begin{array}{r} 67¢ \\ -38¢ \\ \hline 29¢ \end{array}$
16.	50¢	18¢	$\begin{array}{r} 50¢ \\ -18¢ \\ \hline 32¢ \end{array}$
17.	91¢	55¢	$\begin{array}{r} 91¢ \\ -55¢ \\ \hline 36¢ \end{array}$

174 (one hundred seventy-four)

Subtracting money

Correcting Common Errors

Some students may forget to write the cents sign in the answer. Discuss how the cents sign indicates that we are working with money. It may be helpful to students if they write the cents sign first before they subtract.

Enrichment

Tell students to cut 5 items priced less than $1 from newspaper ads. Have them write and solve 5 problems to show how much money they would have left if they had 99¢ and bought 1 of the items. Ask how much money they would need to buy all 5 items.

Practice

Tell students to work the top rows of problems and then solve the money problems by writing and solving a subtraction problem for each. Have students complete the page independently.

Mixed Practice

1. ___ + 5 = 11 (6)
2. 250 ◯ 350 (<)
3. 686, 687, 688, 689, ___ (690)
4. 3 hundreds, 3 tens, 3 ones (333)
5. 13 − 9 (4)
6. 82 ◯ 79 (>)
7. 1 + 8 (9)
8. 10 + 2 (12)
9. 3¢ + 9¢ (12¢)
10. 13 − 5 (8)

Extra Credit   *Probability*

Ask students if they know what is meant by the term **chance.** Explain that chance means by luck, or something over which we have no control, like the outcome of throwing the dice or flipping a coin. Whether you are born a boy or a girl is largely a matter of chance. Ask students in your class to name the number and sex of the children in their families. Write the students' answers on the board.

When the chart is finished, ask students to guess whether there are more boys or girls listed. Then have volunteers count up the number of boys and girls to compare with the class estimate. Ask students to name something else in their lives that can happen by chance.

Adding Money

Objective

To add money amounts less than $1 for sums through $1.99

Materials

dollar, dimes and pennies
hundred-flat
ten-strips and ones

Mental Math

Tell students to name the number that comes next:

1. 18, 20, 22, 24 (26)
2. 10, 9, 8, 7 (6)
3. 163, 173, 183, 193 (203)
4. 708, 710, 712, 714 (716)
5. 7, 9, 11, 13 (15)
6. 165, 170, 175, 180 (185)

Skill Review

Have a student lay out 8 dimes and 4 pennies. Ask the student to talk through the necessary trade to give another student 76¢. Ask how much money is left. (8¢) Have a student write and solve the subtraction problem on the board. (84¢ − 76 = 8¢) Have another student write and solve an addition problem on the board to check the subtraction. (8¢ + 76 = 84¢) Repeat for more subtraction of money amounts.

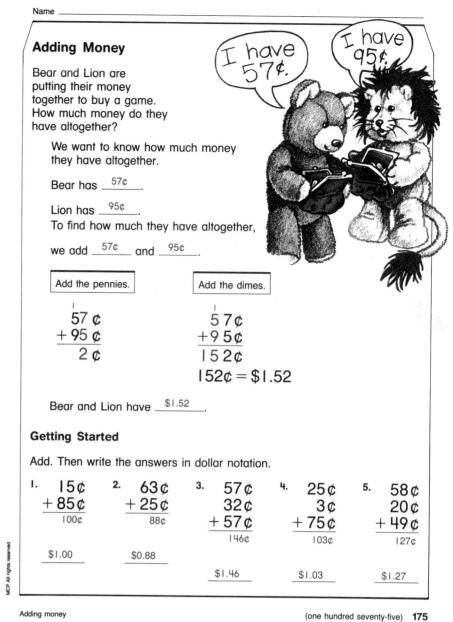

Name _____

Adding Money

Bear and Lion are putting their money together to buy a game. How much money do they have altogether?

We want to know how much money they have altogether.

Bear has ___57¢___.

Lion has ___95¢___.
To find how much they have altogether,

we add ___57¢___ and ___95¢___.

Add the pennies.		Add the dimes.

```
    ¹               ¹
   57 ¢            5 7 ¢
 + 95 ¢          + 9 5 ¢
 ─────          ───────
    2 ¢          1 5 2 ¢
              152¢ = $1.52
```

Bear and Lion have ___$1.52___.

Getting Started

Add. Then write the answers in dollar notation.

1.	2.	3.	4.	5.
15¢ +85¢ ── 100¢	63¢ +25¢ ── 88¢	57¢ 32¢ +57¢ ── 146¢	25¢ 3¢ +75¢ ── 103¢	58¢ 20¢ +49¢ ── 127¢
$1.00	$0.88	$1.46	$1.03	$1.27

Adding money

(one hundred seventy-five) **175**

Teaching the Lesson

Introducing the Problem Have a student read the problem aloud and tell what is to be found. (how much money Bear and Lion have all together) Ask students what information is given in the problem or the picture. (Bear has 57¢ and Lion has 95¢.) Have students read and complete the information sentences. Work through the model with students and then have them complete the solution sentence. Have students lay out 57¢ and 95¢ and add the coins to check their solution.

Developing the Skill Write **120** on the board and have students lay out hundreds, tens and ones to show the number. Now write **120¢** on the board and have students lay out 1 dollar, 2 dimes and 0 pennies. Write **120¢ = $1.20** on the board to remind students that 120 pennies can be written as $1.20. Have students lay out 93¢ and 48¢ and tell how many pennies in all. (11) Remind students that 10 pennies can be traded for 1 dime. Ask students how many pennies and dimes after the trade. (14 dimes, 1 penny) Ask if a trade for $1 can be made. (yes) Tell students to make the trade and then have a student write the sum of 93¢ and 48¢ on the board in total cents and then using the dollar sign and decimal point. (141¢, $1.41) Repeat to find the sum of 68¢, 24¢ and 51¢ ($1.43), 79¢ and 86¢ ($1.65), 48¢, 57¢ and 82¢ ($1.87) and 99¢ and 58¢. ($1.57)

175

Practice

Add. Then write the answers in dollar notation.

1.
$$75¢ \atop + 52¢$$
127¢

$1.27

2.
$$98¢ \atop + 95¢$$
193¢

$1.93

3.
$$61¢ \atop + 89¢$$
150¢

$1.50

4.
$$50¢ \atop + 41¢$$
91¢

$0.91

5.
$$83¢ \atop + 42¢$$
125¢

$1.25

6.
$$92¢ \atop + 69¢$$
161¢

$1.61

7.
$$88¢ \atop + 63¢$$
151¢

$1.51

8.
$$12¢ \atop + 98¢$$
110¢

$1.10

9.
$$55¢ \atop + 45¢$$
100¢

$1.00

10.
$$77¢ \atop + 37¢$$
114¢

$1.14

11.
$$87¢ \atop + 62¢$$
149¢

$1.49

12.
$$56¢ \atop + 39¢$$
95¢

$0.95

13.
$$86¢ \atop 3¢ \atop + 46¢$$
135¢

$1.35

14.
$$14¢ \atop 34¢ \atop + 26¢$$
74¢

$0.74

15.
$$55¢ \atop 11¢ \atop + 45¢$$
111¢

$1.11

Apply

Write the answers on the lines.

☆ Lana has $1.25.
☆ Craig has 37¢.
☆ José has 75¢.

16. Who has the most money? __Lana__

17. Who has the least money? __Craig__

18. How much money do Craig and José have together?

$$37¢ \atop + 75¢$$
112¢

__112¢ or $1.12__

19. How much more money does José have than Craig?

$$75¢ \atop - 37¢$$
38¢

__38¢__

Adding money

Correcting Common Errors

Some students may write money incorrectly because they misplace the cents point. Reveiw with them how 184 cents is the same as 1 dollar 8 dimes 4 pennies and should be written as $1.84, where the cents point separates the whole dollar from the part of a dollar. Be sure they understand that when a cents point is used in money, it is always followed by two digits and no more.

Enrichment

Tell students to cut out 3 items with prices under 70¢ from newspaper ads. Have them draw dimes and pennies to show how much money they would need to buy all 3 items. Then tell them to draw the total amount using a dollar, dimes and pennies.

Practice

Tell students they are to add in each problem, write the sum in cents and then write the amount using the dollar sign and decimal point. In the Apply section, tell student they will be writing names for the first two answers and money amounts for the last two. Assign the page to be completed independently.

Mixed Practice

1. 8¢ − 3¢ (5¢)
2. 6 + ___ = 10 (4)
3. 695 ◯ 705 (<)
4. 11 − 3 (8)
5. 585, 590, 595, ___ (600)
6. 16 − 7 (9)
7. 58 ◯ 158 (<)
8. 0 + 3 (3)
9. 7 hundreds 1 ten 5 ones (715)
10. 7 + 6 (13)

Extra Credit   *Numeration*

Give students large paper, school glue and colored rice or other small seeds. Write the Roman numerals for 1 through 10 on the board. (I, II, III, IV, V, VI, VII VIII, IX, X) Have students draw the Roman numerals with glue on their papers. Dust each paper with rice. Display their colorful numerals.

Problem Solving Money

pages 177-178

Objective

To add or subtract amounts of money to solve problems

Materials

dollar, dimes and pennies

Mental Math

Ask students if they will add or subtract for problems asking:

1. how many in all? (add)
2. how many more? (subtract)
3. how many are left? (subtract)
4. how many all together? (add)
5. how much change? (subtract)
6. what is the sum? (add)

Skill Review

Write **82¢ + 49¢ + 23¢** on the board. Have students work the problem independently on paper and write the sum using the cent sign and then in dollar notation. (154¢, $1.54) Have a student write the sum on the board in each notation. Remind students that amounts of $1 or more are generally written in dollar notation. Repeat for more addition problems of 2 or 3 money amounts.

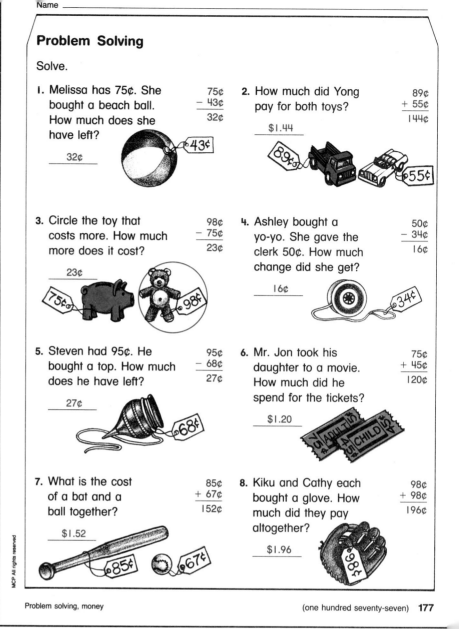

Problem Solving

Solve.

1. Melissa has 75¢. She bought a beach ball. How much does she have left?

   75¢
   − 43¢
   32¢

   __32¢__

2. How much did Yong pay for both toys?

   89¢
   + 55¢
   144¢

   __$1.44__

3. Circle the toy that costs more. How much more does it cost?

   98¢
   − 75¢
   23¢

   __23¢__

4. Ashley bought a yo-yo. She gave the clerk 50¢. How much change did she get?

   50¢
   − 34¢
   16¢

   __16¢__

5. Steven had 95¢. He bought a top. How much does he have left?

   95¢
   − 68¢
   27¢

   __27¢__

6. Mr. Jon took his daughter to a movie. How much did he spend for the tickets?

   75¢
   + 45¢
   120¢

   __$1.20__

7. What is the cost of a bat and a ball together?

   85¢
   + 67¢
   152¢

   __$1.52__

8. Kiku and Cathy each bought a glove. How much did they pay altogether?

   98¢
   + 98¢
   196¢

   __$1.96__

Problem solving, money

(one hundred seventy-seven) **177**

Teaching page 177

Have a student read the first problem aloud and tell what is to be solved as you write **What is to be found?** on the board. (how much money Melissa has left) Ask students what is known as you write **What do we know?** on the board. (She had 75¢ and bought a beach ball.) Ask students what information is needed from the picture. (The ball costs 43¢.) Ask what operation needs to be done as you write **What needs to be done with the numbers?** on the board. (subtract) Have students work the problem. (32¢) Ask if the answer makes sense as you write **Does the answer make sense?** on the board. Have a student write and solve an addition problem on the board to check the solution. (32¢ + 43¢ = 75¢) Tell students they are to write and solve problems on this page and then record the answer on the line below the problem. Remind students to use the questions on the board to help solve each problem. Also remind students to use money to check each addition prob-

lem and check each subtraction problem with money or by adding. Tell students to complete the page independently.

177

Solve.

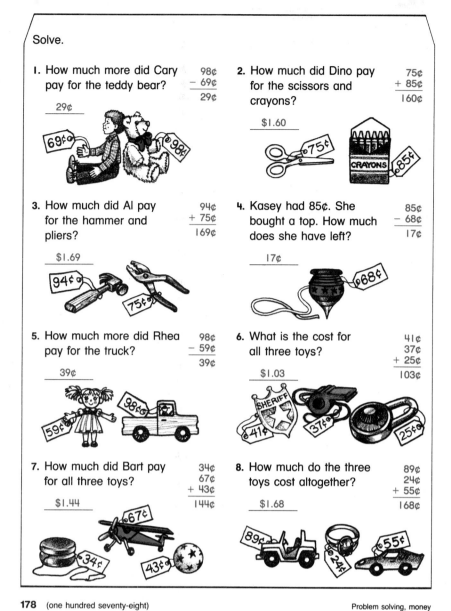

1. How much more did Cary pay for the teddy bear?

$$\begin{array}{r} 98¢ \\ -\ 69¢ \\ \hline 29¢ \end{array}$$

29¢

2. How much did Dino pay for the scissors and crayons?

$$\begin{array}{r} 75¢ \\ +\ 85¢ \\ \hline 160¢ \end{array}$$

$1.60

3. How much did Al pay for the hammer and pliers?

$$\begin{array}{r} 94¢ \\ +\ 75¢ \\ \hline 169¢ \end{array}$$

$1.69

4. Kasey had 85¢. She bought a top. How much does she have left?

$$\begin{array}{r} 85¢ \\ -\ 68¢ \\ \hline 17¢ \end{array}$$

17¢

5. How much more did Rhea pay for the truck?

$$\begin{array}{r} 98¢ \\ -\ 59¢ \\ \hline 39¢ \end{array}$$

39¢

6. What is the cost for all three toys?

$$\begin{array}{r} 41¢ \\ 37¢ \\ +\ 25¢ \\ \hline 103¢ \end{array}$$

$1.03

7. How much did Bart pay for all three toys?

$$\begin{array}{r} 34¢ \\ 67¢ \\ +\ 43¢ \\ \hline 144¢ \end{array}$$

$1.44

8. How much do the three toys cost altogether?

$$\begin{array}{r} 89¢ \\ 24¢ \\ +\ 55¢ \\ \hline 168¢ \end{array}$$

$1.68

Problem solving, money

Teaching page 178

Tell students to write and solve each problem and then record the answer on the line. Tell students to check each problem. Assign the page for independent work.

Extra Credit *Logic*

Read or duplicate for students:

After her lunch break was over, a woman walked up to the cafe cash register to pay her bill. The cashier noticed the woman had carefully drawn a circle, a square and a triangle along the left-hand side of the bill. The cashier immediately looked up and said, "How long have you been a policewoman?" How did the cashier know the lady was a policewoman? (The policewoman was wearing her uniform.)

Review

pages 179-180

Objectives

To review addition and subtraction of 2-digit numbers

To maintain skills learned previously this year

Materials

dollars and coins

Mental Math

Ask students to name the following numbers:

1. 6 tens + 6 tens (12 tens or 120)
2. 2 tens − 9 ones (11)
3. 3 tens + 4 tens (7 tens or 70)
4. 9 ones + 9 ones (18)
5. 12 ones − 4 ones (8)
6. 8 tens + 9 tens (17 tens or 170)
7. 7 ones − 0 ones (7)

Skill Review

Have students mentally tell the sums of dictated 2-digit multiples of 10 such as 10 + 80 + 10 (100), 40 + 90 (130), 70 + 50 + 20 (140), 80 + 90 (170), etc.

CHAPTER CHECKUP

Add or subtract.

1. $38 + 9 = 47$	2. $46 + 21 = 67$	3. $15 + 83 = 98$	4. $24 + 63 = 87$	5. $25 + 38 = 63$	6. $46 + 26 = 72$
7. $87 + 62 = 149$	8. $32 + 77 = 109$	9. $77 + 43 = 120$	10. $69 + 66 = 135$	11. $83 + 58 = 141$	12. $67 + 63 = 130$
13. $86 - 23 = 63$	14. $75 - 14 = 61$	15. $67 - 17 = 50$	16. $93 - 24 = 69$	17. $51 - 39 = 12$	18. $75 - 48 = 27$
19. $23 + 14 + 42 = 79$	20. $10 + 50 + 70 = 130$	21. $13 + 65 + 63 = 141$	22. $43 + 73 + 6 = 122$	23. $45 + 50 + 55 = 150$	24. $32 + 27 + 93 = 152$
25. $34 + 21 + 22 = 77$	26. $53 + 72 + 8 = 133$	27. $32 + 42 + 26 = 100$	28. $20 + 60 + 40 = 120$	29. $40 + 51 + 69 = 160$	30. $16 + 75 + 60 = 151$

Add or subtract. Then write the answers in dollar notation.

31. $35¢ + 75¢ = 110¢$	32. $57¢ + 98¢ = 155¢$	33. $97¢ - 65¢ = 32¢$	34. $75¢ + 50¢ = 125¢$	35. $83¢ - 25¢ = 58¢$
$1.10	$1.55	$0.32	$1.25	$0.58

Chapter review

(one hundred seventy-nine) **179**

Teaching page 179

Tell students to write the sum or difference for each problem. Remind students to look for a ten when adding a column of numbers. Tell students to write each of the sums involving money using the cent notation and then in dollar notation. Ask students how they will write a sum in dollar notation when there are no dollars. (write a zero in the dollar place) Have students complete the page independently.

179

ROUNDUP REVIEW

Fill in the oval next to the correct answer.

1	7 + 6	○ 12 ● 13 ○ 14 ○ NG	8	25 34 + 17	○ 66 ○ 77 ● 76 ○ NG

1   7
    + 6   ○ 12   ● 13   ○ 14   ○ NG

8   25   34   + 17   ○ 66   ○ 77   ● 76   ○ NG

2   8 + 9   ● 17   ○ 16   ○ 18   ○ NG

9   78   − 45   ○ 123   ● 33   ○ 113   ○ NG

3   12   − 5   ○ 17   ○ 15   ● 7   ○ NG

10   91   − 25   ● 66   ○ 74   ○ 76   ○ NG

4   15 − 6   ○ 8   ○ 21   ○ 11   ● NG

11   48 + 35   ○ 82   ● 83   ○ 73   ○ NG

5   ○ 76   ○ 57   ● 67   ○ NG

12   57   + 6   ○ 51   ○ 53   ● 63   ○ NG

6   39 ○ 41   ○ >   ● <

13   71 − 29   ○ 58   ● 42   ○ 52   ○ NG

7   69   + 89   ● 158   ○ 20   ○ 148   ○ NG

[ ] score

Enrichment

1. Tell students to write all the basic addition facts which could be used to tell about 1 dozen eggs.
2. Have students write and solve a subtraction problem which tells the missing addend if 3 numbers have a sum of 91 and 2 of the numbers are 46 and 19.
3. Tell students to write all the even numbers from 279 through 297 in one column and the odd numbers in another column.

Teaching page 180

This page reviews basic addition and subtraction facts, place value, number comparison and addition and subtraction of 2-digit numbers. Tell students to solve each problem and then fill in the oval beside the correct answer. Remind students that the NG is to be filled in only if the correct answer is not given. Have students complete the page independently.

Place Value through 1,000

pages 181-182

Objective

To understand place value through 1,000

Materials

hundred-flats
ten-strips and ones

Mental Math

Tell students to name the next ordinal number:

1. 7th, 8th, 9th (10th)
2. 215th, 216th, 217th (218th)
3. 11th, 10th, 9th (8th)
4. 1st, 3rd, 5th (7th)
5. 4th, 6th, 8th (10th)
6. 100th, 200th, 300th (400th)

Skill Review

Tell students you have 2 dimes and 6 pennies left after buying a book for 89¢. Ask a student to write and solve a problem to show the amount of money you had when you went shopping. (89¢ + 26 = $1.15) Now tell students you started with 8 dimes and 2 pennies and have 4 dimes and 3 pennies left. Ask a student to write and solve a problem to show the amount of money you spent. (82¢ − 43 = 39¢) Repeat for more problems.

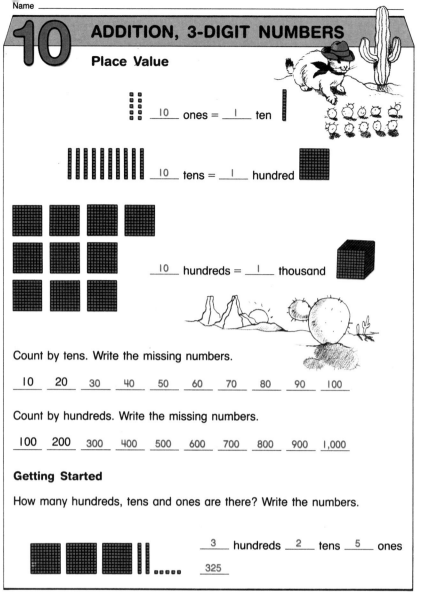

10 ADDITION, 3-DIGIT NUMBERS

Place Value

10 ones = 1 ten

10 tens = 1 hundred

10 hundreds = 1 thousand

Count by tens. Write the missing numbers.

10 20 30 40 50 60 70 80 90 100

Count by hundreds. Write the missing numbers.

100 200 300 400 500 600 700 800 900 1,000

Getting Started

How many hundreds, tens and ones are there? Write the numbers.

3 hundreds 2 tens 5 ones

325

Place value through 1,000   (one hundred eighty-one) **181**

Teaching the Lesson

Introducing the Problem Have students count the squares and complete the number sentences. Have students count by tens and hundreds orally as they fill in the missing numbers.

Developing the Skill Lay out 3 hundred-flats, 2 ten-strips and 6 ones. Ask how many hundreds, tens and ones. (3, 2, 6) Ask students to tell the number. (326) Repeat for more 2- or 3-digit numbers. Write **683** on the board and ask a student to lay out manipulatives to show the number (6 hundred-flats, 8 ten-strips, 3 ones) Continue for more numbers including those with no tens and/or no ones. Help students recognize that 10 hundreds equal 1,000.

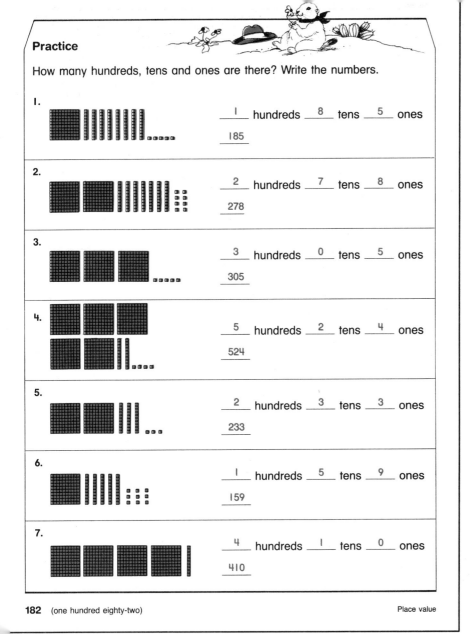

Practice

How many hundreds, tens and ones are there? Write the numbers.

1. ___1___ hundreds ___8___ tens ___5___ ones

185

2. ___2___ hundreds ___7___ tens ___8___ ones

278

3. ___3___ hundreds ___0___ tens ___5___ ones

305

4. ___5___ hundreds ___2___ tens ___4___ ones

524

5. ___2___ hundreds ___3___ tens ___3___ ones

233

6. ___1___ hundreds ___5___ tens ___9___ ones

159

7. ___4___ hundreds ___1___ tens ___0___ ones

410

182 (one hundred eighty-two)   Place value

Correcting Common Errors

If students have difficulty understanding hundreds, tens, and ones, have them work with partners and use hundred-flats, ten-strips, and ones. Give each pair 4 cards, each card with a number on it such as 247. Have them use their place-value materials to model the number.

Enrichment

Tell students to write in a column the numbers from 0 through 1,000 which have 2 tens and 6 ones. Then tell them to make another column of the numbers which have 8 tens and 7 ones.

Practice

Tell students to write the number of hundreds, tens and ones and then write the number. Have students complete the page independently.

Mixed Practice

1. 13 − 6 (7)
2. 17 − 8 (9)
3. 3 + ___ = 12 (9)
4. 695 ◯ 700 (<)
5. 8¢ + 8¢ (16¢)
6. 570, 580, 590, 600, ___ (610)
7. 0 + 9 (9)
8. 93 ◯ 100 (<)
9. ___ + 6 = 10 (4)
10. 3 hundreds 2 tens 9 ones (329)

Extra Credit   *Logic*

Tell students to imagine **themselves** as the city bus driver in the following problem: At the first stop 11 passengers get on their bus. At the next stop 3 get on and 4 get off. At the next stop 7 get on and 2 get off. At the next stop 9 get on and 2 get off. At the next stop 4 get on and 5 get off. Now, ask them to tell you the driver's name. (They are the driver. What is their name?)

182

Adding 2-digit Numbers

pages 183-184

Objective

To review adding two 2-digit numbers for sums through 199

Materials

hundred-flats
ten-strips and ones

Mental Math

Tell students to name the number if they skipped 3 numbers after each:

1. 121 (125)
2. 706 (710)
3. 297 (301)
4. 87 (91)
5. 5, 10, 15, 20 (40)
6. 6, 8, 10, 12 (20)
7. 200, 300, 400 (800)

Skill Review

Have a student use manipulatives to lay out a 3-digit number. Have another student write the next number on the board. Have a student lay out the number that follows the number on the board. Have a student write the next number on the board. Continue for several more numbers and ask students to tell the pattern of the numbers on the board. (counting by 2's)

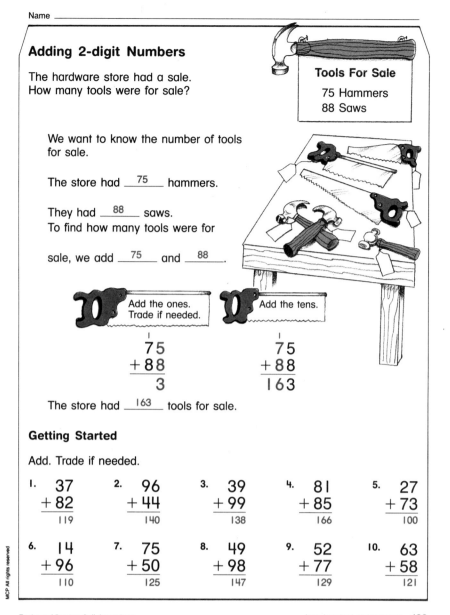

Adding 2-digit Numbers

The hardware store had a sale.
How many tools were for sale?

Tools For Sale
75 Hammers
88 Saws

We want to know the number of tools for sale.

The store had __75__ hammers.

They had __88__ saws.
To find how many tools were for

sale, we add __75__ and __88__.

Add the ones. Trade if needed.

$$75 + 88 \atop 3$$

Add the tens.

$$75 + 88 \atop 163$$

The store had __163__ tools for sale.

Getting Started

Add. Trade if needed.

1. $37 + 82 \atop 119$
2. $96 + 44 \atop 140$
3. $39 + 99 \atop 138$
4. $81 + 85 \atop 166$
5. $27 + 73 \atop 100$

6. $14 + 96 \atop 110$
7. $75 + 50 \atop 125$
8. $49 + 98 \atop 147$
9. $52 + 77 \atop 129$
10. $63 + 58 \atop 121$

Review adding two 2-digit numbers

(one hundred eighty-three) **183**

Teaching the Lesson

Introducing the Problem Have a student read the problem aloud and tell what is being asked. (the number of tools for sale) Ask students what information is given in the problem. (none) Ask what information is given in the picture. (75 hammers and 88 saws) Ask students what operation needs to be done to find the total number of tools. (addition) Have students read and complete the information sentences. Work through the model with students and then have them complete the solution sentence. Have students lay out 7 tens 5 ones and 8 tens 8 ones and tell the total tens and ones to check their solution.

Developing the Skill Have students write the basic subtraction facts which have sums of 10. (9 + 1, 8 + 2, 7 + 3, . . ., 1 + 9) Remind students that 10 ones are traded for a ten and that 10 tens are traded for a hundred. Write **78 + 64** on the board and remind students that 8 ones + 4 ones = 12 ones so 10 of the ones are traded for a ten, leaving 2 ones. Write the trade and the 2 ones. Remind students that 7 tens and 6 tens are added and then the 1 more ten for 14 tens. Tell students that 10 of the tens are traded for a hundred, leaving 4 tens. Write the trade and the 4 tens. Have a student record the number of hundreds. (1) Ask students to read the sum. (142) Repeat for 87 + 88 (175), 53 + 92 (145) and 78 + 99 (177), having students show the trades and write the sums.

183

Practice

Add. Trade if needed.

1. 42
  + 83
  125

2. 95
  + 70
  165

3. 84
  + 29
  113

4. 39
  + 57
  96

5. 79
  + 83
  162

6. 18
  + 67
  85

7. 68
  + 54
  122

8. 86
  + 76
  162

9. 22
  + 54
  76

10. 82
  + 68
  150

11. 56
  + 55
  111

12. 90
  + 53
  143

13. 63
  + 82
  145

14. 97
  + 85
  182

15. 78
  + 79
  157

16. 51
  + 84
  135

17. 68
  + 24
  92

18. 77
  + 89
  166

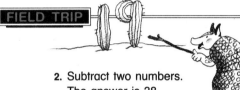

FIELD TRIP

Solve.

1. Add two numbers.
   The sum is 96.
   One number is 35.
   What is the other number?

   61

2. Subtract two numbers.
   The answer is 38.
   The larger number is 96.
   What is the other number?

   58

3. Add two numbers.
   The sum is 91.
   One number is 36.
   What is the other number?

   55

4. Subtract two numbers.
   The answer is 57.
   The smaller number is 19.
   What is the larger number?

   76

Correcting Common Errors

Some students may need additional practice in deciding when to trade and when not to trade when adding 2-digit numbers. Have them work with partners. Give the pair 8 cards, each showing an addition problem, 4 that require trading and 4 that do not. Have them separate the cards into a trading pile and a non-trading pile. Be sure they verbalize how they decided into which group to put the problems. Then have them perform the additions.

Enrichment

Tell students to write and solve problems to show all the numbers from 40 through 60 which, if added to 47, would require trading for a ten and/or a hundred.

Practice

Have students complete the rows of problems independently.

Field Trip

Write **26 + 42 = 68, 68 − 42 = 26** and **68 − 26 = 42** vertically on the board. Remind students that the larger number or the sum in the first problem minus one of the numbers equals the other number. Tell students that the sum of 2 numbers is 41 and one of the numbers is 26. Ask a student to write and solve a problem to find the other number. (41 − 26 = 15 or 26 + 15 = 41) Repeat for an answer of 73 if one number is 38. (73 − 38 = 35 or 38 + 35 = 73) Have students complete the problems independently.

Extra Credit *Applications*

Arrange for an adding machine or cash register to be brought into the classroom. Invite a cashier, salesperson, or company representative to demonstrate the use of the machine. If possible, provide students with the opportunity to work at the machine for awhile. Have students list some of the jobs where they would be expected to know how to use one of these machines.

184

3-digit Plus
1-digit Numbers

pages 185-186

Objective

To add a 3-digit and a 1-digit number with some trading

Materials

hundred-flats
ten-strips and ones

Mental Math

Ask students to name a number that:

1. is less than 219 (218, . . . , 0)
2. has 8 tens (80, 180, 280, . . . , 980)
3. is greater than 468 (469, . . . , 999)
4. means 25 minutes after the hour on a clock (5)
5. has 3 digits and all are the same (111, 222, 333, . . . , 999)
6. reads the same backward and forward (111, 121, 131, etc.)

Skill Review

Write **46 + 6** on the board and have a student talk through the solution as another student records the work. (52) Repeat for 72 + 9 (81), 56 + 5 (61), 83 + 8 (91), 74 + 9 (83) and 68 + 8 (76).

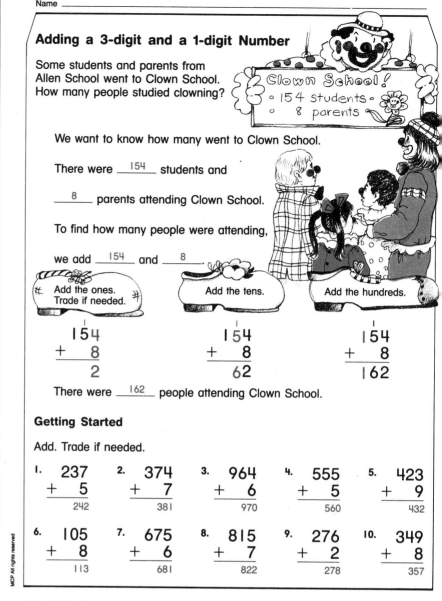

Teaching the Lesson

Introducing the Problem Have a student read the problem aloud and tell what is being asked. (how many people studied clowning) Ask students what information is given in the problem or the picture. (154 students and 8 parents) Ask what needs to be done with the 2 numbers. (add) Have students read aloud with you as they complete the sentences, talk through the solution and complete the solution statement. Have students use manipulatives to check their addition.

Developing the Skill Dictate the following problems for students to write and solve on the board: 76 + 8 (84), 19 + 7 (26), 25 + 5 (30). Now write **252 + 9** on the board and have students show the numbers with manipulatives. Have students tell the sum of 2 and 9. (11) Ask if trading is needed. (yes) Have a student show the trade and record the number of ones left. (1 one left) Have a student tell and record the number of tens and hundreds. (6 tens and 2 hundreds) Ask students the sum. (261) Repeat for the following problems: 456 + 7 (463), 8 + 709 (717), 345 + 4 (349), 7 + 208 (215), 389 + 9 (398). Have students check each problem with manipulatives.

Practice

Add. Trade if needed.

1. 774
    $+\quad 9$
    ___
    783

2. 588
    $+\quad 2$
    ___
    590

3. 517
    $+\quad 9$
    ___
    526

4. 603
    $+\quad 7$
    ___
    610

5. 357
    $+\quad 4$
    ___
    361

6. 282
    $+\quad 7$
    ___
    289

7. 156
    $+\quad 6$
    ___
    162

8. 921
    $+\quad 8$
    ___
    929

9. 813
    $+\quad 9$
    ___
    822

10. 628
    $+\quad 5$
    ___
    633

11. 487
    $+\quad 4$
    ___
    491

12. 307
    $+\quad 5$
    ___
    312

13. 156
    $+\quad 6$
    ___
    162

14. 385
    $+\quad 3$
    ___
    388

15. 906
    $+\quad 8$
    ___
    914

16. $\quad 9$
    $+286$
    ___
    295

17. 986
    $+\quad 6$
    ___
    992

18. $\quad 9$
    $+849$
    ___
    858

19. 383
    $+\quad 8$
    ___
    391

20. 566
    $+\quad 7$
    ___
    573

Apply

Solve.

21. There were 335 tickets to the circus sold. Then 6 more tickets were sold. How many tickets were sold?

    335
    $+\quad 6$
    ___
    341

    __341__ tickets

22. Pat sold 248 bags of popcorn at the circus. Then he sold 7 more bags. How many bags of popcorn did Pat sell?

    248
    $+\quad 7$
    ___
    255

    __255__ bags

Adding 3-digit numbers to 1-digit numbers

Correcting Common Errors

Some students have difficulty understanding trading when they add a 3-digit number and a 1-digit number. Draw a number line from 100 through 130 on the chalkboard with intervals of 1. Circle the decade number on the line; that is, 100, 110, 120, and 130. Tell students that each time a decade number is passed, a trade of 10 ones is made for 1 ten. Write 115 + 9 on the board. Have a student locate 115 on the number line, go 9 spaces forward and tell the number. (124) Ask, "Was a decade number passed?" (Yes) Now write on the chalkboard the addition problem for 115 + 9 in vertical form and discuss the trades as you solve it together. Repeat this procedure for other addition problems.

Enrichment

Tell students to write and solve a problem which tells the day of the year which is one week later than the 313th day.

Practice

Remind students to add the ones first and then the tens and hundreds. Assign the page to be completed independently.

Mixed Practice

1. 2 dimes 1 nickel (25¢)
2. 635, 640, 645, ___ (650)
3. 700 ◯ 600 (>)
4. 13¢ − 4¢ (9¢)
5. 8 hundreds 0 tens 5 ones (805)
6. 7 + 4 (11)
7. 805 ◯ 815 (<)
8. ___ + 5 = 14 (9)
9. 10 + 7 (17)
10. 2 + 9 (11)

Extra Credit   *Creative Drill*

Provide students with copies of this crossword puzzle. Do one across and one down together. Have students finish the puzzle independently.

ACROSS
1. subtract 4 from 38
2. subtract 9 from 26
4. subtract 20 from 60
6. subtract 30 from 50
7. subtract 15 from 39
9. subtract 27 from 42
10. subtract 48 from 62

DOWN
1. 38 minus 7
3. 83 minus 5
4. 70 minus 30
5. 45 minus 13
6. 60 minus 40
8. 65 minus 24
9. 72 minus 58

186

3-digit Plus 2-digit Numbers

pages 187-188

Objective

To add 3-digit and 2-digit numbers with one trade

Materials

hundred-flats
ten-strips and ones
colored chalk

Mental Math

Ask students what 3-digit numbers read the same backward and forward and has:

1. 4 tens (141, 242, . . . , 949)
2. 9 ones (909, 919, 929, . . . , 999)
3. 6 hundreds (606, 616, 626, . . . , 696)
4. 0 tens (101, 202, 303, . . . , 909)
5. 3 ones (303, 313, 323, . . . , 393)
6. 7 tens (171, 272, 373, . . . , 979)
7. 8 hundreds (808, 818, 828, . . . , 898)

Skill Review

Dictate the following problems for students to write and solve on the board as other students use manipulatives: 426 + 9 (435), 204 + 8 (212), 355 + 6 (361), 774 + 5 (779), 563 + 7 (570).

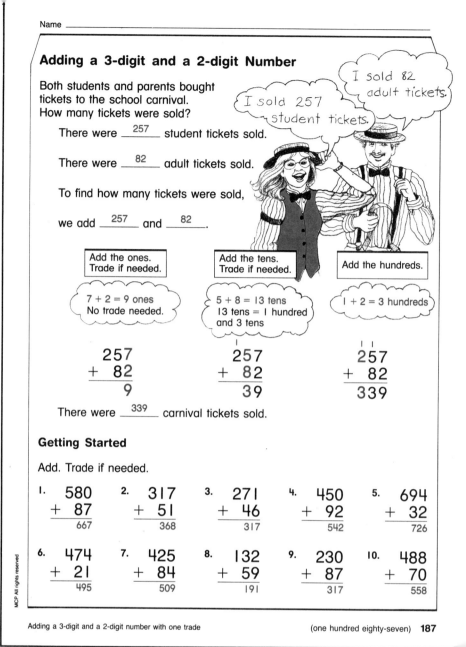

Name _____

Adding a 3-digit and a 2-digit Number

Both students and parents bought tickets to the school carnival. How many tickets were sold?

There were ___257___ student tickets sold.

There were ___82___ adult tickets sold.

To find how many tickets were sold,

we add ___257___ and ___82___.

I sold 257 student tickets.

I sold 82 adult tickets.

Add the ones. Trade if needed.	Add the tens. Trade if needed.	Add the hundreds.
7 + 2 = 9 ones No trade needed.	5 + 8 = 13 tens 13 tens = 1 hundred and 3 tens	1 + 2 = 3 hundreds

$$\begin{array}{r} 257 \\ +\ 82 \\ \hline 9 \end{array} \qquad \begin{array}{r} 257 \\ +\ 82 \\ \hline 39 \end{array} \qquad \begin{array}{r} 257 \\ +\ 82 \\ \hline 339 \end{array}$$

There were ___339___ carnival tickets sold.

Getting Started

Add. Trade if needed.

1. $\begin{array}{r}580\\+\ 87\\\hline 667\end{array}$	2. $\begin{array}{r}317\\+\ 51\\\hline 368\end{array}$	3. $\begin{array}{r}271\\+\ 46\\\hline 317\end{array}$	4. $\begin{array}{r}450\\+\ 92\\\hline 542\end{array}$	5. $\begin{array}{r}694\\+\ 32\\\hline 726\end{array}$
6. $\begin{array}{r}474\\+\ 21\\\hline 495\end{array}$	7. $\begin{array}{r}425\\+\ 84\\\hline 509\end{array}$	8. $\begin{array}{r}132\\+\ 59\\\hline 191\end{array}$	9. $\begin{array}{r}230\\+\ 87\\\hline 317\end{array}$	10. $\begin{array}{r}488\\+\ 70\\\hline 558\end{array}$

Adding a 3-digit and a 2-digit number with one trade

(one hundred eighty-seven) **187**

Teaching the Lesson

Introducing the Problem Have a student read the problem aloud and tell what is to be solved. (the number of tickets sold) Ask what information is known. (257 student and 82 adult tickets were sold.) Ask what needs to be done with these numbers. (add) Have students read and complete the information sentences. Work through the model with students and then have them complete the solution sentence. Have students use manipulatives to check their solution.

Developing the Skill Write **264 + 53** vertically on the board. Have students work in pairs to lay out the 2 numbers. Ask students the sum of the ones. (7) Ask if a trade is needed. (no) Have a student write 7 in the ones answer column. Ask students the sum of 6 tens and 5 tens. (11 tens) Ask if a trade is needed. (yes) Have students make the trade and tell how many tens are left. (1) Have a student record the trade and the 1 ten. Ask students the total number of hundreds. (3) Have a student record the 3 in the answer on the board. Have students read the sum. (317) Repeat for the following problems which require either no trade, a trade of 10 tens or a trade of 10 ones: 815 + 92 (907), 420 + 58 (478), 746 + 83 (829), 278 + 18 (296), 342 + 96 (438).

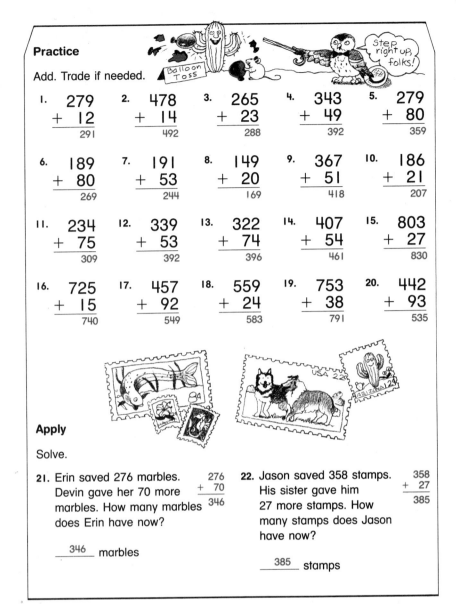

Practice

Add. Trade if needed.

1. 279
+ 12
291

2. 478
+ 14
492

3. 265
+ 23
288

4. 343
+ 49
392

5. 279
+ 80
359

6. 189
+ 80
269

7. 191
+ 53
244

8. 149
+ 20
169

9. 367
+ 51
418

10. 186
+ 21
207

11. 234
+ 75
309

12. 339
+ 53
392

13. 322
+ 74
396

14. 407
+ 54
461

15. 803
+ 27
830

16. 725
+ 15
740

17. 457
+ 92
549

18. 559
+ 24
583

19. 753
+ 38
791

20. 442
+ 93
535

Apply

Solve.

21. Erin saved 276 marbles. Devin gave her 70 more marbles. How many marbles does Erin have now?

276
+ 70
346

346 marbles

22. Jason saved 358 stamps. His sister gave him 27 more stamps. How many stamps does Jason have now?

358
+ 27
385

385 stamps

Adding a 3-digit and a 2-digit number with one trade

Correcting Common Errors

Some students may have difficulty adding a 2-digit number to a 3-digit number because they want to add a number to the hundreds. Have them work with partners and use place-value materials to model the problem.

Enrichment

Ask students to write and solve problems to find out which numbers from 20 through 30 require a trade when added to 274.

Practice

Remind students that a trade is needed in addition only if the sum is 10 or more. Have students complete the page independently.

Mixed Practice

1. 3 dimes, 3 nickels (45¢)
2. 7¢ + 7¢ (14¢)
3. 28 ◯ 82 (<)
4. 15 − 6 (9)
5. 9 + ___ = 17 (8)
6. 170 ◯ 710 (<)
7. 85, 90, 95, 100, ___ (105)
8. 6 + 7 (13)
9. 10 − 2 (8)
10. 13 − 8 (5)

Extra Credit *Numeration*

Write the Roman numerals for one to 10. (I, II, III, IV, V, VI, VII, VIII, IX, X) Select one student to put his head down, while another student erases two of the Roman numerals. The first student then goes to the board and writes in the correct missing numerals. If the student is correct, they can be the one to erase the numerals next, while another student puts their head down. Extend the range of Roman numerals as the students' familiarity increases.

3-digit Plus 2-digit Numbers

pages 189-190

Objective

To add a 3-digit and a 2-digit number with up to 2 trades

Materials

grid paper
hundred-flats
ten-strips and ones

Mental Math

Ask students if a trade is needed in addition for:

1. 7 tens + 1 ten + 3 tens. (yes)
2. 2 ones + 1 one + 6 ones. (no)
3. 5 tens + 5 tens. (yes)
4. 75 + 5. (yes)
5. 60 + 40. (yes)
6. 2 ones + 2 ones + 2 ones. (no)
7. 6 tens + 9 tens. (yes)

Skill Review

Write **6 tens** on the board. Ask student to write on the board the number of tens which can be added to 6 tens without a trade. (0 through 3) Repeat for the number of tens that would require a trade. (4 through 9) Repeat for other numbers of tens or ones.

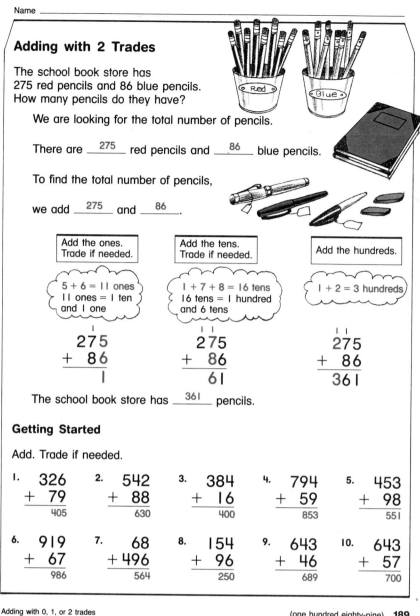

Adding with 2 Trades

The school book store has 275 red pencils and 86 blue pencils. How many pencils do they have?

We are looking for the total number of pencils.

There are ___275___ red pencils and ___86___ blue pencils.

To find the total number of pencils,

we add ___275___ and ___86___.

Add the ones. Trade if needed.	Add the tens. Trade if needed.	Add the hundreds.
5 + 6 = 11 ones 11 ones = 1 ten and 1 one	1 + 7 + 8 = 16 tens 16 tens = 1 hundred and 6 tens	1 + 2 = 3 hundreds

$$\begin{array}{r} 1 \\ 275 \\ +\ 86 \\ \hline 1 \end{array} \qquad \begin{array}{r} 1\ 1 \\ 275 \\ +\ 86 \\ \hline 61 \end{array} \qquad \begin{array}{r} 1\ 1 \\ 275 \\ +\ 86 \\ \hline 361 \end{array}$$

The school book store has ___361___ pencils.

Getting Started

Add. Trade if needed.

1. 326 + 79 405	2. 542 + 88 630	3. 384 + 16 400	4. 794 + 59 853	5. 453 + 98 551
6. 919 + 67 986	7. 68 +496 564	8. 154 + 96 250	9. 643 + 46 689	10. 643 + 57 700

Adding with 0, 1, or 2 trades   (one hundred eighty-nine) **189**

Teaching the Lesson

Introducing the Problem Have a student read the problem aloud and tell what is to be found. (the total number of pencils) Ask what information is given. (There are 275 red and 86 blue pencils.) Ask what operation is used to find how many in all. (addition) Have students read and complete the information sentences. Work through the model with students and then have them complete the solution sentence. Have students use manipulatives to check their solution.

Developing the Skill Write the following problems vertically on the board: **254 + 35** (289), **254 + 39** (293), **254 + 73** (327), **254 + 88** (342). Have students talk through each problem as you record the work. Students will see that the problems progress from no trade, to a trade for 1 ten, to a trade for 1 hundred and then to trade for both 1 ten and 1 hundred. Repeat for the following series of problems: 726 + 33 (759), 726 + 34 (760), 726 + 82 (808), 726 + 87 (813). Repeat for similar problems.

189

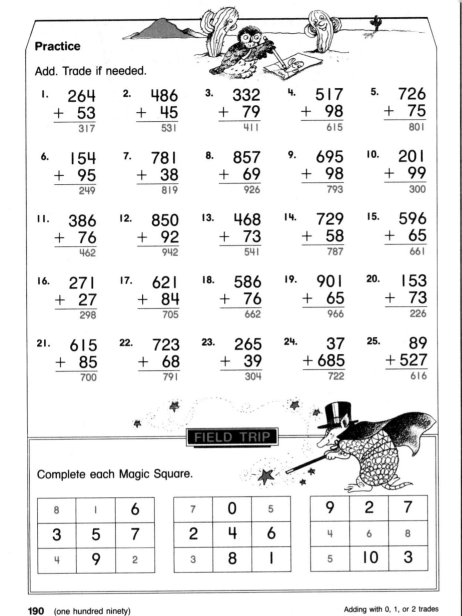

Practice

Add. Trade if needed.

1. 264
   + 53
   ——
   317

2. 486
   + 45
   ——
   531

3. 332
   + 79
   ——
   411

4. 517
   + 98
   ——
   615

5. 726
   + 75
   ——
   801

6. 154
   + 95
   ——
   249

7. 781
   + 38
   ——
   819

8. 857
   + 69
   ——
   926

9. 695
   + 98
   ——
   793

10. 201
    + 99
    ——
    300

11. 386
    + 76
    ——
    462

12. 850
    + 92
    ——
    942

13. 468
    + 73
    ——
    541

14. 729
    + 58
    ——
    787

15. 596
    + 65
    ——
    661

16. 271
    + 27
    ——
    298

17. 621
    + 84
    ——
    705

18. 586
    + 76
    ——
    662

19. 901
    + 65
    ——
    966

20. 153
    + 73
    ——
    226

21. 615
    + 85
    ——
    700

22. 723
    + 68
    ——
    791

23. 265
    + 39
    ——
    304

24. 37
    + 685
    ——
    722

25. 89
    + 527
    ——
    616

FIELD TRIP

Complete each Magic Square.

8	1	6
3	5	7
4	9	2

7	0	5
2	4	6
3	8	1

9	2	7
4	6	8
5	10	3

Adding with 0, 1, or 2 trades

Correcting Common Errors

Some students may trade correctly but then simply drop the renamed value.

INCORRECT	CORRECT
	1 1
248	248
+ 95	+ 95
233	343

Correct by having students work with partners and use place-value materials to model the problems.

Enrichment

Tell students to write and solve problems to show which numbers from 8 through 16 when added to 686 require 2 trades, that require 1 trade and that require no trades.

Practice

Remind students that the problems may need 0, 1 or 2 trades. Have students complete the page independently.

Field Trip

Help students complete the first square by guessing and checking. Have students complete the next 2 squares independently. Then draw the squares on the board for students to write in their solutions.

Extra Credit *Measurement*

Introduce this activity with a recording of "The Inchworm" from the musical "Hans Christian Anderson". Have each child trace, color, and cut out an inchworm made to scale:

Then have each student make 4 marigolds for a class bulletin board garden with stems that are 2, 4, 8, and 16 inches high. Using the inchworm to measure, have the class discuss the progression of height. Point out that if the stems are in sequence, each stem is two times the height of the stem before.

3-digit Addition with Trading

pages 191-192

Objective

To add 3-digit numbers to 2-digit numbers with trading

Materials

*addition fact cards
hundred-flats
ten-strips and ones
grid paper

Mental Math

Tell student to rename the following numbers in hundreds, tens and ones:

1. 999 (9 hundreds 9 tens 9 ones)
2. 182 + 2 (1 hundred 8 tens 4 ones)
3. 206 (2 hundreds 0 tens 6 ones)
4. 480 (4 hundreds 8 tens 0 ones)
5. 100 + 40 (1 hundred 4 tens 0 ones)
6. $1.62 (1 hundred 6 tens 2 ones)

Skill Review

Show addition fact cards in random order. As the card is flashed tell students the fact is tens or ones. Have students tell if a trade is needed, and if so, what the trade would be. For example: 6 ones + 9 ones requires a trade of 10 ones for 1 ten.

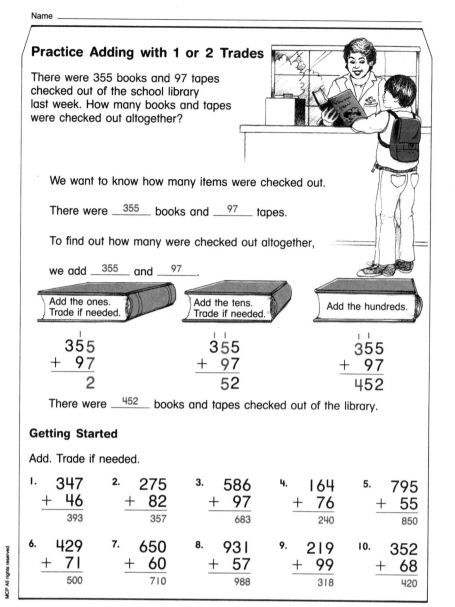

Practice Adding with 1 or 2 Trades

There were 355 books and 97 tapes checked out of the school library last week. How many books and tapes were checked out altogether?

We want to know how many items were checked out.

There were __355__ books and __97__ tapes.

To find out how many were checked out altogether,

we add __355__ and __97__.

Add the ones. Trade if needed.	Add the tens. Trade if needed.	Add the hundreds.
355 + 97 = 2	355 + 97 = 52	355 + 97 = 452

There were __452__ books and tapes checked out of the library.

Getting Started

Add. Trade if needed.

1. 347 + 46 = 393
2. 275 + 82 = 357
3. 586 + 97 = 683
4. 164 + 76 = 240
5. 795 + 55 = 850

6. 429 + 71 = 500
7. 650 + 60 = 710
8. 931 + 57 = 988
9. 219 + 99 = 318
10. 352 + 68 = 420

Adding with 1 or 2 trades

(one hundred ninety-one) **191**

Teaching the Lesson

Introducing the Problem Have a student read the problem aloud and tell what is to be found. (the total number of books and tapes) Ask what information is known. (There are 355 books and 97 tapes.) Ask what operation tells us how many in all. (addition) Have students read and complete the information sentences. Work through the model with students and then have them complete the solution sentence. Have students use manipulatives to check the solution.

Developing the Skill Have students rewrite and solve the following horizontal problems at the board: 476 + 24 (500), 82 + 327 (409), 253 + 86 (339), 89 + 192 (281). Then write **423** on the board and have a student complete the problem by writing a 2-digit addend. Have another student solve the problem and tell how many trades were needed. Repeat for more practice.

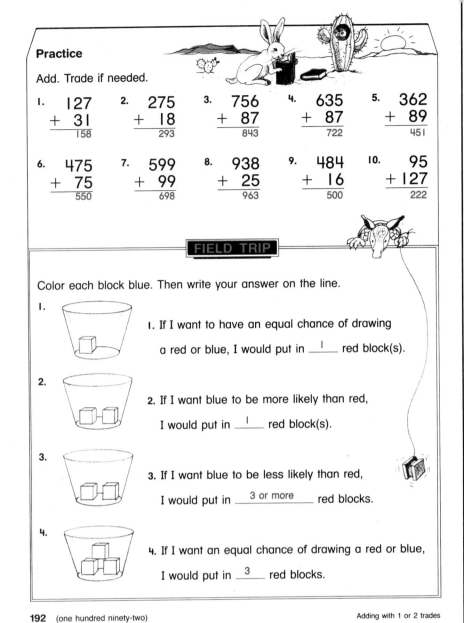

Practice

Add. Trade if needed.

1. 127 + 31 = 158
2. 275 + 18 = 293
3. 756 + 87 = 843
4. 635 + 87 = 722
5. 362 + 89 = 451
6. 475 + 75 = 550
7. 599 + 99 = 698
8. 938 + 25 = 963
9. 484 + 16 = 500
10. 95 + 127 = 222

FIELD TRIP

Color each block blue. Then write your answer on the line.

1. If I want to have an equal chance of drawing a red or blue, I would put in __1__ red block(s).

2. If I want blue to be more likely than red, I would put in __1__ red block(s).

3. If I want blue to be less likely than red, I would put in __3 or more__ red blocks.

4. If I want an equal chance of drawing a red or blue, I would put in __3__ red blocks.

Adding with 1 or 2 trades

Correcting Common Errors

Watch for students who write a renamed ten or hundred, even when a trade is not performed. Remind them to check the ones, or the tens, to see if a trade is necessary. Encourage students to encircle the place value digits that require a trade before they start working the problem.

Enrichment

Tell students to write and solve problems where 99 is added to 99, 199, 299, 399, etc. through 899. Ask what pattern can be seen.

Practice

Remind students that any sum of 10 or more in these problems will require a trade. Have students complete the rows of problems independently.

Field Trip

Discuss the meanings of **equal chance, more likely chance** and **less likely chance** with students. For there to be an equal chance, there must be the same number of each color block. For there to be a more likely chance of drawing blue, there must be more blue than red blocks. For there to be a less likely chance of drawing blue, there must be fewer blue than red blocks. Have students work the first problem using large and small paper clips in a container. Now have students put in 2 large clips and tell how many small clips would need to be added to have an equal chance of drawing a large or small clip. (2) Repeat for 2 large clips in and the number of small clips needed to have a more likely (1) and less likely (3) chance of drawing a large clip.

Have students color each block blue and complete each problem independently.

Extra Credit *Measurement*

Fill a box with styrofoam packing material. Allow students to experiment with volumes of common household packages for example, milk cartons, empty cereal boxes, etc. Have them pour material from one container to another several times until they have a clear understanding of how much each container holds. Have the students make greater than and less than pictures using the information gathered from their experiments. (Hint: Antistatic spray or hairspray will keep the material from sticking.)

3-digit Addition with Trading

pages 193-194

Objective

To add two 3-digit numbers for sums through 999 with trading

Materials

hundred-flats
ten-strips and ones

Mental Math

Tell students to compare the following numbers:

1. 482 ◯ 428 (>)
2. $3.75 ◯ $4.26 (<)
3. 29¢ ◯ $1.29 (<)
4. 901 ◯ 109 (>)
5. 141 ◯ 139 (>)
6. 777 ◯ 862 (<)
7. 311 ◯ 312 (<)
8. $9.00 ◯ $8.99 (>)

Skill Review

Write **473 + 68** vertically on the board. Have a student talk through the solution as another student records the work. (541) Repeat for 721 + 99 (820), 452 + 69 (521), 245 + 38 (283), 690 + 70 (760) and 288 + 46 (334).

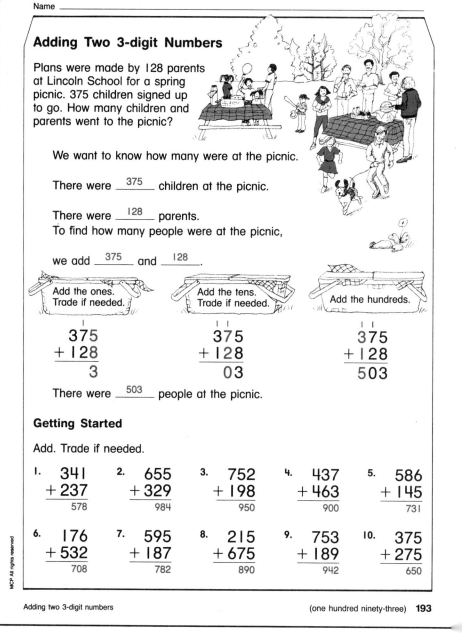

Adding Two 3-digit Numbers

Plans were made by 128 parents at Lincoln School for a spring picnic. 375 children signed up to go. How many children and parents went to the picnic?

We want to know how many were at the picnic.

There were __375__ children at the picnic.

There were __128__ parents.
To find how many people were at the picnic,

we add __375__ and __128__.

Add the ones. Trade if needed.	Add the tens. Trade if needed.	Add the hundreds.
375 +128 ___ 3	375 +128 ___ 03	375 +128 ___ 503

There were __503__ people at the picnic.

Getting Started

Add. Trade if needed.

1. 341 +237 = 578
2. 655 +329 = 984
3. 752 +198 = 950
4. 437 +463 = 900
5. 586 +145 = 731

6. 176 +532 = 708
7. 595 +187 = 782
8. 215 +675 = 890
9. 753 +189 = 942
10. 375 +275 = 650

Adding two 3-digit numbers   (one hundred ninety-three) **193**

Teaching the Lesson

Introducing the Problem Have students tell about the picture. Have a student read the problem aloud and tell what is to be found. (number of children and parents who attended the picnic) Ask what information is given. (There were 375 children and 128 parents.) Ask students what needs to be done with these numbers to find the total. (add) Have students read and complete the information sentences. Work through the model with students and then have them complete the solution sentence. Have students use manipulatives to check their solution.

Developing the Skill Write **473 + 268** vertically on the board. Have a student talk through the addition of the ones as you record the trade and the 1 one left. Repeat for the tens column recording the trade and 4 tens left. Ask students how many hundreds in all. (7) Ask students to read the sum. (741) Repeat for 452 + 358 (810), 376 + 525 (901), 402 + 394 (814), 582 + 209 (791) and 643 + 158 (801).

193

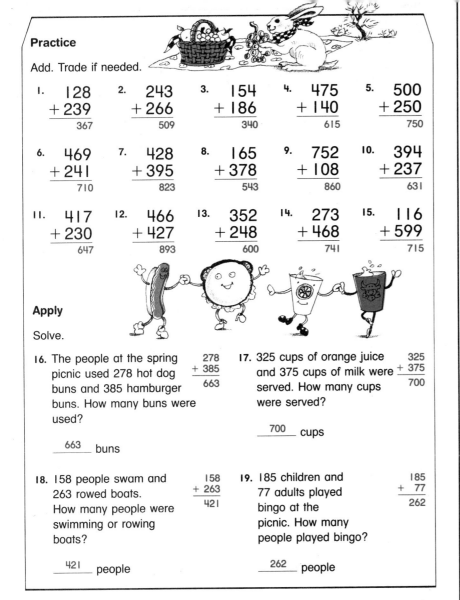

Practice

Add. Trade if needed.

1. 128 +239 367	2. 243 +266 509	3. 154 +186 340	4. 475 +140 615	5. 500 +250 750
6. 469 +241 710	7. 428 +395 823	8. 165 +378 543	9. 752 +108 860	10. 394 +237 631
11. 417 +230 647	12. 466 +427 893	13. 352 +248 600	14. 273 +468 741	15. 116 +599 715

Apply

Solve.

16. The people at the spring picnic used 278 hot dog buns and 385 hamburger buns. How many buns were used?

278
+ 385
663

_663_ buns

17. 325 cups of orange juice and 375 cups of milk were served. How many cups were served?

325
+ 375
700

_700_ cups

18. 158 people swam and 263 rowed boats. How many people were swimming or rowing boats?

158
+ 263
421

_421_ people

19. 185 children and 77 adults played bingo at the picnic. How many people played bingo?

185
+ 77
262

_262_ people

194 (one hundred ninety-four)   Adding two 3-digit numbers

Practice

Remind students to add the ones first, then the tens and then the hundreds. Also remind students to trade only if the sum is 10 or more. Assign the page to be completed independently.

Mixed Practice

1. ___ + 7 = 15 (8)
2. 2 hundreds 9 tens 6 ones (296)
3. 4 nickels, 2 pennies (22¢)
4. 57 + 6 (63)
5. 3 + 6 (9)
6. 795 ◯ 98 (>)
7. 15 − 8 (7)
8. 91 + 5 (96)
9. 68 + 8 (76)
10. 16 − 9 (7)

Extra Credit *Geometry*

Introduce the class to geoboards. If you do not have a classroom set of geoboards, you may want to use one class period to help students make them. Each board is a square of plywood with small nails arranged in a grid. You may make the board any convenient dimension. One common arrangement is a 10×10 grid.

In this first class have students make as many different kinds of triangles as they can using a rubber band to outline the shapes on the geoboard. Have them experiment, and discover and list any other geometric shapes they can make.

3-digit Addition with Trading

pages 195-196

Objective

To add for any 3-digit numbers with trading

Materials

hundred-flats
ten-strips and ones

Mental Math

Ask students where the hour hand is when it is:

1. 7:55. (almost on 8)
2. 2:40. (between 2 and 3)
3. 6:30. (between 6 and 7)
4. 12:00. (on 12)
5. 5:45. (between 5 and 6)
6. 3:50. (almost on 4)
7. 10:58. (almost on 11)

Skill Review

Write **2 hundreds 8 tens 6 ones + 3 hundreds 4 tens 5 ones** vertically on the board. Have students add the ones, trade, add the tens, trade and add the hundreds. Write the sum as **6 hundreds 3 tens 1 one** on the board for students to read and then tell the number. (631) Repeat for more problems of 3-digit addends with 0, 1 or 2 trades.

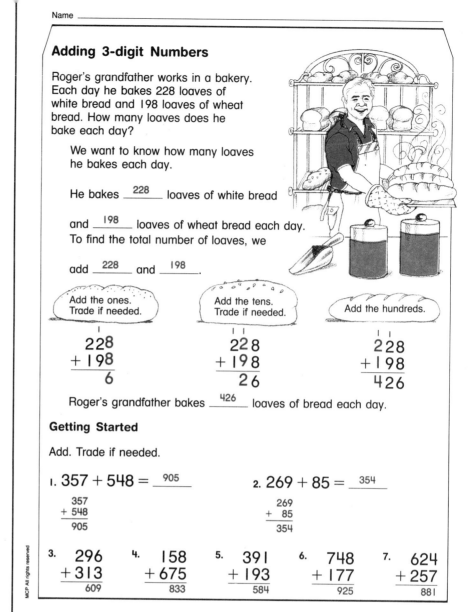

Name _____

Adding 3-digit Numbers

Roger's grandfather works in a bakery. Each day he bakes 228 loaves of white bread and 198 loaves of wheat bread. How many loaves does he bake each day?

We want to know how many loaves he bakes each day.

He bakes ___228___ loaves of white bread

and ___198___ loaves of wheat bread each day.
To find the total number of loaves, we

add ___228___ and ___198___.

Add the ones.
Trade if needed.

$$\begin{array}{r} \overset{1}{2}28 \\ +198 \\ \hline 6 \end{array}$$

Add the tens.
Trade if needed.

$$\begin{array}{r} \overset{1\ 1}{2}28 \\ +198 \\ \hline 26 \end{array}$$

Add the hundreds.

$$\begin{array}{r} \overset{1\ 1}{2}28 \\ +198 \\ \hline 426 \end{array}$$

Roger's grandfather bakes ___426___ loaves of bread each day.

Getting Started

Add. Trade if needed.

1. $357 + 548 =$ ___905___

$$\begin{array}{r} 357 \\ +548 \\ \hline 905 \end{array}$$

2. $269 + 85 =$ ___354___

$$\begin{array}{r} 269 \\ +\ 85 \\ \hline 354 \end{array}$$

3. $$\begin{array}{r} 296 \\ +313 \\ \hline 609 \end{array}$$

4. $$\begin{array}{r} 158 \\ +675 \\ \hline 833 \end{array}$$

5. $$\begin{array}{r} 391 \\ +193 \\ \hline 584 \end{array}$$

6. $$\begin{array}{r} 748 \\ +177 \\ \hline 925 \end{array}$$

7. $$\begin{array}{r} 624 \\ +257 \\ \hline 881 \end{array}$$

Practice adding 3-digit numbers with trading

(one hundred ninety-five) **195**

Teaching the Lesson

Introducing the Problem Have a student read the problem aloud and tell what is to be found. (number of loaves of bread baked each day) Ask what information is given. (Each day 228 white loaves and 198 wheat loaves are baked.) Ask what operation will find the total. (addition) Have students read and complete the information sentences. Work through model with students and then have them complete the solution sentence. Have students use manipulatives to check their solution.

Developing the Skill Write **215 + 326** horizontally on the board. Have a student write the problem vertically on the board. Have a student talk through the solution as another student records the work. (541) Repeat for 4 + 789 (793), 162 + 333 (495), 464 + 187 (651), 385 + 385 (770), 89 + 189 (278) and 101 + 889 (990) having students rewrite each problem vertically and then solve.

Practice

Add. Trade if needed.

1. $166 + 351 = \underline{517}$

$$\begin{array}{r} 166 \\ + 351 \\ \hline 517 \end{array}$$

2. $449 + 276 = \underline{725}$

$$\begin{array}{r} 449 \\ + 276 \\ \hline 725 \end{array}$$

3. $256 + 68 = \underline{324}$

$$\begin{array}{r} 256 \\ + 68 \\ \hline 324 \end{array}$$

4. $159 + 681 = \underline{840}$

$$\begin{array}{r} 159 \\ + 681 \\ \hline 840 \end{array}$$

5.
$$\begin{array}{r} 275 \\ + 323 \\ \hline 598 \end{array}$$

6.
$$\begin{array}{r} 384 \\ + 119 \\ \hline 503 \end{array}$$

7.
$$\begin{array}{r} 525 \\ + 195 \\ \hline 720 \end{array}$$

8.
$$\begin{array}{r} 436 \\ + 297 \\ \hline 733 \end{array}$$

9.
$$\begin{array}{r} 523 \\ + 288 \\ \hline 811 \end{array}$$

10.
$$\begin{array}{r} 35 \\ + 265 \\ \hline 300 \end{array}$$

11.
$$\begin{array}{r} 96 \\ + 875 \\ \hline 971 \end{array}$$

12.
$$\begin{array}{r} 105 \\ + 196 \\ \hline 301 \end{array}$$

13.
$$\begin{array}{r} 57 \\ + 288 \\ \hline 345 \end{array}$$

14.
$$\begin{array}{r} 441 \\ + 82 \\ \hline 523 \end{array}$$

15.
$$\begin{array}{r} 73 \\ + 580 \\ \hline 653 \end{array}$$

16.
$$\begin{array}{r} 394 \\ + 262 \\ \hline 656 \end{array}$$

17.
$$\begin{array}{r} 546 \\ + 254 \\ \hline 800 \end{array}$$

18.
$$\begin{array}{r} 9 \\ + 215 \\ \hline 224 \end{array}$$

19.
$$\begin{array}{r} 751 \\ + 163 \\ \hline 914 \end{array}$$

20.
$$\begin{array}{r} 95 \\ + 438 \\ \hline 533 \end{array}$$

21.
$$\begin{array}{r} 526 \\ + 175 \\ \hline 701 \end{array}$$

22.
$$\begin{array}{r} 253 \\ + 288 \\ \hline 541 \end{array}$$

23.
$$\begin{array}{r} 615 \\ + 173 \\ \hline 788 \end{array}$$

24.
$$\begin{array}{r} 252 \\ + 308 \\ \hline 560 \end{array}$$

Practice adding 3-digit numbers with trading

Correcting Common Errors

Some students may have difficulty keeping the numbers aligned properly when they are adding two 3-digit numbers. Have them work their problems on grid paper using the lines to keep the digits placed in their correct columns.

Enrichment

Tell students to write and solve an addition problem for a 3-digit sum where 2 trades are needed. Then tell them to write a problem requiring 1 trade and a problem requiring no trades.

Practice

Tell students to rewrite each of the first problems vertically. Tell students to solve each problem and record the sum on the line in the number sentence. Have students complete the page independently. Remind students they can check each problem with manipulatives.

Mixed Practice

1. 35 + 28 (63)
2. 4 dimes, 2 nickels, 3 pennies (53¢)
3. 41 + 7 (48)
4. 10 + 4 (14)
5. 573 ◯ 375 (>)
6. 72 + 58 (130)
7. 5 hundreds 3 tens 8 ones (538)
8. 16 − 9 (7)
9. 28 + 9 (37)
10. 14 − 6 (8)

Extra Credit *Applications*

Have students collect cash register tapes from home shopping trips. Cover or remove the totals on the tapes. Tell students they are the calculators and they must find the totals. Begin with shorter tapes and gradually have students advance to longer ones. Extend the activity by covering up some of the numbers within the column instead of covering the totals, and have students find the missing amounts in the problems.

Adding Money Dollar Notation

pages 197-198

Objectives

To add amounts of money for 3-digit sums in dollar notation
To add amounts of money to solve word problems

Materials

dollars, dimes and pennies
hundred-flats
ten-strips and ones

Mental Math

Tell students to name the coins when:

1. 2 coins equal 30¢ (1 quarter, 1 nickel)
2. 2 coins equal 50¢ (2 quarters)
3. 4 coins equal 40¢ (4 dimes)
4. 3 coins equal 75¢ (3 quarters)
5. 3 coins equal 30¢ (3 dimes)
6. 3 coins equal 40¢ (1 quarter, 1 dime, 1 nickel)
7. 3 coins equal 20¢ (1 dime, 2 nickels)

Skill Review

Dictate amounts of money through $9.99 for students to write in dollar notation. Remind students that the word, **and,** is said for the decimal point in reading amounts of money in dollar notation.

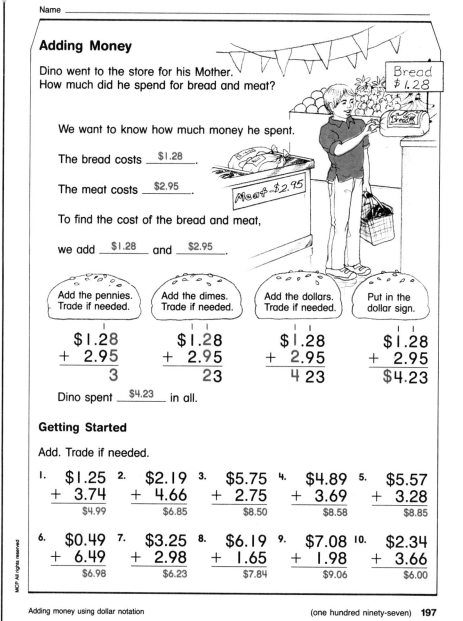

Adding Money

Dino went to the store for his Mother. How much did he spend for bread and meat?

We want to know how much money he spent.

The bread costs ___$1.28___ .

The meat costs ___$2.95___ .

To find the cost of the bread and meat,

we add ___$1.28___ and ___$2.95___ .

Add the pennies. Trade if needed.	Add the dimes. Trade if needed.	Add the dollars. Trade if needed.	Put in the dollar sign.
$1.28 + 2.95 ——— 3	$1.28 + 2.95 ——— 23	$1.28 + 2.95 ——— 4 23	$1.28 + 2.95 ——— $4.23

Dino spent ___$4.23___ in all.

Getting Started

Add. Trade if needed.

1. $1.25 + 3.74 $4.99	2. $2.19 + 4.66 $6.85	3. $5.75 + 2.75 $8.50	4. $4.89 + 3.69 $8.58	5. $5.57 + 3.28 $8.85
6. $0.49 + 6.49 $6.98	7. $3.25 + 2.98 $6.23	8. $6.19 + 1.65 $7.84	9. $7.08 + 1.98 $9.06	10. $2.34 + 3.66 $6.00

Adding money using dollar notation
(one hundred ninety-seven) **197**

Teaching the Lesson

Introducing the Problem Have a student read the problem and tell what is being asked. (amount of money Dino spent) Ask what information is given in the problem. (Dino bought bread and meat.) Ask what information is needed from the picture. (Bread costs $1.28 and meat costs $2.95.) Ask how the total cost of bread and meat can be found. (add) Have students read and complete the information sentences. Work through the model with students and then have them complete the solution sentence.

Developing the Skill Write **$2.64 + 3.46** vertically on the board. Ask students to read each amount orally with you. Have a student talk through the addition as another student records the work. (610) Remind students that the problem is about money and that the dollar sign and decimal point must be in the answer. Insert the signs in the answer. ($6.10) Have students note that the decimal point is placed after the number of dollars and before the number of cents. Repeat for $4.87 + 3.66 ($8.53), $0.28 + 2.45 ($2.73), $6.01 + 0.99 ($7.00), $5.98 + 2.43 ($8.41) and $7.59 + 1.43 ($9.02).

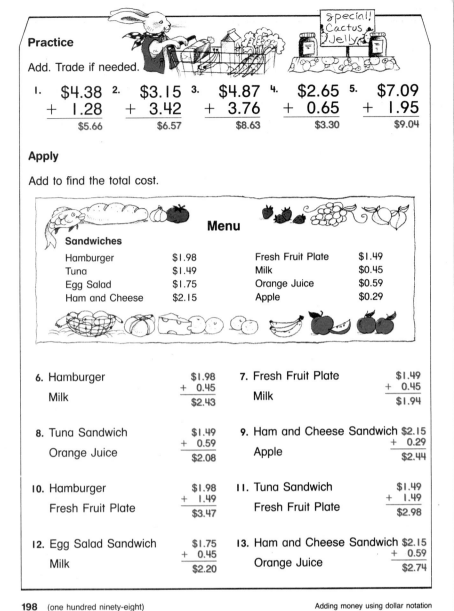

Practice

Add. Trade if needed.

1. $4.38	2. $3.15	3. $4.87	4. $2.65	5. $7.09
+ 1.28	+ 3.42	+ 3.76	+ 0.65	+ 1.95
$5.66	$6.57	$8.63	$3.30	$9.04

Apply

Add to find the total cost.

Menu

Sandwiches

Hamburger	$1.98	Fresh Fruit Plate	$1.49
Tuna	$1.49	Milk	$0.45
Egg Salad	$1.75	Orange Juice	$0.59
Ham and Cheese	$2.15	Apple	$0.29

6. Hamburger
   Milk
   $1.98
   + 0.45
   $2.43

7. Fresh Fruit Plate
   Milk
   $1.49
   + 0.45
   $1.94

8. Tuna Sandwich
   Orange Juice
   $1.49
   + 0.59
   $2.08

9. Ham and Cheese Sandwich $2.15
   Apple
   + 0.29
   $2.44

10. Hamburger
    Fresh Fruit Plate
    $1.98
    + 1.49
    $3.47

11. Tuna Sandwich
    Fresh Fruit Plate
    $1.49
    + 1.49
    $2.98

12. Egg Salad Sandwich
    Milk
    $1.75
    + 0.45
    $2.20

13. Ham and Cheese Sandwich $2.15
    Orange Juice
    + 0.59
    $2.74

Adding money using dollar notation

Correcting Common Errors

Some students may need more practice adding money. Have them work with partners and the menu on page 198 to plan their own lunch. Then have them write and solve an addition problem to find the total cost for the two lunches.

Enrichment

Have students make a menu having 5 or more priced items. Tell them to write 3 customer's orders and have a friend total the 3 bills. They should then check their friend's work.

Practice

Have students read the items and their prices from the menu. Help students complete the first 2 problems and then tell students to complete the top row of problems and the remaining menu orders independently.

Mixed Practice

1. 1 quarter, 2 dimes (45¢)
2. 65¢ + 27¢ (92¢)
3. 275 ◯ 265 (>)
4. 15 − 7 (8)
5. 43 + 18 (61)
6. 45, 50, 55, ___ (60)
7. ___ + 7 = 11 (4)
8. 95 + 8 (103)
9. 26 + 32 (58)
10. 16 − 8 (8)

Extra Credit *Probability*

Just as numbers and colors can be arranged in different combinations, so can letters. Write this on the board: **POT to TOP** and **PAT to TAP.**
Tell students that when the original three-letter words in each pair are rearranged, they take on a new meaning. Mathematicians would call it a permutation. Explain that you want the class over the next 2 days, to list as many such three-letter word pairs as they can. Tell them to ask everyone in the family to help think of words that make sense spelled forwards and backwards.

Problem Solving
3-digit Addition

pages 199-200

Objective

To add 3-digit numbers to solve problems

Materials

dollars and coins

Mental Math

Tell students to name the number that tells:

1. 100 + 900. (1,000)
2. 40 minutes after the hour. (8)
3. 80 − 60. (20)
4. what can be traded for 10 tens. (1 hundred)
5. the total tens in 200 + 86. (8)
6. the value of 7 quarters. ($1.75)

Skill Review

Lay out 2 dollars and 3 quarters in one group and 6 dollars, 4 dimes and 1 quarter in another. Have a student write and solve an addition problem to tell how much money there is in the 2 groups. ($2.75 + 6.65 = $9.40) Repeat for other groups of bills and coins for sums through $9.99.

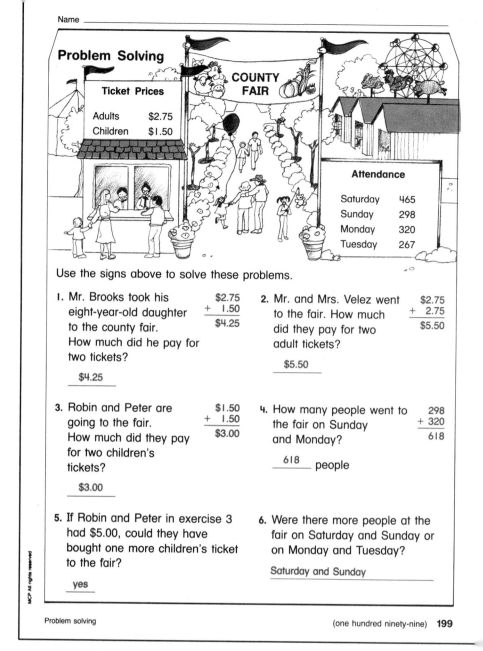

Name _____

Problem Solving

COUNTY FAIR

Ticket Prices	
Adults	$2.75
Children	$1.50

Attendance	
Saturday	465
Sunday	298
Monday	320
Tuesday	267

Use the signs above to solve these problems.

1. Mr. Brooks took his eight-year-old daughter to the county fair. How much did he pay for two tickets?

$2.75
+ 1.50
$4.25

___$4.25___

2. Mr. and Mrs. Velez went to the fair. How much did they pay for two adult tickets?

$2.75
+ 2.75
$5.50

___$5.50___

3. Robin and Peter are going to the fair. How much did they pay for two children's tickets?

$1.50
+ 1.50
$3.00

___$3.00___

4. How many people went to the fair on Sunday and Monday?

298
+ 320
618

___618___ people

5. If Robin and Peter in exercise 3 had $5.00, could they have bought one more children's ticket to the fair?

___yes___

6. Were there more people at the fair on Saturday and Sunday or on Monday and Tuesday?

___Saturday and Sunday___

Problem solving

(one hundred ninety-nine) **199**

Teaching page 199

Have students tell about the picture and then discuss the students' experiences at county fairs or similar events. Have students tell the admission price for a child ($1.50) and an adult. ($2.75) Ask students how many people attended the fair on Monday (320) and then repeat for the other days noted. Have a student read the first problem aloud and tell what is to be found as you write **What is to be found?** on the board. (the cost of 2 tickets) Ask students what information is given in the problem as you write **What do we know?** on the board. (Mr. Brooks and his daughter bought tickets.) Ask what additional information is needed. (the cost of the tickets) Have a student write the cost of an adult's ticket and a child's ticket on the board. ($2.75, $1.50) Ask what needs to be done with the amounts to find the total cost as you write **What needs to be done with the numbers?** on the board. (add) Have students write and solve the problem independently. ($4.25) Tell students to use money to check their answer as you write **Does the an-**

swer make sense? on the board. (yes) Tell students to record the answer on the line under the problem. Help students solve the second problem, if necessary, before assigning the page to be completed independently. Remind students to use the questions from the board to help solve the problems. Remind students to check each solution.

199

More Problem Solving

County Fair
Animals

87 horses
256 cows
107 pigs
127 sheep
148 rabbits

Use the sign to solve these problems.

1. How many horses and cows are shown at the fair?

    87
 + 256
   343

_____343_____ horses and cows

2. How many sheep and rabbits are shown at the fair?

    127
 + 148
   275

_____275_____ sheep and rabbits

3. How many horses and rabbits are shown at the fair?

    87
 + 148
   235

_____235_____ horses and rabbits

4. How many pigs and sheep are shown at the fair?

    107
 + 127
   234

_____234_____ pigs and sheep

5. How many pigs and rabbits are shown at the fair?

    107
 + 148
   255

_____255_____ pigs and rabbits

6. How many cows and sheep are shown at the fair?

    256
 + 127
   383

_____383_____ cows and sheep

200 (two hundred)

Problem solving

Teaching page 200

Tell students to use information from the picture to solve the problems on this page. Also remind students to check each problem and then record the answer on the answer line. Have students complete the page independently.

Extra Credit *Applications*

This lesson will help students learn to follow recipe directions on packages. Begin with a review of oven temperatures, degrees, how to use a timer, and how to measure with a cup measure teaspoon and tablespoon. Bring in several packages of corn muffin mix or other mix that can be simply made. Arrange the packages and the equipment students will need in several stations around the room. Divide the class into groups and assign each group a station. Ask them to work together to read the directions and put the ingredients together. Help them with words and procedures they do not understand. Arrange with the lunchroom to have the muffins baked, so students can enjoy the finished product. Finally, list the number each group made, and have a student count the total for the class.

Review

pages 201-202

Objectives

To review addition of 3-digit numbers
To maintain skills learned previously
this year

Materials

dollars and coins
hundred-flats
ten-strips and ones

Mental Math

Tell students to name the number that
tells:

1. their zip code.
2. their phone number.
3. their phone number area code.
4. their address.
5. the present month in ordinal numbers.
6. yesterday's date.

Skill Review

Write **206 + 48** (254) and **215 + 40**
(255) on the board. Have students
solve the problems and then tell which
answer is greater. (255) Help students
write 254 < 255 and 255 > 254 on
the board. Repeat for more pairs of
addition problems of 2- or 3-digit addends for sums through 999.

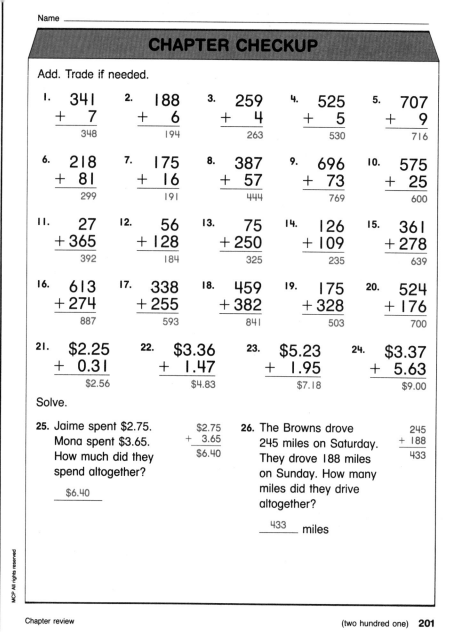

Name _____

CHAPTER CHECKUP

Add. Trade if needed.

1. 341	2. 188	3. 259	4. 525	5. 707
+ 7	+ 6	+ 4	+ 5	+ 9
348	194	263	530	716

6. 218	7. 175	8. 387	9. 696	10. 575
+ 81	+ 16	+ 57	+ 73	+ 25
299	191	444	769	600

11. 27	12. 56	13. 75	14. 126	15. 361
+365	+128	+250	+109	+278
392	184	325	235	639

16. 613	17. 338	18. 459	19. 175	20. 524
+274	+255	+382	+328	+176
887	593	841	503	700

21. $2.25	22. $3.36	23. $5.23	24. $3.37
+ 0.31	+ 1.47	+ 1.95	+ 5.63
$2.56	$4.83	$7.18	$9.00

Solve.

25. Jaime spent $2.75. Mona spent $3.65. How much did they spend altogether?

$2.75
+ 3.65
$6.40

__$6.40__

26. The Browns drove 245 miles on Saturday. They drove 188 miles on Sunday. How many miles did they drive altogether?

245
+ 188
433

__433__ miles

Chapter review

Teaching page 201

Tell students to write the sum for each problem. Ask students to name any problems which must have dollar signs and decimal points in their answers. Ask students if either word problem is about money. (yes, the first one) Have students complete the page independently.

ROUNDUP REVIEW

Fill in the oval next to the correct answer.

1 (clock showing 2:25)
- ○ 1:25
- ● 2:25
- ○ 3:25
- ○ NG

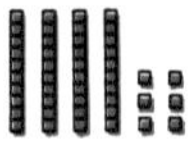

2 (base-ten blocks)
- ○ 36
- ○ 64
- ● 46
- ○ NG

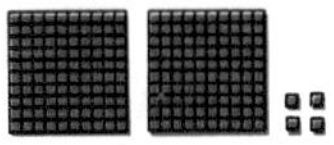

3 (base-ten blocks)
- ● 204
- ○ 240
- ○ 402
- ○ NG

4 38 ○ 52
- ○ >
- ● <

5 (money: bill, coins)
- ● $1.66
- ○ 60¢
- ○ $1.56
- ○ NG

6
$$\begin{array}{r} 98 \\ -\ 26 \\ \hline \end{array}$$
- ○ 124
- ● 72
- ○ 36
- ○ NG

7
$$\begin{array}{r} 84 \\ -\ 47 \\ \hline \end{array}$$
- ○ 47
- ○ 131
- ○ 43
- ● NG

8
$$\begin{array}{r} 91 \\ -\ 27 \\ \hline \end{array}$$
- ○ 74
- ● 64
- ○ 76
- ○ NG

9 38 + 99
- ○ 127
- ○ 1217
- ● 137
- ○ NG

10
$$\begin{array}{r} 75 \\ +\ 85 \\ \hline \end{array}$$
- ○ 150
- ○ 170
- ● 160
- ○ NG

11
$$\begin{array}{r} 346 \\ +\ 73 \\ \hline \end{array}$$
- ○ 319
- ● 419
- ○ 429
- ○ NG

12
$$\begin{array}{r} 638 \\ +\ 267 \\ \hline \end{array}$$
- ● 905
- ○ 895
- ○ 805
- ○ NG

13
$$\begin{array}{r} 135 \\ +\ 396 \\ \hline \end{array}$$
- ○ 421
- ● 531
- ○ 431
- ○ NG

☐ score

202 (two hundred two)

Cumulative review

Enrichment

1. Tell students to write a silly story where the numbers 48 and 92 are added when they should have been subtracted. Then have them tell how the error causes a problem.
2. Have students draw 2 clocks with Roman numerals showing times that are 20 minutes apart.
3. Tell students to find out how many seats are in an auditorium if 276 people are seated and there are 385 empty seats. (661)

Teaching page 202

This page reviews time, money, place value, subtraction of 2-digit numbers and addition of 3-digit numbers. Tell students to solve each problem and then fill in the oval beside the correct answer. Remind students that NG means not given and they should only fill in that oval if none of the given answers is the correct one. Have students complete the page independently.

2 Digits Minus 1 Digit

pages 203-204

Objective

To review subtracting a 1-digit number from a 2-digit number with trading

Materials

*addition and subtraction fact cards
colored chalk
ten-strips and ones

Mental Math

For each of the following tell students to add 2 tens, subtract 5 ones and tell the number:

1. 46 (61)
2. 80 (95)
3. 150 (165)
4. 21 (36)
5. 280 (295)
6. 55 (70)
7. 184 (199)

Skill Review

Write 4 headings across the board: **Sums through 10, Sums of 11 and 12, Sums of 13, 14 and 15** and **Sums of 16, 17 and 18.** Show addition fact cards, have students give the answers and then place the cards on the chalk tray under the correct heading. Repeat for subtraction facts, changing the heading to minuends.

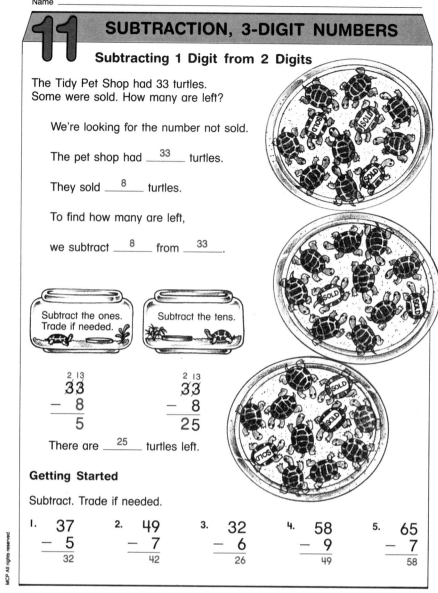

Subtracting 1 Digit from 2 Digits

Name _____

The Tidy Pet Shop had 33 turtles. Some were sold. How many are left?

We're looking for the number not sold.

The pet shop had ___33___ turtles.

They sold ___8___ turtles.

To find how many are left,

we subtract ___8___ from ___33___.

Subtract the ones. Trade if needed.

Subtract the tens.

$$\begin{array}{r} {}^{2}\,{}^{13} \\ \cancel{33} \\ -\ 8 \\ \hline 5 \end{array}$$

$$\begin{array}{r} {}^{2}\,{}^{13} \\ \cancel{33} \\ -\ 8 \\ \hline 25 \end{array}$$

There are ___25___ turtles left.

Getting Started

Subtract. Trade if needed.

1. $\begin{array}{r} 37 \\ -\ 5 \\ \hline 32 \end{array}$
2. $\begin{array}{r} 49 \\ -\ 7 \\ \hline 42 \end{array}$
3. $\begin{array}{r} 32 \\ -\ 6 \\ \hline 26 \end{array}$
4. $\begin{array}{r} 58 \\ -\ 9 \\ \hline 49 \end{array}$
5. $\begin{array}{r} 65 \\ -\ 7 \\ \hline 58 \end{array}$

Subtracting a 1-digit from a 2-digit number

(two hundred three) **203**

Teaching the Lesson

Introducing the Problem Have students tell about the picture. Have a student read the problem and tell what is to be found. (the number of turtles left) Ask students what information is given in the problem. (There were 33 turtles.) Ask what information is needed from the picture. (8 are sold.) Ask what will need to be done with the numbers. (subtract) Have students read and complete the information sentences. Work through the model with students and then have them complete the solution sentence. Remind students that to check subtraction, they should add the answer to the smaller number.

Developing the Skill Write **26 − 8** vertically on the board. Remind students that 8 ones cannot be taken away from 6 ones so a trade of 1 ten for 10 ones is made. Show the trade with colored chalk and have students then complete the subtraction. (18) Provide more problems on the board for added practice in subtracting a 1-digit number from a 2-digit number. Have students tell if trading is needed for each problem.

Practice

Subtract. Trade if needed.

1. $\begin{array}{r} 18 \\ -\ 5 \\ \hline 13 \end{array}$

2. $\begin{array}{r} 27 \\ -\ 3 \\ \hline 24 \end{array}$

3. $\begin{array}{r} 13 \\ -\ 4 \\ \hline 9 \end{array}$

4. $\begin{array}{r} 57 \\ -\ 6 \\ \hline 51 \end{array}$

5. $\begin{array}{r} 41 \\ -\ 8 \\ \hline 33 \end{array}$

6. $\begin{array}{r} 63 \\ -\ 6 \\ \hline 57 \end{array}$

7. $\begin{array}{r} 45 \\ -\ 2 \\ \hline 43 \end{array}$

8. $\begin{array}{r} 77 \\ -\ 8 \\ \hline 69 \end{array}$

9. $\begin{array}{r} 88 \\ -\ 6 \\ \hline 82 \end{array}$

10. $\begin{array}{r} 93 \\ -\ 4 \\ \hline 89 \end{array}$

11. $\begin{array}{r} 25 \\ -\ 5 \\ \hline 20 \end{array}$

12. $\begin{array}{r} 38 \\ -\ 1 \\ \hline 37 \end{array}$

13. $\begin{array}{r} 57 \\ -\ 9 \\ \hline 48 \end{array}$

14. $\begin{array}{r} 47 \\ -\ 3 \\ \hline 44 \end{array}$

15. $\begin{array}{r} 63 \\ -\ 7 \\ \hline 56 \end{array}$

16. $\begin{array}{r} 31 \\ -\ 7 \\ \hline 24 \end{array}$

17. $\begin{array}{r} 87 \\ -\ 8 \\ \hline 79 \end{array}$

18. $\begin{array}{r} 68 \\ -\ 3 \\ \hline 65 \end{array}$

19. $\begin{array}{r} 44 \\ -\ 8 \\ \hline 36 \end{array}$

20. $\begin{array}{r} 55 \\ -\ 7 \\ \hline 48 \end{array}$

Apply

Solve.

21. The pet shop had 42 kittens for sale. They sold 9 kittens. How many kittens are left?

$\begin{array}{r} 42 \\ -\ 9 \\ \hline 33 \end{array}$

__33__ kittens

22. The pet shop had 61 dog collars for sale. Sal sold 7 collars. How many collars are left?

$\begin{array}{r} 61 \\ -\ 7 \\ \hline 54 \end{array}$

__54__ collars

23. There were 55 fish. Trish bought 9. How many fish are left?

$\begin{array}{r} 55 \\ -\ 9 \\ \hline 46 \end{array}$

__46__ fish

24. There were 75 puppies for sale. Walter sold 6. How many puppies are left?

$\begin{array}{r} 75 \\ -\ 6 \\ \hline 69 \end{array}$

__69__ puppies

Subtracting a 1-digit from a 2-digit number

2 Digits Minus 2 Digits

pages 205-206

Objective

To review subtracting a 2-digit number from a 2-digit number with trading

Materials

*addition and subtraction fact cards ten-strips and ones

Mental Math

Tell students to use the following numbers to make a 3-digit number which reads the same backward or forward:

1. 3, 1 (131, 313)
2. 7, 8, (787, 878)
3. 6, 2 (626, 262)
4. 5, 6, (565, 656)
5. 4, 9, (949, 494)
6. 1, 2 (121, 212)

Skill Review

Flash a fact card for a sum from 11 through 18. Have one student give the answer. Call on other students to supply related addition or subtraction facts. Continue with more facts for sums and minuends through 18.

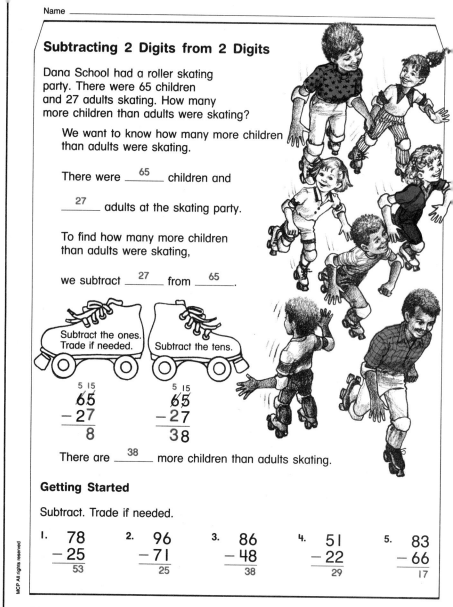

Subtracting 2 Digits from 2 Digits

Dana School had a roller skating party. There were 65 children and 27 adults skating. How many more children than adults were skating?

We want to know how many more children than adults were skating.

There were ___65___ children and

___27___ adults at the skating party.

To find how many more children than adults were skating,

we subtract ___27___ from ___65___.

Subtract the ones. Trade if needed.

Subtract the tens.

$$\begin{array}{r} \overset{5}{}\overset{15}{6\!\!\!/5} \\ -\ 27 \\ \hline 8 \end{array}$$

$$\begin{array}{r} \overset{5}{}\overset{15}{6\!\!\!/5} \\ -\ 27 \\ \hline 38 \end{array}$$

There are ___38___ more children than adults skating.

Getting Started

Subtract. Trade if needed.

1.
$$\begin{array}{r} 78 \\ -25 \\ \hline 53 \end{array}$$

2.
$$\begin{array}{r} 96 \\ -71 \\ \hline 25 \end{array}$$

3.
$$\begin{array}{r} 86 \\ -48 \\ \hline 38 \end{array}$$

4.
$$\begin{array}{r} 51 \\ -22 \\ \hline 29 \end{array}$$

5.
$$\begin{array}{r} 83 \\ -66 \\ \hline 17 \end{array}$$

Subtracting a 2-digit from a 2-digit number

(two hundred five) **205**

Teaching the Lesson

Introducing the Problem Have students tell about the picture. Have a student read the problem aloud and tell what is to be found. (how many more children than adults were skating) Ask what information is given. (There were 65 children and 27 adults.) Ask what needs to be done with the numbers. (subtract) Have students read and complete the information sentences. Work through the model with students and then have them complete the solution sentence. Have students check by adding.

Developing the Skill Write the following problems vertically on the board: **67 − 32** (35), **95 − 54** (41), **52 − 25** (27), **76 − 59** (17), **80 − 11** (69). Have a student record the work for each problem as other students talk through the subtraction. Now have students tell which problems needed a trade of 1 ten for 10 ones. (the last 3 problems) Repeat for more problems, if necessary.

205

Practice

Subtract. Trade if needed.

1. 47 −41 = 6	2. 67 −17 = 50	3. 92 −60 = 32	4. 96 −89 = 7	5. 63 −59 = 4
6. 73 −26 = 47	7. 61 −45 = 16	8. 96 −78 = 18	9. 81 −43 = 38	10. 65 −47 = 18
11. 95 −87 = 8	12. 88 −83 = 5	13. 92 −63 = 29	14. 49 −25 = 24	15. 38 −16 = 22
16. 62 −14 = 48	17. 71 −31 = 40	18. 66 −49 = 17	19. 87 −36 = 51	20. 64 −16 = 48
21. 72 −43 = 29	22. 52 −30 = 22	23. 47 −21 = 26	24. 63 −39 = 24	25. 81 −56 = 25

Apply

Solve.

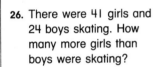

26. There were 41 girls and 24 boys skating. How many more girls than boys were skating?

41
− 24
17

   17   more girls

27. Art skated around the rink 75 times. Ro skated around the rink 57 times. How many more times did Art skate around the rink?

75
− 57
18

   18   times

206 (two hundred six)

Subtracting a 2-digit from a 2-digit number

Practice

Remind students that not all subtraction problems require trading. Have students complete the page independently.

Mixed Practice

1. 45 + 83 (128)
2. 57 − 20 (37)
3. 68¢ + 56¢ ($1.24)
4. ___ + 5 = 12 (7)
5. 39 − 13 (26)
6. 291 ◯ 209 (>)
7. 5 hundreds 3 tens 7 ones (537)
8. 27 − 8 (19)
9. 79 + 4 (83)
10. 38 − 19 (19)

Extra Credit *Statistics*

Introduce the concept of estimating to the class. Explain that some things can be counted exactly. Ask a student to tell how many people are in the classroom. Ask how the answer was calculated. (by counting) Ask another student to tell how many people are in a neighboring classroom. Ask how that number was calculated. (by guessing) Help students see an estimation is made by using any data the student already knows. In the case of how many students in a class, they know about how many students can be in a class. Ask students to gather the following information by estimating:

1. the number of rooms in their home.
2. the number of leaves on a tree.
3. the number of desks in the school.
4. the number of people in their family.
5. the number of pages in their math book.

Then ask which numbers could actually be counted.

3 Digits Minus 1 Digit

pages 207-208

Objective

To subtract a 1-digit number from a 3-digit number with trading

Materials

*colored chalk
hundred-flats
ten-strips and ones

Mental Math

Ask students if they will add or subtract to find:

1. how many are left. (subtract)
2. the total of 64 and 36. (add)
3. how many more. (subtract)
4. the difference. (subtract)
5. how many all together. (add)
6. the sum. (add)
7. how many remain. (subtract)

Skill Review

Have students make 3-digit numbers using the numbers 3, 7 and 2. (327, 723, 237, 732, 372 or 273) Have students tell the number of hundreds, tens and ones in the numbers they created. Repeat for 3-digit numbers using the numbers 9, 1 and 6. (916, 961, 169, 196, 691 or 619)

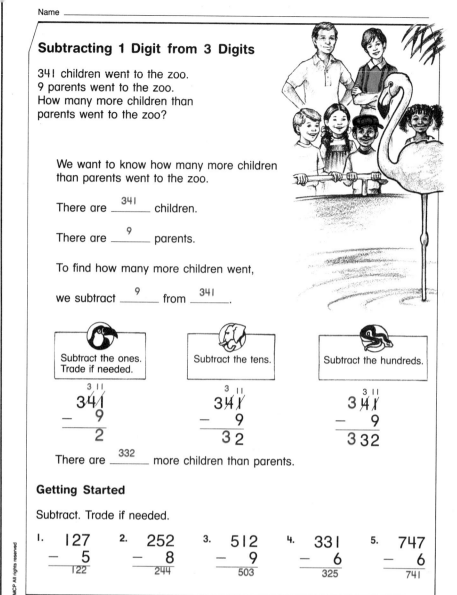

Subtracting 1 Digit from 3 Digits

341 children went to the zoo.
9 parents went to the zoo.
How many more children than parents went to the zoo?

We want to know how many more children than parents went to the zoo.

There are ___341___ children.

There are ___9___ parents.

To find how many more children went,

we subtract ___9___ from ___341___.

Subtract the ones. Trade if needed.	Subtract the tens.	Subtract the hundreds.
$$\begin{array}{r} \overset{3\ 11}{3\cancel{4}\cancel{1}} \\ -\ \ 9 \\ \hline 2 \end{array}$$	$$\begin{array}{r} \overset{3\ 11}{3\cancel{4}\cancel{1}} \\ -\ \ 9 \\ \hline 3\ 2 \end{array}$$	$$\begin{array}{r} \overset{3\ 11}{3\cancel{4}\cancel{1}} \\ -\ \ 9 \\ \hline 3\ 3\ 2 \end{array}$$

There are ___332___ more children than parents.

Getting Started

Subtract. Trade if needed.

1. $$\begin{array}{r} 127 \\ -\ \ 5 \\ \hline 122 \end{array}$$
2. $$\begin{array}{r} 252 \\ -\ \ 8 \\ \hline 244 \end{array}$$
3. $$\begin{array}{r} 512 \\ -\ \ 9 \\ \hline 503 \end{array}$$
4. $$\begin{array}{r} 331 \\ -\ \ 6 \\ \hline 325 \end{array}$$
5. $$\begin{array}{r} 747 \\ -\ \ 6 \\ \hline 741 \end{array}$$

Subtracting a 1-digit from a 3-digit number

(two hundred seven) **207**

Teaching the Lesson

Introducing the Problem Have students tell about the picture and then discuss their own zoo experiences. Have a student read the problem and tell what is to be found. (how many more children than parents went to the zoo) Ask what information is given. (341 children and 9 parents went.) Ask what needs to be done with the numbers. (subtract) Have students read and complete the information sentences. Work through the subtraction model with students and then have them complete the solution sentence. Have students add to check their subtraction.

Developing the Skill Have students solve **357 − 5** (352) and **699 − 7** (692) at the board. Ask students if any trading was needed. (no) Now write **476 − 8** on the board and ask if trading is needed. (yes) Ask why. (8 ones cannot be taken from 6 ones) Have a student use colored chalk to show the trade. Ask if another trade is needed. (no) Have another student complete the subtraction and tell the answer. (468) Repeat for 271 − 8 (263), 906 − 5 (901), 472 − 3 (469), 555 − 6 (549), 338 − 3 (335) and 612 − 7 (605).

Practice

Subtract. Trade if needed.

1.   229
   −   4
   ‾‾‾‾‾
     225

2.   636
   −   8
   ‾‾‾‾‾
     628

3.   399
   −   9
   ‾‾‾‾‾
     390

4.   851
   −   7
   ‾‾‾‾‾
     844

5.   233
   −   4
   ‾‾‾‾‾
     229

6.   137
   −   5
   ‾‾‾‾‾
     132

7.   141
   −   7
   ‾‾‾‾‾
     134

8.   725
   −   6
   ‾‾‾‾‾
     719

9.   911
   −   3
   ‾‾‾‾‾
     908

10. 673
   −   5
   ‾‾‾‾‾
     668

11. 252
   −   6
   ‾‾‾‾‾
     246

12. 341
   −   9
   ‾‾‾‾‾
     332

13. 585
   −   7
   ‾‾‾‾‾
     578

14. 463
   −   9
   ‾‾‾‾‾
     454

15. 224
   −   6
   ‾‾‾‾‾
     218

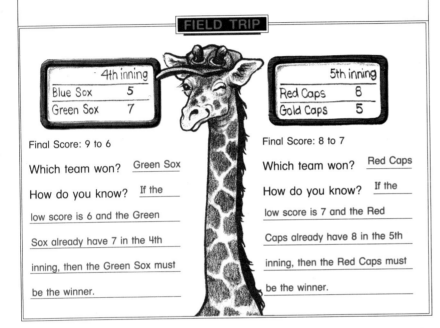

FIELD TRIP

4th inning	
Blue Sox	5
Green Sox	7

Final Score: 9 to 6

Which team won? Green Sox

How do you know? If the

low score is 6 and the Green

Sox already have 7 in the 4th

inning, then the Green Sox must

be the winner.

5th inning	
Red Caps	8
Gold Caps	5

Final Score: 8 to 7

Which team won? Red Caps

How do you know? If the

low score is 7 and the Red

Caps already have 8 in the 5th

inning, then the Red Caps must

be the winner.

208   (two hundred eight)

Subtracting a 1-digit from a 3-digit number

Correcting Common Errors

Watch for students who get confused when a 1-digit number is subtracted from a 3-digit number and try to subtract the subtrahend from all the top digits.

INCORRECT	CORRECT
658	658
− 3	− 3
325	655

Have them work with a partner using hundred-flats, ten-strips, and ones to model the problem.

Enrichment

Tell students to write and solve problems to show all the 1-digit numbers that require a trade when subtracted from 715.

Practice

Tell students that some of the problems on this page do not need a trade. Have students complete the rows of problems independently.

Field Trip

Students are asked to use logic to solve these problems. Have students discuss the information given in the first problem. Help student, if necessary, discover that if the Green Sox had 7 runs at the end of the 4th inning, they could not end the game with only 6 runs. Therefore, they had to win the game with a score of 9. Help students apply the logic from the first problem to see that if the Red Caps had 8 runs in the 5th inning, they could not have 7 runs at the end of the game. Therefore, they had to have won the game with 8 runs.

Extra Credit   *Numeration*

Write the following on the board, or duplicate for students: Find the number that is:

1. the greatest number that has a 4 in the hundreds place and an 8 in the ones place. (498)
2. the least number that has 2 in the hundreds place and 4 in the tens place. (240)
3. the largest and the smallest 3-digit numbers that has the same number in the ones, tens and hundreds place. (111, 999)

Subtracting Multiples of 10

pages 209-210

Objective

To subtract a 2-digit multiple of 10 from a 3-digit number

Materials

*colored chalk
hundred-flats
ten-strips and ones

Mental Math

Ask students if the following are true or false:

1. 3 quarters means 75¢. (T)
2. 6:30 means 6 minutes after 6. (F)
3. A square has 3 corners. (F)
4. A triangle has 3 sides. (T)
5. V means 5 in Roman numerals. (T)
6. 8 + 5 checks 13 − 5. (T)
7. 30 tens is 3 hundreds. (T)

Skill Review

Have students rename the following numbers in tens: 120 (12 tens), 240 (24 tens), 80 (8 tens), 840 (84 tens), 630 (63 tens), 960 (96 tens), 100 (10 tens). Now have students name numbers as you say the numbers in tens.

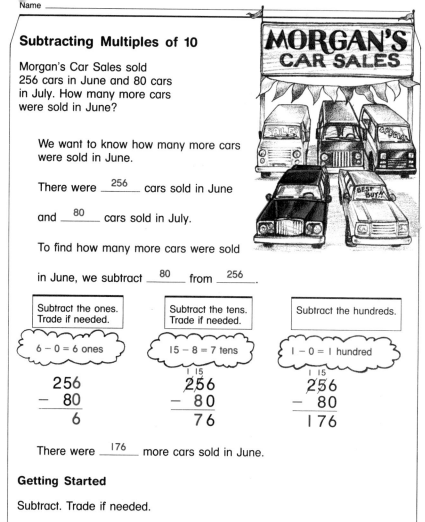

Subtracting Multiples of 10

Morgan's Car Sales sold 256 cars in June and 80 cars in July. How many more cars were sold in June?

We want to know how many more cars were sold in June.

There were __256__ cars sold in June

and __80__ cars sold in July.

To find how many more cars were sold

in June, we subtract __80__ from __256__.

Subtract the ones. Trade if needed.	Subtract the tens. Trade if needed.	Subtract the hundreds.
6 − 0 = 6 ones	15 − 8 = 7 tens	1 − 0 = 1 hundred
256 − 80 6	2⁵⁶ − 80 76	2⁵⁶ − 80 176

There were __176__ more cars sold in June.

Getting Started

Subtract. Trade if needed.

1. 342
− 20
322
2. 563
− 50
513
3. 245
− 40
205
4. 326
− 60
266
5. 681
− 90
591

MCP All rights reserved

Subtracting a 2-digit multiple of 10

(two hundred nine) **209**

Teaching the Lesson

Introducing the Problem Have a student read the problem aloud and tell what is to be found. (how many more cars were sold in June) Ask students what information is given. (256 cars were sold in June and 80 cars in July.) Ask what needs to be done with the numbers to find how many more. (subtract) Have students read and complete the information sentences. Work through the model with students and then have them complete the solution sentence. Have students use manipulatives or add to check their solution.

Developing the Skill Have students use manipulatives to solve each of the following problems from the board: 565 − 40 (525), 385 − 50 (335), 732 − 70 (662) and 428 − 90 (338). Now use colored chalk to show the trade of 1 hundred for 10 tens in each of the last 2 problems on the board. Have students use the colored chalk to show any trade and then solve each of the following problems at the board: 276 − 80 (196), 955 − 90 (865), 104 − 20 (84), 332 − 10 (322), 720 − 60 (660).

209

Practice

Subtract. Trade if needed.

1. 636
    − 80
    ―――
    556

2. 521
    − 20
    ―――
    501

3. 561
    − 80
    ―――
    481

4. 327
    − 50
    ―――
    277

5. 613
    − 20
    ―――
    593

6. 399
    − 30
    ―――
    369

7. 229
    − 50
    ―――
    179

8. 168
    − 70
    ―――
    98

9. 852
    − 90
    ―――
    762

10. 355
    − 50
    ―――
    305

11. 512
    − 70
    ―――
    442

12. 303
    − 50
    ―――
    253

13. 756
    − 30
    ―――
    726

14. 230
    − 30
    ―――
    200

15. 646
    − 60
    ―――
    586

16. 116
    − 20
    ―――
    96

17. 663
    − 80
    ―――
    583

18. 550
    − 70
    ―――
    480

19. 909
    − 40
    ―――
    869

20. 855
    − 60
    ―――
    795

21. 532
    − 50
    ―――
    482

22. 763
    − 40
    ―――
    723

23. 877
    − 90
    ―――
    787

24. 145
    − 30
    ―――
    115

25. 315
    − 70
    ―――
    245

Apply

Solve.

26. During July there were 325 cars and 70 vans sold. How many more cars than vans were sold?

    325
    − 70
    ―――
    255

    _255_ more cars

27. There were 257 used cars on the lot. They sold 80. How many cars were left?

    257
    − 80
    ―――
    177

    _177_ cars

210 (two hundred ten)

Subtracting a 2-digit multiple of 10

Correcting Common Errors

If students have difficulty subtracting multiples of ten, have them practice on a number line from 100 to 300 marked off in intervals of 10. Give them problems such as 256 − 40. They first find 256 on the number line and then count back by tens for 40. (216) Help them see the pattern that the digit in the ones place remains the same.

Enrichment

Tell students to write and solve a problem to find the number of days left in 1 year when 10 days have passed since January 1. Then have them find how many days are left when 30, 70 and 90 days have passed.

Practice

Remind students that when subtracting a multiple of 10, any necessary trade will be a trade of 1 hundred for 10 tens. Tell students to complete the page independently.

Mixed Practice

1. 46 − 31 (15)
2. 56 + 7 (63)
3. 32¢ − 15¢ (17¢)
4. 56¢ + 27¢ (83¢)
5. 92 + 9 (101)
6. 86 − 27 (59)
7. 6 dimes, 1 nickel (65¢)
8. 78 − 53 (25)
9. 527 ◯ 659 (<)
10. 630, 635, 640, ____ (645)

Extra Credit *Measurement*

Have students work in pairs to cut a piece of adding machine tape the length of their bodies and label the tape with their names. Take the students outside in the morning and have them help each other cut a piece of tape the length of their shadow, labeling the tapes with names and "shadow morning." Have them repeat the shadow measurement in the afternoon and label those shadows. Finally, have them measure the 3 tapes in inches or centimeters and compare. Discuss with students why there is a difference between the morning and afternoon shadows.

210

3 Digits
Minus 2 Digits

pages 211-212

Objective

To subtract a 2-digit number from a 3-digit number with one trade

Materials

*colored chalk
hundred-flats
ten-strips and ones

Mental Math

Tell students to name the number that is:

1. the largest 3-digit number. (999)
2. the smallest 2-digit number. (10)
3. the largest 2-digit number. (99)
4. the smallest 4-digit number. (1,000)
5. the smallest 3-digit number. (100)
6. 2 more than the largest 2-digit number. (101)
7. 9 tens more than the smallest 3-digit number. (190)

Skill Review

Have students write and solve problems to subtract each 2-digit multiple of 10 from 760. Have students tell if a trade is needed in each problem.

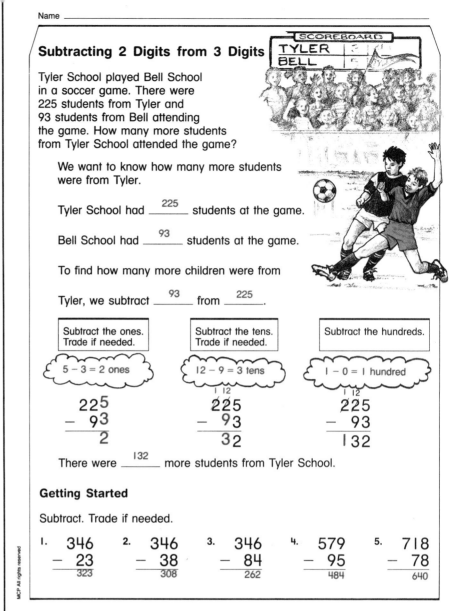

Subtracting 2 Digits from 3 Digits

Tyler School played Bell School in a soccer game. There were 225 students from Tyler and 93 students from Bell attending the game. How many more students from Tyler School attended the game?

We want to know how many more students were from Tyler.

Tyler School had ___225___ students at the game.

Bell School had ___93___ students at the game.

To find how many more children were from

Tyler, we subtract ___93___ from ___225___.

Subtract the ones. Trade if needed.	Subtract the tens. Trade if needed.	Subtract the hundreds.
5 − 3 = 2 ones	12 − 9 = 3 tens	1 − 0 = 1 hundred

$$\begin{array}{r} 225 \\ -\ 93 \\ \hline 2 \end{array}$$

$$\begin{array}{r} 2\overset{1\ 12}{2}5 \\ -\ 93 \\ \hline 32 \end{array}$$

$$\begin{array}{r} 2\overset{1\ 12}{2}5 \\ -\ 93 \\ \hline 132 \end{array}$$

There were ___132___ more students from Tyler School.

Getting Started

Subtract. Trade if needed.

1. $\begin{array}{r} 346 \\ -\ 23 \\ \hline 323 \end{array}$
2. $\begin{array}{r} 346 \\ -\ 38 \\ \hline 308 \end{array}$
3. $\begin{array}{r} 346 \\ -\ 84 \\ \hline 262 \end{array}$
4. $\begin{array}{r} 579 \\ -\ 95 \\ \hline 484 \end{array}$
5. $\begin{array}{r} 718 \\ -\ 78 \\ \hline 640 \end{array}$

Subtracting a 2-digit from a 3-digit number

(two hundred eleven) **211**

Teaching the Lesson

Introducing the Problem Have a student read the problem aloud and tell what is to be solved. (how many more students from Tyler School attended the game) Ask students what information is given. (225 Tyler students and 93 Bell students attended.) Ask what needs to be done with the numbers. (subtract) Have students read and complete the information sentences. Work through the subtraction model with students and then have them complete the solution sentence. Have students check their work by adding.

Developing the Skill Write **488 − 79** on the board. Ask students if a trade for more ones is needed in order to subtract the ones. (yes) Show the trade with colored chalk and have a student then subtract the ones. (9) Ask if a trade is needed to subtract the tens. (no) Have a student complete the subtraction. (409) Repeat the procedure for 488 − 94 where a trade is needed to subtract the tens. Continue to have students solve the following problems where no trade or 1 trade is needed: 263 − 48 (215), 903 − 82 (821), 679 − 42 (637), 333 − 28 (305), 564 − 81 (483).

Practice

Subtract. Trade if needed.

1. 286
− 54
= 232

2. 192
− 78
= 114

3. 375
− 43
= 332

4. 422
− 81
= 341

5. 623
− 42
= 581

6. 518
− 27
= 491

7. 742
− 92
= 650

8. 891
− 85
= 806

9. 566
− 75
= 491

10. 327
− 95
= 232

11. 963
− 39
= 924

12. 462
− 62
= 400

13. 319
− 58
= 261

14. 294
− 85
= 209

15. 601
− 71
= 530

16. 708
− 46
= 662

17. 643
− 28
= 615

18. 840
− 37
= 803

19. 677
− 70
= 607

20. 575
− 49
= 526

21. 350
− 25
= 325

22. 517
− 86
= 431

23. 999
− 95
= 904

24. 741
− 29
= 712

25. 802
− 82
= 720

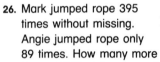

Apply

Solve.

26. Mark jumped rope 395 times without missing. Angie jumped rope only 89 times. How many more times did Mark jump rope?

395
− 89
306

__306__ times

27. Liz sold 329 tickets to the ball game. Harry sold 95 tickets. How many more tickets did Liz sell?

329
− 95
234

__234__ tickets

Subtracting a 2-digit from a 3-digit number

Correcting Common Errors

Watch for students who forget to decrease the digit to the left by one after trading.

INCORRECT	CORRECT
14	1 14
2̶4̶2	2̶4̶2
− 9 1	− 9 1
2 5 1	1 5 1

Have them practice rewriting numbers in the hundreds as 1 less hundred and 10 more tens; e.g. 327 = 3 hundreds 2 tens 7 ones or 2 hundreds 12 tens 7 ones aligning one form of the number under the other.

Enrichment

Tell students to write and solve a problem to find out how many more students than teachers are in their school.

Practice

Remind students to trade in subtraction only when needed. Assign the page to be completed independently.

Mixed Practice

1. 75¢ + 37¢ ($1.12)
2. ___ +8 = 11 (3)
3. 87 + 26 (113)
4. 56 − 39 (17)
5. 75 − 41 (34)
6. 84¢ − 38¢ (46¢)
7. 41 + 93 (134)
8. 921 ◯ 937 (<)
9. 2 quarters, 2 dimes, 3 nickels (85¢)
10. 68 + 40 (108)

Extra Credit   *Statistics*

A fairly common genetically determined trait is the ability to curl your tongue. Ask students to try to curve the edges of their tongues upwards so that their tongues form a tiny circle. Count the number who can curl their tongues and the number who cannot. Put the results on the board. Now ask the class to predict how many tongue-curlers they would expect to find out of every 30 people; out of every 15. (Answers will vary.) Ask them to survey 15 different people, outside the class. Have them keep track of the number of curlers and the number of non-curlers. Compare the results of their surveys. Remind students that this is not a test of skill, nor is it something they can practice. It is an inherited characteristic. They might want to try the test at home to see which members of their families can curl their tongues.

3 Digits Minus 3 Digits

pages 213-214

Objective

To subtract two 3-digit numbers for up to 2 trades

Materials

*colored chalk
hundred-flats
ten-strips and ones

Mental Math

Ask students if the following are true or false:

1. 6 tens + 4 tens is 64 tens (F)
2. 30 + 180 = 220 (F)
3. The present year has 4 digits. (T)
4. 5 hundreds + 10 tens = 600 (T)
5. Subtraction always needs trading. (F)
6. Addition never needs trading. (F)

Skill Review

Write **186 − 49 = 137** on the board. Have a student write and solve an addition problem to check the subtraction problem. Continue for the following problems: 235 − 94 = 141, 379 − 89 = 290, 490 − 68 = 420 (422), 519 − 29 = 490, 360 − 90 = 280 (270). Have students correct and check any problems which have errors.

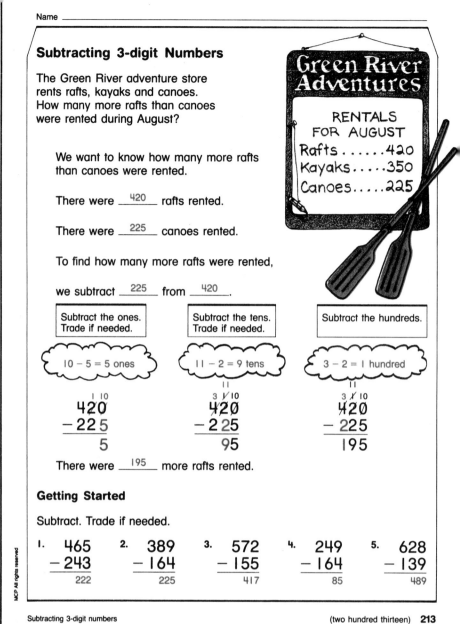

Subtracting 3-digit Numbers

The Green River adventure store rents rafts, kayaks and canoes. How many more rafts than canoes were rented during August?

Green River Adventures

RENTALS FOR AUGUST
Rafts......420
Kayaks.....350
Canoes.....225

We want to know how many more rafts than canoes were rented.

There were __420__ rafts rented.

There were __225__ canoes rented.

To find how many more rafts were rented,

we subtract __225__ from __420__.

Subtract the ones. Trade if needed.	Subtract the tens. Trade if needed.	Subtract the hundreds.
10 − 5 = 5 ones	11 − 2 = 9 tens	3 − 2 = 1 hundred

$$\begin{array}{r} {}^{1}\ ^{10} \\ 4\,2\,\cancel{0} \\ -2\,2\,5 \\ \hline 5 \end{array}$$

$$\begin{array}{r} {}^{3}\ ^{11}\ {}^{10} \\ \cancel{4}\,\cancel{2}\,\cancel{0} \\ -2\,2\,5 \\ \hline 9\,5 \end{array}$$

$$\begin{array}{r} {}^{3}\ ^{11}\ {}^{10} \\ \cancel{4}\,\cancel{2}\,\cancel{0} \\ -2\,2\,5 \\ \hline 1\,9\,5 \end{array}$$

There were __195__ more rafts rented.

Getting Started

Subtract. Trade if needed.

1. 465 − 243 = 222
2. 389 − 164 = 225
3. 572 − 155 = 417
4. 249 − 164 = 85
5. 628 − 139 = 489

Subtracting 3-digit numbers   (two hundred thirteen) **213**

Teaching the Lesson

Introducing the Problem Have students tell about the picture. Have a student read the problem aloud and tell what is to be found. (how many more rafts than canoes were rented in August) Ask students what information is needed from the picture. (420 rafts and 225 canoes were rented in August.) Ask students if the information about kayaks is needed. (no) Ask what operation needs to be done. (subtraction) Have students read and complete the information sentences. Work through the subtraction model with students and then have them complete the solution sentence. Have students add to check their solution.

Developing the Skill Write **376 − 197** on the board. Ask students if a trade is needed to subtract the ones. (yes) Use colored chalk to show the trade and then have a student subtract the ones. (9) Ask if a trade is needed to subtract the tens. (yes) Show the trade with colored chalk and have a student complete the problem. (179) Repeat the procedure for 926 − 278 (648), 453 − 327 (126), 849 − 678 (171), 655 − 432 (223), 895 − 576 (319) and 753 − 269 (484) where 1, 2 or no trades are needed.

Subtract. Trade if needed.

1. 965
− 234
731

2. 782
− 357
425

3. 359
− 165
194

4. 417
− 186
231

5. 531
− 167
364

6. 361
− 172
189

7. 619
− 285
334

8. 999
− 578
421

9. 843
− 357
486

10. 775
− 298
477

11. 375
− 185
190

12. 658
− 459
199

13. 583
− 196
387

14. 417
− 208
209

15. 625
− 357
268

FIELD TRIP

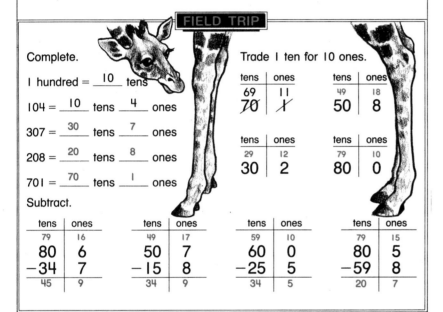

Complete.

1 hundred = __10__ tens

104 = __10__ tens __4__ ones

307 = __30__ tens __7__ ones

208 = __20__ tens __8__ ones

701 = __70__ tens __1__ ones

Subtract.

tens	ones
79	16
80	**6**
−34	**7**
45	9

tens	ones
49	17
50	**7**
−15	**8**
34	9

tens	ones
59	10
60	**0**
−25	**5**
34	5

tens	ones
79	15
80	**5**
−59	**8**
20	7

Trade 1 ten for 10 ones.

tens	ones
69	11
70	**1**

tens	ones
49	18
50	**8**

tens	ones
29	12
30	**2**

tens	ones
79	10
80	**0**

Subtracting 3-digit numbers

Correcting Common Errors

Some students may always write either 10 tens or 10 ones when they are trading and not add traded values to existing numbers.

INCORRECT	CORRECT
10	13
2 $\cancel{3}$10	2 $\cancel{3}$16
$\cancel{3}\cancel{4}\cancel{6}$	$\cancel{3}\cancel{4}\cancel{6}$
−187	−187
123	159

Correct by having students work in pairs using place-value materials to model the problems so they see that 10 tens or 10 ones must be added to the number already in the place.

Enrichment

Ask students if 543 minus 277 equals 276. Tell them to show their work to support their answer.

Practice

Remind students to trade in subtraction only when needed. Tell students that some of these problems will need no trades while some will need 1 or 2 trades. Have students complete the rows of problems independently.

Field Trip

Write on the board: **406 = 40 tens 6 ones.** Have students read the number sentence. Write **503** on the board and ask students how many tens there are. (50) Repeat for 705 (70), 904 (90) and 607 (60). Now write **705 − 137** vertically on the board and ask if a trade for a ten is needed. (yes) Mark through the 70 tens and write **69** above the 70. Show that there are 15 ones and have students subtract and tell the number of ones left. (8) Ask the number of hundreds when 1 is subtracted from 6. (5) Have a student read the answer. (568) Repeat the procedure for 607 − 488 (119).

Have students complete the number sentences and then trade 1 ten for 10 ones in the problems. Tell students to solve the 4 problems in the bottom row by subtracting 1 ten from 80, 1 ten from 50, etc.

Extra Credit *Measurement*

Have students make paper chains that are equal to their height by gluing circular strips together. Ask students to estimate the length of the chain in centimeters or inches. Then have students measure and record their own chain measurement. Connect the individual chains to make a class chain. Have students first estimate the length of the class chain and then measure and record the length.

Subtraction Practice

pages 215-216

Objective

To practice subtraction with trading

Materials

*colored chalk
*addition and subtraction fact cards
hundred-flats
ten-strips and ones

Mental Math

Tell students to complete each statement:

1. A 4-sided figure is a ___. (square or rectangle)
2. A clock tells us the ___. (time)
3. A coin worth 50¢ is a ___. (half-dollar)
4. 726 is ___ more than 696. (30)
5. A 3-sided figure is a ___. (triangle)

Skill Review

Distribute all addition fact cards to students so that each student has several. Show a subtraction fact card and ask students to show the addition fact or facts which would be used to check the subtraction fact. Continue with more cards.

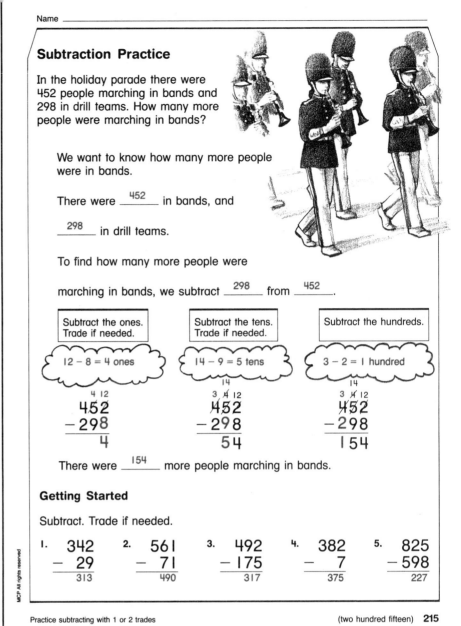

Subtraction Practice

In the holiday parade there were 452 people marching in bands and 298 in drill teams. How many more people were marching in bands?

We want to know how many more people were in bands.

There were ___452___ in bands, and

___298___ in drill teams.

To find how many more people were

marching in bands, we subtract ___298___ from ___452___.

Subtract the ones. Trade if needed.	Subtract the tens. Trade if needed.	Subtract the hundreds.
12 − 8 = 4 ones	14 − 9 = 5 tens	3 − 2 = 1 hundred

$$\begin{array}{r} 4\ 12 \\ 4\cancel{5}2 \\ -298 \\ \hline 4 \end{array}$$

$$\begin{array}{r} 14 \\ 3\ \cancel{4}\ 12 \\ \cancel{4}\cancel{5}2 \\ -298 \\ \hline 54 \end{array}$$

$$\begin{array}{r} 14 \\ 3\ \cancel{4}\ 12 \\ \cancel{4}\cancel{5}2 \\ -298 \\ \hline 154 \end{array}$$

There were ___154___ more people marching in bands.

Getting Started

Subtract. Trade if needed.

1.	2.	3.	4.	5.
342 − 29 = 313	561 − 71 = 490	492 − 175 = 317	382 − 7 = 375	825 − 598 = 227

Practice subtracting with 1 or 2 trades   (two hundred fifteen) **215**

Teaching the Lesson

Introducing the Problem   Have a student read the problem aloud and tell what is to be solved. (how many more people were marching) Ask what information is given in the problem. (452 people marched and 298 were in drill teams.) Ask what operation is used to find how many more. (subtraction) Have students read and complete the information sentences. Work through the model with students and then have them complete the solution sentence. Have students add to check their answer.

Developing the Skill   Write on the board: **423 − 9** (414), **708 − 26** (682), **354 − 296** (58), **966 − 589** (377), **458 − 272** (186). Have students tell if a trade is needed in the first problem and what trade is needed. (yes, 1 ten for 10 ones) Use colored chalk to draw a small arrow above the 3 to denote a trade is needed. Continue through the other problems noting with an arrow where trades are needed. Have students talk through each problem as it is being solved.

215

Practice

Subtract. Trade if needed.

1.
$$342$$
$$-8$$
$$334$$

2.
$$561$$
$$-80$$
$$481$$

3.
$$478$$
$$-96$$
$$382$$

4.
$$658$$
$$-167$$
$$491$$

5.
$$725$$
$$-286$$
$$439$$

6.
$$786$$
$$-451$$
$$335$$

7.
$$892$$
$$-355$$
$$537$$

8.
$$669$$
$$-278$$
$$391$$

9.
$$315$$
$$-192$$
$$123$$

10.
$$669$$
$$-580$$
$$89$$

11.
$$419$$
$$-269$$
$$150$$

12.
$$915$$
$$-400$$
$$515$$

13.
$$643$$
$$-258$$
$$385$$

14.
$$695$$
$$-555$$
$$140$$

15.
$$947$$
$$-589$$
$$358$$

16.
$$456$$
$$-8$$
$$448$$

17.
$$316$$
$$-93$$
$$223$$

18.
$$695$$
$$-636$$
$$59$$

19.
$$721$$
$$-345$$
$$376$$

20.
$$926$$
$$-387$$
$$539$$

21.
$$350$$
$$-75$$
$$275$$

22.
$$736$$
$$-258$$
$$478$$

23.
$$840$$
$$-375$$
$$465$$

24.
$$624$$
$$-398$$
$$226$$

25.
$$261$$
$$-243$$
$$18$$

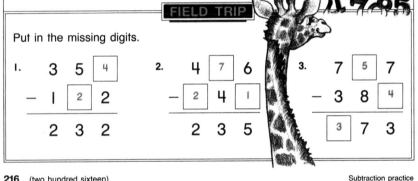

FIELD TRIP

Put in the missing digits.

1.
$$3\ 5\ \boxed{4}$$
$$-\ 1\ \boxed{2}\ 2$$
$$2\ 3\ 2$$

2.
$$4\ \boxed{7}\ 6$$
$$-\ \boxed{2}\ 4\ \boxed{1}$$
$$2\ 3\ 5$$

3.
$$7\ \boxed{5}\ 7$$
$$-\ 3\ 8\ \boxed{4}$$
$$\boxed{3}\ 7\ 3$$

Subtraction practice

Correcting Common Errors

If students have difficulty keeping all three numbers aligned properly and their trades in the correct places, have them work their problems on grid paper so that the lines and columns can help them place everything correctly.

Enrichment

Tell students to write and solve a subtraction problem of two 3-digit numbers where a trade of 1 hundred for 10 tens is needed, but no trade for more ones is needed.

Practice

Remind students to trade only when needed. Have students solve the problems independently.

Field Trip

Write on the board:

$$4\ \ 2\ \ \boxed{[6]}$$
$$-\ \boxed{[2]}\ \ 1\ \ 8$$
$$2\ \ 0\ \ 8$$

Tell students there are 2 missing numbers to be found. Ask students how many ones would 8 ones be taken from to have 8 ones left. (16) Write **6** in ones place and ask students if a ten needed to be traded for ones. (yes) Help students see that 1 ten would be left and 1 from 1 is 0. Ask if 1 of the 4 hundreds was traded. (no) Ask the number of hundreds that would be taken from 4 hundreds to have 2 hundreds left. (2) Record the 2 and help students check the

problem by adding. Tell students to work each problem to find the missing numbers.

Extra Credit   *Graphing*

Explain to students that one way to show a tally of information is with a picture graph. Have students divide a large sheet of paper into three sections. Have them label each with a title: Refrigerator, Freezer, Cupboard. Have them use old magazines, scissors and glue. Tell them to cut out pictures of food, and glue them under the correct category according to how they would be stored. Have them display their finished graphs and discuss: Is it easy or difficult to get information from a picture graph? Which category had the most food? Which items fit under more than one category? etc.

216

Subtraction Dollar Notation

pages 217-218

Objective

To subtract amounts of money through $9.99

Materials

dollars, dimes and pennies
hundred-flats
ten-strips and ones

Mental Math

Tell students to name the number for:

1. the third Tuesday this month.
2. the present year.
3. 1 penny less than $1. (99¢)
4. the number of months until January.
5. 40 more than 68. (108)
6. the last Sunday in next month.
7. yesterday's date.
8. 100 more than 799. (899)

Skill Review

Have students lay out 1 one and tell what piece of money has the same value. (a penny) Repeat for students to relate the hundred-flat and ten-strip to the dollar and dime, respectively. Dictate amounts of money through $9.99 and have students show each amount with money and then with hundred-squares, ten-strips and ones.

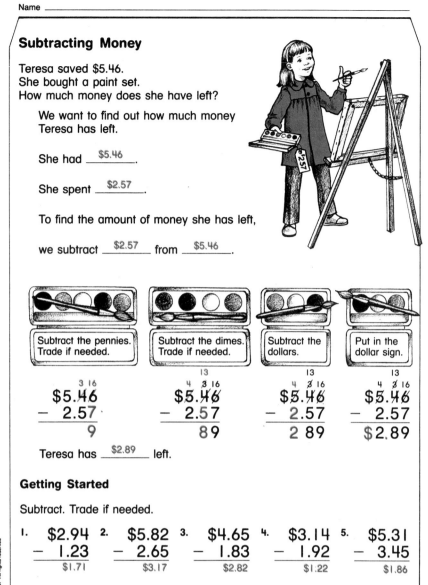

Subtracting Money

Teresa saved $5.46.
She bought a paint set.
How much money does she have left?

We want to find out how much money Teresa has left.

She had ___$5.46___.

She spent ___$2.57___.

To find the amount of money she has left,

we subtract ___$2.57___ from ___$5.46___.

Subtract the pennies. Trade if needed.	Subtract the dimes. Trade if needed.	Subtract the dollars.	Put in the dollar sign.
$5.46 − 2.57 9	$5.46 − 2.57 89	$5.46 − 2.57 2 89	$5.46 − 2.57 $2.89

Teresa has ___$2.89___ left.

Getting Started

Subtract. Trade if needed.

1. $2.94 − 1.23 = $1.71
2. $5.82 − 2.65 = $3.17
3. $4.65 − 1.83 = $2.82
4. $3.14 − 1.92 = $1.22
5. $5.31 − 3.45 = $1.86

Subtracting money using dollar notation
(two hundred seventeen) **217**

Teaching the Lesson

Introducing the Problem Have students tell about the picture. Have a student read the problem and tell what is to be solved. (the amount of money Teresa has left) Ask what information is given in the problem. (She saved $5.46 and bought a paint set.) Ask what information is needed from the picture. (The paint set costs $2.57.) Ask students what operation tells us how much is left. (subtraction) Have students read and complete the information sentences. Work through the model with students and then have them complete the solution sentence. Tell students to add to check their answer.

Developing the Skill Have students lay out $7.47, subtract $3.28 from it and tell the amount left. ($4.19) Have a student write and solve the problem on the board. Remind students that the decimal point separates the dollars and cents and that the dollar sign goes before the number of dollars. Ask students why this answer would not be written using the cent sign. (The amount is more than $1.) Continue for $2.63 − 0.96 ($1.67), $8.98 − 3.59 ($5.39), $7.18 − 4.49 ($2.69), $6.02 − 1.99 ($4.03) and $5.50 − 3.26 ($2.24).

217

Practice

Subtract. Trade if needed.

1. $1.07	2. $4.71	3. $6.35	4. $1.98	5. $7.45
− 0.75	− 1.89	− 2.75	− 0.98	− 1.49
$0.32	$2.82	$3.60	$1.00	$5.96

Apply

PAT'S DINER

Hamburger............$2.95	Salad Plate.......$3.49
Ham Sandwich.........$3.25	Milk..............$0.65
Egg Salad Sandwich....$1.88	Chocolate Milk....$0.75
Tuna Sandwich.........$2.59	Iced Tea.........$0.49

Solve.

6. How much more did Jack pay for a hamburger than an egg salad sandwich?

$2.95
− 1.88
$1.07

$1.07

7. How much more is a chocolate milk than iced tea?

$0.75
− 0.49
$0.26

$0.26

8. How much did Joe pay for a hamburger and a glass of milk?

$2.95
+ 0.65
$3.60

$3.60

9. How much less is a tuna sandwich than a ham sandwich?

$3.25
− 2.59
$0.66

$0.66

10. How much more is a ham sandwich than an egg salad sandwich?

$3.25
− 1.88
$1.37

$1.37

11. How much is a salad plate and a chocolate milk?

$3.49
+ 0.75
$4.24

$4.24

218 (two hundred eighteen)

Subtracting money using dollar notation

218

Review

pages 219-220

Objectives

To review subtraction of 3-digit numbers

To maintain skills learned previously this year

Materials

dollars, dimes and pennies
hundred-flats
ten-strips and ones

Mental Math

Ask students how many:

1. minutes there are between 7 and 8 on a clock. (5)
2. ones are gained in a trade of a ten. (10)
3. cents are in 13 dimes. (130)
4. nickels make $1.00. (20)
5. half-dollars are in $8. (16)
6. tens are in $8.26. (2)
7. digits are after the decimal point in a money amount. (2)

Skill Review

Tell a story of John having $2.70 and losing 23¢. Have a student write and solve a problem to tell how much money John has left. ($2.47) Tell more stories of dollar amounts for students to decide if addition or subtraction is needed. Then have them write and solve the problems.

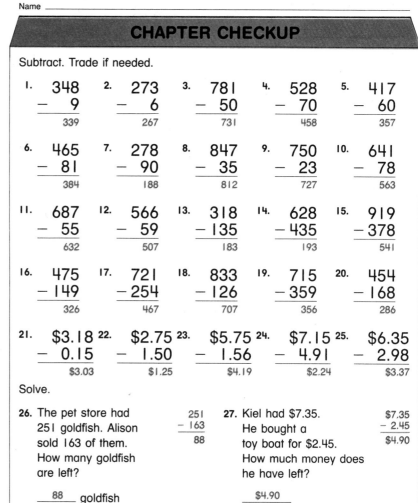

Name _____

Subtract. Trade if needed.

1.	2.	3.	4.	5.
348 − 9 339	273 − 6 267	781 − 50 731	528 − 70 458	417 − 60 357

6.	7.	8.	9.	10.
465 − 81 384	278 − 90 188	847 − 35 812	750 − 23 727	641 − 78 563

11.	12.	13.	14.	15.
687 − 55 632	566 − 59 507	318 −135 183	628 −435 193	919 −378 541

16.	17.	18.	19.	20.
475 −149 326	721 −254 467	833 −126 707	715 −359 356	454 −168 286

21.	22.	23.	24.	25.
$3.18 − 0.15 $3.03	$2.75 − 1.50 $1.25	$5.75 − 1.56 $4.19	$7.15 − 4.91 $2.24	$6.35 − 2.98 $3.37

Solve.

26. The pet store had 251 goldfish. Alison sold 163 of them. How many goldfish are left?

   251
 − 163
    88

   __88__ goldfish

27. Kiel had $7.35. He bought a toy boat for $2.45. How much money does he have left?

   $7.35
 − 2.45
  $4.90

   __$4.90__

Teaching page 219

Ask students which problems on this page require a dollar sign and decimal point in the answer. Remind students to add to check each subtraction problem. Have students complete the page independently.

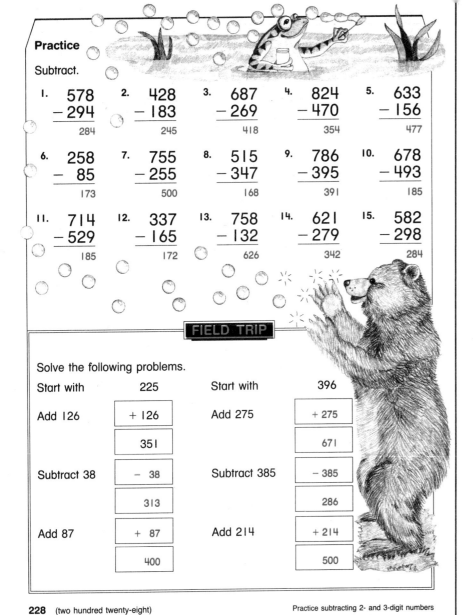

Practice

Subtract.

1. 578 − 294 = 284	2. 428 − 183 = 245	3. 687 − 269 = 418	4. 824 − 470 = 354	5. 633 − 156 = 477
6. 258 − 85 = 173	7. 755 − 255 = 500	8. 515 − 347 = 168	9. 786 − 395 = 391	10. 678 − 493 = 185
11. 714 − 529 = 185	12. 337 − 165 = 172	13. 758 − 132 = 626	14. 621 − 279 = 342	15. 582 − 298 = 284

FIELD TRIP

Solve the following problems.

Start with	225	Start with	396
Add 126	+ 126	Add 275	+ 275
	351		671
Subtract 38	− 38	Subtract 385	− 385
	313		286
Add 87	+ 87	Add 214	+ 214
	400		500

Practice subtracting 2- and 3-digit numbers

Correcting Common Errors

Watch for students who subtract incorrectly because they do not know their basic subtraction facts. Have them work with partners using the fact cards for those facts that give them trouble and practice quizzing each other.

Enrichment

Tell students to cut pictures from catalogs or newspapers to make a store display with a sign that shows there were 550 of one item and 287 of another item for sale. Then tell them to find out how many of each item were left after the store sold 199 of each.

see back of book after p. 305

Practice

Have students complete the rows of problems independently.

Field Trip

Write on the board: **Start with 100, add 264, subtract 78, add 126.** Tell students that to solve this problem, we must go step-by-step. Write **100 + 264** vertically on the board and find the sum. (364) Write **−78** under 364 and find the difference. (286) Write **+126** under 287 and find the sum. (412) Repeat for another example and have students complete the problems independently and then as a group at the board. Have students complete the problems independently.

Extra Credit   *Statistics*

Bring a collection of toy cars and trucks to class. Have students graph the total number of wheels, starting with one car, then adding another and another. Give each student graph paper and help them set up the paper for a bar graph. Have them graph their wheel counts.

```
                  5
number of cars    4
                  3
                  2
                  1
                  4  8  12  16  20  24 . . .
                  number of wheels
```

Pin up all the bar graphs so students can see each other's work. Ask students to describe the pattern made. (The bars increase in length in a constant way. Later, this kind of graph will be called a linear graph.)

228

Checking Subtraction

pages 229-230

Objective

To check subtraction by adding

Materials

*subtraction fact cards
hundred-flats
ten-strips and ones

Mental Math

Ask students how many pennies are in the following:

1. $2.63 (263)
2. 5 quarters (125)
3. 6 dimes (60)
4. 4 half-dollars (200)

Ask how many dollars and dimes equal:

5. $6.90 (6, 9)
6. 340 pennies (3, 4)
7. 4 quarters and 2 nickels (1, 1)
8. 20 nickels (1, 0)

Skill Review

Show a subtraction fact and have a student write the addition fact on the board which uses the same numbers. Remind students that the 2 facts are related and the addition fact is used to check the subtraction fact. Continue for more practice.

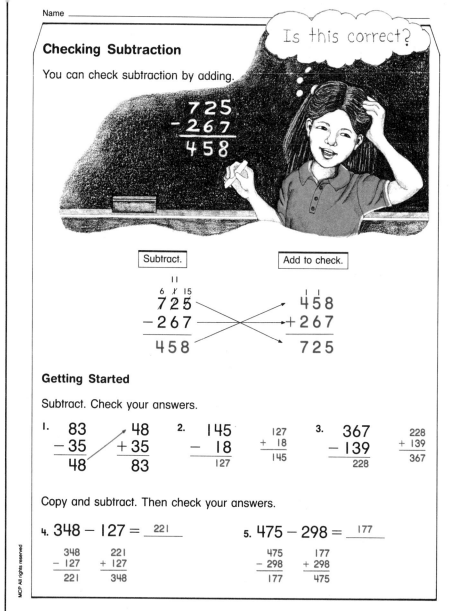

Checking subtraction problems by adding

(two hundred twenty-nine) **229**

Teaching the Lesson

Introducing the Problem Have students read the statement about checking subtraction. Work through the solution of the subtraction problem with students. Ask students what numbers are used in the addition problem to check subtraction. (the answer and the smaller number) Work through the addition problem together and discuss how to find out if the problem is correct. (The sum is the same number as the top number in the subtraction problem.)

Developing the Skill Have students lay out manipulatives to show 132. Tell students to move 64 away and tell the number left as you write **132 − 64** on the board. (68) Have a student show the trades and record the answer in the problem on the board. Tell students to now add the 68 left and the 64 removed to see if the total is 132. (yes) Have a student write and solve **68 + 64** on the board. (132) Ask students how we know that the subtraction problem is correct. (The sum of the number left and the number removed is the same as the number in all.) Repeat the procedure for 375 − 219 (156), 708 − 649 (59), 573 − 386 (187) and 921 − 84 (837).

229

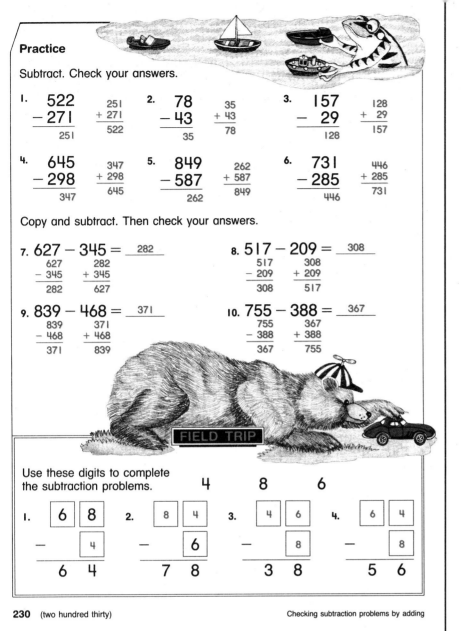

Practice

Subtract. Check your answers.

1. 522 − 271 = 251   251 + 271 = 522
2. 78 − 43 = 35   35 + 43 = 78
3. 157 − 29 = 128   128 + 29 = 157
4. 645 − 298 = 347   347 + 298 = 645
5. 849 − 587 = 262   262 + 587 = 849
6. 731 − 285 = 446   446 + 285 = 731

Copy and subtract. Then check your answers.

7. 627 − 345 = 282
8. 517 − 209 = 308
9. 839 − 468 = 371
10. 755 − 388 = 367

Use these digits to complete the subtraction problems.   4   8   6

1. 6 8 − 4 = 6 4
2. 8 4 − 6 = 7 8
3. 4 6 − 8 = 3 8
4. 6 4 − 8 = 5 6

230 (two hundred thirty)   Checking subtraction problems by adding

Correcting Common Errors

Some students may get confused and simply add the minuend and subtrahend to check. Have them work with partners and place-value materials to model a subtraction problem, such as 456 − 234. After they show 222 as the answer, have them add the place-value materials they have removed, 234, to those left, 222, to get those they started with, 456.

Enrichment

Tell students to write 3 subtraction problems of 2- and 3-digit numbers. Have them solve the problems so that at least 1 solution is incorrect. Tell them to have a friend find and correct any errors made.

Practice

Tell students to solve each subtraction problem in the first 2 rows and then write and solve an addition problem to check the subtraction. Remind students that the next group of problems needs to be written vertically. Tell students to solve each subtraction problem and then check by adding. Have students complete the problems independently.

Field Trip

Write **2, 8** and **3** on the board. Tell students to arrange the 3 digits in the following problem so that each is used only once and the problem makes sense:

[(3)] [(8)]
− [(2)]
3 6

As students experiment with the numbers, show them how to keep a record of which number combinations have been tried by listing each number which does not work. Repeat for (2) (3) − (8)=15. Tell students to solve the problems independently.

Extra Credit   *Creative Drill*

Tell the students they are going to make a Numeral Nancy. Put the following example on the board:

Point out that the three's form the head, the eyes are made with nines and the number eight, and the nose is formed with a zero. Ask students to identify that the mouth, chin and neck are formed with the numbers six, seven and eleven. Ask if all the numbers in the addition problem are used. (yes) Ask the students to add the numbers to find the age of Numeral Nancy. Tell students to make their own numeral person using a column addition problem and trade problems with a partner.

Money, Adding and Subtracting

pages 231-232

Objective

To add or subtract money for sums and minuends through $9.99

Materials

hundred-flats
ten-strips and ones
dollars and coins

Mental Math

Ask students what page would come first in a book:

1. 26 or 35 (26)
2. 310 or 301 (301)
3. 224 or 186 (186)
4. 92 or 116 (92)
5. 15 or 51 (15)
6. 143 or 35 (35)
7. 200 or 315 (200)
8. 90 or 62 (62)

Skill Review

Have students lay out a hundred-flat and then lay out one piece of money that is the same. (1 dollar) Have a student write $1.00 and 100 on the board. Repeat for other 1- through 3-digit numbers to be shown and written as money amounts.

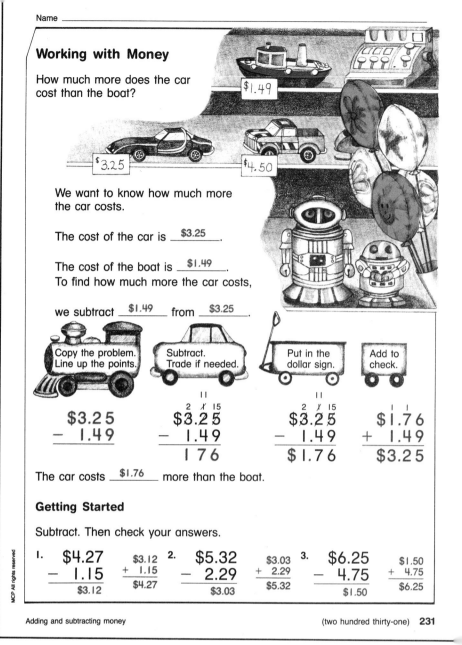

Name _____

Working with Money

How much more does the car cost than the boat?

We want to know how much more the car costs.

The cost of the car is __$3.25__.

The cost of the boat is __$1.49__.
To find how much more the car costs,

we subtract __$1.49__ from __$3.25__.

Copy the problem. Line up the points.	Subtract. Trade if needed.	Put in the dollar sign.	Add to check.
$3.25 − 1.49	$3.2⁵5 − 1.49 1 76	$3.2⁵5 − 1.49 $1.76	$1.76 + 1.49 $3.25

The car costs __$1.76__ more than the boat.

Getting Started

Subtract. Then check your answers.

1. $4.27 $3.12   2. $5.32 $3.03   3. $6.25 $1.50
   − 1.15 + 1.15   − 2.29 + 2.29   − 4.75 + 4.75
   _____ _____   _____ _____   _____ _____
   $3.12 $4.27 $3.03 $5.32 $1.50 $6.25

Adding and subtracting money

(two hundred thirty-one) **231**

Teaching the Lesson

Introducing the Problem   Have a student read the problem and tell what is to be solved. (how much more the car costs than the boat) Ask what information is needed. (the cost of the car and the cost of the boat) Ask what information is given in the picture but is not needed to solve this problem. (The truck costs $4.50.) Ask students what operation is needed to find how much more. (subtraction) Have students read and complete the information sentences. Work through the model with students to solve and check the problem. Then have them complete the solution sentence.

Developing the Skill   Have a student solve the following problem at the board: **326 − 145** (181) Now have a student solve this problem at the board: **$3.26 − 1.45** ($1.81) Ask students how the 2 answers differ. (The second one has a dollar sign and decimal point.) Have students check the problems by writing and solving addition problems at the board. Now write **$2.59 − 0.88** on the board and tell students to subtract the numbers and then insert the dollar sign and decimal point to show the problem is about money. ($1.71) Repeat for more money problems.

231

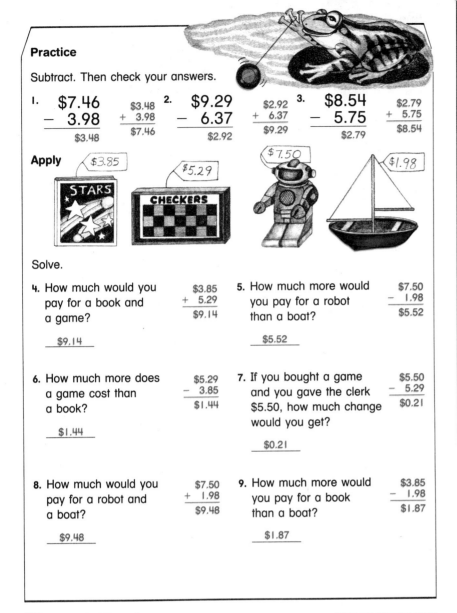

Practice

Subtract. Then check your answers.

1.
$$\begin{array}{r} \$7.46 \\ -\ 3.98 \\ \hline \$3.48 \end{array} \qquad \begin{array}{r} \$3.48 \\ +\ 3.98 \\ \hline \$7.46 \end{array}$$

2.
$$\begin{array}{r} \$9.29 \\ -\ 6.37 \\ \hline \$2.92 \end{array} \qquad \begin{array}{r} \$2.92 \\ +\ 6.37 \\ \hline \$9.29 \end{array}$$

3.
$$\begin{array}{r} \$8.54 \\ -\ 5.75 \\ \hline \$2.79 \end{array} \qquad \begin{array}{r} \$2.79 \\ +\ 5.75 \\ \hline \$8.54 \end{array}$$

Apply

$3.85 STARS   *$5.29* CHECKERS   *$7.50*   *$1.98*

Solve.

4. How much would you pay for a book and a game?

$$\begin{array}{r} \$3.85 \\ +\ 5.29 \\ \hline \$9.14 \end{array}$$

__$9.14__

5. How much more would you pay for a robot than a boat?

$$\begin{array}{r} \$7.50 \\ -\ 1.98 \\ \hline \$5.52 \end{array}$$

__$5.52__

6. How much more does a game cost than a book?

$$\begin{array}{r} \$5.29 \\ -\ 3.85 \\ \hline \$1.44 \end{array}$$

__$1.44__

7. If you bought a game and you gave the clerk $5.50, how much change would you get?

$$\begin{array}{r} \$5.50 \\ -\ 5.29 \\ \hline \$0.21 \end{array}$$

__$0.21__

8. How much would you pay for a robot and a boat?

$$\begin{array}{r} \$7.50 \\ +\ 1.98 \\ \hline \$9.48 \end{array}$$

__$9.48__

9. How much more would you pay for a book than a boat?

$$\begin{array}{r} \$3.85 \\ -\ 1.98 \\ \hline \$1.87 \end{array}$$

__$1.87__

232 (two hundred thirty-two)   Adding and subtracting money

Practice

Tell students that the first 3 problems are to be solved and checked. Tell students they are to use the priced items to solve the word problems and some of the word problems require addition and some require subtraction. Have students complete the page independently.

Mixed Practice

1. 83¢ + 27¢ ($1.10)
2. ___, 120, 130, 140, (110)
3. 91 − 74 (17)
4. 8 + ___ = 13 (5)
5. 651 ◯ 647 (>)
6. 3 quarters, 2 pennies (77¢)
7. 75 + 6 (81)
8. 27 + 13 + 35 (75)
9. 83 − 28 (55)
10. 15 − 8 (7)

Extra Credit   *Numeration*

Have the students cut thirty small squares of tagboard. Number each card from 0 to 9, making three cards that show each number. Then have students write ones under each number in one set, tens under each number in the second set, and hundreds under each number in the third set. Pass out the cards to several students. Have a student call out a 3-digit number. Those students holding the correct number and place value cards to make that number, come to the front of the room and hold up their cards. Check to make sure students have the correct place value and are in the right order. Repeat for each student to call out a number.

Mixed Problem Solving

pages 233-234

Objective

To add or subtract 3-digit numbers to solve problems

Materials

dollars and coins
hundred-flats
ten-strips and ones

Mental Math

Ask if the following are true or false:

1. A square has 4 corners. (T)
2. A circle has 4 corners. (F)
3. Some clocks have Roman numerals. (T)
4. 10 is X in Roman numerals. (T)
5. I, V and Y are Roman numerals. (F)

Skill Review

Write **728** and **169** on the board. Have a student show and tell why it is important to know whether to add or subtract these numbers. (728 + 169 = 897, 728 − 169 = 559, the answers are far different.) Have students make up word problems using the same numbers for each operation. Repeat for more pairs of 2- or 3-digit numbers.

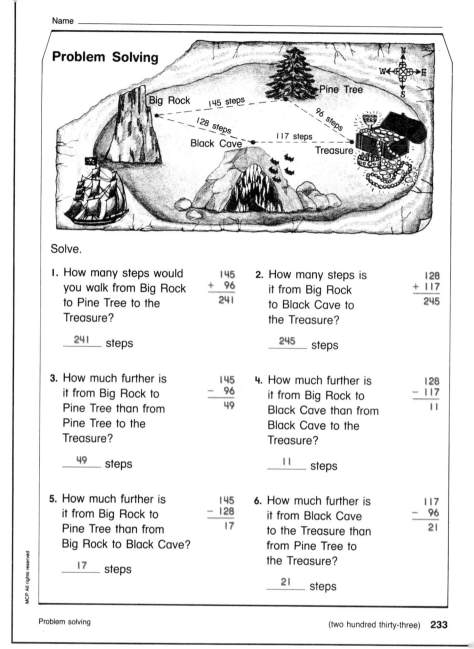

Name _____

Problem Solving

Solve.

1. How many steps would you walk from Big Rock to Pine Tree to the Treasure?

$$\begin{array}{r} 145 \\ +\ 96 \\ \hline 241 \end{array}$$

____241____ steps

2. How many steps is it from Big Rock to Black Cave to the Treasure?

$$\begin{array}{r} 128 \\ +\ 117 \\ \hline 245 \end{array}$$

____245____ steps

3. How much further is it from Big Rock to Pine Tree than from Pine Tree to the Treasure?

$$\begin{array}{r} 145 \\ -\ 96 \\ \hline 49 \end{array}$$

____49____ steps

4. How much further is it from Big Rock to Black Cave than from Black Cave to the Treasure?

$$\begin{array}{r} 128 \\ -\ 117 \\ \hline 11 \end{array}$$

____11____ steps

5. How much further is it from Big Rock to Pine Tree than from Big Rock to Black Cave?

$$\begin{array}{r} 145 \\ -\ 128 \\ \hline 17 \end{array}$$

____17____ steps

6. How much further is it from Black Cave to the Treasure than from Pine Tree to the Treasure?

$$\begin{array}{r} 117 \\ -\ 96 \\ \hline 21 \end{array}$$

____21____ steps

Problem solving

(two hundred thirty-three) **233**

Teaching page 233

Have students use the map to tell the distance from Big Rock to Black Cave (128 steps), Pine Tree to the Treasure (96 steps), etc. Ask students how to get from Big Rock to the Treasure. (go to Black Cave or Pine Tree and then on to the Treasure) Ask students how they could find the total distance from Big Rock through Pine Tree to the Treasure. (add 145 steps and 96 steps) Have a student write and solve the problem on the board. (145 + 96 = 241 steps) Ask students how they could find out how many more steps from Black Cave to Big Rock than from Black Cave to Treasure. (subtract 128 steps from 96 steps) Have a student write and solve the problem on the board. (128 − 96 = 32 steps) Tell students the word problems on this page ask them to solve problems similar to the 2 on the board and that some problems require addition and some require subtraction. Remind students of the 4 helpful

questions they have been using to solve problems. Have students help recall the following questions as you write in a column on the board: **What is to be found? What do we know? What operation needs to be done with the numbers? Does the answer make sense?** Have students solve all problems independently. Remind students to show their work beside each problem and record each answer on the line.

233

Solve.

1. How much more is
936 than 375?

$$\begin{array}{r} 936 \\ -\ 375 \\ \hline 561 \end{array}$$

936 is __561__ more than 375.

2. How much less is
562 than 821?

$$\begin{array}{r} 821 \\ -\ 562 \\ \hline 259 \end{array}$$

562 is __259__ less than 821.

3. How much is
456 and 279?

$$\begin{array}{r} 456 \\ +\ 279 \\ \hline 735 \end{array}$$

The sum is __735__.

4. How much is
312 and 395?

$$\begin{array}{r} 312 \\ +\ 395 \\ \hline 707 \end{array}$$

The sum is __707__.

5. Betsy had $6.35.
She spent $2.98.
How much money
is left?

$$\begin{array}{r} \$6.35 \\ -\ 2.98 \\ \hline \$3.37 \end{array}$$

Betsy has __$3.37__ left.

6. John has $4.50.
He earned $2.75.
How much money
does John have now?

$$\begin{array}{r} \$4.50 \\ +\ 2.75 \\ \hline \$7.25 \end{array}$$

John has __$7.25__.

7. Gary has $3.80.
He earned $2.90
babysitting. How
much money does
he have now?

$$\begin{array}{r} \$3.80 \\ +\ 2.90 \\ \hline \$6.70 \end{array}$$

Gary has __$6.70__.

8. Bre had $8.15.
She spent $3.69.
How much money
does Bre have left?

$$\begin{array}{r} \$8.15 \\ -\ 3.69 \\ \hline \$4.46 \end{array}$$

Bre has __$4.46__ left.

9. What if Gary in exercise 7
spends $1.55 of his money?
How much will he have left?

__$5.15__

10. Read exercise 8 again. How
much more does Bre need to
have $5.00?

__$0.54__

234 (two hundred thirty-four)   Problem solving

Correcting Common Errors

If students have difficulty knowing whether to add or subtract, have them work with partners and take turns re-telling each story in their own words, discussing which words suggest addition and which suggest subtraction.

Enrichment

Tell students to use the map on page 233 to find the distance from Black Cave to the Treasure if one went by way of Big Rock and Pine Tree. Ask how many more steps this is than if one went directly to the Treasure from Black Cave.

Teaching page 234

Ask students which problems on this page will require them to write a dollar sign and decimal point. Have students circle those problem numbers as a reminder. Remind students to show their work to the right of each problem and record their answer on the line.

Extra Credit   Creative Drill

Duplicate the following for students:

Across
1. At the drinking fountain, you usually wait in (line).
2. Jim is tall, Jane is the opposite. She is (short).
3. When we line up against the wall we are in a (straight) line.
4. To find out how long a crayon is, we (measure) it.
5. A foot is divided into (inches).

Down
1. If your pencil is not short, it is (long).
7. Twelve inches is equal to one (foot).
8. We use a (ruler) to measure length.
9. There are (twelve) inches in one foot.

234

Review

pages 235-236

Objectives

To review addition and subtraction of 2- and 3-digit numbers

To maintain skills learned previously this year

Materials

dollars and coins
hundred-flats
ten-strips and ones

Mental Math

Tell students to add 7 tens and 2 ones to:

1. 6 (78)
2. 100 (172)
3. 28 (100)
4. 14 ones (86)
5. 6 hundreds (672)
6. 10 (82)
7. 1 hundred 2 tens (192)
8. 20 ones (92)

Skill Review

Have a student write a 2- or 3-digit number on the board for other students to show with manipulatives. Have students read the number and give its value in hundreds, tens and ones. Repeat for more place value practice.

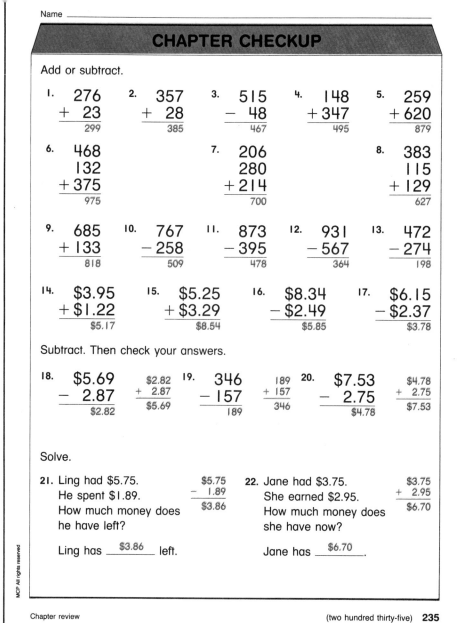

CHAPTER CHECKUP

Add or subtract.

1. 276
   + 23
   ——
   299

2. 357
   + 28
   ——
   385

3. 515
   − 48
   ——
   467

4. 148
   +347
   ——
   495

5. 259
   +620
   ——
   879

6. 468
    132
   +375
   ——
   975

7. 206
    280
   +214
   ——
   700

8. 383
    115
   +129
   ——
   627

9. 685
   +133
   ——
   818

10. 767
   −258
   ——
   509

11. 873
   −395
   ——
   478

12. 931
   −567
   ——
   364

13. 472
   −274
   ——
   198

14. $3.95
   +$1.22
   ——
   $5.17

15. $5.25
   +$3.29
   ——
   $8.54

16. $8.34
   −$2.49
   ——
   $5.85

17. $6.15
   −$2.37
   ——
   $3.78

Subtract. Then check your answers.

18. $5.69 $2.82
   − 2.87   + 2.87
   ——   ——
   $2.82 $5.69

19. 346   189
   −157   + 157
   ——   ——
   189   346

20. $7.53 $4.78
   − 2.75   + 2.75
   ——   ——
   $4.78 $7.53

Solve.

21. Ling had $5.75.
    He spent $1.89.
    How much money does
    he have left?

         $5.75
       − 1.89
       ——
        $3.86

    Ling has __$3.86__ left.

22. Jane had $3.75.
    She earned $2.95.
    How much money does
    she have now?

         $3.75
       + 2.95
       ——
        $6.70

    Jane has __$6.70__.

Chapter review

(two hundred thirty-five) **235**

Teaching page 235

Tell students to solve each addition or subtraction problem and show the work which checks problems 18, 19 and 20. Have students circle the number of each problem which requires a dollar sign and decimal point in the answer. Remind students to decide which operation should be used to solve each word problem. Have students complete the page independently.

Fill in the oval next to the correct answer.

1	7 + 8	○ 1 ● 15 ○ 14 ○ NG
2	16 − 7	● 9 ○ 23 ○ 19 ○ NG
3		○ 326 ○ 263 ● 236 ○ NG
4		● $1.88 ○ $1.28 ○ $1.83 ○ NG
5		○ 4:45 ● 3:45 ○ 9:18 ○ NG
6	85 + 67	○ 12 ○ 142 ● 152 ○ NG

7	238 + 475	○ 703 ○ 603 ● 713 ○ NG
8	91 − 48	○ 53 ● 43 ○ 57 ○ NG
9	315 − 197	● 118 ○ 512 ○ 328 ○ NG
10	563 − 274	○ 281 ○ 311 ○ 399 ● NG
11	$3.25 + 2.75	● $6.00 ○ $5.90 ○ $5.00 ○ NG
12	$5.25 − 2.98	○ $8.23 ● $2.27 ○ $3.37 ○ NG

[ ] score

Cumulative review

Enrichment

1. Tell students to write 2 subtraction problems which are related to 326 + 184.
2. Have students draw 10 coins for a total value of $1.53.
3. Tell students to draw 2 clocks that could show their starting and finishing times if it took 40 minutes to complete your homework.

Teaching page 236

This page reviews basic facts, place value, money, time and addition and subtraction of 2- and 3-digit numbers. Remind students to fill in the oval beside NG only if the correct answer is not given. Have students complete the page independently.

Plane Figures

pages 237-238

Objective

To identify circles, triangles, squares and rectangles

Materials

*different sizes of squares, rectangles, triangles, circles
blank cards

Mental Math

Tell students to name the number:

1. 480 − 6 (474)
2. 20 tens (200)
3. 149 + 5 (154)
4. 770 + 12 (782)
5. 45 + 45 (90)
6. 16 tens + 6 (166)

Skill Review

Give each student 2 cards. Have students write an addition problem and a subtraction problem using 2- or 3-digit numbers. Write across the board: **No trade, 1 trade, 2 trades.** Have students place their problems under the proper heading. Then have each student select 2 cards and solve the problems. Have students replace the cards under their proper headings and then select 2 problems and check the answers.

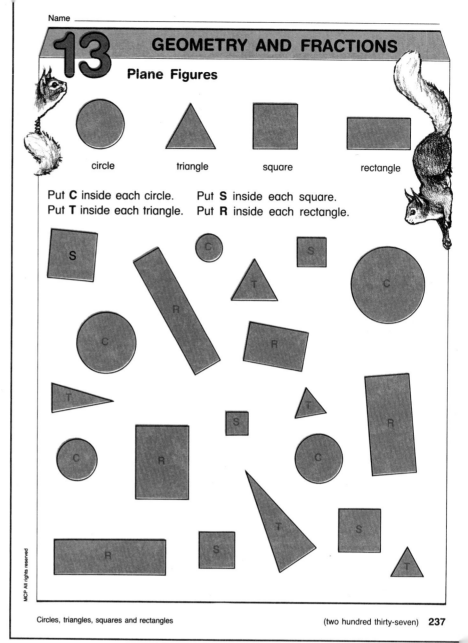

GEOMETRY AND FRACTIONS

Plane Figures

circle   triangle   square   rectangle

Put **C** inside each circle.   Put **S** inside each square.
Put **T** inside each triangle.   Put **R** inside each rectangle.

Circles, triangles, squares and rectangles

(two hundred thirty-seven) **237**

Teaching the Lesson

Introducing the Problem   Display 1 circle, 1 triangle, 1 rectangle and 1 square across the board. Write the name of each figure under or above it, using an upper case letter to begin each shape's name. Help students read each word. Show another circle and have students tell the name of the shape as you place it under the circle. Continue to show more of each shape for students to identify and then place on the chalk tray under its respective sample figure.

Developing the Skill   Hold up one circle. Help students tell about circles as you write the following identifying features of a circle in phrases or sentences on the board: **round, no corners, 1 continuous side, may be different sizes.** Repeat for the other figures, stressing their features as follows: **triangle**–3 sides, 3 corners, may be different sizes; **rectangle**–4 sides, opposite sides are same length, 4 corners, corners are same size, may be different sizes; **square**–a special kind of rectangle, 4 sides, sides are equal, 4 corners, corners are equal, may be different sizes. Leave sample shapes on the board as you mix the other figures and show one at a time for students to identify. Continue until students are readily able to name each shape. Then remove the samples from the board and have students again identify randomly presented shapes.

Read directions aloud to students. Have students complete the page independently.

237

Practice

Color circles green.   Color triangles purple.
Color squares red.   Color rectangles orange.

Circles, triangles, squares and rectangles

Correcting Common Errors

Some students may have difficulty identifying plane figures since their everyday-life experiences are not two-dimensional. Use paper cutouts of the five figures in this lesson as flash cards. Have students identify the figure and then identify an object or, more likely, part of an object in the classroom that has the same shape. Drawing a figure on an overhead may help students to understand how a figure could have length and width, but not depth.

Enrichment

Tell students to cut from magazines or catalogs 4 examples of each of the following: circle, rectangle, square, triangle.

Practice

Tell students to color all shapes as indicated in the directions. Have students complete the page independently.

Mixed Practice

1. 23 + 46 + 31 (100)
2. 253 + 6 (259)
3. 729 ◯ 279 (>)
4. 57 − 29 (28)
5. ___ + 6 = 15 (9)
6. 78¢ + 53¢ ($1.31)
7. 469 + 4 (473)
8. 38¢ + 29¢ (67¢)
9. 65 − 32 (33)
10. 5 + 9 + 5 (19)

Extra Credit   *Numeration*

On the board write a simple code for the alphabet. Assign each letter of the alphabet a number. For example:

A B C D . . .
1 2 3 4 . . .

Tell students to write addition problems using the letters as addends. Tell them to exchange papers with a partner and solve each other's problems. Have them exchange papers again to check. Tell them to try writing more problems, changing the code by varying the numbers assigned to each letter.

Sides and Corners

pages 239-240

Objectives

To identify the number of sides and corners on a plane figure
To identify square corners

Materials

*straightedge
*plane figures with and without square corners
square-cornered paper
cardboard figures

Mental Math

Ask how long Ed worked if he started at 4:20 and ended at:

1. 6:20. (2 hours)
2. 5:00. (40 minutes)
3. 5:10. (50 minutes)
4. 4:47. (27 minutes)
5. 1:20. (9 hours)
6. 5:25. (65 minutes)

Skill Review

Show circles, rectangles, squares and triangles at random and have students identify each figure.

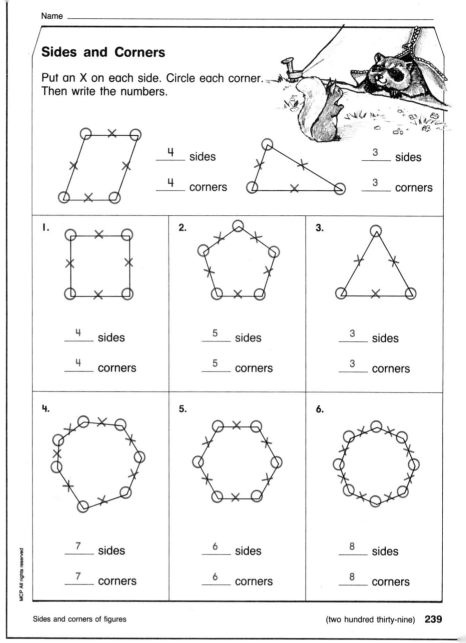

Sides and Corners

Put an X on each side. Circle each corner. Then write the numbers.

___4___ sides
___4___ corners

___3___ sides
___3___ corners

1.
___4___ sides
___4___ corners

2.
___5___ sides
___5___ corners

3.
___3___ sides
___3___ corners

4.
___7___ sides
___7___ corners

5.
___6___ sides
___6___ corners

6.
___8___ sides
___8___ corners

Sides and corners of figures

(two hundred thirty-nine) **239**

Teaching the Lesson

Introducing the Problem Display a triangle, rectangle and square and have students tell how many sides each figure has. (triangle 3, rectangle 4, square 4) Ask students to tell how many corners are in each figure. (triangle 3, rectangle 4, square 4) Now use a straightedge to draw a figure with up to 9 or so sides on the board. Have a student draw an x on each of the figure's sides and then count the x's to tell how many sides in all. Have another student draw a circle around each corner in the figure and count the circles to tell how many corners in all.

Developing the Skill Use a straightedge to draw plane figures on the board for students to tell the number of sides and corners in each. If students have difficulty remembering where they began counting corners or sides on a figure, have students begin with 1 and write the numbers consecutively as they go around the figure. Always use a straightedge to draw figures on the board.

Have students place an x on each side and circle each corner of the 2 figures at the top of the page. Tell students to count the number of sides and corners in each figure and write the numbers. Remind students to begin with 1 and write the numbers in order around a figure to help in counting the sides and corners. Have students complete the page independently.

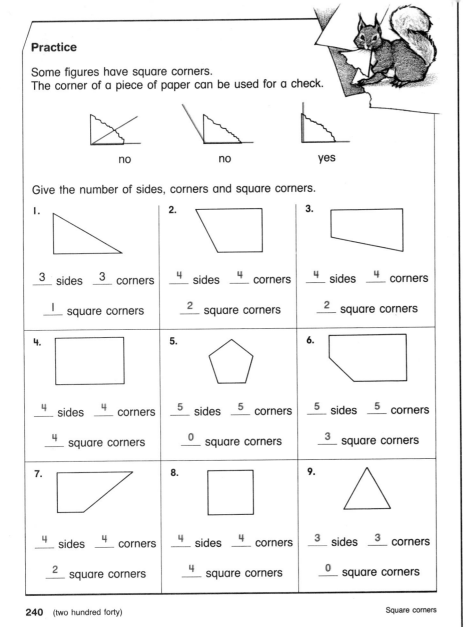

Practice

Some figures have square corners.
The corner of a piece of paper can be used for a check.

no   no   yes

Give the number of sides, corners and square corners.

1.
__3__ sides __3__ corners
__1__ square corners

2.
__4__ sides __4__ corners
__2__ square corners

3.
__4__ sides __4__ corners
__2__ square corners

4.
__4__ sides __4__ corners
__4__ square corners

5.
__5__ sides __5__ corners
__0__ square corners

6.
__5__ sides __5__ corners
__3__ square corners

7.
__4__ sides __4__ corners
__2__ square corners

8.
__4__ sides __4__ corners
__4__ square corners

9.
__3__ sides __3__ corners
__0__ square corners

Correcting Common Errors

Some students may have difficulty identifying sides and corners. Have them work with partners with cutouts of figures similar to those shown in the lesson. Have them use their fingers to trace around each figure and tell the number of sides and corners. Encourage students to place a dot at each corner and an x through each side to make them easier to count.

Enrichment

Tell students to use a square-cornered paper to test corners of objects in the classroom. Have them make a list of the objects, telling the number of sides, corners and square corners in each.

Practice

Display a square on the board. Ask students the number of sides. (4) Ask how many corners. (4) Show the square corners of a piece of paper as you tell students that such corners are called **square corners.** Tell students that a square corner of a piece of paper can be used to check to find other square corners. Show students how to position the paper's square corner on top of another shape to see if they match corner-to-corner. Tell students they are to tell how many sides, corners and square corners are in each figure. Remind students that some figures have no square corners. Have students complete the page independently.

Extra Credit   *Logic*

Draw this on the board:

hamster	dog
cat	bike

Ask students to tell you something about the items. (Three of the things are related. The hamster, dog and cat are all pets.) Ask which item does not belong. (bike) Tell each student to make up three of these diagram games of their own. They may write the names of the objects in each quarter of the diagram, or they may draw pictures of the items. Have students do the work at home, cutting pictures from magazines to illustrate the items for their puzzle. Then have students exchange puzzles and try to guess which item does not belong. Have the author of the puzzle help if no one can guess the answer.

Symmetry

pages 241-242

Objectives

To identify a line of symmetry
To create the other part of a symmetrical figure

Materials

*various sizes of paper
*symmetric paper figures
*asymmetric paper figures
*large sheet of dotted paper
*colored pencils
*plane figures with and without square corners
square-cornered paper
paper and scissors

Mental Math

Ask students when solving a problem, what question is answered by:

1. checking. (Does the solution make sense?)
2. deciding to add. (What operation needs to be done?)
3. finding the numbers given. (What do we know?)
4. telling what is asked. (What is to be found?)

Skill Review

Show various figures and have students tell how many sides and corners are in each. Have students test each corner and then tell how many square corners there are.

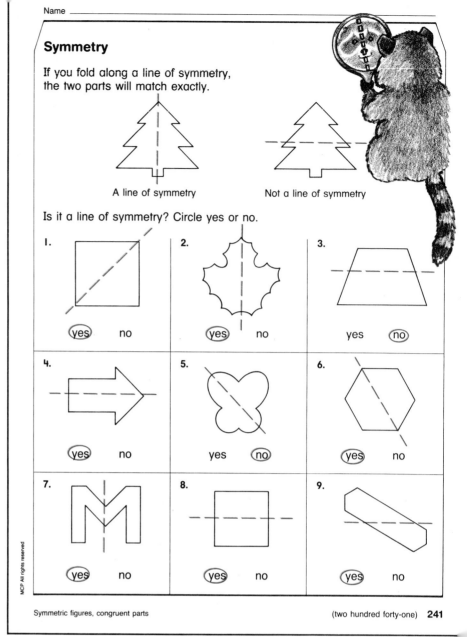

Symmetry

If you fold along a line of symmetry, the two parts will match exactly.

A line of symmetry   Not a line of symmetry

Is it a line of symmetry? Circle yes or no.

1. (yes)   no

2. (yes)   no

3. yes   (no)

4. (yes)   no

5. yes   (no)

6. (yes)   no

7. (yes)   no

8. (yes)   no

9. (yes)   no

Symmetric figures, congruent parts   (two hundred forty-one) **241**

Teaching the Lesson

Introducing the Problem   Demonstrate folding a piece of paper in half and cutting a shape such as a tree or a heart. Open the paper and show students how the part on each side of the fold is the same size and shape. Fold the paper again and run your finger along the edge of the shape to show students that both sides have the same edge. Open the paper and tell students the fold is called the **line of symmetry** because it divides the shape into 2 parts which are the same size and shape. Tell students the 2 parts are called **congruent** because they are the same size and shape. Tell students a figure is called **symmetric** if a line of symmetry can be drawn down the middle to form 2 congruent parts.

Developing the Skill   Fold a rectangular piece of typing or colored paper in half, open it and ask students to name the line of symmetry (the fold) and the 2 congruent parts. (each half) Repeat for more shapes folded in half in different ways to form congruent parts. Now fold paper so that the parts are not congruent and have students tell if each fold is a line of symmetry (no) and if the 2 parts are congruent. (no) Help students fold paper to form congruent parts and then fold paper in half and cut shapes with congruent parts. Have students read the sentences about the 2 tree shapes with you. Then tell students that in each of the problems they are to circle the word **yes,** if the line is a line of symmetry or circle the word **no** if it is not. Have students complete the page independently.

Practice

The line of symmetry in each figure below shows one part of a symmetric figure. Draw the missing part of each figure.

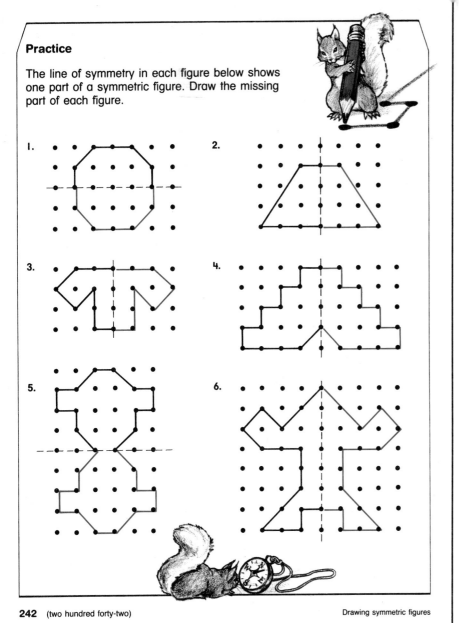

Drawing symmetric figures

Practice

Display the large sheet of dotted paper. Use a colored pencil to draw a vertical or horizontal line to connect some dots. Then use a different-colored pencil to connect dots to draw half of a square on one side of the line. Tell students we want to draw the other half of the square to form congruent parts. Proceed to use a straightedge to connect the dots to show students how to count the dots up and across to be sure the other half is exactly the same size and shape as the first. Repeat for more examples and then have students complete the first problem on this page. If students need more practice, use the dotted paper to give more examples. Then have students complete the page independently.

Extra Credit *Applications*

Illustrate a car odometer on the board.

$$\boxed{1}\;\boxed{4}\;\boxed{3}\;\boxed{4}\;\boxed{1}$$

Tell students it shows the number of miles the car has traveled. Explain that it is made up of little wheels, each with the digits 0 through 9 on it. Ask a student to read the number your odometer shows.

Explain that on the far right of each odometer there is a special wheel which is a different color from the rest. Point out that this shows small parts of a mile, but that you want them to ignore the extra wheel for now. Tell them that their assignment is to read the odometer in their car at home everyday for a week. Give each student a chart they can write the numbers on similar to the one you drew on the board.

When they bring their odometer charts in at the end of the week, use one as an example and show the class how to figure how far that car went each day.

Solid Figures

pages 243-244

Objectives

To identify solid figures
To match solid shapes

Materials

*sphere, cube, cylinder and cone
*various solid figures
dot paper

Mental Math

Tell students to name the number that is:

1. 70 tens + 2 ones. (702)
2. 200 less than 563. (363)
3. 6 hours later than 4:22. (10:22)
4. 1 of 4 equal parts. (¼)
5. 3 half-dollars + 2 quarters. ($2.00)
6. 3 hours past 11:47. (2:47)
7. 36 + 90 tens. (936)
8. 5 dollars + 10 nickels. ($5.50)

Skill Review

Have students draw half of a symmetrical figure on dot paper. Have students exchange papers to complete the figure and draw the line of symmetry.

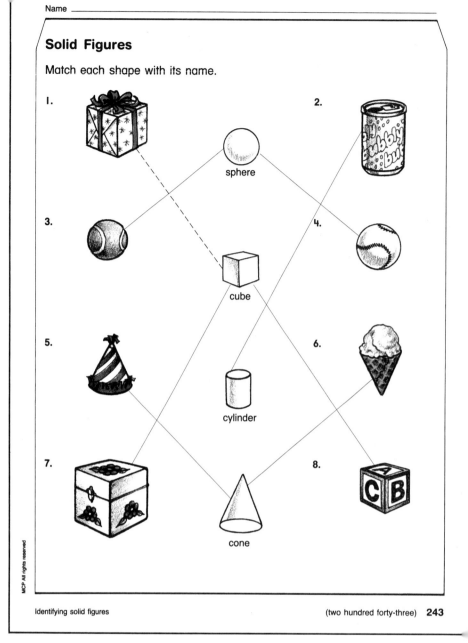

Solid Figures

Match each shape with its name.

1.
2.

sphere

3.
4.

cube

5.
6.

cylinder

7.
8.

cone

Identifying solid figures   (two hundred forty-three) **243**

Teaching the Lesson

Introducing the Problem Display a sphere, cube, cylinder and cone on the chalk tray and write the name of each above it. Have students read the names aloud with you as you hold up each figure. Tell students these are called **solid figures** because they have depth, or space, through them. Have students hold and examine the 4 figures. Then show various solid figures and ask students to match each figure to one of the figures displayed and tell its name. Continue until students can readily match and name the figures. Then remove the examples and have students tell the names of figures shown.

Developing the Skill Have students name other examples of spheres, cubes, cylinders and cones such as the following: spheres—globe, tennis ball, golf ball, etc., cubes—building blocks, dice, some flashcubes, etc., cylinders—some cups, soup cans, pop cans, etc., cones—party hats, ice cream cones, etc. Note: Some boxes are cubes but only if all sides are equal and all corners are squares. Boxes with unequal sides are prisms and cubes are special kinds of prisms.
Tell students they are to draw a line from each numbered object to the figure in the center of the page that matches its shape. Have students complete the page independently.

Practice

Circle the shapes that match the first shape in each row.

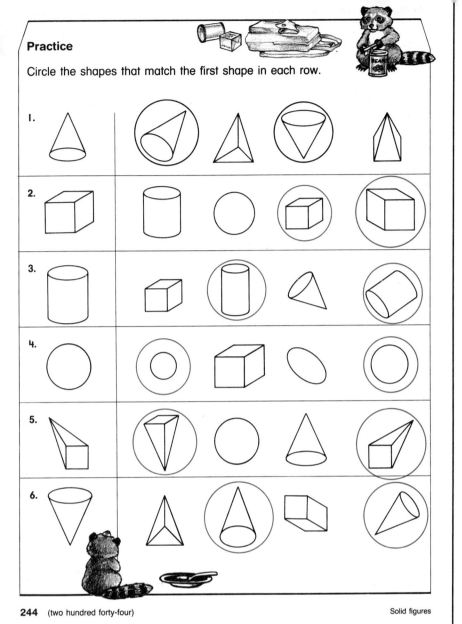

1.

2.

3.

4.

5.

6.

244 (two hundred forty-four)   Solid figures

Practice

Tell students they are to circle all the shapes in each row which are the same shape as the numbered shape. Have students complete the page independently.

Mixed Practice

1. 393 ◯ 387 (>)
2. 83¢ − 29¢ (54¢)
3. 653 + 86 (739)
4. 47 − 9 (38)
5. ___ + 8 = 12 (4)
6. 36 + 15 + 43 (94)
7. 8 + 7 (15)
8. 4 dimes, 5 nickels, 2 pennies (67¢)
9. 6 + 6 + 6 (18)
10. 78¢ + 26¢ ($1.04)

Correcting Common Errors

For students who have difficulty identifying solid figures from two-dimensional drawings, have them work with partners to find and name models of solid figures in the classroom. For each figure, have them write comments to describe it. EXAMPLE: Sphere: smooth, no flat parts, no corners, round like a ball, etc.

Enrichment

Tell students to cut from the magazines or catalogs as many examples as they can of spheres, cubes, cylinders and cones.

Extra Credit   *Geometry*

The Chinese tangram puzzle is made up of seven pieces: two small triangles, a medium size triangle, two large triangles, a square and a parallelogram. At least one tangram set is needed for this lesson. To make individual sets from an original set, trace the pieces carefully, reproduce the tracings and give each student a sheet. Have them cut out the pieces carefully. Give students time to play with the pieces, fitting them together in any way they choose. Then have them make as many squares as they can, using as many pieces as they like. They should be able to make at least two squares using each set of triangles. Some will be able to make larger squares. Challenge the class to make a square using all the pieces.

Unit Fractions

pages 245-246

Objective

To identify ½, ⅓ and ¼ fractional parts of a whole

Materials

*fractional part pieces for ½, ⅓, ¼
paper
paper marked in thirds
scissors

Mental Math

Tell students a nickel is to 5 as:

1. a dime is to ___. (10)
2. a dollar is to ___. (100)
3. a half-dollar is to ___. (50)
4. a quarter is to ___. (25)
5. a penny is to ___. (1)
6. 2 quarters are to ___. (50)
7. 9 dimes are to ___. (90)
8. 3 dollars are to ___. (300)

Skill Review

Have each student fold a sheet of paper and cut a symmetrical figure of their own design. Encourage students to create a unique design to be displayed in the classroom.

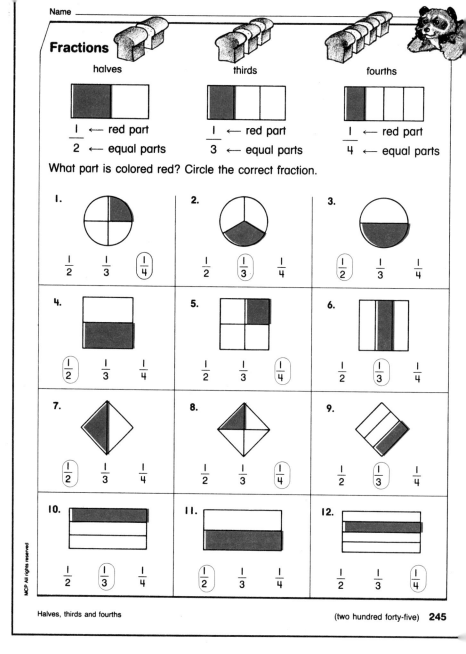

Halves, thirds and fourths

(two hundred forty-five) **245**

Teaching the Lesson

Introducing the Problem Fold a paper in half lengthwise, unfold it and ask students to tell how many parts there are. (2) Tell students that 1 part is 1 part of 2 as you write **½** on the board. Tell students that ½ is called a **fraction** and that fractional parts are always **equal parts.** Fold the paper on the fold to stress that the 2 parts are equal. Now fold the paper in half lengthwise again, unfold it and ask how many parts in all. (4) Tell students that 1 of the parts is 1 part of 4 equal parts or one-fourth as you write **¼** on the board. Now fold a paper into thirds, point to 1 part and ask students the fraction for that part. (⅓) Write **⅓** on the board.

Developing the Skill Tell students that ½, ¼ and ⅓ are called **unit fractions** because we are talking about 1 part of the whole or 1 unit. Help students fold papers to show halves, fourths and thirds. Have students write a unit fraction on each part of each paper to show its part of the whole.

Have students read aloud with you through the illustrated unit fractions at the top of the page. Ask students how many equal parts are in the circle in problem 1. (4) Ask how many parts are red. (1) Ask students which fraction below the circle tells what part of the circle is red. (¼) Have students circle ¼. Tell students to circle the unit fraction under each figure that tells the part of the whole colored red. Have students complete the page independently.

245

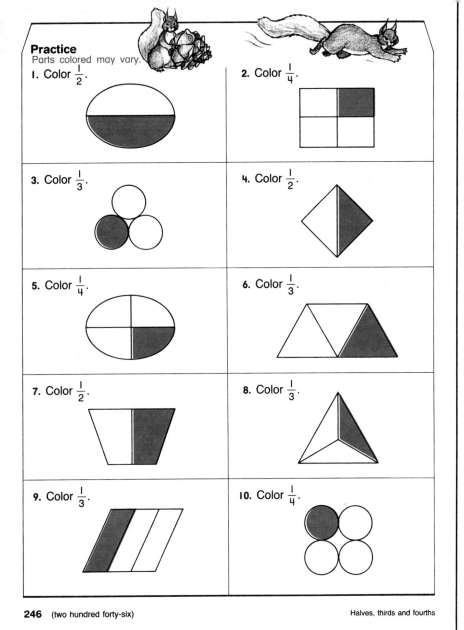

Practice
Parts colored may vary.

1. Color $\frac{1}{2}$.

2. Color $\frac{1}{4}$.

3. Color $\frac{1}{3}$.

4. Color $\frac{1}{2}$.

5. Color $\frac{1}{4}$.

6. Color $\frac{1}{3}$.

7. Color $\frac{1}{2}$.

8. Color $\frac{1}{3}$.

9. Color $\frac{1}{3}$.

10. Color $\frac{1}{4}$.

Halves, thirds and fourths

Correcting Common Errors

Some students may have difficulty understanding the concept of fractions. Have them work in groups of four with 4 equal parts of a circle. Ask, "If each of you takes a part, did anyone get a part larger or smaller than someone else?" (No.) Let them physically compare parts to confirm the answer. Ask, "How many equal parts of the whole does each of you have?" (1) Write ¼ on the board. Ask, "Which number tells how many equal parts in the whole?" (4) "Which number tells how many parts each of you has?" (1) Encourage students to use the fraction ¼ to describe other common situations that exist or may exist in their experience. Repeat this process with other unit fractions.

Enrichment

Tell students to draw objects to show how they could be shared so that the student would have ¼ and then ⅓ and then ½ of them.

Practice

Tell students to read the unit fraction and then color that part of the figure. Help students complete the first problems, if necessary, before assigning the page to be completed independently. Note: Students may color any 1 of the parts in each figure.

Mixed Practice

1. 61 − 43 (18)
2. 58 − 33 (25)
3. 7 hundreds 2 tens 5 ones (725)
4. 68¢ − 42¢ (26¢)
5. 473 + 86 (559)
6. 92¢ − 73¢ (19¢)
7. 39 + 47 + 21 (107)
8. 656 ◯ 566 (>)
9. 46¢ + 28¢ (74¢)
10. ____ +3 = 11 (8)

Extra Credit   *Geometry*

Have students use their tangrams they made in the previous extra credit. Tell them to remove the two large triangles from the set and use the remaining five pieces. Give students paper and pencils and have them work with a partner. Have each student arrange the pieces in a simple pattern, trace the outside of the figure and give the tracing to the other student. When each partner has received an outline from the other, have them try to arrange the five pieces so that they all fit within the tracing. Have students make at least two outlines to exchange and solve. Collect all the patterns and leave them in one spot in the classroom. Allow students time to try to solve the classmates' puzzles.

Fractional Parts

pages 247-248

Objective

To identify a non-unit fractional part of a figure

Materials

*fractional part pieces for halves through eighths
paper marked in thirds, fifths, eighths

Mental Math

Tell students to name the number that is:

1. less than 500 but more than 498. (499)
2. 1 part of 6 equal pieces. (⅙)
3. 1 inch more than 7 inches. (8 inches)
4. corners in a triangle. (3)
5. sides in square. (4)
6. square corners in a rectangle. (4)
7. corners on a circle. (0)

Skill Review

Have students fold papers into halves, thirds and fourths and then cut on the folds. Have student place all pieces in a group and then reassemble the wholes. Ask students to hold up ¼, ⅓, ½ and another ¼, ⅓, etc., as you dictate a unit fraction. Write each unit fraction on the board.

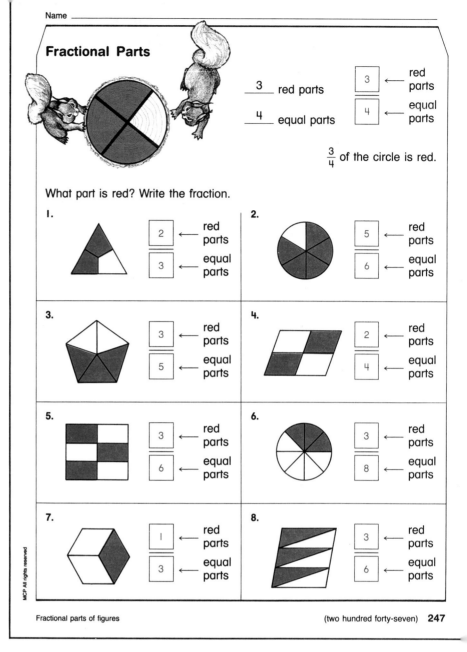

Fractional parts of figures   (two hundred forty-seven) **247**

Teaching the Lesson

Introducing the Problem Have students lay out their cut fractional parts which show fourths. Have students show ¼ of the whole as you write **¼** on the board. (1 part) Remind students that ¼ is 1 part of 4 equal parts. Now have students hold up 2 parts of the whole as you write **²⁄₄** on the board. Tell students that this fraction is not a unit fraction because we are now talking about 2 parts of 4 equal parts. Have students hold up 3 parts of the whole and tell the fraction. (¾) Write **¾** on the board. Have students hold up 4 parts and tell the fraction. (⁴⁄₄) Write **⁴⁄₄** on the board and tell students that ⁴⁄₄ is the whole figure because we are talking about all 4 of the 4 parts.

Developing the Skill Repeat the above activity for halves and thirds. Now have students cut out the parts of the figure marked in fifths and hold up ⅕, ⅗, ⁵⁄₅, etc. Repeat the activity to show various fractions in eighths. Have students look at the top of the page and fill in the answers for red parts (3) and equal parts. (4) Help student complete the first 1 or 2 problems before assigning the page to be completed independently.

247

Practice
Parts colored may vary.

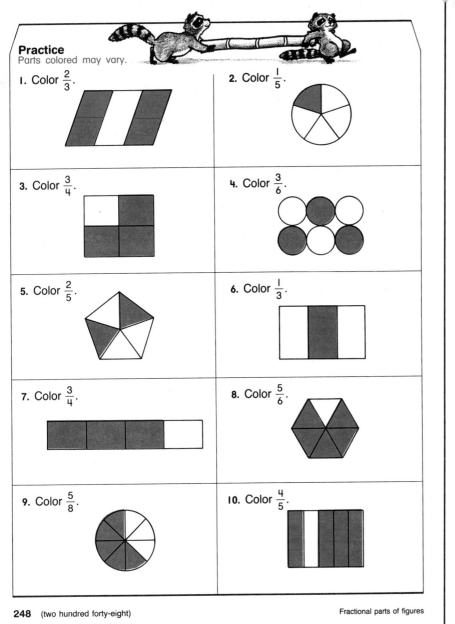

1. Color $\frac{2}{3}$.

2. Color $\frac{1}{5}$.

3. Color $\frac{3}{4}$.

4. Color $\frac{3}{6}$.

5. Color $\frac{2}{5}$.

6. Color $\frac{1}{3}$.

7. Color $\frac{3}{4}$.

8. Color $\frac{5}{6}$.

9. Color $\frac{5}{8}$.

10. Color $\frac{4}{5}$.

Fractional parts of figures

Practice
Ask students what they are to do in the first problem. (color ⅔ of the figure) Ask how many equal parts are in the figure. (3) Ask what number in the fraction tells how many of the equal parts are to be colored. (2) Have students complete the page independently.

Mixed Practice
1. ___ + 7 = 12 (5)
2. 47 − 21 (26)
3. 526 + 318 (844)
4. 76 − 58 (18)
5. 6 dimes, 3 nickels, 2 pennies (77¢)
6. 27 − 20 (7)
7. 755 + 108 (863)
8. 937 ◯ 793 (>)
9. 9 + 3 + 2 (13)
10. 68¢ + 47¢ ($1.15)

Extra Credit *Logic*
On large paper, draw a branching tree like this one.

big little   big little
←red grey→

At the first intersection put a sign indicating red one way and grey the other. At the next intersections put signs that indicate big one way and little the other. Pin the tree on a bulletin board. Then put several cardboard squirrels (red and grey, big and little) at the base of the tree. Have students take turns helping the squirrels up the tree and into the right branch. Let them use thumbtacks to pin the squirrels in place.

248

Parts of a Whole

pages 249-250

Objective

To identify unit and non-unit parts of a whole

Materials

scissors

papers marked in fifths, sixths, eighths and tenths

Mental Math

Ask student how to get from:

1. 462 to 356. (subtract)
2. 75 to 253. (add)
3. 4:00 to 7:00. (add)
4. $3.26 to $9.00. (add)
5. 630 to 603. (subtract)
6. 40 + 6 to 8 tens. (add)
7. 4 hundreds to 9 tens. (subtract)
8. 50¢ to a dollar. (add)

Skill Review

Have a student write the fraction on the board that tells about 2 parts of 6 equal parts. (2/6) Continue having students write fractions as you name the number of parts of wholes.

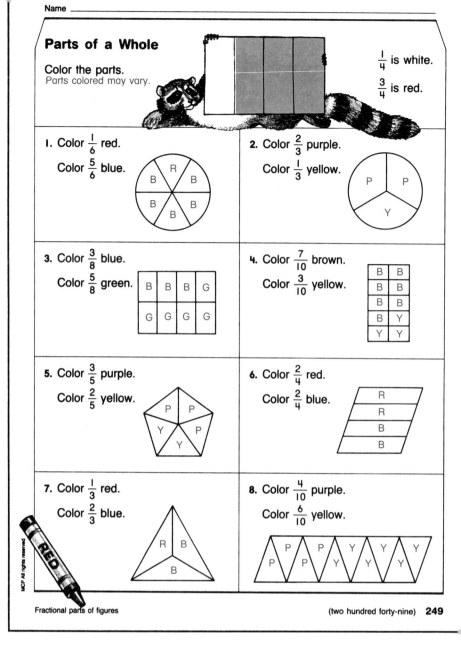

Name _____

Parts of a Whole

Color the parts.
Parts colored may vary.

$\frac{1}{4}$ is white.

$\frac{3}{4}$ is red.

1. Color $\frac{1}{6}$ red.
   Color $\frac{5}{6}$ blue.

2. Color $\frac{2}{3}$ purple.
   Color $\frac{1}{3}$ yellow.

3. Color $\frac{3}{8}$ blue.
   Color $\frac{5}{8}$ green.

4. Color $\frac{7}{10}$ brown.
   Color $\frac{3}{10}$ yellow.

5. Color $\frac{3}{5}$ purple.
   Color $\frac{2}{5}$ yellow.

6. Color $\frac{2}{4}$ red.
   Color $\frac{2}{4}$ blue.

7. Color $\frac{1}{3}$ red.
   Color $\frac{2}{3}$ blue.

8. Color $\frac{4}{10}$ purple.
   Color $\frac{6}{10}$ yellow.

Fractional parts of figures

(two hundred forty-nine) **249**

Teaching the Lesson

Introducing the Problem Have students fold a paper into fourths and cut out the 4 parts. Have students hold up ¼ of their figure and then tell what fraction tells about the other parts. (¾) Now have students hold up 2/4 and tell what fraction tells about the rest of the figure. (2/4) Repeat for showing ¾ with ¼ remaining. Repeat the activity for papers marked in tenths and sixths. Now have students hold up 2 parts of 6 and write on the board the fraction which tells the parts being shown (2/6) and then the fraction telling about the remaining parts. (4/6) Repeat for eighths and fifths.

Developing the Skill Have students read aloud with you about the white and red parts of the figure at the top. Ask students what number in each fraction tells how many parts in all. (4) Ask students what number in each fraction tells about the white and colored parts. (1 and 3) Help students complete the first problem before assigning the page to be completed independently.

249

Practice

Write the fraction that tells which part is red.
Then write the fraction that tells which part is white.

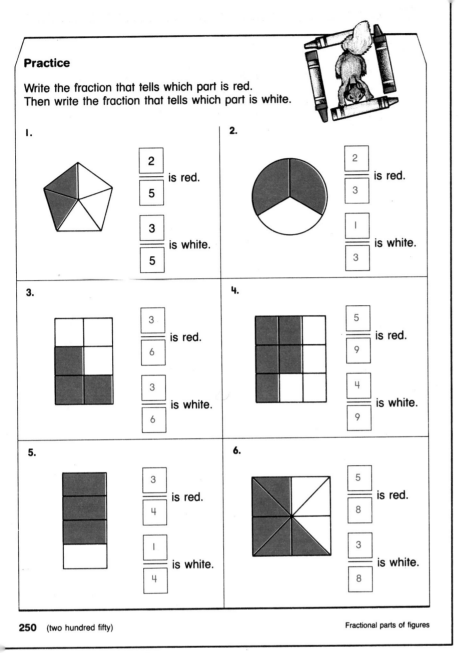

1.

$\dfrac{2}{5}$ is red.

$\dfrac{3}{5}$ is white.

2.

$\dfrac{2}{3}$ is red.

$\dfrac{1}{3}$ is white.

3.

$\dfrac{3}{6}$ is red.

$\dfrac{3}{6}$ is white.

4.

$\dfrac{5}{9}$ is red.

$\dfrac{4}{9}$ is white.

5.

$\dfrac{3}{4}$ is red.

$\dfrac{1}{4}$ is white.

6.

$\dfrac{5}{8}$ is red.

$\dfrac{3}{8}$ is white.

Fractional parts of figures

Practice

Tell students to write the fractions which tell about the red and white parts of each figure. Have students complete the first problem together and then write the fractions on the board. (²⁄₅ and ³⁄₅) Then have students complete the page independently.

Mixed Practice

1. 68 − 37 (31)
2. 84¢ − 36¢ (48¢)
3. $2.59 + 5.36 ($7.95)
4. 709 ◯ 790 (<)
5. 368 + 135 (503)
6. 4 hundreds 8 tens 2 ones (482)
7. 6 + 8 + 3 (17)
8. ____ + 2 = 11 (9)
9. 40 − 27 (13)
10. 305 + 208 (513)

Extra Credit *Statistics*

Survey the class and list on the board how many different things they had for breakfast. Then have a volunteer ask how many students ate each of the foods while a second student writes the numbers on the board. Help them set up a graph with the number of students along one axis and the types of food along the other. Ask them to transfer the information from the board to a bar graph. Extend the activity by discussing nutritious foods, perhaps non-traditional, that should be eaten for breakfast.

Fractional Parts of Groups

pages 251-252

Objective

To identify fractional parts of a group of objects

Materials

*Fractional part pieces for halves through eighths
counters

Mental Math

Ask students the following:

1. What is today's date?
2. What is the present year?
3. What time is it?
4. What ordinal number tells the present month?
5. What is tomorrow's date?
6. What time will it be in 2 hours?
7. What was yesterday's date?

Skill Review

Show students 3 of 8 equal parts and have a student write the fraction on the board. Continue for other parts of wholes.

Name _____

Parts of Groups

Ann has 5 cars.
3 cars are red.
What part of the cars are red?

There are ___3___ red cars. $\dfrac{3}{5}$ of the cars are red.

There are ___5___ cars in all.

1. Color $\frac{1}{2}$ of the apples.

2. Color $\frac{2}{3}$ of the oranges.

3. Color $\frac{4}{5}$ of the bananas.

4. Color $\frac{3}{10}$ of the cherries.

5. Color $\frac{3}{4}$ of the tomatoes.

6. Color $\frac{3}{6}$ of the peaches.

7. Color $\frac{4}{4}$ of the pears.

8. Color $\frac{5}{8}$ of the lemons.

Fractional parts of groups

(two hundred fifty-one) **251**

Teaching the Lesson

Introducing the Problem Have a student read the problem aloud and tell what is to be found. (the part of the cars that are red) Ask what information is given. (5 cars in all and 3 are red) Have students read and complete the information sentences and then write the fraction.

Developing the Skill Draw 6 circles on the board and have a student fill in 4 of them. Ask students how many circles are filled in. (4) Ask students how many circles in all. (6) Write **4/6** on the board and tell students that 4/6 is the fraction which tells that 4 of the 6 circles are filled in. Ask students to tell what part of the circles is filled in as you fill in another circle. (5 of 6 or 5/6) Write **5/6** on the board. Draw 10 x's on the board and draw a circle around 4 of them. Ask students how many x's are circled. (4) Ask how many in all. (10) Write **4/10** on the board and tell students that 4/10 is the fraction which tells that 4 of the 10 x's are circled. Continue with x's or circles to show 5/7, 2/5, 3/8 and 4/9 having students write the fractions for each.

251

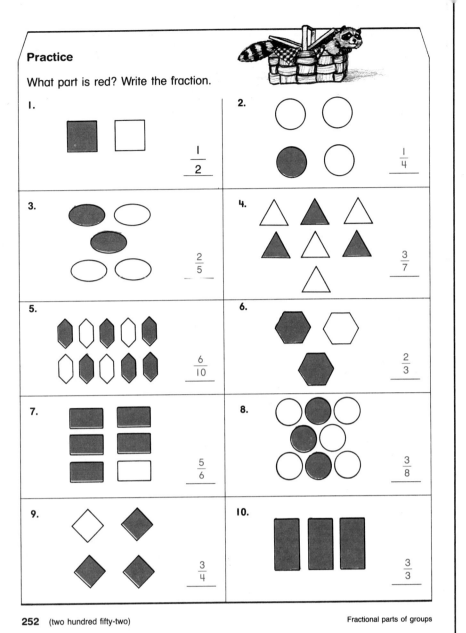

Practice

What part is red? Write the fraction.

1. $\dfrac{1}{2}$

2. $\dfrac{1}{4}$

3. $\dfrac{2}{5}$

4. $\dfrac{3}{7}$

5. $\dfrac{6}{10}$

6. $\dfrac{2}{3}$

7. $\dfrac{5}{6}$

8. $\dfrac{3}{8}$

9. $\dfrac{3}{4}$

10. $\dfrac{3}{3}$

Fractional parts of groups

Correcting Common Errors

Some students may confuse the numerator and denominator when writing a fraction. Encourage them to first count all the objects in the group and write this number as the denominator. The denominator tells them how many there are in the "whole" group. Then they should count the objects that are red and write this number as the numerator. The numerator tells how many parts of the whole are to be colored.

Enrichment

Tell students to draw objects to show ⅝ and ⅜ and tell which fraction is greater and why.

Practice

Tell students to write a fraction in each problem to show what part of the group is red. Remind students that the top number in each fraction tells how many are red and the bottom number tells how many in all. Help students complete the first few problems, if necessary, before assigning the page to be completed independently.

Mixed Practice

1. 15 + 18 + 22 (55)
2. 47¢ + 28¢ (75¢)
3. 270 − 6 (264)
4. 263 + 408 (671)
5. 7 + ___ = 13 (6)
6. 270 ◯ 207 (>)
7. 78 − 30 (48)
8. 73¢ − 37¢ (36¢)
9. $2.95 + 3.08 ($6.03)
10. 94 + 38 (132)

Extra Credit *Sets*

Have students select different but even numbered related items found in the classroom, such as books, boots and shoes, writing and drawing utensils, etc. Tell them to arrange the articles in sets on a table. Ask each student to come up when they have finished other work, and arrange the articles into each of the following parts of each set: ½, ⅓, ¼, etc. Have them list on their papers the corresponding number of objects contained in each fraction of the set. At the end of they day, have students take turns showing each correct fraction by rearranging the objects.

More Fractional Parts of Groups

pages 253-254

Objectives

To practice finding fractional parts of groups

To find fractional parts of groups to solve problems

Materials

*circles, triangles, rectangles, squares

Mental Math

Ask students what fraction tells:

1. 1 part of 10 equal parts. (1/10)
2. 3 parts of 4 equal parts. (3/4)
3. 2 parts of 8 equal parts. (2/8)
4. 6 parts of 7 equal parts. (6/7)

Ask students how many parts in the whole:

5. 6/9 (9)
6. 7/10 (10)
7. 1/2 (2)
8. 4/5 (5)

Skill Review

Show students a square, rectangle, triangle and circle. Have students identify each figure. Lay out more examples of all 4 figures and have students sort the shapes into groups of circles, rectangles, squares and triangles.

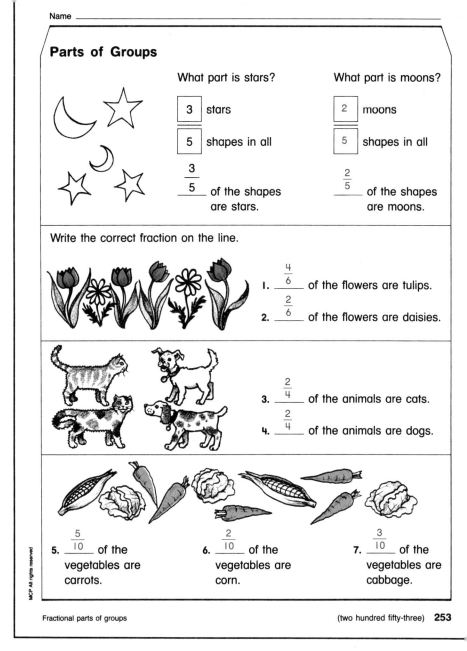

Name _____

Parts of Groups

What part is stars?	What part is moons?
3 stars	2 moons
5 shapes in all	5 shapes in all
$\frac{3}{5}$ of the shapes are stars.	$\frac{2}{5}$ of the shapes are moons.

Write the correct fraction on the line.

1. $\frac{4}{6}$ of the flowers are tulips.
2. $\frac{2}{6}$ of the flowers are daisies.

3. $\frac{2}{4}$ of the animals are cats.
4. $\frac{2}{4}$ of the animals are dogs.

5. $\frac{5}{10}$ of the vegetables are carrots.
6. $\frac{2}{10}$ of the vegetables are corn.
7. $\frac{3}{10}$ of the vegetables are cabbage.

Fractional parts of groups

(two hundred fifty-three) **253**

Teaching the Lesson

Introducing the Problem Draw 5 circles and 4 x's on the board. Ask students how many objects in all. (9) Ask how many objects are x's. (4) Write 4/9 on the board. Tell students that 4/9 is the fraction which tells what part of the whole group of objects is x's. Now ask students how many objects are circles. (5) Write 5/9 on the board. Tell students that 5 of the 9 objects are circles so 5/9 is the fraction which tells what part of the group is circles. Add 2 more x's and have students tell how many objects in all. (11) Ask how many of the objects are x's now. (6) Write 6/11 on the board and ask students what this fraction tells. (that 6 of the 11 objects are x's) Have a student write a fraction on the board to tell what part of the whole group is circles. (5/11)

Developing the Skill Draw 3 circles and 5 x's on the board. Ask how many objects in all. (8) Ask how many objects are circles. (3) Have a student write the fraction that tells what part of the whole group is circles. (3/8) Ask how many objects are x's. (5) Have a student write the fraction that tells what part of the the whole group is x's. (5/8) Repeat for more examples, if needed. Note: Although simplifying fractions is not included here, students may notice that 4/8 of the group is also 1/2 of the group. Have students read aloud with you as they complete the fractions to tell what part of the group of objects is stars and what part is moons. Help students complete the first problem and then have them complete the page independently.

253

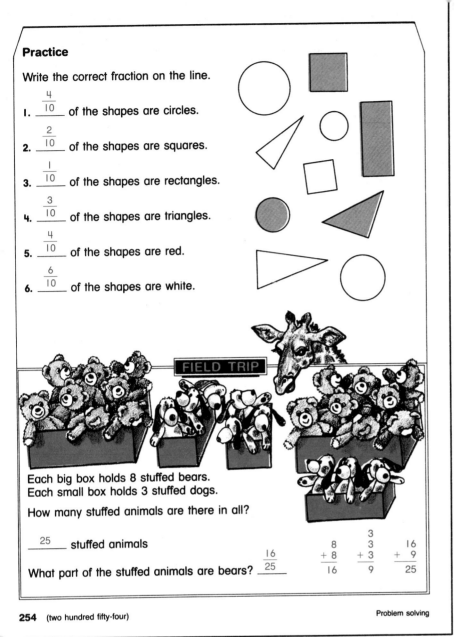

Practice

Write the correct fraction on the line.

1. $\dfrac{4}{10}$ of the shapes are circles.

2. $\dfrac{2}{10}$ of the shapes are squares.

3. $\dfrac{1}{10}$ of the shapes are rectangles.

4. $\dfrac{3}{10}$ of the shapes are triangles.

5. $\dfrac{4}{10}$ of the shapes are red.

6. $\dfrac{6}{10}$ of the shapes are white.

FIELD TRIP

Each big box holds 8 stuffed bears.
Each small box holds 3 stuffed dogs.

How many stuffed animals are there in all?

$\underline{25}$ stuffed animals

What part of the stuffed animals are bears? $\dfrac{16}{25}$

$$\begin{array}{r} 16 \\ +\ 9 \\ \hline 25 \end{array}$$

$$\begin{array}{r} 8 \\ +8 \\ \hline 16 \end{array} \qquad \begin{array}{r} 3 \\ 3 \\ +3 \\ \hline 9 \end{array} \qquad \begin{array}{r} 16 \\ +\ 9 \\ \hline 25 \end{array}$$

254 (two hundred fifty-four)

Problem solving

Practice

Have students tell the shape of each figure at the top of the page. Ask students how many shapes in all. (10) Ask students how many of the shapes are circles (4), rectangles (1), triangles (3) and squares (2). Ask how many shapes are red (4) and how many are white (6). Tell students they are to complete each sentence with a fraction.

Field Trip

Draw 3 large circles and 2 small circles in a row across the board. Have a student draw 4 x's in each large circle. Have another student draw 3 sticks in each small circle. Ask students to add the x's. (12) Ask students to add the sticks. (6) Ask a student to write an addition sentence to tell how many x's and sticks in all. (12 + 6 = 18) Ask what part of all the marks are x's. (12 of 18) Write **12/18** on the board. Ask what part of all the marks are sticks. (6 of 18) Write **6/18** on the board. Have students complete the problem independently.

Extra Credit *Applications*

Draw pictures on the board of various items that can be bought in a cafeteria. Lable these items with prices and names.

apple 75¢   milk 50¢   hot dog $1.00
soup $1.25   granola bar 45¢   banana 30¢
ice cream 65¢   salad 99¢

Tell the students they are taking two friends to lunch, but they have only $10 to spend. Tell them to write each name including their own, and list below each the items they might order for lunch and its cost. Tell students to add the prices to find the total cost for each lunch. Remind them to stay within their budget.

Review

pages 255-256

Objectives

To review geometry and fractions
To maintain skills learned previously
  this year

Materials

*symmetrical paper shapes
*asymmetrical paper shapes
square cornered paper

Mental Math

Have students name the figure with:

1. 4 square corners _____. (square or rectangle)
2. congruent parts, a line of _____. (symmetry)
3. no sides _____. (circle)
4. 3 sides _____. (triangle)
5. 4 equal sides _____. (square)
6. no corners _____. (circle)

Skill Review

Show students a paper shape and ask if it is symmetrical. Have a student fold the shape in half to check. Ask students to identify the line of symmetry for each symmetrical shape. (the fold) Ask why the fold is not a line of symmetry for some of the shapes. (The 2 parts are not congruent.)

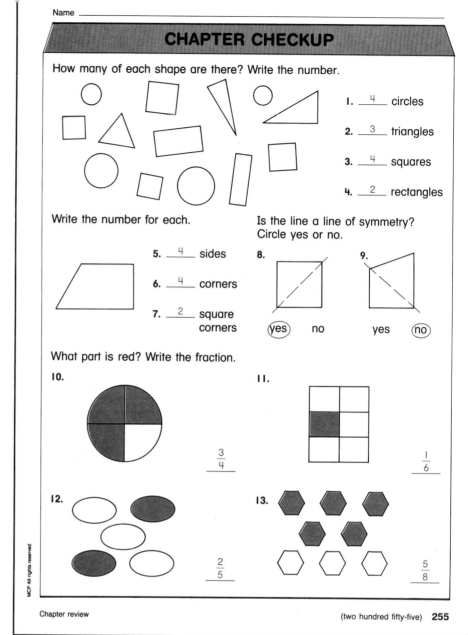

CHAPTER CHECKUP

How many of each shape are there? Write the number.

1. __4__ circles
2. __3__ triangles
3. __4__ squares
4. __2__ rectangles

Write the number for each.

5. __4__ sides
6. __4__ corners
7. __2__ square corners

Is the line a line of symmetry?
Circle yes or no.

8.   (yes)   no
9.   yes   (no)

What part is red? Write the fraction.

10. $\frac{3}{4}$

11. $\frac{1}{6}$

12. $\frac{2}{5}$

13. $\frac{5}{8}$

Chapter review

(two hundred fifty-five) **255**

Teaching page 255

Have students tell what they are to do in each section. Remind students to use a square cornered paper to check for square corners. Remind students that the top number in a fraction tells how many parts are being asked about and the bottom number tells how many parts in all. Have students complete the page independently.

255

ROUNDUP REVIEW

Fill in the oval next to the correct answer.

1 5 + 7	○ 2 ◖ 12 ○ 13 ○ NG

2 15 − 8	○ 23 ○ 3 ◖ 7 ○ NG

3	○ 352 ○ 235 ○ 523 ◖ NG

4 35 + 27	○ 52 ○ 8 ◖ 62 ○ NG

5 473 + 75	○ 448 ◖ 548 ○ 398 ○ NG

6 265 + 376	◖ 641 ○ 631 ○ 541 ○ NG

7 85 − 26	○ 61 ◖ 59 ○ 69 ○ NG

8 526 − 85	○ 561 ○ 541 ◖ 441 ○ NG

9 725 − 298	○ 573 ◖ 427 ○ 537 ○ NG

10 What part is red?	◖ $\frac{3}{4}$ ○ $\frac{4}{3}$ ○ $\frac{1}{4}$ ○ NG

11 455 + 345	◖ 800 ○ 750 ○ 700 ○ NG

12 $4.59 + 2.82	○ $7.31 ○ $6.41 ◖ $7.41 ○ NG

13 $7.15 − .48	◖ $6.67 ○ $6.77 ○ $7.33 ○ NG

□ score

256 (two hundred fifty-six)

Cumulative review

Enrichment

1. Tell students to draw a picture which shows the fractions 4/6 and 2/6.
2. Tell students to draw a picture of an outdoor scene that includes 2 things that are symmetrical.

Teaching page 256

This page reviews basic facts, place value, addition and subtraction of 2- and 3-digit numbers and fractions. Remind student to fill in the oval next to the correct answer and fill in the NG only if the correct answer is not given. Have students complete the page independently.

256

Inches and Half-Inches

pages 257-258

Objective

To measure length in inches and half-inches

Materials

*paper
*large ruler
6-inch rulers
paper strips cut into inch and half-inch lengths through 6 in.
objects that are exact to the inch or half-inch
scissors

Mental Math

Tell students to name the number for:

1. 42 more than 410 (452)
2. 90 − 25 (65)
3. 7 hundreds − 699 (1)
4. 5 parts of 7 equal parts ($\frac{5}{7}$)
5. 45 + 100 + 5 (150)

Skill Review

Show students a piece of paper folded in half lengthwise. Ask if the 2 parts are congruent. (yes) Write ½ on the board and remind students that 1 part of 2 equal parts is written as ½. Have students identify ½ of more papers folded in half in different ways.

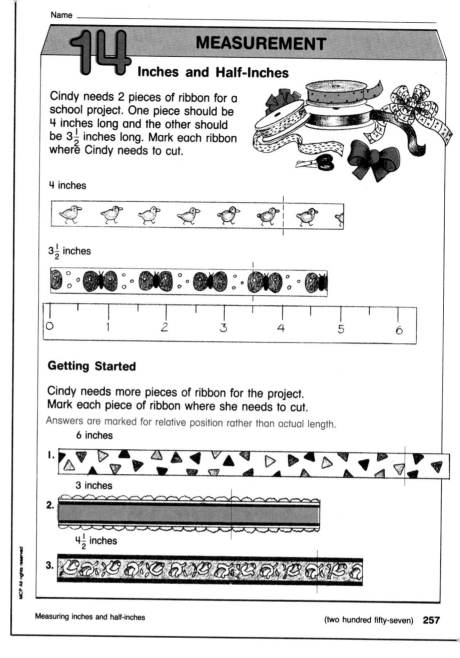

MEASUREMENT

Inches and Half-Inches

Cindy needs 2 pieces of ribbon for a school project. One piece should be 4 inches long and the other should be $3\frac{1}{2}$ inches long. Mark each ribbon where Cindy needs to cut.

4 inches

$3\frac{1}{2}$ inches

Getting Started

Cindy needs more pieces of ribbon for the project. Mark each piece of ribbon where she needs to cut.

Answers are marked for relative position rather than actual length.

1. 6 inches

2. 3 inches

3. $4\frac{1}{2}$ inches

Measuring inches and half-inches

Teaching the Lesson

Introducing the Problem Have a student read the problem aloud and tell what is to be found. (where Cindy needs to cut the ribbons) Ask what is known. (Cindy needs a piece 4 inches long and a piece 3½ inches long.) Have students note that the left edge of each ribbon is placed at zero on the 6-inch ruler. Help students find the 4-inch mark on the ruler and go up to trace the dotted line on the first ribbon. Help students see that the dotted line on the second ribbon is halfway between the 3 and 4 on the ruler. Have students trace the dotted line to show where to cut the ribbon for 3½ inches.

Developing the Skill Discuss the need for a standard unit of measure. Tell students that the **inch** is a standard unit of measure. Have students find the 1-, 2-, 3-inch marks, etc., on their rulers. Place a large ruler on the board and show students how you start at zero or the edge of the ruler to draw a bar 5 inches long. Continue for 2-, 3-, 4- and 6-inch bars. Now show students the **half-inch** marks on the ruler for measuring half inches. Draw a bar which is 1½ inches long and have several students measure to check your work. Repeat for more lengths. Have students measure various objects and tell the length of each in inches or half-inches.

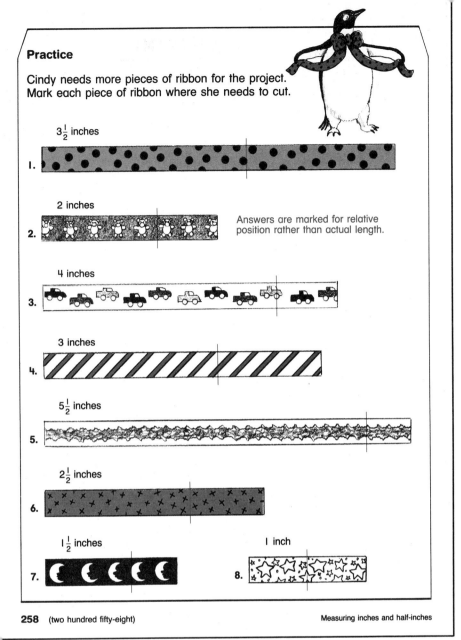

Practice

Cindy needs more pieces of ribbon for the project.
Mark each piece of ribbon where she needs to cut.

1. $3\frac{1}{2}$ inches

2. 2 inches

Answers are marked for relative position rather than actual length.

3. 4 inches

4. 3 inches

5. $5\frac{1}{2}$ inches

6. $2\frac{1}{2}$ inches

7. $1\frac{1}{2}$ inches

8. 1 inch

258 (two hundred fifty-eight)   Measuring inches and half-inches

Correcting Common Errors

Some students measure incorrectly because they do not properly align the end of their rulers or the mark for 0 with the end of the object that they are measuring. Have these students work in pairs to measure line segments, checking each other to make sure that the ruler is correctly placed.

Enrichment

Tell students to cut string, ribbon or paper strips for every inch and half-inch measure from ½ inch through 6 inches.

Practice

Tell students to mark each ribbon where it is to be cut. Help students mark the first ribbon and then tell students to complete the page independently.

Mixed Practice

1. 8 + 5 + 9 (22)
2. 26 + 18 + 21 (65)
3. 565 − 20 (545)
4. 1 quarter, 1 dime, 1 nickel (40¢)
5. 295 + 430 (725)
6. 91 − 37 (54)
7. 372 − 80 (292)
8. 78¢ + 45¢ ($1.23)
9. 650 ◯ 560 (>)
10. 6 + ___ =10 (4)

Extra Credit *Probability*

One way probability is used in everyday life is in the prediction of the weather. Explain that the prediction is usually made in terms of percents. Point out that 100% means that something is certain and that 0% means that something is completely unlikely. The weather forecaster might say that there is a 90% chance of rain. Ask class to explain why the numbers between 0 and 100 show increasing probability, so that 90% is very likely, while 10% is very unlikely. Ask students to listen to the nightly weather report and record any probabilities given. The next day have individuals report on the weather forecast and ask the class if the weather report was accurate after looking at the day's actual weather conditions.

A good book to read to the class with this activity is Judy Garrett's *Cloudy With a Chance of Meatballs.*

Measuring to the Nearest Inch

pages 259-260

Objective

To measure length to the nearest inch

Materials

*large rulers
*objects to be measured to the nearest inch
*paper strips
objects that are exact to the inch or half-inch
6-inch rulers

Mental Math

Ask students how many:

1. more than 10 is 60. (50)
2. months between May and September. (3)
3. hours from 2:00 to 12:00. (10)
4. days between Monday and Saturday. (4)
5. objects in a dozen. (12)
6. days in a year. (365)

Skill Review

Review how to place the ruler edge or zero mark at one end of an object when measuring length. Have students measure various objects 6 inches or less in length and tell each length in inches or half-inches.

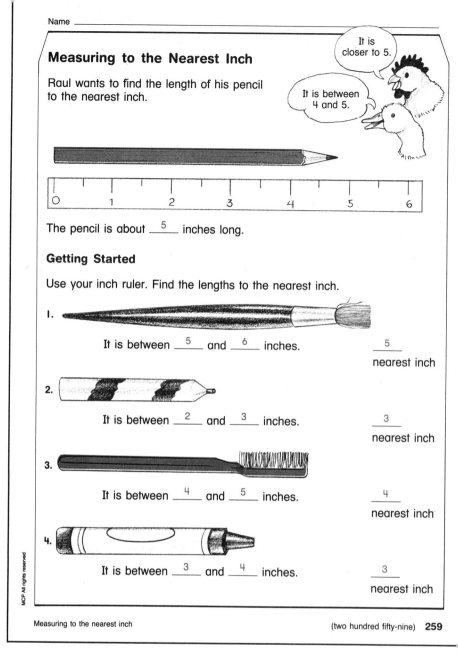

Measuring to the Nearest Inch

Raul wants to find the length of his pencil to the nearest inch.

It is closer to 5.

It is between 4 and 5.

The pencil is about __5__ inches long.

Getting Started

Use your inch ruler. Find the lengths to the nearest inch.

1. It is between __5__ and __6__ inches.   __5__ nearest inch

2. It is between __2__ and __3__ inches.   __3__ nearest inch

3. It is between __4__ and __5__ inches.   __4__ nearest inch

4. It is between __3__ and __4__ inches.   __3__ nearest inch

Measuring to the nearest inch   (two hundred fifty-nine) **259**

Teaching the Lesson

Introducing the Problem Have a student read the problem aloud and tell what is to be found. (the length of the pencil to the nearest inch) Ask what is known. (The pencil is between 4 and 5 inches in length.) Ask students to tell the length of the pencil to the nearest inch. (5) Have students read and complete the solution sentence.

Developing the Skill Tell students there are times when we do not need to know the exact length of an object and that knowing it is **about** 4 inches or about 6 inches is enough information. Attach a 4¾-inch strip of paper to the board or bulletin board. Use the large ruler to measure the strip and ask students if the paper is exactly 4½ inches. (no) Ask if it is exactly 5 inches. (no) Tell students that the paper is between 4½ and 5 inches so it is closer to 5 inches than to 4 inches. Tell students we say that the paper is about 5 inches long to the **nearest inch.** Now show students a paper which is 4¼ inches long and ask if it is closer to the 4-inch mark or the 5-inch mark. (4-inch) Tell students that the paper is between 4 and 4½ inches so we say it is about 4 inches long. Tell students the paper is about 4 inches to the nearest inch. Have students use their rulers to measure more strips of paper to tell each length to the nearest inch.

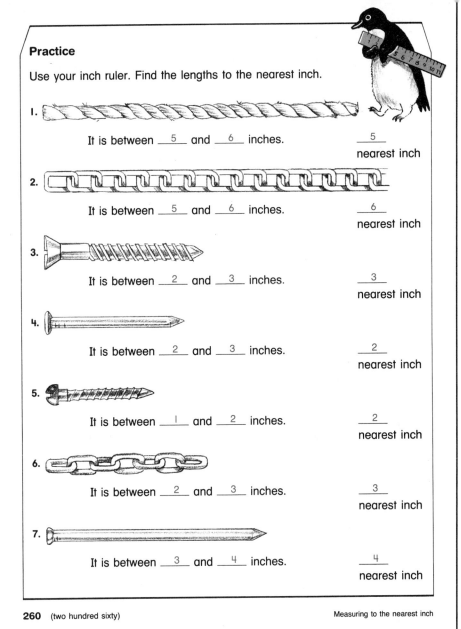

Practice

Use your inch ruler. Find the lengths to the nearest inch.

1. It is between __5__ and __6__ inches.

__5__
nearest inch

2. It is between __5__ and __6__ inches.

__6__
nearest inch

3. It is between __2__ and __3__ inches.

__3__
nearest inch

4. It is between __2__ and __3__ inches.

__2__
nearest inch

5. It is between __I__ and __2__ inches.

__2__
nearest inch

6. It is between __2__ and __3__ inches.

__3__
nearest inch

7. It is between __3__ and __4__ inches.

__4__
nearest inch

Measuring to the nearest inch

Correcting Common Errors

If students have difficulty telling to which of two numbers of inches a measure is closer, have them place their finger at the end of the object. Then have them move their finger back and forth across the ruler to determine whether the end of the object is to the left or to the right of the half-way mark between the inches. If it is to the left, they choose the smaller number of inches; if it is to the right, they choose the larger number of inches.

Enrichment

Tell students to locate 4 objects that are about 6 inches to the nearest inch and 4 objects which are about 2 inches to the nearest inch.

Practice

Help students complete the first problem, if necessary, before assigning the page to be completed independently.

Mixed Practice

1. 207 ◯ 270 (<)
2. 63 + 21 + 15 (99)
3. 438 − 246 (192)
4. $3.56 + 4.94 ($8.50)
5. 16 − 5 (11)
6. 105, 110, 115, ____ (120)
7. 195 − 168 (27)
8. 326 + 53 (379)
9. 68 − 15 (53)
10. 306 − 219 (87)

Extra Credit   *Numeration*

Display a chart on the chalkboard that assigns a dollar value to each letter of the alphabet:
A = $1, B = $2, C = $3, . . . Z = $26.

Ask students to find:

1. the value of their name
2. the value of the teacher's name
3. the most expensive 3-letter word
4. the least expensive 3-letter word
5. $10 words
6. $100 words

Centimeters

pages 261-262

Objective

To measure length in centimeters

Materials

*10-centimeter paper strip
objects with lengths in whole centi-
    meters
centimeter ruler
6-inch ruler
paper strips
scissors

Mental Math

Tell students to name the ordinal number for:

1. the tenth plus eighteenth. (twenty-
   eighth)
2. the month of October. (tenth)
3. today's date.
4. your age in order in your family
   from the oldest.
5. 5 less than twentieth. (fifteenth)
6. 11 more than eighty-eighth.
   (ninety-ninth)

Skill Review

Display several paper strips which are
not exact to the inch. Have students
measure the strips to the nearest inch
and tell about how long each strip is.

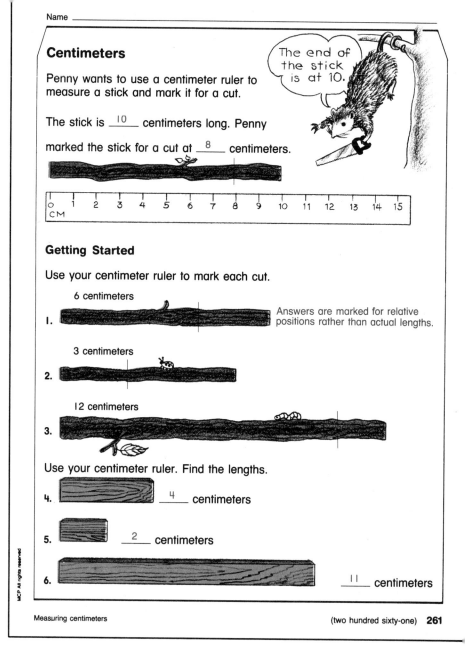

Centimeters

Penny wants to use a centimeter ruler to measure a stick and mark it for a cut.

The stick is __10__ centimeters long. Penny

marked the stick for a cut at __8__ centimeters.

The end of the stick is at 10.

Getting Started

Use your centimeter ruler to mark each cut.

1. 6 centimeters

   Answers are marked for relative positions rather than actual lengths.

2. 3 centimeters

3. 12 centimeters

Use your centimeter ruler. Find the lengths.

4. __4__ centimeters

5. __2__ centimeters

6. __11__ centimeters

Measuring centimeters

(two hundred sixty-one) **261**

Teaching the Lesson

Introducing the Problem Have a student read the problem aloud and tell what is to be done. (find the length of the stick in centimeters and the new length once it is cut) Have students read to find the length of the stick (10 cm) and the new length at the cut (8 cm) and then complete the sentences.

Developing the Skill Tell students that the **centimeter** is a metric unit of measure. Have students read the numbers in order across a centimeter ruler. Have students work in pairs to measure various objects and record their measurements. When all students have had time to measure several objects, have students measure each object as other students check their work. Attach a 10-centimeter paper strip on the board or bulletin board and ask a student to measure it and tell its length in centimeters. (10 centimeters) Have another student measure and make a mark on the strip at 8 centimeters. Continue for 5 centimeters, 9 centimeters, 3 centimeters, etc.

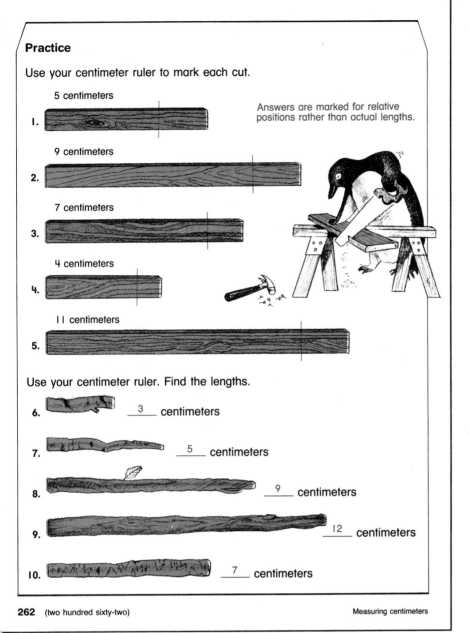

Practice

Use your centimeter ruler to mark each cut.

Answers are marked for relative positions rather than actual lengths.

1. 5 centimeters

2. 9 centimeters

3. 7 centimeters

4. 4 centimeters

5. 11 centimeters

Use your centimeter ruler. Find the lengths.

6. ___3___ centimeters

7. ___5___ centimeters

8. ___9___ centimeters

9. ___12___ centimeters

10. ___7___ centimeters

262 (two hundred sixty-two)

Measuring centimeters

Practice

Tell students to make a cut mark on each length in the first group of problems and then measure and write the centimeters for each length in the last group. Assign the page to be completed independently.

Mixed Practice

1. $6 + 8 + 4$ (18)
2. $\$7.02 - 5.31$ ($\$1.71$)
3. $96 - 27$ (69)
4. 87¢ + 46¢ ($\$1.33$)
5. 226 ◯ 262 (<)
6. $175 + 225 + 108$ (508)
7. $368 + 402$ (770)
8. 9 hundreds 2 tens 5 ones (925)
9. $408 - 28$ (380)
10. $756 - 235$ (521)

Extra Credit *Applications*

Ask a local restaurant to let you use a current or no longer used menu. Tell students that they each have $12.00 to spend on breakfast, lunch and dinner for the next day. Have students use the menu, and plan their meals. Tell them to write out their choices, the prices and the total bill for each meal. Have them add all meals together, for a day's total. Have them make note of any things that strongly influenced their decisions on how to spend the money. Remind them if they go over budget, they may have to wash dishes.

Nearest Centimeter

pages 263-264

Objective

To measure length to the nearest centimeter

Materials

*paper strips not to the exact centimeter or half-centimeter
*small objects
*straightedge
centimeter ruler

Mental Math

Tell students to name the closest hour to:

1. 2:03. (2:00)
2. 6:48. (7:00)
3. 12:40. (1:00)
4. 9:25. (9:00)
5. 11:57. (12:00)
6. 7:35. (8:00)
7. 10:15. (10:00)
8. 1:01. (1:00)

Skill Review

Use a straightedge to draw the following lengths on the board: 5 centimeters, 9 centimeters, 4 centimeters, 1 centimeter, 11 centimeters. Have students measure and record each length. Repeat for more lengths in centimeters.

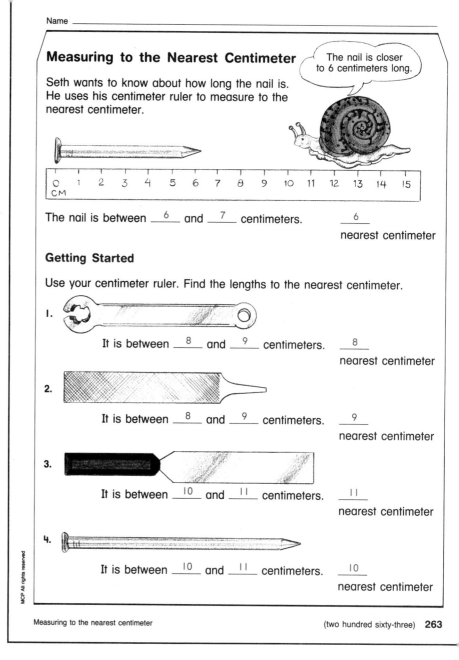

Measuring to the Nearest Centimeter

Seth wants to know about how long the nail is. He uses his centimeter ruler to measure to the nearest centimeter.

The nail is closer to 6 centimeters long.

The nail is between __6__ and __7__ centimeters.

__6__
nearest centimeter

Getting Started

Use your centimeter ruler. Find the lengths to the nearest centimeter.

1. It is between __8__ and __9__ centimeters.

   __8__
   nearest centimeter

2. It is between __8__ and __9__ centimeters.

   __9__
   nearest centimeter

3. It is between __10__ and __11__ centimeters.

   __11__
   nearest centimeter

4. It is between __10__ and __11__ centimeters.

   __10__
   nearest centimeter

Measuring to the nearest centimeter

(two hundred sixty-three) **263**

Teaching the Lesson

Introducing the Problem Have a student read the problem and tell what is to be found. (about how long the nail is) Ask what is known. (The nail is more than 6 centimeters.) Have students read the caption and then complete the sentence. Have students check the centimeter ruler to see if the length of the nail is closer to 6 or 7 and then write the nearest centimeter on the line. (6)

Developing the Skill Have students find the mark between 2 and 3 on the centimeter ruler. Tell students that the mark is halfway between 2 and 3 and means a measure of 2½ centimeters. Have students locate other half marks on the ruler and tell each length. Give each student a paper strip which is slightly longer than 8 centimeters. Have students measure and tell if the length is exactly 8 centimeters. (no) Tell students we then look to see if the length is closer to 8 or to 9 centimeters as you write **between 8 and 9 centimeters** on the board. Tell students that if the length is between 8 and the 8½ mark, then it is closer to 8 centimeters but if it is between the 8½ mark and the 9, it is closer to 9. Ask students which whole centimeter is closer to the end of the strip. (8) Write **nearest centimeter** on the board and have a student write 8 on the board. Repeat with more paper strips.

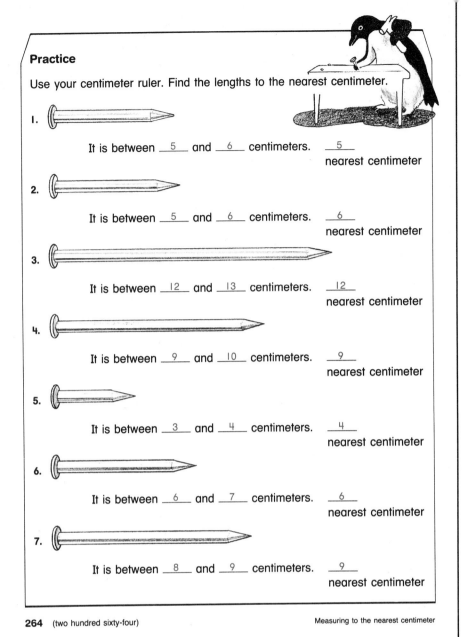

Practice

Use your centimeter ruler. Find the lengths to the nearest centimeter.

1. It is between ___5___ and ___6___ centimeters.
   ___5___
   nearest centimeter

2. It is between ___5___ and ___6___ centimeters.
   ___6___
   nearest centimeter

3. It is between ___12___ and ___13___ centimeters.
   ___12___
   nearest centimeter

4. It is between ___9___ and ___10___ centimeters.
   ___9___
   nearest centimeter

5. It is between ___3___ and ___4___ centimeters.
   ___4___
   nearest centimeter

6. It is between ___6___ and ___7___ centimeters.
   ___6___
   nearest centimeter

7. It is between ___8___ and ___9___ centimeters.
   ___9___
   nearest centimeter

Measuring to the nearest centimeter

Correcting Common Errors

If students have difficulty measuring objects to the nearest centimeter, have them work with partners to measure paper strips. If they put the paper strip very close to the edge of the ruler, it will be easier to see where the end of the strip meets the ruler and to which of the two numbers of centimeters it is closer. A ruler is also easier to read if the person using it sits squarely in front of and looks down over the ruler.

Enrichment

Tell students to draw a 5-sided figure and then measure each side to the nearest centimeter and record the length.

Practice

Tell students they are to measure each length to the nearest centimeter. Assign the page to be completed independently.

Mixed Practice

1. 773 ◯ 377 (>)
2. 651 − 68 (583)
3. 83 − 41 (42)
4. 205, 210, 215, ___ (220)
5. $3.93 − 2.96 ($0.97)
6. 5 dimes, 1 quarter, 1 nickel (80¢)
7. 27¢ + 46¢ (73¢)
8. 63 + 29 + 42 ($1.34)
9. 17 − 6 (11)
10. ___ + 7 = 15 (8)

Extra Credit *Applications*

Discuss with the class the reasons for planning ahead and budgeting when handling money for a family or business. Make sure students understand what a budget is. Invite someone who works with budgeting daily, such as an accountant or homemaker, to speak to the class about how they deal with planning and budgeting in their jobs. Encourage them to ask their parents about their family budget.

Perimeter

pages 265-266

Objective

To measure to find the perimeter of a figure in centimeters

Materials

*straightedge
*square corner
*figures having sides in exact centimeters
centimeter ruler
dotted or graph centimeter paper

Mental Math

Ask students to solve the following:

1. 100 + 6 (106)
2. 64 + 9 (73)
3. 6 + 6 + 6 (18)
4. 24 − 16 (8)
5. 40 + 50 (90)
6. 6 + 5 + 10 (21)
7. 50 + 70 (120)
8. 120 − 90 (30)

Skill Review

Have students find the total length of 2 ribbons that are 8 cm and 5 cm long. (13 cm) Repeat for adding 2 lengths of various sizes using centimeters.

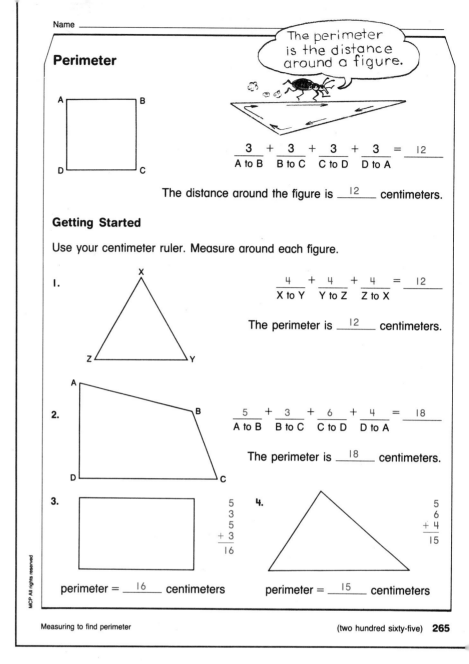

Measuring to find perimeter

(two hundred sixty-five) **265**

Teaching the Lesson

Introducing the Problem Ask students to identify the shape at the top of the page. (square) Have one student read the caption aloud and tell what is to be found. (perimeter) Tell students that **cm** is the abbreviation for centimeter. Ask them the measure of each side. (3 cm) Have students fill in the measure of each side and then find the total. (12 cm) Then have students complete the solution sentence.

Developing the Skill Use a straightedge and square corner to draw on the board a rectangle with sides of 8 centimeters and 4 centimeters. Ask students how many sides and corners are in the figure. (4,4) Label the corners **A, B, C** and **D**. Write **Sides** on the board and the following under that: **A to B, B to C, C to D** and **D to A**. Have a student use a centimeter ruler to measure the length from A to B and record the distance on the board. Repeat for the other sides. Tell students to find the total distance around the figure. Tell students the **perimeter** is the total distance

around a figure as you write **perimeter** on the board. Tell students we must add all 4 lengths to find the perimeter as you write __ + __ + __ + __ = __ **centimeters** on the board. Have a student write the measurements of the sides in the number sentence and find the sum. (8 + 4 + 8 + 4 = 24 centimeters) Display labeled figures which have sides measured in exact centimeters and have students find the perimeter of each.

265

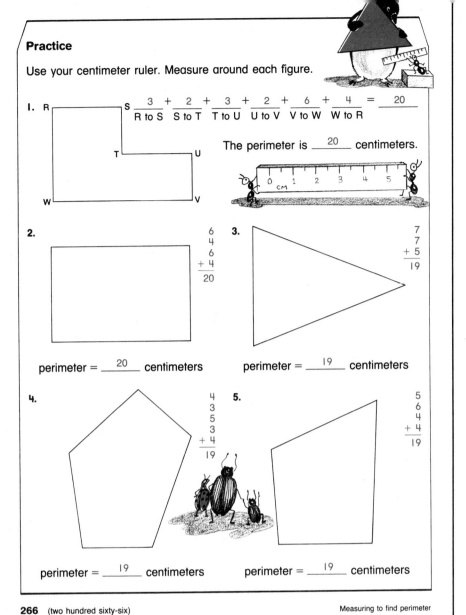

Practice

Use your centimeter ruler. Measure around each figure.

1. R $\underline{\quad 3 \quad}$ + $\underline{\quad 2 \quad}$ + $\underline{\quad 3 \quad}$ + $\underline{\quad 2 \quad}$ + $\underline{\quad 6 \quad}$ + $\underline{\quad 4 \quad}$ = $\underline{\quad 20 \quad}$
R to S   S to T   T to U   U to V   V to W   W to R

The perimeter is __20__ centimeters.

2.
$$\begin{array}{r} 6 \\ 4 \\ 6 \\ + 4 \\ \hline 20 \end{array}$$

perimeter = __20__ centimeters

3.
$$\begin{array}{r} 7 \\ 7 \\ + 5 \\ \hline 19 \end{array}$$

perimeter = __19__ centimeters

4.
$$\begin{array}{r} 4 \\ 3 \\ 5 \\ 3 \\ + 4 \\ \hline 19 \end{array}$$

perimeter = __19__ centimeters

5.
$$\begin{array}{r} 5 \\ 6 \\ 4 \\ + 4 \\ \hline 19 \end{array}$$

perimeter = __19__ centimeters

266 (two hundred sixty-six)

Measuring to find perimeter

Correcting Common Errors

Watch for students who forget to measure every side of a figure. Have them first count the number of sides on the figure and then make sure they have that number of measures, or addends, before they add.

Enrichment

Tell students to draw 3 figures and find the length of each side to the nearest centimeter. Then tell them to find the perimeter of each figure.

Practice

Tell students to measure each side in centimeters and then add the numbers to find the figure's perimeter. Tell students to record the sum on the answer line. Have students complete the page independently.

Mixed Practice

1. 91 − 8 (83)
2. 303 + 28 (331)
3. 295 + 308 + 125 (728)
4. 408 + 390 (798)
5. 600 ○ 60 (>)
6. 870, 880, 890, ___ (900)
7. $4.70 − 1.58 ($3.12)
8. 46¢ + 38¢ (84¢)
9. 391 − 68 (323)
10. ___ + 8 = 17 (9)

Extra Credit   *Measurement*

Set up a fulcrum balance. Choose an object, such as a rock, to be the weight constant. Have each student bring in objects daily to compare with the constant. Each day, have students estimate whether the new object will weigh more or less than the constant. When all of the students have made an estimate, weigh the objects. Have students keep a chart and record both their estimate and the outcome. When finished, have students tally the number of correct estimates made.

266

Area

pages 267-268

Objective

To find area by counting square units

Materials

blank cards
centimeter graph paper
centimeter ruler
inch ruler
scissors

Mental Math

Tell students to name the number that equals:

1. days in a week + 1 dozen (19)
2. greatest 1-digit number − 3 (6)
3. minutes in 1 hour + your age
4. 1 dozen − your age
5. people in your family + all class-mates
6. months in a year + 1 dozen (24)
7. wheels on a car − 2 flat tires (2)

Skill Review

Draw lengths on the board for students to measure each to the nearest inch and the nearest centimeter.

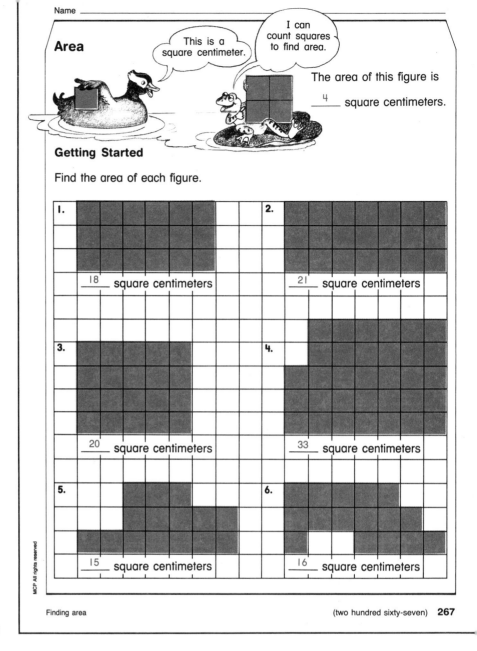

Teaching the Lesson

Introducing the Problem Have a student read the first caption aloud to learn about a **square centimeter** and then measure each side of the square to see that each is 1 centimeter long. Have a student read the second caption aloud to learn about **area.** Tell students to count the square centimeters in the figure to find the area. (4) Have students read and complete the solution sentence.

Developing the Skill Have students cut out 12 square centimeters from graph paper. Give each student a 3 centimeter by 3 centimeter card. Help students cover the card with square centimeters. Ask how many square centimeters it takes to cover the card. (9) Tell students that 9 square centimeters is called the **area** of the card. Repeat for more cards of various sizes. Now have students mark an x on the first 6 squares across the top row of graph paper and continue to mark 6 x's across on the next 3 rows. Have students outline the 6 by 4 rectangle and tell its area. (24 square centimeters) Continue for more squares and rectangles and then have students outline odd-sized figures and find each area by counting the square centimeters.

267

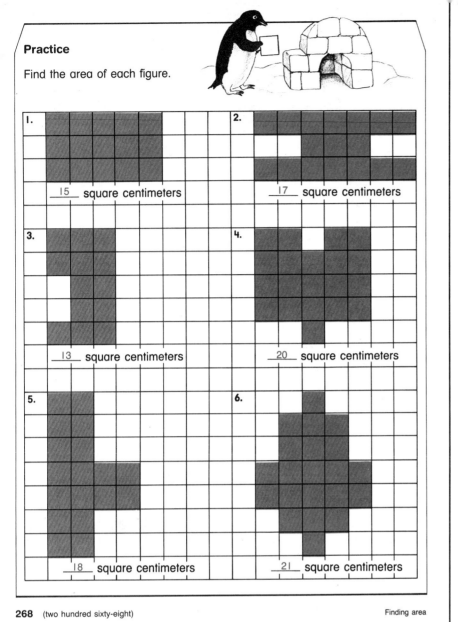

Practice

Find the area of each figure.

1. __15__ square centimeters

2. __17__ square centimeters

3. __13__ square centimeters

4. __20__ square centimeters

5. __18__ square centimeters

6. __21__ square centimeters

Correcting Common Errors

If students need additional work with area, have them work in small cooperative groups with centimeter grid paper. Have each member draw a polygonal figure with an area of 12 square centimeters. Then have them compare their shapes to see that not all figures with the same area have the same shape. Repeat the activity drawing figures that have 20 square centimeters for area measurements.

Enrichment

Tell students to use centimeter graph paper to draw a square that is 13 centimeters on all sides. Have them draw a square inside that square that has sides of 9 centimeters. Then have them find the difference in the 2 areas.

Practice

Tell students to count the square centimeters in each figure and write the number under the figure. Have students complete the page independently.

Extra Credit   *Creative Drill*

Duplicate or draw the following on the board.

```
                              1.
          2.          3.      _
          _           _ _ _
   4. _ _ _ _         _       _
      _ 6.  7. _   8. _
   5. _ _ _ _ _ _ _ _
      _       _    _        _
      _       _    _        _
      _       _    _
      _       _    _
           9. _ _ _ _ _ _
```

Across
3. The distance between two points is a (line).
4. 35 is (more) than 27.
5. The side of a square is a (straight) line.
9. A foot is (smaller) than a yard.

Down
1. 256 is (less) than 526.
2. Twelve inches equal 1 (foot).
3. If your pencil is not short, it is (long).
5. The opposite of tall is (short).
6. You measure length with a (ruler).
7. (Inches) are smaller than feet.
8. There are (ten) digits from 0 to 9.

268

Pounds and Ounces

pages 269-270

Objective

To estimate weight in pounds and ounces

Materials

*balance scale
*1-pound and 1-ounce weights
*items weighing about 1 pound and
   about 1 ounce
inch graph paper

Mental Math

Have students tell the perimeter of a figure whose sides are:

1. 4, 3, 6 centimeters. (13 cm)
2. 50, 50, 40 inches. (140 in.)
3. equal and 1 of 4 sides is 2 inches. (8 in.)
4. 1, 2, 3, 4 and 5 centimeters. (15 cm)
5. equal and 1 of 3 sides is 5 centimeters. (15 cm)
6. 1, 2½, 2½ inches. (6 in.)

Skill Review

Have students use inch graph paper to draw figures with areas of 12, 9, 16, 18, etc., square inches.

Pounds and Ounces

A pound is a unit for measuring weight.

This weighs I pound.

1 Pound

BUTTER

This tennis ball weighs less than I pound.

My dog weighs more than I pound.

An ounce is also a unit for measuring weight.

9 pennies weigh about I ounce.

16 ounces = 1 pound

Getting Started

Circle the better guess for the weight.

1.
(More than I pound)
Less than I pound

2.
More than I pound
(Less than I pound)

3.
(2 pounds)
2 ounces

4.
4 pounds
(4 ounces)

Estimating weight   (two hundred sixty-nine) **269**

Teaching the Lesson

Introducing the Problem Have students read the captions and sentences aloud. Ask how many **ounces** are in 1 **pound.** (16) Ask students if a dog or a tennis ball weighs more. (dog) Ask if 9 pennies would weigh more or less than a dog. (less) Ask how many ounces the butter would weigh. (16)

Developing the Skill Tell students that one unit we use to measure the weight of an object is the **pound.** Have students hold the 1-pound weight to get a feel for its weight. Place the 1-pound weight on the balance scale and tell students that the scale will tip to the side of the heavier object. Show several items weighing about 1 pound and have students place each on the scale to see if they weigh more or less than 1 pound. Have students group the objects for more than and less than 1-pound. Repeat for the 1-ounce weight and objects which weigh about 1 ounce. Now have students hold the pound weight in one hand and an object in the other and tell if the object feels to be more or less than 1 pound. Repeat for 1 ounce. Show 2 books and ask students if the books might weigh 2 pounds or 2 ounces. (2 pounds) Repeat for students to estimate if objects would be weighed in pounds or ounces.

Practice

Circle the better guess for the weight.

1.
More than 1 pound
(Less than 1 pound)

2.
(More than 1 pound)
Less than 1 pound

3.
More than 1 pound
(Less than 1 pound)

4.
(More than 1 pound)
Less than 1 pound

5.
3 pounds   (3 ounces)

6.
(20 pounds)   20 ounces

7.
(21 pounds)   21 ounces

8.
1 pound   (1 ounce)

9.
3 pounds   (3 ounces)

10.
(15 pounds)   15 ounces

Correcting Common Errors

Some students may have difficulty deciding whether an object weighs more or less than a pound. Have them work in cooperative groups with a bag of sugar or loaf of bread weighing one pound. Let each of them, in turn, hold it in one hand and another object in the other hand to determine whether the object weighs more than or less than one pound. Then have them work together to make a list of 5 objects in the classroom that weigh more than one pound and 5 objects that weigh less than one pound.

Enrichment

Tell students to make a list of items in their bedrooms which would be measured in pounds and items measured in ounces.

Practice

Have students tell which measure of weight would be the better guess for each item. Have students complete the page independently.

Mixed Practice

1. 397 + 18 (415)
2. 600 − 173 (427)
3. 3 dimes, 3 nickels, 5 pennies (50¢)
4. 105 + 306 + 219 (630)
5. 38 + 46 (84)
6. 75 − 48 (27)
7. 410 − 38 (372)
8. 5 hundreds 0 tens 0 ones (500)
9. $2.56 − 1.77 ($0.79)
10. 6 + ___ = 14 (8)

Extra Credit   *Geometry*

Have each student trace their right hand on a piece of graph paper. Have students count and label the number of squares covered by their hand. Tell them to count every square that is included or drawn through, as one whole square. Have students repeat the process for their right foot. Ask students to compare the areas of their hand with that of their foot. Discuss the results. Ask students for the mathematical problem that would be a way to find the area of a pair of hands and a pair of feet.

Cups, Pints, Quarts

pages 271-272

Objectives

To compare the capacities of cups, pints and quarts

To estimate capacities of a cup, pint and quart

Materials

*various-sized containers

cup, pint and quart containers

water or Styrofoam packing filler

Mental Math

Tell students to name the day or month:

1. 11th month (November)
2. last month of the year (December)
3. last day of the week (Saturday)
4. month between March and May (April)
5. fifth day of the week (Thursday)

Skill Review

Write on the board: **16 ounces = 1 pound.** Have the student add 16 and 16 to find out how many ounces are in 2 pounds and write in on the board. (32 ounces = 2 pounds) Have students find the number of ounces in 3, 4, 5, etc., pounds.

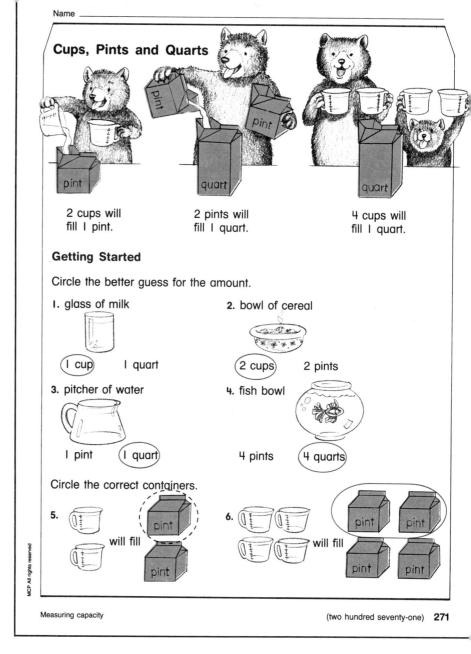

Name _____

Cups, Pints and Quarts

2 cups will fill 1 pint.

2 pints will fill 1 quart.

4 cups will fill 1 quart.

Getting Started

Circle the better guess for the amount.

1. glass of milk

(I cup)   I quart

2. bowl of cereal

(2 cups)   2 pints

3. pitcher of water

I pint   (I quart)

4. fish bowl

4 pints   (4 quarts)

Circle the correct containers.

5.   will fill

6.   will fill

Measuring capacity

(two hundred seventy-one) **271**

Teaching the Lesson

Introducing the Problem Ask students to read the 3 sentences silently. Ask how many pints will fill 1 quart. (2) Ask how many cups will fill 1 pint. (2) Ask how many cups will fill 1 quart. (4)

Developing the Skill Show students the cup and pint containers. Have a student fill the cup with water or Styrofoam filler and pour it into the pint. Ask if the pint will hold more. (yes) Have the student pour another cupful into the pint and tell how many cups equal 1 pint. (2) Repeat for filling the quart container from a pint container. (2 pints = 1 quart) Continue for students to see that 4 cups equal 1 quart. Repeat each measurement and write the following on the board:

$$2 \text{ cups} = 1 \text{ pint}$$
$$2 \text{ pints} = 1 \text{ quart}$$
$$4 \text{ cups} = 1 \text{ quart}$$

Ask students how they can use these measurements to find out how many cups are in 2 pints. (add 2 cups and 2 cups) Write on the board:

$$\begin{array}{l} 1 \text{ pint} = 2 \text{ cups} \\ \underline{+1 \text{ pint} = 2 \text{ cups}} \\ 2 \text{ pints} = 4 \text{ cups} \end{array}$$

Continue to find how many cups are in 2 quarts, pints in 2 quarts, etc. Now show students various-sized containers to estimate the capacity each would hold. Have students measure to check each estimate.

271

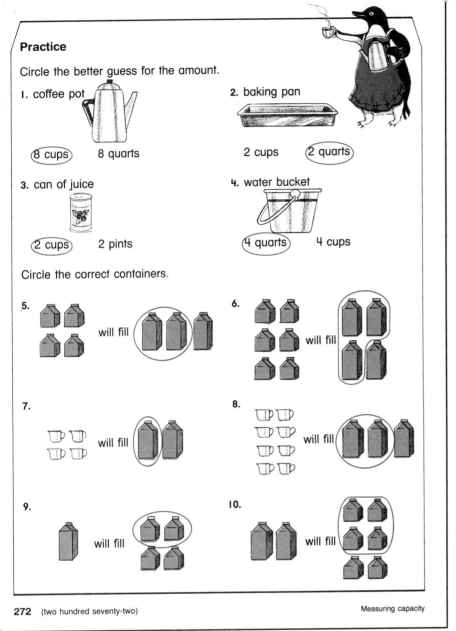

Practice

Circle the better guess for the amount.

1. coffee pot

   (8 cups)   8 quarts

2. baking pan

   2 cups   (2 quarts)

3. can of juice

   (2 cups)   2 pints

4. water bucket

   (4 quarts)   4 cups

Circle the correct containers.

5.   will fill

6.   will fill

7.   will fill

8.   will fill

9.   will fill

10.   will fill

Practice

Ask students if the coffee pot would hold about 8 cups or 8 quarts of liquid. (8 cups) Have students circle the correct answer. Tell students to look at the first problem in the bottom section and tell how many of the quart containers can be filled with the contents of the 4 pints. (2 quarts) Have students circle any 2 of the quarts. Tell students to estimate the better guess of measurement for problems in the top section and then find which containers can be filled in problems in the bottom section. Have students complete the page independently.

Correcting Common Errors

Some students may have difficulty choosing the appropriate unit to measure liquid capacity. Have them work in cooperative groups with models of a cup, pint, and quart. Have them use water or sand to see how many of each unit it takes to fill the next larger unit. Then, let them fill various non-standard containers with water or sand from the models. This provides everyday-life models for estimating and comparing capacities.

Enrichment

Tell students to cut from magazines or newspapers items which are commonly measured in cups, pints or quarts. Have them use the pictures to make a chart telling the number of cups in a pint, pints in a quart and cups in a quart.

Extra Credit   *Measurement*

Give each student a drinking straw and tell them to cut it to any length they want. Tell them they have created a new non-standard measuring unit, that they must then name, ex. "Squinch." Tell students to measure items you name, such as: desk top, length and width of a textbook, their forearm, etc. with their non-standard unit of measure, and record each measure. Then have them repeat each measurement, using a standard unit of measurement, and record data. Have students compare and discuss their 2 sets of measurements. Ask them to explain why standard units of measurement are necessary.

272

Temperature

pages 273-274

Objective

To read Fahrenheit and Celsius thermometers

Materials

*Fahrenheit and Celsius thermometers cup, pint and quart containers

Mental Math

Have students tell the change that would be received from $1 if they spent:

1. 15¢. (85¢)
2. 92¢. (8¢)
3. 75¢. (25¢)
4. 20¢. (80¢)
5. $1. (none)
6. 19¢. (81¢)
7. 50¢. (50¢)
8. 9¢. (91¢)

Skill Review

Have students draw pictures to show how many cups are in 1 pint, cups in 1 quart and pints in 1 quart. Allow students to use the cup, pint and quart containers to remember the equalities.

Temperature

Thermometers are used to measure temperature. This is a Fahrenheit thermometer.

This is a Celsius thermometer. It measures temperature using a different scale.

70°F

20°C

We read this __70__ degrees Fahrenheit.

We read this __20__ degrees Celsius.

Getting Started

Write the temperature.

1.

__30__ °F

__0__ °C

Fahrenheit and Celsius temperatures

(two hundred seventy-three) **273**

Teaching the Lesson

Introducing the Problem Have students tell about the picture. Have students read the paragraph aloud with you. Ask a student to read the temperature on the Fahrenheit thermometer. Write **70°F** on the board and tell students we write the number, the degree notation and an **F** to tell the degrees as shown on a Fahrenheit thermometer. Tell students to write the temperature on the line before the degree notation and complete the solution statement. Be sure students understand that the °F is written out in words in the solution statement. Repeat this procedure for the Celsius example.

Developing the Skill Display the Fahrenheit thermometer and tell students that the **Fahrenheit** thermometer is one of 2 kinds of thermometers used to measure **temperature.** Tell students that temperature is the amount of heat or cold in the air. Have a student find the zero on the thermometer. Tell students that zero degrees Fahrenheit is very

cold weather and that the numbers below the zero are for showing even colder temperatures. Have a student find and read the highest number on the thermometer. Tell students this number is for a very hot temperature. Have students find other temperatures.

Display the Celsius thermometer and tell students that temperature can also be measured on a metric thermometer called a **Celsius thermometer.** Have a student find the zero as you tell students that a zero degree temperature is cold and the numbers below the zero are for even colder temperatures. Have a student find and read the highest number on the thermometer for an extremely hot temperature. Have students find various other temperatures.

273

Practice

Write the temperature.

1.

75 °F   25 °C

2.

50 °F   10 °C

3.

95 °F   35 °C

Fahrenheit and Celsius temperatures

Review

pages 275-276

Objectives

To review units of measure
To maintain skills learned previously
this year

Materials

6-inch ruler
centimeter ruler
inch graph paper

Mental Math

Tell students to name the number for:

1. 4 + 4 + 4 (12)
2. 17 − 9 (8)
3. 6 + 4 − 3 (7)
4. 7 + 0 + 11 (18)
5. 18 − 9 + 1 (10)
6. 200 more than 6 (206)
7. 15¢ + 40¢ (55¢)
8. 26 − 19 (7)
9. 100 − 94 (6)

Skill Review

Have students draw on graph paper a
rectangle with sides of 8 and 6 inches.
Have students find the perimeter (28
inches) and the area. (48 square
inches) Repeat for perimeters and
areas of more squares and rectangles.

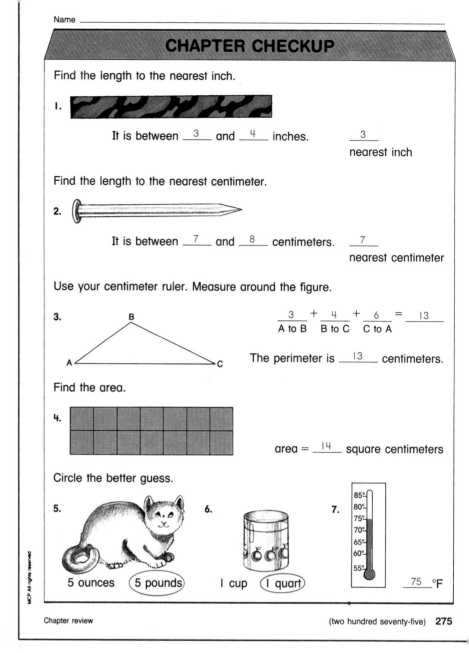

CHAPTER CHECKUP

Find the length to the nearest inch.

1.

It is between __3__ and __4__ inches.   __3__
nearest inch

Find the length to the nearest centimeter.

2.

It is between __7__ and __8__ centimeters.   __7__
nearest centimeter

Use your centimeter ruler. Measure around the figure.

3.

$$\frac{3}{\text{A to B}} + \frac{4}{\text{B to C}} + \frac{6}{\text{C to A}} = \frac{13}{}$$

The perimeter is __13__ centimeters.

Find the area.

4.

area = __14__ square centimeters

Circle the better guess.

5. 5 ounces   (5 pounds)

6. I cup   (I quart)

7. 85° 80° 75° 70° 65° 60° 55°   __75__ °F

Chapter review   (two hundred seventy-five) **275**

Teaching page 275

Have students tell what is to be done in each problem or
group of problems. Then have students complete the page
independently.

ROUNDUP REVIEW

Fill in the oval next to the correct answer.

1	7 + 5	○ 2 ● 12 ○ 13 ○ NG	

8 Name this shape.
○ square
○ rectangle
● triangle
○ NG

2	17 − 8	○ 8 ○ 25 ○ 11 ● NG

9 What part is red?
● $\frac{2}{3}$
○ $\frac{1}{3}$
○ $\frac{2}{4}$
○ NG

3	○ 365 ● 356 ○ 653 ○ NG

10 3 pints = _____?_____ cups
○ 2
● 6
○ 4
○ NG

4	38 + 96	○ 124 ○ 62 ● 134 ○ NG

11 What part is red?
○ $\frac{3}{4}$
● $\frac{1}{4}$
○ $\frac{1}{3}$
○ NG

5	346 + 275	● 621 ○ 611 ○ 511 ○ NG

12 Which is the better guess?
● more than 1 pound
○ less than 1 pound

6	75 − 49	● 26 ○ 34 ○ 36 ○ NG

7	524 − 135	○ 499 ○ 411 ● 389 ○ NG

score

276 (two hundred seventy-six)

Cumulative review

Enrichment

1. Tell students to make a chart of the number of cups and pints in 1, 2, 3, 4, 5, 6, 7, 8, 9 and 10 quarts.
2. Tell students to write five 3-digit numbers that have the same number of tens and ones.
3. Have students fold or cut a sheet of paper to show eighths and then color ⅝ of the figure.

Teaching page 276

This page reviews basic facts, place value, addition and subtraction of 2- and 3-digit numbers, geometry, fractions and measurement. Have students solve the problem and then fill in the oval next to the correct answer. Tell students to fill in the NG oval if the correct answer is not given. Have students complete the page independently.

276

Multiplying by 2

pages 277-278

Objective

To multiply by the factor 2 through 2 × 5

Materials

3 × 5 cards
counters

Mental Math

Ask students to identify each:

1. I have 3 sides. (triangle)
2. I have 3 tens and 6 ones. (36)
3. I am 3 parts of 7 equal parts. (³⁄₇)
4. I hold 2 cups. (pint)
5. I tell the distance around a figure. (perimeter)
6. I have 1 digit and mean none. (0)
7. I am used to find the total. (addition)
8. I am a mark halfway between 2 numbers on an inch ruler. (half-inch)

Skill Review

Have students count by 2's through 200 with each student saying 5 numbers in order and the next student counting on for the next 5 numbers, etc.

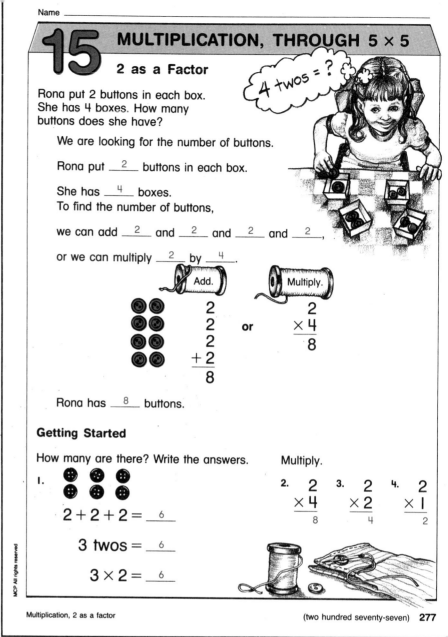

MULTIPLICATION, THROUGH 5 × 5

2 as a Factor

4 twos = ?

Rona put 2 buttons in each box. She has 4 boxes. How many buttons does she have?

We are looking for the number of buttons.

Rona put __2__ buttons in each box.

She has __4__ boxes.
To find the number of buttons,

we can add __2__ and __2__ and __2__ and __2__,

or we can multiply __2__ by __4__.

Add.

$$\begin{array}{r} 2 \\ 2 \\ 2 \\ +2 \\ \hline 8 \end{array}$$

or

Multiply.

$$\begin{array}{r} 2 \\ \times 4 \\ \hline 8 \end{array}$$

Rona has __8__ buttons.

Getting Started

How many are there? Write the answers.

1. $2 + 2 + 2 =$ __6__

3 twos = __6__

3 × 2 = __6__

Multiply.

2. $\begin{array}{r} 2 \\ \times 4 \\ \hline 8 \end{array}$ 3. $\begin{array}{r} 2 \\ \times 2 \\ \hline 4 \end{array}$ 4. $\begin{array}{r} 2 \\ \times 1 \\ \hline 2 \end{array}$

Multiplication, 2 as a factor

(two hundred seventy-seven) **277**

Teaching the Lesson

Introducing the Problem Have students tell about the picture. Have a student read the problem aloud and tell what is to be found. (how many buttons Rona has in all) Ask what information is given. (Rona has 4 boxes with 2 buttons in each box.) Have students read and complete the information sentences. Work through the model with students and then have them complete the solution sentence. Have students count the buttons in the picture to check their solution.

Developing the Skill Draw 3 groups of 2 x's each on the board. Ask students how many groups. (3) Ask how many x's are in each group. (2) Tell students we want to know how many in all. Tell students that adding 3 twos is one way to find the total. Have a student write and solve the addition problem for a sum of 6. Tell students there is another way to find the total of 3 two's. Tell students we can **multiply** 3 times 2 as you write **3 × 2** both vertically and horizontally on the board. Ask students to write the answers to both problems. (6, 6) Write **3 two's =** ___ and have a student solve the problem. (6) Draw another group of 2 x's on the board and repeat the procedure to multiply 4 times 2. (8) Repeat for 5 × 2 and 2 × 2.

277

Practice

How many are there? Write the answers.

1.

$2 + 2 + 2 + 2 = \underline{8}$

4 twos = $\underline{8}$

$4 \times 2 = \underline{8}$

2.

1 two = $\underline{2}$

$1 \times 2 = \underline{2}$

3.

$2 + 2 = \underline{4}$

2 twos = $\underline{4}$

$2 \times 2 = \underline{4}$

4.

$2 + 2 + 2 + 2 + 2 = \underline{10}$

5 twos = $\underline{10}$

$5 \times 2 = \underline{10}$

5.

$2 + 2 + 2 = \underline{6}$

3 twos = $\underline{6}$

$3 \times 2 = \underline{6}$

Multiply.

6. $2 \times 2 = \underline{4}$

7. $3 \times 2 = \underline{6}$

8. $1 \times 2 = \underline{2}$

9. $4 \times 2 = \underline{8}$

10. $5 \times 2 = \underline{10}$

11. $4 \times 2 = \underline{8}$

12.
$$\begin{array}{r} 2 \\ \times 2 \\ \hline 4 \end{array}$$

13.
$$\begin{array}{r} 2 \\ \times 4 \\ \hline 8 \end{array}$$

14.
$$\begin{array}{r} 2 \\ \times 1 \\ \hline 2 \end{array}$$

15.
$$\begin{array}{r} 2 \\ \times 3 \\ \hline 6 \end{array}$$

16.
$$\begin{array}{r} 2 \\ \times 5 \\ \hline 10 \end{array}$$

Multiplication, 2 as a factor

Correcting Common Errors

Some students may not make the connection between multiplication and repeated addition. Have them work with counters to model arrays. For example, to find 3 twos, or 3×2, have them lay out 3 sets of 2 counters and skip count to find the total; e.g., 2, 4, 6.

Enrichment

Tell students to draw pictures to show that 4 two's is the same number as 2 four's.

Practice

Remind students that adding $2 + 2 + 2 + 2$ tells us the total of 4 two's. Have students write the sum of the addition problem. (8) Have students read the 2 multiplication sentences aloud with you as they write 8 for each answer. Have students complete the page independently.

Mixed Practice

1. $3.27 - 1.56$ ($1.71)
2. $308 - 36$ (272)
3. $283 + 472$ (755)
4. $657 - 421$ (236)
5. $75 - 7$ (68)
6. $323 \bigcirc 332$ (<)
7. $63 + 21 + 38$ (122)
8. $4.76 + 2.75$ ($7.51)
9. $98 - 21$ (77)
10. 7 dimes, 2 nickels, 9 pennies (89¢)

Extra Credit *Probability*

Give each student paper and a set of four objects, each a different color. Wooden cubes or beads in red, blue, green and yellow would work well. Ask students to arrange the objects, two at a time, all possible paired combinations in different ways as they can. Have them illustrate each arrangement with crayons. Explain that if they make one arrangement, for example red-blue; that the opposite pair, blue-red, is different. Have students demonstrate and display all the possible arrangements, as a volunteer writes them on the board. (possible 12; If R = red, B = blue, Y = yellow, G = green; then; RY, YR, RG, GR, RB, BR, GY, YG, GB, BG, YB and BY).

278

Multiplying by 3

pages 279-280

Objective

To multiply by the factor 3 through 3×5

Materials

3×5 cards
counters

Mental Math

Have students name the amounts:

1. 2 dimes. (20¢)
2. 2 quarters. (50¢)
3. 2 two's. (4)
4. 2 pennies. (2¢)
5. 2 three's. (6)
6. 2 half-dollars. ($1)
7. 2 fours. (8)

Skill Review

Draw 3 groups of 2 circles each on the board and have a student write and solve an addition problem to tell the total. $(2 + 2 + 2 = 6)$ Have a student write and solve the multiplication problem. $(3 \times 2 = 6)$ Continue to draw groups of 2 circles for students to write and solve addition and multiplication problems.

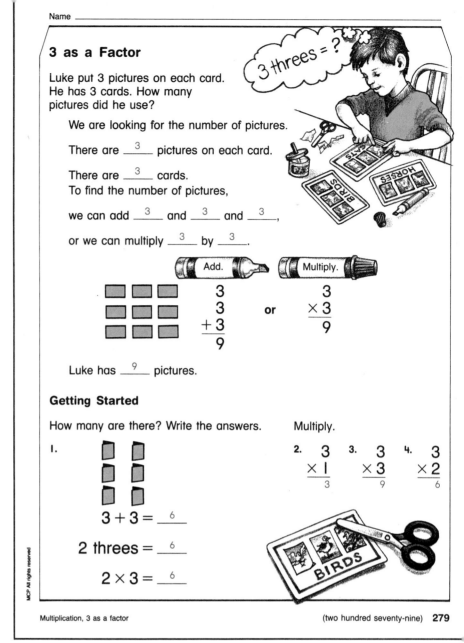

3 as a Factor

Luke put 3 pictures on each card. He has 3 cards. How many pictures did he use?

3 threes = ?

We are looking for the number of pictures.

There are __3__ pictures on each card.

There are __3__ cards.
To find the number of pictures,

we can add __3__ and __3__ and __3__,

or we can multiply __3__ by __3__.

Add.

$$\begin{array}{r} 3 \\ 3 \\ +3 \\ \hline 9 \end{array}$$

or

Multiply.

$$\begin{array}{r} 3 \\ \times 3 \\ \hline 9 \end{array}$$

Luke has __9__ pictures.

Getting Started

How many are there? Write the answers.   Multiply.

1.

$3 + 3 =$ __6__

2 threes = __6__

$2 \times 3 =$ __6__

2. $\begin{array}{r} 3 \\ \times 1 \\ \hline 3 \end{array}$ 3. $\begin{array}{r} 3 \\ \times 3 \\ \hline 9 \end{array}$ 4. $\begin{array}{r} 3 \\ \times 2 \\ \hline 6 \end{array}$

Multiplication, 3 as a factor   (two hundred seventy-nine) **279**

Teaching the Lesson

Introducing the Problem   Have students tell about the picture. Have a student read the problem and tell what is to be found. (how many pictures Luke has) Ask what information is known. (Luke has 3 cards with 3 pictures on each.) Have students read and complete the information sentences. Work through the model with students and then have them complete the solution sentence. Have students count the pictures shown on the cards to check their solution.

Developing the Skill   Have students lay out 3 counters in a group and then lay out another group of 3 counters. Ask if the groups are equal. (yes) Have students count to tell the total in both groups. (6) Write **2 threes = 6** and **3 + 3 = 6** on the board. Have students read the number sentences aloud with you. Now write **2 × 3 = 6** on the board as you tell students this is a multiplication fact. Repeat for students to lay out 4 groups of 3 each and 5 groups of 3. Help students write on the board and solve the multiplication facts for 3 through 5 × 3.

Practice

How many are there? Write the answers.

1.

$3 + 3 + 3 + 3 = \underline{12}$

4 threes = $\underline{12}$

$4 \times 3 = \underline{12}$

2.

I three = $\underline{3}$

$1 \times 3 = \underline{3}$

3.

$3 + 3 + 3 = \underline{9}$

3 threes = $\underline{9}$

$3 \times 3 = \underline{9}$

4.

$3 + 3 + 3 + 3 + 3 = \underline{15}$

5 threes = $\underline{15}$

$5 \times 3 = \underline{15}$

5.

$3 + 3 = \underline{6}$

2 threes = $\underline{6}$

$2 \times 3 = \underline{6}$

Multiply.

6. $\begin{array}{r} 3 \\ \times 2 \\ \hline 6 \end{array}$
7. $\begin{array}{r} 3 \\ \times 1 \\ \hline 3 \end{array}$
8. $\begin{array}{r} 2 \\ \times 2 \\ \hline 4 \end{array}$
9. $\begin{array}{r} 2 \\ \times 4 \\ \hline 8 \end{array}$
10. $\begin{array}{r} 2 \\ \times 1 \\ \hline 2 \end{array}$

11. $\begin{array}{r} 3 \\ \times 4 \\ \hline 12 \end{array}$
12. $\begin{array}{r} 3 \\ \times 5 \\ \hline 15 \end{array}$
13. $\begin{array}{r} 3 \\ \times 3 \\ \hline 9 \end{array}$
14. $\begin{array}{r} 2 \\ \times 3 \\ \hline 6 \end{array}$
15. $\begin{array}{r} 2 \\ \times 5 \\ \hline 10 \end{array}$

Multiplication, 3 as a factor

Correcting Common Errors

Watch for students who add instead of multiply when they see the multiplication fact. For example, when seeing 2×3, they think $2 + 3 = 5$ instead of $2 \times 3 = 6$. Have them work with partners to draw arrays to model the problems.

Enrichment

Tell students to use their multiplication fact cards for 2's and 3's to find 2 facts which use the same 2 numbers. Then they should make a drawing to explain why the answers are the same.

Practice

Remind students that 3×2 means 3 two's or $2 + 2 + 2$. Encourage students to use counters when needed as they complete the page independently.

Mixed Practice

1. $308 + 36$ (344)
2. $406 + 143 + 227$ (776)
3. 3 hundreds 7 tens 4 ones (374)
4. $65 - 27$ (38)
5. $78¢ + 17¢$ (95¢)
6. $820 - 46$ (774)
7. $570 - 126$ (444)
8. $491 \bigcirc 501$ (<)
9. $\$9.23 + .61$ ($9.84)
10. $\$8.07 - 6.38$ ($1.69)

Extra Credit *Probability*

Ask students to think about all the different things they have for lunch. List the possibilities on the board. Try to limit the list to no more than ten items. Now ask students to arrange the lunch foods into whole meals. For example, if they listed: peanut butter sandwich, hard-boiled egg, apple, milk, soup, these could be formed into different meal combinations. Have them check each other's work for duplicate meals. See who can find the most different lunches.

Multiplying by 4

pages 281-282

Objective

To multiply by the factors 4 through 4 × 5

Materials

3 × 5 cards
counters

Mental Math

Tell students to name the number:

1. 5 × 2 (10)
2. 2 + 2 + 2 (6)
3. 3 × 4 (12)
4. 5 × 3 (15)
5. 3 + 3 + 3 (9)
6. 3 + 5 (8)
7. 3 five's (15)
8. 3 three's (9)

Skill Review

Have a student write and solve a multiplication problem to tell the number of fingers on 2 hands. (2 × 5 = 10) Repeat for problems to find the following: wheels on 3 bicycles (3 × 2 = 6), cents in 3 nickels (3 × 5 = 15¢), perimeter of a triangle whose sides are all 3 inches (3 × 3 = 9), tires on 3 cars (3 × 4 = 12), etc.

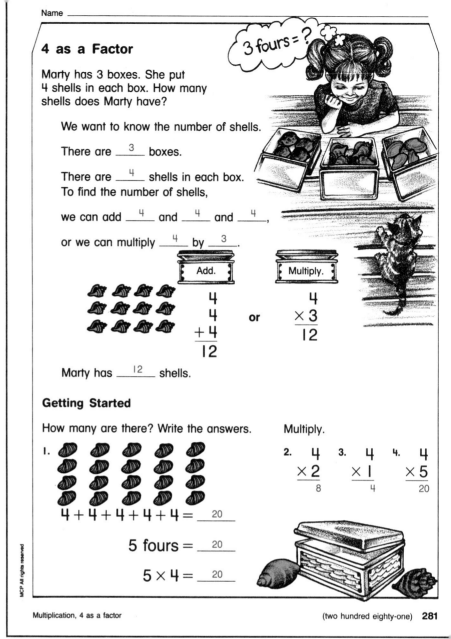

4 as a Factor

Marty has 3 boxes. She put 4 shells in each box. How many shells does Marty have?

We want to know the number of shells.

There are ___3___ boxes.

There are ___4___ shells in each box. To find the number of shells,

we can add ___4___ and ___4___ and ___4___,

or we can multiply ___4___ by ___3___.

Add.		Multiply.
4		4
4	or	× 3
+ 4		12
12		

Marty has ___12___ shells.

Getting Started

How many are there? Write the answers.   Multiply.

1.

4 + 4 + 4 + 4 + 4 = ___20___

5 fours = ___20___

5 × 4 = ___20___

2. 4
× 2
8

3. 4
× 1
4

4. 4
× 5
20

Multiplication, 4 as a factor

(two hundred eighty-one) **281**

Teaching the Lesson

Introducing the Problem Have students tell about the picture. Have a student read the problem and tell what is to be found. (how many shells Marty has) Ask what is known. (She has 3 boxes with 4 shells in each.) Ask students what operation needs to be done. (multiplication or addition) Have students read and complete the information sentences. Work through the model with students and then have them complete the solution sentence and count the boxes in the picture to check their work.

Developing the Skill Have students lay out a group of 4 counters. Tell students to lay out 3 more groups of 4 counters each. Write **4 + 4 + 4 + 4** on the board for students to tell the sum. (16) Write **4 fours = __** and **4 × 4 = __** on the board and have students read and complete each. (16, 16) Remind students that the sum of 4 + 4 + 4 + 4 is the same as multiplying 4 times 4. Repeat for 4 × 5. Help students write and solve the multiplication facts for 4 × 1 through 4 × 5 on the board.

Practice

How many are there? Write the answers.

1.

$4 \text{ fours} = \underline{16}$

$4 + 4 + 4 + 4 = \underline{16}$ $4 \times 4 = \underline{16}$

2.

$4 + 4 = \underline{8}$

$2 \text{ fours} = \underline{8}$

$2 \times 4 = \underline{8}$

3.

$1 \text{ four} = \underline{4}$

$1 \times 4 = \underline{4}$

Multiply.

4. $3 \times 2 = \underline{6}$ 5. $2 \times 2 = \underline{4}$ 6. $1 \times 3 = \underline{3}$

7. $4 \times 3 = \underline{12}$ 8. $5 \times 4 = \underline{20}$ 9. $4 \times 2 = \underline{8}$

10. $\begin{array}{r} 3 \\ \times 5 \\ \hline 15 \end{array}$
11. $\begin{array}{r} 2 \\ \times 5 \\ \hline 10 \end{array}$
12. $\begin{array}{r} 3 \\ \times 3 \\ \hline 9 \end{array}$
13. $\begin{array}{r} 4 \\ \times 1 \\ \hline 4 \end{array}$
14. $\begin{array}{r} 4 \\ \times 4 \\ \hline 16 \end{array}$

Apply

Solve.

15. The farm has 3 pens. There are 4 pigs in each pen. How many pigs are there?

$\begin{array}{r} 4 \\ \times 3 \\ \hline 12 \end{array}$

$\underline{12}$ pigs

16. Stacy made 5 stacks of books. There are 4 books in each stack. How many books does she have?

$\begin{array}{r} 4 \\ \times 5 \\ \hline 20 \end{array}$

$\underline{20}$ books

Multiplication, 4 as a factor

Correcting Common Errors

Some students may have difficulty with facts of 4. Have them work with partners and make multiplication-fact cards for 1×4 through 5×4. Then write $4 + 4$ on the chalkboard and have students show the multiplication fact for this addition problem. (2×4) Have students give the answer. (8) Repeat for the following:

$4 + 4 + 4$ $(3 \times 4 = 12)$
$4 + 4 + 4 + 4$ $(4 \times 4 = 16)$
$4 + 4 + 4 + 4 + 4$ $(5 \times 4 = 20)$

Enrichment

Have students lay out the multiplication problems for the factors 2, 3 and 4. Tell them to make a list of all the facts which use the same numbers. Tell them to then make a list of all the other facts.

Practice

Tell students to write the answers to multiplication problems for the factors 2, 3 and 4 on this page. Assign the page to be completed independently.

Mixed Practice

1. $495 + 42$ (537)
2. 2×8 (16)
3. $450 + 127 + 203$ (780)
4. 220, 230, 240, ___ (250)
5. $108 - 89$ (19)
6. 4 nickels, 8 pennies (28¢)
7. $6.50 - 2.84$ ($3.66)
2. 2×5 (10)
9. $695 - 108$ (587)
10. $409 \bigcirc 490$ (<)

Extra Credit   *Logic*

Arrange desks in your room to form gates like the boxes below: the first gate indicating red one way and blue the other; the next two showing smiles one way, frown the other; and the last showing boys one way, girls the other.

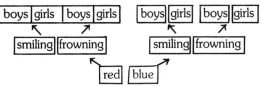

Make a number of cards coloring half-red, half-blue, half with a smiling face and half with a frowing face. Ask students to line up at the first gate and have one student pass out the cards. As each receives a card they should start through the gates. At each one they will have to choose the right direction. When all the students have negotiated this maze they should be divided into eight groups: smiling red boys, smiling red girls, frowing red girls, etc. Have students in each area compare their cards to see if they maneuvered correctly.

282

Multiplying by 5

pages 283-284

Objective

To multiply by the factor 5 through
5 × 5

Materials

3 × 5 cards
counters

Mental Math

Tell students to name a multiplication
the fact for:

1. 16 (4 × 4)
2. 20 (4 × 5 or 5 × 4)
3. 12 (3 × 4 or 4 × 3)
4. 6 (2 × 3 or 3 × 2)
5. 4 (2 × 2)
6. 8 (2 × 4 or 4 × 2)
7. 9 (3 × 3)
8. 10 (5 × 2 or 2 × 5)

Skill Review

Lay out 3 groups of 3 counters in
each group and a group of 4 counters.
Ask students if the groups are equal.
(no) Remove 1 from the group of 4
counters and ask if the groups are
equal. (yes) Ask a student to write a
multiplication fact on the board to tell
about the number of counters in all.
(4 × 3 = 12) Repeat to review multiplication facts for 1 through 5 groups
of 2's, 3's and 4's.

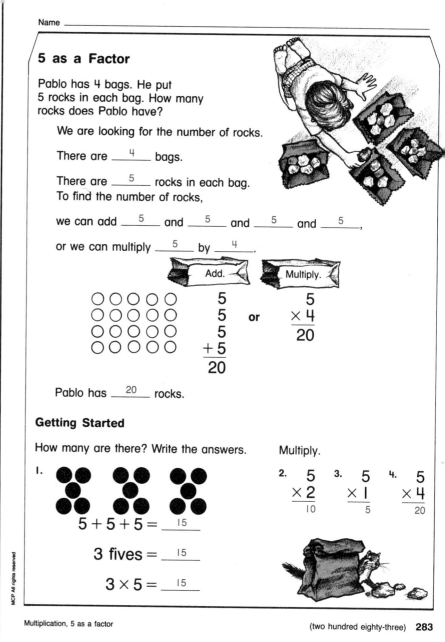

Name _____

5 as a Factor

Pablo has 4 bags. He put
5 rocks in each bag. How many
rocks does Pablo have?

We are looking for the number of rocks.

There are ___4___ bags.

There are ___5___ rocks in each bag.
To find the number of rocks,

we can add ___5___ and ___5___ and ___5___ and ___5___,

or we can multiply ___5___ by ___4___.

Add.   Multiply.

○○○○○   5   5
○○○○○   5   or   × 4
○○○○○   5   ___
○○○○○ + 5   20
        ____
         20

Pablo has ___20___ rocks.

Getting Started

How many are there? Write the answers.   Multiply.

1.

5 + 5 + 5 = __15__

3 fives = __15__

3 × 5 = __15__

2. 5   3. 5   4. 5
   × 2   × 1   × 4
   ___   ___   ___
    10   5   20

Multiplication, 5 as a factor

(two hundred eighty-three) **283**

Teaching the Lesson

Introducing the Problem Have a student read the
problem aloud and tell what is to be found. (total number
of rocks Pablo has) Ask what information is known. (Pablo
has 4 bags of 5 rocks each.) Have students read and complete the information sentences. Work through the addition
and multiplication with students and then have them complete the solution sentence. Tell students to count the rocks
in the picture to check their solution.

Developing the Skill Tell students that the total number
in several groups of 5 objects can be found by multiplying
the number of groups by 5 or by writing an addition problem. Lay out 5 groups of 5 counters and ask a student to
write and solve a multiplication problem to find the total
number of counters. (5 × 5 = 25) Tell students that counting by 5's is another way to remember that 5 × 5 = 25.
Have a student write and solve an addition problem to find
the total number of counters. (5 + 5 + 5 + 5 + 5 = 25)
Repeat the procedure for finding 2 fives, 3 fives and 4 fives
using addition. Now have students write and solve the problems for 1 five through 5 fives using multiplication on the
board.

283

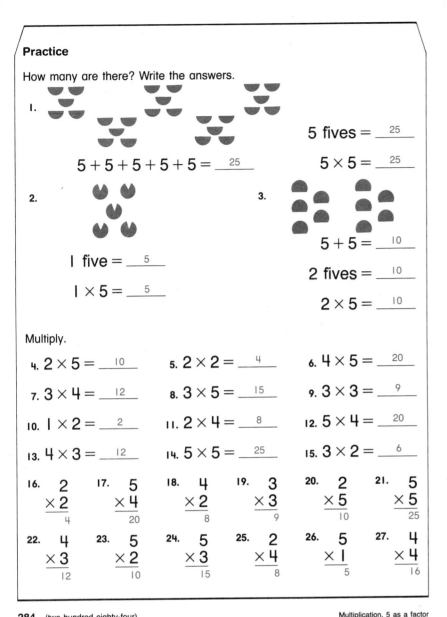

Practice

How many are there? Write the answers.

1.

$5 + 5 + 5 + 5 + 5 = \underline{25}$

5 fives = $\underline{25}$

$5 \times 5 = \underline{25}$

2.

1 five = $\underline{5}$

$1 \times 5 = \underline{5}$

3.

$5 + 5 = \underline{10}$

2 fives = $\underline{10}$

$2 \times 5 = \underline{10}$

Multiply.

4. $2 \times 5 = \underline{10}$ 5. $2 \times 2 = \underline{4}$ 6. $4 \times 5 = \underline{20}$

7. $3 \times 4 = \underline{12}$ 8. $3 \times 5 = \underline{15}$ 9. $3 \times 3 = \underline{9}$

10. $1 \times 2 = \underline{2}$ 11. $2 \times 4 = \underline{8}$ 12. $5 \times 4 = \underline{20}$

13. $4 \times 3 = \underline{12}$ 14. $5 \times 5 = \underline{25}$ 15. $3 \times 2 = \underline{6}$

16. $\begin{array}{r} 2 \\ \times 2 \\ \hline 4 \end{array}$ 17. $\begin{array}{r} 5 \\ \times 4 \\ \hline 20 \end{array}$ 18. $\begin{array}{r} 4 \\ \times 2 \\ \hline 8 \end{array}$ 19. $\begin{array}{r} 3 \\ \times 3 \\ \hline 9 \end{array}$ 20. $\begin{array}{r} 2 \\ \times 5 \\ \hline 10 \end{array}$ 21. $\begin{array}{r} 5 \\ \times 5 \\ \hline 25 \end{array}$

22. $\begin{array}{r} 4 \\ \times 3 \\ \hline 12 \end{array}$ 23. $\begin{array}{r} 5 \\ \times 2 \\ \hline 10 \end{array}$ 24. $\begin{array}{r} 5 \\ \times 3 \\ \hline 15 \end{array}$ 25. $\begin{array}{r} 2 \\ \times 4 \\ \hline 8 \end{array}$ 26. $\begin{array}{r} 5 \\ \times 1 \\ \hline 5 \end{array}$ 27. $\begin{array}{r} 4 \\ \times 4 \\ \hline 16 \end{array}$

Multiplication, 5 as a factor

Correcting Common Errors

If students have difficulty multiplying with 5, have them work with partners and use counters to model the problem. For example, to find 3×5, they should think "3 fives" and put out 3 sets of 5 counters each, and skip count to find the total; i.e., 5, 10, 15.

Enrichment

Tell students to write numbers by 5's through 25. Then tell them to write a multiplication fact for each number they wrote. Ask if they can write the facts for the next 4 numbers when counting on to 45 by 5's.

Practice

Tell students to solve the problems on this page independently.

Mixed Practice

1. $8 + 5 + 7$ (20)
2. 3×7 (21)
3. $\$9.53 - 7.28$ ($2.25)
4. $602 - 248$ (354)
5. $93 - 46$ (47)
6. 2×7 (14)
7. $105 \bigcirc 510$ (<)
8. $490 - 103$ (387)
9. $\$2.78 + 4.08$ ($6.86)
10. 6 hundreds 2 tens 8 ones (628)

Extra Credit   *Numeration*

You will need counters of three different colors. Draw this conversion chart such as this one using red, blue and yellow on the board:

one red = three blues
one blue = two yellows

Now arrange a display of simple objects that students can buy with the counters you will give them. Label each item with a price. (one blue and one yellow; or two blues; or one red and one yellow, for example) Give each student two red counters. Explain that before they can buy anything, they must visit the exchange counter to get the correct change. Have students act as shopkeepers and bankers often exchanging roles. Give each student an opportunity to exchange counters and to purchase an item.

Order in Multiplication

pages 285-286

Objective

To understand the order property in multiplication

Materials

*multiplication fact cards through 2×5, 3×5, 4×5 and 5×5
counters
nickels and pennies

Mental Math

Ask students the following riddles:

1. 4 of me equals 20. (5)
2. 3 of me equals 12. (4)
3. 2 of me equals 6. (3)
4. 5 of me equals 20. (4)
5. 3 of me equals 15. (5)
6. 4×4 equals me. (16)
7. Me $\times$ me equals 9. (3)
8. 5×5 = me. (25)

Skill Review

Have students give answers for multiplication fact cards as you show them in random order. Help students work to increase their speed of recall.

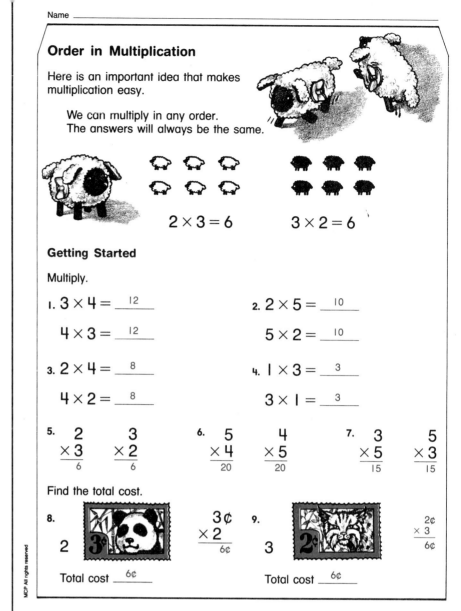

Name _____

Order in Multiplication

Here is an important idea that makes multiplication easy.

We can multiply in any order.
The answers will always be the same.

$2 \times 3 = 6$ $3 \times 2 = 6$

Getting Started

Multiply.

1. $3 \times 4 =$ __12__   2. $2 \times 5 =$ __10__

   $4 \times 3 =$ __12__ $5 \times 2 =$ __10__

3. $2 \times 4 =$ __8__   4. $1 \times 3 =$ __3__

   $4 \times 2 =$ __8__ $3 \times 1 =$ __3__

5. $\begin{array}{r} 2 \\ \times 3 \\ \hline 6 \end{array}$ $\begin{array}{r} 3 \\ \times 2 \\ \hline 6 \end{array}$
6. $\begin{array}{r} 5 \\ \times 4 \\ \hline 20 \end{array}$ $\begin{array}{r} 4 \\ \times 5 \\ \hline 20 \end{array}$
7. $\begin{array}{r} 3 \\ \times 5 \\ \hline 15 \end{array}$ $\begin{array}{r} 5 \\ \times 3 \\ \hline 15 \end{array}$

Find the total cost.

8. 2 $\begin{array}{r} 3¢ \\ \times 2 \\ \hline 6¢ \end{array}$ 9. 3 $\begin{array}{r} 2¢ \\ \times 3 \\ \hline 6¢ \end{array}$

Total cost __6¢__   Total cost __6¢__

Teaching the Lesson

Introducing the Problem Have a student read aloud the sentences about order in multiplication. Talk through the 2 problems.

Developing the Skill Have students lay out 8 counters. Tell students to place the counters into groups of 2 and tell how many groups. (4) Ask the total of 4×2. (8) Write **4 × 2 = 8** on the board. Ask students to group the 8 counters into groups of 4 and tell how many groups. (2) Ask the total of 2×4. (8) Write **2 × 4 = 8** on the board. Have students note that the same 3 numbers are in both facts and that the answer is still 8 whether there are 2 groups of 4 or 4 groups of 2. Repeat for 20 counters to show that $5 \times 4 = 20$ and $4 \times 5 = 20$. Continue for 3×1 and 1×3 and then 3×5 and 5×3. Now have students work with coins to work similar problems. Remind students that the cent sign must be written in all problems using cents.

285

Practice

Multiply.

1. $5 \times 4 = \underline{20}$

 $4 \times 5 = \underline{20}$

2. $1 \times 5 = \underline{5}$

 $5 \times 1 = \underline{5}$

3. $4 \times 1 = \underline{4}$

 $1 \times 4 = \underline{4}$

4. $3 \times 5 = \underline{15}$

 $5 \times 3 = \underline{15}$

5.
$$\begin{array}{r} 5 \\ \times 2 \\ \hline 10 \end{array} \qquad \begin{array}{r} 2 \\ \times 5 \\ \hline 10 \end{array}$$

6.
$$\begin{array}{r} 4 \\ \times 2 \\ \hline 8 \end{array} \qquad \begin{array}{r} 2 \\ \times 4 \\ \hline 8 \end{array}$$

7.
$$\begin{array}{r} 3 \\ \times 4 \\ \hline 12 \end{array} \qquad \begin{array}{r} 4 \\ \times 3 \\ \hline 12 \end{array}$$

Find the total cost.

8. 5
$$\begin{array}{r} 3¢ \\ \times 5 \\ \hline 15¢ \end{array}$$
Total cost __15¢__

9. 3
$$\begin{array}{r} 5¢ \\ \times 3 \\ \hline 15¢ \end{array}$$
Total cost __15¢__

10. 3
$$\begin{array}{r} 4¢ \\ \times 3 \\ \hline 12¢ \end{array}$$
Total cost __12¢__

11. 4
$$\begin{array}{r} 3¢ \\ \times 4 \\ \hline 12¢ \end{array}$$
Total cost __12¢__

12. 4
$$\begin{array}{r} 5¢ \\ \times 4 \\ \hline 20¢ \end{array}$$
Total cost __20¢__

13. 5
$$\begin{array}{r} 4¢ \\ \times 5 \\ \hline 20¢ \end{array}$$
Total cost __20¢__

286 (two hundred eighty-six)

Order in multiplication

Problem Solving Multiplication

pages 287-288

Objective

To multiply to solve problems

Materials

Mental Math

Ask students what operation to use to find:

1. tires on 4 cars. (multiplication or addition)
2. how much more. (subtraction)
3. the sum. (addition)
4. the difference. (subtraction)
5. 4 groups of 5. (multiplication or addition)
6. wheels on 5 bikes. (multiplication or addition)
7. how much change. (subtraction)

Skill Review

Help students recall the 4 problem solving questions as you write on the board: **What is to be found? What do we know? What operation is to be done? Does the answer make sense?** Help students create a word problem and then answer each question to solve the problem.

Problem Solving

Solve.

Each chair has 4 legs.

1. 2 chairs have ___8___ legs.

2. 5 chairs have ___20___ legs.

3. 3 chairs have ___12___ legs.

4. 4 chairs have ___16___ legs.

Each bird has 2 legs.

5. 3 birds have ___6___ legs.

6. I bird has ___2___ legs.

7. 2 birds have ___4___ legs.

8. 5 birds have ___10___ legs.

9. 4 birds have ___8___ legs.

10. 2 hands have ___10___ fingers.

11. 4 hands have ___20___ fingers.

12. 3 hands have ___15___ fingers.

13. I hand has ___5___ fingers.

14. 5 hands have ___25___ fingers.

Each hand has 5 fingers.

Problem solving

(two hundred eighty-seven) **287**

Teaching page 287

Work through the first two or three problems together, showing students how to use the illustrations to solve the problems. Have students complete the page independently.

287

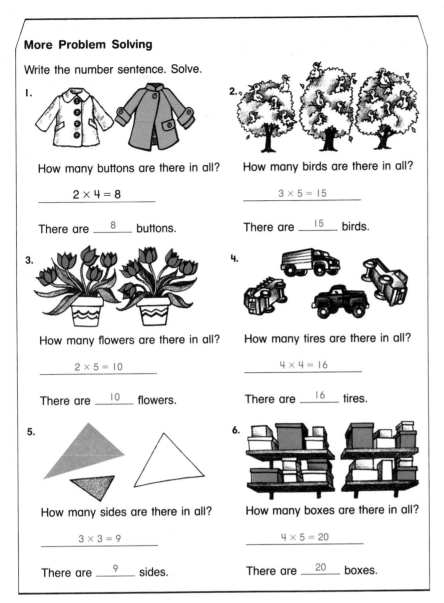

More Problem Solving

Write the number sentence. Solve.

1. How many buttons are there in all?

   $2 \times 4 = 8$

   There are ___8___ buttons.

2. How many birds are there in all?

   $3 \times 5 = 15$

   There are ___15___ birds.

3. How many flowers are there in all?

   $2 \times 5 = 10$

   There are ___10___ flowers.

4. How many tires are there in all?

   $4 \times 4 = 16$

   There are ___16___ tires.

5. How many sides are there in all?

   $3 \times 3 = 9$

   There are ___9___ sides.

6. How many boxes are there in all?

   $4 \times 5 = 20$

   There are ___20___ boxes.

Problem solving

Correcting Common Errors

Some students may have difficulty understanding when multiplication can be used to solve a problem. Have these students work with partners to create a word problem that requires multiplication. For example: How many panes are there in 3 windows of our classroom?'' They then can write the multiplication fact that can be used to solve it, recognizing that an addition sentence with equal addends also could be used.

Enrichment

Tell students to draw a picture of a rectangular table with 4 chairs on each of the long sides and 3 chairs on each shorter side. Have them write and solve problems to find out how many legs are on each side of the table. Then tell them to find out how many legs are on all the chairs plus the table.

Teaching page 288

Tell students they will be writing a multiplication number sentence to solve each problem. Work through the first problem together and then have students complete the page independently. Remind students to write each answer in the solution sentence.

Extra Credit   *Creative Drill*

Give each student 10 toothpicks. Have students glue toothpicks onto paper to form various shapes that have the same perimeter. Broken toothpicks may be used to make interesting shapes, without changing the perimeter. Have students use a centimeter ruler to measure the perimeter of each figure and compare the results. Display their toothpick creations on the bulletin board.

Picture Graphs

pages 289-290

Objective

To interpret picture graphs using multiplication

Materials

*multiplication fact cards through 2×5, 3×5, 4×5 and 5×5

Mental Math

Ask students how many:

1. cups in a pint. (2)
2. eggs in a dozen. (12)
3. wheels on 3 tricycles. (9)
4. sides on 3 doors. (6)
5. hands on 5 people. (10)
6. wheels on 4 bicycles. (8)
7. days in 1 week. (7)
8. sides on 4 squares. (16)

Skill Review

Have students give answers to multiplication fact cards randomly shown. Have students place cards in pairs when possible to show that the answer is the same regardless of the order of the 2 numbers.

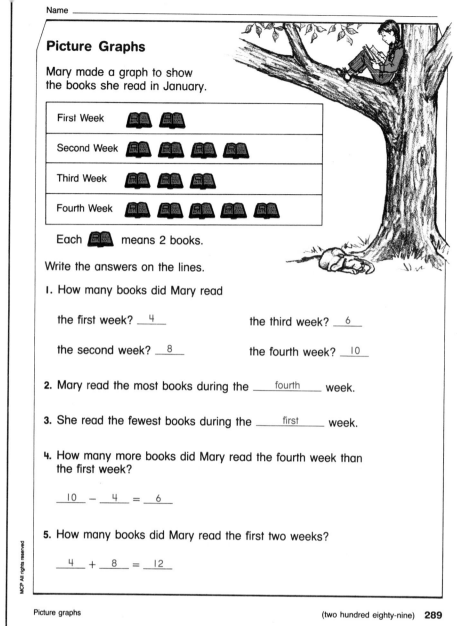

Picture Graphs

Mary made a graph to show the books she read in January.

First Week	
Second Week	
Third Week	
Fourth Week	

Each ▥ means 2 books.

Write the answers on the lines.

1. How many books did Mary read

    the first week? __4__   the third week? __6__

    the second week? __8__   the fourth week? __10__

2. Mary read the most books during the ___fourth___ week.

3. She read the fewest books during the ___first___ week.

4. How many more books did Mary read the fourth week than the first week?

    __10__ − __4__ = __6__

5. How many books did Mary read the first two weeks?

    __4__ + __8__ = __12__

Picture graphs

(two hundred eighty-nine) **289**

Teaching page 289

Have students read the sentence about Mary's graph aloud. Tell students that each book pictured on the **picture graph** means 2 books, so 1 pictured book means 1 two as you write $1 \times 2 = 2$ on the board. Tell students that 2 pictured books mean 2 twos as you write $2 \times 2 = 4$ on the board. Have a student write on the board and solve the multiplication fact for 3 pictured books. ($3 \times 2 = 6$) Ask students to tell how many books were read each week as shown on the graph. (first week 4, second week 8, third week 6, fourth week 10) Have students complete the page independently.

289

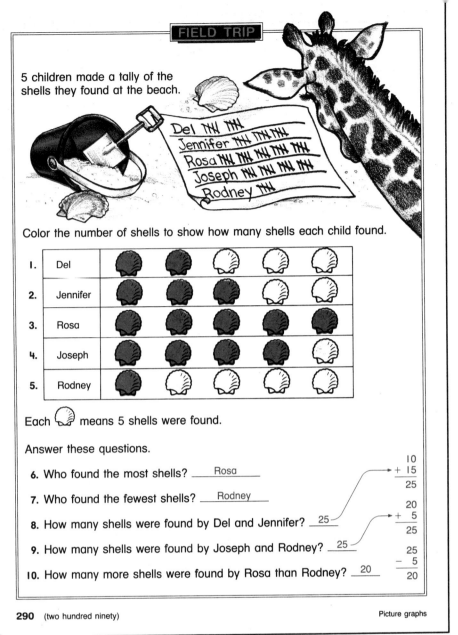

FIELD TRIP

5 children made a tally of the shells they found at the beach.

Del 𝈀𝈀
Jennifer 𝈀 𝈀 𝈀
Rosa 𝈀 𝈀 𝈀 𝈀 𝈀
Joseph 𝈀 𝈀 𝈀 𝈀
Rodney 𝈀

Color the number of shells to show how many shells each child found.

1.	Del					
2.	Jennifer					
3.	Rosa					
4.	Joseph					
5.	Rodney					

Each 🐚 means 5 shells were found.

Answer these questions.

6. Who found the most shells? ___Rosa___

7. Who found the fewest shells? ___Rodney___

8. How many shells were found by Del and Jennifer? _25_

9. How many shells were found by Joseph and Rodney? _25_

10. How many more shells were found by Rosa than Rodney? _20_

```
   10
 + 15
 ────
   25

   20
 +  5
 ────
   25

   25
 -  5
 ────
   20
```

290 (two hundred ninety)   Picture graphs

Teaching page 290

Field Trip

Have students read the first sentence aloud. Tell students that 4 tally marks are crossed by a fifth tally mark to make it easy to count the tallies by 5's. Have students count by 5's to tell how many shells each child found. (Del 10, Jennifer 15, Rosa 25, Joseph 20, Rodney 5) Have students read the directions for the picture graph aloud. Ask students how many shells each picture represents. (5) Ask how many shells will be colored for Del. (2) Repeat for the other names on the graph. Have students color the necessary shells. Then tell students to answer the questions at the bottom of the page independently.

Correcting Common Errors

Watch for students who always think that a symbol on a picture graph represents 1. Correct by having them write the number that a symbol represents on each symbol on the graph.

Enrichment

Tell students to use the picture graph on page 289 to find out how many books in all were read in the 4 weeks.

Extra Credit *Creative Drill*

Make up a scavenger hunt that requires students to find things in your classroom by measuring linear distance accurately.

Give the students a direction sheet and a meter- or yard-stick. Create directions that refer to specific things in your room. Tell students they must complete each measurement and record the name of each object as they locate it. This could be done as a timed activity. Directions might include:

1. Two yards from the pencil sharpener you will find a blue _____.
2. There are five _____ lying 2.5 centimeters from the upper right-hand corner of the teacher's desk.
3. _____ is hanging 1 meter from the tip of the flag.

Have a small reward or prize at the end of the hunt, that the students can find if they solve the last clue correctly.

Review

pages 291-292

Objectives

To review multiplication facts through 5 × 5

To maintain skills learned previously this year

Materials

counters

Mental Math

Ask if the following are true or false:

1. Temperature is told in degrees. (T)
2. 2 pints equal 2 quarts. (F)
3. 660 is 10 more than 650. (T)
4. Buying lunch, you subtract to find your change. (T)
5. Area is the distance around a figure. (F)

Skill Review

Tell students a story of 5 groups of 3 children in each. Have a student draw stick figures to show the problem on the board. Have a student write and solve a multiplication fact to find the total number of children. (15) Have students draw and solve more story problems using multiplication facts through 5 × 5.

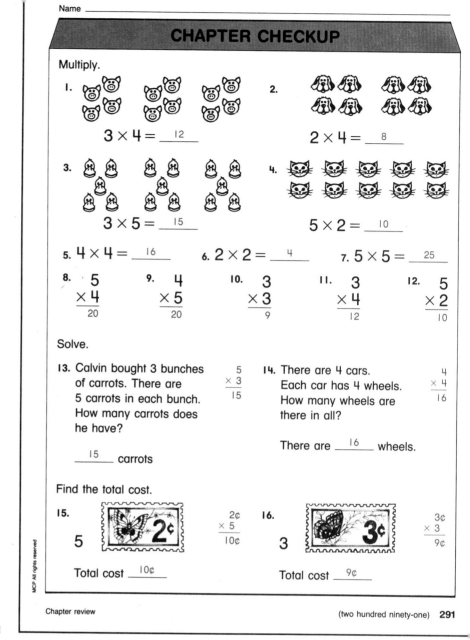

Name _____

CHAPTER CHECKUP

Multiply.

1. $3 \times 4 = \underline{12}$

2. $2 \times 4 = \underline{8}$

3. $3 \times 5 = \underline{15}$

4. $5 \times 2 = \underline{10}$

5. $4 \times 4 = \underline{16}$ 6. $2 \times 2 = \underline{4}$ 7. $5 \times 5 = \underline{25}$

8. $\begin{array}{r} 5 \\ \times 4 \\ \hline 20 \end{array}$ 9. $\begin{array}{r} 4 \\ \times 5 \\ \hline 20 \end{array}$ 10. $\begin{array}{r} 3 \\ \times 3 \\ \hline 9 \end{array}$ 11. $\begin{array}{r} 3 \\ \times 4 \\ \hline 12 \end{array}$ 12. $\begin{array}{r} 5 \\ \times 2 \\ \hline 10 \end{array}$

Solve.

13. Calvin bought 3 bunches of carrots. There are 5 carrots in each bunch. How many carrots does he have?

$\begin{array}{r} 5 \\ \times 3 \\ \hline 15 \end{array}$

_____15_____ carrots

14. There are 4 cars. Each car has 4 wheels. How many wheels are there in all?

$\begin{array}{r} 4 \\ \times 4 \\ \hline 16 \end{array}$

There are ___16___ wheels.

Find the total cost.

15. 5

$\begin{array}{r} 2¢ \\ \times 5 \\ \hline 10¢ \end{array}$

Total cost ___10¢___

16. 3

$\begin{array}{r} 3¢ \\ \times 3 \\ \hline 9¢ \end{array}$

Total cost ___9¢___

Chapter review   (two hundred ninety-one) **291**

Teaching page 291

Have students tell what they are to do in each section. Then have students complete the page independently.

291

Fill in the oval next to the correct answer.

1	$\begin{array}{r} 7 \\ + 8 \\ \hline \end{array}$	○ 16 ○ 1 ● 15 ○ NG	7	$\begin{array}{r} 81 \\ - 55 \\ \hline \end{array}$	○ 36 ● 26 ○ 34 ○ NG

2	13 − 6	● 7 ○ 13 ○ 19 ○ NG

8	$\begin{array}{r} 623 \\ - 298 \\ \hline \end{array}$	● 325 ○ 335 ○ 435 ○ NG

3
○ 3:45
● 8:15
○ 8:03
○ NG

9 What part of the figure is red?
○ $\frac{2}{4}$
○ $\frac{1}{4}$
● $\frac{3}{4}$
○ NG

4
● 85¢
○ 80¢
○ 75¢
○ NG

10 $\begin{array}{r} 5 \\ \times 3 \\ \hline \end{array}$
○ 8
● 15
○ 2
○ NG

5 $\begin{array}{r} 37 \\ + 54 \\ \hline \end{array}$
○ 23
○ 81
○ 83
● NG

11 $\begin{array}{r} \$8.35 \\ - 4.26 \\ \hline \end{array}$
○ $4.11
○ $4.19
● $4.09
○ NG

6 $\begin{array}{r} 356 \\ + 575 \\ \hline \end{array}$
● 931
○ 921
○ 821
○ NG

12 4 × 4
○ 8
○ 20
○ 12
● NG

☐ score

Cumulative Review

Enrichment

1. Tell students to draw 3 coins to show their change from $2.00 after spending $1.25.
2. Tell students to draw 12 fruit bars and show how they would share them equally with 3 friends.
3. Tell students to draw pictures to show that $5 \times 4 = 20$ and $3 \times 4 = 12$ have a difference of 2×4.

Teaching page 292

This page reviews basic addition and subtraction facts, time, money, addition and subtraction of 2- and 3-digit numbers, fractions and multiplication facts. Tell students to solve each problem and fill in the oval beside the correct answer. Tell students to fill in the NG oval if the correct answer is not given. Have students complete the page independently.

292

Review

pages 293-294

Objective

To review basic addition and subtraction facts

Materials

counters

Mental Math

Tell students to name a related fact for:

1. 6 + 6. (12 − 6)
2. 17 − 8. (17 − 9, 9 + 8, 8 + 9)
3. 14 − 7. (7 + 7)
4. 16 − 9. (16 − 7, 9 + 7, 7 + 9)
5. 6 + 8. (8 + 6, 14 − 8, 14 − 6)
6. 0 + 9. (9 + 0, 9 − 0, 9 − 9)
7. 10 − 4. (10 − 6, 6 + 4, 4 + 6)
8. 9 + 4. (4 + 9, 13 − 9, 13 − 4)

Skill Review

Write **5 × 4, 5 + 4** and **5 − 4** vertically on the board. Have students tell which fact has an answer of 1. (5 − 4) Ask which has an answer of 20. (5 × 4) Ask which has an answer of 9. (5 + 4) Ask students to read the multiplication fact (5 × 4), the addition fact (5 + 4) and the subtraction fact (5 − 4). Repeat for groups of facts such as 3 − 2, 3 × 2, 3 + 2 and 5 + 5, 5 − 5, 5 × 5.

Add.

1.									
0 +5 5	3 +2 5	0 +4 4	2 +1 3	0 +7 7	3 +4 7	3 +1 4	3 +8 11	1 +1 2	1 +6 7
2.									
1 +5 6	0 +1 1	8 +2 10	7 +3 10	6 +5 11	7 +1 8	1 +4 5	6 +0 6	5 +1 6	0 +8 8
3.									
9 +8 17	0 +3 3	4 +0 4	6 +7 13	5 +3 8	0 +2 2	5 +7 12	4 +1 5	2 +2 4	0 +6 6
4.									
8 +0 8	9 +0 9	1 +8 9	6 +3 9	5 +6 11	2 +4 6	1 +7 8	6 +1 7	4 +7 11	3 +0 3
5.									
4 +8 12	7 +9 16	7 +0 7	1 +2 3	2 +6 8	5 +5 10	7 +4 11	1 +9 10	1 +3 4	4 +3 7
6.									
2 +9 11	3 +7 10	0 +0 0	3 +5 8	7 +2 9	8 +9 17	9 +5 14	1 +0 1	4 +5 9	7 +5 12
7.									
6 +9 15	7 +6 13	4 +6 10	3 +3 6	9 +9 18	9 +4 13	8 +1 9	9 +3 12	2 +0 2	6 +4 10
8.									
8 +6 14	4 +2 6	5 +2 7	2 +3 5	2 +8 10	3 +6 9	8 +3 11	9 +7 16	2 +7 9	3 +9 12
9.									
6 +6 12	9 +2 11	2 +5 7	6 +8 14	5 +0 5	0 +9 9	8 +5 13	4 +4 8	7 +7 14	6 +2 8
10.									
5 +4 9	8 +7 15	9 +6 15	4 +9 13	7 +8 15	5 +9 14	8 +8 16	8 +4 12	5 +8 13	9 +1 10

100 addition facts

(two hundred ninety-three) **293**

Teaching page 293

This page of addition facts can be used as a timed test. Have students correct any incorrect answers. You may want to have students rewrite problems in horizontal form and then solve each problem.

Subtract.

1.	2 −1 ― 1	3 −2 ― 1	5 −1 ― 4	6 −6 ― 0	9 −8 ― 1	5 −0 ― 5	2 −0 ― 2	5 −4 ― 1	11 − 3 ― 8	2 −2 ― 0
2.	4 −3 ― 1	8 −6 ― 2	8 −1 ― 7	7 −0 ― 7	8 −2 ― 6	11 − 4 ― 7	8 −0 ― 8	9 −3 ― 6	3 −1 ― 2	10 − 3 ― 7
3.	10 − 7 ― 3	6 −3 ― 3	10 − 1 ― 9	13 − 4 ― 9	7 −1 ― 6	9 −9 ― 0	7 −2 ― 5	6 −4 ― 2	11 − 5 ― 6	15 − 8 ― 7
4.	0 −0 ― 0	6 −1 ― 5	4 −4 ― 0	4 −2 ― 2	14 − 9 ― 5	15 − 6 ― 9	9 −7 ― 2	4 −1 ― 3	8 −7 ― 1	8 −3 ― 5
5.	8 −5 ― 3	3 −3 ― 0	12 − 5 ― 7	14 − 5 ― 9	14 − 6 ― 8	4 −0 ― 4	6 −0 ― 6	9 −5 ― 4	9 −2 ― 7	6 −2 ― 4
6.	12 − 7 ― 5	5 −2 ― 3	7 −3 ― 4	16 − 8 ― 8	17 − 9 ― 8	7 −4 ― 3	1 −1 ― 0	10 − 8 ― 2	5 −5 ― 0	8 −4 ― 4
7.	16 − 9 ― 7	6 −5 ― 1	7 −5 ― 2	12 − 9 ― 3	13 − 9 ― 4	8 −8 ― 0	7 −7 ― 0	13 − 5 ― 8	10 − 6 ― 4	11 − 8 ― 3
8.	9 −0 ― 9	10 − 9 ― 1	11 − 6 ― 5	10 − 5 ― 5	15 − 9 ― 6	15 − 7 ― 8	11 − 2 ― 9	13 − 6 ― 7	5 −3 ― 2	9 −6 ― 3
9.	12 − 6 ― 6	12 − 3 ― 9	16 − 7 ― 9	12 − 4 ― 8	11 − 9 ― 2	10 − 4 ― 6	10 − 2 ― 8	1 −0 ― 1	13 − 8 ― 5	12 − 8 ― 4
10.	17 − 8 ― 9	14 − 7 ― 7	9 −1 ― 8	11 − 7 ― 4	18 − 9 ― 9	14 − 8 ― 6	9 −4 ― 5	3 −0 ― 3	7 −6 ― 1	13 − 7 ― 6

100 subtraction facts

Enrichment

1. Tell students to write all the addition facts that are doubles.
2. Tell students to write all the subtraction facts that are related to doubles.
3. Tell students to use page 294 to write all the facts that have a difference of 8 or 9.

Teaching page 294

This page of subtraction facts can be used as a timed test. Have students correct any incorrect answers. You may want to have students rewrite problems in horizontal form and then solve each problem.

294

Alternate Chapter 7 Checkup

Objective

To review addition of 2-digit numbers with and without trading

ALTERNATE CHAPTER 7 CHECKUP

Add. Trade if needed.

1.	2.	3.	4.	5.	6.
43 + 6 49	65 + 9 74	76 + 7 83	70 +40 110	20 +90 110	50 +60 110

7.	8.	9.	10.	11.	12.
53 +45 98	83 + 9 92	27 +77 104	59 +50 109	45 + 6 91	98 +61 159

13.	14.	15.	16.	17.	18.
28 +27 55	69 +74 143	88 + 5 93	36 +36 72	17 +44 61	64 + 8 72

19.	20.	21.	22.	23.	24.
40 +87 127	55 +98 153	91 +71 162	73 +68 141	54 +53 107	87 + 8 95

Add. Then write your answers in dollar notation.

25.	26.	27.	28.	29.
57¢ + 8¢ 65¢	80¢ +50¢ 130¢	74¢ +13¢ 87¢	85¢ +22¢ 107¢	97¢ + 7¢ 174¢
$0.65	$1.30	$0.87	$1.07	$1.74

Solve.

30. There were 72 girls and 69 boys in the swimming pool. How many children were swimming?

72
+ 69
141

___141___ children

31. Tony has 99¢. Young Mi has 85¢. How much money do they have in all?

99¢
+ 85¢
184¢

$1.84

295

Name _____

Alternate Chapter 8 Checkup

Objective

To review subtraction of 2-digit numbers

Subtract. Trade if needed.

1. $\begin{array}{r} 47 \\ -3 \\ \hline 44 \end{array}$
2. $\begin{array}{r} 85 \\ -9 \\ \hline 76 \end{array}$
3. $\begin{array}{r} 76 \\ -7 \\ \hline 69 \end{array}$
4. $\begin{array}{r} 61 \\ -5 \\ \hline 56 \end{array}$

5. $\begin{array}{r} 70 \\ -20 \\ \hline 50 \end{array}$
6. $\begin{array}{r} 90 \\ -50 \\ \hline 40 \end{array}$
7. $\begin{array}{r} 40 \\ -10 \\ \hline 30 \end{array}$
8. $\begin{array}{r} 55 \\ -31 \\ \hline 24 \end{array}$

9. $\begin{array}{r} 74 \\ -15 \\ \hline 59 \end{array}$
10. $\begin{array}{r} 92 \\ -45 \\ \hline 47 \end{array}$
11. $\begin{array}{r} 67 \\ -38 \\ \hline 29 \end{array}$
12. $\begin{array}{r} 75 \\ -45 \\ \hline 30 \end{array}$

13. $\begin{array}{r} 91 \\ -15 \\ \hline 76 \end{array}$
14. $\begin{array}{r} 87 \\ -69 \\ \hline 18 \end{array}$
15. $\begin{array}{r} 48 \\ -19 \\ \hline 29 \end{array}$
16. $\begin{array}{r} 56 \\ -38 \\ \hline 18 \end{array}$

17. $\begin{array}{r} 64¢ \\ -25¢ \\ \hline 39¢ \end{array}$
18. $\begin{array}{r} 71¢ \\ -54¢ \\ \hline 17¢ \end{array}$
19. $\begin{array}{r} 38¢ \\ -29¢ \\ \hline 9¢ \end{array}$
20. $\begin{array}{r} 95¢ \\ -56¢ \\ \hline 39¢ \end{array}$

Solve.

21. Jason saved 57 marbles. He gave Sonja 18 of them. How many marbles did he have left?

$\begin{array}{r} 57 \\ -18 \\ \hline 39 \end{array}$

__39__ marbles

22. The pet store had 84 hamsters. They sold 39 of them. How many did they have left?

$\begin{array}{r} 84 \\ -39 \\ \hline 45 \end{array}$

__45__ hamsters

Alternate Chapter 9 Checkup

Objective

To review addition and subtraction of 2-digit numbers

ALTERNATE CHAPTER 9 CHECKUP

Add or subtract.

1.	2.	3.	4.	5.	6.
63 + 9 72	58 +31 89	23 +76 99	41 +48 89	57 +34 91	62 +19 81

7.	8.	9.	10.	11.	12.
26 +45 71	83 +38 121	63 +77 140	14 +88 102	45 +46 91	98 +61 159

13.	14.	15.	16.	17.	18.
76 −22 54	52 −31 21	91 −47 44	65 −58 7	74 −19 55	86 −68 18

19.	20.	21.	22.	23.	24.
44 15 +26 85	58 21 +43 122	72 16 +33 121	27 35 +68 130	54 62 +19 135	67 26 +55 148

25.	26.	27.	28.	29.	30.
16 69 + 8 93	32 21 +49 102	47 43 +14 104	86 33 +28 147	63 68 +53 184	27 19 +42 88

Add or subtract. Then write the answers in dollar notation.

31.	32.	33.	34.	35.
57¢ +18¢ 75¢	82¢ +59¢ 141¢	74¢ −27¢ 47¢	85¢ +36¢ 121¢	97¢ −18¢ 79¢
$0.75	$1.41	$0.47	$1.21	$0.79

Chapter review   (two hundred ninety-seven) **297**

Name _____

Add. Trade if needed.

1. $\begin{array}{r} 543 \\ + 6 \\ \hline 549 \end{array}$ 2. $\begin{array}{r} 666 \\ + 7 \\ \hline 673 \end{array}$ 3. $\begin{array}{r} 432 \\ + 9 \\ \hline 441 \end{array}$ 4. $\begin{array}{r} 715 \\ + 5 \\ \hline 720 \end{array}$ 5. $\begin{array}{r} 136 \\ + 5 \\ \hline 141 \end{array}$

6. $\begin{array}{r} 329 \\ + 60 \\ \hline 389 \end{array}$ 7. $\begin{array}{r} 455 \\ + 16 \\ \hline 471 \end{array}$ 8. $\begin{array}{r} 376 \\ + 29 \\ \hline 405 \end{array}$ 9. $\begin{array}{r} 528 \\ + 73 \\ \hline 601 \end{array}$ 10. $\begin{array}{r} 409 \\ + 54 \\ \hline 463 \end{array}$

11. $\begin{array}{r} 48 \\ + 333 \\ \hline 381 \end{array}$ 12. $\begin{array}{r} 26 \\ + 178 \\ \hline 204 \end{array}$ 13. $\begin{array}{r} 77 \\ + 460 \\ \hline 537 \end{array}$ 14. $\begin{array}{r} 143 \\ + 109 \\ \hline 252 \end{array}$ 15. $\begin{array}{r} 321 \\ + 538 \\ \hline 859 \end{array}$

16. $\begin{array}{r} 177 \\ + 304 \\ \hline 481 \end{array}$ 17. $\begin{array}{r} 326 \\ + 176 \\ \hline 502 \end{array}$ 18. $\begin{array}{r} 265 \\ + 416 \\ \hline 681 \end{array}$ 19. $\begin{array}{r} 531 \\ + 199 \\ \hline 730 \end{array}$ 20. $\begin{array}{r} 428 \\ + 275 \\ \hline 703 \end{array}$

21. $\begin{array}{r} \$2.37 \\ + 0.42 \\ \hline \$2.79 \end{array}$ 22. $\begin{array}{r} \$3.42 \\ + 1.39 \\ \hline \$4.81 \end{array}$ 23. $\begin{array}{r} \$4.11 \\ + 3.79 \\ \hline \$7.90 \end{array}$ 24. $\begin{array}{r} \$5.28 \\ + 3.72 \\ \hline \$9.00 \end{array}$

Solve.

25. Kathy spent $3.74. Matt spent $4.33. How much did they spend altogether?

$\begin{array}{r} \$3.74 \\ + 4.33 \\ \hline \$8.07 \end{array}$

____$8.07____

26. The Jacksons drove 313 miles on Tuesday. They drove 178 miles on Wednesday. How many miles did they drive altogether?

$\begin{array}{r} 313 \\ + 178 \\ \hline 491 \end{array}$

____491____ miles

Alternate Chapter 10 Checkup

Objective

To review addition of 3-digit numbers

298

Alternate Chapter 11 Checkup

Objective

To review subtraction of 3-digit numbers

ALTERNATE CHAPTER 11 CHECKUP

Subtract. Trade if needed.

1. 432 $-\ \ \ 6$ $\overline{426}$	2. 833 $-\ \ \ 7$ $\overline{826}$	3. 715 $-\ \ 10$ $\overline{705}$	4. 168 $-\ \ 50$ $\overline{118}$	5. 917 $-\ \ 60$ $\overline{857}$
6. 329 $-\ \ 81$ $\overline{248}$	7. 456 $-\ \ 92$ $\overline{363}$	8. 376 $-\ \ 35$ $\overline{341}$	9. 528 $-\ \ 38$ $\overline{490}$	10. 401 $-\ \ 78$ $\overline{323}$
11. 177 $-\ \ 89$ $\overline{88}$	12. 326 $-\ \ 27$ $\overline{299}$	13. 265 -174 $\overline{91}$	14. 534 -243 $\overline{291}$	15. 428 -278 $\overline{150}$
16. 483 -365 $\overline{118}$	17. 258 -179 $\overline{79}$	18. 734 -585 $\overline{149}$	19. 672 -433 $\overline{239}$	20. 916 -558 $\overline{358}$
21. $\$2.75$ $-\ 0.24$ $\overline{\$2.51}$	22. $\$5.64$ $-\ 2.42$ $\overline{\$3.22}$	23. $\$7.17$ $-\ 1.58$ $\overline{\$5.59}$	24. $\$4.12$ $-\ 3.23$ $\overline{\$0.89}$	25. $\$3.45$ $-\ 2.98$ $\overline{\$0.47}$

Solve.

26. The music store had 765 CDs. Lucy sold 177 of them. How many CDs are left?

765
$-\ 177$
$\overline{588}$

__588__ CDs

27. Sam had $8.42. He bought a book for $3.85. How much money does he have left?

$\$8.42$
$-\ 3.85$
$\overline{\$4.57}$

__$4.57__

Name _____

Alternate Chapter 12 Checkup

Objective
To review addition and subtraction of 2- and 3-digit numbers

Add or subtract.

1.	2.	3.	4.	5.
465 + 34 499	638 + 38 676	313 − 49 264	752 +139 891	278 +610 888

6.	7.	8.
329 143 +333 805	251 227 +295 773	406 118 +276 800

9.	10.	11.	12.	13.
593 +248 841	888 −359 529	656 −447 209	451 −167 284	923 −278 645

14.	15.	16.	17.
$6.95 +$2.24 $9.19	$4.37 +$3.33 $7.70	$6.14 −$2.69 $3.45	$8.21 −$3.54 $4.67

Subtract. Then check your answers.

18.		19.		20.	
$3.49 − 1.67 $1.82	$1.82 + 1.67 $3.49	852 −564 288	288 + 564 852	$6.21 − 2.45 $3.76	$3.76 + 2.45 $6.21

Solve.

21. Soo had $5.35.
She spent $4.58.
How much money does
she have now?

$5.35
+ 4.58
$9.93

Soo has __$9.93__ .

22. Mike had $3.42.
He spend $1.58.
How much money does
he have left?

$3.42
− 1.58
$1.84

Mike has __$1.84__ left.

Alternate Chapter 13 Checkup

Objectives

To review geometry and fractions

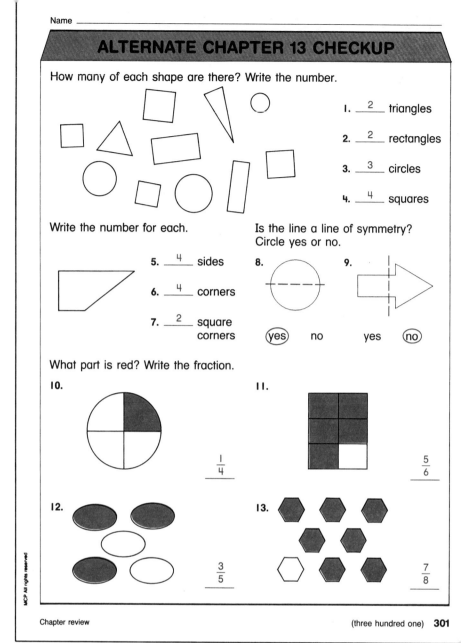

How many of each shape are there? Write the number.

1. __2__ triangles

2. __2__ rectangles

3. __3__ circles

4. __4__ squares

Write the number for each.

5. __4__ sides

6. __4__ corners

7. __2__ square corners

Is the line a line of symmetry? Circle yes or no.

8. (yes)   no

9. yes   (no)

What part is red? Write the fraction.

10. $\frac{1}{4}$

11. $\frac{5}{6}$

12. $\frac{3}{5}$

13. $\frac{7}{8}$

301

Name _____

Find the length to the nearest inch.

1.

It is between __2__ and __3__ inches.   __2__
                                          nearest inch

Find the length to the nearest centimeter.

2.

It is between __8__ and __9__ centimeters.   __9__
                                                nearest centimeter

Use your centimeter ruler. Measure around the figure.

3.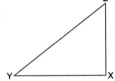

$$\frac{4}{\text{X to Y}} + \frac{5}{\text{Y to Z}} + \frac{3}{\text{Z to X}} = \underline{12}$$

The perimeter is __12__ centimeters.

Find the area.

4.

area = __12__ square centimeters

Circle the better guess.

5.    **6.**   **7.**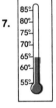

4 ounces   (4 pounds)   1 cup   (1 quart)   __65__ °F

Alternate Chapter 14 Checkup

Objective

To review units of measure

Alternate Chapter 15 Checkup

Objective

To review multiplication facts through 5×5

Multiply.

1.

$3 \times 3 = \underline{9}$

2.

$2 \times 3 = \underline{6}$

3.

$3 \times 4 = \underline{12}$

4.

$4 \times 2 = \underline{8}$

5. $5 \times 4 = \underline{20}$ 6. $4 \times 4 = \underline{16}$ 7. $2 \times 5 = \underline{10}$

8. $\begin{array}{r} 2 \\ \times 4 \\ \hline 8 \end{array}$ 9. $\begin{array}{r} 5 \\ \times 5 \\ \hline 25 \end{array}$ 10. $\begin{array}{r} 3 \\ \times 5 \\ \hline 15 \end{array}$ 11. $\begin{array}{r} 4 \\ \times 3 \\ \hline 12 \end{array}$ 12. $\begin{array}{r} 2 \\ \times 2 \\ \hline 4 \end{array}$

Solve.

13. Peter bought 4 bunches of grapes. There are 5 grapes in each bunch. How many grapes does he have?

$\begin{array}{r} 4 \\ \times 5 \\ \hline 20 \end{array}$

$\underline{20}$ grapes

14. There are 3 cars. Each car has 4 wheels. How many wheels are there in all?

$\begin{array}{r} 3 \\ \times 4 \\ \hline 12 \end{array}$

There are $\underline{12}$ wheels.

Find the total cost.

15. 4

$\begin{array}{r} 2¢ \\ \times 4 \\ \hline 8¢ \end{array}$

Total cost $\underline{8¢}$

16.  5

$\begin{array}{r} 3¢ \\ \times 5 \\ \hline 15¢ \end{array}$

Total cost $\underline{15¢}$

Glossary

.dend A number that is added.
In 7 + 2 = 9, the addends are 7 and 2.

.ea The measure of a surface surrounded by a boundary.
For example, the shaded part of the square is its area. ■

.sic fact A number sentence that has at least two one-digit numbers.
The equations below are examples of basic facts.
4 + 3 = 8; 12 − 5 = 7.

.rdinal number A number, such as three, used to count or to tell how many.

.lsius scale A temperature scale naming 0 degrees as the freezing point of water, and 100 degrees as its boiling point.

.rcle A plane figure with all of its points the same distance from a given point called the center.

.ngruent figures Figures of exactly the same size and shape. For example, △ and ▽ are congruent triangles.

.nominator The number below the line in a fraction. In 3/5, 5 is the denominator.

.fference The answer to a subtraction problem.

.git Any one of the ten number symbols: 0, 1, 2, 3, 4, 5, 6, 7, 8 and 9.

.llar notation The symbols $ and a decimal point in money problems.

.quation A mathematical sentence that uses the = symbol.
16 − 4 = 12.

.en number A whole number with 0, 2, 4, 6 or 8 in the ones place.

.ct family The related number sentences for addition and subtraction that contain all the same numbers.
2 + 4 = 6   6 − 4 = 2   4 + 2 = 6   6 − 2 = 4

.ctor A number to be multiplied.

.hrenheit scale A temperature scale naming 32 degrees as the freezing point of water, and 212 degrees as its boiling point.

.action A number less than one which names part of a figure or group.

.eometry The branch of mathematics that studies points, lines, plane figures and solid figures.

.raph A picture of relationships among numbers and quantities.

.reater than (>) A relationship between two numbers with the greater number given first.
10 > 7; 1/2 > 1/4

.ss than (<) A relationship between two numbers with the lesser number given first.
2 < 4; 1/4 < 1/2

Line of symmetry A fold line of a figure that makes the two parts of the figure match exactly.

Minuend A number from which another number is subtracted. In 18 − 5 = 13, 18 is the minuend.

Multiple The product of a number and a whole number. Some multiples of 3 are 3, 6, and 9.

Number sentence An equation or an inequality.
3 + 2 = 5; 4 < 7

Numerator The number above the line in a fraction.
In 3/5, 3 is the numerator.

Odd number A whole number with 1, 3, 5, 7 or 9 in the ones place.

Order property of multiplication The order in which numbers are multiplied does not affect the product. Also called the commutative property of multiplication.
For example, 4 × 6 = 6 × 4.

Ordinal number A number, such as fifth, used to tell order or position.

Perimeter The distance around a shape that is the sum of the lengths of all of its sides.

Place value The value of the place where a digit appears in a number.
In 137,510, the 7 is in the thousands place and is worth 7,000.

Plane figure A shape that appears on a flat surface. For example, circle, square, and triangle.

Product The answer to a multiplication problem.

Rectangle A four-sided plane figure with four right angles.

Right angle An angle that measures 90 degrees.

Roman numerals An ancient system of numeration using I, V, X, L, C, D, and M to express numbers.

Sequence Numbers following one another in a pattern.

Side One border of a plane or solid figure. For example, a triangle has three sides.

Solid figure A solid shape. For example, sphere, rectangular prism, and cube.

Square A plane figure with four sides of equal length, and four right angles.

Subtrahend The number that is subtracted from the minuend. In 18 − 5 = 13, 5 is the subtrahend.

Sum The answer to an addition problem.

Symmetry The characteristic of a plane or solid figure that allows it to be cut into two identical parts.

Trading The renaming of two adjacent place values.

Triangle A plane figure with three sides.

Whole numbers Those numbers used in counting and zero.

Index

Addition
  column, 49–50, 52, 165–166,
    169, 171–172, 223–224
  doubles, 40
  fact families, 8, 28, 42, 50, 71
  missing addends, 34, 130, 224
  money, 15, 31, 43–44, 51–52,
    139–142, 175–178, 197–198
  multiples of 10, 133–134, 142
  sentences, 171–172
  sums through 10, 3–6, 11,
    13–14
  sums through 12, 21–24,
    29–30
  sums through 19, 38–42, 45–
    48, 71–72, 293
  three-digit numbers, 185–198,
    221–224
  trading, 129–132, 135–136,
    163–166, 183–198, 221–224
  two-digit numbers, 127–136,
    138, 163–166, 169–172, 183–
    184

Calendar, 94, 109–112

Choosing the operation, 18, 30,
  33–34, 43–46, 53–54, 68, 72

Counting, 1–2, 85

Fractions
  of figures, 245–250
  of groups, 251–254

Geometric figures
  fractional parts, 245–250
  plane, 237–242
  sides and corners, 239–240
  solid, 243–244
  symmetrical, 241–242

Graphs, 160, 289–290

Measurement
  area, 267–268
  capacity, 271–272
  centimeters, 261–264
  inches, 257–260
  perimeter, 265–266
  temperature, 273–274
  weight, 269–270

Money
  adding, 15, 31, 43–44, 51–52,

69, 139–140, 175–178, 197–
198
  counting, 51, 83–84, 113–122,
    150
  multiplication, 285–286
  notation, 83–84, 119–122
  subtracting, 16, 32, 69–70,
    157–158, 173–174, 217–218,
    231–232

Multiplication
  factors through 5, 277–286
  order, 285–286
  problem solving, 287–288

Numbers
  comparing, 89–92
  counting sets, 1–2
  in sequence, 2, 77–78, 82, 85,
    87
  ordinals, 93–94
  Roman numerals, 104
  skip counting, 85, 87–88, 181
  word names, 37–38, 77–78,
    95–96

Ordinal numbers, 93–94

Place value
  comparing, 89–92
  expanding numbers, 37, 79–82,
    86, 181–182, 214
  three-digit numbers, 79–82, 86,
    91, 181–182
  through 100's, 181–182
  two-digit numbers, 37, 77, 89,
    91

Plane figures, 237–242

Probability, 166, 192

Problem solving
  adding, 5, 13, 15, 17–18, 23,
    33–34, 39, 43–46, 48, 53–56,
    66, 69–70, 73–74, 128, 132,
    134, 137–138, 140–142, 152,
    158–159, 164, 169–170, 176–
    178, 184, 186, 188, 194, 198–
    200, 218, 222, 232–234
  choosing the operation, 5, 13,
    15–18, 23, 33–34, 39, 43–46,
    48

money, 15–16, 18, 33, 55–56,
  69–70, 121–122, 128, 152,
  158, 176–178, 198–199, 218
  multiplying, 282
  numeration, 86–88, 90, 96
  probability, 166, 192
  subtracting, 13, 16–18, 27, 33–
    34, 43, 56, 59–61, 69–70,
    73–74, 121–122, 140, 146,
    148, 152, 154, 156, 158–159,
    168–170, 176–178, 184, 198–
    199, 204, 206, 210, 212, 218,
    226, 232–234
  time, 103–106

Roman numerals, 104

Skip counting, 85, 87–88, 181

Solid figures, 243–244

Subtraction
  checking, 155–156, 229–230
  fact families, 8, 28, 71
  minuends through 10, 7–10,
    12, 14
  minuends through 18, 25–30,
    57–60, 63–68, 71–72, 294
  missing subtrahends, 34, 216,
    230
  money, 16, 32, 157–158, 173–
    174, 217–218, 231–232
  multiples of 10, 209–210
  sentences, 171–172
  three-digit numbers, 207–218,
    225–232
  trading, 147–156, 167–170,
    203–216, 225–230
  two-digit numbers, 145–156,
    167–172, 203–206

Symmetry, 241–242

Time
  calendar, 94, 109–112
  days of the week, 109
  months of the year, 110
  progressed, 103–106
  to five minutes, 101–102
  to the half-hour, 99–100
  to the hour, 99–100
  to the minute, 107–108

ROUNDUP REVIEW

Fill in the oval next to the correct answer.

1 $\begin{array}{r} 7 \\ + 8 \end{array}$	○ 16 ○ 14 ● 15 ○ NG	**7** $\begin{array}{r} 57 \\ + 38 \end{array}$ ○ 21 ● 95 ○ 85 ○ NG
2 $13 - 6$	● 7 ○ 3 ○ 19 ○ NG	**8** $\begin{array}{r} 35 \\ + 68 \end{array}$ ○ 915 ○ 33 ● 103 ○ NG
3	○ 55 ● 145 ○ 154 ○ NG	**9** $\begin{array}{r} 275 \\ + 465 \end{array}$ ○ 630 ● 740 ○ 730 ○ NG
4 (clock showing 2:18)	● 2:18 ○ 2:08 ○ 3:18 ○ NG	**10** $\begin{array}{r} 71 \\ - 24 \end{array}$ ● 47 ○ 53 ○ 57 ○ NG
5 (coins)	○ 42¢ ○ 57¢ ○ 47¢ ● NG	**11** $\begin{array}{r} 93 \\ - 27 \end{array}$ ○ 74 ○ 76 ● 66 ○ NG
6 (dollar bill and coins)	○ $1.51 ● $1.76 ○ $1.71 ○ NG	**12** $\begin{array}{r} 435 \\ - 162 \end{array}$ ○ 333 ● 273 ○ 373 ○ NG

☐ score

220 (two hundred twenty)

Cumulative review

Enrichment

1. Tell students to find 3 numbers greater than 122 that can be subtracted or added to 335 without any trading.
2. Have students write and solve a problem to find how many days are in 2 years and 2 months.
3. Tell students to find 3 numbers greater than 122 that require trading when they are subtracted or added to 335.

Teaching page 220

This page reviews basic addition and subtraction facts, place value, time, money and adding and subtracting 2- and 3-digit numbers. Remind students to fill in the oval beside NG only if the correct answer is not given. Have students complete the page independently.

220

3-digit Sums

pages 221-222

Objective

To add two 2- or 3-digit numbers for sums through 999

Materials

hundred-flats
ten-strips and ones

Mental Math

Ask students what should be done:

1. first in addition. (add ones)
2. to find how many more. (subtract)
3. to show a money amount. (use cent or dollar notation)
4. to check subtraction. (add)
5. to find how many are left. (subtract)
6. first in subtraction. (subtract the ones)
7. when there are not enough tens to subtract. (trade 1 hundred for 10 tens)

Skill Review

Write **284** on the board. Have students write and solve problems on the board to add various multiples of 10 to 284. Dictate the multiples of 10 as 12 tens, 24 tens, 6 tens, etc.

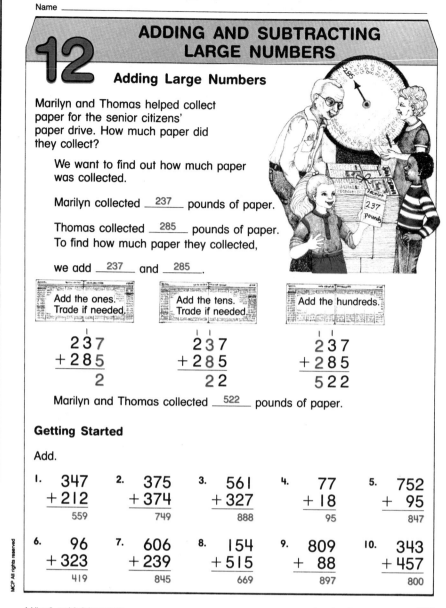

Name _____

Adding Large Numbers

Marilyn and Thomas helped collect paper for the senior citizens' paper drive. How much paper did they collect?

We want to find out how much paper was collected.

Marilyn collected ___237___ pounds of paper.

Thomas collected ___285___ pounds of paper. To find how much paper they collected,

we add ___237___ and ___285___.

Add the ones. Trade if needed.	Add the tens. Trade if needed.	Add the hundreds.
237 +285 ———— 2	237 +285 ———— 22	237 +285 ———— 522

Marilyn and Thomas collected ___522___ pounds of paper.

Getting Started

Add.

1. 347 +212 = 559
2. 375 +374 = 749
3. 561 +327 = 888
4. 77 +18 = 95
5. 752 +95 = 847
6. 96 +323 = 419
7. 606 +239 = 845
8. 154 +515 = 669
9. 809 +88 = 897
10. 343 +457 = 800

Adding 2- and 3-digit numbers

(two hundred twenty-one) **221**

Teaching the Lesson

Introducing the Problem Have students tell about the picture and then discuss reasons for recycling paper or other products. Have a student read the problem aloud and tell what is to be found. (total amount of paper collected) Ask what information is given and where. (The picture shows that 237 pounds and 285 pounds were collected.) Have students tell what operation is needed to find the total. (addition) Have students read and complete the information sentences. Work through the model with students and then have them complete the solution sentence. Have students use manipulatives to check their answer.

Developing the Skill Write **6 + 7** on the board. Have students lay out 6 ones and 7 ones, trade for a ten and tell the number. (13) Write **66 + 47** on the board and have students lay out 6 tens and 4 tens and tell the total number of tens and ones. (11, 3) Ask if 10 tens can be traded for 1 hundred. (yes) Have students make the trade and tell the number. (113) Write **266 + 447** on the board and have students lay out 2 hundreds and 4 hundreds and tell the total number of hundreds, tens and ones. (7, 1, 3) Write **592 + 389** (981) on the board and repeat the process. Continue to develop more addition problems.

221

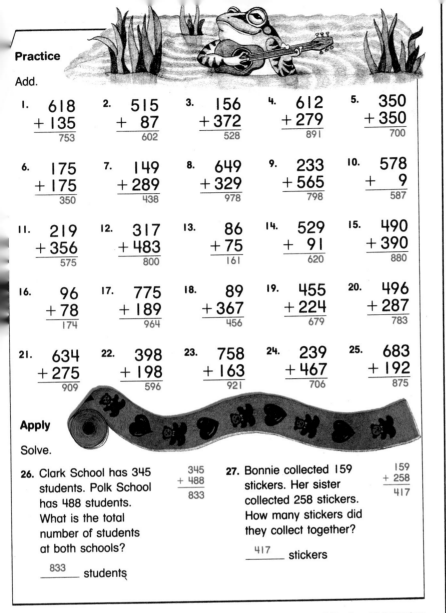

Practice

Add.

1. 618
  + 135
  ___
  753

2. 515
  + 87
  ___
  602

3. 156
  + 372
  ___
  528

4. 612
  + 279
  ___
  891

5. 350
  + 350
  ___
  700

6. 175
  + 175
  ___
  350

7. 149
  + 289
  ___
  438

8. 649
  + 329
  ___
  978

9. 233
  + 565
  ___
  798

10. 578
  + 9
  ___
  587

11. 219
  + 356
  ___
  575

12. 317
  + 483
  ___
  800

13. 86
  + 75
  ___
  161

14. 529
  + 91
  ___
  620

15. 490
  + 390
  ___
  880

16. 96
  + 78
  ___
  174

17. 775
  + 189
  ___
  964

18. 89
  + 367
  ___
  456

19. 455
  + 224
  ___
  679

20. 496
  + 287
  ___
  783

21. 634
  + 275
  ___
  909

22. 398
  + 198
  ___
  596

23. 758
  + 163
  ___
  921

24. 239
  + 467
  ___
  706

25. 683
  + 192
  ___
  875

Apply

Solve.

26. Clark School has 345 students. Polk School has 488 students. What is the total number of students at both schools?

    345
    + 488
    ___
    833

    _833_ students

27. Bonnie collected 159 stickers. Her sister collected 258 stickers. How many stickers did they collect together?

    159
    + 258
    ___
    417

    _417_ stickers

Adding 2- and 3-digit numbers

Correcting Common Errors

Watch for students who are trading incorrectly because they are adding from left to right.

INCORRECT	CORRECT
1 1	1
495	495
+ 852	+ 852
258	1,347

Have students use counters and a place-value chart to show the two addends. Then have them join the counters in each place, from right to left, trading as they go along. Remind them to work toward the operation sign rather than away from it.

Enrichment

Tell students to find the greatest 1-digit number which can be added to 643 without requiring a trade. (6) Then tell students to find the greatest 2-digit number which, when added to 643, requires no trade. (56)

Practice

Remind students to add the ones column first. Tell students that some of the problems on this page need no trading while others will need 1 or 2 trades. Remind students to record each word problem answer on the line under the problem. Have students complete the page independently.

Mixed Practice

1. 72¢ + 38¢ ($1.10)
2. 16 − 8 (8)
3. 65 + 9 (74)
4. 38 ◯ 380 (<)
5. 48 − 32 (16)
6. 270, 280, 290, ___ (300)
7. 31 + 57 (88)
8. ___ + 6 = 15 (9)
9. 3 + 5 + 7 (15)
10. 48 + 93 (141)

Extra Credit *Probability*

Ask students to tell the last four digits in their telephone numbers and list these on the board in columns. Have the class look at these numbers to see if they can find any pattern. (Except for the fact that each is four digits long, the numbers will be unrelated.) Explain that these are random numbers. Many things in the world are random. Ask students if they all have the same arm span, or reach? (no) Point out that although they are all in the same grade, they each have a slightly different arm length. There is not one arm length for a second grader, but rather an average calculated by measuring the random arm spans of many children and calculating the most common. Demonstrate the random distribution of arm spans by having all the students line up and mark their farthest reach, from outstretched arms, with chalk on the board. From their seats, have students look at the collection of random spans. Ask them to pick one reach that seems to be an average.

Adding Three 3-digit Numbers

pages 223-224

Objective

To add three 2- or 3-digit numbers for sums through 999

Materials

hundred-flats
ten-strips and ones

Mental Math

Tell students to repeat these numbers in order and tell the sum:

1. 4, 6, 3 (13)
2. 9, 2, 8 (19)
3. 11, 6, 1 (18)
4. 7, 7, 2 (16)
5. 9, 3, 5 (17)
6. 8, 9, 2 (19)

Skill Review

Write **7 + 3 + 2** in a column on the board. Remind students that in column addition, it is helpful to find a sum of 10 if possible. Have a student talk through the addition of 7 and 3 for a sum of 10 and then 10 and 2 for a sum of 12. Remind students to add up the column to check the sum. Have students find more sums of three 1-digit numbers whose sums are less than 20.

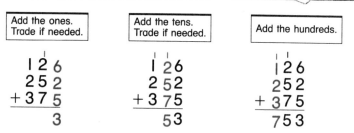

Adding Three Numbers

How many baseball cards did Bobby, Cathleen and Keith collect together?

We want to know how many cards were collected.

Bobby collected ___126___ cards.

Cathleen collected ___252___ cards.

Keith collected ___375___ cards.
To find how many cards in all,

we add ___126___ , ___252___ and ___375___ .

Add the ones. Trade if needed.	Add the tens. Trade if needed.	Add the hundreds.

$$\begin{array}{r} 1\ 2\ 6 \\ 2\ 5\ 2 \\ +\ 3\ 7\ 5 \\ \hline 3 \end{array}$$

$$\begin{array}{r} 1\ 2\ 6 \\ 2\ 5\ 2 \\ +\ 3\ 7\ 5 \\ \hline 5\ 3 \end{array}$$

$$\begin{array}{r} 1\ 2\ 6 \\ 2\ 5\ 2 \\ +\ 3\ 7\ 5 \\ \hline 7\ 5\ 3 \end{array}$$

They collected ___753___ baseball cards together.

Getting Started

Add.

1.	2.	3.	4.	5.
113 231 +442 786	143 46 + 51 240	314 122 +351 787	442 136 + 55 633	165 225 +365 755

6.	7.	8.	9.	10.
251 315 +178 744	423 74 +186 683	142 436 +219 797	323 265 +188 776	504 193 +268 965

Adding three 3-digit numbers

(two hundred twenty-three) **223**

Teaching the Lesson

Introducing the Problem Have a student read the problem aloud and tell what is to be found. (the total number of baseball cards collected) Ask what information is given. (Bobby collected 126 cards, Cathleen collected 252 and Keith collected 375.) Ask students what operation is used to find the total number of cards. (addition) Have students read and complete the information sentences. Work through the model with students and then have them complete the solution sentence. Have students add up each column to check their answer.

Developing the Skill Write **168 + 222 + 537** vertically on the board. Ask students the total number of ones. (17) Remind students to look for a ten when adding a column of numbers. Talk through the addition of 8 and 2 for 10 and then 10 and 7 for 17. Ask if a trade for a ten should be made. (yes) Have students trade 10 ones for a ten and tell how many ones are left as you record the trade and the

7 remaining ones. Continue the procedure for adding the tens, trading for 1 hundred and adding the hundreds. Ask students the sum of the three 3-digit numbers. (927) Have students add up each column with you to check the addition. Repeat the activity for 710 + 139 + 87 (936), 215 + 333 + 345 (893), 649 + 28 + 170 (847), and 452 + 327 + 206 (985). Note: The sum of the ones or tens column does not exceed 19.

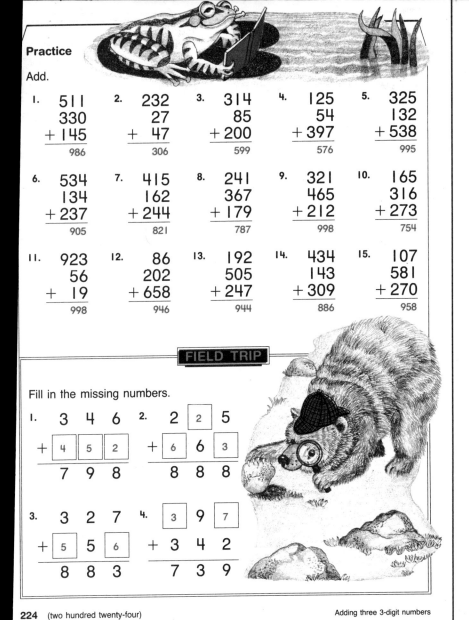

Practice

Add.

1.   511
    330
 +145
  986
	2. 232
	    27
	 + 47
	  306
		3. 314
		    85
		 +200
		  599
			4. 125
			    54
			 +397
			  576
				5. 325
				    132
				 +538
				  995

6.   534
    134
 +237
  905
	7. 415
	    162
	 +244
	  821
		8. 241
		    367
		 +179
		  787
			9. 321
			    465
			 +212
			  998
				10. 165
				    316
				 +273
				  754

11.   923
    56
 + 19
  998
	12. 86
	    202
	 +658
	  946
		13. 192
		    505
		 +247
		  944
			14. 434
			    143
			 +309
			  886
				15. 107
				    581
				 +270
				  958

FIELD TRIP

Fill in the missing numbers.

1.
```
   3 4 6
 + 4 5 2
 ───────
   7 9 8
```

2.
```
   2 2 5
 + 6 6 3
 ───────
   8 8 8
```

3.
```
   3 2 7
 + 5 5 6
 ───────
   8 8 3
```

4.
```
   3 9 7
 + 3 4 2
 ───────
   7 3 9
```

Adding three 3-digit numbers

Correcting Common Errors

Some students will have problems doing column addition because they become confused going from one partial sum to the other. Suggest to them that they can help themselves by thinking of only two digits at a time and by writing down partial sums so they won't forget them.

Enrichment

Tell students to write and solve problems to show all the ways that three 1-digit numbers can have a sum of 19.

Practice

Remind students to check each answer by adding up the columns. Have students complete the page independently.

Field Trip

Write on the board:
```
      2 5 8
 + (5)(2)(3)
 ──────────
      7 8 1
```

Ask students what operation is to be done. (addition) Ask what number is added to 8 to have 1 one (3) Write **3** in ones place, trade the 10 ones for 1 ten and record 1 one left. Ask what number is added to 5 + 1 to have 8 tens. (2) Record the 2 tens and ask what number is added to 2 to have 7 tens. (5) Record the 5 and help students check by adding again.

Help students complete the first problem, if necessary, and then have students complete the problems independently.

Extra Credit   *Geometry*

Draw a pentagon on the board and ask students to copy the five-sided figure on their geoboards with a rubber band. Tell them to make as many different pentagons as they can and copy them onto graph paper. Show them how to take a pentagon and divide it up into triangles using more rubber bands. Have them illustrate these dissected pentagons on the graph paper as well. This activity is preliminary to later work in geometry in which students will show that many-sided plane figures can be made rigid by dividing them up into triangles. Have students collect their work, staple it together, and label it the "pentagon book".

Subtracting Large Numbers

pages 225-226

Objective

To subtract from 3-digit minuends

Materials

addition and subtraction fact cards
hundred-flats
ten-strips and ones

Mental Math

Have students complete each comparison, that 2 is to 5 as 7 is to 10 as:

1. 61 is to __ (64)
2. 23 is to __ (26)
3. 8 is to __ (11)
4. __ is to 22 (19)
5. 253 is to __ (256)
6. __ is to 45 (42)

Skill Review

Have students help sort the subtraction facts into groups of facts related to sums through 10, facts related to sums 11 through 18 and facts which are doubles. Then have students find and show a subtraction fact related to an addition fact you show. Repeat to pair more related addition and subtraction facts.

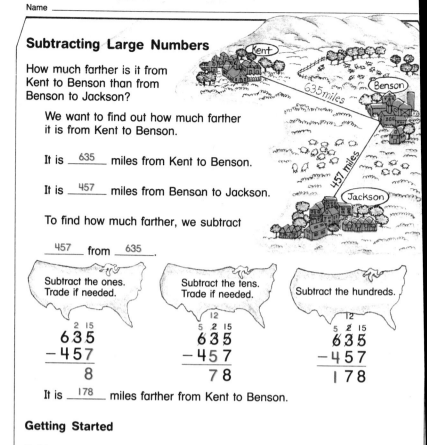

Name _____

Subtracting Large Numbers

How much farther is it from Kent to Benson than from Benson to Jackson?

We want to find out how much farther it is from Kent to Benson.

It is __635__ miles from Kent to Benson.

It is __457__ miles from Benson to Jackson.

To find how much farther, we subtract

__457__ from __635__.

Subtract the ones. Trade if needed.

$$\begin{array}{r} {\scriptstyle 2\ 15} \\ 6\,3\,5 \\ -4\,5\,7 \\ \hline 8 \end{array}$$

Subtract the tens. Trade if needed.

$$\begin{array}{r} {\scriptstyle 5\ 2\ 15} \\ 6\,3\,5 \\ -4\,5\,7 \\ \hline 7\,8 \end{array}$$

Subtract the hundreds.

$$\begin{array}{r} {\scriptstyle 5\ 2\ 15} \\ 6\,3\,5 \\ -4\,5\,7 \\ \hline 1\,7\,8 \end{array}$$

It is __178__ miles farther from Kent to Benson.

Getting Started

Subtract.

1.	2.	3.	4.	5.
347 −212 135	845 −428 417	561 −327 234	877 − 18 859	752 − 95 657

6.	7.	8.	9.	10.
275 −198 77	323 − 96 227	515 −154 361	457 −289 168	635 −436 199

Subtracting 2- and 3-digit numbers

(two hundred twenty-five) **225**

Teaching the Lesson

Introducing the Problem Have students tell about the map. Have a student read the problem aloud and tell what is to be found. (how much farther it is from Kent to Benson than from Benson to Jackson) Ask what information is given. (It is 635 miles from Kent to Benson and 457 miles from Benson to Jackson.) Have students read and complete the information sentences. Work through the subtraction model with students and then have them complete the solution sentence.

Developing the Skill Ask students how to find how much greater 9 is than 6. (subtract) Have a student solve the problem on the board. (9 − 6 = 3) Repeat to find how much greater 26 is than 19 (7), etc., for more subtraction problems of 1-, 2-, or 3-digit numbers. Have students check their subtraction by adding. Remind students that questions of **How much farther? How much greater? How many more? What is the difference?** etc., will require subtraction. Present more dictated problems using the above questions for students to gain practice in writing and solving the problems. Help students recognize that in subtraction problems, the larger number of the 2 must always be the minuend, or the top number. Have students continue to check each problem by adding.

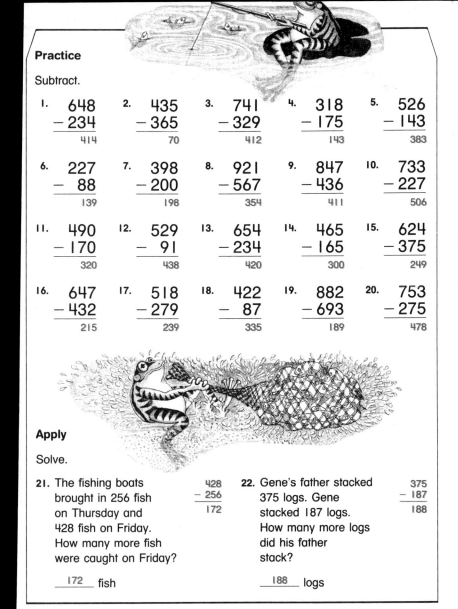

Practice

Subtract.

1. 648
− 234
414

2. 435
− 365
70

3. 741
− 329
412

4. 318
− 175
143

5. 526
− 143
383

6. 227
− 88
139

7. 398
− 200
198

8. 921
− 567
354

9. 847
− 436
411

10. 733
− 227
506

11. 490
− 170
320

12. 529
− 91
438

13. 654
− 234
420

14. 465
− 165
300

15. 624
− 375
249

16. 647
− 432
215

17. 518
− 279
239

18. 422
− 87
335

19. 882
− 693
189

20. 753
− 275
478

Apply

Solve.

21. The fishing boats brought in 256 fish on Thursday and 428 fish on Friday. How many more fish were caught on Friday?

428
− 256
172

___172___ fish

22. Gene's father stacked 375 logs. Gene stacked 187 logs. How many more logs did his father stack?

375
− 187
188

___188___ logs

226 (two hundred twenty-six)   Subtracting 2- and 3-digit numbers

More Subtracting Large Numbers

pages 227-228

Objective

To subtract 2- and 3-digit numbers

Materials

hundred-flats
ten-strips and ones

Mental Math

Ask students to supply answers for the following:

1. 6:42 means (42) minutes after 6.
2. 54 is (6) more than 48.
3. The difference of 100 and 75 is (25).
4. The total of 8 and 90 is (98).
5. 2 dimes are (5¢) less than a quarter.
6. 4 hours later than 2:15 is (6:15).
7. 6 + 18 is 2 more than (22).

Skill Review

Help students make a list of questions on the board which are commonly found in subtraction word problems. The list may include, but not be limited to, the following: How much more? How many more? What is the difference? How much greater? How much older? How many are left? How much change?

More Subtracting Large Numbers

During the spring sale, the Sports Store sold 325 baseballs and 179 footballs. How many more baseballs were sold?

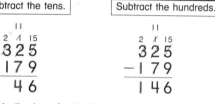

We want to know how many more baseballs were sold.

There were __325__ baseballs sold.

There were __179__ footballs sold.

To find how many more baseballs were sold,

we subtract __179__ from __325__.

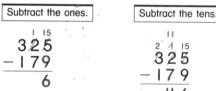

Subtract the ones.	Subtract the tens.	Subtract the hundreds.
1 15 3 2 5 − 1 7 9 6	11 2 1 15 3 2 5 − 1 7 9 4 6	11 2 1 15 3 2 5 − 1 7 9 1 4 6

They sold __146__ more baseballs than footballs.

Getting Started

Subtract.

1.	2.	3.	4.	5.
465 − 128 337	819 − 96 723	752 − 329 423	530 − 156 374	738 − 299 439

6.	7.	8.	9.	10.
561 − 9 552	678 − 496 182	788 − 298 490	937 − 447 490	825 − 466 359

Practice subtracting 2- and 3-digit numbers

(two hundred twenty-seven) **227**

Teaching the Lesson

Introducing the Problem   Have a student read the problem aloud and tell what is to be found. (how many more baseballs than footballs were sold) Ask what information is given. (325 baseballs and 179 footballs were sold.) Ask what operation is used to find how many more. (subtraction) Have students read and complete the information sentences. Work through the model with students and then have them complete the solution sentence. Have students check their answer by adding.

Developing the Skill   Have students work in pairs at the board to gain practice in writing and solving subtraction problems as you dictate problems such as: How many more than 127 is 642? (642 − 127 = 515) How many miles farther is a town that is 306 miles away than a town that is 88 miles away? (306 − 88 = 218) How much greater is the number 990 than the number 694? (990 − 694 = 296) Have one student solve the problem and the second student check the problem with manipulatives or by adding.